Forty-five
Books I and II

by

Brent Chichester

DORRANCE PUBLISHING CO., INC.
PITTSBURGH, PENNSYLVANIA 15222

ISBN# 0-8059-4134-7
Printed in the United States of America

First Printing

For information or to order additional books, please write:
Dorrance Publishing Co., Inc.
643 Smithfield Street
Pittsburgh, Pennsylvania 15222
U.S.A.

Dedication

I had gone to lower Kinnear Park, from which Neptune's water can be seen, each February 13. The conspicuous rock in the path was circled, bowed to, and a small stone placed on it. The ritual was executed thirteen times, with a total of thirteen stones. Then on February 14, fourteen times, and so on through the 21st, the ancient period. This had to be done, though it was unexplainable why. Vaguely—in a craziness— I thought with such hocus pocus a demon in the rock would give me magic and protection. And that it did. But only after doing this faithfully for four or five years. It was then the realization came that Kinnear means Kin-near, the rock represented a grave mound, and the stones brought to it were Jewish flowers. Who knows? Maybe there was someone buried below centuries ago. Still, the souls of deceased persons since the beginning of time were being honored. This is for the spirits of the dead, all of whom were winners. Each finished the race, though some were more racial about it than others.

> *The written words cannot be erased,*
> *Now retribution must be faced*
> *For having bad-mouthed the dead,*
> *No works will carry me ahead.*
> *The Code of the Di Manes is the dread,*
> *Nothing voiced or written should be said.*
> *Nothing even under your breath,*
> *But the name, date of birth, and of death.*

For Robyn too

Contents
Book I

Hermes, the "Good Shepherd." Leonardo da Vinci born at 4.5. Vincenzo Perugia steals Mona Lisa. Michelangelo, the Pietá: damaged by Laszlo Toth. St. Peter's built over a cemetery: Di Manes. Both Pope Julius II and Michelangelo connected to the Parentalia. Jean Calment: the oldest documented living person born on the Feralia, as was General Santa Anna. President Zachary Taylor, a peer sacrifice. President Andrew Johnson connected to February 21, as was President Richard Nixon. John Quincy Adams had stroke on February 21, becoming the first peer sacrifice. Captain Cook's burial on February 21, in what would later become U.S. territorial water. Washington Monument stolen on February 21. Washington died on "Mausoleum Day," equivalent to February 14, St. Valentine's Day. Last battle of the Civil War won by "Rip" Ford on May 13 (1865), equivalent to the Feast of the Dead. Howard Carter escaped Tutankhamen's curse by honoring the second sacred ancient period. Martha Washington consented to the removal of George Washington's body to a national mausoleum, then left the impression she had been put under pressure when making the decision. Body should have gone to Washington Monument, as indicated by February 21 and February 22 dates, the Feralia-Caristia, Pisces sign of fish going in opposite directions. Mexican War's ominous dates: May 13, 1846, to May 30, 1848. Lee's estate, via Mary Custis, becomes a cemetery. First St. Peter's built by Emperor Constantine, connected to May 21 and May 22: crosses painted on horses' heads, death symbols of departure. Roman Catholic Church moved Feralia date. Di Manes countered by increasing their power by three. February, previously the last month of the year, retains same meaning, and December parallels February to some extent. February 21/22 connected to Mahatma Gandhi and wife. President Kennedy assassinated twenty-one days after the South Vietnam coup on November 1, equivalent to Feast of the Dead; chickens had come home to roost. The Arlington flame. "Salute." Snake medicine. Lake View Cemetery: Bruce and Brandon Lee. The number 9, a necromancy number: aluminum tip on Washington Monument is 9 inches.

Book II

Foreword

If Hermes is a god of derring-do,
He's gotta be a god of detectives too.

Jesus H. Christ. JHC = 21. *Jesus Holy Christ* CHTHO-I-
(NC) or CHTHOnIc. Chthonic (thón′ ik) relates to gods
and spirits of the nether world. Hermes could travel in
either world, above or below. Thus part of his divinity
was to be a god of travelers.[1-A]

The picture of Christ as the "Good Shepherd" was fleeced from the
Tanagra statue of Hermes (whose name probably means "he of the stone
heap") carrying a goat. But if Hermes is a god of thieves, Christians aren't
to worry about the theft or—if not that—the cunning deception of bor-
rowing the theme. For Jesus said, "Let him who is without sin among you
be the first to throw a stone..." (Jn 8:9). Buried in a new tomb hewn of
rock, he had died between two thieves, a name which encompasses all
sinners. By extension, this includes any prisoners: those in jail (St. Peter,
of the fetters) who are sinners, and those prisoners—not necessarily from
sin—who are trapped in their minds or bodies.

But most importantly, to catch a thief—the biggest thief of all was
stealing the souls right back.[1-B]

Leonardo da Vinci, born in a fourth month (April 15 [4.5], 1452) and
dying in a fifth (May 2, 1519), was a gentle soul who detested wars. He
designed a flying machine and was noted for buying caged birds so he
could set them free, as well as for having painted *The Last Supper* and the
Mona Lisa.

On August 21, 1911,[1-C] the latter—the most famous painting in the
world—was stolen from the Louvre Museum in Paris. Over two years
later, when trying to sell it, Vincenzo Perugia was arrested and confessed
to the theft. As if a conspirator, "the lady with the magic smile" who has

a primordial *rock* in her background, had traveled to Italy, spending ten days in Florence, where she was born, before returning to France on December 31, 1913. Perugia, who had been sentenced to a little over a year in prison, was set free in a little over seven months.

Michelangelo, a contemporary of da Vinci, produced the *stone* sculpture of the mourning Virgin holding the body of Christ on her lap. This, one of the most famous pieces of all time, is called the *Pietá,* a word meaning pity or compassion and which describes the devotional image of several works. It was carved out of a block of Carrara[1-D] marble and is the only statue Michelangelo ever signed.

On May 21, the beginning of the Mercury period, in 1972, a Hungarian emigre to Australia, a traveler, pulled out a hammer at St. Peter's[1-E] Basilica in Rome and severely damaged the masterpiece.

Julius II, who had commissioned Michelangelo, more or less against his will, to paint the frescoes on the ceiling of the Sistine Chapel, died on February 21, the Feast of the Dead, in 1513, the anniversary of the day "Julius the Colossus" was set in place in 1508 (the statue, with the exception of the decapitated head, was later destroyed). Julius II is the most famous pope to date. He laid the stone for the second St. Peter's Basilica. Michelangelo later lamented that he himself had spent his youth "chained to a tomb." It seems highly unlikely that the death-date numbers were by chance or that Michelangelo's remark was chance either. This is even less so when considering that Michelangelo received advance payment for work to begin on the Sistine Chapel on May 10, 1506, the eve of the second Lemuria day. In 1512 on October 31, Halloween (equivalent to eve of the Feast of the Dead), the first Mass was celebrated in the reopened chapel. But the most important thing not to forget is that St. Peter's Church, the largest in the world, was built over a necropolis.[1-EE]

That the remains of St. Peter could be there might or might not have been part of the reason the original church was built. But in the main there were older "Parentalia" forces at work. That one of the largest collections of ancient art lies within the Vatican isn't just coincidence, nor is the fact that the catacombs (caves excavated deep within the ground for burial) lie around the original perimeter of ancient Rome. Despite what others say, Julius II's death of *February 21* was the consecration of St. Peter's by Parentalia forces, and the feast of St. Peter's Chair (at times in history given as *February 22*) strengthens this view, as does the *May 13,* 1981, shooting of John Paul II.

In Roman antiquity, *February 21* was the Feralia, the end of the nine-day period from February 13–21. That Jeanne Calment, born *February 21,* 1875, is entered in the *Guiness Book of Records* as the oldest living person whose birth can be documented, is not by accident.

Michelangelo died on *February 18,* 1564. Martin Luther, the great

Protestant reformer, had died on *February 18*, 1546, eighteen years earlier. That both Pope Julius II and Michelangelo died within the ancient celebration period is curious. Perhaps even stranger is that the emigre will shout during the attack, "I am Jesus Christ," when his name was actually Laszlo Toth, which sounds remarkably close to Lazarus Thoth, sometimes spelled Thot (some say Lazarus died for the second time in A.D. 63 on December 17, equivalent to the middle of the Parentalia). Thoth was believed to be the author of the *Book of the Dead*.

On *February 21*, 1794, Antonio Lopez de Santa Anna was born. General Santa Anna lay siege to the Alamo on *February 23*, 1836. He defeated the Texans there but was captured by General Sam Houston on *April 21*, 1836. It was General Santa Anna's fate to preside over the loss of Texas and the American Southwest to the United States. He, by the way, was defeated at the Battle of Buena Vista on *February 22–23*, 1847, by the forces of General Zachary Taylor.

It was Zachary Taylor's fate, however, to have been groomed for the sacrifice as far back as *May 15*, 1814, when he received the regular commission of major in the twenty-sixth U.S. infantry. Keep in mind he became famous in the war against Mexico, declared by Congress on May 13 (linked to the Feralia, May 13 would also become the last day of the last battle of the Civil War), 1846, and which would end on May 30 (a date later to become the traditional Memorial Day), 1848.

At first they'd planned to lay the cornerstone to the Washington Monument on February 22, 1848. This was postponed to July 4. (Four, coincidentally, is the number associated with Hermes.) But there was no sacrifice then, and who would be deemed worthy of sacrifice so that the monument would eventually pulse and breathe? Certainly only one who had been connected closely to *February 21* and who as president was Washington's peer.

On July 4, 1850, President Taylor (whose mother had been born on *December 14*, 1760, and died on *December 13*, 1822, and whose son-in-law had been Jefferson Davis)[1-F] attended ceremonies at the Washington Monument (to be linked to February 21–22) when he began to complain of the heat, giddiness, and a headache. He stuck it out, however, until the benediction. He then stood, *walked around the monument,* and went to his carriage, the horses of which in Roman times were symbols of death. Now remember this was on the fourth. He returned to 1600 (4 P.M.) Pennsylvania Avenue. Five days later Dr. Weatherspoon (Washington's last writing before he died on *December 14*, 1799, was to record the mercury) pronounced him dead.

It's also likely Lincoln, whose first vice-president, Hannibal Hamlin, died on July 4, 1891, was to be a later sacrifice. At the ceremony for laying the cornerstone on July 4, 1848 (21), were James Buchanan; Andrew Johnson; and Abraham Lincoln, then a little-known congressman.

Lincoln's birth on February 12, 1809, is a transposition of *February 21*, and the ZA in Zachary is a transposition of AZ. Where President Taylor got sick on the fourth day and died five days layer, President Lincoln simply died at 4.5. Andrew Johnson, Lincoln's second vice-president, found all his troubles began in his presidency on *February 21*, 1868, when he fired Secretary of War Stanton. Johnson's mother died *February 13*, 1856. (Had he not resigned, President Nixon, linked to February 21, probably would have been the second president to face impeachment proceedings.)

It would seem that of the three men sitting at the cornerstone ceremonies, only James Buchanan wouldn't have to pay a stiff penalty for the presidency. Not so! He had been paying on the presidential installment plan for the preceding twenty-eight years and would continue to pay to the end of his long life at age seventy-seven and after. For nothing in this world is quite so durable as gossip, if not a scandal.

In 1819 Buchanan was engaged to Ann Coleman, the daughter of a millionaire. It would be as naive to think he hadn't considered her wealth as it was for his critics not to consider he might have loved her too. Anyway, this and other things drove a wedge between the two, at least so far as the unstable Ann was concerned. She penned off a hasty note to him breaking off the engagement. Not long after, she died suddenly. Suicide was a possibility, though there seemed to be no hard evidence. Ann Coleman's friends called him a murderer, and her parents shunned him. He was devastated for awhile and couldn't get her out of his mind, as most certainly he had considered her money, so besides a genuine grief, he must have felt guilt, too.

Was her mysterious death a sacrifice in advance?

On February 21, 1848, John Quincy Adams—then a member of Congress protesting honorary swords be awarded to generals who had participated in the "most unrighteous war" with Mexico—had a stroke on General Santa Anna's birthday. Adams, whose wife had been born on *February 12*, 1775, and who had named his first son after George Washington, died on February 23, two days later. Before his death, he was designated to give the Washington Monument Cornerstone oration, moved from *February 22* to July 4; thus it appears he too was a peer sacrifice.

The U.S. had declared war against Mexico on May 13 (equivalent to the Feast of the Dead), 1846, and it ended on May 30 to become Memorial Day after the Civil War, 1848. General Winfield Scott led the army in the field in the Mexican War. At the beginning of the Civil War, Scott was commanding general of the U.S. Army, but his age was beginning to tell. On October 31, 1861, he requested retirement. On November 1 (both October 31 and November 1 are equivalent to the Feast of the Dead), President Lincoln and his cabinet went to Scott's home, where Lincoln read a eulogy. Scott was retired on this day with full pay and allowances.

He died on May 29 (later to become Memorial Day eve and the day John F. Kennedy was born), 1866.

Winfield Scott, Zachary Taylor, Jefferson Davis, Abraham Lincoln, Albert Sidney Johnston (the second in rank of the Confederate generals in the Civil War), and Robert Anderson took part in the Black Hawk War in 1832. Black Hawk died October 3, 1838. He was buried seated on the ground, according to Sac/Sauk custom. In 1839 his sepulchre was violated, and his severed head and other parts were carried away. Later his bones were found in the possession of a Quincy, Illinois, physician and restored. Ultimately, by consent of his family, they were placed in the Historical Society of Burlington, Iowa, but the building burned down. The desecration (at odds with the Parentalia, the Di Manes) might have influenced (or been synchronized with) someway the outcome of the lives of the six men taking part in the Black Hawk War. Lincoln was assassinated; Zachary Taylor became a peer sacrifice; Jefferson Davis was the losing head of the Confederacy; Winfield Scott (whose wife died in Rome in 1862) was too old to command because of infirmities; General Johnston was killed in battle in 1862; and Robert Anderson commanded at Fort Sumter on April 12–13, 1861, and so lost the first battle of the Civil War.

On the night of *February 21*, 1855, the Washington Monument was "stolen" by the "Know Nothings," the American Party, which was strongly anti-Catholic. They broke into the office of the Washington National Monument Society, took its records and books, kicked out the former owners, and voted in their people to office. The "Know Nothings" was the same group suspected of stealing nearly a year before (March 5, 1854) the "Papist" gift of marble (brought from the Temple of Concord in Rome), smashing it to bits with sledgehammers and disposing of it in the Potomac.

Two years after stealing the Washington Monument, the "'Know Nothings' fell into disrepute. The monument was returned to the official society, which Congress incorporated as the Washington National Monument Society on February 26, 1859.[1-FF]

On February 21, 1885, the Washington Monument was dedicated. Why on the twenty-first, when the anniversary of Washington's birth was on the twenty-second? Even today it seems peculiar, this one-time shot appearing not to have been gotten right. The reason they gave—and which they apparently believed—was that more people were likely to attend on Saturday the twenty-first than on Sunday, when it might be an inconvenience. It was the right date, of course, but the wrong real reason, for which the people were ignorant.

When the Washington Monument was nearing completion, Congress passed a joint resolution pertaining to the dedication ceremonies which were to take place on February 22, 1885. This was approved on *May 13*,

1884. Since May 13 corresponded with *February 21*, it had to be the Feralia, for that's what it was all about: the Parentalia-Caristia.

And on February 21, 1787, Congress had called for a constitutional convention to meet on May 14. The first regular session was on May 25.

On the Washington Monument's completion date (December 6, 1884), the nine-foot pyramidal "capstone was finally set" and the nine-inch pyramid-of-aluminum tip "was put in place" amidst a "howling gale." (On dedication day *February 21*, 1885, a keen wind made those in attendance uncomfortable.)

Since aluminum is one of the lighter metals, non-corrosive, and a good lightning conductor, it was ideally suited. But lightness, quickness to attract and safely divert (protect), and wind suggest Hermes. Now consider that the atomic number of aluminum is 13.

> 13-21 (9 days), the Parentalia.
> 13-22, the Parentalia-Caristia.

There are three thefts associated with the Washington Monument. You are aware of the disappearance of the Pope's gift and the actions of the "Know Nothings." In 1934–1935, the monument was cleaned for the first time and there was scaffolding up. Right in plain sight of those from miles around, a set of platinum-tipped conductors disappeared, a daring theft worthy of the "Master Thief."

On *February 21*, 1779, the Feast of the Dead, Captain James Cook, the discoverer of Christmas Island, was buried in part and parts at sea (now the U.S.). He had been butchered on February 14 (4514 - Dead). The remains for burial had been recovered after being cooked and offered up in high places by priests. Though Captain Cook never claimed to be the natives' god, he did little to deny it. It was the month of purification, of which Neptune is the guardian.

On *February 21*, 1852 (New Style, March 4), Nikolai Gogol, the famous Russian author, died. He lived a dozen years *in Rome*, where he wrote stories and worked on his famous novel *Dead Souls*. *Chich*ikov, the main character, was a swindler who got rich by buying up the "souls" of dead serfs whose deaths had not yet been officially recorded and thus were still carried on records. Some say Gogol, a fanatical mystic, ruined his health and caused his death by extreme fasting, but on *February 11*, 1852 (old style) he, now nearly half mad, burned Volume Two of *Dead Souls*.

On *February 21*, 1924, J.S. Sargent's painting "The Synagogue" was vandalized when ink or paint was thrown on it at the public library in Boston, Massachusetts. The same day in Pawtucket, Rhode Island, ninety-nine tombstones in Mt. St. Mary's Cemetery were wrecked by vandalism (a vandal is defined as a member of a Germanic tribe which sacked

Rome in A.D. 455). Far off in Egypt, the government granted the Countess of Carnarvon a new permit (the old one was canceled on *February 20*) to excavate King Tut's tomb (the following day, *February 22*, Egyptian officials broke the locks), where the previous year her husband—now dead—had very carefully removed the faint seal impressions dotting the door to the inner tomb of King Tut, on *February 15*, the Lupercalia.[1-FFF] On *February 16*, 1923, the sepulchral chamber was entered, and on *February 17*, the dismantling of the burial chamber blocking wall occurred. On *February 23*, Lord Carnarvon visited Howard Carter to try to reconcile differences. *February 15, 16, 17, 20, 21, and 22* are days within the Parentalia-Caristia period.

Lord Carnarvon, the fifth earl, died on April 5 (4–5 or 5–4), 1923, less than two months after breaking the dotted seals on the Lupercalia. His body was sent home and buried in an unmarked grave on the estate overlooking his castle on the day of Walpurgis Night (April 30).

Not to be overlooked is the fact that he had died on the anniversary of the christening of George Washington, born *February 22* (new style), 1732, the *parent* of his country. (Booker T. Washington was born April 5, 1856.) Washington had been a mercury checker most of his life. It was the last thing he had written about before his death on "Mausoleum Day."[1-FFFF] Martha, his wife (born June, or *May 22*, old style, 1731) died on *May 22*, 1802, the anniversary of the mutilation of the Hermae busts in ancient Athens.

The death date is curious. She'd given her consent for George Washington's body to be buried in the proposed national monument. Then later she apparently left the impression that her consent was "extorted from her by the ejaculations of public grief in 1799." This must have infuriated the Di Manes, who caused her death on the anniversary of the day small monuments to Hermes were mutilated, a sign of betrayal. Bushrod Washington, George's nephew who inherited the estate and was a Supreme Court justice, declined in 1816 to consent to the eventual transfer on the ground that it was committed to the Mt. Vernon vault in conformance with his wish. On Bushrod's death, "the house and immediate grounds" went to his nephew, John Augustine Washington, who in 1832 replied similarly to a proposition by Congress.

Logically the body should have gone to the mausoleum in Washington which was made for it. This is suggested by his birthday of *February 22* (new style) and the dedication date of the Washington Monument on *February 21* (1885). The Feralia and Caristia go together. There had been no date for honoring the dead prior to the Civil War, possibly brought about by the Di Manes for the hundreds of years of neglect and to show their anger of the separation of body and monument in the separation of the states. The Mexican War's ominous dates are just too close to the Civil War not to be linked someway, as well as the fact that General Winfield Scott retired on *November 1*, 1861.

Lee married Mary Custis, heiress to the Arlington estate and great granddaughter of Martha Custis Washington. (See Book II, footnote 146.) In choosing Lee—one of whose forebears had been a crusader—to vent their anger, the Di Manes probably caused the Civil War and certainly influenced its outcome. This was made clear by Confederate Colonel Rip Ford winning the last battle on May 13, 1865, equivalent to the Feast of the Dead and a meaningless battle as the South lost the war, being buried figuratively. In beautiful irony, Lee's property became Arlington National Cemetery, where the Lupercalia mast of the *Maine* (Le Maine, Le Mans, Di Manes) is now.

We should not forget too that the first man buried at Arlington Cemetery—where countless crows now line the oaks at sunset—was a Confederate soldier whose last rites were conducted in 1864 on Friday, May 13, equivalent to the Feast of the Dead. It was also the third Lemuria Day and the day Hermes led Persephone back to earth from Hades. She, of course, had changed somewhat, as is suggested by the miracle of Fatima on May 13, 1917 (Francisco and Jacinta died in the influenza epidemic of 1918–1919, and Lucia later wrote down the Lady's "secrets" of 1) a vision of hell and 2) a possible reference to World War II); the economic collapse of Germany on "Black Friday," May 13, 1927; the birth of Jim Jones on May 13, 1931; and the attempted assassination of Pope John Paul II on May 13, 1981.

On *February 12,* 1924, the anniversary of Lincoln's birth, the lid to Pharaoh Tutankhamen's sarcophagus was opened, revealing a golden mummy case.

Howard Carter always had been mercurial and impulsive. This in itself can be a curse most times, but on the day following the raising of the lid, it was a blessing. He'd been greatly agitated with the Egyptian ministry's ruling that the wives of the workers wouldn't be allowed in the tomb to see the relics. In a snit, he cut power lines, slammed the steel door shut, and locked it with a sturdy padlock which only he had the key to. The ministry be damned! He'd show them. And in a mighty huff, he tore out to the Winter Palace Hotel in Luxor and posted the following on its bulletin board:

NOTICE

Owing to the impossible restrictions and discourtesies on the part of the Public Works Department and its Antiquity Service, all my collaborators in protest have refused to work any further upon the scientific investigations of the discovery of the tomb of Tutankhamen. I am therefore obliged to make known to the public that immediately after the press view of the tomb this morning between 10:00 A.M. and noon the tomb [was] closed and no further work can be carried out.

(signed) Howard Carter
February 13, 1924[1-FFFFF]

The Parentalia association to King Tut's tomb doesn't seem too far-fetched, furthermore, when considering that Pope Alexander VI (created as cardinal *February 22*, 1456) had commissioned Pintoricchio and his group to paint the Vatican Borgia apartments. The similarity between the Borgia symbol of a peaceful ox and the sacrificial bull of Osiris—the Egyptian god of death and lord of the underworld—could not have escaped the Borgias, nor the fact the Vatican was built over a graveyard. The ceiling of one room is embossed stucco with painting illustrating the myth of Osiris. Deification of the bull suggests the "exaltation of the House of Borgia." (Phillipps, Evelyn March, *Pintoricchio*, 1901, George Bell and Sons, 1901, London.)

Howard Carter, like Lord Carnarvon, had been a marked man for violating the tomb the previous year in the Parentalia. Even if acting like a little cunt, though showing concern for the underdog, Howard Carter effectively averted the curse upon himself by preventing the desecration of King Tut's tomb the second time around, beginning at *12:00 noon, February 13* and lasting through the *twenty-first*, the sacred period in ancient Rome.

Seven were killed at the St. Valentine's Day Massacre in Chicago on *February 14*, 1929. The following year on *February 21*, 1930, the mercury in Chicago broke all existing records, registering at 67F (13C). Also on this day in *Florence*, Arizona (admitted as St. Valentine's Day, the forty-fifth day), Mrs. Eva (5) Dugan (4), who had killed A.J. Mathis, was *beheaded* by the noose when hanged. And in England, *parent* Lord Westbury (Lord Carnarvon's friend) who had items in his apartment from King Tut's tomb, jumped to his death three months after his son, who had been one of the excavators, died mysteriously. Many Londoners felt it was all linked to King Tut's curse. Howard Carter, excavator of the tomb, thought any such speculation was nonsense and wired newspapers "a heated denial." Apparently no one linked Westbury's death to the Feralia. Then four days later (*February 25*, 1930) when Lord Westbury's hearse was going to the cemetery, it struck down Joseph Geer, age eight, of *Battersea*, he died on the way to the hospital. The death of Edgar Steele, a British Museum employee who had handled the Luxor relics, was also announced this day, raising to thirteen the total deaths connected to the pharaoh's tomb.

The sudden wealth discovered at the tomb was secondary to the rediscovery of the Parentalia and the assertion of Hermes' numbers

9

running counterpoint. Born on the first Lemuria day (5–9), Howard Carter would be buried in grave number 45 with nine mourners present. Again Lord Carnarvon, the fifth earl, died at 4–5. Note the numbers 4, 5, and 9. In 495 B.C. in Rome, on the Aventine overlooking the Circus Maximus, a temple to Mercury was dedicated.

In keeping with the god of thieves, Carter had stolen art objects from King Tut's tomb, and later he left the bulk of his estate to his niece Phyllis *Walker* (Hermes is the god of walkers). Fate smiled ironically too when, on *February 22*, 1940, Howard Carter's books were auctioned at Sotheby's.

Washington; Lincoln; the two Roosevelts; and Prime Minister Winston Churchill, whose mother was American; were—among many others— linked to the ancient period.

An Egyptian obelisk stands in the middle of the piazza of St. Peter, whose church is connected to the Parentalia-death days of Pope Julian II and Michelangelo "chained to a tomb," *February 21* and *February 18* respectively.

But now we return to May 21, a day associated with St. Helena and Emperor Constantine the Great in the Eastern Church. Constantine had been born on *February 27*, "probably in the later A.D. 280s." He died on May 22, 337. Of interest here is May 21–22 (2122) which brings to mind February 21–22, the Feralia-Caristia. Do not forget that on May 22, 415 A.D., there was the mutilation of the Hermae busts in Athens. Had it just been this, there might not be much to think about, but you see Constantine had built the first St. Peter's Basilica. John Paul II had been pope at the time the statue was damaged on May 21. Then John Paul II (born May 18, 1920) would later be seriously injured in an assassination attempt at St. Peter's Square on May 13, 1981, by Mehmet Ali Agca (already condemned to death for a February 1, 1979, murder) from Turkey, the home of Istanbul, formerly called Constantinople ("New Rome" dedicated May 11, 330, the second Lemuria day). May 13 in olden days was the date the very ancient Feralia had been changed to by the Church, finally to become November 1, All Saints' Day, originally called in England Allhallows, or Allhallows Eve, Halloween.[1-G] So it appears that February and May are linked to Hermes. Now add April, the fourth month. February 21 and May 21 have been mentioned. According to tradition, Rome was founded on April 21, 753 B.C.

On *February 21*, Albert Einstein (A.E., atomic energy, born March 14 [a Pisces], 1879, twenty-one days after the Feralia, of Jewish parents) became a citizen of Zurich (noted for the graves of the beheaded Felix, Regula, and Exupernatus) and a citizen of Switzerland (noted for its *time* industry; any hand of a clock is a radius. In a lecture at Columbia University in 1921 on April 15 [4.5], Einstein "called time the fourth dimension").

In a 1939 letter to President Roosevelt (connected by blood to the Parentalia), Einstein pointed out the danger of the Nazis' developing a uranium bomb. This letter also led somewhat to the development of the first U.S. atomic bomb. On *February 21*, 1944, the day when Mahatma Gandhi's drunken son Harilal had to be escorted away from his mother's deathbed, U.S. forces seized Eniwetok. (Note Harilal's mother died the following day, the Caristia, and Gandhi was assassinated on January 30, 1948. His funeral pyre was lit twenty-one days before the Feralia.) On *November 1*, 1952, at Eniwetok, the U.S. detonated its first hydrogen bomb. (But November 1 = May 13 = February 21.) On May 21 (the beginning of the first Mercury period), 1956, the United States' first airborne hydrogen bomb was dropped on Namu, Bikini Atoll, in the Pacific. Thirty-five years previously, Andrei Sakharov, collaborator on the first Soviet atomic and hydrogen bombs, was born in Moscow.

On November 22, 1963, President John F. Kennedy was assassinated while riding in a Lincoln (named for the bookend president to the Parentalia), *21 days after November 1*. (November 1 being equivalent to the Feast of the Dead in ancient Rome and the anniversary of the date [1755] that a tremendous earthquake, flooding, and fire nearly destroyed most of Lisbon, built—like Rome—on seven hills. Tens of thousands died, and escaped convicts and galley slaves caught looting were left hanging from gallows for days as a warning. People puzzled over the meaning of the disaster. Why on All Saints' Day? Why had both bad and good been killed indiscriminately?) This suggests the 2122 of the Parentalia-Caristia and Washington, the other bookend president. But the U.S. had withdrawn support of South Vietnam's President Diem, which served as his death warrant. For anyone to think differently is absurd. The coup d'etat by Diem's generals on *November 1*, 1963, previously had been "acquiesced to" by U.S. Ambassador Henry Cabot Lodge. On November 2 (equivalent to the Caristia when differences between relatives were smoothed over), 1963, Diem and his brother (both, ironically, Roman Catholics like the assassinated President John F. Kennedy and later his brother Robert) were murdered. Since the U.S. had withdrawn its support of Diem, thereby supporting the coup, President John F. Kennedy was ultimately responsible for the coup and the murders.

> The Arlington flame,
> Lights the Kennedy shame,
> For ploughing ahead,
> On the Feast of the Dead.

> It's no sin to die,
> But don't ask me why,
> That is in requiem to say,
> Jackal-ine died on the nineteenth of May.

Salute

A sadness of the pariah war,
No Kipling along the way,
To sound the bugle call just right,
To make it go away.

Worst of all
After searching wide,
Is the thought that God
Was on the other side.
Or maybe hell's own
Is to be counted on the list,
To believe and pray to God,
Who really doesn't exist.

Or to find He did,
And saved them when they cried,
Only to learn years later,
'Twould been better if they died.

For good luck, there must be bad,
That's how they survived.
So kill them now with perfect
Nam insanity: Their buddies died.

You of the days for the dead,[1-GG]
With vets' contempt you're driven,
Your fate not to have been right or wrong,
And forever unforgiven.

Proudly lift your glass to the Viet vets,
As men should always do,
Owning to the gap,
Not wishing to pass through.

This isn't an easy book. Go no further if you aren't prepared to tackle a mountain of trivia in numbers, facts, and associations. History was written by the numbers. If you can't deal with them, go. Just don't come back crying me a river about your damn luck, as if I'm suppose to baptize you in your own tears. Complain directly to Hermes (Mercury), god of luck, numbers,[1-GGG] and measurement, or call 911. I don't run interference.

Why is it impossible for us strutting and fretting our hour upon the stage to conceive of a world beyond where there's no balance requiring entry? Simple enough. We're first and foremost little pipsqueak measurers. Horology at least is older than the oldest profession. Though the word pertains to the measurement of time, we might coin a word from it to cover all our processes of measurement, like saying man-the-robot is a "hor." Our world is nothing more than numbers and measurement: more, less, same; win, lose, draw; rich, poor, middle class; saints, sinners, and the unforgiven; love ("How do I love thee? Let me count the ways") and hate; hour, minute, day, week, and year; the measurement of the senses; the vital signs; the number of brothers and sisters; gallons of gasoline, more miles per gallon; cooking; basketball and football scores, yardage; and so on. Offhand, I can think of nothing which can't be measured one way or another. And we're constantly improving, finding newer and better ways of computing. You'd think we'd grow tired of it, always taking someone's measure or having them take ours. Sometimes we do, but we can't escape it. How much I got, how much you got, how much they got. Fortunately for Albert Einstein, he predicted Mercury would wobble in a certain way. Rather cryptically, the last thing George Washington (the father-*parent* of his country) wrote was describing the wind and what the mercury said the night before he died,[1-H] and Jesus was a measurer. Lincoln of "four score and seven years ago" was noted for asking tall people their height. Had others paid such attention to measurement, the *Titanic* never would have been sunk. The radius of 4.5, the anniversary of Lincoln's April 15 death, confirms this.

Teachers measure their students, and students take measure of their parents, saying their teachers never taught 'em nothin'. Children are believed by their parents, never realizing that the only channeling their little demons ever did was 2, 5, and 13, with 7-11 lunch breaks. It's always numbers. If you don't agree, then "Sound off: 1, 2, 3, 4."

A friend says there are only so many numbers and only so much room in space. "That explains your coincidences," he squelches. This same friend believes anything written about flying saucers and visits from people from outer space. If I were to tell him without bursting out laughing that I'd been taken aboard a spaceship last night and an alien said, "Take me to your alienist," he'd believe me.

There are bonafide coincidences. More often than not what we dismiss as being a coincidence is the result of having a lazy mind, a condition we all have now and then. Maybe we'll never get any rest if we don't use this coincidence-classification, a dustbin for our sweepings. It's so much easier to sit back and leave the thinking to others, to accept what they say, who in turn have accepted what someone higher up the ladder has said as being the truth but which often confused with the majority opinion. Because that person is preeminent with credentials, a shining star, even the heavenly bodies seem to support him.

Since no group—except perhaps ministers and priests—can be more self-righteous sometimes than medical doctors, dentists, and nurses, it would be comic, were it not so tragic, that it took physicians so long to realize that most ulcers can be cured with antibiotics. Sure everyone makes mistakes, but the same one for every day for fifty years? This, to my thinking, is more scandalous than the S & L crisis. It's the stuff from which Aesop's fables were made.

Wasn't that fun watching the fizzing from baking soda and vinegar with my childhood chemistry set? the general practioner muses. But he can't seem to recall now whether he poured the beaker of acid into the bicarbonate-of-soda solution or vise versa. It's important sometimes acid-to-base or base-to-acid, you know. Finally he remembers he was about to recommend Maalox or Mylanta to the priest sitting in front of him, so he must have poured the baking soda into the vinegar. He prides himself now that after all these years he's still got it together, the deductive reasoning that set him apart from some of the schmucks in his profession.

Now looking at the priest, he thinks, *This guy ain't got faith to cure himself, let alone move a mountain. Oh well, maybe that's his cross to bear in life.* He barely strangles this thought by telling the priest that though he could prescribe something, Maalox or Mylanta would probably work just as well. The priest is told to return if he doesn't feel better in a few days, in which case he will run a few tests. The priest feels slightly better because the snake doctor hasn't prescribed an expensive drug, hasn't ordered expensive tests, and has not scheduled another costly appointment just to be told he's okay. God is merciful.

After repeating religiously the acid-base fizzing that propels him two weeks along burping away, the priest even feels worse, if possible. When he returns to the doctor's office still complaining, tests are done, and it's found that he has an ulcer. No malignancy—God is merciful. The doctor treats him unsuccessfully for half a year. Nothing seems to help, so the doctor must make the decision whether to refer him to a surgeon or a psychiatrist. If he sends him to a surgeon, that doc will cut out two-thirds of his stomach on an odd day and one-half on an even day. The patient now sitting in front of him is shaking; he appears nervous and anxious. The GP opts for an alienist rather than a surgeon. God is merciful.

The shrink talks to the priest and deduces the ulcer stems from the fact that the priest believes his mother beat him on the odd days while his father beat him on even days. He writes back on the consult that in his opinion the priest, who is not very insightful, doesn't yet fully understand that it was just the opposite: His mother beat him on the even days and vice versa. Until the priest can think and reason this out for himself, he will have the ulcer. Hopefully with three years on the couch (maybe less) it can be cured.

The psychiatrist offers the priest hope. God is merciful. And even though God is merciful, the priest prays for a miracle, wondering if praying for such is in some way a conflict of interest with God being merciful. But miracles do happen, you know. The priest probably will be canonized someday, showing that things really do work out in the end.[1-I] It's this very positive message I wish to impress upon you.

Anyway fifty years after the introduction of antibiotics (the priest had long since died; God was merciful) a miracle occurred when a doctor in Australia—not even a stomach specialist—refused to accept the fact of coincidence.

Integrity now requires that you step forward and accept your lumps, you snake doctors, you wielders of the caduceus. After that, you qualify for life—rather than eternal—memberships in the Dumb-Fuckers' Club. God is merciful.

It's doubtful in relationship to Thoth being the god of measurement, calendars, and reckoning that 45 B.C. would be just a random year when the process began that every *four years in February* there would be an extra day added. In 45 B.C., Julius Caesar and the Julian calendar, both having the initials J.C., were clearly signposts. Of course the new style calendar under Pope Gregory XIII changed this, but not much. Every four years most Februaries still have twenty-nine days.

Shavuot, the Jewish Feast of the Weeks, is a moveable date each year in May-June. One book[1-J]—possibly using the date usually thought of—gives it as May 25. This is interesting since it probably also is connected to Mercury (or Hermes, "he of the stone heap"). The Jewish Shavuot celebrates Moses' return from the top of Mt. Sinai where he was given two tablets of *stone* on which were written the Ten Commandments.

Part of this book's purpose is to show that there are coincidences that suggest Christ's origin might be different than generally thought. None of this can be proved beyond a *sombra* of a doubt, just as no one can say with absolute certainty that Jesus ever existed historically, or if he did, that he was the son of God, and so the sombrero for man to stand in the sun.

In places where quotations are more than a phrase, full credit has been given to the author or source. Other places, when paraphrasing was used (sometimes paraphrasing what these authors themselves have paraphrased), I've tried to give full credit to the source or author. This doesn't mean I'm quoting them verbatim, which is usually more clearly and more precisely written should the reader have more interest or some doubt and wish to refer directly to what was used. Mistakes made in interpretation and writing were unintentional. There were no outright lies—maybe a few half-truths—except in instances where names were changed for protection of individuals. This excludes, of course, things of a mystical nature and literary license. Some things weren't mentioned. Enough's enuf.

You may have wondered why "spirits of the dead" are spoken of in the dedication. It's in keeping with the Feralia, the Roman All Souls' Day. Still I wondered about it myself at first: why a retirement in the Pacific Northwest, and why every few days for nearly three years I'd stolen five or nine flowers from Volunteer Park (the park sort of volunteered them) and then walked to the adjoining Lake View Cemetery whose office is across the street at 1554 (Hermetic numbers: 44 [5]/55 [4]), the crossroads corner of Fifteenth Avenue East and Garfield Street East. President Garfield, you might recall, was assassinated when President Lincoln's son, Robert Todd Lincoln, was nearby.

Once inside the cemetery, a huge chess set with many pieces, I put a flower on this or that grave as the spirit moves me or the caw of a raven.[1-K] At times when I'm walking along, someone in a car will stop and ask where Bruce Lee (phonetic LI) and his son Brandon are buried. I just point in the general direction and give them my impersonation of Boris Karloff or put on my best sepulchral face, neither of which is all that difficult.

In fact, when I'd forgotten to do either/or one day, somebody wanting directions asked me seriously if I were the caretaker of the cemetery. A few minutes later, catching up to where they're still wandering about looking, I felt obliged to go over and show them exactly. It seemed a lot of time could be saved if better directions had been given. This is how I stumbled on the fact that both father and son were Hermetic characters.

About thirty-three paces from their graves and above them is a huge, roughly hewn stone obelisk (inscribed Hunter). To its left is a large, rugged, roughly hewn stone cross. To the obelisk's right is another obelisk (stone), which is smooth-faced. There are, in fact, five or six obelisks in proximity to the graves. But if you drew a line from the largest, you would find it nearly bisects the graves of the father and the son. An open, black book, as well as a marker, marks Bruce Lee's grave. Were it just these Thoth-Hermes symbols, I wouldn't have thought much about it, but you see the name Brandon could very well have been derived from Bran, or raven.[1-L] This I knew previously, having done research on the name Bran.

Swiftness and deception (Mercury) are associated with the martial arts. The grandfather, the father, and son were actors (eloquence certainly in body movement for all three). Though Bruce Lee and Brandon were dragons, Brandon was borderline, being born on February 1, 1965, the snake period for that year began on February 2, 1965. The snake is a "chthonic" being, and in alchemy, magic, and mythology, the snake and dragon are closely linked. Ancient Egyptians painted them together in a circle, biting each other's tails, to instruct that they sprang from one thing. You will read later that both Poe, the author of *The Raven*, and Lincoln were borderline dragons. Poe's parents were actors, acting in Boston at the time he was born. Lincoln was assassinated by an actor.

Not having followed Brandon's death, I was surprised to read he had the lead in the film *The Crow*, being filmed by the Crowvision movie production company at the time of his death. Since Brandon was shot by a .44 caliber cartridge on set, the bird fit the superstition in this case of being ill-omened. Many other mishaps plagued the production. The raven (crow) also has an air of mystery about it, and I wonder if Brandon, being a borderline case, could have brought about his father's death too, which was called "death by misadventure." You might recall *Wheatfield with Crows* was the last painting Vincent Van Gogh was doing when he shot himself to death.

Bruce Lee was taught Tai Chi by his father, and possibly Brandon had been taught this by Bruce. A peculiarity here is that legend has it that Tai Chi got started when its originator saw a crane (a wading bird like the ibis) and a snake fighting. As they feinted, they were wearing each other down, and so Tai *Chi*. But both the wading bird and the snake are in *Chi*chester heraldry. You will see a similarity to the Chinese offerings at graves to those in ancient Rome and perhaps Greece too (see footnote 12-A). Though the old sage Confucius may have objected to the comparison, there was a touch of Hermes in him.

The bottom line is that: The two graves are a macabre reminder that a bullet, fired even unintentionally, is swifter than martial arts and just as deadly.

Well anyway, you might have wondered why I visit the cemetery, a necropolis, whose office's location and number are appropriate, so I'm tellin' yuh. After nearly a lifetime, a calling had been found. Why I eventually moved so much closer to the graves is something else. Certainly there was no thought of this in mind when I was moving.

"It's because you're sick, man. You need help!"

This is true too, though not that simple really. As certain as you are that there's not a full deck here, I'm just as certain the cards weren't shuffled thoroughly for a reason. Medicine would be the easy way, but it would also defeat the purpose of my existence, which was of the deads' making. First, before explaining, let me quote author Suzanne White's sketch of people like me:

> This deep thinker is bubbly and graceful but only on the strict surface. Underneath roil philosophies and perceptions too otherworldly to share with any but the most enlightened. Pisces/Snake feels everything profoundly and intuits each situation with such force and lucidity that he seems to wince at the power of human contact. Sensitivity takes on a whole new meaning in case of the Pisces/Snake. Intuition is redoubled, second sight emphasized and presentiment too powerful as to be considered a gift. Pisces/Snake is a kind of witch in sheep's clothing.

Trouble is, the world is no fit place for sentient souls. There are no jobs for witches currently. Oh, I suppose these people might choose astrology or crystal ball gazing if they had their druthers. But Pisces/Snake people are decidedly not "druthers" type. They don't want to impress anyone with their importance, and they have no axes to grind in the big bad world.[1-M]

Of course I have to admit making a statement about the dead and me sounds a wee morbid and a mite cozy. It may seem even necrophiliac perhaps, which it isn't, to the writer of a supermarket scandal sheet, or maybe bananas, though when I tell you a lot of work and planning on their part through time was necessary for me to come together.

For instance, my name is Brrrrrent Chichester. I am the B.C. (5) to the A.D. (5), though the book is really about the number 45. I've lived the last third of my life in Washington, named of course after Jorge Lavadaton, and suffered mentally most my life (no different from millions of others) but worst when in Washington, D.C.,[2] which I see now was necessary. Long before knowing anything about the dead, I'd climbed the steps of the Washington Monument, gone to Ford's Theater, and the Lincoln Memorial. But in truth, it meant nothing to me then because I wasn't ready.[3] What's being said is that dues have been paid in order to talk about certain arcane things, which are important for you to know.

General Washington had premonitions of death, and Jefferson felt Washington was "inclined to gloomy apprehensions" about most things in life. In some ways then, it strikes me that Washington and Lincoln were a lot alike.[4] But you have to figure General Washington lost many good men in the Revolutionary War and President Lincoln in the Civil War (as well as President Jefferson Davis), and thus their credentials are impeccable. It is not so much that they were responsible for the deaths exactly, but the suffering, sadness, and grief (which is what death is about) was a tremendous burden for them to carry.

I (born at 10:00 P.M.) am the 21 to Washington's 22 (born at 10:00 A.M.),[5-A] as was Lincoln and one of my brothers. My birth will come only after the sacrifice of 7, and the depression will follow. Sorry, but it was necessary to bring you full circle around to more of an awareness of commerce and its importance in your lives. (Hermes, god of commerce, industry: persona peace.) Also you had failed to revive the ancient Roman custom in February, the month of purification. For what other reason were you given the two presidents and the name "American" but as a reminder of this.

The depression could end only when my brother, who was ten years older than I, would die. It was the ninth death. Thoth was "lord of the city of eight,"[5-B] or 1 + 8 = 9. Quetzalcóatl ruled over the ninth hour. Odin hung himself for nine nights for the runes of wisdom. In necromancy there's an old belief that there are nine spheres the soul must pass through from life to death. The river Styx flows nine times around, separating the worlds of the living and the dead. The angelus rings nine times;[6-A] in the ninth hour Jesus yielded up his spirit and the earth shook; most ley lines are nine miles in length;[6-B] the Parentalia is nine days; in ancient Rome, a sacrifice was made to the dead nine days after burial; the Lemurs (the mischievous spirits of the dead) were told nine times in ritual to go; and the period of human gestation is roughly nine months. There are nine muses. Nine is a sacred sign in China. Ramadan in Islam is the ninth month of the lunar year. The most well-known magic square contains the numbers 1 - 9.[6-C]

Nine appears more than any other number in the Vedic Square (*twenty-one* times). The alphabet is broken into units of nine in modern numerology. The Seal of the City of the Dead shows nine captives—excruciatingly bound—kneeling in front of the god Anubis, manifested as a jackal. Clementine, whose shoes (feet) were number nine, is "lost and gone forever."[7-A] Maybe, and a cat has nine lives. It was on the ninth of April that Lee (phonetic LI) surrendered at Appomattox and the HMS Hermes was sunk. The atomic number of Einsteinium is 99.[7-B] The coven circle is nine feet in diameter,[7-C] making a radius of 4.5. A span, an English unit of length, is 9 inches, made from the belief that this is the distance from the thumb to tip of the little finger. The aluminum tip of the Washington obelisk is 9 inches, or 5 (digits) times 9 = 45. But for now remember only that Washington is simply washing-stone, in spite of what others might say about his name's derivation,[8-A] and the LA in Lavadaton and the LI in Lincoln,[8-B] signifying the Lupercalia and the Luperci respectively, and that there's a synchronicity.

Chapter One

A wretched thing
With polyethylene clothes,
A stained, frayed collar,
And a big, red nose.
Whatever happened to my youth?
Gone like a tooth.

The winter solstice had come on the 21st of December in 1990. Just before this, Seattle had been hit by the worst snowstorm anyone could remember. Just after—on Saturday morning, December 22—I climbed the hill to the Fourth Avenue library. Off to the side of a slick path, the thought came that somehow the footprints[9] in the snow were like flowers to a grave, a winter pall and all, an ancient ritual. I began looking around, ashamed, to see if someone had seen me hear these thoughts, the damned ideas of a schizoid. No, no one was watching. A book said later that December *21* was the day of the final entombment of Osiris, chief god of the underworld in Egyptian mythology.[10-A]

The boots—a dumb idea! It would have been safer to have worn sneakers, but the thermal underwear, Levis, shirt—once a Woolworth special—and padded jacket were cool. As in some incantation, 'twas colder than a witch's tit, a well-digger's ass, or a banker's heart. Radiation scars on my lower face and neck stuck out like red lines on a road map. I had walked a long distance over an icy area, retreating within; my eyes were vacuous, my expression was dissipated, burned out, appropriate somehow for the ice associated with death.

The long-winded signal to cross to the temple of knowledge was forever. What might have been taken for a sign of life was breath hitting the cold air, or it might have been taken for steam from something which 'ad just plopped. No! Not really. I'd had to feel better before dying.

Something was behind me. I turned, seeing a man silently snickering. Caught 'im looking me up and down as if he'd paid for a ticket and damned-well intended to get 'is money's worth at the wax museum. Well fuck him!

"What you laughing at?"

"Just laughing at...the crazy motorists, the way they're driving in this weather," he managed.

"Okay," not really convinced but willing to let it go.

He began to walk across the street ahead of me and muttered without looking back, "Okay, Frankenstein!"

"What did you say, creep?" I yelled.

He acted like he didn't hear me. Being a pussycat, I was almost happy he didn't respond. After all, he was a tough-looking mother, about twenty, or less than one-third my age. Yet I felt compelled to chase after him in rage, Frankenstein over the ice.[10-B]

"What did you say, creep?" I repeated.

"What?" he said turning.

"What did you say?"

"I was just laughing at what the drivers were doing. That's all."

"Okay," I repeated, letting it pass again.

A game player. Though saying no more, he'd lied and now was walking away, while I still seethed. What good was it for me to know I had, if nothing else, pushed him closer to an abyss being dug by his own mouth and actions? Or that in ridiculing or humiliating someone publicly, it's accounted to him (in the Talmud) that he has spilled human blood. This could be fifty years or more or never.

At the time, were it not for dignity, I might have agreed with him about being formed in the laboratory by the mistake of an incompetent assistant who'd taken parts from two piles so that they didn't seem to fit exactly, giving me jerky, uncoordinated movement and an ungainly appearance. Then, too, there was always the feeling that something happened before my birth. Well ah...not exactly what you're thinking, nor that three wise men from the east came bearing gifts, though in a sense this was true. It's more like something was held back—like maybe Lizzie Borden, with her crazy fondness for forty, had been a great aunt or that a passing gypsy had muttered something, half of it now fulfilled, the other half unheard. This was hardly an obsession since it didn't dominate me, nor was it delved on. Actually it was seldom thought of, but when doing so, it was as if pieces to a puzzle fit, yes and no.

Any uncles and aunts who may have known something had long since died. One brother who might have had some idea passed away a year or two ago. But being reticent by nature, he seldom discussed anything with me much more than the ranch news: Each year there was less profit in raising beef. There had not been enough snow, probably making a water shortage. Calving, branding, haying, or cleaning out irrigation ditches was keeping him busy. His inner feelings, thoughts, and suspicions couldn't have been more closely guarded at Fort Knox. The only surviving brother seemed to have escaped whatever it was. He not only looked physically different but also acted more outgoing and self-assured. Obviously he could tell me nothing. Besides, it would have been ridiculous for me to write and ask, "Hey bro, can't tell you what it is, but can you tell me what I want to know?"

Settled in the library, I caught up in my reading. There was that word *feral* again. I could remember in great detail looking it up, yet when it came to pronouncing it, there was a blank. Common sense should have said to avoid it—or even better, to forget it—it not being essential. But like the stutterer who motorboats on with the relentless "S", I plough ahead with "feral" (be), and invariably some asshole says, "I think you mean 'feral' (pier) or 'feral' (pet)." But are these people hated like the plague? No, rather they're hated so much that if it could be arranged they'd die of the plague. No matter how much effort is made, you'll never be more to them than a monkey trying to imitate a man. Oddly enough the ones who pronounce a word are the most savage. It figures then that when some of us use a dictionary, we're really praying.

Yeah I know, "Oh my goodness gracious!" which is just another form of snobbery.

Beneath *feral* was *Feralia*. These were the public ceremonies in ancient Rome to honor the dead on the last day of the Parentalia. Who cared? Why'd they put all this old crap in a modern dictionary? Anyway Parentalia must have had something to do with parents. Right? Thus it was only to gratify a Neanderthal ego and intelligence, to prove to myself I was smarter than I looked, that the trivial pursuit began.

At least that's the way it was way back then, and I often wonder *why me*? of my oh-dear delicate sensitivity, who wanted not so much of life other than to dig a hole, crawl in it, and hide. The answer lay in the ground rules set before entering the library that first day. Never would I be given relevant information thereafter than just prior to it there'd been some humiliation, ridicule, or depression. A nemesis? A reward? *Quid pro quo*? Who knows.

The Parentalia was a public period set aside to venerate the spirits of deceased family members, who were believed at this time to be able to leave Hades and visit the living. Decorations and other offerings were put on graves.[12-A] It began at 12:00 noon on the thirteenth ($4.5 + 4.5 = 9 + 4.5 = 13.5$, or 12:00 noon on the thirteenth) and ended on the twenty-first of February, the Feralia, when all the dead were honored and there was a feast. During the Parentalia, temple fires were extinguished, and most temples closed. No gods were honored this way, as the Romans had other days for that. You couldn't get married. Magistrates appeared without their insignias, and nearly all magisterial functions ceased. So what ya gonna do for nine full days whun everthang closed? Doan know.

> No coke ta take,
> No Bud to drink.
> All ya gotta do
> Is think?

But don't pooh-pooh all this, my friend, like saying, "Some shit!" The Romans took things seriously, and they believed the souls of the dead could cause them a lot of trouble in the coming year if they didn't do right by them. In fact, there was sometimes the sobering thought: If you can't beat 'em, you might as well join 'em.

The family included those presently living, those yet to be born, and those who had passed on. In many homes hung grim death masks of the Di Manes, the kindly shades.[12-B] * * * * And far off in China, Confucius (551–478 B.C.) would start a whole system of ethics and moral values based on ancestor worship, which seemed to work. Do not forget, too, that divine ancestors were venerated by the Celts.

The Parentalia took on an added importance because it was believed that during this period all punishment in Hades was suspended. All spirits of the dead could enjoy their rest and liberty. The friendly spirits then were most likely to have gone to their grave sites.

What caught my attention wasn't any of this, however. It was the fact that even though in ancient Rome February was the last month of the year, the period of celebration was from the thirteenth at noon to the twenty-first. And the twenty-first, the Feralia, just happened to be when I was born. It also was the birthday of my oldest brother, Ralph, who died at the height of his youth, like in some ancient, sacrificial rite meticulously executed in detail. And somehow my mother, father, and infant sister were involved in the overall mystery. What was wondered about— that there had been some unknown occurrence—began to crystalize. The last day of the Parentalia represented both the beginning and the end for me, my final years. For the first time I was on to something. But what?

Nearly nothing at this point was known. The Parentalia had to do with those who were dead, as well as those who were alive. There was a hunch that four other family members, now dead, were also directly involved someway. But was this really a hunch? Or was it a thinly disguised desire to have a place somewhere—if not in the sun, then a murkiness at the expense of relatives? Doubtful. Just trying to make it down the road seemed so long. Please, no heaven no hell, just let me cease. But for those who must have a heaven and hell, be prepared for a microchip, what with so many saints and sinners.

The day following the Feralia was called the Caristia. It was important, too, and it can't be compartmentalized off by itself, separated completely from the Parentalia. Hermes, by virtue of his caduceus, is logically the god of the Parentalia-Caristia. Ma and Pa Roman surely couldn't rest easy in their graves or the netherworld if their children—who had been the purpose of their lives—were fighting each other tooth and nail. The Caristia then was a time for living relatives to settle or smooth over disputes between themselves. Once having made peace with the dead and peace with the living relatives, they would find peace within themselves to begin another year.

By comparison, this makes our New Year's resolutions, such as giving up chocolate and exercising more, seem exceedingly selfish. Vain, inane, insane.

Thus if my brother and I were to be born on February 21, my father had to die on February 22 (2122).

People in ancient Rome and Greece were superstitious, sure, as we are (If you trip over a stone, go back and touch it; otherwise, it's unlucky), but they weren't dolts, shallow characters in Hollywood extravaganzas. Science hadn't progressed to the point it has nowadays. But certainly, other than this, they were every bit as keen and alert as we are. If they felt there were forces out there, which they chose to think of as gods, then perhaps there might have been and still are. Tidy, simplified explanations are nice to have, but we weren't there at the time. What we (me, you, or anybody else) know or think we know are often two different things.[13-A]

The reason marriages were banned and temples closed, etc., was that the days were considered to be ill-omened. Harper and Brothers, New York: J.J. Rose (*Religion in Greece and Rome*, 1959) states that the Lupercalia and Quirinalia (Festival of Quirinus, god of assembly, on February 17) were the only two days, however, the courts didn't meet and legislative assemblies were not held. The question might well be asked, "If the Di Manes were thought to have been so powerful and to be taken seriously, why did the Roman Empire decline?" A guess would be an erosion of Parentalia belief, vitality, and observance.

Chapter Two

Since Christian, Jew, or Muslim would likely give silent prayer to God on visiting the grave of a loved one, it seems reasonable—most men and women having religious and/or superstitious fears—that ancient Romans would have invoked Mercury. Pluto, the ruler of the underworld, was indifferent to prayer,[13-B] but Mercury traveled between the two worlds and would be able to see the spirits. To offer a small prayer to Mercury on behalf of the dead would have been honoring them, which was what the Parentalia was about—that and having the spirits' good will for the following year.

The idea that Mercury might have been petitioned in one's mind at least, when none of the other gods was during the Parentalia,[14-A] is reenforced by the fact that in ancient Athens between the eleventh and thirteenth of the month corresponding to February (some say February-March roughly), there was held a festival in honor of Dionysus[14-B] called the Anthesteria. The last day, known as the Day of Pots, cooked food was offered to Hermes (Mercury) on behalf of the dead.[15] Clearly the Greeks weren't as intense in their belief in the spirits of the underworld as the Romans.

In my journey, starting with the Feralia, into the unknown, there were no books to guide me, that is, ones which plotted some sort of course. I had to select what chronology and facts I, as a low-watt mystic, felt a sympathy with or an affinity to. Since no one can stand outside himself, there's no doubt that, in some cases, meaning that wasn't really there was read into things. Yet with equal certainty is the conviction of being right more times than wrong.

The word *herma*, meaning heap of stones, is probably where Hermes got his name. He invented measure, and stones in ancient Greek marked judgments or boundaries of property. A pile of stones (cairn) was symbolic of him, and it was considered good luck for a traveler to place a stone (or rock of ages) on the heap as he passed.

A tall stone, furthermore, was used as a grave marker, and frequently the grave mounds were of smaller stones. This is consistent with the belief that Hermes travels between two worlds. Hades, his uncle, was deaf to human prayers, took a shine to Hermes, and commissioned him to take his own place conducting the departing spirits to the underworld, a job that is considered a kindness to mortals. Hermes brings back souls to be born. Zeus, his father, made him a messenger[16-A] of the gods, maybe to keep him busy, for he is the shrewdest, the most cunning, the master of strategy. He had personal charm and was as much loved by the gods of the netherworld as those above it.

Since sleep is a brother to death, Hermes is also a sleep[16-B] and dream god, as well as a god of boundaries and the breaking of boundaries, crossroads, highways, and travelers. He was a fertility god, and through his son had a connection to androgyny. Hermes was the "darling" of servants,[16-C] peasants, and the simple people. Most times he would make them laugh, sometimes cry, but he never bored them. He was called Hermes the Helper, the protector. They had good reason to like him, of course, for though each of the gods had a favorite mortal now and then or a favored city perhaps (Athena: Athens), only a few gave a damn about mankind in general.

Most notable of these were Hermes, Prometheus, Demeter, Dionysus, and Aesculapius (Asclepius, though not an immortal, had godlike healing powers). From what we know, they were all sufferers except, it would seem, for Hermes. While bound, Prometheus will have his liver torn away each day by an eagle. Demeter will suffer in the winter, having been saddened that her daughter Persephone was now in Hades for one-third the year. Dionysus will suffer from the hacking away of his vines and the winter too. Aesculapius will be slain by Zeus.

Some say Prometheus was contemptuous of Hermes, the "messenger boy" who came to reason with him to yield to Zeus. Why? Did Prometheus know something about Hermes that Hermes didn't then know about himself? That Hermes must suffer and so was linked even closer to Prometheus than he could understand then? Certainly to be the god of sacrifice, Hermes, unless he was a hypocrite, must be willing to sacrifice himself and so become the god of reconciliation.

Since Hermes invented firesticks (some say fire, too) and sacrifice, he becomes a natural rival of Prometheus who, for giving fire to man, will suffer daily. Though others may see Prometheus or Dionysus as Christ, in the end neither one fits the picture. Prometheus wasn't the son of Zeus. Dionysus, though a benefactor of man at times, could also be cruel.

Loss and gain (luck), kindliness and mischief square with our concept of the reality of life. It has to be this way or measurement and commerce would be static.

Indeed, Hermes represents the world. In the profoundness of the divine, he likes different people for different reasons. This includes, on the one hand, saints, the righteous, and good. On the other, it includes thieves, rogues, and the irresponsible. If you pray to him, however, he will usually guide and protect you from those of the other hand—but not always. Sometimes he guides those of both hands to the path of chance, luck, and so learning, to be able to accept the bad with the good. Rarely, if ever, is Hermes, a death god, praised for being a god of deception, yet this facet is really a kindness to human beings. Few would want to know in advance the time and circumstances of their death or that of a loved one.

Hermes is the son of Zeus and Maia. Zeus is the supreme deity in Greek mythology. Maia is a nymph, the oldest of the seven daughters of Atlas and Pleione, and addressed by Zeus as the great goddess of the night. The name Maia is probably the Latin origin for the name of the month of May. There might be controversy over whether the month was named after this Maia or a more obscure one. For my purpose, it's important only that May can be traced back to the name Maia, which happens to be what Hermes' mother is called.

It is said that Hermes was born in a cave[17-A] on Mt. Cyllene[17-B] in Arcadia at *dawn* on the fourth of the month.[18] Thus the day and number were sacred to him, and he is a wind god. A multiple of four would seem to suggest him too. He was a precocious child, and by noontime of his day of birth he had spotted a tortoise; killed it; and by using the shell as a backboard and sheep gut (or reeds) for strings, he invented the lyre.[19] Soon he left his new plaything and was up to mischief stealing cattle[20] from his older and more powerful half brother Apollo. Hermes disguised his own tracks by fashioning out of twigs what resembled "a kind of snow-shoe." This might also have been done to prevent him from sinking in the sand[21]—sandals. He made the cattle walk backwards.[22]

When confronted, he denied it. Still it was clear to Apollo what Hermes had done. Zeus was amused by his new son's antics. Apollo was fiercely angry: He threatened to treat this infantile delinquent as an adult; to put him in prison forever; to cast him into Tartarus, a place of punishment in the lower world. But Hermes played the lyre and figuratively sang the magic words "goo-goo" to his older brother, whose anger waned like a wave into the sea. When it had stopped, Hermes gave him the lyre as a present. Here was a true con man, for then Apollo, in a shower fitting only for a god, gave his baby brother: (1) the cattle he had stolen; (2) the divine office over flocks; (3) a golden-winged staff that brought harmony to strife, which Hermes tested between two fighting snakes;[23] and finally (4) the gift of prophecy by teaching him how to interpret signs, omens, and occurrences,[24-A] as well as, some say, prediction from dice.[24-B] He stipulated, however, that *Hermes must never reveal the future in words*, as he could do.

IT'S SAID THAT HE WHO CAN UNDERSTAND OR INTERPRET
THESE SIGNS WILL BE CONSIDERED LUCKY.

Hermes obviously had figured out beforehand that Apollo and Zeus wouldn't be taken in by the ruse. If Hermes were precocious, he knew their character through and through and what the consequences would be. Yet by lying (deceiving) at day one, he was showing, paradoxically, an honesty and forthrightness. He was putting them on notice like a superstar belting out a song. Though he'd play by their rules thereafter, he wouldn't be taken in by the mishmash of self-deception in others. All pap to the contrary, he knew how the world was run. Indeed there must have been some truth to this, considering the gifts Apollo gave him and that Zeus made him a messenger and, on occasion, his traveling companion. This was a good choice since Hermes could hold those to whom he spoke spellbound—especially with words—and was the merriest of the Olympians.

As a pre-Greek pastoral god (in a sense ageless), Hermes was a protector of cattle and sheep, and he was considered the god of crops in many places. He's associated with vegetative deities and nymphs, and there are several myths concerning him as the wind in connection with the stars, sky, sun, and moon.

As a messenger of the gods, he's represented in early art as a powerful man with a beard, long tunic, broad-brimmed or winged hat, winged boots or winged sandals, and a shepherd's staff. In later art, he is depicted as a lithe, beardless young man with an intelligent and friendly bearing. Possibly because of his uncanny speed and flight, he was one of the patron gods of athletes. The Olympiad was at an interval of four years by which the Greeks measured time. He was a god of measurement and connected with any type of game where any one or combination of luck, agility, or cunning is required.

Certainly today base-stealer athletes, who have speed in their legs and larceny in their hearts, would be under him as well as the *fourth* estate, the postal service, airlines, merchant marines, prisoners, gypsies, and psychiatrists; for after all, "life is but a dream"—a dream to fulfill the unfulfilled dream of a parent. Failing that, it is to have a child or children to fulfill a dream, or to turn to a moment's respite in a dream that is a form of self-destruction.

He is capricious at times but mainly serves as a god of good fortune. Since he's identified with the Egyptian god Thoth, there's the syncretic Thoth-Hermes. Thoth was believed to be the inventor of writing and the patron of writers. He also had to do with magic, astrology, and judgment.[24-C] Hermes is the god of commerce and the patron of musicians (along with Apollo) and writers. He is said to have invented the alphabet (A-Z).

It seems the closest thing we have today to the Parentalia is the three-day Memorial Day weekend on the last Monday in May. The Lemures (unfriendly spirits of the dead) were appeased on May 9, 11, and 13. Newer books agree that May 15 was celebrated by merchants in honor of Mercury and Maia, while older ones25 use the date of May 25. This contradiction probably is explained by the calendars used. Though possibly Maia might have been honored on May 15 for reasons having nothing to do with the fact she was one of the Pleiades, they appear in the sky in the middle of May, signifying that good weather has come again.

Chapter Three

On August 17, 1924, the *San Francisco Examiner* published an article suggesting that the drawings on some rocks on a hill about thirty miles south of Yerington, Nevada, predated Egyptian hieroglyphs. This so-called assumption was based on the alleged opinions of experts who had studied the writing and drawings. In time, however, the work was found to be that of earlier Paiute Indians.

My first knowledge of the area near Yerington came from a *Nevada* magazine July/August 1993 article by Harry A. Chalekian, titled "Yesterday: Was the Garden of Eden Located in Nevada?" In the same issue of the magazine was an article on snakes. This might be expected since the Garden of Eden had a serpent. What's harder to explain, however, is that the cradle-of-civilization deception was typically Hermes, occurring four to five years before the excavation at Ras Shamra, and so four to five years before my birth at Yerington.

Since the *San Francisco Examiner* was a Hearst paper, William Randolf Hearst, Sr. (whose father made a fortune *mining*), aided and abetted the 1924 journalism.

Name	Common	Difference
HERMES	HERS	ME
HEARST	HERS	AT

HERMES AT HEARST

Patricia Hearst, born in the Parentalia on February 20, 1954, was one of five daughters of Randolph A. Hearst. She was kidnapped from her Berkeley apartment on February 4, 1974, and took part in two bank robberies. Both she and I had attended the University of California at Berkeley though at a different time.[26]

Topaz (AZ) Lake is southwest of Yerington, and it's in both southern Douglas County, Nevada, and Mono County, California.

The name *topaz* is thought to come from a Greek word meaning "cross." The stone, symbolic of the planet Mercury in astrology, was—and perhaps still is in some places—believed to prevent the wearer from sleepwalking.[27] This is curious as Hermes is both a god of sleep and of wayfarers. The gems vary in color, but the one usually thought of is a tawny yellow.

Irrigation ditches, nearly straight as leylines, run toward the lake. Sometimes if the sun is right, the water in them is this color; other times, a reddish brown; or most often, clear with darting minnows fighting the flow. When the water's held back by boards, it seeps into the fields, eventually making the hay grow and the cattle fat. But long before this the barriers are removed, and some of the water in an ancient rite flows back into the ditch, as it has already several times before on ranches up the valley, touching myriad things: the decay of vegetation; crushed grasshoppers, bugs, flies, and other insects; dead field mice; the remains of birds; snakes; the nearly burned-out carcasses of horses and cattle; the droppings of a thousand creatures; and now the fresh sacrifice of a few minnows. It's tainted water that carries with it both a blessing and a curse, since it travels between two worlds. Because of this, my father didn't want me ever to swim in the cross-boundary lake of Topaz. For this reason, too, he never thought the barren hills surrounding the lake would ever become valuable property. He'd been born in California; I, in Nevada. The Hermetic overtones of the slot machines nearly at the lake's edge—the kinship of gambling and death—would have escaped him, but expressed as the "uncertainty of life" he would have understood it. He was a dumb-jerk rancher who couldn't see past his nose—or maybe he was not that at all and knew more than I'll ever know or hope to know. For one hot summer day I went swimming in it. In any case, he couldn't have prevented this. The game had long since started, and whoever heard of a batter—once a ball has been hit inside the baseline—refusing to travel around the *diamond or square*, touching all the bases?

The *Reno Evening Gazette* and *Time* magazine carried articles. I missed these, and just as well, as the Haman-Fairfield claim would have meant nothing to me years ago. Then just recently the April (fourth month) 1991 *Nevada* magazine published a brilliantly written story called "Cloud Rustlers" by Richard Moreno. The content, the locale, and the timing of it was itself another sign. For when I begin to have doubts of the mystique and my spirits sink, it's as if being fed more information to reassure me of not being insane, at least not completely.

In 1947, Dick Haman, architect-rancher, and his partner, Freeman Fairfield, who made millions drilling oil in Long Beach, California, filed a claim to the water clouds over their 12,300 acres of land near Topaz Lake. The two men had hoped to seed the clouds with dry-ice pellets. It was both a clever and cuckoo idea at the same time—not as far out as persons putting in claim stakes for vast stretches of ocean outside of territorial waters—but certainly Haman's belief that the water was his that might have fallen on the property of others was stretching things a bit.

Arizona (AZ) Cloud Ropers, Inc. planned to lasso the clouds and rustle them off from Nevada to Arizona. The clouds were, figuratively, milk cows, and Cinnabar[28] Ike, a folksinger, wrote lyrics about cloud rustlers, but perhaps the real significance of the happening was missed entirely. He was singing and playing on a guitar, the grandchild of the lyre. The cattle Hermes had stolen from his brother Apollo, the sun god,[29] have long since been thought to be rain clouds. My story, some of which takes place at or near Topaz, the Mercury Topaz, is documentation of occurrences, omens, and signs before and after the Haman-Fairfield affair. Moreover, my father—who lived in Topaz—was a brand inspector.

Chapter Four

For some, keeping clean is partly busy work to feel time's not being wasted. It's money in the bank; it's being ready—to pass an inspection, to get praise. It's to avoid judgment, the damning criticism by your peers that on at least one occasion you had bad breath, dandruff, stinky feet, armpit armor, or smelly clothing. They'll never let you forget this, that you polluted their space, even if it happened before the flood. So better it is in the long run to change your friends than to change your clothes.

Often, keeping clean has the opposite effect, making people feel uncomfortable for having been so profane as to cause you more work to clean up the area, for just living and breathing. It gives them anxiety in knowing that death is just a fart away.

The whole damn batch of clothes could have been washed almost effortlessly at the laundromat every week or so, but this will not do. It has to be done on a daily basis. Why? Oh, to be ready to go instantly. To go where? Oh, just to be ready to go and to perform ablutions, to atone for the sins of the day. The cleaner you are, the more sins you have washed away. If you have no sins for that day then for yesterday, for which has already been atoned—okay, sins two or three years from now, which is money in the bank. In the old days society would have isolated itself from people like this by sending them off to a monastery or convent. Science with all its technology will never develop a cheaper fuel than guilt, but there are few monasteries and convents left. So what yuh gonna do with 'em when you can't cure 'em in their youth? The answer is nothing.

Old age will right things. The body eventually rebels saying, "Fuck you!" that it's just too tired to worry about all this nonsense, the silly rigmarole. The venetian blinds with their hundred or so slats, back and front two hundred sides, become nursing notes that show your daily progress in curing yourself, which is really old age. So keeping clean could be the most obvious reason that you don't want to get ostracized and/or all of the above.

I'd gone down the hall to take a shower. When I returned the digital clock had just come up with the red numbers 444, like on a slot machine. I know what you're going to say even before you say it: This ain't no burning bush, a stigmata, or a parting of the Red Sea. But being a small fish, maybe that was all that was forthcoming. I might have been a small fry, but there was still a huge doubt. It would take more than a parlor trick, if indeed that's what it was. And it was certainly cheap, because whoever it was could have managed a few nickels down below.

The blinds banging woke me up early in the morning. Irritated, I thunked down the window as if it were a guillotine carrying all the way to the sill of the window below. The old lady the previous day had complained to the manager—instead of coming to me—that food was being tossed down to the pigeons on the flat roof her window opened up on, and that she was sick, sick, sick of the pigeon-shit smell that wafted through the open window and that it was the health hazard.

It was the first time in two years I ever recall closing the window. The slats of the blinds always lay like horse latitudes on a map, flyspeckled and dusty. And though the room itself may not have been hermetically sealed, it was so close to it that it really didn't make any difference. The *Seattle Times* for December 28, 1990, reported:

Since midnight Washington was experiencing winds
20-to-40 miles an hour as the temperature combined to
create a wind-chill factor of 10 degrees below zero.

Yet for me this still wasn't enough. That morning I went to the Fourth Avenue library to check out a story heard only vaguely a few weeks before but which seemed to be nagging at me, something about a rock dropping on a car. Nothing more came to mind. This is what was learned.

Early Saturday morning on December 8, 1990, Lester L. Miller, a fifty-five-year-old Lynnwood, Washington, man, traveled to work at Boeing Company in his 1990 Honda CRX on State Highway 525. When he reached a point below the 148 Street Southwest overpass, a rock that weighed 16 (8 + 8) pounds came crashing through his *wind*shield killing him. The car skidded off the highway and plunged down a 64-foot (8 x 8) culvert.[30] The rock was thought to have been part of the landscaping close to the overpass. Later two boys, one twelve and the other thirteen, were arrested and set to be tried.[31]

Remember now, Hermes is a herald of death, and he's said to have invented measure. In addition to being a god of night, of commerce (the Mercury dime),[32] and travelers, he is also a wind god, a god of flight, of roads (public safety on roads), of crossroads, and is said to have cleared the roads of rocks. Because of this, piles of stones (herms) were made along the roads as monuments to him. He is associated with squareness and roundness, nowadays represented by a car's chassis (Latin *capsa*, a box) with four wheels (five tires).

34

So we have darkness, a traveler, commerce, flight, highway, pound, wind, rocks, overpass, mischief of two boys, double trouble, and at least five multiples of four. Chris Brecher, a talk show host for King Radio, had a caller who wondered what two boys would be doing up at 4:00 A.M.? At this point I was convinced, but you probably won't be. How about this then? The license plate of Mr. Miller's Honda CRX (45)[33] read: AGE LES.

Chapter Five

No one knows for sure how the state of Maine got its name. Most feel it's probably French in origin. An ancient province of western France was called *Maine,* and the city of *Le Mans,* or La Maine, is well-known today. But how did the word Maine or Le Mans originate in France? France was part of the Roman Empire. A good possibility is that the name came from *Di Manes* (sometimes called *Di Parentes*), "the good ones," a collective name for spirits of the dead honored during the Parentalia in ancient Rome. The *Di* suggests a godly cast.

"Oh, but you can't just jump from France to Italy like that to make your case," you protest.

"Oh but I can, the same way I can go from Salem, Massachusetts, to the state of Maine.[34] But even then it wouldn't be jumping, for Maine was part of Massachusetts until 1820 when it was admitted to statehood on the Ides of March, the day about which Julius Caesar was warned. More importantly he was connected to a day which fell within the Parentalia, and that day, in my opinion, augured the coming of Jesus. This will be explained in more detail later.

For my money, both the witch hunters and the so-called witches in seventeenth century New England were right in that they sensed something, but neither knew exactly what and so their imaginations and actions took over from there. It wasn't what Cotton Mather did or didn't stand for that was important but rather the day and month of his birth and the day and month of his death, the clues we were given but failed to understand.

When a new town was built in Italy, a round pit[35] was dug, and a stone called a *lapis manalis* was placed in it. Then, varying in dates from town to town, the stone would be removed to allow the *Di Manes* to go between the worlds.[36] The *Di Manes* were usually benevolent but could be angered if not shown proper respect, withdrawing their support for the coming year. In very ancient times, blood sacrifices were made at these sites. Then some time later it's probable the sophistification of gladiator combats were instituted to replace this, becoming commercial, as has Christmas and Easter, which are also linked to blood sacrifice.

Daniel Chase Duren, my maternal grandfather, was born and grew up in Maine. Most everyone figured Chase was a family name. He married Annie L. Cameron.[37] A rough and inaccurate genealogy sheet handed down to me said Annie's mother's maiden name was McDonald.

Could we have been related to the Chases of the Chase-Manhattan bank? Was this just ol' McDonald who had a farm or the granddaddy of the founder of the billions-upon-billions sold hamburger chain; world-wide and now spreading even to Japan with *etai-etai-O*? Shur I'd na sa no tae mutch walth.

It's unknown where Daniel and Annie married, but it was probably in the Dakota Territory, where my mother Frances May was born.[38] Later they moved to Montana[39] and had three more daughters: Nellie Isabelle on May 27, 1890; Edith M. in March 1892; and Dollena Dorothy on March 15, 1900.[40] Genevieve was born in Washington around 1904. In about 1906 the family moved to California where Granddad lived the last forty years of his life, working at least some years before retiring as a pumper for Standard Oil Company.

The few times I, as a young squirt, saw Granddad, he seemed ancient. All over his face and the back of his hands were sun and liver spots, now his legacy to me. We'll both have lichen on our tombstones.

He and Ida May, his second wife, visited us in Bakersfield for a few weeks one spring. I was interested in knowing about him and asked what he could tell me about the wild west, cowboys, and Indians. Did he ever travel in covered wagons? He answered these questions without saying much, which is probably why not much can be remembered today of what he said. Yet now, forty-five years later, on reading his death certificate, I see the doctor listed under other conditions "senility." This then probably accounted for it, or I've reached that stage myself. Norma Beth, my cousin who knew him when he was younger, described him as follows:

> I remember Granddad very well. He was a wonderful old man, with a terribly good disposition. He wasn't very tall, but your brother Robert is practically a carbon copy of him in looks. When we were living in Long Beach, and he and Ida, his second wife, would visit us, he would go down to the barber shop for a shave every morning. He was also rather slow in speech but liked to talk.... I'm sure you remember Ida, a slow-talking, slow-moving Southern belle from Tennessee.

Ida had a phobia that she couldn't sleep without a light burning. And when we visited them one time when I was very young at their small farm in Woodlake, California (before they had retired at Long Beach), she would make toast for the whole family for a week or more at a time, which seemed mighty peculiar. Who in his right mind would want to eat toast for breakfast made up a week earlier? I was certain then that some of my insanity came from her. As a little shit, I hadn't reasoned that genetically she and I weren't related. About the time of figuring it out, I'd already locked into this illogically somehow. It wasn't until nearly a half century later that an old timer told me people living out in those days often toasted loaves of bread to slow down the molding process. So it was nice to know there wasn't the cross of madness to bear after all but just my own stupidity.

Yet there are things which happen in life that are little understood and worse than either. With more maturity, I now see Ida as a pleasant woman who never gave me a hard time. Possibly because she had sort of a stooped posture; was slow moving; and, to the best of my recollection, had curly, grey and orange-red hair, she was patronized sometimes behind her back, perhaps undeservedly.

Chapter Six

My paternal grandparents, George and Elizabeth, I never knew. They were returning from a visit to England when he, then sixty, had a heart attack aboard ship, either dying at sea or shortly after in New York in 1910 on November 22, or 21 days past November 1, equivalent to the Feast of the Dead. His body was brought back and buried in the cemetery at Coleville, California. My grandmother lived on until she was eighty-four in the white house they had built nearly sixty years before with "its picket fence and lovely green orchard surrounded by a hedge of hope, reminiscent of Elizabeth's home in England." Here at least three of their six children were born, including my father Frank William.

According to the 1900 census, George Chichester was born in England in 1850 (the tombstone reads July 3, 1850); his U.S. immigration was 1873. Both dates are difficult to substantiate.[41]

The dates of birth of my great grandparents Mary Anne (Ann) Moon[42] and Henry Mills are presently unknown. Ditto for the day of their marriage. What's known is that they lived in Mereworth,[43] East Peckham, County of Kent, England. LDS records show—unless I missed someone someplace—that they had ten children. Below are Mereworth christening dates except for Alice *Alexander* (sic), who was christened at Halling, and the only one whose middle name was given:

I.	Ellen.	.October 21, 1838
II.	Anne	.November 22, 1840
III.	Thomas	.February 19, 1843
IV.	Mary.	April 27, 1845 (snake)
V.	Williams.	.October 31, 1847
VI.	Elizabeth.	March 10, 1850
VII.	Frederick.	January 18, 1852
VIII.	Matilda.	.June 11, 1854
IX.	Emma.	January 20, 1856
X.	Alice Alexander. . . .	.June 25, 1865

Elizabeth Mills Chichester was my grandmother. Though a sixth child, she was also the fourth of seven daughters and was born on the fourth of February 1850. Her father, Henry, was a farmer and bailiff, and Mary Moon Mills went to registrar John Leeds on March 5, 1850, to have Elizabeth's birth recorded. Mary indicated what she told him was true by making her "X."

Both Elizabeth Mills and George Chichester were 21 and living in England at the time of the Chicago fire, which began around 8:00 P.M. on October 8, 1871, when Mrs. O'Leary's cow (Hermes, dominion over cattle and inventor of fire) is suspected of kicking over a lantern so that straw caught fire in a barn. Fanned by *winds* described as "gale-force,"[44] the fire continued to burn until October 10. Only a few buildings survived, but rebuilding was quick.

George Chichester was twenty-two or twenty-three when he came to the U.S. in 1873, and Elizabeth Mills came in 1874. Where exactly each lived is unknown. Presumably one or both lived in or near the Chicago area or possibly Elgin, Illinois, twenty-five to thirty miles away.

Two of Elizabeth's older sisters, Mrs. Mary Hardy and Mrs. Silvester, had already settled in Antelope Valley, California. So immediately after their marriage in Elgin on September 24, 1877, George and Elizabeth set out for there. Elizabeth would be near her kin, whom she missed, and they would be able to advise and give some assistance to the couple in getting started.

It was probably October that their train climbed slowly over the ground that those in the Donner Party had walked and struggled over thirty years before. Could they have had any inkling of this at the time? Had they ever even heard of the earlier pioneers, or did it just pass unnoticed? The numbers in Elizabeth's life[45] would lead me to think that she had, and because so much of George's life is clouded in mystery, he might have been very well aware of it, too.

They wouldn't have known then, of course, that my father, their fourth child, would be born during a Mercury period (MP) or that he would die on February twenty-second, the anniversary that the first of four rescue parties either arrived at or left Donner Lake.

In 1958 Elsie Chichester, an aunt, described my grandparents' journey as follows:

> The year 1877 was an important one also in the life of the nation, which had just celebrated its first one hundred years. The gold stake, driven by Leland Stanford at Promontory Point, Utah, marking the completion of the first railroad to be laid across our continent had occurred only eight years before. It was on this same railroad that George and Elizabeth made their way west. After some

ten days of weary train travel, the Chichesters reached the frontier town of Reno, where they changed to the Virginia and Truckee railroad that brought them to Carson City. Here they boarded a stagecoach pulled by four horses, and traveled fifty miles south to Coleville.

The description below, as well as that previously of their home, is also Elsie Chichester's:

There were opportunities waiting for the young couple in Coleville. The booming mining camps of Aurora and Bodie lay to the south of them. Their populations, taken together in 1880, have been estimated at about ten thousand people. Supplies for these camps had to be freighted in great wagons drawn by sixteen to twenty animals, either from the railroad or across Sierra Nevadas from Folsom, California. Part of the freight wagons, those bound for Aurora, turned eastward and went by way of Wellington, Nevada. Those bound for Bodie came through Coleville. So at Coleville the Chichesters set what was called in the early days a "station." Here were food yards for the animals that pulled the freight wagons and rooms and meals for the teamsters who drove them, as well as for the general traveling public who rode in the Concord stages.... After a few years the Chichesters sold their station and bought a ranch just south of Coleville.

Here my father will be born and later two of his brothers. Ralph A., if the twins are alphabetized, will be a fifth child, while Ralph Haven Chichester, his nephew and namesake (though a second child), will be the first of four sons.

These were the children of George and Elizabeth:

1. Bruce H.   April 1879 – 1947
2. Mabel Louise (snake)   July 8, 1881 – March 30, 1888
3. Annie C. (Mullin)   May 12, 1883 – January 11, 1914
4. Frank William   September 10, 1888 – February 22, 1958
5. Ralph A.   December 20, 1890 – January 20, 1901
6. Roy G.   December 20, 1890 – 1967

The house faced the road, which is now 395, close in front. In February 1934, it "burnt" down. When it had cooled enough where a search could be made, they found my grandmother's body. Her head had been crushed, and none of her jewelry could be found in the ashes. Other than this, there was little to go on. She had lived by herself. It could have been an accident, but you would have had a hard time convincing the people of this then living in the area. Most thought it was the work of a murderer and thief passing in the night. While suspecting this is true too, I do know one fact they missed. She had died four to five days, or exactly halfway into the Parentalia, before my fifth birthday; i.e., I was still four to five years old. Ralph died five years following her death[46] (See Book II, 308-B).

Years later Aunt Elsie wrote wondering if I, then about fifty, knew that my grandfather had sailed before the mast[47] at fourteen from Devonshire, England; spent much of his youth at sea; and that my grandmother had been a nurse. I hadn't. This struck her, as well as me, as curious that after going into the army at seventeen, I'd request and be given a first duty station aboard an army hospital ship and following that, spending many years in medical work and one-third or more of my life sailing.

She previously had written that George's and Elizabeth's home had been "fifty miles from a railroad where the only connecting link with the outside world was an unimproved road." My grandfather "used to make one trip a year to Carson City with a big wagon and there purchase all the supplies for the family that they needed, except those raised locally or on their ranch." When his sons expected his return, "they mounted horses and headed north waiting for the dust of his wagon on Alkali Hill. Somewhere in the vicinity of Alkali Lake, they would meet and escort him home." And somewhere in this vicinity, too, the mustangs ran wild.

I wondered if George, as he sat sweating and driving his team, ever made the comparison that his provisioning for a year was like when he sailed, the ships taking on supplies for a year-or-more voyage in those days.

This mysticism, seen in George and Elizabeth's occupations and mine, seems to have happened too in another way beyond my ken, a hecklingly vague association with three famous men. The similarity that each was born in 1809 first occurred to me in 1948, nothing more. Then forty-four years or so later, I had the conviction that I was on to something about them but not knowing just what. There's no presumption of my being in their league; nor with equal sureness, I don't see any one of them as a father figure.

They were born within twenty-five days of each other: Edgar Allan Poe on January 18 and both Charles Darwin and Abraham Lincoln on February 12.[48-A]

Poe's parents were *actors, playing in Boston at the time of his birth*. Though undoubtedly a genius, he had a neurotic instability. His poems and stories show he was preoccupied with morbid and bizarre themes. Yet *The Raven* is possibly the most widely read poem in the English language today. The first draft was outlined in 1844 and published in 1845, a snake year (SY). One source gives the month as February.

Darwin suffered from bad health for "forty-five years" following his trip on the *HMS Beagle*.[48-B] There's no way of knowing for certain what caused his symptoms. But historians generally agree it was probably Chagas' disease along with psychological problems, signs of which seem to have been present before he sailed.

Lincoln, whose forbears are believed to have come from Massachusetts, had a personality which alternated between low and high moods. He married Mary (4) Todd (4) on November 4, 1842. They had four boys, only one of which survived to adulthood. Lincoln was the sixteenth president and *would be shot while attending a performance at Ford's (four) theater by an actor* on the fourth month, fourteenth day in 1865. Mrs. Lincoln throughout most her life was high-strung and had fits of temper. After his assassination, she eventually was declared insane and committed to an asylum for a time.

It was as if in order for each of these men to achieve greatness or renown he had to pay the pendulum price at the other extreme of some psychological or physical problem, which paradoxically might have aided him to some extent, too.

Again, I've no notions about being in the big leagues, yet we had some things in common, e.g., our birthdays were in a relatively close spread of thirty-four days, mine being nine days from Lincoln's and Darwin's. Both of Poe's parents died before he was three; Darwin's mother, when he was eight; and Lincoln's mother, when he was nine. None of us had religious affiliations to any extent, if at all, yet not precluding a belief in God. Though Poe, Darwin, and Lincoln were technically dragons, they came very close to being earth-snakes. The snake cycle occurs every twelve years. Within this classification are five types; each of these comes around every sixty years. I, being born in 1929, one hundred and twenty years after Poe, Darwin, and Lincoln, would be an earth-snake. A rule is that snakes born in warmer months will be happier, but it's not ironclad. Alfred Tennyson, born August 6, 1809, was unstable, a drunk, morbidly shy, extremely sensitive to criticism, and an "indefatigable walker" (*Collier's Encyclopedia*). My personal life, as with these four men, will be clouded.

In addition my maternal grandfather, possibly a snake, was a fourth son and fourth child. My father was a fourth sibling. I was the fourth son and fourth surviving child[49] of five children and would be brought up for the first seventeen years of my life by an aunt who was the fourth of five daughters and an uncle who was the fourth son and sixth child. I was born in Nevada, a state destined to be the gambling capital of the world, at 10:00 P.M. on February 21, *ten* years to the day after the birth of my brother Ralph.

My mother died on the twenty-sixth of February, four to five days following my birth, and was buried on the twenty-eighth. According to a newspaper article, she had come down with influenza *ten* days prior to her death. Other contributing causes listed on his death certificate were bronchopneumonia and my birth (*Febris, Februa, Februus*), which was followed by the Ras Shamra revelations and the Great Depression.[50] The latter didn't end until *ten* years later, the year Ralph *Haven* Chichester died. Could this have been some sort of sacrifice? Possibly. For if Ralph were the haven (refuge, shelter, port, harbor), I was the raven,[51] both names having "ave," hail and farewell.

Why the five tens? My father, born September *10*, 1888,[52] was forty years old at my birth. If there were some sort of scheme or logic to this, wouldn't my mother have been forty years old, too? Ralph's birth certificate, however, says she was twenty-nine at his birth (and so thirty-nine at mine). This is substantiated by a newspaper article and also her tombstone which reads "Frances 1889–1929." A person doesn't argue with a gravestone where a line between two dates makes everything right with God—the gravestone to which men and women in ancient times spoke, feeling that it was a conductor for communication between the two worlds. Hermes, persona communication.

In a way this was a relief, for had she been forty too, I'd feel irrevocably locked into a fate, having no idea what it meant.

Still a boundary had been broken with my birth or shortly after, and now it was necessary symbolically to cross another, though I'm sure the two aunts who brought me by car from Yerington, Nevada, to Long Beach, California, when I was just a few days old,[53] were not aware of what they were doing, which was much the same as a Christian child being baptized.

Chapter Seven

It's funny looking back. The script had been written long before my birth, so being judgmental is ridiculous. But as a "know-nothing" for the first sixty-one or sixty-two years, I'll write with a critical eye, as things were seen then.[54]

In Shakespeare's *Julius Caesar*, the soothsayer bids Caesar to "beware of the Ides of March." For some who are superstitious, this has become an unlucky day, much like Friday the Thirteenth. The significance of the thirteenth possibly comes from the ancient Roman calendar[55] too. For by definition, the Ides are the fifteenth of March, May, July, and October and the thirteenth of the other months.

Dollena Dorothy Duren (444) Fry, my aunt, was born on the Ides of March 1900, and Burton Carlson (B.C.) Fry, my uncle, was born of the thirteenth (a Saturday) of October 1900. Though not on the Ides, it was a day which seems to have been almost a calculated counterbalance. Burt was the fourth son and sixth child, while Dot was the fourth of five daughters. They would take me to bring up, and, though being told my origin at an early age, I'd come to think of them as Mom and Dad and of Robyn, their daughter, as my sister. Curiously the only thing retained from this early period after living out of suitcases for years is this slightly battered card of measurement:

Four years old and Oh! so tall,
Put your height upon the wall,
When another Birthday comes,
See how big you have become.

45

Certainly Long Beach had been written into the script with the very respectable earthquake[56] killing 133 and injuring thousands, on March 10, 1933, the day "Old Ironsides" got damaged and Lemuria-and-Lupercalia Mayor Anton Cermak was buried, as much as it had been written into the lives of millionaire Freeman Fairfield and billionaire[57] Howard Hughes, a flier, a loner who did much for Nevada and built the "Hughes H-4 Hercules,"[58] commonly called the "Spruce Goose,"[59] which sits at Long Beach at this time. Having *eight* engines, the "flying boat" could carry 700 passengers. A considerable part of it is constructed of wood. Hughes, born on December 24, 1905,[60] was a wood-snake. Both the snake and the goose hiss, and the goose has a long, snaking neck.

Dad quit Shell Oil Company in Long Beach. In June 1935 we traveled to Avenal, California, where he worked for Perkins and then Haliburton Oil Company.

Both *Avenal* and *Nevada* are Spanish names. Avenal means a field sown with oats, or an oat field. Nevada means snow-clad, snowy land, snowy; take your pick. At first there doesn't seem to be much similarity in the two other than Avenal and certain parts of Nevada can be hot hell-holes some summers. But when you look closely at the names, you find that five of the letters in each are the same:

A V E N A - D
A V E N A - L

D - L, devil? L - D, living deity? Mercury's temple in Rome is said, by one author, to have been on Aventine Hill. Since weather authorities begin and end their day with liturgies about the weather such as, "It don't supposed to be this warm today," let's settle on Mercury, the god of measurement, gamblers, and commerce.

La Neva is the name of Avenal High School's yearbook. Besides that, a fair share of those living in Avenal spend some of their amusement money at gaming tables in Nevada. It's hardly a one-way street though with relatives both in California and Nevada. The latter spend a small fortune taking their kids to Disneyland (dreams) and out-of-state ball-park meccas (games). When it boils down, we're talking about commerce in the form of travel, food, rest, and amusement. It's not money wasted; there's much in return. It fights off boredom, which is always safe, well scrubbed, robot-like, lawful—and insidious. We don't just have crime on our streets but a pendulum which has swung back with a vengeance.

Perhaps the biggest boredom of all in life comes from no love. It's great to receive but often costs something of oneself to give. Here's an expenditure, a drain, and so money in a sense. Yet love is like a bicycle or puppy: There's only one year it means something to a kid. You can try the following year to make up for having missed by buying a thousand bicy-cles and puppies, but they're not the same as when the need was most. The Dance of Love, both for young and old, is the most important of all commerce. If you miss your timing, the piece will never sound just right. The song goes wrong not because there was a lack of love in most cases but in expression of the timing.

Maybe this is the best reason there's no waiting period and no blood tests and why marriage ceremonies are wide open to improvisation in Nevada. It's the spontaneity, the feeling that by improvisation the couple will be jinxing the clutch of planned boredom that ruined their parents' marriages. Most states have overlooked or really don't understand what the lovers are saying: "Let's just do it!"

The name St. Valentine is associated with two martyrs having the same name, or possibly it is the same man, a confusion of facts which are shaky at best.

One story is that Emperor Claudius II felt that married men made poor soldiers because they didn't want to leave their families, and, once leaving them, they were too careful, remembering they had obligations. This, if not the same, is similar to the recent situation where the marine corps said it would take only single men on a first enlistment, incurring a political flap that resulted in superseding instructions.

The answer seemed simple enough for Claudius II: Abolish marriage, which he did. But Valentine, bishop of Interamna, now Terni, went to the emperor's door:

> Knock! Knock!
> "Who's there?"
> "Marion."
> "Marion who?"
> "Marion makes it legal!"

(This joke's even older than you thought. Right?)

Valentine, being rather bullheaded (if you'll pardon the papal pun) continued to perform marriages and so was beheaded, becoming the legendary patron saint of engaged couples, young people, beekeepers (honey being one of the offerings to Hermes), and travelers.

Some say this took place on February 24, about A.D. 269 or 270. Yet Valentine's Day today is February 14, one of the days in the pagan Parentalia when no marriages were to be performed, and, of course, there's a closeness of the Parentalia and May, when it was considered unlucky to marry. Maybe because of the head-chops, it's okay now to marry on February 14, or maybe it was rather a dire warning, the blood-letting on the ground like the handwriting on the wall.

Possibly because of the nonreligious customs that became associated with St. Valentine's Day, the Catholic Church stopped celebrating it as a feast day, and it's no longer on the Roman rite calendar. So who's winning? And who are the good guys and the bad guys? You don't have enough to worry about without someone playing head-games, right? But you'll think about it.

The dubious distinction of being the divorce capital of the world has been hung on Nevada. Did you know that in 1992, there were nearly ten times more marriages than divorces?[61] Now you may have wondered what this is leading up to, and in truth I've wondered that myself.

There are more marriages in Nevada on St. Valentine's Day than at any other day in the year. Second place might go to President's Day weekend.[62] Why these days when it's so damn cold, some Christmas bills are yet to be paid, and income-tax payments are coming up in April? The answer, in my opinion, lies in the fact that both St. Valentine's Day[63-A] and President's Day lie within the Parentalia. The Parentalia is as inseparable from Mercury as is Nevada, which has some special dispensation—maybe.

Las Vegas has the greatest number of marriages—"up to eight hundred couples"—on St. Valentine's Day. Of course, it's Nevada's largest city, but don't discount Vega, May 15, Caesar's Palace, or the Luxor.[63-B] And don't forget that Nevada's first reported marriage, occurring in 1853, was done with a worn *cookbook* in place of a Bible and that in each case a *silver* spoon wrapped around the fingers, stood for a ring.[64] But isn't Nevada really four fingers and a thumb?

In Latin Avéna means reed, straw, or Shepherd's Pipe–the latter being a symbol of Hermes. Perhaps then it wasn't by chance that Avenal became the location of a state prison, a place for those who have broken boundaries and are under his concern. Nor was it by chance the Desert Bighorn sheep became the adopted animal of Nevada in 1973. The ram is another Hermes symbol, and Avenal once—before the drilling (not too dissimilar from mining) and breaking of earth boundaries for oil in the nearby Kettleman Hills—was a pastoral place with flocks of sheep.

It would simplify things to be able to stick to the one god Hermes. But the fact of the matter is that the similarities of Hermes, Jesus, and Quetzalcóatl, are far greater than their differences. As with Hermes, the number four is significant in Aztec (AZ) religion. Two very ancient gods had four sons, from whom all the other gods sprang. The universe was created and destroyed four times, and every person is assigned to one of four directions. Each direction represents one of the four gods. Quetzacóatl, being one of these, is also "Lord of the House of Dawn" (remember dawn was when Hermes was born) and the wind god called Ehecatl, whose calendar name is ce[65] acatl (one reed).

A V E N A - Shepherd's pipe made of corn (Spanish).

A V E N A - Reed (Latin).

A C A T L - Reed (Aztec).

The first Footprints in Avenal, after the native Indian, were Hispanic. When younger, I recall only two or three Mexican wives living there. Given then *Avena, Avena, Acatl*, it's interesting that today Hispanics are now Avenal's largest minority.

Compared to Long Beach, Avenal the summer of '35 was a nearly beaten desolation of withering trees which looked like stage props[66]—camouflaging, pretending, but not having even the dismal hope of a mirage. Refusing to drop when they seemed dead, they will be resurrected someday to a place alongside the willow and poplar at the gates of Hades.[67] We called them tamaracks then, but that might have been a misnomer. If not, tamarack sounds close to tamarisk, of which Hermes' sandals were made. They were made of that and myrtle (sacred to Venus, Venus being the second planet from the sun) branches. Tamar in the Bible suggests trickery and fertility.

There were no sidewalks, except maybe for a block downtown, and no way to get around without a car or bike other than *walking*. As always, children were outgrowing their shoes, which weren't cheap. If they were going barefoot (Footprints) in the summer, they'd tear of the searing asphalt road—where the heat could be seen shimmying up at times—to the mistaken refuge of the parched ground to the side. Here snaking weeds ruled, hugging and defending their turf with painful bites of thorns. Deciding then where they were was worse than where they'd been, the shoeless kids went back and forth in a devil's dance to their destination, which couldn't have been far. Had they gone on for a few miles in one direction, they'd have reached what was and is down Highway 33, Devil's Den, though some may argue today it should be designated "Devil's Den south," so as not to be confused with the prison[68-A] to the north.

The downtown area around Kings Street had a no-frills movie house with four flimsy walls and a ceiling open to the sky. Here perhaps twenty people might attend while sitting in hard-back wooded or folding chairs and benches, waiting patiently for the projectionist to change reels. Nearby was a barbershop, Stewart Nill's drugstore, a small department store, a couple of hotels, and a few shops and offices including Dr. Levin's. Then businesses and companies, nothing fancy by today's standards, spread out along Skyline two miles or so to the hills.

Dad bought a small plastic fan with cloth blades for safety to try to help him sleep between jobs. A dingy, brown icebox melted a block of ice, as if its sole purpose was to level the ice posthaste rather than to cool the food. There were drop-cord lights, and at first a few cockroaches from previous tenants skittered about. In short, the sweltering, plain, and cramped little house we moved into would have had no distinction whatsoever had it not been for the lady next door. She had opened a small shop down the street to try to support herself and her son. We liked them well enough. They were never any problem, but it was rumored that she was insane, and the stories got juicier with each telling, sometimes among the children, always with the gossips, but most surprisingly among grown men of little compassion. Catching the smell of blood, the sharks circled, moving in for the kill. Occasionally they jeered, laughed, and hooted. A grammar school kid sent anonymous letters that frightened the poor woman out of her wits. Later she was admitted to an asylum. Ah, the milk of human kindness in the rustic simplicity of a small town!

In about a year's time, we moved into a house they had financed to have built. It had two bedrooms, a bathroom, a front room, a kitchen, and a utility area and screened porch behind. *Better Homes and Gardens* it wasn't, but it was brand new and ours.

Here we had our first electric refrigerator, and much of the furniture was bought on time, as were our Christmases, from the Montgomery Ward catalog. No sooner had they paid off one year than they had the yoke of debts for the following year. This they could have managed well enough in their planning had they not been hit with all kinds of medical problems in a space of a few years. If many families still don't have medical coverage today, there were a hell of a lot more in those days. I had an appendectomy in the fourth grade, which my father in Topaz paid for. Then, not necessarily in this order, Dad was laid up for weeks with severe burns on his legs which he'd gotten on a job. Mom had a hysterectomy, and Dad had a hernia operation. So it's easy to see why many oil field families become drinkers—the paycheck is nearly gone before it ever arrives.

Our Avenal teacher decided to take her fifth grade class on an outing for nature studies, and everyone was told to bring a bag lunch. It was a beautiful, spring day in the 1930s, and we were driven by bus to an area in front of a mountain with many lupine68-B bushes in bloom on it and beneath a small brook. There the teacher found a harmless, baby green snake about seven inches long and insisted each of pass the supreme test of holding it for a minute apiece, which she timed with her watch.

"Don't be afraid," she said. "You see it won't hurt you."

I doubt if it ever occurred to her that the snake being passed around was far more uncomfortable than we were. Indeed it had snake eyes and was shooting craps. That's how I know I was the one. Just think it had chosen me out of the twenty. Why me? It was the first of three snake omens.68-C

If I'd had any presence of mind, I'd have wiped my hand on the teacher's dress: "Don't be afraid. See it won't hurt you."

Instead, I rinsed it off in the brook. "Brent is always so kind and considerate!" Besides, she was bigger than I.

Dad was gone two, three, or four days at a time, working without much sleep on rigs. When finishing a job, he was exhausted, sleeping and resting ten or twelve hours, followed by several more hours of reading, listening to sports on the radio, and playing cribbage. Then he'd take the shopping list, go buy groceries or whatever we needed, and drop by the company he worked for to clean equipment or get ready for the next job. Both he and Mom were heavy smokers and drinkers, mainly port wine but also beer. They seldom drank hard stuff because it cost too much. He could handle his better than she, whose mouth when she was soused turned down in a grimace. Yet he would not escape the effects completely, dying in old age from a very painful cirrhosis of the liver.

Once in awhile, he'd get irritated at something, but usually he was good natured. Working hard all his life until retirement, he paid every cent owed and never got in trouble with the law or had a hint of scandal. I always knew he was a good man. Not until after his death did I realize he was better than I thought.

His blind spot was that he hadn't seen through Mom soon enough. Belay that! He'd seen through her all right but was defeated by the system—you know, the people who mean well, the fixers and do-gooders who're going to get their credit with God when, if they'd just left things alone, they might have worked out better in the long run.

He must have loved her very much at first, and then after that he just sort of got used to her. It was a bonding in that she was part of his life. If she left, a large part of his life was finished. He was dependent upon her, so he let her have her way on most things, and in a way this was wrong. For as the years passed she became increasingly willful and began to lie. I say that in a way this was wrong for him to do because nobody really knows where she might have ended if he had forced the issue and got a divorce.

He once wrote me that I should be willing to forget a couple of bad years later in Bakersfield.69 Because he was gone so much of the time or sleeping, he failed to realize things had started much earlier than that. Two of these, not pertaining directly to me, might be given some thought.

First, Avenal in those days had little traffic. It would have been very easy for her to have gotten a driver's license. It made no sense whatsoever that he had to spend part of his short time between jobs shopping for groceries. Even when cars became easier to drive, she never drove. Though I'm sure he would have been glad for her to go along with him on short jobs, she rarely did. Could it have been fear by one or the other that a driver's license might have opened up Pandora's box?

Second, she belonged to a bridge club. The ladies would meet periodically at one another's home during an afternoon. When a long time had passed since she had been called, she phoned one of the members and heard, "Didn't they tell you when we'd be meeting? I thought someone called you."

When this happened again, she began to realize they didn't want her. It was learned indirectly the reason was that she took over, ran things, and tried to star. But then, I never heard her side of it.

Though we had a duck, a cat, goldfish, and canaries, it's the wonderful dog that is remembered most. She was a mixture of chow and collie, having the protective and fighting instinct of a chow and the even temper and intelligence of a collie. Wisely they'd let her have one litter of pups before getting her spayed. So she wasn't craving for affection, jumping up on people, edging her rear end over to be patted, rolling over on her back, or pissing all over herself. We never had any worry about her biting someone or senselessly barking on and on, yet she let no other dog get near us or any person she sensed might have had ill intent.

Her coat was smooth and long, a dark orange, sort of like around the sun very early in the morning (see Nescafé Sunrise). But it wouldn't have been right to call her Dawn, though they'd not reasoned this out when they called her Ginger.

My bond with her was pure love. She watched over Robyn and me with single-mindedness, as if we were the only purpose for her existence. She always knew when we got out of school and would be a block or two up the street waiting.

She did have one fault, however. She'd suffer patiently while we washed her with perfumed soap. Then when finally released she'd shake her coat of water all over us and dash off to roll in manure.

When she got old, she couldn't see as well as she used to. I'd gone to the ranch one summer for three months, shooting up nearly a foot. When I got back, she didn't recognize me and began barking.

"What's the matter, Ginger? Don't you know me?" I asked.

She stopped barking and looked startled and surprised. Then all of a sudden she tore out and began circling me, round and round, for at least five minutes, whimpering before letting me touch her. Then she wouldn't leave my side for the next few days.

Every family should be blessed with at least one pet like her, but there was more to it than that. They'd got her as a small puppy in 1928, four months before I was born. She eventually got so crippled that she had to be put out of her misery. Of course, I'm inclined to believe there's no hereafter, or maybe Hermes takes us to Hades, but if there is and no god, friend, or relative will take the job, I'd sure like to be shown the way by that old dog.

The divine right from Mom's nurse's training was to probe and invade the privacy of another's mind, sort of patronizing and well-meaning at the same time. Was it just her way? Or did she have good reason for concern? Could something have happened to me when I was younger? A dream one night made me wonder. Still many dreams are foolishness and deceptive. Not having had it since, I'll discount that.

It's perhaps symbolic in breaking boundaries that when Dad was bound I'd be subjected to an enema too, as if she still had a quota to meet on a practical factors card in the school she had dropped out of fifteen or so years before.

I can't remember that she ever laid a hand on me. Probably she had slapped me a few times, but it really wasn't her style. She thought of herself as being much more progressive and well read. It was certainly wrong to beat your kid; this bordered on child abuse, like holding a hand over a flame or starving and locking a child in a closet. Such things were not only medieval but extreme evil. Rather a parent should talk to and reason with the child, but don't make it easy. A stern lecture was required so that there would be no mistake about the meaning. Where she often broke boundaries, however, was to make it a complete catharsis for herself. She threw in whatever she could think of—any cheap shot, criticism, or passing remark that any neighbor, friend, relative, or acquaintance had made. In doing this, she effectively robbed the person of self-esteem, making him feel like a complete shit. Then after making the case that she somehow was the abused person, she might ask if I didn't love and feel sorry for her? Growing older, I truthfully replied once of not feeling sorry for her. She then called up her tank to kill a gnat: "Don't you have any love for me at all? How can you ever, ever talk to me like that when I took you when your mother died, and I changed your diapers as a baby. For this you can never repay me, even if you lived a million years."

It was a shit opera, a soap opera, and an onion opera rolled up into one. All I could think of at the time was that I wished I was some other place and that she was done.

"And your Aunt Nell," she went on, "said when your mother died that you would have been better off it you died with her. Oh yes, your Aunt Nell who you think so much of! But I took you, and I cared for you. So how dare you talk to me like that!"

Aunt Nell was always my favorite aunt. She had long since figured her sister would be telling me this and explained before it happened that she had meant only that it was a shame a baby should have to come into a world without its mother.

"What's the matter with you?" Mom sometimes probed.
"Nothing."
"Oh yes there is, and you're going to tell me what. Do you hear me?" On stage everybody.

At these times in Avenal she could be anywhere; out working in her rock-and-cactus garden with its wagon wheels and bleached cattle skulls, cleaning out a fish pond, cooking dinner, or lying in a bathtub while sipping wine and puffing on a cigarette. So if anything had been eating me, I'd tell her, but even if nothing was wrong, I wasn't going to be let off the hook until telling her something. Then that thing which had no importance to me before would become something to reckon with after a case had been made out of it. And if by chance I could think of nothing, she would.

When Dad's two-week vacation came one summer, we traveled south over the old Ridge Route. There were cars and trucks whizzing by in each direction. Occasionally we passed a collision with police or ambulance in attendance. We saw Okie families with their mattresses and other belongings piled so high that you wondered how they could trundle off to Bakersfield and beyond. Cars had broken down along the way or were stopped, as we had, to let their radiators cool so they could make the grade.

Some friends we stayed with one night in Los Angeles had a girl about ten or eleven years old. I was about seven or eight. Both being very young, we apparently shared one bed. A month or so following our return to Avenal, Mom confronted me with the story that the girl told her mother she and I played with one another. I couldn't even remember sleeping with her, let alone playing with her, so I denied it. What else? But Mom was willing to accept her word over mine. Did something happen I'd forgotten about? Or was it a fishing expedition to make something out of nothing?

A few years later when being irritated or under the weather or both, she told me I was just like my mother, who she said was a loner and had no friends, as if to imply that I should be ashamed of this and perhaps more. Aunt Nell, not knowing she'd said this, would tell me my mother was "a handsome woman and the best of the five daughters." So who to believe? The aunt who raised me as a son or her sister whose opinion was respected more.

As it happened, this was cleared up for me some years later. Phyllis, Aunt Nell's daughter, visited my father's ranch one summer. My Aunt Elsie remarked how much she reminded her of my mother. I was happy to hear this, since Phyllis was a sweet, pretty girl who was just as bright as she could be and could sit and be pleasant without feeling she had to be the center of attraction.

We never starved. There was always meat, potatoes and some other vegetable, and maybe a salad on the table. Milk, cheese, eggs, pickles, olives, Coke, and Kool-aid were in the refrigerator. But in order to have this, it was necessary for Dad to be a careful shopper, checking out the best values and buying things on sale. He deprived himself while Mom felt it was part of my training at an early age to emphasize that everything cost money. Neither one can be faulted on this, as they'd had the Depression at its worst to deal with and the operations toward the last for which to pay. But it no doubt left a lasting impression on me.

I recall as a small kid going into Dad's room when he was sleeping and stealing some of the change from his pockets. I also stole some non-perishable food and bars of soap, etc., then buried it all about a hundred yards from the house in open land. I was getting quite a cache when the thievery was discovered. I readily admitted it and returned everything, which had been squirreled away so they'd have something when times got hard. If they couldn't save for themselves, then I'd do it for them. Dumb kid! I should have stolen something out of my own greed, which probably most kids at that age do at one time or another in a normal childhood. But I was off in some goody-goody world then, and even today I have never returned to planet earth.

Being 99 and 44/100ths percent pure ideologically, I float. I would have made an ideal communist, so perfect, in fact, in all the commie charismatic qualities of being self-serious, intense, and intractable that they'd have done me in out of jealousy. Failing that, they'd no doubt have given me a dacha on the Black Sea in my old age. If I'd continued on with my honesty and "inta-gri-tee" in Japan, why, those suckers would have made me a corporate head, at which time I'd have connived, schemed, lied, stolen, and bribed for country, company, and myself, not necessarily in that order.

It's hard for people to grasp the idea that God might like thieves for different reasons than he likes saints, though I'd have a long way to go to be successful in the pursuit of either one.

I couldn't be comfortable living around affluence or spending much on myself,[71] not that something wasn't spent now and then but never extravagantly. Had there been a Renoir or van Gogh on the wall in my room, it wouldn't have been noticed half the time, while the other half, I'd have worried it would get stolen or damaged before giving it away to a museum. Wasn't so much that it was wasteful for me to have much more than a warm room, bed, and a place to clean up as it was there was no yearning for luxury. So on retirement, I'd accumulated considerable wealth and gave most of it away. But don't get all blurry-eyed about that. It had nothing to do with love for humanity, and blah, blah, blah. I just couldn't be worried about it.

Once on a freighter where the food was excellent and paid for, an old passenger used to ask for two slices of bread at lunch and, loading them up with catsup, would make a sandwich. This disgusted me, until another passenger said this is what many people had done during the Depression. It was just a carryover. Then and only then did I understand.

Only a fool would think economizing isn't necessary or that man's welfare in general is not important.

> But communism was doomed,
> A prune waiting for a rain
> That never came.[72]

Mom was a natural cook with a feel for seasoning; seldom did she look at a cookbook. Good biscuits and rolls were made almost effortlessly, as well as gravies. Never did she stand over a stove beating lumps to death or strain them through a cloth, or make much of a mess. Even people outside the family commented on her good cooking. But if like anyone else, including executive chefs, she fouled up once in awhile, or perhaps leftover spaghetti was coming out our ears, you had the right to remain silent so that nothing you said could be used against you. She could make a big issue out of things.

Yet before I could read, she read to me a chapter or two each night from books like *Treasure Island*, *Oliver Twist*, and *Tom Sawyer*. This encouragement to read helped me more than anything else—an escape from sleeplessness or worry, costing little or nothing.

Robyn was nearly six years older than I, so our worlds were very different. The room we shared most of the year was plastered with her posters and mementos. She had her homework and was caught up in her high school activities, jitterbugging, cheerleading, majorette, etc. Then later she would marry her high school boyfriend and have three children. These children would then marry and have children themselves. But in high school, Robyn bought each issue of a magazine that had the words to all the latest songs. These she sang while washing the dishes, which I was to dry and put away. Seldom did we do this than we didn't scrap, but there was never any jealousy or resentment. I'll always have love for and good things to say about her.

Chapter Eight

If the summers were broiling in Avenal, the early spring made up for it. There were miles of flat land, hills, foothills, and mountains to roam and old, abandoned ruins to explore. I suspect that long before oil was discovered this had been, in the spring at least, an area shepherds found pleasing.

Bags of lush mushrooms[73] that an average, weekly check wouldn't be enough to pay for today could be gathered in a couple hours. We brought back from the ravines interesting rocks, seashells, horned toads, and turtles, some of which were much older than we.

Great stretches were aflame with wildflowers.[74-A] One color sometimes went on unbroken for a mile or two before being taken up by another. Families on Saturday and Sunday outings drove from miles around just to take this in. If we missed the vast buffalo herds and huge flocks of birds of a century or two before in North America, at least we saw this: nature unspoiled. It seems ironic that one of the flowers stretching in patches for hundred of yards was called the Indian Paintbrush. Years later I could appreciate what Lady Bird Johnson was trying to do in Texas. Now, of course, all this has changed due to man, farms, pollution, drought, and dust—progress!

Still not all progress has been bad. Many diseases in the 1930s and later were suffered without much real help until nature took its course. A vivid remembrance is the agony of those with ulcers (Book I, pages 13-14).

Only a few sulfa drugs were in use toward the end of the decade. Penicillin wouldn't be ready for injection until the early 1940s. Thermometers, now disposable, had to be put into a green soap solution for some time after each use, then washed and placed in an alcohol solution for another period of time. Rubber gloves, now discarded, were washed in soap and water, tested for holes, hung up to dry, flipped inside-out for drying again, powdered, repacked, and autoclaved. Syringes and needles were boiled and reused, and some of those needles got very dull before discarding. If nurses and paramedical people ran out of something to do, there was always a need for more swabs. They would sit down with a box of sponge sticks, a roll of cotton, and a glass of water. Once a canister had been filled, it was sent off for sterilization. If there is any silver lining to the AIDS epidemic today, it's that it came when it did rather than this period, during World War II, or the Korean and Vietnam Wars.

Housewives did most of their own baking and much canning. Pies and cakes were made from scratch. There was little frozen food. Most families couldn't afford butter (probably a blessing in disguise), so coloring had to be squeezed through white oleomargarine. Nobody ever heard of wash-and-wear clothing. Women still had scrub boards built into their sinks. If they were lucky enough to have a washing machine, chances are it only washed. The clothing was fed through a wringer and put into rinse water. Then back again through the wringer. Inevitably a woman would hear, "Don't get your tit caught in a wringer now!"

Much of the clothing had to be starched and then wrung through a wringer again. All was hung out to dry on clotheslines that first were wiped down for rust. If it rained or was a cold or cloudy day, the clothes were brought in to dry in the garage or draped over furniture in the house. When finally dry, much of it had to be sprinkled down and rolled into balls which were stuck in a basket until ready for ironing. A woman with a family could expect two full days of work each week from washing and ironing alone.

If you had a small savings account at some bank and wanted your interest brought up to date, you had to wait while the teller located some old ledger where the interest was recorded by pen, and then this was transferred by pen into your passbook.

A person damn well had better have learned to hold his/her stick shift car on a hill while waiting for a light to change. There was no microfilm to scan newspaper articles. No fancy machines for locating books, just card catalogs. No copy machines. Think about this someday when you go to the library, that what you're copying in less than a minute we had to write out in longhand. There were no televisions or pocket calculators. Answers were figured out laboriously by one process or a combination of addition, subtraction, multiplication, and division and then rechecked to make certain of the answer. Students in high school had homework assignments to complete satisfactorily if they ever expected to be advanced. Those planning to enter a university or college of good standing usually spent a minimum of three hours studying every night.

Each man, woman, or child had individual problems, as they do nowadays. Yet I never heard one of them grouse about "how much harder we have it today than they used to have." We all knew—which many don't know now—that, generally speaking, we had it much easier than the people before us.

Chapter Nine

When I was nine I was sent to my father's ranch in northern California one summer. It was several hundred miles away, a trip by car and roads today taking much less time. As a little, citified dude, a snot-nosed brat, I didn't know what to expect. Certainly there'd be something special when returning to my roots for the first time.

We neared Topaz, our destination, late one afternoon. To our left on 395 were mountains. On reaching a point where one seemed just another mountain in the range, we turned to the right across a Walker River[74-B] bridge and down a country road for two miles or so to the ranch, barren of trees. Here my father and brothers lived in a small, two-room cabin. Its wood on the outside was old, dark, coarse, and splintery. The inside was no better, being chilly in the early morning and hot in the afternoon. Saddles, saddle blankets, bridles, hackamores, ropes, oats, feed bags, kerosene lamps, old school books, etc., filled the screened porch in front.

Far behind the cabin was an outhouse; it had a bird's nest inside at the top with the mother flying in and out through a hole in the door. As I stood up on the sides of the two-holer to examine the nest, it fell down into one of the holes, the wrong one. Damn! The baby birds, skinny little things down there in no-man's land, began a fearful chirping. That's how the expression got started, "Everything he touches turns to shit!" Thought for a minute of reaching down three feet below to try to get them out then rationalized that the smell the mother would have the same problem taking them back as I did thinking about their rescue. In those days, there were no telephones nearby, and even if there had been, there was no 911 to call the police. Or is it the fire department? A jurisdictional dispute, each claiming that it's the others responsibility? Anyway, the bird's nest was finished. Just wished they'd die quickly—mercifully for me—so I wouldn't have to listen to their epirbs that they were sinking: beep, beep, beep.

Thus the all-important litmus test for character in life was failed. George Washington admitted to cutting down the cherry tree so a slave wouldn't be punished; Lincoln walked several miles to return a few cents; but no way was this one reaching down in that crap, which might have grabbed ahold of his arms and pulled him in too. How the west was won!

I never could fathom how anyone could sit unconcernedly and browse through the crapper-paper catalogue when the mierda monster lurked in its pit just a few feet below. If the top of its prison is removed on Halloween night, it will break loose, wreaking havoc on humans for all the shit it has taken over the years.

In one of the cabin's rooms were several cases of canned goods. On arrival my father pulled out a can of peaches. This was the first meal on returning to my roots? What happened to the cook in all those Saturday afternoon movie matinees who came out clangin' the delta noisemaker and hollarin', "Come and git it," while a cow mooed in the distance? Where were the fresh-baked pies sitting in the window for the cowhands to filch? Where was it they all went to sit around a long table with heaping platters of steaming food that made your mouth water? This wasn't how the west was won. Can peaches! Phooey!

There was an ax and wood for chopping but not much cut for a few days or weeks to come. Rather, when needed, they chopped an armload. A few chickens more or less ran wild, and every day was an Easter-egg hunt, as well as a Wester, Norther, and Souther. You were never sure the eggs you found were laid yesterday or a month before until you cracked them. A cow was milked twice a day, and there were pans of milk sitting with their scabs of cream and two of three flies buzzing and crapping around.

Conditioned as a squeaky wheel, I'd been afflicted with the worst disease known to man: the double-helix, double-whammy whine gene:

"Hey Pops, I don't like this thin, warm crap, I want cold, pasteurized or homogenized milk!"

"Tough titty!"

To the right of the cabin was a silent spring, level with the field and nearly hidden by growth. As with everything else, it was in full view of the mountain, yet between the mountain and the spring, there was a special relationship. This could only be intuited but not explained rationally. As close as I can come—and this would be just a guess—the mountain watched the spring-trap for footprints to see who might yet fetch a bucket of water without sinking and slogging in the ground around it. Or maybe it cared not who could do this but was interested only in the footprints, for the following year when the new house was built the spring was gone.[75-A]

My father and mother married on May 20, 1916.[75-B] He had gone into the sheep business in Smith Valley, Nevada, where he's bought a home with ranges on the East Walker River. They had five children. My three brothers, Ralph, Robert, and Warren, were ten, eight, and six respectively at the time of my mother's death. Helen had been born before us all on April 25, 1917, and she died in infancy of meningitis on November 8, 1917.

Her name, like my mother's middle one, can be associated with a name in Greek mythology: Helen of Troy, a crosser of boundaries, was Hermes' half sister. Both had Zeus for a father. Helen and Menlaus' only child (by some accounts) was a daughter called Hermione, and again Maia was the mother of Hermes. Dorothy is derived from theos (Greek for placer or arranger) and *doron* (Greek for gift). Thus Theodora, when reversed, comes close to Dorothea or Dorothy. Doll and Dolly are further derivatives. Helen is also name of Greek origin. Two derivatives of the name Helen are Lena and Nell. Dollena Dorothy (Mom) and Nell were the names of the two aunts who brought me from Nevada to California.

Prior to my birth, or maybe shortly after, Frank decided to give up the sheep business and began making payments on a ranch near Topaz, California, not too far from the California-Nevada boundary. There was no money for a hired hand. Payments were not easy to make. Cows had to be milked. The boys went to school some distance away. Fences had to be built, irrigation ditches dug, and calves castrated, dehorned, and branded; cattle inoculated; horses shoed; wood hauled in and cut; chickens fed; eggs gathered; animals killed for meat; and horses rounded up and harnessed. Most everything was still being done with teams of horses, including haying. Any neighbor asked to help during the stacking of hay was probably paid off in a return favor. There was no barn, just two big stacks in one of the fields which they used for winter feed. My brothers worked on the ranch then without wages for the most part. If they were ever to have anything more than board and room, be that what it may, they had to rope and break mustangs to sell, work for neighbors on nearby ranches or the county on road construction, hunt, fish, and trap for pelts. It was harsh conditions for them to grow up under. Nevertheless, with their help, Frank managed to meet his bills, take out some insurance on himself, and build in a period of ten years or so a herd of two hundred and fifty to three hundred head of cattle, which was about all his land could support along with thirty to thirty-five horses, half of which were mustangs they'd roped. This was many more than the actual number of horses they needed, but they were cowboys.

My first summer at the ranch, Ralph was nineteen; Robert, seventeen; and Warren, fifteen. Frank, having become an excellent horseman, was close to fifty. He was reticent and honest, a natural for the area's brand inspector, yet for me he was almost a stranger. It was hard to call him Dad and easier to think of him as Uncle Frank, so both names were avoided. Also I was uncomfortable in using the term "my real father" when referring to him. I never really knew him—the less-worrying and carefree nature he might have had when he was younger—and to some extent this was true until his death. We rode together here and there on horses, usually something to do with ranching, but riding was what he enjoyed and perhaps hoped I would, too. He smiled once in awhile. If he corrected me, it wasn't severely, yet I can't recall if he ever gave me a compliment and there's the uncertainty whether he really ever liked me. In a sense, Ralph's horse and I were a lot alike. Our welfare would be looked after because it was a duty, obligation, or a promise. But he never could or would—or perhaps didn't know how to—bond himself to me, or I to him, whatever. We would never play games, just me and him, or do something outlandish or crazy or fuck up and laugh about it later.

Ralph was off working on a dude ranch in Bridgeport or some other place. Warren, the youngest son next to me, had suffered most from the conditions he had to adapt to at an early age. He was a quiet and dutiful son, going to bed and getting up with the chickens. He worked like an ox. He endured because it was the manly thing to do, but somehow it was at a cost. To my knowledge, he was never happy-go-lucky. He held most of his feelings inside himself, became a private person, and so was really hard to know. He'd have been the last gone to if one was wanting to talk something over personally.

Robert was more outgoing. I was his brother from the beginning, and that was it. He gave me one or two mustangs he'd broken and felt I could handle a saddle, a saddle blanket, a bridle, and a tie rope. He made sure I had some pocket money if we went to the store. He played tricks on me. He told me right from wrong but not severely. He didn't clobber me when I broke his best bridle or even make an issue of it.

At one level—if I'd been raised on the ranch—if anybody could have helped me, it was him. I saw him only two or three summers, and then he was in the army, off in Iran and France during World War II. At another level, nobody could have helped me anymore than they were able to help Helen, my mother, and Ralph. We'd all been marked someway. Since in the end death comes to all, there's no certainty whether this is good or bad. One thing is for sure, a person can't change the hand he's been dealt.

The first summer I was bucked off once or twice because the horse sensed the rider didn't know what he was doing. When it was necessary to wash up, I'd ride to the Walker River, where my horse (you know, Slippery, Bucephalus, Traveller, Winchester, and Snorts Chichester) managed to slip away from me three times. I'd go running after him, hoping to catch him before he got back to the ranch and my brothers would see what happened. But no matter how fast I'd go, Snorts always stayed twenty-five yards ahead. If I speeded up, he speeded up. If I slowed down, he'd slow down until we got back to the ranch's gate. There he'd stand, saddled and bridled, waiting patiently for me to open the gate so he could get back in. On this damn horse I frequently used a hackamore because a bit would be too uncomfortable. This damn horse I never cinched up too tight because I felt sorry for him. Then later I'd find the saddle, the saddle blanket, and myself slipping down his side and would have to ask the other riders to stop while getting off, pushing everything back up again, and cinching him tight. This damn horse never failed to get a bag of oats at the end of each ride.

Finally realizing that by dropping the reins Snorts wasn't going to stand there like horses do in the movies, I decided the tie-rope was too much trouble to rewind each time and tie in place. It seemed faster and easier to tie him up by the reins (after all, they do it this way in the movies too). He then pulled back, breaking them, and trotted off with "Little Wind Cussing Behind," a name any Paiute in the area would have hung on me for life. If my brothers had failed to see the Chichester Downs race with Feedbag in the lead and Windbag bringing up the rear, they couldn't have missed the broken reins of Bob's best bridle, taken without permission.[76]

At least once I forgot to close a gate (boundary). The cattle and horses in one field mingled with those in another. Sometimes one brother on horseback would chase the horses in from a distant field. I'd close the gate they passed through and then run to stand just beyond the corral's entrance so that they would turn in. Shouting and raising my hands to scare them, I'd see them thundering toward me at a full run. Then just before the last few seconds, I'd move out of their way fast with hardly the grace of a matador. I might have been a little coward, but I wasn't crazy. My brother on horseback would cuss like hell as he rode past to chase them around once more to the entrance, where upon they'd bluff me out again. "Home, home on the range...Where seldom is heard a discouraging word." So it was that it took me half a summer to learn that if I stood my ground, the horses would turn into the corral at the last second.

About the only thing left which hadn't happened to me was getting kicked. This good luck is owed to my father and brothers who would have bet it was just a matter of time but nevertheless felt obliged to warn me constantly not to walk behind one. In short, much was still being learned the hard way on things which would have been second nature to any kids living in the area, who were much tougher. During haying season, after doing maybe eighteen bunches all day, I was pooped, while any one of my brothers did three times that amount and still had plenty of stamina.[77-A]

One day we watched a man in a fancy new car drive up to the gate, open it, drive through, close it, and drive up to the cabin. He'd noticed our "fine, white horse" grazing not too far away. The more he looked at it, the more he was convinced it was perfect, large enough and suitable for Errol Flynn to ride in his next picture. Bob and he were discussing it, and it looked as though a sale might go through, when little ol' inta-grit-ee had to give his two-cents worth: "But you don't want to buy that worn-out plug, mister; that's just one of our old work horses. You don't want him to ride something like that!"

When he left, Bob remarked," Why did you have to tell him that? If he thought the horse was good enough, what difference does it make? Now he'll never come back," which was true. Everything I got near turned to shit.

At dusk one evening, I got mad about something and decided to run away. If I could get to 395, there'd be no trouble catching a ride. Starting out through the gate, I got two-thirds of the way to the main ranch at Topaz when two or three skunks appeared on the dirt road, blocking the way and stinking up a storm. (Everything he gets near turns to smell.) Running along one side of the road was an irrigation ditch, too wide to jump across; to the other side was a marsh area with reeds and God only knew what else crawling around at night. There was no way to get around the skunks. It was dark when I returned to the cabin. My brothers either hadn't noticed my disappearance or were unconcerned, knowing I wouldn't have gone far.

By the next summer, Frank William had remarried. He met Anita McElroy,[77-B] who worked as a secretary in San Francisco, when she'd taken her vacation on a dude ranch in Bridgeport. He built for her, my brothers, and himself a new house behind the cabin. It was a plain, white, cracker box without adornment and minimal finish. Three bedrooms about the same size and monotonously rectangular opened into a living room. There was a small bathroom (the sons were still to use the out-house) and a small kitchen leading to a little utility space and a backdoor. But for the first time in nearly ten years, each brother had a room to himself or one he shared with only one other. They had electricity, hot and cold running water, and a telephone, even if it was only a party line that several people around the area could listen in on.

Anita was a devout Catholic and my father a Protestant. At thirty-six or thirty-seven she was somewhat set in her ways, as my father was set in his. It was her first marriage. She was efficient, had supported herself well enough, and had a certain independence by upper-middle-class assets and money she'd inherited from her father. She lived in the city all her life and knew little about rural living. My three brothers still remembered my mother and had got along without Anita before she came, so by all odds, it shouldn't have been but was a very successful marriage.

She loved animals, riding, cooking, and took to ranch life like the proverbial duck to water. In addition to this, she ran successfully for two terms as county superintendent of schools, resigning shortly before her last term was finished. If my brothers still remembered our mother, the grandchildren who came later had not, and to them Anita was unqualifiededly "Grandma."

The first summer of her marriage, she had to return to San Francisco on business. Since the World's Fair at Treasure Island was being held then, she took me along. Her idea, she must have thought, but many of the family dates were long since in place.

It was a first for me on a train. At the end of one meal, the steward put a small, silver bowl of water down for me to drink. She stopped me, explaining the fingerbowl's use. When she got up to go, slightly ahead, she'd left a lot of money in change on the table. I scooped it up quickly and ran behind her yelling, "Anita, Anita, you left this money on the table!" The steward for some reason looked as if he could kill me and muttered a curse to himself that this little b——— would end up a waiter someday.

"No, no," she explained, "you must go put it back." I did, but by then it was too late.

Two days later, we were walking down a ramp from a ferry. Many people were getting off and I'd gone ahead. Then not seeing her, I went back to look. She was bending down. The garter holding up one of her hose had broken, and the stocking was hanging limply on her shoe.

"Go away! Go away!" she cried in embarrassment. "Pretend you don't know me."

Such a contrast to some of the progressive ladies today who even if the elastic in their panties broke wouldn't have batted an eye, gingerly stepping out of them and hardly missing a stride. Nor would they go back to fetch them.

Years later Anita, then in her seventies moved to Santa Rosa, California, not wishing to be a burden to the families on the ranches. I casually remarked once that she must have missed city life when she married my father.

"Oh no!" she exclaimed. "I wouldn't have traded those years on the ranch for anything in the world." There was no question in her mind: God had blessed her.

Chapter Ten

"The Death of a Cowboy on a Country Road" could be a western song, a ballad, a Greek tragedy. Roping and breaking mustangs, hiring out as a ranch hand, Ralph scraped much of his life to get together two thousand dollars, which was still not enough. He liked animals and hoped some-day to attend college and then the University of California at Davis to become a veterinarian. The money was used instead for his burial, and I suppose—looking back to his birthdate—this was fitting in ways people might not have understood then.

Horses in a rodeo string were up for sale, and the one Ralph cottoned to was cheap. He thought that with patience the horse would come to trust him and be made into a fine animal. But my dad was against this from the beginning.

"Any horse that has been beaten and spurred and maybe drugged over and over to make him buck can only be crazy. Bad news. Forget him!"

Ralph wanted nothing to do with this old-lady caution. His dad would always be a worrier as well as a Republican with a Chevrolet. Indeed the faces on Mt. Rushmore would smile before these things ever changed.

And who knows? Maybe Ralph was right about the horse, or his atti-tude was right and that was all which really mattered to a god or gods. But you may see it as fate or destiny.

We were sitting in the living room, where Anita's old, ornate clock was ticking away, a metronome for silence, which had come abruptly on us. Bob, who was looking out the window, uttered, "There's Ralph's horse. Something must have happened to Ralph!" He bolted for the door, jumped into the Chevy and drove to the gate. The horse stood in front of this on the dirt covering the pipe through which the irrigation water flowed. He was saddled and bridled, waiting to get in much like Snorts the previous summer and this was the reason I hadn't thought much about it.

A mile or so up the road, Bob found Ralph lying on the ground, conscious but with his neck broken. He was able to tell Bob the horse spooked suddenly, throwing him. Ralph was brought back to the house and taken to Reno, where he was operated on and then died a day or two later. But before this, he exacted the promise that the horse wouldn't be destroyed, harmed, or gotten rid of,[78-A] insisting it wasn't the animal's fault. The horse lived out its life on the ranch without ever being saddled again. It was always there, a constant reminder of Ralph's death and its link to it.[78-B]

Had Ralph lived, he would have been a quadriplegic (again the number four). Had he not met with the accident, another fate just as grim might have awaited, being among the first to be called up in World War II. At least, that's what some said, like it was going to make things not so bad that it happened sooner. But to my way of thinking, there was no alternate fate for him. At his burial, he was the only one in the cemetery I could remember when alive. And through the years though shelving the accident as one of those things which happens in life, I came to idolize Ralph, my mother, and baby Helen. They were something out of Camelot, people I'd heard about who lived in a far-off world.

For fifty years, I had only the remembrance that his horse shied suddenly. Hadn't someone said that when Ralph fell he'd hit his head on a rock? Maybe that was something just dreamed up. Primitive thoughts of Hermes, Zimbabwe, "houses of stone," animism, and ancestor worship soak in now like a heavy rain at night. A graceful goddess of theater holds two masks with her right hand. The Romans of a certain period used to have the death masks of relatives on the walls of their homes. There is some connection, you know,[78-C] but to have had any of these thoughts in those days would have been real crazy. We'd both been born on the same day of the month. The number of years apart were unknown, as well as anything about the Feralia. I knew my mother was the eldest of five sisters, but I hadn't known her middle name May was similar to Maia, the eldest of seven sisters, nor that my sister Helen bore the same name as Hermes' half sister.

With the connections now made, it seemed important to know more about Ralph's accident. What made his horse shy? Did his head hit on a rock when he fell?

At sixty-one I'd kept in touch with one of Bob and Rhoda's sons and his wife more than with them and asked Bobby and Monica if they'd check with Bob concerning the circumstances of the accident as he remembered. Their letters finally came in reply and, understandably, were classics relatives might write to another who, sadly, they weren't quite certain was all there:

Postmarked: 11 Jan 1991

Dear Brent:

Sorry I have taken so long to write back, but it took me some time to reflect and do some research.

No. 1! Dare I say this? You may never write again. But I have to tell you, do not get carried away over superstition. I am probably as superstitious as anyone. I don't walk under ladders ever. When a black cat crosses my path, I always feel uncomfortable and feel bad luck is on the way. And you never step on a grave. But this is all a good excuse for being born under an unlucky star. Ha Ha!

Anyway you worry me with this letter you have written, and I want to know who, what, where, when, and why has put you on this venture. And I want you to write me back as soon as you receive this letter and answer these questions! O.K.!

All right I had to B.S. Bob, Sr. a little to get some of this information. I told him you were writing about the Chichester history. So if he ever asks, tell him that.

I. Ralph Chichester: Born February 21, 1919. Died Sept.[79] 1939. I do not know the exact day. Dad couldn't remember. He was thrown from his horse into a rock pile and broke his neck. A rattlesnake spooked his horse.

II. Great Grandma Chichester died when her house burned. After the fire they checked the remains and found her skull crushed but could find no remains of her jewelry. So no evidence was ever produced, but everyone suspected it was a murder by a person passing through the area.

Okay that is all I can tell you for now. If you need any more information, please let me know. Keep in mind superstition is superstition. Don't plan your life by it. I want you to tell me how you got turned on to this information. It is very interesting. Write soon. Bob

Just a quick note from me to say hi. We're cold and dry here. Sure need some rain. We were in the fog for a week! I don't know what we will use this summer to grow hay.

All is fine, and we are finally back to normal after the holidays. Now sports start with basketball on Saturday and then baseball in April.

Not much new so will close. Take care and go easy with all your thoughts about what-if. Monica

When first describing Anita's clock as a "metronome for silence," I hadn't known that Hermes invented measurement or how his presence was believed to be signaled. People thought that if silence suddenly fell in a conversation, Hermes had come in.

He is spoken of as the "Rambearer" and is represented with a ram (or he-goat) either over his shoulders or under his arm. Some say he saved the city of Tanagra from pestilence by carrying a ram around its walls. Following this on the day of the feast of Hermes, the most handsome boy was selected to carry the ram around the city's walls to commemorate the *protection and healing power*.

Ralph was a fair and handsome youth whose middle name, Haven, once again means refuge or shelter, implying protection, the salient attribute of Hermes. This, Ralph had given before and after his death to the horse. I can only conclude then that his death was some sort of consummation. The signs were clear: a rider (traveler); a previously beaten and abused horse; a heap of stones (cairn); a rattlesnake; the number four both in quadriplegic and quadruped; and unlikelihood that I, also of the Feralia, would be present at the time,[80-A] sitting in the silence; and the fact that he will cross a boundary (state line) to die and be returned to be buried.

In relation to the Feralia, Ralph's birth and death, it's perhaps important to remember that one of the most common ornaments representing death on tombs in ancient Rome was a horse's head, symbolizing departure. Death was seldom represented in a direct manner.[80-B] Both the horse and the lion, two animals under Hermes' dominion, have a mane.

As Ralph left the ranch, he would have seen Topaz Lake in the distance. Turning right, he rode in a direction perpendicular to and away from the ever-present and—what always seemed to me—mysterious mountain, in front of which hundreds of travelers passed each day on 395, the highway which skirted the ol' Walker River that just keeps travelin' along and figured prominently in one of its branches or another in my family history.

Why, you might ask, would a god, gods, or God have done something like this? It has long been my conviction that Eli, who fell over backward from his seat, breaking his neck and dying and who had judged Israel for forty years, saved himself when he said, "It is the Lord; let him do what seems good to him" (1 Sam 3:18).

My brother's death on the twenty-first of the eighth month was exactly six months Janus from his and my birthday, or twelve months total. Could this stand for the twelve gods of Olympus to whom Hermes made the first sacrifice? It also fell on the eve (the day before) of what would have been the anniversary of our mother's birthday—the day possibly representing Hermes' share of the sacrifice, or one-twelfth. Another idea is that her birthday was the same as Maia's (now unknown), or it could be it doesn't mean anything at all. I would tend to believe the latter had it not been for the fact that the date recurs, fitting in like the last piece of a jigsaw puzzle. That it had not been chipped in stone, like the Ten Commandments, where I would have noticed it before the age of sixty-two is what makes it more believable and cabalistic.

Chapter Eleven

Where one book says Brent is derived from Bran (raven, death, mystery), another gives it as "burnt."

The mountain doesn't loom off in the distant clouds, a forbidding presence. No, it's a hovering magnate, always there in any picture called to mind of Topaz. Most pass it by in one sweep: nothing remarkable, a silent sentinel missed. It's scarcely the highest point—if that all—of a range which spreads to its sides like giant arms. It sits as it has for eons, watching man come and go and the valley where by grandparents, my father, uncles,[80-C] aunts, and neighbors raised their children. It sees and feels the river bathing its feet, the unending flow of highway travelers in unconscious obeisance, the country road straight ahead, and lake to its left, and the cemetery at Coleville to its right. It scans the fields, the herds of cattle and horses grazing, the birds, the water, the trees, and on most days a clear sky.

A deceptive plainness, at its top are two or three sparse trees, barely holding their own, like the last remnants of hair on a very old, bald head. Because of this and the fact it's too steep to climb and yet not high enough to attract mountain climbers, it effectively prevents its desecration. Perhaps no one has ever climbed it—or should try to do so if the iniquity of the father can be visited on his children to the fourth generation.

It is strange never to have wondered what was behind it and then to find out in such a way. So maybe it was taboo for me to go there or even with somebody. There is a higher valley which was then—and still might be—government grazing land.[81] Many from the valley where we lived sent cattle there. These were looked after by one or two cowboys who bunked in a small cabin. Turns were taken by the ranchers to send provisions, and when our time came, Warren readied a pack horse. I saddled Porter, a dependable and faithful mustang they'd caught years before, and followed along with no idea where we were headed other than a place called Slinkard. We then rode toward the mountain, crossed the bridge, and turned right on 395. Here we traveled to the side of the road until the mountains, decreasing in size, had a pass to the left that we could use to get into Slinkard. We eventually broke out of this into a flat valley surrounded by hills and mountains. It was a scenic grazing area with few trees and occasional pockets of sagebrush, called wormwood in the Old World.

I was behind Warren and the pack horse, the price to be paid for old Porter's reliability and faithfulness. Warren had ridden right on by and missed seeing the three-foot rattler in the grass, twenty yards away. It wasn't coiled or any threat to us and was moving in the opposite direction. But you must know by now—that everything I touch or see turns to shit.

"Hey Warren!" I shouted. "Look back there at that snake!"

He turned, seeing it then, and we stopped, getting off the horses. We looked for rocks to kill it, but *there were none*. By this time, it'd outsmarted us and slithered into the protection of the dense sagebrush. Damn thing!

Warren pulled out and lit a match to a bush to smoke it out, but we couldn't see it crawl away anyplace. A small wind blew and spread the fire, and we realized sinkingly what we'd done and what was happening. It was out of control now and had to be reported. The quickest way back seemed to be to ride further into Slinkard, past the steep mountain to a smaller one we could climb with the horses. What god was this of riders and horses, of two brothers, death, of stones or no stones, fire-sticks and fire, sudden wind, flight, mountains, and snakes or *snake*?[82]

We pushed our horses up, up, up, and finally over and down a rugged mountain and swiftly back to the ranch, where they were sweating, lathered, and exhausted. Warren quickly told our father, who immediately called the forest service. The fire already had been reported, but they'd not known how it started. What a contrast to many a parent today who would say, "Don't be a fool! You don't know nothin'. Dummy up." Warren then had to go back and fight it for nearly twenty-four hours before the fire was put out. It must have been very hard for him, but he didn't flinch or complain. Being too young to go, I, a ne'r do gooder blamed for everything, fought the fire in my own way: "It was Warren who lit the match? I had nothing to do with it," I sniveled.

"Shut up!" Bob snarled. "Stand up and take the blame right along with your brother! Hear me?"

Why was he getting hot at me? If he wanted to blame somebody, blame his own great, great great grandparents. Hadn't Grandpa Adam and Grandma Eve passed down to me how to deal with the problems of a serpent? Don't get mad at me, big bruddha, for being a chip off the ol' block, a little weasel.[83-A]

The story was carried in a Carson City newspaper. But either out of respect for our pa, our ages, or both, names were never mentioned. It began something like this: "Two young boys were riding...."

Bob decided to take a few days and rope mustangs at Alkali Flat. Of all things western, I'd wanted to do this most, but because of Ralph's death, my father wouldn't let me. Yet a neighbor's kid who was about my age was allowed to. I was expected to understand that the ranch kid was much more experienced and that it was for my safety. But it was too much to expect my father to understand it was more important for me to have gone than any of the horses they could have roped. Hell, I'd have ridden ol' Porter and stayed a safe distance behind just to be part of it. (The young caretaker of the graves, he of the Feast of the Dead, must be protected at all costs, especially in the exclusion of horse symbolism.)

Somehow this was an instant replay of Mom about not quite measuring up. As long as an explanation was given that could be understood, *she would achieve for herself* in some crazy, mixed-up, vicarious way a saintliness from St. Francis of Assisi's dictum, "It is better to understand than to be understood."

The company Dad worked for transferred him from Avenal to Bakersfield. We eventually moved from Oildale to a la-de-da sounding tract called Highland Manor. Here Robyn married and was off most of those years with her husband, who was in the Coast Guard.

In grammar school I worked for awhile in the school cafeteria for lunches and lined baseball diamonds or basketball and volleyball courts after class. A few second, third, and fourth place ribbons were won in track. Nobody came away without something. After all, our teachers had taken child psychology courses which taught them to make each student feel like a winner and he or she will become a winner, whereupon either the teacher or student can write it up someday for submission to *Reader's Digest*. Exception: The music appreciation teacher gave me a D always, certain I'd never be able to carry a tune. She was, of course, right about me but wrong about Bing Crosby, whom she detested. Anyway if she had just made me feel like a winner, I would have settled for just being filthy rich. I worked harder by singing louder. A poem was published in the school paper. So far this is all there's been in print, which just shows that some people are educated far beyond their intelligence:

> If I had one wish,
> I'd wish for more.
> I'd wish for a tire,
> And the end of the war.
> I'd wish for an airplane
> To fly to Berlin,
> And hit Herr Hitler
> Right on the chin.

(Never got to Berlin by plane, but Hitler died on the day of Walpurgis a few years later.)

Sometimes it was hard to figure what was disliked more: going to the ranch in the summer, where I never seemed to measure up and which was Dullsville and hard work, or staying home with Mom on nearly a one-to-one basis.

My father's idea of a good time—except for a Reno rodeo on the fourth of July—was to go horseback riding or maybe to buy a milkshake at Coleville, where he'd say, "Make mine thick now. I'll pay extra. Don't like those runny things." Could he ever have had the clap? Shut up, Mr. Hyde! That's Doctor Jekyll's business.

Again television hadn't been invented. A movie house might have been in Bridgeport or Gardnerville, but there wasn't one in Coleville. Neither Warren nor my father played cards or games. Other than working nets during haying season on our ranch and one nearby, Warren and I seldom, if ever, did much together. He never seemed enthusiastic about anything, like saying, "Come on, Burnt, help me do this," or "to hell with cutting thistle (let's go wet our whistle)," or "cleaning the irrigation ditch, that can wait a few days. Have you ever been hunting or fishing? No? Well, let's me and you take off a couple days, and we'll catch a limit apiece."

He is easier to understand if you stop to think that he had a hard life beginning at an early age. It was necessary to pull his own weight against two older brothers. Who could he cry to? They weren't much older than he. To him I must have seemed a useless individual who bad luck seemed to follow in at least three instances.

There is one other factor to this equation. Aunt Nell told me once that Anita had commented that my father never seemed to compliment his sons enough or show much affection. This doesn't mean my father's and Warren's intentions weren't good, but generally you were supposed to read their feelings from the fact that they were present and/or doing the work and paying the bills. It's fair to say that neither one was very demonstrative, not, at least, in my case. How they might have related to others could have been very different, depending on their ages at the time, worries, etc. A constant for each throughout his life was honesty.

When Warren married, he bought property on 395, closer to the mountain. There he and Lola brought up their children.

Chapter Twelve

Mom was forever in shorts, showing off her shapely varicose veins and wearing heavy rouge and lipstick. The fact of the matter is that people with varicose veins got just as hot in Bakersfield as anyone else, and women in those days wore more cosmetics than they do today. And if a man or woman begins to sag in places or get gray hair and false teeth, is he or she suppose to drop dead? Mom was in her forties in the forties. Not that forty is old, but it's getting there. And a person not growing old gracefully is like someone hungry, begging on the street. It's a sadness, and it was hard to imagine her as a young girl trying to grow up.[83-B]

Both Dad and she and the next-door neighbor, Mal, and her friends drank and smoked heavily. There was often two or three of them sitting around drinking when I got home from school. This sometimes continued on into the evening. When I'd get up in the morning, usually the front-room air was stale, reeking of wine and cigarette smoke, though she might have emptied the ashtrays and taken the wine glasses out. I was expected to get my own breakfast, fix a lunch to pack with me, do my dishes, make my bed, and clean the bathroom thoroughly. This meant cleaning the bathtub, if dirty; the sink; and the toilet. "And remember to clean around in back of the toilet, and put your hand down in the water when you clean it. It won't hurt you. I did it in nurse's training." All this was to be done while being reasonably quiet so she could sleep in 'til 9:00 or 10:00 A.M.

Being a dumb kid—and kind of afraid she would embarrass me—I told her a couple days before grammar school graduation, "You know, Mom, you won't be able to smoke in the auditorium."

Mein gott in himmel! She flew into a rage, informing me she certainly had sense enough to know that, and she went on and on. It happened that Hoyt, before he married Robyn, had bought a new watch for himself, so they bought his old one for me for graduation.

"It's a perfectly good watch, and you understand we just can't afford to buy you a new one."

74

Sure I understood, as she expected, but the problem, seen now with more perspective, was that I was exploited too much to understand, to look deeper.

Someday, if not done already, a bright psychology student will do a Ph.D. thesis on what gardens reveal about the mind of the gardener. Laugh if you want, but it's not necessarily a crackpot idea, worthy therefore of being funded by taxpayer dollars. In some cases, it would tell more than the Rorschach.

As in Avenal, she threw herself with a mania into her yardwork. She had Dad sink posts around the perimeter of the back. He connected chicken wire to these, making a fence with gates. The area at the time really deserved better than this, but anything else would have cost more than they felt they could afford. Sure it kept the dogs in, but it also kept them from composing doggerel in somebody else's yard, as any smart animals worth their keep will learn to do.

"If you want these animals, you're going to have to look after them," she harped. It almost seems like yesterday going around daily with a shovel and picking up the dog flop and dumping it into the compost pit.[84]

At times the flowers bloomed and were rich in color, and of course she loved this, but it was so damned hard to maintain. Bakersfield isn't Seattle, where the ground is fairly easy to turn over and which has summer rain and only three or four hot, uncomfortable days most years. Her garden probably influenced my writing, which sandwiches anything and everything that comes to mind. To hell with your criticism that it's a flea market with secondhand thoughts, vague connections, and meanderings. In my best Peter Lorre, "Won't you please try to understand?"

At times the yard was a nightmare jungle, as if she were trying to appease some implacable, vegetative deity in spite of overwhelming obstacles of constant watering and rampant devil grass and weeds. Maybe that's why she drank so much. She knew something the rest of us didn't, and her mouth sometimes turned down into a wine-stubborn meanness or grimness as she tried to bring in some order and beauty.

It was a wandering thing, gypsy, ornate, disparate, Bohemeian, cramped into a flat lot, nearly even with the street. Just in the backyard alone, which wasn't large, was a clothesline, a weeping willow,[85] and other deciduous trees. Roses, boysenberry bushes, and grapevines crept over the fence. Several varieties of squash, including the notorious zucchini which feeds an army, climbed up the lattice arbor, nearly filled with a table, chairs, a portable charcoal broiler, two doghouses, and several pans sitting around with water or remnants of their last meal, and a hammock. There was a victory garden, compost pit, flower beds, shrubs, cacti, a wagon wheel, Chinese, wind glass-tinkler, a sundial, a bird house, birdbath, and several cheap statues. To this could be seen most days, a wheelbarrow, a shovel, rake, hoe, motorless lawnmower, and hoses and sprinklers attached to the end.

The worst of the campaigns were those in the spring and hot summer when Bermuda grass grew fast and furious and weeds gained more and more ground. Fortified with wine, she counterattacked savagely, maiming and killing without mercy for two or three days. Neither the old nor young were spared, and often she called up the reserves (me) to help. Then either beaten or feeling the situation was under control, she retreated to the inside, licking her wounds for three or four days, save for watering.

All the homes surrounding us had only two or three trees apiece, a few rose bushes, lawns, and no fences. Nobody but nobody in all Highland Manor certainly—and perhaps even farther—fought the pitch battles we did. It was twenty years or more before Agent Orange and an unstoppable cancer that grew and grew when she pitted herself and me at times against. Nothing could save us except heroic treatment: massive doses of radiation. In this case, a thermonuclear bomb. So if in your travels you might/ Come across some man's home/Peculiarly protected by a concrete sea/ Think of me.

But that's just one perspective. Fifty years later I wonder about being the serpent in the garden. The betrayal of writing lay dormant, which she sensed even then.

The stones next to the street made a demarcation of property. There's nothing wrong with that really, but we were the only ones in a tract of many homes who had this, so typically Hermes that any Greek traveler from millenniums before would have felt compelled to add a stone in passing for luck.

Come to think of it, maybe that's why Ralph of the Feralia lost his life. He had not known about this, that he somehow related to another time, another place. Far-fetched? You're probably right.

Still there'll always be some question in my mind of why Dot and Burt Fry took off in his company pickup one day. They'd gone someplace where a building was being torn down and salvaged a large, rectangular urinal, approximately four feet by twenty or more inches. She had no trouble finding a conspicuous place for it in the backyard and soon added water lilies and goldfish: water, lilies, and fish.

A young cousin coming to visit gasped in surprise: "Isn't that a...a...a...?" Embarrassed, I cut her off with a curt, "Yeah," making it very clear the discussion had ended. Dad in his old age commented that he hated it, too. "But you know how she was," he wrote. At a young age and at the time I took it seriously. Now I'd probably post a sign next to it saying, "Please don't piss in our pool. We don't swim in your toilet."

It seems amusing that the god was just laughing at us all along, having his little joke on how we propel ourselves through life with vanity and pride. And yet there was a sadness that if he cut it off, he would bring each of us to suicide. He could have had rectangular stones with human heads and erect phalli sticking out to represent him as a fertility god, but times had changed.

Nothing fantasized could have been better than being a composer. Musica, the universal language. The instrument, a piano. For this, like some Chekhov character, I'd have given up ever seeing, hearing, or touching another human being. To have known that only the piano and I existed and nothing more as meals were put through a door.

Naturally at first I'd not have known what the piano was for, jumping back both surprised and scared when pressing its keys. Then realizing it wouldn't hurt me, I'd bang on it over and over to make more noise. Perhaps this would go on for months and months as one piano after another wore out. Then maybe I'd experiment, plunking away at single sounds and discordant notes. How beautiful to be completely ignorant of Bach, Beethoven, Brahms, Chopin, Liszt, Wagoner, and Tchaikovsky. To never have heard another sound other than what I'd made myself. One day through dumb luck, I'd hit upon three or four notes which intrigued me, and very slowly I'd learn to express my thoughts and feelings through the keyboard. And for all, though not knowing it at the time, I'd reach down into my soul to find a different music, never before heard, which heals and brings peace.[86] So you see me as the idealist, the day-dreamer, and not much has changed in this respect over the years. Maybe Mom was right: "You understand we just don't have the money for you to take piano lessons."

Like she expected, I understood. It wasn't until years later that it occurred to me they'd had money for Robyn to take tap-dancing lessons when she was growing up, though for me there was no resentment toward Robyn. They did, however, send off for a self-teaching course. It wasn't the same as having someone teach and correct on fundamentals. Eventually I'd mow a piano teacher's lawn, four hours of work for one hour of instruction. What with wanting to make a grade-point average to get into college, a certain amount of work to be done around the house; mowing lawns for pocket money, I found my motivation began to wane. Yet it cost nothing to sit at the piano and imagine myself as José Iturbi.

Dad's mother, Matilda, then in or nearing her eighties, was visiting us for a period. She had one of the twin beds in the bedroom, and I the other, or very possibly I slept on the front-room couch or in the garage. Relentlessly practicing Chopin's *Minute Waltz*, a piece far beyond my capabilities, I'd made little progress, missing every fourth note but nonetheless finishing in one minute. This was repeated over and over. Matilda by this time was in a snit. Unable to put up with one minute one minute longer, she said peevishly, "You'd think as many times as you've practiced that, you'd have it right by now!"

Implicit in her tortured eyes was: "What am I to do?" I'd think *What are you to do? Why do the Minute Waltzing Matilda? What else?* Reading her: "What am I to do now that you have driven me up a tree?" *What are you to do? Why jump and pull your ripcord*, I thought but said only, "Okay Grandma," and stopped practicing. I was always deferring to relatives, friends of the family, and older people.[87] I was such a nice, understanding little boy then that now considerable empathy can be found with Charles Whitman, who climbed the Texas University tower on August 1, 1966, and sniped away, killing fourteen and wounding thirty. I'm not saying I'd do this. What's being said is that after awhile all human beings look pretty much alike. The essence of life for each is: I have or have not; you have or have not; we have or have not. It's pure measurement coupled with need and/or greed.

Of course Matilda was right. Even my uncle Norm wrote me a note once:

> I remember your music
> So well rendered.
> Like grease from cracklings
> So harshly surrendered.

Still, sometimes I think had there been proper training soon enough....

Was the world dark, without form and void before Nintendo and television? No. We played games: checkers, Chinese checkers, dominoes, monopoly, Hollywood poker, cribbage, rummy, hearts, solitaire, double solitaire, etc. I knew then and have forgotten more about blackjack and poker than most adults know today. Curiously we never played Chess, nor would I have known how had we a board and pieces.

Dad's work routine in Bakersfield was the same as in Avenal. Had he an 8:00-5:00 workday, the marriage probably wouldn't have lasted. Again, he was gone two and four days at a time. My problems, however, were on a daily basis. Sometimes when I got home from school, she'd hear the bus or the front door opening and call me into the bedroom where the blinds were pulled, and she was lying in bed. She didn't feel well, she'd say, and begin to tick off what was supposed to be done. Go peel the potatoes, put them on to boil, do this, and do that, but first get her a glass of water, which I'd do. She usually didn't look sick, and so I'd leave her without saying a word, without any commiseration. If her indignation at this was any gage at all, then she usually proved my point. It was a year-in and year-out pattern for her to lie around for a couple days saying she was sick. The doctor, to my knowledge, could find nothing wrong with her. Certainly he never seemed to prescribe anything, but she remarked that he'd once said she might have the Valley Fever.

There was no Valium or Prozac in those days. Today a person would probably get a prescription for one of these or something similar without the stigma of having to go to a psychiatrist, making oneself more vulnerable to the pecking order, and many expensive hours of sessions.

Then when the period of sickness was over, she'd get up and work like hell for three or four days, followed by a couple more on the phone telling Ruth, the wife of one of Dad's coworkers, how hard she'd been working, and sit around with Mal and/or other friends drinking.

She chipped away at my self-esteem—especially by saying if I was defying or criticizing her, I was ungrateful. That was rich! Chances are my only reason for wanting to be a doctor was to make her proud so she'd have some feeling her life had some importance. There were fleeting and perhaps sincere moments when she said she and Dad loved me and all they wanted for me out of life was to be happy. This confused me even more as I understood. Maybe, but I think she expected more. Phyllis, who probably could see into this, remarked to me one time, "Brent, you don't have to set the world on fire."

A suspicion or perhaps insight to writing this book is the inherited or learned mania to excel from the bright sisters. Unfortunately their brainpower didn't accompany it, for only a dim wit would choose to dig up a past which should have been buried and long forgotten. What purpose would it serve? It won't change things. No one's perfect, least of all me, thinking back of life. A tyrannical or domineering parent isn't uncommon. For an adult to whine he had one is much like a man who tells a friend he's been cuckolded. There's pity perhaps, but a certain mockery and contempt lie just beneath the surface, to be ready to use in the war of words if he should ever cross that person. This may sound cynical, but it's also a realism in life. Anybody who thinks differently is living in a Walt Dizzy-Reader's Digested world. A certain detachment can be reached only if a person regards life as a learning experience. None of us learns at the same rate. Judgment is foolish, yet even in knowing and seeing this clearly, I will have judged someone or thing before the cock[88-A] crows just once. Judgment is simply betrayal and the nature of the beast. Brent is always so understanding!

> So now you'll understand
> That down deep inside
> Is Mr. Hyde
> Growing stronger by the day.
> The end of life will be photo-finish,
> If he doesn't break away.

Chapter Thirteen

Dollena Dorothy was twelve when her mother, Annie, died of breast cancer in 1912. Robyn wrote that Mom had mentioned seeing one or two times the "deep hole in her breast or chest when she peeked through the bedroom door when the dressings were being changed by the doctor or nurses," and Mom told me that Annie—when talking of death—had said to her one time, "Oh you'll get over it, and in four or five days, you'll hardly think about it." "This was true," Mom said. Life goes on.

Annie, if not dour, was likely a stern woman and a disciplinarian, or so two cousins had heard or surmised. The one, nearly fifty years ago, mentioned also that she felt our grandmother had instilled in her daughters (or perhaps it was an inherited trait) that they somehow were a little better or perhaps made for better things, that they must be achievers.

A letter, dated August 22, 1991, from Columbia University in New York City sums up my mother's education:

> Frances Mae Duren attended the Graduate School of Arts and Sciences during the Spring 1914 term (January–May). Miss Duren registered for two courses, one in history and one in social economy...previous education notes "Leland Junior/Stanford, California" where she was awarded the B.A. degree and 8 points graduate study (1908–1912).

Aunt Nell graduated from Stanford too, and Aunt Edith, an accomplished pianist, graduated from the College of Pacific. Aunt Gen, the youngest, was in some respects—but certainly not all—like Mom and would marry and raise a family. Late in life, when her children had long since married and had children, Aunt Gen went to college and got a degree. It's guesswork, but it's a good bet she felt compelled to do that.

Scholastically it probably took more effort to make it through college before the twenties than it does nowadays. Possibly Dollena Dorothy was overshadowed by her three older sisters who were respectively eleven, nine, and eight years older than she. Remember, too, she was still in grammar school when Annie died, while her older sisters were in or near-ly out of college. She was certainly as smart as they, but she wasn't per-severing (nor was I for that matter) and maybe competed for her father's love, recognition, and attention the only way she knew how—with her imagination by trying to be entertaining, different, unique. She told me several times it was she who was her father's favorite, and she said he used to say, "Oh Dolly (Dottie), you're the one, so cute and clever."

In this respect, as if vying for her father's attention, she dealt with oth-ers, as if trying to be a star, if only for a minute while it fell. But that's just my opinion of what she thought.

It's only fair to add Robyn's recollections and perceptions which dif-fer somewhat from mine:

> I can never remember Mother saying she was Granddad
> Duren's favorite. But, as I see her in my memory, she
> always wanted to be the attraction of the family X-mas
> and holiday get-togethers. She wanted the attention
> focused on her, so I wouldn't be surprised if she thought
> she was her daddy's favorite, although it's usually the
> last child born that is the baby always through life and
> made over by the parents. I agree with your conclusions
> that she was vying for everybody's love, not just grand-
> dad's love. Brent, honest to God, I don't remember ever
> hearing her say anything demeaning about her sisters.

Robyn, of course, wouldn't have heard the comments because they were made in Bakersfield during the four years or so when she was gone. I stand by what's said. Indeed, Aunt Gen might have got the attention. This would have put Mom in the left-out position all the way around, and she could have fantasized or read more into her father's remarks than was meant. All this, of course, is only supposition. But there has to have been something that happened back then to explain or justify her later erratic behavior in life.

As previously stated, Mom filed away in her memory and then, fifteen years or so after my birth, tried to stir up trouble by making much more out of Aunt Nell's remark than was intended at the time. Mom sniffed both at me and my mother as having no friends, being loners, and per-haps something more. She said my father had misled my mother into thinking he had more than he really did. Since Gen had never been a threat to Dollena, that left only Edith, who she thought put on airs, to take down a peg or two. This aunt of mine never failed to send Mom expen-sive figurines she otherwise couldn't have afforded on her birthday and at Christmas.

It came to pass that when Mom visited this sister and her husband in Long Beach in the 1940s, there was a young man staying with them as a guest. Mom, probably reading meaning into something that wasn't there, or projecting her own feelings, whispered that her sister was having an affair. Even at the worst, if true, it certainly wasn't her business to spread this as she herself lived in a very fragile glass house. When word had gotten back to the aunt and uncle what she was saying, they were mortified and disgusted. A few years following this, when Mom died, Edith was the only one not attending her funeral, giving ill health as a reason. Previously her husband had called Mom a "psychopathic liar." He might have been right.

Any arguments she and I had when Dad was gone she told him about later. There was always an element of truth in what she said, but it was usually slanted. He believed her like a man under a spell.

As a favor to a friend who had once given us a purebred puppy, we took an old cocker spaniel off his hands. Gypsy had had several litters of pups before, was high-strung, and tended to growl and snarl if made to do anything she didn't want, such as being put out of the garage into the yard. One day she ran out the front door and got into a fight with the neighbor's English bull. I went over and got them separated. No one was hurt, including the animals. There was nothing to the incident whatsoever, or at least there shouldn't have been. Mom heard the noise, and as I brought Gypsy back in, she asked what happened.

"The two dogs got into a fight. That's all."

"Was it on our property or hers?"

"Neither. It was right in between."

"Well, I'm going over there when she gets home and have this out with her. I'll put a stop to this."

"A stop to what?"

"That she's got to do something about her dog and biting you."

Jesus! Neither dog had bitten me, and this was explained again to her. If one had, it would have been our black cocker, not the white, English bull who, making no qualms about a gas attack at times, would have died before biting me.

"You shut up! Their dog bit you, and that's what you'll say."

So she broke off relations with the lady next door who had been our friend for four or five years and wasn't a drinker to any extent, if at all. She was a divorced woman who had to have transfusions for leukemia from time to time and worked hard at a job downtown to support herself and her two teenage children. Furthermore, she had always been nice to me. Her kids and I shot baskets over their garage door and played Ping-Pong and tennis together. I'd slept over at their house before, eaten with them many times, and been invited to their parties.

For at least a year or more, no one spoke, and we pretended we didn't know each other. It was an awkward situation to be in for all. Funny but I never put together just what happened before this writing. Maybe because it was better to forget those years. Dad, who was putty in

Mom's hands, died without ever knowing the reason, and evidently the lady next door never figured it out either. I was mowing the lawn of a neighbor on the other side of her house one day when she spoke from her kitchen window.

"Well, Brent, it's a good thing there's not another dogfight going on, or you'd be stupid enough to pull them apart and get yourself bit."

Now I recall Mom muttering in her drunkenness one time that she thought Dad was interested in the woman next door.

"He doesn't think I know what's going on. But I know!"

So she had fooled us all as to her reason. Whatever happened–or whatever she could imagine–made the end justify the means. If this weren't a case of cunning, psychopathic lying, then I don't know what would be.

Robyn came home to live with us. Her husband had been transferred to the war zone in Alaska or the Aleutian Islands. Mom and I got into another fight. She was going to have her way no matter what. Maybe at the time, she wouldn't have gone through with it. Still she put on a very convincing performance as she staggered with a threatening voice, menacing eyes, a mouth turned down in grimness and resolve, and a black vase raised to smash down on what she reasoned was a thick skull. Here there might be some confusion of the details of one episode with another as they were all pretty much alike. So I grabbed her arms to prevent this. My skull might have been thick, but there was no pea brain underneath— or maybe it was. When Dad got back, she told him I'd hit her. Move over, Joseph.

Robyn, who had seen the whole thing, stuck up for me by saying it wasn't so. Nevertheless, Dad wouldn't believe me or his own flesh-and-blood daughter, who didn't drink or lie. Such was the hold his wife had on him that sometimes you wondered if they'd spent their honeymoon in Haiti.

Robyn was told to move out. It's ironic that the idea was put into Dad's head by Mom, without him realizing that with Robyn gone, me at school all day, and him being gone for days at a time, Mom once again had the house free in the daytime to socialize with Mal's male friends.

In later life, he wouldn't have me or Robyn living at home to bear the brunt of Mom's episodes, which he could come back to and smooth over, acting as a judge after the fact. He then would have to face her squarely himself. My understanding is that they had many fights, one violent or at least when he smashed to smithereens hundreds of phonograph records which would have been worth a small fortune today. Welcome to the club, Daddy!

Many years later, after Mom died, I went back to Avenal when Dad wasn't home, threw out my things, and left on the bus, never to return. It was the wrong thing to have done to Dad—he deserved better—but it was the right thing for me to have done for myself at that age. I refused to spend the rest of my life apologizing for what I'd become. Steeped in Christian ethic, there was always guilt: "Honor thy father and thy mother."

So you see it wasn't even a good soap. It never would have made *Hard Copy*, *Inside Edition*, or *A Current Affair*. No blood was drawn, no bodies were chopped up, and there were no untidy, unpaid bills or cords of wood and cases of relish and catsup from doing it the safeway. This was by the grace of God who, nevertheless, decided to inflict upon me a never-ending stream of Christendom's Peter Lorres with their benedictions: "Please, you must try to understand and to forgive." And who give a new dimension in meaning to: "Good understanding giveth favor, but the way of transgressors is hard."

That is, good understanding gives favor, but when you push it too much in others to further your own ends, it's wrong.

But I've gotten ahead of myself.

One Friday she and Dad took off to Taft to pick up Grandma Matilda and bring her to Bakersfield for a visit. I fed the animals, watered, and did high school homework. But what goes around comes around. The house was a mess when she left, and she was madder than a wet hen that I hadn't cleaned it up, worked in the yard, and had the evening meal cooking when they returned Sunday afternoon.

Summer session saw me taking courses in typing and English. The latter consisted entirely of diagraming sentences, as if in the beginning "The word was God," every word that followed was related on a holy, begatting genealogical chart. Practically speaking, it made you tongue-tied when you began to write. It had been put together in the devil's workshop and was itself a six-week sentence.

When I gave the record cards to Dad and went outside, he handed them to his brother and wife who were visiting and bragged, "Why I don't even have to look at these. He always gets such good grades." Surprise: a pair of D's. There was no concern for me or wondering why a student who usually got A's and B's would suddenly get D's. Mom, as to be expected, lectured how I had embarrassed Dad in front of his brother and his wife. The low marks affected my overall grade average very little. The damn credits weren't needed. Why the summer school? It made no sense.

From time to time, Mom would break into her facetious refrain, "I'm just a poor ol' broken-down, workhorse, grey-haired mother." She was more than this, but that might very well have been the way she saw—or didn't see—herself at times. Mom had good points, too. It's this that makes it hard to mention only what was wrong, an unfairness in some ways. I can remember many little caring things she did, such as heating up bricks and wrapping them in cloth, then putting them in our beds for our feet on a cold winter's night when we were very young. In her defense, it's only fair to add too that one woman who had a multitude of children commented that snakes were by far the hardest to bring up.

Probably the reason she didn't ever say, "I wish I hadn't done this" or "It was bad for me to have said what I did, " was that she usually didn't acknowledge wrongdoing on her part and so never had any personal regrets about her behavior. Don't get me wrong. She would have been the first to admit a mechanical error *sometimes*. In so doing it would have proved beyond a doubt that, after all, she was very human and made mistakes. But did it really? Or was it just a decoy both to herself and others? There was an ambience that she felt she had class and was somehow "more together" than the rest of us. But she could never be quiet when it came to getting first credit for pointing out the flaws, weaknesses, imperfections, or suspicions about somebody else. In all the above of this paragraph, Robyn's mother and ex-husband were alike. Each, in my opinion, were lacking in this dimension for real depth.

Compounding my problems were good, strong teeth—for a vampire, that is. Riding in my cousin's car one day with her three, small children:

"Mommie, why do his teeth stick out like that in front?"

"Shhh!"

"But Mommie?"

"Shhh! That's enough."

"But Mommie?"

"I'm not going to tell you again now!"

I could hardly go for his jugular with her sitting right there. He was too young for me to give him my best Bela Lugosi: "Oh you hauve such bea-U-tiful blood!" Couldn't smile back sweetly, as that might have triggered another outburst. I wasn't completely bad. W.C. Fields was right.

"We don't have the money for braces," Mom said. "Besides they don't look that bad."

I understood.

Dad drove hundreds of miles each week in his work. Driving for him was second nature. He must have been half asleep at times; still he never had an accident. Sometimes he would take me on a short trip to keep him company, but it was much like horseback riding with my father in Topaz. Both occasions were similar to going on a bus: You weren't doing anything much, just traveling. We never did anything together—just me and him alone—except maybe play cribbage, which he enjoyed. I mean things like fishing, camping, hunting, playing baseball, shooting baskets, taking an engine apart, or changing the oil on a car.

When I was fifteen or sixteen, he did take me out to a flat area one day to teach me to drive. He explained the name of everything, but I didn't grasp it all at once. So when getting behind the wheel, I let out on the clutch before shifting gears completely or something else. The pickup bounced around while he yelled to do this or that. He's excited; I'm excited. When we finally stop, he explains things again with nearly the same results. He doesn't comment, and we go home.

Soon Mom comes in alone to talk to me.

"Your dad says you'll never to able to drive."

But all wasn't lost, maybe. She had read about some famous violinist who couldn't drive. Her meaning was clear, through in so many words. Perhaps there was still some hope. They might yet plumb a depth and discover something that would make them proud of me. Even an idiot savant would be better than nothing. But if not, she wanted me to understand she understood, that she loved me.

Being unusually dumb in the ways of the world (too much effort was being spent on trying to understand), I could only get smarter, and then only by the divine intervention of Hermes. Dad was hired by Hughes Tool Company to go to work in Avenal. How to get out of this? How to get away? It was then that the D's paid off handsome DiviDenDs. I figured that with these two courses it would be necessary only to complete one semester the senior year to graduate. Click! Here was a way of getting out from under. Click! Click! I wrote my father in Topaz that it would mean an awful lot to me to be able to finish up with the students I'd known throughout high school (a half-truth) and that, besides, Mom and I weren't getting along too well (a truth and a half). Would he pay Bakersfield high school my room and board for one semester?

Hallelujah! He would. The D's were a blessing in disguise, an unnoticed sign of the cabala, as well as help from my snake-cousin Howard. My father sent exactly the amount the school specified. In all fairness, that's all which was asked. Money for paper, pencils, haircuts, toilet articles, meals the school didn't provide, amusement, etc., hadn't been taken into consideration. This was money not be push my luck to ask him to send; for though he was my father, he wasn't. A job after classes had to be gotten.

Chapter Fourteen

The high-school employment desk referred me to a nearby Catholic hospital.

"Hope you'll let me work here, sister, because I'm studying to be a medical doctor someday," I said proudly, while gawking in awe. She stood like a statue with her hands folded, eyes radiant, and a beautiful smile. She wore the old-style habit. A tight wimple framed the beads of perspiration on her face. How hot she must be with all that! Did nuns really shave their head as some people say? The errant thought was quickly dismissed as inappropriate and unworthy. This was the closest an unbaptized Protestant background could come to a penance.

The job paid forty cents an hour. *Forty* in biblical terms is supposed to mean a great amount, but even by 1946 standards, it wasn't much for scrubbing the white-tile floors in the operating rooms. If they had electrical equipment for doing this, I never saw it. It was generally work with long-handled brushes and on hands and knees sometimes, followed by mopping with a bucket and wringer. She got her money's worth, for as you recall I'd put in a long apprenticeship under an exacting woman who'd been a nurse trainee. Besides, the sister seemed pleased, often complimenting and asking me to work an extra hour.

She always smiled like an angel, her hands held together, and addressed me as "little boy," though I stood a head taller than she and was seventeen. It's doubtful she could recall my name without referring to a record. Yet I remembered hers to see if she were canonized someday. Of course nobody wanted to rush things, but the suspense was killing me.

If I'd been unbelievably naive for my age in wondering only that she shaved her head—but not thinking about other things—and then feeling as if I was committing a mortal sin, she in her naivety managed a one-upmanship.

"Little boy," she demurred, calling me over to where she was drawing some lines on a paper. Maybe she wanted to play tic-tac-toe and have some good nun fun. But it soon was clear she didn't have that in mind, as I saw a five-stick drawing, one for the torso, two for the arms, and two for the legs. Maybe it was voodoo. Over the torso and just below she then drew two parallel lines:

———————
———————

She stood there in her black-and-white habit, which was nearly all black and very little white, and placed in front of me a straight razor and a piece of paper with a hospital room on it. No sister! I can't do it. Had she made a circle or used the word *genitalia* or *pubic hair*, it might at first made it easier to understand. But only "little boy" and "shave" were righteous for the ceremony. Indeed, some things required of her as a nurse must have been a terrible burden.

So armed with a straight razor, having never used one before, emesis basin, two by two's, and a tincture of green soap, I headed to the hospital room. If such things as accompanying me the first time to see that the razor was used correctly and that the man was prep'ed properly were beyond her, her cross to bear. I'm sure the fist time to do it shakily by myself was my penance for wondering if she'd shaved her head. Just what the patient had done is unknown, but it must have been something terrible. Any surgery to follow could only have been a piece of cake.

Most times after working two or three hours—and especially if I'd missed supper—I'd stop by a bakery to buy a fresh sweet roll. But this cost one-third the hourly wage. I was getting nowhere on forty cents an hour and so asked for a ten-cent increase. The sister said she would talk to the mother superior, who agreed to the raise. They continued to be satisfied with my work, and everything slipped into routine.

Then one afternoon after classes, I was about to go up the dormitory stairs when one student standing in front said, "Hey Brent, the cops are up there going through your things."

"Yeah sure!"

"No, I'm not kidding," he said seriously.

I couldn't ever remember talking to the police before. They, like the sister, were sort of holy.

Entering the sleeping room with several beds, I saw they'd tossed by clothing around.

"What you doing with my stuff?"

"This is yours?"

"Yes."

"Before you say anything, let me tell you we have every right to make this search. The school is public property."

"Why are you doing this?"

"The sister you work for at the hospital has found many surgical instruments missing. She said you told her you wanted to be a doctor and thinks you took them."

They then left. Everything was strewn around. Not a word was said like, "Sorry about that." Guess it would have made it so much easier for them if I'd been guilty.

It threw me for a loop. What could be wanted with surgical instruments which were not known how to use? And I wouldn't have known for at least seven or eight years, provided all the hurdles financially, scholastically, etc., could be met. It was clear that logic had less to do with it than the credentials of a nun's aura. What amazes me, looking back, is that I never thought of telling her to take the job and cram it, which she certainly deserved to be told, making a mockery out of her religion. What a dumb kid for my age! My only thought, pumped up and leaving for the hospital, was to tell her I wasn't going to work for her anymore.

She wasn't in surgery. The nurse who was there could see my agitation and asked what was wrong. I blurted out what happened and about quitting. Would she tell the sister?

"That woman!" she frowned, shaking her head. "Those instruments have been missing for a long, long time, and this is the first she's held an inventory in years."

As I was leaving, the sister came through the door.

"Oh, little boy," she smiled. "I'm so glad you have come by. Guess what? I was looking through the paper and see where they need an ambulance driver at another hospital. Since it pays so much more than you are making here, you really ought to take the job. I wanted to tell you about it."

She didn't mention that she's set the police on me, nor did I. She didn't ask if I had a driver's license, which I didn't, or if those hours could be worked, so intent was she in doing God's work.

"I've come to tell you I'm quitting, sister."

"Well, little boy, you go see about this job I have found for you," she said, as if deserving thanks.

"Goodbye, sister."

"Goodbye, *little boy*" (the name of the bomb dropped on Hiroshima, and if she'd dropped "little," I might have passed for black), she beamed, her eyes clearly saying, A crazy "I love you."

About fourteen years later, it was important to have someone to talk with immediately. A Catholic priest made time for this. So when seeing myself clear, I returned to him saying that I wished to give a donation of five hundred dollars to some charity he suggested. Realizing I didn't make a great deal of money, he said emphatically, "No, it is not necessary. Keep your money." However, I pressed on until he relented.

"Again, it's not necessary at all that you do that. I want you to think it over carefully. Possibly you will change your mind, which is fine. If after a period you still insist on doing it, there's a boys' school here in the city. Though run by the Catholic Church, it's nondenominational, taking in needy boys of all faiths or none. I will write down the director's name and address for you."

A vow had been made. There was nothing to think over. I withdrew the money in cash from an account and went to the school's office, asking to see the director, who was not there. The money was left. The thought never occurred really that the money would help someone but myself to be out from under. This was one more debt or obligation paid.

Months later, when living in another city during income tax preparation, I realized for the first time that some credit could be given for a charitable deduction. It seemed foolish not to take it. The school was written to for a receipt. The father in charge sent it immediately. He said he was sorry he hadn't been there at the time I came but would like to thank me personally, explaining how much it helped one child. Would I be his guest for dinner some evening?

I wrote back that the time he suggested was fine, that I would drive down, and then I added a postscript: "Though the Scriptures say, 'Do not neglect to show hospitality to strangers, for thereby some have entertained angles,' I want to tell you right off I'm no angel."

"That's good," he replied. "I'm not used to entertaining angels."

The father was personable, and like the priest I talked with before, he represented God well. In the course of the evening, I mentioned my experience as a youth with the sister in Bakersfield. He said he was familiar with the people who had worked at the hospital at the time and asked the nun's name, which I told him. He then said she'd died.

"But you might be interested to know that my mother couldn't stand the woman. She hated to be near her. Small world!"

We laughed. Funny how you find real people sometimes in the strangest places.

Toward the end of the high school semester, I, like a lot of others, wondered what to do next. Good grades had been made, but they hadn't come easy. That was a problem. Obviously I couldn't work and put myself through college. If you're asking, I'm sure Mom and Dad didn't have the money to send me nor did my father. Had they had the money, their help wouldn't have been accepted. As a youth then, I was long on stubbornness; short on looks, personality, skills; and filled with academic nonsense. I could recite Hamlet's advice to the players. I could have told you Egbert was the first king of England. I could quote Alexander Pope: "To err is human, to forgive is divine." I knew George Bernard Shaw said, "He who can does. He who cannot, teaches." This latter piece of information, however, I couldn't attribute to my instructors who hardly would have taught it but picked up myself. To it might be added, "He who can do neither, joins the service." So I fled into the army.

Being seventeen, a parent's signature was required. A birth certificate, required and sent for, said my full name was Francis Chichester. I'd gone through life as Brent Fry. Everyone knew me as Brent. Now I wasn't even that. I had known about the other name but thought it was Francis Brent Chichester. Had it been, it would have been left at that. But my masculinity wasn't secure enough to be Francis alone, even if it meant dishonoring the memory of my mother. Why couldn't the name be changed to Brent Chichester. With an old, English baronial name, who needed a middle one? It figures my father wasn't happy about this but had it changed without comment. Frankly, Frank, I didn't give a damn whether you liked it or not, you knew where you were coming from.[88-B]

Brent as a first name in those days was odd, and Brent Chichester had the ring of a firm in the New York stock exchange. Why couldn't it have been a simple name like Joe Smith? Why was life so fucking complicated?

Yet what did it matter really? In mental makeup I was just a jerk and could imagine Mom hollering for me at the front step each night.

"Dilbert! Oh Dilbert! Where are you, Dilbert?"

No answer.

"Dilbert, if I've told you once, I've told you a thousand times, you are to be in here at nine o'clock. You get in here now! Do you hear me, Dilbert?"

"Coming, Mother," my voice cracking.

In truth I regret not so much in life being a jerk as the untold hours wasted trying not to be a jerk. If you're a jerk, be yourself.

Chapter Fifteen

One weekend in basic training at Fort Ord, California, each of us who didn't have a duty of some kind stood in line on Saturday morning waiting to recite the general orders whereupon one would get his pass. Finally getting away around noon, I hitchhiked to Avenal to see the folks, whom I had not seen for six months. Absence makes the heart grow fonder. This was a mistake after taking orders for weeks. Besides it probably never sunk in on Mom—her ego was such—that the last semester in Bakersfield was to get out from under her, and maybe this was my fault for emphasizing it as the lesser of two reasons .

"You come outside. I'm going to take some pictures." she said.

"No, I don't want any taken."

"Why that's ridiculous! Now you come out here!"

"No, I don't want any taken." Again her insistence.

This led to my saying I wouldn't have her ordering me around anymore. I didn't tell her about hating my image. No way would I have told her that, letting her get her hooks in even more. A person is entitled to the privacy of his own thoughts. Anyway if I'd mentioned that to her, she'd have overruled me saying it was ridiculous or something similar, so I left.

Robyn wrote as follows in 1991:

> As for me thinking you are crazy for what you're writing, well I can't wait to read whatever you have come to see or deduce from you sleuthing. As to my feelings being hurt that you might change some of the wording of what I write concerning Mother, I won't be. You have my permission to write my words anyway you choose, as what I am saying is the truth as I remember it.
>
> Some things I am writing are to answer your questions. Others may or may not fit in, or help you to come to a better understanding.
>
> When we lived in Ventura, I don't know how old I was, but it had to be before I was five. Mother had an affair with

some man, and Dad was going to take me and leave her. But Aunt Lil was there and talked them out of it. That's all I can remember about that.

From there we moved to Long Beach and then to Avenal in June 1935, where there was a rock garden—quite large—and some cactuses. It was there our beloved "Ginger," a chow-collie mix, was buried. We had gotten her about four months before you were brought to California from Nevada.

As to the rocks and retaining wall in Bakersfield, I don't know. What with Mother's drinking, my marriage, and subsequent leaving for San Francisco, I just barely recall the names of the neighbors on each side. I remember your police dog "Flicka" that you had loved and taught many tricks. You used to hide from her, and she would search until she found you. Then when they got "Gypsy" she made you give up your dog. I think the reason was jealousy and possibly to hurt you.

When my husband had been transferred to Ketchican, Alaska, I came home pregnant to stay. Jesus! Those days were terrible, as you know. I remember well the fight we three had in the kitchen one day. She was drunk on wine and had come in for more, berating you and me over some damn thing. After she had refilled her wine glass, I told her that if she'd lay off the wine, things would be a hell of a lot better around there. Then I grabbed the glass out of her hand and crashed it into the sink. She cried in her drunken state, called Dad at work on the phone, then went out to the back door and sat sobbing. He came home immediately mad and enraged at us for "upsetting her." "This isn't your home anymore," he told me, "and you can leave any time." So I called my husband's mother and father in Avenal. They came and got me, and I lived with them for awhile.

After I had moved to San Francisco to live with my husband, she also had another affair in Bakersfield. She told me about this later when Dad and she moved to Avenal. In her words, she and the guy used to go out to the Kern River for their trysts. Then also he would stop by the house to see her when Dad was out on a job. She thought she was in love with him and told me she was thinking of getting a divorce. As I always had been closer to Dad than her, and being young then, it naturally angered me. I told her that if she went through with her plans I would never love her or let her see her grandchildren again. Whether she was really in love or just infatuated with this guy, I don't really know. But she called it off, and they lived not so happily ever after.

Following my daughter's birth, I was confined in a maternity hospital in Bakersfield. Mother had ridden down there from Avenal with my husband to see me. He told me later on the way home—after much talk—she said she often wondered how he performed sexually, implying she wouldn't be adverse to the idea. My Mother was a very passionate woman, and if he agreed to her implications, he didn't tell me. However, I hated him for telling me the other. If she really said those things, I don't know. It was a shock to think your own mother would suggest such a thing. I couldn't bear to believe it. But why would he say it if it wasn't true?

I really believe that after the time we had the trouble in Bakersfield and later in Avenal, she was "unbalanced" for awhile. She believed she was in love with her doctor. While in Coalinga Hospital for something, she was examined by a psychiatrist. She said he told her (not Dad) she was as sane as anyone. But I wonder. One thing for sure, she was theatrical.

You have asked about Avenal State Prison, which was officially opened in January 1987. Having many guard towers and fifteen-foot fencing with rolls of razor-edge wires atop, it seems to be much more than the "minimum security," which I understand the city council was told at first. Possibly the state changed its plans for completion, and now it is designated as a "low-medium" security prison. At present it has 4,194 prisoners. One hundred and four of these are women, who are being phased out. Then it will contain men only. It is situated one and one-half miles south of Avenal on Highway 33.

Yes, there were and still are sheep being run here. Shepherds live in small, high-wheeled trailers drawn from area to area. I see them and their dogs when I drive in any direction. There are little, natural grasslands left, so they also make use of picked fields: melon, lettuce, tomato, and barley and wheat stubble.

Chapter Sixteen

It wasn't any great feat graduating at the top of a class of medical technicians. That's not why it's mentioned but to point out that because of this I was able to choose a hospital ship at Ft. Mason, California, as a duty station. Recently when making the February connection to Hermes and Poseidon, I began to think it wasn't so much my choosing the ship as it was where I was supposed to be and would have gone there anyway if not allowed the choice.

Louis is recalled after forty-five years of oblivion. Why? The best that comes to mind is that my contact with him was one of the first signs which went unheeded. Understanding right from the beginning would have saved me and others a lot of trouble through the years. Some are meant to be loners. It might be called unloving, uncaring, or self-centered. It might be all these, or part, or none. It could also be an unconscious protective measure for others, as well themselves. The Sister then might have felt the means—any means—justified the end. Who knows? She still may be canonized, rather than cannonized.

Louis was either naturalized or born in the United States with parents of Chinese ancestry. One thing for sure, there was no conscious malediction. He'd been my first friend when going aboard ship, showing me how to get from Fort Mason to Van Ness to Market Street and where to catch buses and streetcars. Then he went his way; I went mine.

But at sea he wanted someone with whom to play chess. I begged off, explaining my ignorance. Besides it was a game for the high and mighty. No matter, he'd teach me. He was an excellent player, carefully considering the consequences of each move, while I couldn't be bothered with such an approach. Life was too serpentine as it was. Games were made for quick and simple fun and escape. A different attitude might have come in time, but it's doubtful. Like love, if there's no spontaneity, if everything is calculated, analyzed, and criticized, what fun is it? So they weren't even good matches. We were more like travelers bowed at the altar of the same god—two acolytes with snaking-eight caducei on their collars, "pieces of eight," and parrot feathers.

One day, out of the blue, he walked up to the radio shack to send J. Edgar Hoover, F.B.I., a message purporting the ship was a hotbed of communist conspirers. Louis is recalled now standing in the ship's psychiatric ward, with his hands raised like claws, face contorted and terrible, as if by sheer expression someway he would kill or neutralize his tormentor, the wind god, who had tricked and deceived him into being a frantic animal in a cage.

Could he have been fooling? The psychiatrists didn't think so, nor did I. For he had no way of knowing he was being observed at times.

All things considered, a private makes more money today than then, when only two things really mattered: One was to get my teeth fixed, the other, to get a driver's license.

Some say the "eye tooth" gets its name from being in line with the eye above it. This is wrong. If you ever had these sticking out, you'd have noticed the eyes of others are instantly magnetized to them for a beat or two, like a frightened rabbit immobilized by a cobra, before they can break away from the force and look you directly in the eye. That's why there are no orthodontists in Transylvania: They long since have been proselytized. And the service won't correct the problem in any of their personnel, for they realize it gives the fighting man an edge in combat.

An orthodontist I'd gone to downtown had misgivings about doing the work when he heard I'd be gone thirty or more days at a time. But finally he agreed to it, sending me to another dentists to have the tooth pulled behind each fang and the wisdom teeth in back. In eighteen months he accomplished a rubberband miracle, as anyone who has ever had the problem can tell you.

A driver's license wasn't needed (being at sea most of the time and having no immediate plans to buy a car) but to prove Dad wrong, as well as to reject Mom's understanding tit. Many hours beyond the basic course were planned for. Certainly, I thought, the course would have to be repeated several times. The bridge was crossed before getting there that the school would kick me our and—in this case—there were still several others listed in the phone book. The basic course went without a hitch though. No extra hours were needed. Both the written and driving tests were passed the first time. Years later, I'd even have a navy driver's license.

If I could learn to dance, there'd be a better chance of meeting girls. A well-known dance studio downtown gave a free test to prospective clients, administered by an attractive woman who would rate them. Naturally anybody—even someone with two left feet—was told he had a special talent which would be damn shame not to develop. It just so happened in my case the lady was right. There *was* a special talent—for being gullible—and it would have been a damn shame for her if I hadn't been. Three hundred dollars in savings were withdrawn to pay for the basic course, then two hundred more for an advanced course. There's some truth to the statement that students find it much easier later to dance with their instructors and other students than anybody else. Sailing for long periods, I failed to follow through and still can't dance a step. Yet the courses weren't a complete loss. At the bargain-basement price of just five hundred smackeroos, it became a terrific conversation piece. Finally there was consolation in knowing that there were many others just as gullible. From time to time through the years, different commands issued bulletins warning service personnel about signing contracts. Where I'd paid in advance, many hadn't.

Hard liquor: yuck! A glass of wine or two at a meal was something to be tolerated with those friends who felt it showed refinement. One glass with a wine snob showed you had class. Okay, but beer, now that was something else. One or two, sometimes none, and on rare occasions three or four might have made me high but hardly staggering drunk. The problem at these times was that it also made me sleepy, even without pouring a libation to Hermes, the sleep and dream god, though there'd probably been enough slopped around to satisfy the requirement. But why didn't it work in other respects too? Too late in life the knowledge came that these weren't some cheap bar gods. They had feelings too. They don't want some grimy paw spilling the beer, followed by the afterthought: That's for you, like for a dog, not a god. No! You're suppose to go wash your hands first and then come back and pour it out respectfully.

If I was able to stay awake to meet girls at bars, I'd have to drink something other than beer. Someone said to try Tom Collins. So one night six or seven of these were downed. Jesus Innocencio! They were terrible. No problem about going to schleep. I experienced something far worse. All aboard for the roller coaster! My head way, way up there, making me dizzy to look down where my stomach was and then looping the loop. It was worse when lying down. The only thing to do was kneel in front of the toilet bowl the rest of the night to puke. Of course there was a hangover the next day, but there aren't too many around who still don't feel good the second day after a drunk.

A repeat performance with too much beer at another time was enough to convince me there was no drinker here, and so I was a disgrace to those who raised me, a wimp. On listening to me bemoan my lot in life, a doctor friend remarked, "You don't know how really lucky you are with a built-in control."

When I was younger, the *Iliad*, the poem about the Trojan War,[89] often seemed stupid. Were we to believe thousands risked their lives for one Helen of Troy? She might have been the most beautiful woman in the world, but they weren't going to sleep with her. And certainly half the gossip said the lady was a tramp, who'd taken off willingly.90 Come on, Homer, give me a break! But Homer was smarter than that. He could have been saying that one of the fuels for fighting a war is always sexual. Probably sexuality is so well insinuated in what are given as economic and other precipitating causes that it can never be unraveled.

This isn't to say that if Attila the Hun is swooping down on you, you shouldn't fight back. What's being said is that Napoleon might have been just as correct if he'd remarked that an army rolls on its balls rather than travels on its stomach. This is precisely why wars are obscene, hypocritical, and religious wars are the most insane of all.

There is, of course, no way to prove this, to make a correlation coefficient between war and sexuality. What would be used as variables? But most men will know in their hearts that this is true, even if their minds reject it.

Obviously armed forces are needed. But who would ever voluntarily enter if each man's head was shaved like a bird's nest and the uniform looked much like a monk's garb? The average person going in and making a career is soon caught up in the vanity (the saluting, the medals, and ribbons, the service record) and possibly consumed by it. The parents, perhaps regular churchgoers, prefer to think of all this as achievement rather than vanity, and so see no harm or contradiction.

Still if anyone was immune to being part of humanity, it wasn't me. I was no better than Mom or the nun. I could see my own devils in others and did my share of name calling and whispering. With any luck at all, I should have been able to travel through an uncomplicated life without any problems, shifting gears as smoothly as most in doublethink. Unfortunately this wasn't to be. I saw that most often the psychological blades cut both ways, that the world was largely comprised of macho men with women's mouths and feminine women spewing a vile torment, and both sexes are like drunks speeding away from themselves and the child they'd just run down in the intersection. But maybe this is the only way. Of the great observations about life, possibly the most astute is ECCLES 1:18: "...in much wisdom is much vexation, and he who increases knowledge increases sorrow."

Chapter Seventeen

What follows isn't meant to compete in the gore of war, as one vet outdoes another, a race for me where qualifying requirements couldn't even be met. A few experiences show how I, years later (but no assumption at the time), came to believe in being protected throughout, for better or worse I sometimes wonder. Only as such do they seem to fit into a longer journey.

Much has been written about the first year of the Korean War. Despite what some legal beagles might dig up in fine print on contracts, most in the services had joined to fight for their country, to defend it. Had they been mercenaries, they would have joined the French Foreign Legion. Most congressmen and most presidents, so adroit in word games, pontificating and dispatching someone else, can never seem to get this through their thick skills when they commit American troops overseas. And not to forget Mr. and Mrs. American Fix-it, who can solve everyone else's problems but their own (see Taft quote concerning rules of conduct, Book II, page 422). The do-gooder bullshit usually ends with "Yankee Go Home," the reverse Midas, a bitterness and ingratitude as if we were personally responsible for everything that happened to them before we got there, during the time we were there, and after we left. This happened with the French twice, the Philippinos, the Koreans, the former South Vietnamese, the Afghans to whom we sent some money and equipment, and the Somalians in the hunger war.

All things considered, the troops did fairly well. Writing about the Korean War—the only one known about firsthand—I'd say in nearly every instance there was a platoon leader who stayed with his men and whose judgment the men respected, you had people of whom to be proud. But the generals were wrong to expect men in such wars to stick around and fight when in some instances the platoon leader managed to go back to battalion for orders at the crucial moment the fighting was about to begin. The radios never seemed to work at this time for some reason. In the same way, the men could trust the platoon leader and the platoon sergeant if the withdrawal was done with some small order. But when "bug out" is given as if it's every man for himself, don't blame the men for having little confidence "in fighting for their (the foreigners') country," especially when their foreign ally is giving an even worse performance. In the end, the shit shoveled into the tide has to go right back to the American people who can be brainwashed so easily by the right turn of a phrase by presidents and congressmen who can agree on nothing quite so much as their own "golden parachutes" for a prosperous landing.

If the platoon leader has very conveniently gone back to battalion for orders when his platoon is about to be overrun, the equipment shouldn't be abandoned. If abandoned, it should be destroyed or rendered useless.[91-A] But failing all this, the bottom line written into all regulations should be that the next NCO in line takes charge giving whatever help he can to the medic or corpsman in getting the wounded out. Of course, it's not always that easy in some instances of combat, which are chaotic. What's being said is that there were times in Korea where it could have and should have been done. Don't expect the medic and corpsman to scour an area being overrun in the middle of the night by himself to look for wounded he doesn't even know exist, like the trusty St. Bernard who comes with a flask of brandy. Then you ask him the following day after the bug-out order is given, "How many wounded did you treat last night, Doc?" It sucks!

If knowing a man was wounded, I tried to get to him. But it makes no sense to draw fire on a wounded man out in the open who has already had some treatment but with no place to take him until a roadblock is broken and a convoy moves out. If hearing a wounded man had already been taken care of by another medic, American or foreign, I wasn't about to go into a dangerous area to look for him. This was only common sense and a two-way street.

There were a lot of rewards which came from little things. You hear the company commander has made a special trip to collecting to try to get you promoted. You take a wounded man back to the rear when the outfit is moving forward. When at night you finally reach your company, you find your people have taken care of you: They picked out a good place for you to sleep and laid out your sleeping bag. At another time, your platoon has been assigned to a rifle company. It's dark. Their company has sent up coffee and doughnuts. Only a few go over to the line at one time. When your turn comes, you are getting a full, canteen-cup of coffee, while those on each side only get a half cup. You get eight doughnuts on your mess tin, while those about you only get two apiece. You look surprised. You don't know these people. Why are they doing this? Then one man says, "We remember the night you took care of our wounded in Chechon, Doc."

In November, the mortar company of the thirty-eighth infantry regiment set up its CP and mess tent at the base of a mountain in North Korea. Very near this was a dry river bed that showed signs of having overflowed, surged, and raged, perhaps two or three times a century for eons so that it had cut a flat area one-half or three-quarters mile to the higher ground on the other side.

In a previous inspection, the CO had called down a private for not having a haircut, to which the private just shook his head in disbelief at what he was hearing and replied, "Why worry about all that crap? I might be dead tomorrow." Maybe for some getting their hair cut is bad luck.[91-B]

In retrospect, I think he should have added, "And it gets mighty cold down there, sir." At the time, most of us were regular army and could only be contemptuous. For if he couldn't follow orders, show discipline, he could only be a coward. It never occurred to us that in making such a remark to a person as exalted as the CO, the private was a risk-taker, while the rest of us were cowards. Besides, in our minds, the war was over or nearly so. There was nothing to worry about really but the freeze. Who would have known for sure what the temperature was? You only knew that your feet, like slabs of meat, got awfully cold. If your gloves were off when washing mess gear in the cans set up for that purpose, your hands stuck to the metal. The cold had its own art of demoralizing. As soon as darkness came, it was just too damn miserable to be out in it if you didn't have to be. You only wanted to crawl into your sleeping bag, at first assuming an almost fetal position.

For days conversations and thoughts had been about rotation. It couldn't be far off. Some figured it would be based on a point system. Those closest to the front lines (the riflemen, their medics, the forward observers) and who had been in Korea longest would go first. It was only fair, and maybe some credit might be given for decorations.

"Jesus, Doc, you remember that round at the Naktong, causing the bunker to cave in, making my arm bleed. You remember, Doc, you bandaged it. I don't want the Purple Heart, but it was a wound—sort of—and if rotation is going to be based on points, well I want whatever I can get."

High up on the mountain, a private is grousing to his partner: "If the war's almost over, why the fuck they need more than one outpost up here? Shit, some of us could be out of this fuckeeng cold and asleep. You know what I think? I'll tell yuh. It's the CO and the rest of his dickhead, suckass officers. That's what I think. They're all alike. 'Yes sir, Colonel, we got the ridges well-covered, sir. No sir, no one ever told me before now, but I figured you must have been an enlisted man at one time, Colonel. It shows, sir...Well no sir, I didn't mean it like that. What I meant, sir, is that my men will be happy to hear you were once an enlisted man yourself, Colonel. Oh thank you, sir! Oh one other thing, sir, please give my regards to your wife, Mrs. Colonel Sir, when writing. Oh thank you, Sir!'"

At the base of a mountain in a cellar, I was melting, melting, melting. I'd just reached nirvana where the feet and shoulders and neck were warm at one time. There was a spurt of firing off somewhere. It ain't nothin'. It can't be nothin' because I didn't want it to be. It had to be two trigger-happy GIs spooked by a cow in some bushes. Think positive. Don't worry! Be happy.

"Doc!" someone shouting. "They need you in the mess tent quick. A man's been shot bad."

I unzip the sleeping bag and tear out, as if one minute's going to make all the difference in the world, helmet slightly lopsided, boots untied, and in hand a cartridge belt with a medical bag.[92-A] Jesus! It's freezing. I'm tripping over boot laces and stop to tie them quickly. No longer is it a child's game of "king of the mountain" but it is dead serious as the tempo increases like the crescendo to "The Hall of the Mountain King," an uppity description, vulgar and profane. What GI would ever know of halls and kings and Grieg, much less think of them at such a time for godsake. Still it's appropriate in a macabre way. It matches the pompous reason heard, like sour notes for the dying. Maybe more fittingly someday taps will be played off key, as a reminder to those living that they must think harder and look deeper.

The cooks had left the stoves running to provide heat for themselves as well as Cody, the switchboard operator, and the tent with its warmth was a haven, a blessing no less, for the wounded who were carried in and left, since there's little that can be done for them at night in extreme cold on a steep mountain riddled with frenetic firing and confusion other than to pack them off to where they can be attended. This was quite a feat in itself. Some were carried or helped by buddies, some by the other medic who worked his ass off making trips up and down the mountain. Though his work was harder than mine, far more dangerous and worthy of recognition, there was a clear need for both of us doing what we did. Someone had to attend the wounded who were brought in, and someone had to do what he could on the mountain.

Where both the wounded and I were lucky was that Cody was literally running back and forth between keeping his calls going through and helping me. I'd give morphine if indicated, and make out EMT (Emergency Medical Treatment) tags if needed. (Sometimes this had been done by the other medic as best he could under fire on the mountain.) But Cody helped me with almost everything else: applying tourniquets, cutting away clothing, splinting, treating for shock, getting stretchers and blankets, etc. It must have crossed his mind once or twice, as it had mine when the firing intensified, that a Chinese might burst in at any time spraying us with a burpgun. It's strange, but in a way you felt foolishly safe in the tent but in another way very vulnerable. I see now that we and the wounded owed our lives to the men who held on the mountain.

We had little idea what was happening outside other than, from the noise and steady flow of wounded or dead, that we were being clobbered. A few might have been able to wait until dawn to be evacuated, perhaps then it might have been safer. But most were in bad shape and needed STAT help of the battalion aid station, then collecting and clearing stations. And, of course, the flickering hope that begins in a wounded man when he first thinks someone has heard and is going to help must be maintained by reassurance and continued action, getting him back as quickly as possible.

Someone backed up a two and one-half ton truck. It had no top. We carried out the ten or so we had, setting litters in some cases; others were bundled in blankets. The metal was peeling-cold for them. It was like taking something out of the comparative warmth of a kitchen and shoving it in the freeze unit of an icebox and then closing the lids, the tailgate. The driver took off like a bat out of hell. For the first minute or two as he sped away he was clearly in view of one or two points the Chinese had taken on the mountain. He cut sharply to the left and barrel-assed straight down the center of the riverbed—and making it, and making it, *and making it*! Goddamn!

I ran back to the cellar to get something forgotten earlier and had returned to within fifteen yards of the mess tent. Two explosions came near. Dumbly I thought, *The world's rocking. Those shells can't do that, there's nothing that powerful.*

Out of nowhere, Brooks and Ed are supporting Davenport who's hobbling along on one leg. Brooks is shouting above the noise. "Benny's been hit, Doc. We're taking him to the aid station."

They're ten feet away now, heading for a jeep. I hadn't had a chance to examine Davenport, but his lower leg dangled. No blood showed on his trousers, nor did he seem to be in shock or overwhelmed with pain. It was just a feeling that he could wait until it was safer. The mess tent was less than ten yards away.

"Look, Brooks, he can wait until the company moves out together."

"No! If Benny's hit, I'm getting him to the aid station now."

As the three moved closer to the jeep, Ed shouted, "Are you coming with us or not, Doc?"

Christ! The thick challenge of his tone you could cut with a knife. It hung in the air: "It's your job, fucker, not ours. If you're too chickenshit, screw you! But before God and all else, you ain't got a hair on your ass!"

"Okay, I'll go."

Ed was in the back with Davenport, whose leg was partially supported by me, next to Brooks who drove. He took off down the path leading to the riverbed and began going straight across toward the road that skirted it three-quarters mile or so at the other side. The chatter of a machine gun could be heard over the rifle fire. Now in the flat area in front of the mountain and under the moon, you felt vulnerable, naked, spotlighted, like some small, slow animal caught in the open and still having a long way to move to safety. Somehow in stupid logic—the firing was coming from behind us, and we were moving away from it. What difference? We had to keep going.

Maybe they were playing with us. We moved to the incline leading up to the road where bushes and trees would have hidden us once we turned. Brooks looked over at me and said, sort of matter-of-factly and polite-like,[92-B] "Doc, I've been hit! What do I do?"

"Keep going!" What else could I say? This was no place to stop, and he didn't sound too bad.

The jeep went up the incline to the road, just starting the turn, then snaked back down into the riverbed's rocks, bouncing to an abrupt stop and throwing us all forward. Brooks layover the wheel, maybe dead. We pulled him out. Ed tried to start the engine, which wouldn't turn over. The white rocks we were in, though big enough to stop the jeep, weren't big enough for cover. They outlined us. We were still in the moonlight very close to where Brooks had been shot. It was hard to know where some of the firing from the mountain was aimed. Some of it could be seen passing in front of us toward the road. No time to think of rightness or wrongness, fairness or unfairness. We had to get the fuck out fast.

"You take Brooks. I'll take Davenport," I blurted, lifting him into a fireman's carriage. Jesus! He was heavy in the cold. It was all I could do just to keep going for about thirty yards before setting him down. Though not seeing Ed with Brooks, I assumed they were coming. We could still see the dark mountain clearly, so it figured that the enemy up there could see us even better. We had some rest sitting there, waiting and wondering.

A mile or more far into the darkness of the riverbed someone was yelling and pleading at the top of his lungs, "I've been hit. Don't leave me. Please don't leave me here to die!"

I threw Davenport over the shoulders again, and off we went two or three times more. The man now had stopped yelling. No outline of Ed with Brooks could be seen. We couldn't worry about that. He had his problems, I had mine. We were making it but slowly. Then we could hear the gunning and roaring of an engine, like someone shifting gears not too smoothly, and saw in the distance behind us a truck bearing down. I jumped up running closer to its path and waved my arms. If he'd just stop.... He didn't see me. Shit! He saw all right. How could he have missed me? The motherfucker, the piece of shit, was going right on by us to save his own ass. To hell with him! Then very suddenly, he braked, stopping way beyond us while I got Davenport over. Lowering a tailgate or arranging a limp leg in the cab would have taken time. Davenport himself suggested that he stand outside, supporting himself by holding on to the machine-gun ring. We hauled ass. The driver had never driven before in his life.

Two or three miles beyond we looked for the aid station. Where the hell was it? There was no sign of it where someone said it was. Shit! Then up ahead could be seen several vehicles, buttoned up severely like a cheerless black coat at a cemetery. One function was completed. The men had to dig in somewhere else, more bodies. At its end followed a couple litter jeeps and a jeep trailer covered by a tarp just starting to pull onto the road behind them. It was the last of a dreary-and-weary aid station, heading farther back. I yelled to an exhausted medic.

"Christ! We're full up. We have no more room" he pleaded.

Then he thought and said, "Put him on the back of the jeep trailer there."

And that in the grimness was the last I saw of Davenport.

It made no sense to wander around in the dark in the early hours of morning in a deteriorating situation, finally to cross again the flat, open riverbed. Remnants of the company already had begun to gather about a hundred yards ahead, back toward the mountain. The rest would be along soon.

This is brought up because there must be after any god-game of war many (men who saw worse than I certainly) who can never forgive themselves for not having the god-wisdom of being able to discern the sometimes fine line between cowardice and common sense or to forgive themselves for not being wounded or being wounded or for not dying. The fact is there never has been or ever will be in war anyone who—if completely truthful—can say with 100 percent certainty in many, many situations that he always clearly saw the fine line of distinction. Realizing this, my platoon leader (a damn good officer who'd received a battlefield commission in the war) will refuse to testify against a master sergeant of another platoon, who nevertheless was busted to private, and I will be asked to help get rid of the sergeant's platoon leader medically, which we did.

It was too dark for fires. I found a blanket in a truck and lay down, trying to rest and get warm. Someone was saying, "Where's Doc?"

"He's sleeping over there. Do you want me to wake him?"

"No. I was gonna have him look at a couple cuts I got. But they can wait 'til later."

I played possum.

It seemed like it was only an hour or two before dawn. The rest of the company had withdrawn, leaving a couple of tents and mess stoves. But at sunrise the Chinese withdrew, and the company was able to retrieve these.

Ed is telling me he hadn't brought Brooks back, that they had to go get his body, that the first sergeant is really pissed off at him.

"He said I should have brought Brooks out, Doc. God, I didn't want to die bringing him back when he was dead. You know I wouldn't have left him if I thought he was alive. Doc, tell the first sergeant you think he was dead."

I believed him and told the first sergeant.

What followed was a demoralizing and at times a harrowing withdrawal. Riflemen and forward observers as always had it worse, but if the rifle platoons couldn't hold or were overrun before we got a march order, we were in deep shit. The weight of the heavy mortars and ammunition was such that it couldn't be carried any great distance on foot. Trucks were needed for hauling, and roads—or at least flat areas—were needed for trucks. The heavy mortar platoons just couldn't pick up and walk across country or over this or that hill. The men at times were very vulnerable, captive to their own equipment. Each platoon's job was to set up its mortars, dig in, and fire missions in a delaying action at the advancing Chinese and North Koreans. Often they would unload the mortars, set them up, and fire missions only to withdraw again in an hour or so. This doesn't sound like much with time and distance when one is sitting peacefully in a warm room reading about it, but it was bleak, grave, and exhausting for days and nights on end, sometimes without a break. Along with the expected war wounds, cold injuries took their toll.

It was about this time that a letter was received from Mom. She'd been to a psychiatrist and thought he'd helped her. Both she and I, she felt, should have gone to one years ago. "Bye now. Love, Mom."

Damn her hide! Damn her Hyde! Didn't she have any sensitivity? Had she no sense of what was appropriate to write at such a time? And she was all wet about me and a shrink. I never needed one in my entire life. What I really needed was a frontal lobotomy.

Looking back years later, I'd realize my sensitivity wasn't all that great either at the time. To describe the incident as an incredible lack of tact would charitable. A weak defense at twenty-one would be that the pimple on my shoulders had not yet come to a head. I was a jerk, though well meaning.

We'd been relieved for a couple days. This was a period to clean up weapons, resupply, eat hot meals, go to a shower point, drink a few beers, and get some rest at night. For the other medic and me, it was a time to look at feet, check mouths to see if malaria pills had been swallowed, and to refer gnawing complaints to collecting for evaluation. The platoon sergeant told me to report to the CO.

What the hell did he want? I wondered, walking to the CP.

"You asked to see me, sir?" I saluted.

"Yeah, Doc. Could you tell me what happened a few weeks ago on Sergeant Davenport?"

I explained.

"Are you sure it was Davenport you took there?"

Shit! What was he getting at? Did he think I lied?

"If you don't believe me, sir, call in the driver who was with me."

"I'm not doubting your word, Doc. But it's strange. I just got a letter from his mother who's very worried, saying she's not heard from him. I wonder if you would write telling her what happened?"

Responding to my letter, Mrs. Davenport was distressed and saddened by Brook's death. "Greater love has no man than this, that a man lay down his life for his friends," she quoted.

It was a heartfelt prayer. But it was also an incantation, trying to say something magical to work a magic, to make things right. She'd gone to the tinderbox and struck a spark as surely as if she'd lit a candle. A prayer is a fire then, for whatever purpose, and we aren't, for all our denials, any different from the less articulate primitive people who built a roaring fire to their god and danced around it. The many fires we made all over Korea brought warmth and comfort. There was beauty in them, a hypnotic effect. They could also be destructive and deadly if approached too closely. All this can be explained by professors in chemistry texts, like prophets in the Bible, but they somehow fall short of capturing the mysticism.

We checked the aid station and learned that the convoy, buttoned up severely like a gloomy, funeral coat that night, later split up, one part being ambushed. This seemed to be the most likely reason she'd never heard and possibly never would. The whole damn thing started when Davenport was wounded, or rather from the moment I got involved to helping him on the jeep trailer (and so touching the tarp) led only to death, misery, and sorrow. I'd never realized this until the third revision of the book, but it's there like a miasma. I'll leave the explanation made earlier in the following pages stand, though I understand now that it was a two-sided coin with both sides coming up.[92-C]

Ed, who had been with Brooks and Davenport in barracks duty before the war, said that he'd heard them talking. The gist was that Davenport had knocked up a girl he didn't want to marry. Ed wondered if he'd disappeared for awhile until things blew over.

Davenport was a young, popular sergeant, well respected by the riflemen who saw him as a forward observer. He'd been decorated and had a promising career if he wanted. It made no sense that he'd throw it away over a pregnancy and hide out in North Korea nursing a wound. But there might have been something to the thought he was lying low, not writing until he figured things had cooled. Yet sooner or later his name would turn up on army records. Maybe he needed only a little time. It offered a small hope anyway, so I wrote this.

A few years from then it seemed preposterous such a thing was said. But now very many years later I am not so sure that even an airheaded youth can't bumble into a greater wisdom. To steal from Wordsworth, a child (or the possibility of a child) more than anything else offers declining man hope and forward-looking thoughts. Perhaps the only ones qualified to answer about the rightness or wrongness of such a remark are the many grieving parents whose sons have been lost in wars. Even then there'd probably be disagreement. One thing is for certain, I should have been more tolerant of the jerks I met later in life.

At one time, when being sent back to the lines, the regiment was told there'd be more retreating. Things had been carefully planned, and this time we'd hold, come hell or high water. But even with our planes bombing and strafing them ahead, the Chinese came in the daytime, overwhelming the riflemen. Our vehicles, along with those of other outfits, including the Turks, were soon caught in a roadblock for many hours into a night of terror for the men and the wounded. When it was finally cleared, the vehicles split up at a fork in the road. The convoy I was in made it safely out. The other was ambushed, and it wasn't the first time I'd made it through one like that. I always had this bittersweet luck.

Months later the platoon set up its mortars in an orchard, then sat around in or near the trucks eating C-rations. The explosion of incoming rounds could be heard down the way but well concealed by the trees, which seem to lull many into a false sense of security. The battalion commander passing through hollered, "If I were you, men in mortar company, I'd start digging in!"

I got my entrenching tool and began to dig maybe 10 yards away, while the others kept on eating, when two rounds exploded, wounding five where I'd just been a minute or two before. These rounds could have lit where I was just as easily, but they didn't.

A lot of people had been killed or wounded up to then and still more would be. Yet all that will come from this, on both sides down the line, is theater, movies, and books. Doesn't matter much if the old cast of characters is no longer around. There's always young blood to take its place, fantasizing for vicarious thrills of audiences. Carnage: That's entertainment.

Maybe the Romans with their coliseums were more honest, accepting what was inevitable, choosing the lesser of two evils. Judaism, Christianity, and Islam have never been able to stop wars and one way or another have been part and parcel. The greatest obscenity isn't war itself but the scrubbed textbooks later on both sides. Not telling the whole truth, they list only the political, geographic, or economic factors causing and fueling a war when they also should have given the entertainment-sexual nature of man, which is there, at first at least, like the tip of an iceberg. Until all people come to grips with the truth in its entirety, man will never be able to prevent them.

Outside of wounding and killing, nothing sells like rape, and there was plenty of that going on. Nobody wants to hear about the beauty in the world in a war story. That's soft, unmanly, suspicious, cowardly.

In May 1951 much time had been spent digging foxholes and constructing sturdy bunkers for an expected Chinese offensive. We'd gone to the shower points through the winter months, but it was the first time it was warm enough to soap up in a creek, to stretch out and bask in the sun. Everything had begun to turn green, and here and there on the mountains, flowers were blooming, many of which looked like different-colored lupines. One time a small stag with impressive antlers93 looked regally down. Butterflies were out. Like sparkling new toys, freshly painted red and green, young frogs seemed to come from nowhere all at once. Nature's playthings were a delight to watch as they plopped around. Sometimes overnight as many as twenty or thirty fell into a single foxhole. Someone then with nothing better to do while waiting would set them free. Another soldier with a mischievous grin would pull those apart which were coupling or playing a variation of leapfrog.

"How'd you like for somebody to do that to you?" I asked.

"Frogs give warts, Doc. I'm just trying to stop them from gettun venereal warts."

Ask a stupid question, get a stupid answer.

We tried to have some frog races like in Calaveras County. Each soldier putting up for a bet—winner take all—a can of C-rations, which just so happened to be the one he liked least. But the frogs were still too young and undisciplined or maybe just not impressed with the stakes.

This soon fizzled as interest turned to the prank played on Levine. Battalion wanted to know why he'd received two duffle bags full of mail. Someone purporting to be him had written a New York paper saying he'd been brought up in an orphanage and no one to write him. Would the paper tell its readers?

"Doc, I don't know what I'm gonna do, all these people writing thinking it's so. Here's one from a nice old couple who want to adopt me, for Christsake!" Eventually he answered a few of the letters, farmed some out, and left the rest go.

May 13 is the day Hermes is said to lead Kore (Persephone) from the underworld to Demeter, her mother. My time as a medic, along with four from mortar company, had come up to go from Korea to Japan on R and R. We traveled for a half day to an airport where we about froze one night waiting for a plane the following day. If my memory serves me right, it was to Camp Drake where we were flown. Here the army did it up nice. We were given uniforms that had been cleaned and pressed and which fit perfectly. If they didn't, alterations were made immediately. And they gave us a feast: anything we wanted from turkey with trimmings to steak with the works.

Being impressed with the pitch of a Japanese man who came up to us in Yokohama, we decided to go to the Twin Palms Hotel, which from the business card seem to suggest something very worldly, or otherworldly, depending on how your fantasies ran. That's why it was sort of disappointing to see two little, dwarf palms in pots in front of a very plain door to a one-story cracker-box house. Oh well, here we were, and here we would stay. And the palms and the name would be remembered to this day without knowing why.

We had no trouble choosing who we wanted to be with, and we all had a good time, if too short, as the days raced by. Mom-a-zon, who owned the joint, must have been a yakuza's great aunt: She was old as mold and long in the tooth of gold. Each of us had paid her five days in advance for a girl and a room. With that money she now had carpenters constructing a new room the following morning. Why did they start hammering so fuckin' early? Well, you know, business is business: Either expand or go under.

The second night I'd gone to the small kitchen to ask her about something and tripped over one from our group, passed out about a foot from where she was working at the sink. What was he doing here with a blanket thrown over him? I checked his room and found it was now occupied by another solider and girl.

"Who's that in the room and why ain't he in there?"

"He don't know. He stinko, Sergeant; he don't care."

She was pulling a fast one, and the others agreed.

"Move 'im out and heem back in, Mom-a-zon, or yawl know what we gonna do?" one of the mortarmen asked in a deadly drawl. "Why we gonna call the MPs and have this place shut down."

"Okay. Okay. I move. Christsake! You no understand. We still friends. Okay?"

Sure, she lost the skirmish. But make no mistake about it: The Japanese won the Korean War, proving once again that both the North and South Koreans were the Mortimer Snerds of the Far East. And the U.S.? Well, Go race your rat, Charlie!

We had left Korea some time after the thirteen of May, missing most of the offensive in which several in the company were wounded. On the night of the sixteenth or seventeenth of May, one hundred thirty-seven thousand Chinese Communist Forces and thirty-eight thousand North Koreans attacked in what was called the second impulse of the fifth phase offensive. Their objective was to destroy 6 ROK divisions and the second infantry division. On the twentieth of May, the second was hit hard but held against the twelfth and fifteenth armies. Interesting too is that the CCF had 1) been plagued with "dysentery" and 2) consumed the last of their rations on the twenty-first of May, which they had been issued on the twelfth of May to last the duration of the offensive. By the twenty-third of May, the CCF had begun to withdraw in places.

As previously noted, May and spring are the month and season of the snake in Chinese astrology. In ancient Rome, May in many respects was a funereal month, with the Rosalia (May 21 and 23) and the Lemuria (May 9, 11, and 13). Merchants apparently also celebrated the last day of the Lemuria to insure good luck, as they would on the fifteenth. The girl I was with in Japan was called Amy, an anagram, and I thought I loved her.

Chapter Eighteen

Continuation of the letter from Robyn written in 1991:

Mother, the kids, and I had been over to the Armistice Day Parade in Coalinga. It was chilly, and when we got home, she said she wasn't feeling very well. That she felt cold and was coming down with the flu, maybe. I dropped her off and went home as I had ironing to do. When I called her later asking how she felt, she said, "Just cold." Dad was in Riverside on a job. It came out later that she had been to a neighbor's house and that they had been drinking together. She then came home, threw up on the bathroom rug, rinsed it out, and hung it over the backporch rail. She shut the doors into the living room and either passed out on the divan, or just lay down and passed out. The gas took her before she woke up. It always seemed strange to me that she was naked, if she was cold as she said she had been all day long.

But the sheriffs and the coroner thought she had just taken a bath and came into the living room since she was ill, meaning to get up later and dress. Who will ever know! They weren't able to establish the real time she had died because of the terrible heat affected rigor mortis. But they said possibly she had expired before midnight, so that would make her death November 11, 1951.

Returning from Korea in July 1951, I was stationed at Camp *Stoneman*, California. When Robyn called telling me of Mom's death, I went to the Red Cross to ask to have it confirmed in order to get a furlough, but the lady was busy with other people. Sitting there waiting my turn, the more irritated I became, and I impulsively took off. It was the Red Cross later, however, confirming the death and my company commander backdating furlough time to cover my six or seven days of being AWOL, which helped me. Certainly then if there'd been a few bum deals in the army, this compensated for them.

112

Robyn, Aunt Lil (a long-time friend of the family), and I went to the mortuary to view the remains and drop off some clothing the day before the funeral. It was such a shock seeing her—not so much that she was dead, but that her arms were crossed in sternness and her mouth turned down at the sides—like in the drinking grimness seen so often when I was younger, that I laughed hysterically, feeling embarrassed and torn up inside for doing so. It was a boundary I'd not wished to cross and could almost hear her saying, "See, this is the way you are and always were. I knew you would."

We talked to the funeral director. He arranged her arms so they were at her side and changed the facial expression so that she looked in peace.

> Continuation of Robyn's letter 1991:
>   You remember how sarcastic Dad could be, and also how he blew up when you and I objected to having Mother cremated. "It's none of your goddam business," he said, "what you think or do not think about burial details. We both made a pact, and we are going to be cremated." Aunt Lil corroborated his story that she had heard Mother say that is what she wanted, so we went along with the plans.

I too had heard Mom say this. Had she been a different personality, there'd have been no objection to the cremation, but she frequently had to be different, to set a fashion, to take up a progressive thought, as if to show everybody she was far ahead of her time. Did she really know what she wanted? Or was she like a little child who didn't know how to go out or to come in? Somehow in respect to this and the culture, it seemed more fitting she be buried. Burying her properly signified to God that we forgave her, loved her, and were asking for His love and mercy. A cremation in her case was like you were trying to purge, destroy, and rid the world of an evil forever. It wasn't all that simple.

When I was younger she often said she didn't want to live to be old and helpless and hoped she died when she was about fifty, so at fifty-one she was close. She also remarked at one time she nearly had been overcome by carbon monoxide and remained a cautious person, always cracking a window. It seemed odd, on the one hand, that she hadn't done so. On the other, maybe not, since carbon monoxide poisoning will cause impairment of judgment, in addition to nausea and collapse.

Whatever, it was a wind god's death. The time of death given on her death certificate is 1:00 A.M. on the thirteenth of November 1951. This was the Ides of November, four or eight Ides (depending on how you want to look at it) from her birthdate on the Ides of March.

Dad (or B.C. as Mike, his grandson, refers to him) would later marry the neighbor Mom had drunk with just before her death. This second wife died within a short time. He then married a childhood girlfriend, who had also been one of our neighbors in Bakersfield. Though he outlived his third wife too, this was probably his happiest marriage. He wrote me when he was dying of cirrhosis of the liver that had he known of the pain he'd have to go through, he never would have drunk. I always knew he was a good man, but only in my old age was it realized he was a better man than I'd thought.

The sample of Mom's handwriting submitted for analysis in 1991 was about all that remained except for a couple of signatures. It had been written in the mid-1920s before my birth. Mom and Dad's lives had a dimension mine didn't, and it was important to have a more objective opinion of them, even if it were only for a period of their lives "frozen in time."

As with many other people, there was clutter in my mind, better left undisturbed like things in an attic, locked away gathering dust and cobwebs. No matter what, you can't completely divorce yourself from them, but if you've learned nothing else, don't try to freshen your memory in certain areas. It serves no purpose. Leave things alone, and they'll leave you alone. Buy the time to get through life, maybe not first class, but making it nonetheless.

Introspection, which can be self-flagellation, was the last thing needed; it had taken its toll. What's more, if I'm into this, someone invariably rolls his eyes and sighs dryly, "Oh dear. Oh my goodness!" The facial expression of Rodin's *Thinker* will certainly change in a few years if he keeps this up much longer.

With the awareness late in life of a strong Hermes influence, there was no choice but to climb the Attica steps to the past, for it seems to be part and parcel. In doing so, one becomes the rider of a turtle, and an old and slow one to be sure. What had swept by before, because there was no way of interpreting it, finally caught up. This is mentioned even at risk of being thought harebrained and having a pathological obsession with the past, an egomaniac writing his autobiography.

Handwriting Analysis Report on Dollena Fry

If a theme song could have been selected to describe Dollena during the years of her entries in the baby book it might have been, "Don't Fence Me In!"

This is an emotionally charged person who wants to move through life with lots of varied activities to feed her need for involvement. She is a spurter rather than a plodder. She will have some ups and downs because of some energy lapses and also because she has some moodiness to contend with. She tries to retain an optimistic view of life but sometimes she just cannot.

Her emotions reach out to others, and she will do for them but the feelings have to be there to motivate her—she would not be moved just because it may seem like the right thing to do. However, she has some reservations, and she subconsciously sets some limits about how close she wants to be to people so she does not crave constant contact and will put some distance between herself and others. She could be with them but be feeling inward reserve, perhaps melancholy. So she does not have to have the limelight, but neither is she unduly inhibited.

She has a sense of pride that makes it important that she appears at best advantage, and if her feelings are hurt it helps her cover her reaction so others who do not know her well may not be aware.

Her thinking pattern shows a naturally curious mind and is quite capable of learning quickly but is usually satisfied with a general smattering and an overview rather than doing a thorough, in-depth probe. Heavy technical information would not be of much interest. [Actually the incoming television age of news broadcasting just new to the world at the time of her death would have been a format she would have enjoyed: Learn a lot about a lot of things and do it quickly.]

She is a woman who wants to be in the know but she is not consistently open-minded in entertaining others' opinions that might influence her. She is selective in what gets through, but she has come up with a code of living that seems right to her, and she is loyal to that view. In fact, if her emotions come into play more than a little, she will dig in and stand her ground and stubbornly hang on to her contentions no matter what the arguments to the contrary.

One of her most outstanding characteristics is her expansive imagination. It greatly affects everything she thinks and does. As far as her thinking goes, it opens up so many possibilities and options and creates a resourceful pot of ideas. So that if one strategy doesn't produce what she wants to happen she has a plan B in the works. More conservative and inhibited people probably note and see her do things with style and are impressed. She's not afraid to try, and she will take some risks. She can get things done. That is not to say that she can pull of consistent successes—sometimes the idea sounds good, but for one reason or the other depend on her emotional feelings at the time and since they are not consistent, things in the works may fizzle out. Her thinking processes are greatly affected by her imagination also. Unfortunately, because it is a fertile environment, along with all those good ideas comes the tendency to lose whatever hope there is for an objective consideration of the matter. Her imaginative style will make amplification so easy, and then comes possible exaggeration—so that some of what she perceives is embellished. She may hear more expansively than a no-nonsense literally minded person. Her emotional nature means that she judges matters more by her heart than by her head. But when her head joins the party, her remembrance and subsequent retelling could amplify the facts somewhat. That's just the way she sees it. There is minor evidence of the desire to intentionally deceive and manipulate, but neither are strong traits at this point.

She does not like hum drum routine and will avoid it like the plague. She could never stick with such a life for long. Somehow she will seek and find a release. If she did not feel like something was worth the effort, she could show a rather cavalier attitude and call it quits. She likes to keep a lot going on at once, and she can handle it—except that on a bad day her energy may be scattered and she can feel frazzled by too much pressing in on her. She likes to move physically.

She shows a need and enjoyment for money and the things it can buy, and more than likely she will indulge her desires and not do without. Again her imagination comes into play, and she will want to put things together well and enjoy the whole process. She probably loves to shop and enjoys color and design. She will show some flair because she is not terribly conservative in her outlook.

A few fears inhibit her. She has trouble making some decisions easily—again perhaps the effect of that fruitful imagination that is constantly producing options so that the final choice may be difficult. She simply frets about some decisions she must make.

She can be touchy but may cover the feelings successfully. She does not know what it is to feel hurt. While she may feel self-confident about her abilities, she may not always feel self-worthy. There is some fear of not being loved for who she is. Some resentful feelings have been there for a long time about something from her past, and she has not dealt with them. She shows some repression of hurt feelings, and she has a tendency to worry.

She has adjusted to life by relying on a good sense of humor and an independent way of doing things. She will give in to her desires and may justify her actions—probably verbally as well as to herself.

She is sensitive to injustice and will feel that for others as well as herself because she does care. She can be witty and she talks easily and enjoys it. Oh, she is not above a little verbal sparring and will try to hold her own in an argument.

Her best release from tension is to put lots of variety and change into her life. [Maybe that fact accounts for the Robin-Robyn switch?] She loves to get away from it all by seeing things and people. It would appear that she likes surprises and to pull them off for others as well. She enjoys music and she has a literary bent that shows up in her writing. [Hopefully, she knew that too and gave it a whirl.]

All in all, Dollena is an interesting woman and a talented one as well, who cares and is basically trying to face her world pretty honestly. While she has some tendency to not see all the facts of a situation (that is a pretty human characteristic that almost always shows up in some degree in handwriting), she has a great capacity to feel and she gets into the action of life without undue fear.

Observations:

This analysis is based on the writing in the baby book. Since I had to work from the original I regret that the edges are more frayed than before, despite some care to preserve it. It is good to remember that handwriting shows what is happening in the writer's life at the time of the writing, and since people do change it may reflect something different about the writer than the readers of the report may know. It is as if the writer is frozen in time.

The graphoanalysis report is based on measurements of the writing to ascertain the tension-release factor. For example, some people are tense mentally—that is to say, sharp and exacting while in some area they may be quite uninhibited. Let's take a person like Albert Einstein; his writing shows emotional inhibition and great ability to concentrate (a form of controlled tension) but a conceptually broad creative imagination (release in that area).

A note on the last signature on the legal document:

It indicated that she had become even more emotionally reactive than in her earlier years and somewhat more past dependent, almost as if she were leaning or looking backward in time and the healthy, if not somewhat excessive, imagination she had shown in the 1920s had shriveled to a clannish desire to not include very many people or activities in her life. However, that is based on just two signatures on the deed and without more writing to consider could be inconclusive in revealing much how much more she had changed.

My questions:

Was there a sister or someone close to her to whom she felt compared?

Were her mother and father together?

And if so, were they happy as a couple?

Which one had the greatest influence on her?

Did she have any illnesses?

How did her life end?

Handwriting Analysis Report on Burton Fry

This analysis is based on the June 23, 1961, letter and therefore reflects the traits found to be most prevalent in Burton's personality at that time. The later note reflected such a serious physical deterioration that I didn't think it to be typical of him. However, there is evidence even in the letter of July 23 of unsteadiness that indicates some physical problems.

> Burton is a complicated person whose emotions seesaw and show considerable tension. The strokes are not fluid, rather they are jerky, and since writing is really brain-writing and a reflection of emotional condition as well, we see a person here who is under strain of some type which is impairing the nervous system.
>
> He is a man of pride and dignity but still retains the common touch. No big illusions about himself—although perhaps not greatly introspective anyway—his focus tends to be away from himself. He finds it hard to deal with some of the unpleasant things that have happened to him, and he has buried them away. It would do him good to face them, but he can't. So as a result, he doesn't know himself too well.
>
> His thinking processes are interesting. He has a sharply analytical mind that could tend toward a critical bent. He likes to learn, and he can see way beyond the obvious. But he is more likely to trust sound logic and thinking things through than to trust too many hunches. He analyzes everything and has his own opinions to match his conclusions. His recollections of the past very much influence his present thinking and feeling. He is not without his prejudices about some things, so he is no pushover. He will let others have their say, but he likes to good argument from time to time so

there will be some rebuttal, and he will like getting the last word. If pushed he could be a mite bossy.

He is not wishy-washy about his aims. He has practical judgment and can get enthusiastic once he gets into the swing of things. At this point in his life he is showing some hesitancy about plunging into things and will appreciate some warm-up time. It may be a reaction to fear and lack of confidence due to age and its accompanying worries.

He is missing attention from others, and he needs to have it. He suffers from some guilt feelings over something, and he has a jealous streak that nags at him somewhat. [In the letter prior to his death, he showed a greater degree of being very sensitive to anticipated hurts, so he may have felt very vulnerable then.] He can be suspicious.

He needs people around him and is, in fact, somewhat emotionally dependent. It would not be surprising to learn that he remarried fairly quickly after his first wife's death. If he didn't, he would have wanted to. In this letter there is evidence of some depression and fatigue.

He is a conservative person [incidentally, it looks like Alma was more on his wavelength on that score than Dollena was—true?] and counts his resources and is nobody's fool. He is generous but not with abandonment. He is by no means extravagant, especially with himself. He improvises due to a degree of resourcefulness.

He likes to be a doer and maybe try new things, but it is not as important to him as it was to Dollena. But he likes to get away from it all as dull routine is not especially to his liking.

At this writing he is anxious and tense, but he still has his eye on the big picture and can still shoot for some of his aspirations. He is pulled to the past by his memories, but he is still setting goals for the future.

For the most part he is an honest communicator and so tells it like it is. He will not be universally liked by all because his critical opinions could be abrasive, and he is not an easygoing person. He seems to mean well and is not intentionally unkind. His feelings run deep, and he will be able to express them pretty frankly, perhaps with more verbal detail than some people might appreciate.

Like almost everyone, except those rare one-dimensional people, (and there are some—their handwriting is boring too!) Burton is complex and this in no way sums up all the facets of his character in detail—but it is a thumbnail sketch of a person who wanted good things out of life. Here's hoping he got them.

My questions:

There is evidence that his relationship with his mother was much better than with his father. In fact, could it be that his father was an incidental influence on him—either because of absence or separation or lack of support?

No one always has complete objectivity to reason that under precisely the same circumstances (genes and all) he or she would have acted the same way. True, we all should have this detachment.

Possibly then the biggest piece of bullshit ever foisted on mankind is that of psychiatrists and clergy who say they are not judgmental.

All the prophets and disciples throughout the Bible were judgmental at one time or another. Now we have those with their holy-holy veneer, quoting the Scriptures, "Judge not, that you be not judged," but leaving unsaid hanging in the air: "But be my hitman, Lord."

The psychiatrists are saying the fact they themselves are not judgmental (they have no god complex) is what differentiates them from God.

Right along with the two groups are the so-called good wiccas, asserting that they always use their powers for doing good. More shit! If they are being pursued, undeservedly and relentlessly, sooner or later they're going to use their powers for their own good and to get even.

So the psychiatrist or clergyman who says he or she *tries* not to be judgmental seems more credible and less Messianic, as well as the wicca who says, "I *try* to use my power only for doing good for others."

The graphoanalyst began the report on the 1920s sample of Mom's handwriting by saying, "If a theme song could have been selected to describe Dollena during the years of her entries in the baby book it might have been, *Don't Fence Me In!*"

This might give the idea that high up on Mom's priorities was a plan to go on an ocean voyage or to buy a trailer and take off on vacations to parts unknown in Canada and Mexico. Not so. They usually took their vacations in California, possibly because it was what they could afford and because traveling any great distance wouldn't have been much of a vacation for Dad, who traveled many miles in his work.

I'm not saying that if they had had the money they wouldn't have gone. But it wasn't an overriding desire which would cause her to skimp and save or get a job. Most jobs she could have qualified for, by the way, would have been a humdrum existence for her, a Catch 22. But strictly as a mental thing, rather than geographical, the title was appropriate for the years I knew her and probably throughout her whole life.

Where I would strive for perfection and make "trivia a parcel of reckoning," she could get things done in half the time. She had a good imagination, and some of her ideas were excellent. But compared to Albert Einstein and his tension-release factor, she had few barriers or fences in which to channel. Her follow-through was terrible, especially on things not physical that involved a certain dedication over many weeks and months. In this respect, she was like the wind that was here and there and some other place, pausing where something interested her briefly and then moving on. Where it undoubtedly complemented her appeal when she was younger, it didn't necessarily do so when she reached forty.

She followed some new idea for a few days or weeks, and it made a terrific conversation piece, showing that she was indeed the bright and clever one (certainly no bore), then she would pick up on something new when the novelty of the other wore off and her interest began to wane. She failed to realize that the interest could be rekindled by putting forth more work and study, that the feeling of drudgery and boredom might in time be replaced by a consuming interest followed by a measure of satisfaction and fulfillment.

If a neighbor had a large demitasse collection, Mom would start one. Where the neighbor's was forty or fifty and still growing, hers would reach four or five and stop. If the neighbor had a large collection of salt and pepper shakers, she began one too, winding up with four or five maybe. If it were the thing at the time to make a rag rug, tying little strips of cloth around heavy twine or rope, she would make two or three. Dad's mother, Matilda, who came from Sweden, was an expert at crocheting. Mom quickly learned the basics from her, made two or three things, and that was that. She knew how to can peaches, pears, peas, jams, and jellies, if she felt like it. She could play the piano by ear—monotonous style, chords thumping away. Still it was better than I could do. Both she and Dad read library books, worked crossword puzzles, and played cards. The piece which won't fit is how she could sit by herself at times and play solitaire over and over. Yet maybe this is not so strange.

The writer of the report said there were indications that she had a "literary bent." This was true, but she didn't bend it very far. She decided to write a novel, which was to tell the real story of the oil fields. No doubt Maricopa, Taft, Long Beach, Avenal, and Bakersfield would have figured prominently. I can only speculate—since she at times tended to be melodramatic—she would have been the main character in it, thinly disguised as a true-to-life Stella Dallas or perhaps an I-don't-give-a-damn-either Scarlett O'Hara, who, along with Helen Keller, Bette Davis, George Sand, and Eleanor Roosevelt, was one of her heroines. If, incidentally, you made a list containing the names of people who had actually lived or were fictional characters and asked her to select the one on it whom she felt was her kindred spirit, she undoubtedly would have picked Ellen Berent in Ben Ames Williams's *Leave Her to Heaven.*

A friend of mine, a graduate of the University of California at Berkeley School of Journalism, was a talented writer. She got his address and wrote to ask if he would help her on the novel. This he agreed to, and that was the last heard of it.

A few months ago I wrote Robyn to see if she would send me something with Mom's handwriting. She replied there wasn't much left from her later life, a period we both were interested in knowing about and why she went "dipsy doodle." Robyn said she was sorry now that after Mom's death she had thrown away her notes on the novel. But who would have ever thought then they might be important someday for handwriting analysis? Certainly as something of literary merit, the novel never got off the ground. I can see her in my mind defending herself: "Sure, mine never got off the ground. But you wasted many years on yours, and it never flew either."

"*Touché*, Mom!"

"She had listed," Robyn said, "the characters she would use, their future or present husbands, and offspring. I read it and can't tell you now what it was about, as she hadn't really got into much writing on the story line. It was just an outline more or less."

Along these lines too of starting and stopping, Mom wasn't going to be content until Dad bought her an exer-cycle. It cost about three hundred dollars, a lot of money in the early to mid-forties. She must have ridden it a half dozen times and then put it out in the garage where it gathered dust for years. Never mind that, she thought perhaps she'd start a fitness-training school with it someday.

Later in Avenal she decided she would open a home day-care center or nursery. She did get one or two required licenses, but it never actually began.

The analyst pointed out that her handwriting in the 1920 shows "she enjoys color," that "she will show some flair because she is not terribly conservative in outlook," and that "she likes to move physically." All three clearly were combined in her gardening, both in Avenal in the 1930s and in Bakersfield in the 1940s.

As with many oil-field people in those days, much of their entertainment-luxury money—with the exception of that saved for a two-week vacation—was spent on wine, beer, and cigarettes. Lucky Strike, Wings, and Dominoes were supplemented at times by those I would make on a cigarette roller. There was a bird cage with two canaries, pictures on the walls, and figurines, most dime-stone variety dust-collectors. A miniature, rustic hut hung on one wall. If it were to be a clear day, an idyllic scene showed but if cloudy or rainy, an old witch. Flowers were arranged in vases.

Though teaching us to pray when we were younger, her religion, like most everybody else's, was tailored to suit her needs and wasn't meant to be an inconvenience. "You don't have to go to Church to pray or believe in God." How much praying she actually did in her mind is unknown. I am sure she believed in God and Jesus but was turned off by the hypocrisy and/or dullness of religion as practiced sometimes and its judgmental nature most times: the mind-set, the lock-step, the Stepford wife, the Stepford religion. She did go to church on Easter when I was younger and then never when I was older. Still as a person who really isn't superstitious will, when spilling salt, throw some over his shoulder so as not to take any chances, she subscribed to the "Upper Room," a small pocket-size, monthly publication which had a quotation from the Bible for each day, followed by two or three paragraphs. She no doubt would lapse for a few days in reading it. Then read all she had missed and perhaps ahead for three or four days.

She found flowers were more meaningful and easier to understand. The stark beauty of their colors gave zest to her life. It had to have been so or she never would have worked so hard in her garden at times. I doubt if she ever put it into words that they were her church and religion. Where others performed their abolitions, penances, and denials, she preferred to wash herself in beauty. In a week or two, the penitents would have forgotten what they were penitent over, but the beauty of her flowers would still be there to see and in which to bask. This was probably her thinking at its best.

If a polster had asked, he would have found she was sympathetic toward the blacks, the Okies, the Jews, the American Indians, the Chinese, and others. All these she knew firsthand from *Uncle Tom's Cabin*, *Gone With The Wind*, what she had read about the holocaust and the Nuremberg trials, *The Story of Hiawatha*, and *The Good Earth*. That they didn't live next door wasn't her fault nor was the fact that she couldn't or wouldn't drive. Her volunteer charity was, for the most part, a lip service and then not even hers:[94] "Now you eat everything on your plate! Just think of all those millions of starving children in China!"

To her credit, I don't recall her or Dad ever going to some charity line, nor do I ever remember her making any slurs about minorities. But then again, she never actually rubbed elbows to get into impossible traps such as, "What are you staring at?"

"I'm staring at you because you're staring at me."

She had a Ouija board and a book in which she could look up her dreams to tell what they augured. Another told her what her astrology forecast for the day was. There was a container with bamboo sticks in it. When shaken, one would fall out. A number printed on the end would tell what to look up in a book, giving predictions of things to happen. But all these were just games, not to be taken seriously, conversation pieces at most. They added fillips of interest to the day, much the same as fortune cookies do and about as long lasting as Chinese food.

As far as is known, she didn't have any deep belief in any of it, nor was she any dripping mystic. Still, in spite of her shortcomings in this area, there is little doubt that she would have been happier in life as a gypsy. No group is more under the Hermes influence.

Though she had no gift, they could have taught her to read palms, tell fortunes from cards, and fake it with a crystal ball to make money. She was clever enough that she could have carried this off well. Any qualms she might initially have had about dishonesty would have perished by the thought that people were paying for her performance. How well they paid was its touchstone. Hell, here's where inspired performances, high drama took place, not Hollywood where acting paled in comparison. They might have given best supporting Oscars (Noscars, whatever) to the most convincing/convinced victim. Don't you see how simple it is? You get what you pay for, and bad actors usually give the best performances.

In nature—dawns, sunsets, trees, and animals—she would have been closer to the God with whom she could identify. The romance and adventure on the roads and highways would have suited her perfectly, sitting in front with one of the drivers while telling him both lies and damaging truths about one of her rivals of whom she was jealous while manipulating someway or other to get her way.

When the caravans pulled into an area by a stream or river near a town, she'd hop out and wash up, pick some wildflowers, maybe find an interesting rock, and then cook—or help cook—the meal for all over an open fire. When in the evening the stars and moon had come out, Dollena Dorothy Dolores Del Rio could apply her rouge and lipstick, take the prettiest flower she'd picked earlier, put it in her hair over her ear, and take a swig of wine. Then while an accordion or guitar was playing dolefully or joyfully in the background, she would slip away, finally tearing out and trotting up the trail to meet her lover. Early in the morning after a quick cup of coffee from a blackened pot over an open fire, they would all be on the road again with new places to go and see.

Isn't this what life's all about though—to try to find someplace where you can be happy? No doubt she loved Dad, Robyn, and me in her own way, but it was like letters in the mailbox. Sometimes they were there, sometimes they weren't, and a lot of it was junk mail. In return she felt she was due her letters whether she wrote any or not.

If the theme song is valid, why didn't she leave? There's some truth to the fact that she was getting older and less sure of herself. She might have considered she could be getting into something worse than she had. Robyn's threat might have had some impact, but when it came down to her own happiness, none of these seemed to have been a very compelling reason for her to stay.

Ominously a blueprint to the magic hung on one of the walls. It's the only picture really remembered, and it leads me to think that unconsciously Mom might have known something. Certainly for Dad it was just another picture, for me, no more than a rectangular dust collector. It's strange that it would flash into my mind today, something not thought about for decades, and that it's the only picture recalled though there were others.

124

With only a dim recollection, I went to the art section at the Fourth Avenue Library to see if someone there could give me a clue about what it was called or who the artist might have been. From only the vague description, the librarian suggested the name Maxfield Parrish (I thought she said "Paris"). Then several books were brought from the back room to look through, but it wasn't in them. The books were returned. Another librarian was now at the desk. That should have been it, but curiously she very helpfully suggested she go to the back room to see if she could find something else which might have been overlooked. Eventually then in a large, old dusty book which was coming apart at its seams was found *Circe's Palace*.

This shows a sorceress bending over a large vessel or caldron, between four columns, making her magic brew. Seeing the picture again, I realized the sympathy in Mom's dress (blouses, slacks, bracelets) and Circe's attire, as well as her stance. The enchantress will lure *travelers* to Aeaea (Note the *AEA* similarity in AvEnAl; NEvAdA; and AmEricA, born on the fourth of July). What's even more eerie, however, is that it will be Hermes who will provide Ulysses, whose ship can be seen in the background, with the knowledge to combat her.

Chapter Nineteen

Both Mom and Dad were under an Hermes influence. The home was her prison, from which she couldn't escape for long anymore than Dad could get a divorce. They were two fours cast together and fated for life, as much as if they'd been in a Greek tragedy. At the end when Dad is dying and the potion or charm has begun to wear off, he will ask to be buried next to his third wife in a cemetery on the way to Coalinga (about thirteen miles from Avenal), breaking the pact that he and Mom had made years before about being cremated. Sadly he had written to me concerning Mom: "I wonder now if I really ever loved her."

She had entered nurse's training at Seaside Hospital in Long Beach and later married Dad. Possibly before the marriage she might have gotten pregnant. She never mentioned this, however, so chances are the reasons for her dropping out of training were both love and escape. Many, of course, having put in so much time would have continued on upon marriage until they graduated. Robyn wrote on June 22, 1991, as follows:

> In an earlier letter you asked a question about Mother and the stillbirth or births. She told me once when I was younger (maybe 9–13 years old) that she had lost a baby before I was born in 1923. I had always thought they were married in 1920, but I found the announcement sent by Granddad Duren that says they were married December 16, 1921. So—given how soon she had got pregnant and how long she was in pregnancy, and then later pregnant and carrying me nine months—if she had another pregnancy, it would have had to been after me if she ever lost another baby. She had an 18–24 hour labor with me, so I'm not sure if she did or did not. Seems like she told me at the time she had. She said that one of those babies was a boy. But she called it a miscarriage. These days any baby after so many months has to be buried, but there was no grave around that I ever knew about. I

really think she just had a miscarriage before me and never another. But with her dramatics, who knows what she might have dreamed? She did tell me that if they had performed more Caesareans in those days, she would have had one done due to long labor and difficult delivery. The boy part is probably true though, because she and Dad were so thrilled when she brought you home from Nevada and finally had a son.

"Frank," she was said to have urged, "you can't possibly look after the other children, the ranch, and a newborn baby at the same time. Let us take him. We can give him better care."

Overcome with grief, my father saw that what she said was right. He agreed to this but only after exacting the promise that an adoption would never be sought.

Clearly it was meant that they were to take me, but it had to be packaged in reasons that humans can think out for themselves and that make some logical sense. My coming along fulfilled a wish and helped shore up a marriage. Dad's motives can't be faulted. He wanted a son and another child. Mom wanted this too first and foremost. But knowing her so well later in life, I believe layered beneath this in a small part was the feeling that she was showing her father and older sisters that she was the one who had it together when things really counted, that advanced academic education was comparatively nothing. Possibly as a young girl she had rebelled at being cast in the same mold as her older sisters. She just wanted to be herself, and this she did, but she couldn't completely separate from the stamp of childhood.

One of the first memories of Long Beach when I was three or four is that of a police station, an early sign of precocity. Move over Hermes! Dad's brother and his wife had taken me to the beach where I'd wandered off. Nothing whatsoever is remembered about this other than their coming to get me. But you can't trust the cops, you know. The reason nothing is remembered is that I've probably been suppressing it all these years. It's time to sue.

The earthquake, when I was four, seemed like the Pike merry-go-round horses going up and down. Whee! Later, downtown, I saw the shattered buildings, broken windows, glass, naked manikins, and areas roped off.

One recollection is of being very scared one night in my room in back of an apartment on Obispo, a feeling that something or a presence was near. I got up and went down what seemed a long hallway to the front and told Mom. She came back, took a quick look, said there was nobody there, and without further words went off and left me.

When in the fourth grade I had appendicitis, which might have caused me to throw up earlier in life because after the operation I don't remember being sick again. There's the memory at three or four of Mom saying, "You made the mess! Now damn it, you clean it up. I'm tired of cleaning up after you."

So I got the mop. Of course she'd been out of nurse's training for a number of years by then. It could be that she was far ahead of her time, as many nurses nowadays don't want to do anything but carry the keys, issue narcotics, and squawk about not getting paid enough.

There's only myself to blame for not putting her on the right track early on. Should have scraped up the barf and wolfed it right back down. Well, don't look so shocked or act so righteous. Didn't your baby spit out the Gerber's which deposited around its mouth, nose, and chin? This you scraped off with a spoon and shoveled it right back in. It was nasty! Disgusting! Just because you weren't going to open another can. Later you have the gall to wonder why your baby grew up to be tight, lazy, and uncouth, exactly in that order. Don't you see? Your little darling was learning from you even then.

Anyway, there were a few distant drums that nobody heard except me, and nobody would have believed me amidst the good care and coddling at other times.

I'd read *Leave Her to Heaven*[95] in 1944. Forty-seven years later, there was no recollection of what the novel was about but only that Mom had identified with a main character. Rereading the story recently, I was struck by the many similarities between Mom and Ellen Berent:

1) Each was devoted to her father.
2) Where Ellen had seen her adopted sister as a rival, Mom saw her older sisters as such, in my opinion.
3) Each was willing to lie to get her way and to subordinate the wishes of others.
4) Both had recurrent illnesses which were hard to diagnose, or at least to figure out what caused the symptoms.
5) Neither wanted to live to be old, and each wanted to be and later was cremated.
6) Both Ellen and Dollena (again the Greek *ele* root) lost to some extent—but not completely—in influencing what happened after death.
7) Ellen had suspected that after her own death, her sister would become her husband's next wife. Though Mom might not have known or suspected whom Dad would marry if she died, she had known both women who would become, after her death, the second and third wives.

Besides there is a curiousness in more-than-random parallelism, unaccountable things in and about the story itself that suggest a link between them and my life. Examples of this are below:

1) The book was published in 1944 (a multiple of four), not 1941, 1942, 1943, 1945, 1946, or 1947.
2) Hermes is the patron of writers. The main character happened to be a writer. The story took place in part on a ranch near some mountains. Here there are horses, rocks, a cairn, and traveling. Later in the story there will be fire, wind, and flight. Ellen Berent personifies deception and lying.
3) One of the main characters is the daughter of the brother of Professor Berent. The name sounds close to Brent.
4) Professor Berent had a hobby of collecting specimens of dead birds and preserving them. Here is symbolism of death and afterlife—Hermes.
5) Both had a brother and sister-in-law (relatives) who die figure prominently in the story.
6) A mystery to be solved remained after death.

Finally it seems strange that since Ellen Berent was an unsavory character, Mom identified with her in some way.

A distant cousin lived in downtown Bakersfield in a white, clapboard house, constructed before the turn of the century, dwarfed by a huge camellia tree, and nearly surrounded by modern buildings. She owned a richly made afghan; older than she and perhaps grandfather's clock too, it was a collector's item. Since Mom always admired it, the old lady willed it to her when she died.

"Of course," Mom said, "your Aunt Nell wanted this too, but she left it to me." Unspoken yet hanging heavily in the air just the same: "I was the one she really cared about."

Mom did "like surprises and to pull them off for others as well." She conned me into believing they couldn't afford to get me a bicycle one Christmas. She knew my heart was set on it, so this was the reason she was telling me in advance not to be disappointed. What a surprise then when there was a bicycle next to the tree Christmas morning.

Yet not all occasions turned out happily. She overreacted at times, making an issue of something that wasn't called for. To be able to explain this succinctly in adult terms forty-five to fifty years later doesn't perhaps do justice to the degree of importance it had to a kid who hadn't figured all this out.

She spoiled grammar school graduation by making more of something than was necessary. One birthday she tried to bake me an angel food cake, and so the undertaking was doomed from the beginning. It never rose up but just lay there flat, dog-flop dead, and undisguised by a thick layer of frosting. It was so tough, it brought to mind a jackhammer. It could have been a prop for a practical joke, something out of "The Three Stooges," or a first offering from a grammar school home economics class. If you ignored it, it wouldn't go away. The only thing to do was laugh about it good-naturedly. Yet when I did laugh, she became unglued, ugly, reminding me of the parody, "If I'd know'd you were comin', I'd 'ave baked a snake."

One summer a friend lent us his mountain cabin to use at the Jack Ranch for a two-week vacation. As Mom and I got into it, I would get in our Desoto and listen to the radio. Either I left the radio running or the battery ran down from so much listening. Later when they tried to pull the car uphill, something happened to the fluid drive, causing even more problems. There's no other way to describe it than to say she had a way of making me feel like a complete shit. Looking back in my age of Medicare, I see her as a woman of complex emotions, some of them interwound and contrary, not completely free of my suspicions that in her later years she might still have been trying to get back at her older sister through me. The *Leave Her to Heaven* recall then is unsettling.

No doubt "Don't Fence Me In" is apt for the period of the sample used. To try to apply it without some explanation to the years which followed, however, would be misleading. The title seems to suggest a casual, corsetless picture: a romantic, wanderlust person, a free spirit roaming here and there as the mood strikes her. But if you extend the thought, "Don't Fence Me In" can mean a disregard for natural fences and boundaries others have put in their minds to preserve a privacy and dignity.

An analogy to understand Mother, me, or anybody else is to say that each person has two family bank accounts of emotions. If one becomes short and going in to make withdrawals, he might find the balances are extremely low because his mother and father had to borrow heavily. In fact, they were probably plugging up their emotional holes at times with tits from a boar hog. Things become mixed as they become more frantic, so they borrow from their children. It becomes more complicated than the national debt, yet in some ways it is an exact parallel. Churches aren't taxed, so it's easy for them to say pithily, pitilessly, and pissily, "Everyone is responsible for his own actions." But it's not that simple. It's not that there's blame or no blame. It's just the way things are. Brent is so understanding!

Robyn, nearly six years older, was a wholesome, pretty girl whose grades came easily, a cheerful person interested in school activities, and would later marry her high-school boyfriend. Though the marriage ended in divorce, she poured a lot of love into her kids and had "true grit" by hanging in when things got tough. As a result, all three of her children turned out well. I knew, of course, that after she married, Robyn was well aware of Mom's behavior. Not known until recently, however, was that her high school days hadn't been as carefree as I'd imagined.

She wrote:

> I guess you thought my letter rambled on, but I had never been able to talk to anyone about Mother's indiscretions and all I told you. I, too, think she was a bitch in her treatment of Dad and you. She ruled his life, nagged, and made his life miserable most of the time. She never went to the store. He did all the shopping. I had to clean house every Saturday. I don't really know what she did—probably ironing, etc., and worked in the yard. She never came to high school to see me the three years I was cheerleader and majorette for the band. It hurt me, and I never knew why she didn't.... Possibly the reason was that she was drinking. I'm sure you remember the parties at our house on Seventh Street where friends came, played the piano and horns, sang, and got drunk on red wine all night. She had, of course, the hysterectomy in 1937 or 1938 and almost died from complications, so she might not have felt like coming to see me some of that time. But for three years?
>
> All the years they were here and after Avenal built the hospital, they needed nurses and LVNs especially. She probably could have gotten work at an LVN, or at least it wouldn't have taken her long to get some training in order to get a job. But she never considered it. That would have taken her mind off herself and maybe given her a brighter outlook on life. Oh well, like you, I wish her well wherever she is now.

It's all conjecture what went through Mom's mind, and no one will ever know for certain. Mom, though loving her, might have seen Robyn as she grew older more as a rival, as she possibly saw her older sisters earlier in life.

Money was short, and she often complained about that. Since she always talked such a good story about what she could or couldn't do, I too wondered why she never look for a job. The observation that she did "not like hum drum routine and will avoid it like the plague" probably held true for her later years and explains this. But these are possibly packaged explanations which seem plausible.

One spring my grandfather, who was around eighty-eight or eighty-nine, and his second wife, Ida, visited us in our two-bedroom house in Bakersfield. They were given my bedroom, while I slept in the garage. No problem. While he was with us, he had a stroke. He might have gone to a hospital for a short time, but it couldn't have been more than a few days. Mom wanted none of that. She had been drinking, raised her voice, and cussed. Aunt Nell had more class than to get into it with her younger sister, nor did she ever bring it up to me later. Still there was the distinct impression at the time that Aunt Nell knew her well and wasn't completely taken back by the outburst.

Though Mom hadn't completed her nurse's training twenty or more years earlier or kept up with it afterwards, she felt compelled to bring him home from the hospital. Aunt Nell, who had urged her not to do this, thought it was unnecessary, the four sisters should share equally in the hospitalization. Mom went ahead with her plans anyway. She rented a hospital bed and moved it into the bedroom. She saved money doing this, and I believe her care was good. But at what expense in strain to herself and others as he lingered on several weeks before dying? Ida, of course, was with us, possibly sleeping on the couch in the front room, and I, in the garage. Remember also that two of his daughters had come from Long Beach to see him, as well as other relatives in and out. Here again was one of the gray areas: devotion certainly to her father, while showing her sisters that in the end, she was the one. Maybe too there were other factors: one that went way back to her childhood when her mother died at home in Maricopa and another that she was justifying her nurses training, showing that the money her father had put out for her hadn't been completely wasted.

Of course, all this is what's packaged for us to believe. As far as things go, I think what's said is true at one level. It's also true, though not too probable, that Granddad will have his stroke[96] in the "enchanted garden" he used to sit in, that he, the fourth son and fourth child (possibly born a fire snake), will die near Mom, his fourth daughter and fourth child; his son-in-law, a fourth son; and me, his grandson, a fourth son, as if written that he must be there so something could be passed on.

Recalling Mom's death, Robyn wrote as follows:

> The sheriff and the people that go over death scenes, taking pictures, etc., were here over five hours going through every drawer looking for a possible suicide note. On not finding one, they declared it was an accident, not suicide. And of course Dad's story that he had been out at a job site was thoroughly checked out by the detective and sheriff's department. So I know he never had anything to do with her death as I think he still loved her in a way, and I know my father couldn't have done such a terrible thing. The men that were here said that a suicide about always left a note, and I truly believe

that as dramatic as Mother was she would have played it all for what it was worth and to the hilt.

As to Alma—Aunt Lil [the friend of the family who had helped to salvage the marriage years before] didn't like her and years later when she and I were discussing Mother, Aunt Lil wondered if Alma could have given her anything in her wine or in any way contributed to her death. She thought Alma might have done something that night when Mom went over to her place. But as Mom had vomited on the rug, which had been washed and hung out over the backstairs, maybe there wasn't enough contents in her stomach for an autopsy to tell. And I don't think Aunt Lil realized how much they were all drinking then. Anyway, who will ever know but God?

Though not personally knowing Alma too well, I would give less credence to her involvement than to suicide. Most likely it was accidental. Still in my mind there was a lingering doubt. True, Mom could be emotional when she was drinking, but at other times she could be very calculating. To have committed suicide without leaving a note would have been just that. She'd been complaining about being cold, and yet she was found naked. She hadn't wanted to live to be old. She and Dad were drinking heavily and having more and more fights. She threatened divorce, and she wasn't discreet: Alma had walked in, so she said, on Mom and her lover having an affair one time. Besides, Mom had nearly been overcome by carbon monoxide poisoning once before in her life. She had told several people about this over the years and repeatedly pointed out the fact that she always left a window cracked. The thermostat was broken. I've little reason not be believe Dad was receiving comfort from Alma. So Mom's death, as with Ellen Berent's, could have been meant to cast suspicion, for in a year or so, Dad married Alma.

They were married for three or four years, and probably he was happier with her than Mom. But it's questionable if he ever had anything close to real happiness until Alma died and he married for a third time. Concerning this Robyn wrote:

He and Mal were sweethearts before he ever married Mother. After or before he married Mother, they broke up. I'm not sure of the story. It was something that he told me after he had gone up to Oregon a couple times to renew their friendship, and they eventually married. They were really happy, and Dad went down slowly after Mal died. I think he truly loved her best. His love for Mom, I believe, died slowly after her big romance started in Bakersfield.

It's human nature for people to visit graves yearly of those who have meant something in their lives, to take flowers and sort of commune in thought. But it's hard to do this with a small urn of ashes on a mausoleum shelf or in a bank vault. Mom, not realizing the possibility that Dad would ever change his mind about being cremated and placed in an urn next to hers, probably would have been happier with her ashes, like those of Ellen Berent, scattered over the ground. Somehow she did fence herself in and isolate herself off. Very likely it was a Grecian urn, not of her own choosing. Who really knows? Her epitaph might well have been LEAVE HER TO HEAVEN, since the circumstances surrounding her life and death have been packaged into reasons for us to consider and possibly believe. There's still the feeling that something is missing. Who knows? Could be it's a natural feeling that comes with the deaths of those you'd known well, a spook factor with religion being the natural progression. Without death, there would be no religions, no worship of a god or gods.

On returning from Korea in 1951, I visited Dad and Mom. Though I hadn't asked, suggested, or even wanted their help, Mom said she and Dad planned to help me get through college in whatever my major was, be it music or pre-med. Then a few months later at Camp Stoneman, Pittsburg, California, I received a call saying Dad and she were in town. This was very surprising—a first, unusual not only that they had come to visit me but had traveled so many miles. Instead of being the often ballsy woman I'd known in earlier years, she had changed and had become mellower. She was pleasant and enjoyed being there and seeing me.

Over a half century since then, I see now the potion or charm was just beginning to wear itself off. Mom possibly had a presentiment that something was going to happen and came to pass on whatever and to say goodbye as she really was and wanted to be remembered. Two weeks later she was dead.

Burt Fry, like the three women he married and stuck with until their deaths, was a heavy drinker. He died on January 30, 1973, of a circulatory failure, one of the contributing causes being cirrhosis of the liver. (Note: This date was twenty-two days before the Feralia; Mom's birth on March 15, 1900 [a leap year], was twenty-two days after the Caristia.) From the time I knew him, I saw no indication of any jealousy. As far as is known, he had no problems with his brothers and sisters, who he saw from time to time when they were living. I never saw his father, nor did Dad ever speak of him to me or any part of his earlier life. Robyn, however, saw her granddad only once in her life and wrote what she's heard about him:

> He was always a prospector—for oil in those days of
> the 1800s and when Dad was born in 1900. He was in the
> crew that brought in the first oil well in Pennsylvania,

using hand-cable tools. Matilda Carlson was eighteen years old when she arrived from Sweden. I don't know when. Granddad and she were married, but—as family stories go—he was gone a lot, only home enough to get her pregnant with six kids.

The handwriting analyst was correct in saying Burt Fry "was by no means extravagant, especially with himself." He had to worry about paying bills and being the provider and probably felt it was easier to be harder on himself than on the rest of us. His way was to shop for cheaper things, the best value, to be thrifty. Money was seldom lavished on anything, but keep in mind both Dad and my father were depression-era people. Each had a certain integrity about himself that he always paid his debts and didn't accept charity. The same person who might have called them tight usually was the one who was a sponger or welsher when his or her money ran out.

And though Dad drank heavily, he bore his yoke of work like a man. You would never have heard him whine, "I'm so damn tired of this shit, working myself to death night and day, just to keep food in your belly and clothes on your back."

Where he failed in part as a father was not that he didn't love me. He delighted in the naiveté and antics of a dumb kid who took him literally when he said he was "going to see a man about a horse" and was disappointed when he didn't come back with one; who thought he could easily outrun a pickup going ten miles an hour and was soon left panting far behind; who, if he thought he was unobserved, would duel an imaginary pirate with a wooden sword; and when told he didn't "know his ass from a hole in the ground" would always guess the wrong one of two circles drawn on the ground to prove it.

The failure was that he didn't take time to work with me in areas where there might have been trouble dealing with the world. If asked to show me how a car engine worked, he would give me a definition of this or that part, as if I were to understand this. Instead of taking the time—making the time—when things had gone wrong with the car to make certain I had a hand in repairing it and so begin to understand and get an interest, he would go ahead and do it himself, figuring he could do it much faster, which was true. But there's no recall of anything we built together.

In those years, Joe Louis was the heavyweight boxing champion of the world and to Dad and Mom's credit, they never made racial slurs. One Christmas they'd given me a pair of boxing gloves. Then he matched me with a kid my own age (about eight or nine whose father had worked with his son). I was humiliated, of course, and Dad was disappointed. It was clear to him I'd never be a boxer. Instead of working with me to build confidence in myself and give a better performance next time, he probably rationalized that I really wasn't his son but only a nephew by marriage.

Who knows? Life's life. What happens, happens. So not too much do I speak from bitterness but that someday someone might read this where it might make a difference—that is, if in their life they are dealing only on one level.

Robyn wrote:

> As to Dad not doing many things with you—he never did much with me either. He came up to high school to see me cheerlead a few times, depending if he was home and not out on a cement job. He never took a seat in the bleachers though, just stood at the chain-link fence for fifteen or twenty minutes and watched me. That's more than Mother ever did...if she was ever jealous—I think she might have been over how much Dad seemed to love me. He always took my part when she and I would get into arguments or when she nagged me to do the housework that I think he felt she should have been getting done herself. But I don't know. I remember one time after she had given me a belting over something, I told her that I knew my Dad was my real Dad, but I thought she was my step-mother.

The graphoanalyst had said, "He needs people around him and is, in fact, somewhat emotionally dependent. It would not be surprising to learn that he remarried fairly quickly after his wife's death."

Unaware of this statement, Robyn had written concerning his last few years with mother, "...he was not a happy man and was lonely, though after mother's death I think any woman would have made him happy!"

Looking back, I can remember Dad coming home tired and sweating after being on a job for two or three days in grueling summer heat in Bakersfield. He'd go over to the doorway or someplace that stuck out and move side to side scratching his back while the wall rumbled and windows rattled. In time the plaster or wood wore down an inch or two in those places. Now I never see someone do this, scratch his back like an elephant against a tree, that I don't think of Dad and laugh.

136

Chapter Twenty

U.S. Naval Hospital,
Oakland, California 1954

Those who can sleep comfortably in a well-lighted area at night have to be strange, even if this was hardly the place to say it. (Don't even think it!) They were expected to sleep but were cuckoo for doing so under bright lights, or we might also be wacko for expecting them to. As a compromise, dim, overhead nightlights were left on so those from inside the nurse's station could see out into the ward, if not too clearly, while the patients could see us fairly well. Should one of them be watching during the wee hours of the morning, he might have thought it odd that the hospitalman could sleep not only under bright lights but also standing for three or four seconds, at which time he'd start to fall and wake up.

If ever there were a dream, it was to sleep. I had been going to a University of California summer session in the daytime, taking upper-level courses, one in anthropology and the other in classics. It seemed like a good idea when enrolling, but waiting and traveling one and one-half hours each day each way on buses began to get old fast, fasting from sleep.

Being an NP technician, Snake was in charge of the graveyard shift on the brig ward. I was second in charge, which wasn't such a big deal when you stop to think there were only two of us and that third in charge might have been more impressive position since it would have been a chain of command to go through. So you see now why the brig rats sometimes outsmarted me. Some had already outsmarted several people before outsmarting themselves. Others were just babes in the woods caught up in their mental problems. They all had disciplinary action pending. Some typical diagnoses were: passive-aggressive behavior, immaturity reaction, emotional instability, obsessive-compulsive behavior, etc. If once in awhile a schizophrenic or manic-depressive turned up, the reason probably was that the psychiatrist felt the individual's case wasn't too severe.

It wasn't unusual to see a diagnosis changed once or twice. If you didn't know, you'd be misled into thinking the psychiatrists were a bunch of bungling incompetents who didn't know doodly shit, couldn't make up their minds. The problem here is that many times there are several diagnoses that intertwine in the mind. The admitting doctor in a quick interview sees only one of these or puts down the one he thinks is most significant at the time. Later, after more observation and testing, he or another doctor realizes another diagnosis is most typical or representative and so the change.

Besides being required to keep watch for anything suspicious, we were supposed to make and log at least one round hourly. I took off making the first one as soon as we'd come on duty. The ward was quiet; the patients seemed to be sleeping. I returned the keys and was putting the flashlight down when Snake did his takeoff of one of the psychiatric nurses who baby-talked the patients: "Now you sit right down there, and good nurs-ee is going right now to get you a great, big paper cup of good, cold water. Won't that be nice?"

"Present company excluded," I said, almost seeing the phrase as if writing it in class and wondering if we all were condemned in life to share certain words, like a piece of gum stuck to the underside of a table, to pull off when needed, then stuck back for someone else to break off and mouth later....

"Where was I? Oh! Present company excluded," the phrase hung there like steam from breath in cold weather, "some of us are a little flakier than others." Maybe that wasn't exactly true about present company. "How are we helping patients—if we really do—when each of us has some individual problem he or she can't solve and probably never will?"

I wasn't Napoleon or Jesus, for Christsake, just the professor at the lectern earlier that day. "Maybees we need 'em, so it'll be we and they, or us and them, more than they need us," I lectured, warming to the subject.

"The impression of reading case histories sometimes is that the psychiatrist or psychologist is writing with an eye to having it published in a journal or to impress navy brass or his peers with how astute and sharp he is. What's just as bad, I do this, pandering on the nurse's notes to make myself look good, at the expense of someone's peculiarities. Everything is seemingly couched in objectivity, but it's there—a little ratfink to the doctor and the navy. It's a clandestine, spy-gathering operation behind a front saying, 'We're the good guys. Trust us. We have only your interest at heart.'

"Sure some of it has to be written down, but most of it sucks, a lot of garbage to be preserved forever. Chances are before becoming a canonized weirdo off somewhere in a medical-records depot, the patient manages somehow, someway, sometime to see his supposedly locked-up records. He realizes that our front was a bunch of bullshit, and nobody—

you, me, or anybody else—is ever going to have his confidence again. And so he's paranoid for being distrusting. Jesus!

"At least that's my feeling sometimes. Other times I see the observations and comments as clues to making some headway in helping the patient. If the reason for our own motives for making a notation are suspect once in awhile, what's written isn't necessarily wrong. What I'm trying to say is that with big brother Navy watching and influencing, the patient's interests can be compromised."

"Give me a break!" Snake pleaded.

"Why's that? Doesn't the Constitution guarantee freedom of speech?"

"I don't think they had you in mind when they wrote that in."

"Well there's more to come. I'm just getting my second wind."

Mordecai, I almost translate in spoof of the classics professor, now would be beaming at the class, very pleased with himself and his little witticism.

"Whoa! Hold it right there! How many winds are there?"

"Wait and see." Now where was I?...We'd just finished cleaning up one day after lunch when the nurse came to the ward. The first thing she does is go over and check the refrigerator, and then she looks up meowing, "What happened to the chicken that was left over?"

"There wasn't any."

"What?" she asks.

"There was no chicken left. Nada. The patients ate it all. What's wrong? You look like somebody who's just missed lunch."

"Oh no! Oh no!" she chokes.

"I couldn't see her face as she turned away. I think she's putting me on. Then there are tears streaming down her cheeks. Sure there is chicken little, but the sky's not falling. The sun's out. We haven't been invaded by the Martians, yet somehow her world has fallen apart."

"What am I going to feed my little babies now?" she sobs.

"Now you know and I know, Snake, and COs put out bulletins that they're trying to get rid of the damn cats under the ramps and wards, and they're not to be fed. But this means nothing to Sister Catty Nation who will defy the admiral and risk getting nothing from her twenty years of naval service if need be to right the social injustice of a no-cathouse."

"Are you finished?" Snake asked.

"No. Wall to wall quack-quacks never run down. Now get this. When I worked on the NP admission ward, the nurse there brought in some roses she had picked one morning at her home. She places them in a container and tells me to put some water in it. I take it to the back of the ward and fill it with tap water, which was neither hot nor cold. When I bring the flowers back to her, she feels the temperature and becomes agitated that ice water hadn't been used for her b-u-ti-ful roses. 'But you should have known better!' she raves. Could she have been having a psychotic break right on the spot? They were just a bunch of damn roses! A 'Rose is a rose is a rose is a rose.'"[97-A] I then felt compelled to add a stuffy, cutsey bit of erudition: "An Oakland rose, that is."

If the professor wasn't teaching much about basic myths, he still somehow managed to proselytize with his pomposity and pedantry. The university will be sued one of these days for this permanent disability.

"How can Miss Rosebud help anybody?" I went on.

"Sure I know what you're saying," Snake agreed. "She lets little things get to her. Her favorite expression is, 'If I've told you once, I've told you a thousand times'. You should see her in action, though, when things really get touchy on the ward. Where many others would fall apart, she's cool, organizing, and getting things under control in no time. In fact, all the nurses we've been talking about are damn good in their work. If they weren't a little flakey, they wouldn't be here. Most of the so-called normal nurses you get working on these wards don't like it and won't stay. They can't relate and have no real empathy, in spite of what they say. A person doesn't have to have the same problem or even one related. But it's better there be something, a few scars, so the patient can sense that maybe you might have some understanding. Being admitted to the hospital for mumps or a broken leg is over when it's over. But just having been admitted to a hospital for psychiatric observation—regardless of the diagnosis—will take its toll on the person for the rest of his or her life."

Snake made and logged the second round. In an hour I took off to make the third. That was odd: One of the patients hadn't changed position in two hours. Even in sleeping, he seemed lifeless. Was he sick or dead? Jesus, we didn't need a suicide, especially on our watch. I went closer, called his name and asked if he was okay. Then it hit me: The son of a bitch! He'd stuffed a pair of hospital pajamas with blankets and sheets. A light-orange basketball—somewhat deflated and looking much like a head—was partly covered by a sheet.

"Snake! A patient's gone. There's a dummy in the bed."

"What?"

He got up from the desk, flipped on all the ward lights, and unlocked the barred door which separated us from the patients. There was not only one but two missing. Another dummy was in his place. A screen in front of a window and which needed a key to open was slightly ajar. This we relocked. The night nurse, then on another ward, was notified, as well as hospital security, which wanted written statements from of us.

For once I was wide awake, couldn't have slept if I wanted to, picturing the hospital's security officer shaking his head while taking my sweated-over statement to the CO in the morning: "Well, Admiral, we not only found two dummies in the beds last night on the brig ward but also had two on duty. Maybe four, as the two patients were probably gone before the one watch began. We've got to make an example. They weren't doing their jobs properly, sir."

The hard facts of the case, stripped of all the bullshit, were 1) two patients had escaped, and 2) they weren't discovered missing for at least two hours. This deserved a captain's mast at least.

The ace in the hole again: My great, great, great, grandparents Adam and Eve (yep, there'd been a Snake in this picture, too), they counseled, "Don't just leave it like that, the naked truth, try to hide behind a CYA paragraph." So it was pointed out—what the admiral knew anyway—that there was a contradiction in working on a brig mental ward. Though prisoners, they were also mental patents. A person couldn't very well flash a light in their faces every hour or reach over and wake them up or one might come flying out of his bed swinging. The night lights were on. But if all the lights had been on, the patients would have complained they couldn't sleep, requiring more medication. Clarence Darrow and Melvin Belli could only stand in awe.

What really saved our arses wasn't the sophomoric attempt at white-wash but the return of the two escapees. Just before 6:00 A.M., when the lights would have been turned on for all the patients to get up, the two, hoping to sneak back in unnoticed, found the screens locked. They had no choice then but to buzz the ward to get back in. They'd gone to San Francisco to get their ashes hauled.

Of course, that's the truth as far as it goes. But the real, real reason (there's always a real, real reason buried away) I suspect we weren't hung is that the Navy couldn't afford to let the Army, Air Force, Marine Corps, and Coast Guard know it had people that stupid carrying keys.

One of the escapees said they figured if anybody discovered them missing, it would have been me. Some consolation! A complete and thorough search of the ward was made two or three times to try to find what they'd used for a key. Nothing turned up. We couldn't figure out where they'd hidden it. Then a few weeks later, when the disciplinary action against one of the patients had been dropped and he was being discharged, he handed me a completely new and flawless tube of Colgate toothpaste and said, "Here's the key you wanted. We'd made it out of a toothbrush and later hid it inside the tube. You and the others had it in your hands when searching."

Throughout we were dealing with people who had broken boundaries. There was a degree of slyness in us all, patients, doctors, nurses, and hospital corpsmen. In grandness of radar sweeps from our minds, we always underestimated the fact that the patient's radar was effectively sizing us up too. Though they hadn't written down their observations, they were there, nonetheless, in the back of their minds. On way or another, we were all linked to the caduceus, and very improbably, the NP technician went by the nickname Snake. The one patient who handed me the key at the end was from Chicago, and his name, when broken down, came close to meaning "son of a robber." The other patient had the letters *mury* of Mercury in his name. A graveyard shift, sleep, prisoners, deception, and travel were involved.

In good conscience, no connection to Hermes could be built on just this alone, what could only be construed by others to be a flimsy interpretation at best. Most troubling in 1991 was the fact that the pedantic professor had been no more impressed with me than I with him. Certainly as a sign, Hermes would have seen to it that I'd gotten an A in a course which dealt mainly in Greek mythology. An A, though, wouldn't have stood out in retrospect thirty-seven years later but rather a D, not even a D plus. Curiously, astrologers assign D natural to the planet Mercury, and the Greek letter for delta is associated with medicine. More than any other letter, the lower-case delta resembles a snake, the most mystical of creatures. The triangle, pyramid, tomb. $\Delta\delta$ delta

A psychiatrist on one of the other locked wards had given three patients permission to have coffee at night anytime they wanted, be it eleven, twelve, one, two, or whenever. It sounds as crazy now as it did then, since all patients on the ward were very sick and some extremely violent at times. But he was testing these three someway. Then finding out what he wanted to know, or that it wasn't going to work, or possibly to see just what their reaction would be when the coffee was cut off, he discontinued the privilege three weeks later. This was within a day or so after my transfer to the ward for night duty. Since the other corpsman on watch had been there for several weeks, he was the good guy until a chicken-shit like me came along and said, "No more coffee!"

The following morning, two of these psychotics out for revenge escaped from the ward. They found the barracks where the other corpsman was sleeping, roused him awake, and demanded to know where I slept. He lied, saying he didn't know: "Honest fellas!" As they had no beef with him, they stormed off looking through the other barracks. By this time, security had sent out a group to catch them. They were hauled back to the ward. I hadn't known anything about any of this until going to work that evening. Thanks to the protector, sleep god.

Most of the psychiatrists were sharp. They stonewalled any attempt at being manipulated by their patients. Yet they saw no inconsistency in their own behavior in manipulating the Department of the Navy as much as they could get away with for their patients' benefit. It was one of the navy's finest hours.

When there was a riot, a patient or two or three had to be put in a cold pack, sedated, or placed in a padded cell to prevent him from hurting himself and others. No doubt in a long history of any psychiatric institution, there can be found isolated instances of abuse, but I never saw this or even a hint of such a thing in my many months working there. No one fried a brain to get even or kept a patient under drugs any longer than necessary. Nor did I ever see a doctor, nurse, or hospital corpsman mistreat or take advantage of a patient in any way.

One marine hadn't spoken to anyone since he'd been admitted to the neuropsychiatric center several weeks before. Wasn't that what he'd been taught? When in the hands of the enemy, give only your name, rank, and serial number. He wouldn't even to that. Not by any stretch of the imagination could the marine corps, navy, or anyone connected to them be considered his friend. He was tough. That I can attest to having been thrown easily over his shoulder in a ward riot. It took three of us to finally subdue him. The marine corps had taught him well.

Frank, another corpsman, and I got him a pass one weekend when we weren't working. The three of us took off in uniform for San Francisco. I'd had some misgivings when we began, seeing there were many places he could duck out on us before we realized what happened, yet there was nothing to do but go ahead with it once we'd started. From about Saturday at noon, we went to fun land, ate and snacked, took in a few sights, saw a movie or two, stayed at the downtown YMCA overnight, then went out again the following day, returning to the ward late Sunday afternoon. Though he understood what was said, he hadn't spoken to us throughout. The following morning on the ward, a dam broke as he began to talk. The nurse said she believed he'd have been talking about that time whether we'd taken him on a pass or not. Could be. Still it was one of those things where the doctor had taken a chance on a patient, and it worked, with the patient tacitly saying, "See Doc, you can trust me. I didn't run away, didn't make no trouble."

Shortly after, orders came through for training at Camp Pendleton, California, for eventual assignment to the Fleet Marine Force (FMF). One day one of the instructors read aloud a letter of commendation, signed by the rear admiral at the Oakland Hospital, which had just come. Surprise! When he came to a part about showing a fine "sensitivity to needs of the patients," I should have stood up, pretending to talk through a mike: "Hi, Ma. Was a great fight, but I won. I owe it all to you."

Chapter Twenty-one

It's AX-iomatic: The higher an officer goes, the stiffer the competition. There are slots only for so many admirals, generals, lieutenant commanders, majors, etc. Promotion depends largely on evaluations; fitness reports; recommendations; and, like all ladders, making one's boss look good. Less obvious is that once in awhile an enlisted man—or even another officer—can get steamrolled in the process. The balance of justice sometimes has the heavy thumb of getting even pushed down on one side so that the man being weighed was neither as good as he should have been or as bad as they would make him out to be.[97-B]

The company I was assigned to in middle camp, Camp Fuji, usually won or came out near the top during battalion and regimental sports competitions. Usually too it had the highest venereal disease rate—Japan's gross national product at the time. Marines being marines, the company's VD should have averaged out in the long run. This wasn't the case. The only conclusion to be drawn was that the VD talks given by me and the other company corpsman weren't as effective as those given in other companies. Yet after talking with some of their corpsmen, I felt our own material and presentation were just as good in most cases and in some even better.

Maybe the talks were getting dull: The marines had tuned out. More reading was done and the material was reworked, hoping we could make a strong impression. For all the trouble nothing changed.

A book published in the 1920s had large pictures in color showing the havoc caused by advanced cases of VD. They were by far the grisliest pictures ever seen before or since and were almost certain to give each marine a nightmare. These were cut out and posted in conspicuous places in the barracks with a warning beneath: USE RUBBERS! Surprisingly the company's rate each month was still highest.

Statistics! Now there was a lead. Since the company was proud of its standing in sports, all that had to be done was to make a game out of it, appeal to their spirit of competition and pride in winning. Dale Carnegie 'em! They wouldn't even know what was happening. Two large graphs in color were made and posted. They showed the company's standing each month in comparison to the others. It was soon clear that not even this was going to turn the yellow tide. When the new statistics were posted each time, the marines would laugh and say, "See Doc, this proves we're not only the greatest warriors in the regiment but also the greatest lovers." Shit!

The services had come a long way since I'd gone into the army in 1947. The thirty-day medical quarantine, which was more disciplinary than medical, had been narrowed to a week or less in most cases. Regulations, even in 1947, clearly stated that contracting venereal disease was not punishable if reported. It was a good thing too, for there was no reason left for a person to try to hide his or her symptoms or to seek medical treatment outside military jurisdiction, say in a third-world country, which in those days was as likely to be inadequate or quackery as competent. The regulation was a trade-off, as much to the service's advantage to catch a disease before it spread as it was to the individual to get adequate diagnosis and treatment in the early stages. So the marines were advised to use rubbers if they were going to play around, and in most cases it wasn't "if" but "when." If too rather foolishly they hadn't taken precautions and got a disease, no disciplinary action was to be taken, the medical necessity of adequate treatment overriding the cost and inconvenience to the person and service in lost time. The regulation, in effect, had become a bond as great as confidentiality.

Of all stupid things to get was a tattoo. Bateman[98] got two on his right arm. One was the Marine Corps emblem: the world with an anchor and an eagle perched on top, and *Semper Fidelis* back to the language of ancient Rome. Below this, *Death Before Dishonor*, your honor, with a skull and crossbones. The marines would have made excellent Parentalia Romans.

"How'd ya ever find time to get those? Out there spitshining your shoes two or three hours every night. Of course it's clear why you do it. You can't help yourself, hoping that someday in the Marine Corps lottery you'll win first prize, a place on a navy ship where you can wax and buff our decks."

"Whooo-eee! That's some shit, Doc!"

"Not too swift getting those either," I needled.

"If you're ever under suspicion for anything and there's some doubt, you automatically win the prize for pinning the tail on the donkey. You're Rudolf the red-nosed reindeer helping nice Santa to put a noose around your neck."

"I ain't gonna get in no trouble. Why don't you admit it, Doc? Getting to wear our uniform was the best thing that happened to you in your whole miserable, fuckeeng life. You'll probably get a Semper-Fi tattoo yourself tonight. Eat your heart out, Doc."

"That'll be the day!"

"You know who the two most dangerous people are in the marine corps, Doc?"

"No."

"A second lieutenant with a fountain pen and a corpsman with a forty-five."

I decided to let that zinger pass.

"There's pus draining from one of your tattoos. Is that what you're here about?"

"Is a bear bare-assed?"

"Put this thermometer under your tongue."

"Jesus H. Christ! I ain't got no temperature."

"I know you ain't got no fever. Just protects me if you walk out the door and drop dead, especially after treating you."

"That's what I hear. Nobody walks away."

"No, no, no! Don't sit on the bunk. Sit on the chair. I don't wanna get the crabs."

There was some inflammation, but no red streaks going up the arm or swollen lymph nodes in the armpit. It was my considered opinion, considering something had to be done, that he should put compresses on it from a warm salt solution three or four times a day, followed each time by a clean dressing. He'd just had a tetanus toxoid booster.

"There's some good news and some bad news. What do you wanna hear first?"

"Give me the good news, Doc."

"The good news is you're not being sent to the aid station where they'd probably saw off your arm to prevent you from dying of gangrene."

"And the bad news?"

"If you don't follow my instructions exactly and it gets worse, you might still end up going there."

"That's what we like about you, Doc. You're always so cheerful."

That was the last Bateman was seen on sick call other than sending him to the aid station once for a urethral discharge. Now over a month later, the battalion is in formation, and he stands out front. He is given an undesirable discharge. The order sounds, "Buh-tal-yun...about face!" Executing the order sharply, the battalion turns its back on him and we're being dismissed. Jesus, he must have felt terrible. He wasn't a close friend, but it was a surprise like when you hear somebody you see from time to time has died.

"What he'd do, Sergeant?"

"He had clap three times, Doc."

"But they can't do that. It's against regulations."

"Oh that's not the reason for the record. He's being discharged for unclean habits."

"They can't do that!"

"You go tell the captain, the battalion, and regimental colonels they can't."

"Sure, sure, Sergeant, like the captain has already told me once this week he's directly responsible for the health of his company, and I'm responsible under him, like some goddamn bug he has to squash."

"You know, Doc, you take these people's part on the impression you get of them in sick bay, which is often altogether different than the corporal's or sergeant's who has to deal with them most of the time. They've got two sides, you know."

"Don't we all!"

Bateman's medical records, like everybody else's, were kept at the aid station. It wasn't important for me to know the amount of times he'd had VD. I believed what I was told. Very likely if you'd asked the average marine in the company below staff NCO why Bateman was discharged, he's have said, "Oh, he was a crud." The average marine believed what he was told.

Since when was the sergeant or corporal so considerate he'd not dropped off one of his men's BO problems on the company corpsman to take care of? I am not saying the NCO didn't have the authority to handle the problem or couldn't have handled it himself. But since the corpsman had to give the hygiene-and-sanitation talks regularly, it was far easier to give a thankless and perhaps enemy-making task ("Look at it as a challenge, Doc") to the medical (in this respect the Marine Corps was no different than the army or navy) to deliver the bad news: "Your breath cuts like a blowtorch; your feet stink worse than Hogan's goat; and even though your armpits smell like ape-shit, you ain't Tarzan."

Maybe it wasn't such a big deal though. The services have films to cover every situation. Some genius figured out that all a person has to say is, "You know for just a ten-cent bar of soap, you can be as clean as the richest man in the world."

And all your-their problems will go *away*, like in some idiot television commercial echoing, *stay away*, stay away, stay away.

"Why'd they do that to Bateman?" I groused to a corpsman from another company. The girl had brought the beer.

"You buying?" he asked.

"Okay."

"You're all right," he said, adding, "sometimes."

He waited while I forked over the money. The girl walked off. He followed her with his eyes.

"Wouldn't touch this stuff but for reasons of health. Coffee and tea will stain your teeth. Oh the sacrifices we're require to make these days for our country! Still, 'Cheers' for the white, red, and blue."

"Cheers," he said, guzzling down half the glass, in the days it was okay to drink beer rather than to "take a pull" on it like a lamb sucking on a tit.

"How can a person be so smart and so fuckin' dumb at the same time?"

"Who ya talkin' about?"

"You, for Christsake! You pass every goddamn competitive test for promotion and proficiency pay. Right?"

"So far at least. But with a hell of lot more studying than most," I said defensively.

"Too bad you didn't pay more attention to the real world you live in and what you got to do to get along and make life easier for everyone. You're just a machine."

"I don't get ya."

"No. Don't suppose you do. You're thick up here." He tapped his head. "Nobody home."

"All that shit you were doing in your company didn't make a goddamn bit of difference. You know why?"

"No. It should have paid off."

"Well I'll tell you. They'd all figured out whether or not they were going to use a rubber long before a hotshot like you came along, and nothin' you could have said would have made any difference in most cases. If you accept this, then one company's VD rate should be about the same as another's. Right?"

"Right."

"The only answer is that other corpsmen were treating some of their cases off the record. A slide is taken each time and diagnosed. Then maybe the company corpsman got the medicine and treated the man himself, or maybe he went to the doctor and talked some shit, explaining how it could ruin the man's career. You see a lot of the officers in the clubs in Gotemba playing around. How many times do you think VD is going in their records, especially if they've got a lot of juice?"

"I didn't know that."

"You didn't know that!" he parroted.

"I didn't even know Bateman had gonorrhea twice in his record."

"You should have found out."

"We're still friends?"

"Are you still buying the beer?"

"Sure." I waved to the girl to bring another round.

"We're friends," he said doubtfully, shaking his head, "even if you are a dumb fucker."

I said nothing, peeling off the label on the bottle in small pieces, a nervous habit bartenders hate.

"Holy Christ! Didn't know you were so fuckin' sensitive. You must have skin as thin as that label."

"Sensitive my ass! Just wondering about the cost and trouble to train Bateman and then to train somebody else. Must be expensive. Don't they have any salvage? They have the Salvation Army. Why not the Salvation Marine Corps? Couldn't he have been sent to a special class or school? By his lights, all he was trying to do was increase his macho image by being a man, a marine, a tough guy. You know the saying, 'Using a rubber is like washing your feet with your socks on.' And when it comes right down to it, a rubber is sort of a prissy-assed thing."

"Loyalty up begets loyalty down," he said. "When they went around the regulation, it was two-faced. They lied. This guy will likely distrust the VA, the police, the Internal Revenue Service, Congress, and the government at all levels for the rest of his life. And he might be right."

"Maybe not. Like me, he might not have understood really what was happening. He'd just got a couple tattoos, Marine Corps pride things. How will he deal with them now?"

How long does it take for *Semper Fi* to become as unnoticeable and meaningless as a brand on an old hi-fi? But maybe people who get tattoos immunize themselves to life someway, develop a don't-give-a-damn attitude, and so are tougher in or out of the service.

Chapter Twenty-two

Very early one morning, two sailors returning to their LST passed through the gate at the U.S. Naval Station, Long Beach, California. Each had lost his hat. One held his neckerchief in his hand and fumbled around to find his liberty card. Both were sloppy drunk, loud, and belligerent, which was enough to piss off the marine guards, who—to sailors in general passing through gates—always manage to convey their belief that marines are the Brahmans of a caste system.

"Go ahead, fucker," one sailor weaved defiantly, "put us on report. We don't care. Nothin'll come of it. *hic*! You know? *hic*! Our skipper can't stand your asses! That's why. You goddamn jarheads! *hic*!"

Reading the report later that morning, the ship's captain frowned when he came to the part that quoted his men word for word. He phoned the ship's office, and the two men were ordered over the PA system, "Now hear this! Now hear this," to report to his quarters.

As they stood at attention in front of his desk, he noted that though they were sober, in correct uniform, and had shaved, they both looked tired and hung over. That was too damn bad. They could sweat for awhile as he glared, registering his displeasure. He began to see in their bloodshot eyes that they were not only uncomfortable but worried. He added three more minutes for the hell of it, then began, "You know and I know I don't like the Marine Corps. But goddamn it, you didn't have to tell'em that! I'm not going to put this in your record, but don't let me see you up before me again. Now get out of here!"

Besides loathing the Marine Corps, the skipper, who was a short man, didn't like tall people, or at least that was the scuttlebutt. When coming aboard, I'd no way of knowing this. Nor was there any way to change my six feet by trying to look five-nine, which only made it worse, or that I was just coming from the Fleet Marine Force for independent duty. But I might have had sense enough not to talk much about the former duty and to have replied when asked: "Hated the jarheads with a passion, Captain. Like they say, 'The army's got its mules, the navy, the Marine Corps.'

Believe me, sir, it's great to be back with the navy again." Or at least a noncommittal shrug might have been given. But to tell the truth means to talk, and talking on and on is becoming expansive and so it is to be even more honest and truthful, which is better.

It also means for some to have been cursed by the hoof-and-mouth disease: "For the most part, I really liked it, Captain. Hope to get the duty again someday." So much for the whiz-kid psychologists who counsel not to knock your last employer to a prospective or new one. Sometimes they don't know shit from Shinola. Looking back, too, it might have helped to wait until he was halfway up a ladder to ask him a question. That way he'd have been towering over me.

As a lieutenant commander, he hoped like hell to be selected for commander. Some said he'd been passed over once before, and this was his last chance. But who knows? At that level it takes, besides competence, a large element of luck, and in a way you make some of your own luck. If he wasn't watchful, some turkey might come along and do something that would cook his goose.

The main job on independent duty was to handle medical emergencies until they could be seen by a doctor and to hold routine sick call. Equipment had to be maintained and supplies ordered and kept at a certain level. Every cent had to be accounted for on class recap sheets. Weekends of my own time had been spent more than once tracking down a dollar or less. Syringes and needles needed to be sterilized and immunizations given. Suture sets, swabs, gloves, etc. had to be autoclaved. First aid and VD talks were given, and a sanitation inspection was held once each week.

The biggest problem on the latter was cockroaches. If you came down the ladder from the galley to the mess deck at night and flipped on the light, you would see them scurrying for cover. The problem existed long before I came aboard, and I, like the others before me, made recommendations for cleaning and spot-sprayed with Lindane.

Just as long as the little beasties had the good sense to come out only in the dark at night, they and the crew lived in peaceful coexistence. And if by chance *someone else* found one in his food, that was a good joke, ja? It was a little supplementary protein, a good backslapper. Besides, the crew had more important things on their mind that the afternoon launch led them to. Any real detailed cleaning to get rid of *la cucharacha* could be matched with *manana*. "You're always going to have a few, Doc," was the endemic response. But the executive officer, a former hospital corpsman, and I knew differently: There didn't have to be any roaches.

In addition to regular duties, I was told to make daily inspections of the mess area. This wasn't a job I'd wanted, since once a person's made a few sanitation inspections, he's made them all in a sense. It takes no special talent to point out what's wrong, nor does a thrill come from making someone look bad if he or she deserves it. Furthermore, the supervision and cleaning were the responsibilities of the second-class master at arms. Now I was supposed to tell him what was wrong within reason, and he was to see that it was corrected. There was resentment then, although it was not expressed openly. He never understood the job hadn't been asked for, nor had it been suggested that inspections be made by anybody but him. Anyway there was only one or two things (maybe nothing) for him to have his men correct each day. Whatever it was, it could be accomplished, in an hour or less. Some things were done, and some things weren't. For the most part, his was passive hostility. That was okay with me. I couldn't have cared less except then what was the use of making the inspections? Was it just some idiot exercise to channel out my energy? If so, my time could have been better spent.

When the second class was told the ladder where the men slopped food on bringing their trays down from the galley had to be cleaned, he ignored it two or three times. This was over a period of a few days. I talked to the man on a personal level, but that didn't cut any ice. You could spray forever, but without getting the food particles cleaned up, it was ineffective. Finally it was brought to the attention of the XO. He in turn told me to tell the second class it was an order from him that the ladder and back part were to be cleaned before he went ashore. The XO told me to report back if it hadn't been done.

Several hours had now passed since being told what the XO had said. The second class hadn't bothered about having it cleaned. It was an hour before liberty call. Still time enough for him to have it done and make the liberty launch. Did he have to be reminded again? There was a feeling that if it was not done, he'd say he misunderstood, and maybe he had. He replied, however, he didn't give a damn what I or the XO had said, he wasn't going to do anything about it. That he hadn't cleaned it was later verified by the XO and the supply officer.

Again, it's doubtful he ever understood I didn't want the job of overseeing his work nor hinted that someone do it. There was no doubt he deserved to go on report, but I hated like hell to write him up. All the years in the services, I'd never had to do this. It was vanity, as well as perhaps the self-deception of a weak leader. Maybe by talking to the chief master at arms, he'd figure out a way where it could be handled differently. The second class, being mess-deck master at arms, was under him. After explaining what happened, I asked straight out, "Is there any way it can be avoided putting him on report, Chief?"

Certainly he'd say, "Let me handle it this time, Doc. He's not a bad guy. Then if he doesn't square away, we'll lower the boom."

But the chief was emphatic: "He's a fluff-off. He shouldn't have talked to you like that. Put him on report."

The captain was on leave at the time. The XO was hot that a second class hadn't only disregarded my authority as a first class but his too, when ample time and warning had been given. Also the second class had many years in the navy and should have known better. So as acting commanding officer, the XO recommended a summary court martial (maybe even a special court martial; it's been so long now I forget) be given, which surprised me at the time. The reviewing authority kicked this back, feeling justice could be served just as well by a captain's mast. This order came down about the time the captain returned from leave. At most it was a difference of opinion, and that's why they had a reviewing authority.

The captain—though having nothing to do with the court martial that had been recommended—was pissed off by it, apparently feeling somehow it could be misconstrued as an error in his judgment. Then too the less disciplinary action a command has, the better its leader looks for promotion. The chief master at arms sensed the way the wind was blowing. He hadn't been in the navy for nearly forty years without learning something. So when the captain asked his opinion of the second class at the mast, he replied, "Why he's always been an excellent man, Captain, and done excellent work. I just don't understand."

The chief didn't mention my trying to find a way out of the report chit, that he could have stood up for his man at the time if he'd thought so much of him, that he himself was the one who called his man a "fluff-off," and that he said to go ahead and to write him up.

With the only other two people at the mast hostiles toward me, there was no way this could be brought up. Doing little more than slapping the second class's wrist, the old man lowered his quarterly marks (4.0 curiously being the highest mark that can be given) in two areas. Clearly in the captain's mind I was Claggart and "The poor thing was Billie Budd/ Who'd done nothing worse than chew his cud/ And pull on his...Bud," though he was as old or older than I and had as much or more time in the service. The captain wasn't impressed with his XO's decision nor with me for having opened up a can of roaches. If anything, it was confirmed what he'd known all along about tall people and the Marine Corps. It would have been easier to have taken a brush, soap, water, and in twenty minutes cleaned the space myself. Fuck pride! But there was no way this could have been done, especially with sufficient help and time to do the job. It would have made me look even more ridiculous.

There were in the beginning three choices:
1)   See that the order was followed through or report it.
2)   Pretend the problem didn't exist. Don't rock the ship. Shit doesn't stink until you stir it.
3)   Lay the blame on myself. To reason there was a compelling need to create a situation, to be noticed. This would have given some justification for not following through and somehow a way out.

But that was bullshit. It wasn't to my advantage to create a situation for it could be construed as not demonstrating persuasive leadership and reflected in my marks.

Two or three years after this, a first class who was a friend commented when I made a decision, acted on it, and then worried later about being wrong, "Chief, you've got a good mind but not a practical one."

"What do you mean by that?" I asked.

"You usually always make the right decision at the right time and act on it quickly, but instead of forgetting about it, you keep going over it in your mind, wondering if you'd been right."

A logo on T-shirts has a message for people who can't make a decision without analyzing it to death: JUST DO IT!

Here's one that should be designed for another group of persons like me: "Once you've done it, forget it."

But that was two or three years later, and I'm getting ahead of myself.

The chief cook had the galley scrubbed out, and everything was well-secured for spraying one evening. If we were ever to get rid of the roaches, it had to be thorough. All cracks, crevices, and openings for pipes in the overhead and bulkheads of the galley on the old LST were supersaturated with Lindane, as well as behind and under things. Only two or three were scurrying out, but they weren't shimmying. Maybe they'd built up a resistance to the spray or the infestation wasn't as bad as believed.

I could imagine the caption to a news item: "Corpsman tries to rid ship of cockroaches: They survive. He dies. Navy refuses burial in Arlington National Cemetery stating inhalation of insecticide not in the line of duty."

The chief cook, who'd arrived earlier than usual to wipe up before preparing breakfast, said he'd swept up well over a hundred. Several days following this, many more kept falling or could be found dead here and there. With this and cleaning and spraying in other areas, we finally got rid of them. Or at least no one mentioned seeing any. The silence might have sprung from some fear, like a kid getting his mouth washed out with soap for saying a dirty word, that he himself would get sprayed if he had.

That was my thinking at the time. But now having mulled over this for thirty or more years...you know what was really at the root of the problem? Those cockroaches were part of the food supply and just didn't taste good no more when pickled in insecticide.

The influence had always been there, but I'd have balked then at any suggestion of the existence of Hermes. There was only God in the traditional sense. I couldn't swallow hook, line, and sinker—like a good fish—

everything read in the Bible. The ego is always suspect, and there were just too many egos involved for the whole truth and nothing but the truth. In order to forgive, which is good, you've got to judge, which is bad, a catch-22. Moreover, Christianity is like an onion. If you peel away one skin, you might find love; another, forgiveness; and so on layer after layer, faith, hope, charity, etc. But at the very last is ol' greed. What's in it for me? What's my reward?

In a very unforgiving and inconsistent way, a Christian can't simply and benevolently let one die in peace after a lifetime of suffering, where the swords of junk mail, taxes, and death hung over one's head. He or she promises eternal damnation if one fails to jump on the bandwagon. It may not be blackmail, but it's so close it really doesn't make any difference.

"Certainly I don't want to go to hell. How do I believe in Christ?"

"Start out first by pretending you believe in him."

"Okay. I've pretended my belief. Nothing. So doesn't it show a certain honesty and integrity after doing this to hold back if one does not truly hear within his or her heart?"

"Oh no! This is the divine way of winnowing out."

Christians are so slickly patronizing. Despite their protest, I never met one who gave a hoot about my eternal soul. Yet I usually obliged them by listening politely and taking pamphlets as they could complete their practical factors, another step toward promotion as they saw it. It would have blown their minds to know I considered this a Christian act.

Self-deception is a part of man's nature. So why not believe in an aspect of God that understands this—can even be amused by it—rather than believing in God as one who expects more out of man than he is capable of? Being realistic is somehow more truthful.

If in the unlikely event this book ever gets off the ground, I'm certain to be vilified as Christendom's Salman Rushdie. What can be lost then be cackling, "Double, double, toil and trouble; fire burn and caldron bubble?" Hermes is supposed to have invented measure. If you double two, you get four. Any double, doubled number is dividable by four. Each day hundreds of millions of Christians make the four points of the cross. As you see after all these ages, I'm still rattling cages, possibly my own. Just doing for my country while not asking what it can do for me; *ding ding*, the bells begin to chime.

Regulations required that a narcotics inventory be held each month by two officers and the medical department representative. These were usually ensigns (flag officers?) or a Lieutenant (jg) and an ensign. In practice one officer made the inventory with me while the other took our word for it and three signed the report. Everything checked with the morphine and other drugs, though there were three opened bottles of barbiturates, each having a thousand count originally, that looked too intimidating, too time-consuming to even think about counting when first going aboard. So the inspecting officer took my word and the other officer both our words, as I had the chief's before me; obviously no one knew for certain. When there was time to spare, I decided to count them. I couldn't believe it at first, and so I counted them again with the same results. In one bottle alone, there were over one hundred capsules missing. In the others, thirty or sixty variously. Holy Jesus! The three of us had already signed our names on two monthly reports that they were there. Figuratively we'd made Xs for our signatures, or maybe the sign of our crosses to bear. Why'd the chief done this to me. I could have kicked myself in the ass for being so trusting.

The facts had to be faced: They weren't there. They couldn't be accounted for. The only way to make it right—and the sooner the better—was to report the truth. A formal letter of disclosure, initiated and written by me, was then submitted to the ship's office for forwarding through channels.

Within an hour or two, I was told over the PA system to report to the captain's quarters amid the bantering of other crew members: "Hey Doc, in the next life be short, and don't, for Christsake, do duty with the Marine Corps. But for now, let this be a lesson to you, go up and get your ass chewed."

He began by telling me that though he'd read my letter, he had no intention of forwarding it.

"Captain, the barbiturates are old. There are many damaged capsules, some completely empty with granules at the bottom. But even being generous in trying to account for the damaged ones, I come up with at least a hundred short in one bottle alone. The reporting of this isn't optional. Regulations are clean that BuMed (Bureau of Medicine and Surgery) and ONI (Office of Naval Intelligence) will be notified simultaneously when any discrepancy occurs."

"I just told you I'm not forwarding it. Who would have taken them? Certainly not me, and I'm sure the captain before me didn't either. We were the only ones who had the combination to the safe, other than you and the chief. So who would have taken them?"

"I don't see where you have any choice but to forward the letter, Captain. Having the combination to the safe, you're no more above suspicion than I."

That was an unfortunate choice of words, for he became as red as a beet and glowered for several beats until I finally said uncomfortably, "I guess I'm supposed to be embarrassed by all this, but I'm not."

"Well neither am I. Dismissed!"

Everyone on a small ship knows what's happening. A good-natured humor was seen in some wag's adept cartoon takeoffs on *Gunsmoke* and posted near the sickbay. I was drawn as Chester Goode. You remember—

Matt Dillon's well-meaning deputy, who brewed "a mean cup of coffee," walked with a limp, and was forever twanging "Mr. Dillon."

The captain appointed a survey board of three officers and myself to destroy the barbiturates. They were written off the books as the incorrect count given in the previous inventory. At the time my little-old-lady sense of propriety thought this was improper, though they'd probably been missing for years, some bottles being very old. The peculiarity of three big bottles for such a small ship might have been the result of larger ships being decommissioned in World War II. There was a truth, as I'd seen it then and yet on occasion thought nothing of circumventing to help an underdog, and there was common sense, which should have told me the captain himself was an underdog. That mistakes had to be corrected and incompetence dealt with, I make no qualms. But there are shadow lands of the devil where the writer of a report of investigation scavenges from error and misfortune. There are red herrings of a sort. In the deception of so-called truth, logic, and objectivity, good men have been ruined and possibly thousands of careers advanced.

The cramped, little sick bay between the mess deck and the crew quarters on one side had an examining table but no beds, which there wouldn't have been room for anyway. So the wardroom was designated as medical's battle station. Being bigger, it was more practical and stocked with first-aid supplies and blankets. When the GQ alarm sounded one day, I went to the battle station and was directed by the captain to report with the resuscitator to the con. On reaching it, I saw the captain in battle helmet and life preserver making a big show of looking down at his watch and then up at me. He was hot that it had taken me five minutes to come up only two or three ladders when it should have taken only two minutes at the most with the resuscitator. We were underway, and he was chewing me out in front of rated and non-rated alike.

My mind blanked out for the reason of the delay, though I had set out immediately when word was received. Then after the drill, it came to me what had happened. Someone had dogged the door necessary to get through very tight and then taken off with the dogging wrench. It meant a few minutes were lost kicking the dogs loose. At first it occurred to go to the captain's quarters and set the record straight but then thought better of it. Doc wasn't exactly one of the likable seven dwarfs, and absence could only make the heart grow fonder. Besides, hadn't he just come down on me the day before for what someone told him had been taught at a first-aid talk?

The *Handbook of the Hospital Corps*, an ABC warfare five-day school for all ratings, taught that if in a large disaster first-aid supplies were scarce, they must be used where they could do most good. Simply put, this meant that if there was only one bandage and two wounded—one who was certain to die and the other seriously but had a chance—the bandage was to be used on the latter. It was only common sense, but the captain didn't feel it was appropriate to tell the men this, even though the law of the jungle applied to me as well if wounded. You could only wonder who he thought was going to handle the first aid in a major disaster if the corpsman were killed. And if there were many casualties, did he think Doc was going to be able to handle them all—by himself?

The squadron medical officer had mentioned one time that his commanding officer came to him with a simple cold and wanted penicillin for it. Patiently the doctor explained that penicillin wasn't indicated since it didn't touch the cold virus. But his CO, who made up the doctor's fitness report, was insistent, and so the doctor had little choice but to give him what he wanted, though he was indignant for having been pressured.

It was clear from this anecdote that others had problems too, that no one had smooth sailing completely unless he was an idiot, which might have been. Yet I'd have sold my soul to get off the ship, but the truth of the matter was that even though it was offered, neither one wanted it, kicking it back and forth among themselves.

SATAN: I'm going to be generous today and give this one to you.

GOD: No, no. Be my guest. You take him.

SATAN: I insist.

GOD: You're too generous, but I can't really.

I couldn't very well put in for a transfer on the grounds that I didn't like the CO but could request independent duty school, upon completion of which there'd by a new duty station. Probably half the requests for schools in the navy (or any other service, for that matter) are motivated by this reason (i.e., they're trying to get out of a situation they don't like) as much as for getting more training. Since I'd been aboard only a short time, however, it was unlikely orders would come through for a year or more. What choice was left then but to try harder?

As stated the captain wasn't seen as an underdog in the barbiturate count. In this I was wrong; I didn't believe he'd taken them. They'd probably been missing for years. Certainly the disclosure would have made some hotshot investigator's day and possibly ruined the captain's career. This was never considered as a consequence, nor was the report submitted with malice toward him. Remember, I was wrong too. It was sort of an achtung (respect) response to a higher authority, a vicarious god way up there to whom I was saying, "Bless me, Father, for I have told the truth." In short, I was a serious, loyal, stubborn, rigid, little pissant. In my defense, there were some inconsistencies of character, a few cracks in the facade, a glimmer of hope:

1) Regulations required that if a man had to be restrained, it was to be reported to the officer of the day so a log entry could be made. If the reason for the restraint was due to alcohol, the man would almost certainly

get a captain's mast. But there were no regulations that required you to notify the O.D. if you were merely moving a man by litter a few feet on the ship. If a wire-basket litter were used, he would have to be strapped in so he wouldn't fall out. This was restraint too, not requiring notification of the O.D. since your main purpose was to transport the man. And if it took three hours to go twenty feet, so what? You got busy.

A sailor came back drunk one night, loud and noisy, raising hell and smashing his fists into the bulkhead. This was brought to my attention to handle. When sober, he and I had good rapport. He was strong; trying to restrain him physically could have caused injury to him as well as to those trying to do it. He was given the choice of being put into a straight-jacket, in which case he'd be logged, or voluntarily be strapped into the wire-basket for a few hours until he sobered up, and nothing would be said. He agreed to the latter. A first-class suggested paraldehyde be given, but I wasn't sure how it would work when he already had alcohol, a central nervous system depressant in him. Besides, any medicine administered would have had to have been entered in his record, and he'd still have to been watched, which was done in sick bay by reading a book and keeping an eye on him, while he was being transported.

2) Before dawn one morning in port when most everyone was asleep, a first-class, nearing retirement, snuck down into the engine room. He needed a drink bad and had heard they kept a bottle of ethyl alcohol there for engine purposes. He was unfamiliar with the space and saw an unmarked bottle of clear liquid which he figured must be it. Tilting it up, he got a mouthful of acid, which he realized immediately, spitting it out before swallowing any. Then he rinsed his mouth out quickly several times. When seen later, there seemed to be little damage, if any at all. There was no reason to record this.

3) One Sunday evening ashore, I ran into a crew member, the son of a full captain on active duty in the navy. I knew the man was AWOL but that it could be smoothed over if he reported aboard before quarters the following morning. An attempt was made to try to talk some sense to him, but he said no way was he going back.

"Why not?"

He explained that as a mail clerk he'd stolen and spent about one hundred and seventy dollars of ship's money which had been entrusted to him. The loss would be noticed the following morning. It happened that I had a locker downtown. The owner of the club, a former navy man, lent me the money for twenty-four hours until making it to the bank the following day. The mail clerk then returned the money to the ship, paying me back in time, and no one was the wiser.

4) A first-class got gonorrhea. He claimed it was the first time he'd strayed in twenty years of marriage. He'd been diagnosed and treated aboard a nearby hospital ship. The problem was that he had intercourse

with his wife several times before he realized what he had. Though he was now cured, she was more than likely infected.

"You better go ahead and tell her the truth," I counseled, "and take her in for an examination."

"I can't do that. There's no way she'll ever forgive me. I know her too well. She will get a divorce. I love her and don't want that. You've got to help me, Doc."

"How could I help you?"

"If you'd just give me something for her to take."

"You can't be serious. I could be court martialed for doing what you ask. Even if I agreed to help you, which I can't, she'd put two and two together. She'd damn well know what'd happened."

"No, she wouldn't Doc. My wife doesn't think that way. She believes what I tell her. She wouldn't suspect anything."

"Maybe she doesn't even have it. She should be diagnosed and have follow-up blood tests for syphilis. In fact, she should have a blood test maybe before being treated."

"Doc, you've got to help me. She gets tests every year with a physical."

"Shit! There are so many things which could go wrong. What if she were allergic to the medicine given her? What if she took a letter written to her to the navy?"

"I know she's not allergic to anything, Doc. I swear I'll bring the letter right back to you."

It was, unfortunately, one of my character flaws that I'd have made a better jewel smuggler than a hospital corpsman. A letter was typed and signed for him to give to her. It probably sounded very professional to someone who had no medical knowledge but certainly couldn't have fooled anybody else. Briefly it stated that her husband, through no fault of his own, had developed an infection in his urethra, a nonspecific urethritis. It was non-venereal, and only in extremely rare cases could it be transmitted. But just to be on the safe side, though it really wasn't necessary, I requested that she take the medicine as instructed for several days.

The *Merck Manual* and other textbooks were consulted. She was given five days of a broad-spectrum antibiotic, and I very carefully made up a dilution of potassium permanganate, then prescribed for douches, and sent along a plastic bulb syringe.

The following day he returned the letter to me, and I breathed easier. He said she suspected nothing and was carefully following the instructions. In five days he reported she had completed the treatment, and so they lived happily ever after.

For those who aren't content unless everyone gets his or her punishment or retribution, I believe the sailor suffered and worried a great deal over it. It wasn't right, of course, to take advantage of trust and naivete— yet I can honestly say I never used my position or rate for personal gain, a kickback, or *quid pro quo*, or purposely gave a bad shot or lost a shot record, and so on. Though willing to take a lie-detector test on this, I see it also as a vanity, as much as saying, "I never bummed a nickel on the street in my life." Well whoop dee do! Aren't you the great one now? What did you do?

The lumbering *LST*, now the flagship with the commodore aboard, was headed north along the California coast with four mine sweeps. A sailor reported to sickbay with nausea, pain in his lower abdomen, and rebound tenderness. The commodore wanted to be notified within an hour if the man should be sent to a hospital. Any time within that period he could order his ships to change course so they would be near a northern port where a boat would come to pick up the sailor.

This wasn't an easy decision to make, for if it weren't anything serious, I'd have felt foolish to have advised him to get the man off. On the other hand, if it were an appendicitis and I hadn't diagnosed it correctly, the results could have been disastrous if he were kept aboard. I hadn't done a complete blood cell count since basic hospital corps school several years before. A few cells could be identified, but being competent in doing a CBC was something else. I had, however, kept up to some extent with the white blood cell count and ran three slides, taking the average. Since all were elevated above the normal range, there was justification in recommending the man be taken off. An icebag at this point was about all that was called for in treatment. The sailor was operated on in an army hospital. A day or two following the appendectomy, he wrote a letter thanking me and said the army doctor had been impressed with the write-up.

When the annual administrative inspection came, the commodore remarked that sickbay looked "like it used to in the old navy." Overall, medical got an excellent rating, as well as the ship's office (personnel records, administration) which the XO was over. The other divisions of the ship got very satisfactory and satisfactory.

In time the captain's promotion to full commander came through. He was being sent to Washington D.C. On leaving he made a point to say goodbye, shaking my hand. He said, though never doubting my competency, he felt I pushed harder than the average man could adjust to. I let that lie. He then remarked that if he could help me in some way in his new job, to write him a letter. After he had left, the personnel office showed a letter of accommodation he'd put in my service record.

It was inevitable then that the old joke about the skipper hating tall people and the marine corps, not necessarily in that order, be replaced with another. Both the new "old man" and the new executive officer were competent and likable. But this didn't stop the crew from laughing that their ship was the only one in the fleet which had a nut for a captain and a moron for an executive officer—the new captain's last name being Nutt, and new XO's, Moran.

As already pointed out, once an officer makes lieutenant commander or major in the service, the competition becomes much stiffer. A lot depends on luck. The joker is always there to pop up, sometimes when least expected. The snafu of an enlisted person or even a junior officer can ruin a career. So it's easy to understand the vexation of one of these officers over an enlisted's well-meaning ignorance, as it is to see how an enlisted man might develop the old sergeant's syndrome, where he hates without prejudice any and all officers.

The new CO had hardly been aboard a month when the LST came in from a routine exercise one day and docked. One of our sailors, having come from the east cost, hooked us up to the water system. As I understood it, the designated color of the fittings on the east coast was different than on the west coast, with the result that we pumped salt water into the entire freshwater system of the nearby hospital ship. Since I had ship's business to attend to on the hospital ship anyway, our skipper asked if I'd check to see if they planned to report it. "You probably can talk to medical people better than I," he said. The hospital ship's captain later told me he had to make out a report, but "you can tell your captain I don't intend to make an issue of it."

Chapter Twenty-three

My father was dying of cancer in a Reno hospital. Reno had come into being on the first Lemuria day May 9, 1868. I got leave, arriving one bleak Parentalia morning, and walked around to keep warm while waiting for visiting hours. Anita, however, had come earlier. For weeks she'd been doing this, spending most of the daytime and part of each evening at his bedside before returning to her hotel. She'd been a faithful and loving wife, married to him even longer than my mother. It was very hard on her, especially his last few days when he could recall at times only the earlier periods of his life and called out, "Frances, Frances."

I'd wondered on the bus how to make some feelings show, to handle the awkward moments, to reach down into a well where there was nothing and to come up with something:

> His irony was the serious flaw
> In my criminal mind.
> They just look to find
> What they want to know.
>
> Twould been better to
> Look him in the eye
> And twinkle a convincing lie.
> Can't get away with nothin'.

Some thought was given to what he'd leave me, as I recalled again on seeing him, an emaciated and weak old man making a great effort to be pleasant. This wasn't about money or material things. I was hoping he'd tell me—now that he was near death—who I was (if he could or would) and maybe like an old patriarch give me his blessing. He'd never told me about himself or my mother. It was like being born with an old baronial name but not having any birthright or heritage other than duty. Though not thinking of it at the time, I see now in old age my feeling toward him as he was dying mirrored exactly what his feelings were toward me, that is, duty and obligation, without love, without hate.

Perhaps he had loved me in his own way. If so, he never really communicated it. Two or three times a year when I was younger, he'd write a note at Christmas or on a birthday; enclose a small check; and sign, "Love, Dad," It was easier for him to write this by mail perfunctorily while hundreds of miles away than to express it when near. Yet he and my brothers did visit me every two or three years. He paid for an appendectomy when I was in the fourth grade. He bought me a vizor and boots when going to the ranch, but he also trimmed and shod his horses's hoofs. He worried they'd get hurt, and he worried the same about me. For all of it, though, he was as much a stranger to me as I to him, being nearly fifty years old and still putting in long, hot tiring days when I first went to Topaz. The spontaneity, carefreeness, and daredeviltry of his youth had long since burned out.

Not only that but he had a hearing problem and refused to wear a hearing aid because it made him nervous. Had he been asked, "Hey padre Pancho, *Cómo está* today?" He'd have turned toward me, cupping his hand over one ear and said, "What?" I'd repeat it louder, whereupon he'd say, "You're going to have to speak louder than that." So I'd raise my voice, nearly shouting and enunciating everything very carefully while explaining he was just being asked how he was in Spanish and that Pancho meant Frank. Finally he'd understand and probably sigh, "Oh!" while wondering why he'd been put through all that when it really wasn't necessary. By that time, I'd wondered myself. Now he's probably rolling over in his grave, laughing about my hearing loss, not so severe, and that his little brat has become an even bigger stick in the mud and cold fish. A retribution? And maybe I caused his deafness, like the willow witches did to Yerington, and maybe his death too and that of Ralph, born *February* 21.

He died on *February* 22, 1958, a few days after the visit. The date clearly marks him as being caught up in the mystique. He'd be brought back across the state line to be buried. My mother died on *February* 26, 1929, and was also brought across the state line to be buried. My father's mother, Grandmother Elizabeth Mills Chichester (who had been born in February) died on *February* 17, the middle of the Parentalia, 1934, apparently of violence. Grandfather George Chichester died in 1910 near the end of a voyage from England to New York, which was long before I was born and not in February. But as February is connected to Neptune, so Neptune is connected to water. George's body was brought back across the United States.

Speculation is that my father, like my brothers, felt I'd killed my mother. They probably thought it wasn't my fault. Still how could they have helped but reason that life had been so much pleasanter and full before my birth? If you argue that it's ridiculous for me to have guilt feelings over my mother's death, you're repeating what I told a shrink once that he was reading in something which wasn't so.

"Whether you accept this or not, " he said emphatically, "it's clearly there in many ways. Your recurrent dream of a dead dog and blood being just one of them."

He was possibly right at the time, a cocoon of guilt, or maybe it was never there. Now it's academic, having metamorphosed beyond that. Of course I killed her. There was no other way to bring communication from the dead to you. Don't even try to understand it, this necromancy thing on the ninth day through a circle on the Feast of the Dead. When fuel began to run out, there was Ralph labeled *Feast of the Dead*. When that ran out, my father had to die on the Caristia. It was kindred embraced. The reason for the murders overrode any arguments you might have, my personal feelings, the scandal, the disgrace of insanity, the living in an alien world, the dying without the peace of anonymity that comes with a tombstone. Yet the world must return to honoring the dead during the ancient period, or there's no hope.

> The crazy are always messengers,
> Wanting your donation,
> And that you readily give,
> Grasping at any straw to live.
> Or that you readily do,
> Making you just as crazy too.
> But maybe not,
> For now I've been thinkin'
> Better to be anything,
> Than dead, rotten, and stinkin'.
> You're wheat for bread of gods,
> Movies for their VCR,
> A god yourself in the next world,
> Driving a brand-new car.

The wheel was rigged with numbers and dates to come up, starting at least for me to take notice in 1991, and it's not for me to interpret so much the future as the past.

Were it, however, I'd speculate that had the human race rejected the idea of individual salvation as being immature and selfish, it might have seen God, if he exists. But as it is now, man is only his brother's keeper so far as he can be used as a stepping stone into heaven. Even into righteousness, it has become an evil. We are inextricably tied to what has been done to us and what we do to others. There should be no saints or martyrs with special places. What talent each had should have been used for the good of all mankind. Without resorting to fanaticism, violence, cruelty, and the like, each has the responsibility to try to leave the world a better place than he found it. This was to be the beauty of the human flower. If man is to see God, all must see him together or not at all. Since man can never come to terms with this thinking, he propagates his own destruction.

Chapter Twenty-four

Wise words about facing what happens in life were those of a black friend who suffered a stroke in early old age, just after retiring.

"It doesn't seem fair," I said, "why this had to happen to you."

"Why not?" he replied. "If it had to happen to someone, why not me?"

Shit happens. So it was about being gay. Pardon me for being one that Hitler missed. (Hitler will die on the day of Walpurgis, a collective effort.)

The stigma was something to be dreaded and hated. Never in a million years would the life have been picked for myself. Had there been a button to push to change things, it would have been done. Still, like the man said, if it had to happen to someone, why should I have been exempt—or anybody, for that matter? May you come back in the next life to take your turn. This may not square with your judgment, but it's what's fair.

Excerpts of Dad's letter written in 1963:

> To get to matters closer, I have loved you ever since the moment Dot and Aunt Nell brought you home from Nevada as a seven-day-old infant after your sweet mother passed away following your birth. I wanted to adopt you then and there, but your own Dad would not consent although we argued and talked for about three days up at Twin Lakes out of Bridgeport. He won out as he had a stronger argument that I had, being your natural father. My concern and definitely my love for you is as deep today as before your letter came yesterday. I won't or cannot say it wasn't a surprise, but your candor and truthfulness in the reason for your discharge from the service show a lot of courage, and I am very proud of you son, regardless.

What might happen was uncertain. Didn't want the burden—along with everything else—of how disgusted relatives might feel or come to depend upon a tenuous charity in thought which could change in a flash with an argument, the ball being viciously slashed back into your court.

The best way, it seemed, was to change my name to one that was common. In time I could forget them and they me. In order to do this, it was necessary to write to the county of my birth. The lawyer to whom the letter was referred advised that in addition to appearing in court, it would be necessary to run an ad in a local paper for a period of time telling what the new name was to be. The area where this would have taken place wasn't heavily populated. It might have been noticed by a few with tongues wagging in speculation causing embarrassment to kin, so it was left. Checkmate, destiny.

Dad had known only it was my intention to have the name changed, not that I'd heard from a lawyer, when he wrote:

> As to you changing your name, can I suggest you take my name, the name you used up to the time you entered the service? It is an easy name to spell and write. If you did, it would make me very happy. It is the best I can offer, and I am only too glad to share it with you. Please come home or at least write. You are always welcome here with Mal and me. We both send our love and wish you the best of luck in the world.

Letter written by Anita to me in 1963:

> I am heartsick to learn of the trouble you are in and only hope that I can do something to help in any possible way.
>
> It occurs to me that after so many years in the service it will be a tremendous adjustment for you to get back into civilian life. Since this is bound to take some time, how about coming out here for a visit until you have a chance to get your bearings and come to some decision regarding your future plans? The task of making a new start after seeing all your plans for the future completely shattered must seem overwhelming, but I am sure that with God's help you will be able to come out all right. Should you decide not to visit now perhaps you would like to later on. You are always welcome, and your room will always be ready. If you don't come, please keep in touch and let me know how you are getting along. Just remember, no matter where you are, you are my son, and I love you.

Though not thinking so at the time, calling it "sour grapes" then, getting discharged was the best thing which could have happened. Security and vanity had become deadly. Navy posters spoke of travel. You got that and then in a sense stopped traveling and were in a rut.

It's academic, of course, but I sometimes wonder (and no doubt he'd call it preposterous) whether it was the same-o same-o MacArthur was rebelling against in the end. It seemed madness what he wanted to do then, and it could very well have been.

For me there was a world to see once more under the protection of the god of travel. From being mocked and ridiculed would come insights, perspectives, and understanding that never would have come from praise and accolades. I couldn't see this then but knew it necessary to keep busy: Work had to be found immediately. If I stopped to brood, there'd be quicksand, and that's what they'd have wanted. But now I can pause to say,

> To you who were so clever and good,
> Your old age and death
> Come like a lost friend,
> With a levelling revenge.

From savings, a life insurance policy was paid up in full. Small payments from property being sold were signed over to Dad so he'd have something besides his social security check. After that, there wasn't much left. I got Blue Cross, budgeted, economized, and lived in cheap hotels. There were times those in charity lines were eating much better, but I didn't get in them. That's what they would have wanted, confirming what they believed. The pride is seen now as just another form of vanity, not an attribute.

There was the belief that honesty on applications would work. Christians would take into consideration that they hadn't been lied to. What naivete! It worked against me in all cases. Christian charity is nearly always sanitized and compartmentalized. Please don't try to tell me these people really weren't Christians. They were as Christian as 99 percent. Perhaps it's their saving grace they really weren't the gods they aspired to be after all but just part of humanity themselves.

One interviewer told me, "Why didn't you just lie about that? I don't give a damn personally. But if something comes up later, not even connected, they'll come back to me saying, 'You should have never hired him in the first place.'"

A general discharge under honorable conditions had been given. (Many years later this was changed to an honorable discharge.) There was then still Cal-Vet entitlement. It paid for the barber-training course and tools but nothing beyond that.

All beginners went to work in the back room. So what if each person who sat in the chair later looked like a dog in advanced stages of mange.

I was thirty years ahead of my time, right? Couldn't he see I was trying as hard as possible? And he got the haircut for free, for Christsake! What indeed would I have known about Auschwitz?—especially then that it too was connected to *February 21*? I was fed up with their insults. Something inside was dead, but within three days after starting, I arose from the grave and saved humanity by quitting.

"No way will I ever come back to this!" the instructor heard. "Sell the tools, and we'll split the money."

This was on a Thursday or Friday. I would look for work on Monday, but that didn't stop a long weekend of worry. When Monday came, I'd gone a full circle, realizing that being temperamental wasn't a luxury to be indulged. Like a dog with his tail between his legs—a retribution for the mange—I went back to see if it was still okay to continue.

"Sure," the instructor said, "didn't sell your tools. Figured you might change your mind."

Passing the first state board at the end of the six-month course, I got work, though few shop owners wanted to hire an inexperienced apprentice. My attitude toward barbering was no different. If I dropped out and then changed my mind again later, I'd have to complete the school once more and pass another apprentice board. Eligibility for the journeyman test would be in eighteen months. By passing that, I could leave barbering any time and still be licensed, provided the renewal fee was paid every few years. This license was bread and butter, maybe necessary to fall back on. So fueled by negative motivation (I hate it, I hate it), I passed the first journeyman test and barbered only a few months longer, though keeping up the license for fifteen years.

Picking Cucamonga lemons, with the perk you can eat all you want while picking; hanging fliers; and washing pans, I existed. A statistics correspondence course was completed from the University of California. It seemed like a good idea to return to the full time, whipping more than three years miscellaneous credits into a B.A. Two semesters of university credit had been given for three years of high school Spanish, and two semesters of German with A's previously had been taken on campus. The language requirement was stamped completed on my records. Now returning after many years, I was told by the registrar's office that the university would no longer accept the language requirement completed in two languages but required it be done in one language only. It also wouldn't accept an American history and institutions course completed at its correspondence section and which had previously satisfied the requirement.

Since no language was required for my major, it seemed preposterous. Most of the language taken nearly twenty years before was forgotten. This meant, in effect, a new language would have to be started from scratch for four semesters, or old courses would have to be audited two semesters, to be able to continue on for two more semesters—another obstacle course. Obviously some new-clothes professor—who himself probably couldn't pass a proficiency test in the foreign language he'd taken as an undergraduate—had pontificated his influence, and it was hard to figure out who had more shit for brains, he or the kowtowing, rubber-stamp academic group who went along with him.

But look who's talking. Aside from that, though, it was an insult to my "intelligence"! Taking the well-known advice, I left. There's some truth, of course, to what Harry Truman said about the heat in the...volcano? And there's some truth to what I've been saying.

A few years later, I was walking through the campus and browsed through the current curriculum catalog. The requirement had been changed back, allowing the students to fulfill it in two languages. An uproar must have led to this common sense.

An acquaintance suggested going to sea. It was necessary to have Coast Guard papers (Merchant Mariner's Document) and, for all practical purposes, to belong to a union. To my thinking, there was no use applying to a union unless Coast Guard clearance was given first. Fat chance!

You might shrug and say, "What the hell! All they could do is say 'no.' No big deal!" But I hated going to the Coast Guard and putting myself in that position as much as I hated to think of them sifting through my records, finally to say "no." No way can you fully understand this unless you'd been down that same road yourself.

Routinely each applicant waited six weeks. There was no hope for clearance, so I'd forgotten about making out the application. Indeed when the Coast Guard card came—*Coast Guard? What could they be writing me about?* I thought. It took me several beats to realize what they were saying. I could pick up my seaman's papers. It took several more minutes to get used to the idea and finally be happy.

As it worked out, getting Coast Guard clearance was much easier than getting into the union, which said no. The reason given: thirty-eight was over the hill, too late to begin its retirement program, with the decrease in ships, there were less jobs, and shipping was slow. The only thing to do was give up on the idea.

I was working in a car wash two years later when Wayne, a friend, suggested another attempt be made.

Having reached forty and been turned down once, I wasn't too eager. Through his help, I talked to a different union official who said he'd try to get me in but could do nothing at present since the union's school already had too many people. He suggested calling him once a week. This sounded promising. You'd think if he had no intention of helping me, he'd have said so or, "Don't call me. I'll call you." Wouldn't he?

Come, come whoever you are,
Wanderer, worshipper, lover of leaving,
It doesn't matter.
Ours in not a caravan of despair.
Come even if you have broken your vow a thousand times.
Come, come yet again, come.

—Mevlana Jelalu'ddin Rumi

After five months running from car to car, I began to have doubts about this and decided to tell the union official to forget it. Just when this was about to be done, he asked if a physical had been taken yet.

"No."

"Well you'd better come down here tomorrow so we can get that out of the way."

The union wasn't going to waste money on a complete physical examination if it didn't plan to take me.

Anything had to be better than waiting tables, which I'd been trying to do for a week. It was trying both for me and the bottomless pits. Why couldn't they be good sports and eat what they got, whether they ordered it or not? So when the instructor over the storeroom said he had an opening and wondered if I were interested, I jumped at the chance. Having figured out there was no executive position with a high salary and few hours available, it was either that or wait tables.

Storekeeping didn't have the bullshit area which depended on others. The work was either done or not, and there were pieces of paper to prove it. The job was okay. The problem was that to get the storekeeper designation it was necessary to complete the books at the end of some month. There were two who were senior to me, which meant three months off. Besides, there were only so many assistant storekeeper jobs on ships. This could have added a month or two beyond that, possibly more. Money was running out and became a worry, even though board and room were provided by the union. Maybe the supervisor could get me out as a scullion or porter. If not that, a messman (hopefully not).

This all sounds pretty finicky, but when you've spent considerable time and effort climbing two or three ladders, you burn yourself out and become skiddish. You want to run. It's a worker's skidrow syndrome, for lack of a better term.

About this time, two passenger ships had come and gone, nearly clearing out the hall. When a third one arrived where seventeen waiters were quitting over a beef with the chief steward, the union hall had problems and fell back on the school. By the time four or five of us sent from Santa Rosa got to the hall in San Francisco, it was after hours. A patrolman was still there to process us, however, along with two or three office personnel. He explained he would be working on our shipping cards while one of the ladies worked on the forms to be filled out for Coast Guard papers. As it was unusual for a student to have a seaman's document, it seemed common sense to remind her about it, rather than her saying,"You should have told me so I didn't have to go to all this work." True, the school probably had noted it on my record. When I started to say something, a big black man jumped on me.

"Where you from?" He knew. The doors were locked. There were only a few of us there.

"From school, sir."

"What school is that?" he asked in a real smartass tone.

"Why a...a...Santa Rosa."

"Santa Rosa! Ha! Ha! Ha!" he laughed, shaking his head. "And you expect to go aboard ship?"

"Yes sir."

"Well," he said, looking around to milk whatever laughter he could from the office personnel, "I sure wish you a lot of luck. Ha! Ha! Ha!"

Shining it on with the greatest performance of humility in my life: "Thank you very much, sir."[100]

Within a year or so, this patrolman was shot aboard ship, killed by another union member, a white man, which just shows the uncertainty of life for any of us. We're here today and gone tomorrow.

Being assigned as a first class waiter, I reported to the chief steward, a grey-haired man with a pot belly protruding from a spotless white, starched uniform, representing wisdom, cleanliness, and a living testament that there was good food to enjoy. He sized me up too, in spite of his benign appearance which might have suggested otherwise. It seemed best to tell him immediately about knowing next to nothing when waiting tables in hope he might have me working at something else. But he replied affably, "Well I'll give you a try." Shit!

It was soon clear to the headwaiter and the assistant headwaiter that I'd told the truth, nothing but the truth, and that only God could help me. They had no choice but to put me in kindergarten. Some of the stewardesses skipped breakfast. Two never came down for any meals. The others at lunch or dinner stopped by the galley to pick up a salad with dressing and maybe a dessert before coming into a dining room. So the only thing required was to get each an entrée and perhaps coffee. Even then one commented, "Honey, you'll never be a waiter. You should try something else."

The tailor, who sat next to the printer on a deuce, had a speech problem. It wasn't in my makeup to mock him but hating him was. There's no other way to describe him than to say he seemed to be a Donald Duck with feathers ruffled, perpetually exasperated. He made sounds to the printer, thereby calling the attention of those at tables nearby, then pointed to me, turning his thumb down, and squawking and shaking his head. The headwaiter would later ask me what was wrong, saying the tailor had asked for somebody else to wait on him. I'd reply I didn't know why. He was given exactly what he'd pointed to on the menu, then he wouldn't eat it. He was just a goofy fucker!

Still I worried more about the tailor than all the others together. No matter who had been sitting there longer, he would be waited on first. That he had to wait seemed the most likely reason for his irritation, then maybe that he'd got the wrong order, and finally that the food was cold. But no matter how much effort was made to make sure his order was right, to get it to him quickly, and to make sure it was piping hot (hot water would be run on his plate so it would only be held with a side towel when the food was dished up), he invariably would stand up and turn to put it on the small flat area between the deuces and, of course, squawking and pointing the whole time.

I'd think *wait just one damn minute here. You ordered that food. There's nothing wrong with it or your service.* Even a two-year-old could see what he was up to. When enough food had piled up, he was going to call the headwaiter over and tell him he'd not ordered the food and that I wouldn't even clear it away. Not being born yesterday, I'd go over and whisk away the evidence while he squawked furiously. *"Ha! Outsmarted you. Didn't I?"* Then I'd walk to the galley area, dump the food, and leave the dishes. When I returned each time, he was gone. Thank God for small blessings!

Finally after a week or two, another waiter told me he thought the tailor might have had an operation and couldn't eat the food when hot and put it up there to cool. On realizing this—that I was Daffy Duck and he wasn't out to get me—I and the tailor began to get along fine. There were no more problems—at least not with him. Yet why hadn't he written on a piece of paper what he was trying to tell me?

Because of four passengers during second sitting had said good things, I was promoted the next trip to a better station. This was a table of eight and a deuce. Pursers sat at the table during the first sitting, and seven ladies in the seventies and one lawyer getting there filled the table during the second sitting, when the lights were dimmed to give the dining room atmosphere.

Two of the ladies couldn't read the menu and their cry was, "Why do they have to turn the lights down so low?" To which I almost replied, "So you can't see what you're eating," but thought better and said, "I don't know either" and read the menu to them each time. As a result, I was always the last of twenty-two or twenty-three waiters getting away from the starting gate.

If that weren't enough, there was trouble trying to figure out who the eldest old lady was to be served first. One wrinkle looked much like another. I wasn't about to say, "Now would you open your mouth, ladies, so I can see how long in the tooth you are?" One lady, sensing and adding to the confusion, kept referring to the woman who sat next to her as "Mother," though they were obviously near the same age.

Finally I decided to forget it all and took at first the lady sitting next to the lawyer. But the number one chair used for first sitting was different than the one she sat in. This confused me even more. How amenable would they be if asked to stand and move three seats to the right? They'd still be sitting next to whomever they wanted, and it would make it so much easier. But circumspection prevented this circular movement.

Trying to write quickly in a very slowly developing shorthand, I'd later puzzle over the scrawl in the galley, where there were various realms of chefdoms and stations. A further hindrance was that I just had to be the personality kid, deciding it would be flattering to the passengers if each name was learned right off. But when finally getting out of the galley (through a door that swung open automatically and would swing back knocking the tray of entrees off your shoulder if you didn't walk briskly through) and back to the table, I found Mrs. Koulasouski had changed places with Mrs. Michelmore. Or was it Mrs. Dyson? No Dyson was sitting in what was the number three chair for first sitting, so that made it what my second sitting?

The only solution seemed to be to lift the covers off each of the eight entrées and ask who had ordered what, hopefully before the nearby strolling band got to the table and could see what was being done.

"Who ordered the medium-rare prime rib?"

One taker.

"Who ordered the Salisbury steak?"

No reply. Again, "Who ordered the Salisbury steak?"

"I'll take that, honey."

"Who ordered the veal Parmesan?"

I ended up with one order, and one lady didn't have an entrée. But she said, "What happened to my Salisbury steak?" The other lady had accepted it out of kindness and already had eaten two or three bites. Now it couldn't be snatched away from her. Shit!

So it was that each meal was a disaster, though less so than the preceding one. Still the old ladies liked me, probably would have eaten dog food and died before breathing a word of my nincompoop-etence. But the lawyer was something else! Just because he always got his food last in a lottery of sorts and that it was usually cold, the big baby complained to the headwaiter, with whom I'd previously got into a shouting match over disputed overtime. The upshot was a demotion back to kindergarten, in which I could show and tell entrées.

It was clear waiting tables was for the birds. I'd been happier washing pans on the beach and intended to get off at the end of the voyage. A funny thing happened, however. About a month later, the headwaiter came up to me one day and said, "Brent, I know you plan to quit at the end of the trip, but don't feel you have to do it because of me. You're going to make it okay. You just need more time."

The following voyage, I drew a hard station, a table of six and a table of four near the dining room entrances. Waiters and passengers passed between the side stand and me. I just barely managed to muddle through. Then things got progressively easier, largely due to the help of many waiters. The tailor motioned me over one day. Riveting the attention of half the dining room with two or three loud squawks, he pointed to me and smiled, giving a thumbs up. Then turning toward his new waiter who was going toward the galley, he squawked furiously, cooked him with a laser glare, flipped him a bone, and gave a loud raspberry.

Four of us were quartered in a small room one voyage. Music blared from a speaker on a locker next to my head. I asked that this be turned off at 11:00 P.M. The others were younger, partiers, and couldn't have cared less. One in his drunkness cussed me out and threw a light bulb against the bulkhead. The others, though not as rowdy, were on the same wavelength.

No one in the other quarters wanted to change. Even though the reason was downplayed, they were all smart enough to say no. And so without fail, the partying at night continued. There was a stewards' lounge only two or three decks directly above for that purpose and which no one used. They never considered going up there if they wanted to party. So I'd take a blanket and pillow to the lounge and sleep for a couple hours on a wooden bench. Then around midnight, I'd return to the room. If they were still awake, I'd go up to the lounge for another hour or two. This went on for weeks.

Each morning they were all dead to the world when it was time to get up for work. I refused to wake them. By their book, this was chickenshit. So be it. Finally there were less than two weeks left on the voyage. Hallelujah! Someone in the other quarters certainly would be getting off, but the yeoman said this was not so. No one was quitting, taking a trip off, or being fired. The situation now took on different proportions. Like the *Flying Dutchman*, it could go on forever. Two days before we reached Honolulu inbound, the yeoman found a room steward who was willing to change. What a relief to move into a space where people went to bed at night or were quiet. As far as I was concerned that was the end of it.

But Nick, one of the four in the room just vacated, was arrested trying to take what looked like an unopened carton of cigarettes ashore. This proved to be marijuana. The customs officer made a careful search of the room and then doubled back for a surprise re-search within twenty-four hours. Nick lost his seaman's papers, and the other two were harassed and under suspicion of customs. Something or someone had been looking after me. Must have been the sleep-and-dream god.

Since customs had known what Nick looked like coming down the gangway and called him over by name, it obviously had to have been an inside job. I'd asked Nick one day why he was always burning incense in the room. He replied he liked the smell of it.

About six months later, I had to work closely with a room steward who claimed to be one of the original members of "Our Gang." I couldn't figure out why he'd always give me a hard time and gone out of his way to make his opinion clear. He said it was because I'd finked on Nick. This wasn't true. Nothing had been said about the use of drugs when trying to move from the room. I never saw it. How could I? Still it's very possible to be in a room where marijuana or other narcotics are being used and not be involved. But you're never going to be able to convince customs or the Coast Guard of this.

Anyway, my denial was useless until saying, "There's no way of proving to you I had nothing to do with Nick's arrest. Tell you what we can do then. I'll put up ten thousand dollars and you match it. We'll go to some disinterested place which gives lie-detector tests. If it shows I'm lying, you get my ten thousand dollars. If not, I get yours. Loser pays for testing." This was enough to convince him.

More than one man has remarked, "It's not the work which wears at sea so much as personalities." This has always been and will be, and most problems—though by no means all—have to do with someone not doing his work for one reason or another: drunkenness, incompetence, ignorance, laziness, lack of integrity. You name it.

If both the official and unofficial records of each person who sailed many years were examined closely, it undoubtedly would be found that he or she had failed to make it to work for one reason or another, be it oversleeping, accident, sickness, family problems, car breakdown, drunkenness, jail, etc. One or even two of these excuses might reasonably be expected in a twenty-year period for not making it to work or missing the ship. No one's perfect, though some might think they are.

But there's also the sea lawyer who goes to the doctor in the morning at some choice port and then never returns until the beginning of the next day, though the medical was accomplished in two hours, early the day before. There's the mariner at sea who gets temperamental or has feelings hurt, giving illness as an excuse for not working two or three days, though the purser can find nothing wrong or only something minor or vague. There's the drunk who you've got to help get through his shift. You don't mind this too much if it's somebody you like and it only happens once in awhile, but it can be a pain in the ass otherwise. Finally there's the mariner who has a chronic complaint which can be turned on (or off like hot and cold running water) when he or she doesn't like something about shipboard work or a personality and flies home for medical reasons.

In short, it's often the alibi-Ike person who beats you out of time you had planned to have off. By itself, this might sound trivial, but when you stop to consider the normal workday for someone in the stewards department is ten hours, probably over a longer spread, seven days a week, month-in and month-out, the extra hours added to this by someone's shenanigans can get old fast.

One mariner summed it up as follows: "I don't give a damn who or what a person is or isn't out here. That doesn't bother me in the least. What matters is that he just do the job he signed on to do. I'm sick of doing someone else's work. Sure, at times you *might* get paid more. But it's all blood money."

Taking drugs, other than those prescribed, has in years past been solid grounds for revoking a seaman's papers permanently. It's felt that taking drugs is just one step away from smuggling them aboard for personal use and profit. Nowadays most are given a second chance after a drying-out period and counseling of some kind. The reasoning is, what good is it to ruin a man for life so that he has little reason to control himself later? This makes sense. Yet the Coast Guard's current policy of saying no to a third chance is right also. There are just too many hiding places on a big ship, not large enough for one man working by himself to make a million-dollar haul in one trip but very possible for him to make many thousands of dollars.

It's only fair to add that most sailors are competent, reliable people who do a good job.

Chapter Twenty-five
India, 1980

A smug sun/ condescending in/ its purity that/ all be roasted. The taxi edged slowly along a hot, stifling backroad through animals, children, and adults until coming to a stop. Moorthy, who worked at a watchman aboard ships in Madras Harbour, pointed across the road to a brown; drab, but sturdy, windowless; one-story, tenement building, having as much appeal as a pillbox ready to be charged. It was totally cheerless, completely shrubless, and called the unlikely name of K.M. Garden.

There were no odors. Expecting worse, still I shored: You wanted to come, now make the best of it. Moorthy said pleasantly, "You first from ship I ever want to bring to my home," making me feel like the wrong man in a parable.

A long, narrow corridor divided small, doorless rooms occupied in some cases by a family or a couple. From one came the slight smell of incense. We passed two or three people with hands pressed together in the traditional Indian greeting. Moorthy's home was a room about six by nine feet. Kalyani, his wife, smiled and greeted *namaste*. She spoke no English nor I Tamil, and so the three of us went to join others in a small entrance area at the back of the building.

With only a few words known in English, he began to introduce and explain who each was by relationship rather than by name. This was just as well as it wouldn't have stuck the first time anyway. I understand that Kalyani's mother, father, and sister were visiting from Bangalore, and they along with Moorthy's aged father and mother, a sister, his elder brother, and several curious children of neighbors slowly crowded in. They'd been told a guest would be coming. Some of the women had dressed in their best, with rings on their toes and nose ornaments, metal bracelets, and *tilaks*. On the walls were solemn family photographs, as if there were no dignity in smiling, and colorful pictures of Lord Muruga, the god from whom Moorthy's father, Murugasen, probably got his name and perhaps Moorthy too.

The only chair, borrowed from a neighbor, was a nearly reclining, canvas, folding type. I didn't want to sit in this; it seemed ridiculous while Moorthy's ancient parents stood, as well as some adults who were much older than I. And meaning well as a good host, Murugasen insisted on fanning me, though I told him over and over it wasn't necessary, for it was I who had weathered Madras West—Avenal, California—and read that Funston had measured a 165 degree Fahrenheit in Death Valley, which ought to have counted for something.

Finally it was clear no one was going to be content until the guest of honor sat. So with Murugasen's *pukka* of sorts going, Lord B-r-r-r-ent Chichester plunked himself down, down, down as the old canvas chair r-r-r-ripped through to the floor. Shit! Ac-tu-al-ly not a very auspicious beginning.

Had this happened in the U.S. where some self-styled, foreign-baboon bigshot was holding an audience, most would have cracked up laughing at pure slapstick, wishing they had it on film—but not India. No one laughed or even snickered, not even the children. The tyranny of the *raj* is hard to dispel.

Shortly someone came in with another chair and handed me a Coke. It was too expensive for the others to have except for Moorthy, who shared his with his mother and father. His elder brother, whose children had long since married and had children, spoke English very well; Murugasen and Moorthy's father-in-law spoke a little. But mostly the captive speaker was Wind-chester, delivering a speech to a captive audience, while Murugusen, fanning away, must have thought: *Wind in wind out.* Yet somehow the good intentions prevailed.

When it was time to leave, the elder brother said, "Come, I would like you to see something," He showed me his room, there on the wall as a large cross with Christ and a statue of the Virgin Mary. We looked at each other and laughed. Where else but India could this happen?

By the time deductions were taken, Moorthy, who was then thirty-five, took home the equivalent of forty-five dollars U.S. per month, or what I made in one day, not counting food, lodging, overtime, vacation pay, and other benefits. This was to support Kalyani, himself, Rajaseka (his son), and to give partial help to his parents. Later he and Kalyani would have two more children, Anita Bhuvaneswari and Gunasekar, and most of the responsibility toward his father and mother.

His and Kalyani's dream—for that's what it was for most parents in third-world countries—was to see that their children had a better education than they themselves had. Because of the poverty, the potential from one generation to the next vaporized away like water from a tea kettle, as one Indian poet put it. Education then was their first priority when using what little help was first sent. Their children were put in Catholic schools in which the instruction was in English and the fathers and sisters refused to send anyone to a higher level before examinations were passed.

Their second priority was to buy a lot and build a structure, providing a home for them as well as some income. This they did in Anna Nagar, then an up-and-coming neighborhood in Madras. It consisted at first of three units, each of sixteen feet and having a bedroom, living room, small kitchen, and storeroom. Most of the work he did by himself after his shifts on ships. But some of it had to be hired to be done.

June 18, 1982
Madras, India

I shall try to complete the house somehow by the end of this month and try to make the entrance and occupation of same by the owner. According to custom here it is bad sign when venomous snakes enter one's premises; so it happened when a cobra which had taken shelter in the heap of brick jelly for over 8 months got out and tried to enter the premises. Though sighted yet we could not harm it for fear that bad omen is to be anticipated. I asked the workman to let it go free, but those around had killed it and set fire to the dead. To propiate the bad omen, I had to perform the pooja in temple, thinking that is happen bad is being averted. But another one had emerged to everyone's surprise. That too had been killed.

M. Moorthy

They sent their kids to Catholic schools because the education was far superior to that in public schools. Though they were able to do this and still remain Hindu, there's no doubt that the children over the years had been influenced by their teachers and that the Church had kept hammering away at them. It was from the pressure from their kids, I believe, that Moorthy and Kalyani agreed to the conversion.

It wasn't really that difficult for them ideologically. Throughout their lives they had followed the Hindu equivalents of most of the Ten Commandments. Christianity had no franchise on ethics. As Hindus they believed it was the same god who answered all prayers. Practically speaking, Christ had long since been assimilated in most Hindus' thinking as another god.

All five family members were baptized, and Moorthy and Kalyani were remarried in the Catholic Church. Moorthy thereafter would be known as Moses, Kalyani as Stella. Rajasekar kept his name. Anita Bhuvaneswari became Anita (or Anitha), and Gunasekar became George.

When Moses wrote telling of their conversion to Christianity, he thought I'd be pleased. There was neither pleasure nor displeasure. If it made them feel better, fine. Besides the Catholic Church influence on the children, money—beyond which he could have earned in a lifetime—was given to him by an American who must have been Christian since one Christmas in Madras he'd brought presents for the children.

But the fact is I was part Jew, part Muslim, part Hindu, and part Christian, though purists in each religion are quick to bridle that this isn't possible. Not forgetting the positive aspects of Christianity, I hoped the conversion wouldn't spoil them.

Several families were followed in my travels and for a few years after retirement. These were in India, Pakistan, Bangladesh, and the Philippines, but none, including my own relatives, were given more than the family in Anna Nagar. Now that there's been time to see things in relationship to the caduceus, I wonder if it was Moorthy's attitude concerning the two cobras, as opposed to that of the Hindu workers, which brought him and his family good fortune and, indirectly, raised the number of snakes to five. And in passing, in respect to hypnopompous, I've seen an unknown, levitated Hindu staring down in amused and intelligent eyes and several times the head of a Bengal tiger, perhaps watching or guarding. Once the entire body was surrounded by a reddish aura, but it was not blood red, as if to convey no harmful intent.

Two families needing help didn't work out too well. One in the Philippines will be discussed in another chapter. The other, an Afghan refugee family, was a disappointment and learning experience that our immigration laws often work against those who try to work within the system, while those who don't, while circumventing the laws, get what they want without much trouble. The immigration mess is often biased while cloaked in the guise of fairness. The bottom line is often political: votes.

For at least fifteen years after the Vietnam War, and possibly still, people from the former South Vietnam had only to be on a boat at sea in some shipping lane to the United States and be rescued, at which time they were taken in at American taxpayer expense. I.e., whether you or I wanted to sponsor them or not, a part of our taxpayer dollar was taken out for this program. Why? Guilt, though it often took on the proportions of the far-fetched. The South Vietnamese forces were better equipped and better trained than those in the North. When there, U.S. forces fought for them and gave them muscle while losing tens of thousands, and we probably have that many today troubled by bad dreams and addiction (drugs obtained by the South Vietnamese and sold to the Americans at a good profit). We'll be paying for our backing in that war well into the next century, and yet we are to feel guilt-ridden forever to the former South Vietnamese?

There was much trouble trying to open an account in an Afghan refugee's name at any bank in Karachi, Pakistan, so that checks could be sent, but there was no other way. Who could the illiterate trust to see all the money sent for his family got to him? Even Abdul Zahir was well aware of the possible trickery, for he told me that when he sent a letter he would enclose a small picture each time to show that the letter was written by someone he trusted. If there was no picture, then I was to disregard the letter.

The Pakistani had an ambivalence toward the Afghans who fled into their country. Religion was taught to help their fellow Muslim brothers in need, but some Afghans were now taking jobs where their own poor found trouble finding work, and the refugees were costing the country much more in taxes. The Pakistani just wished the refugees would disappear. If banks gave them bank accounts, they might never return to Afghanistan when the war was over. So it was only through the influence of a very rich Pakistani, partly out of good motives and partly because he saw me as a potential for more wealth, that Abdul Zahir got an account. Later, of course, refugees didn't have this trouble.

The USSR was becoming increasingly involved in the war, while the United States gingerly worked indirectly. In other words, the Afghan resistance fighters were performing a feat at greater odds than we'd done in Vietnam. This is not to make light of the Vietnam horror stories or to forget the Afghans—a historically fierce people—were fighting for their own soil. Still they inspired my admiration, if not the U.S. as a whole. Afghanistan would later become Russia's Vietnam. The little indomitable people managed in a way to do what no other country had—to bring Russia to her knees, a debt the free world soon forgot.

But long before this, I'd asked a Pakistani taxi driver (whose family I followed) to select some refugee needing help. I didn't want to get involved in choosing between one or another and wanted to keep it objective. He in turn drove by a restaurant where refugees were known to beg at the front from those leaving. Here he got out and talked to a lady who looked much older than her years by the name of Noor-bibi. He learned that she had children with her, her three youngest sons. She'd lost her husband and one older son in Afghanistan, both as freedom fighters in the conflict. Abdul Zahir, another older son, had been wounded in the war and went back and forth across the border to fight. His wife had been wounded from shrapnel, and their baby was born cross-eyed. It was Zahir I hoped to sponsor, or his brother, who worked in a refugee camp for nothing and was more fluent in English. Both were in their mid or late twenties. Sponsorship of either one would have given the family some hope.

I went to a lot of trouble trying to do this, obtaining bank statements showing over two hundred thousand in accounts. Since I was sailing most of the time, it was my plan to set up a fund so that whoever was sponsored had a permanent room with some Islamic family or nearby. I had checked with the Islamic center in Seattle to make certain there would always be people around to counsel him. Money would be provided for food and clothing, etc. Also a Blue Cross plan would have been taken out. If this weren't enough to make sure he wouldn't become a burden at tax-payer expense, I agreed that my own social security money (later for retirement) could be taken.

The problem here was that Abdul Zahir, his wife, and baby were not really Afghan refugees. An Afghan refugee was defined by the Reagan administration as a person who could meet one of the requirements:

1) He or she had attended a college in the United States before the war began (Afghanistan was a poor country).
2) He or she had a relative living in the United States who was willing to sponsor him or her.
3) He or she had worked for an American company in Afghanistan before the war (many records of proof had been lost).

It was bureaucratic bullshit, a slick variation on the ol' Marie Antoinette ploy, "If there's no bread, give them cake." Again, the South Vietnamese had only to get on a boat in a shipping lane and qualified many times simply because they'd been born in South Vietnam. Today there are probably many trying to work within the system but will come to realize how ridiculous the government really is when reading the article titled "Welfare for Illegal Aliens" by Randy Fitzgerald in the June 1994 *Reader's Digest*.

Chapter Twenty-six

There was no doubt. The beaters of the bushes and the rail-birds were preening and reassuring themselves they weren't creeps by sniping. "Oh he never goes ashore," or "Hasn't been ashore all trip," even if it was not strictly true, as if a person were his own living-dead tombstone, which might have been. Never mind that some of them hadn't been ashore, or that sometimes when you didn't want to go because you were not feeling much like it and had seen the port numerous times before, you found your self going just to say you had, to chalk up credit with the beaters-of-the-bushes and the rail-birds.

India was different. Mark Twain knew it. No prodding was necessary to get me off in Bombay, where the sweltering heat steeped the a) mysticism, b) romance, c) culture, d) allure, and where to participate in all the above required certain ablutions and sacrifices to the gods, such as peeling off the sweat-soaked clothes put on clean a few hours before and taking a shower and changing into other clothing for going ashore for a few hours only to repeat the whole drill—shower and clean clothes—later for serving the passengers. All this was to be done besides breaking your ass to catch the next boat, to hassle with the taxi drivers inside the gate or the pedicabs outside, to worry then about changing your money legally when the banks were closed—or later if you hadn't that customs would hold a surprise inspection before sailing, to undergo the test of giving to someone who was a damn nuisance or to somebody who nearly broke your heart, to rush back so as not to miss the last launch to the ship before sailing, and then to sit and sweat and wait and wait on the quay, wondering if you had missed it until the reassuring appearance of other shipmates.

It's insane to go through just to drink two or three nearly warm beers, a hundred times or so if you already had ice-cold ones aboard ship within an arm's reach. If you look at it that way, if the gods hadn't shown you that the golden sun and jeweled sky over India below are the ceiling of an enormous temple. That's if they like you. They either do or don't;

there's no in between. If found lacking, you will be told not to come back, though you are made to think you yourself rejected India not the other way around. It's the etiquette of the gods, the kindness of the Hindu.

Within the vast temple are hundreds of smaller ones, beautifully crafted, enshrouded in mysticism. If you can't feel it, you'll never understand the reverence of the cow and other life. "It's a stupid religion," says the etiquette of the gods, the kindness of the Hindu.

There's the communion of beer (Noah would have liked it here), the acceptance of life as it is, the comparative lack of judgment. Hundreds of millions seem to pray just by going about their lives, by being themselves, and pass on to those of us favored by the gods the feeling when you look them squarely in the eyes: "Yes. I am yours, sir, but you are mine," as if knowing something we don't yet understand.

I'd seen Ali shortly after arrival before lunch but only to exchange greetings. Then after lunch, the purser nailed me before we had a chance to talk.

"Say, I need someone to help inventory your delegate's gear. He's going to the hospital."

Aw shit! "Can't it wait until tomorrow when we're at sea?"

"No. I want to get it done while he's here to watch."

Knowing I was about to say I planned to go over, he quickly cut me off: "When I asked Mike if he had any friend aboard who could help me, he said 'no' he had no friends. Then thinking it over, he said, 'Well maybe Brent.'"

Making a face and giving a finger, I knew I'd been had. Some consolation indeed that God loves simple people.

Ali stood in the passageway, wondering when we'd be done. No telling. We were up to our elbows in artifacts, clearly unimpressed by the thought that archaeologists a thousand years thence might call them the find of the century. I'd catch him later. It went without saying.

We went back maybe ten years. A half-assed friendship between a messman and a watchman who emptied the pantry garbage for any leftover food. It would, of course, have been easier and much faster to dump our own garbage by the time you figured what leftover food could be put in containers for the watchmen. Still you'd have to have been a real shit to deny them this.

If you sailed often to one port, then you'd see the same watchmen over and over. So I'd asked about his family once back in day one, telling him of helping some others and, once seeing myself clear, that I might help him and his family someday. No promises—someday, somewhere over the rainbow, that sort of thing. It was a double-think really, as I hated people who did that, big-dealed the low man, though it wasn't that exactly, but I was trying to offer some hope. Then finally figuring it out or putting it together two or three years previously, I began to follow through.

Sometimes we had two or three beers at a bar near one of the gates, and once by taxi we visited his family, forty minutes away, past mile upon mile of human hutches thrown together like small kids might do some Saturday afternoon in a vacant lot next door. There was a difference here though that nary a blade of grass grew or a bush or a tree to shade or hide behind, where both men and women squatted in the street's gutter to piss, where occasionally a man, or woman with a baby, or a child might crawl out of their warren and stand very erect in defiance of the dust, flies, odors, and lousy life.

It was miserably hot, a fierce, bright sun that plays shimmery tricks. Still they didn't shield their eyes, grimace, or even seem to mind, which, of course, they must have. I wondered what they'd think if they knew I admired and envied them. Maybe they did know. There was something there as they stared back, something they either didn't know anymore about than I or perhaps a great deal more, for this was India with all its mysticism. Whatever, it seemed to be a mutual liking, very real at the time. Now I wonder if it mightn't have been just the craziness that comes with the sun, that they stood staring after our taxi until it disappeared, much like a person at sea watching a small boat pass until it is lost in the distance.

Ashik Ali Khan had come to Bombay from an area near Lucknow, not too far from Nepal. At times a simple conversation with him in English could be as exasperating as reading a book where a page or two are missing and where, no matter how hard you look, you'll never find them. He understood about 80 percent of what was said but was always stumped by the two crucial adverbs "how" and "why." I could never get him to take these two words into his vocabulary, even though I went to the trouble a couple times of having someone fluent both in English and Hindi explain their meaning to him. Never let it be said we Americans aren't good. I mean after all I was like somebody in the Peace Corps bestowing two English words on him that would change his whole life—the ingrate. My failure proved embarrassing.

Now as we were approaching his home in Baignwadi Govandi, a section of Bombay, I asked him *how* he met his wife. He looked puzzled, so I reworded the question three or four times, using phrases such as "before marriage" and "before Mymoonisa (phonetic) became wife." He still didn't get it. I raised by voice: "Before meet wife, before you and wife meet." There wasn't a glimmer of understanding, of hope. I shouted, "Before you and your wife come together," netting my fingers to make the point.

"Oh!" he exclaimed, his eyes filling with understanding and shock.

"Sir, I can talk about old girlfriends but not my wife. She is close here," he emphasized thumping his heart.

Something had been lost in the translation. Somehow, someway the unspeakable had been spoken. Rather than pick that card up again, I decided to let it lie right there in the quicksand. Besides, his tendency to volunteer more information, though less sensitive, than necessary, as well as to answer a question not really understood, reminded me of someone else I knew: myself.

There was no disagreement anyway. Home was where his heart was and vice versa. It was the people who lived there really, not the structure, a small room having front and back entrances shielded by light curtains. He entered first telling them who would be coming and pulled back the curtain.

Mymoonisa drew her head wrap closely at the neck as we were introduced. She wasn't any better at meeting people than I. Had we bumped into each other two minutes later on the street, there would have been no recognition by either of us. Outside, of course, she'd have covered her face. But she had more to worry about than all that now as she went about taking care of a family of eight counting one still in the oven. There was Gul (flower) Mohammed, a six-month-old boy who had to be held and cuddled; little Akalaque (good behavior, educated) whose eyes were edged with kohl (powdered antimony) in belief it would protect from eye diseases and who toddled about with only a T-shirt on; and Afasana (story) Began (queen, wife, respected woman), now eight, besides two other children.

Mymoonisa never seemed to get caught up. There was always something to be done—even to thanking Allah for the blessings of her family at least once a day, if not five, and now especially Afasana, her older daughter, rushing outside to get a rag then back in, smiling shyly while she wiped where little "good behavior" has just piddled. Poverty and practicality ran hand in hand.

For my benefit an old fan was plugged into a long extension cord, connected to an outlet somewhere, and it began to whir a passing thought that electricity was costly. Old containers, which we'd have thrown away aboard ship, were still being used, piled up neatly on shelves high up on the walls. I'd given Ali these years before, along with used menu covers, now fading, taped on a small cupboard. Other than this, there were no decorations. Poverty and religion ran hand in hand. The room was spotless.

Hungry India wants heavy milk and sugar in its tea, for it's food that way, not like hot water, which is "no good." Richer is better, more respectable. Certainly with a guest it would be poor taste not to add these if one had them. So without asking, very generous amounts were heaped into mine. I gulped it down like a trooper, but now I wish to testify before God, the world, and the senate investigating committee that it's a blatant lie they be tellin' our poor, innocent children on Teli these days that "a spoonful of sugar makes the medicine go down."

We talked, Ali and I. The older children, though possibly amused, didn't understand. English wasn't taught in public schools. There was merit to the idea that Hindi would become the national language, but the poor were still penalized to some extent by this in that those who had a foundation in English would in the end probably get better jobs. Ali couldn't afford to send his children to a Catholic one where most classes were conducted in English. That someday he might be able to send one of his sons to it and that Mahabooh (beloved) Khan, then eleven, and his oldest, might become a customs officer were foolish dreams he mustn't think about.

I'd brought a box filled with food, toys, candy, Band-Aids, soap, etc. But now we had to leave almost before we arrived. The 3:30 launch back to the ship would get me to work at 4:00 P.M. I had doubts that we could make it even then. "Don't wharee, sir," the taxi driver, who'd been waiting, said, but I did. He was like a stubborn burro you had to keep urging to go faster. To save time, he took a shortcut, driving up to a gate he shouldn't have, then asked me for money to bribe the guard. Finally reaching the quay with less than two minutes to spare, he decided he was entitled to much more money than he'd originally agreed upon because he had to drive faster coming back. I would have given him a fat tip for that anyway, but what he wanted now was highway robbery. I'd no time to argue, forking it over in disgust. He was a slick bastard, a bandido. Maybe in his own mind he was just a poor man with a grievance, but in mine he'll always be "that bastard."

Two very old couples were assigned to one of my tables. Nearing the end of the evening meal, the next day following my trip to Ali's, one lady looks up, as if regretting very much what she's going to say, as if there had been some gross impropriety which she, nevertheless, felt compelled to mention.

"Brent," she began haltingly, "there's something we've all agreed we must speak to you about."

"Sure."

I couldn't recall messing up in their orders. The cabinet pudding, though, they'd scarcely touched, and it really didn't look to be top drawer. Or maybe that was the problem; if it really was, in which case I'd reply that 1) I was sorry to hear it, 2) all of our food was generally excellent except that sometimes it was more excellent than at other times (I'd been programmed), and 3) I'd be happy to get them something else if they wanted.

"Well you see we stood waiting awhile for the boat today at 1:30. When it finally came, we had almost withered from the heat. We walked down the gangway and got on. I don't know how we did that. It was bouncing around so, and the ride over was so taxing for us at our age, you know. By the time we got up the wharf's steps, we thought we'd better stop to catch our breath for a moment or two. An Indian man came over to us, carrying four Cokes he'd bought at a stand nearby. We didn't know him and wished he hadn't done that but tried to pay him anyway. But he said "no" and that his name was Ali. He asked if we knew Brent, and we answered that you were our waiter. He said you'd been out to his home yesterday, that you and he were friends, and that he wouldn't charge us too much if we'd like to go visit his home today."

Tell me it's not true. In my mind I could see the captain calling me in, then fuming that I was to stop immediately the Bilk-the-Passenger-Tour scheme—something I knew nothing about but wouldn't be able to convince him differently. "A fine mess you've got us into" Ali.

It took some explaining, but fortunately the passengers understood. Later that evening when I'd got back to my room and thought it over, it was funny. Not by any stretch of the imagination could I have believed Ali would become an entrepreneur and then so quickly. It was crazy.

But that was then and this was now, another voyage. Mike was in pain, sweat pouring off him. He alternately rested and got up, making trips back and forth to the laundry room washers and dryers, while trying to give the purser and me instructions on what he wanted put in a small bag carried with him. The rest would end up in a van returned to Seattle. Like many mariners, he was a pack rat, always dragging something back each time he got into a storeroom. Nothing was too insignificant. Everything was important for the seven years of famine to come. Never had he any intention of stealing. It would remain on the ship when he left. Still if the ship were sinking, he'd have been hindered by it all in locating his survival suit or life preserver and seaman's document. Maybe that was it. He couldn't have cared less; he was pharaoh with treasures intended for afterlife.

There were tiers of sets of linen for room changes, bed spreads, white jackets and trousers, a deck chair, bars of soap, matches, and ice buckets up the yin yang. Besides this there was the usual stuff sailors have: personal items such as suitcases, clothing, toilet articles, a radio clock, a pocket calculator, odds and ends of foreign currency, a stack of *Playboy* magazines, etc.; broken cases of soft drinks, candy, cigarettes, and other things bought from the ship's store; a stack of union papers and forms; calendars; and books and pocket books, some his own, some belonging to the crew library. Then there were the things he'd bought during the trip requiring customs forms: Three large ship wheels, one medium, and two small ones; a bunch of carvings; a coffee table; and Japanese gadgets. The two illegal, fake Rolexes he'd bought in Taiwan couldn't be declared, and he wondered what he'd do about them. But most intimidating of all for the purser and me to consider were two VCRs with a hundred films, a television set, a cassette with twenty or thirty tapes, headsets, and all kinds of tools. After all any idiot could go to sea and be miserable, but it took a brain to make the trip enjoyable.

Sorting it all out, the inventory and packing took two and a half hours.

By then it was nearly time to go back to work, back from work. I'd forgotten about Ali. He had as a watchman other things to do anyway. That he mightn't have been working never occurred to me. Now looking back, I can imagine what he could have felt: "Here's my friend. No, the person who I thought was my friend, who I was so happy to see earlier, who I've talked with many hours and drunk with, who I've had out to my home, now keeping me standing here like a dog waiting for his master. I'm going ashore to buy whiskey for the sailors. This money I must make while I can."

Damned if the beaters of the bushes and the rail-birds wouldn't be having their day in court again. Forget the extenuation and mitigation crap; it was a fine point in distinction about really wanting to go ashore this time, that age was catching up, that worry can be exhausting, that there's a contradiction between "Don't worry" and "You should have thought about that!"

To hell with it! The evening meal's over. Now to wind up the family's business, and I'm done, done, *done*! Praise the Lord and pass the malnutrition!

"Where's Ali?"

"I tink he go ashore, sir," the old Indian replied with the same even respect he gave crew members and officers alike.

"Are you sure?"

He looked at the other gangway watchman who nodded.

"Yes sir. He go ashore."

"Will he be back?"

"I do not know, sir. I tink maybe."

It had taken some planning and time to put together the box. The receipts of Safeway and other purchases made in the United States were taped on the outside to forestall accusations from the chief steward and customs officer that the items had been stolen from the ship, suspicions which probably came from personal experience. Pork items and those requiring refrigeration were out, as well as rice, which if not coal to Newcastle was Sacramento to Patna. Canned items such as tuna, salmon, fruit, and evaporated milk were in, as were cheese spreads and boxes of processed cheese which didn't spoil quickly; black-eyed peas and beans; Ritz crackers, cookies, and jams; Tang; Country-Time lemonade, and instant coffee; two large cans of Almond Roca and other candy; medical supplies like Band-Aids, cotton swabs, cough medicine, and a large Vaseline Intensive Care lotion; toothpaste, toothbrushes, soap, deodorants, and disposable razors; pens, pencils, paper, Scotch tape, crayons, and coloring books; and ship store items such as a carton of cigarettes and a box of Hershey's.

There was also three hundred dollars in cash to be given Ali, the yearly amount for his family. You are told this not to give an example of "Brent the Magnificent, MCMLXXXVI" but that you might understand my anger at the moment toward him. Even then you yourself would first have to take such a box through a gate in India to appreciate it fully.

There never would have been any objection on my part to completing the paperwork and paying the duty if the procedure had been accomplished quickly and efficiently. But in India, it's often slow, filled with runarounds, delays, and inaction. It's a snail in molasses with a tacit, "Come now! You know how to speed this up. You're not really that naive are you?"

To hand a box full of things to someone at the last minute before sailing is stupidity. Half of it will end up in the pockets of the customs officer, the gate guards, and the taxi driver. A few customs officers are scrupulously honest and fair and refuse any gratuity for being so. But in most cases, it's Indian roulette with all chambers loaded except one. The Indian government can rightfully boast at being even more democratic than England, Japan, Canada, or the United States in that in India the little man gets part of the graft too. No wonder that Ali, who passed a customs office twice each day, would dream that Mahaboob might someday become part of it—the crisp, white uniforms; the status and authority; the steady salary and security; the kickbacks.

There's a meanness about taking the last drop in a bucket meant for a poor man. So the only reasonable way was to make several trips, going through one gate one time and a different on the next, appealing to the sympathetic and charitable nature of the customs officer and guards rather than pandering to their greed. But time had run out for doing this. Were Ali to return and grab everything at the last minute, he would have two choices.

The first was more daring: he would strike a deal with a taxi driver he knew he could trust. This would be costly because even a friend didn't want to risk a heavy fine and the loss of his gate-entry permit for nothing. The box would be put on the floor next to the backseat. They would drive past the customs shack to the gate. The motor would be left running. When the first guard came over, Ali or the driver would quickly and slyly hand him a wad of rupees, a "go-man-wadi," before the other guards knew what had happened, then push down on the gas peddle and balls it through. If by chance another guard had opened the truck before this happened, the driver would wait until he heard the trunk door slammed shut, and then speed off. The one guard would tell the other that it was okay in front. He'd seen it.

Even playing Indian roulette, there's still the risk of the one empty chamber. So the second choice, being safer, is clearly preferred: The taxi driver stops near the small customs office and waits while Ali carries the box and sets it in front of the door. It's better to look-see first if the officer is busy with someone than to barge right in. The customs officer who has seen him comes to the door quickly.

"Yes?" he asks in English. Then noticing the box, he scowls, taking in the guard shack near the gate to see what guard is on duty and if he'd seen the man come with the box.

"What is this?"

Before an answer can be given, he demands that it be brought inside. He's haughty. Ali thinks at first he's a high-caste Hindu or maybe he has a bellyache or that he is expecting the port commissioner of customs at any moment. There's a peevishness about him which does not auger well.

"An American. He give this to me, a poor man, sir, for my family."

"But he should have taken it through the main customs office himself," he scolds in the typically didactic, Indian cadence.

"Yes sir. He give it to me only when ship go. Now too late for main customs. I know not what to do until it tomorrow opens."

"But this must be declared. You should have declared it."

"The American did not give...."

"Yes. Yes. Yes. I know all that."

"What I am doing now, sir. I am declaring. I am giving money for duty."

"This is all very irregular, you know. I am not certain what to do. But while you are here, I suppose I might as well look at what you have."

He picks up the money and puts it away. Whether it's to be used as evidence against him or to be taken as a bribe, Ali doesn't know. He's sure only that an intricate game has begun.

When everything has been taken out of the box and placed on the table, the officer picks up a can of Almond Roca.

"What is this?"

"Candy sir."

"Choc-o-lates?"

"Yes sir."

"Oh my little boy loves choc-o-lates," he suddenly chortles, looking angelic.

"Please take for your little boy, sir."

"Thank you."

It's no longer a game but a scripted farce. Ali has only to remember his cues.

The officer looks over the items again, then settles on a two-pound box of cheese. He places it to the side.

"My wife likes cheese," he explains, sparing Ali this time the elaborate thanking ritual of telling the officer he enjoyed kissing his ass, a small blessing. Besides Ali can't believe his good fortune: He still has the carton of cigarettes, which he himself would have taken first.

"I'll take these too," customs says, putting the cigarettes and instant coffee in his briefcase and the rest of the items back in the box.

The other can of Almond Roca is on the surface, crying out "save me," and the customs' eyes keep darting back to it. He hesitates but in a second plunges his hand back into the box.

"This too," looking as if he might give it mouth resuscitation right on the spot.

"But my children like chocolates too, sir!"

"All right, all right," he concedes, throwing it back in. He can afford to be generous.

"Well you have no toys or electrical things, which is good. The rest is okay. I am letting you take this to show kindness and understanding for the nice cause your friend has. Just tell the guard at the gate that I said it is all right."

He waves Ali off grandly, then waggles his head, as if very pleased with himself for having done his good deed for the day.

Ali carries the box to the back seat of the taxi. They drive twenty-five yards to the gate and stop. The guards are young soldiers. One looks in the trunk. The other, a corporal, sees the box.

"What is that?"

"It is for my family."

"Do you have paper?"

"The customs officer says to tell you it is okay."

"But I must have paper telling what is in box. He must give you paper," he insists.

Ali hands him two dollars in rupees. The corporal takes it, while turning so that he's not seen.

"I still must look in box."

He spies the can of Almond Roca.

"May I have?"

Ali nods.

The corporal picks up the bottle of lotion.

"What is this?"

"For dry skin."

He opens the top, smells it, then rubs a small amount on his skin.

"I take this?"

"Okay."

He then wants some of the Hershey's. The box is opened, and he is given six. Two other guards have wandered over, making four in the party altogether. They peer through the windows and smile. The three others are given two apiece.

"You have cigarettes?" the corporal asks.

"No."

"No cigarettes?" he frowns and looks disappointed.

Then as if to say "Oh well," he waggles his head, meaning "Okay to go."

The covered wagon, having been visited by the Indians, rolls down the trail. Ali breathes easier. The longer he remained in their clutches, the greater the possibility he could have been searched, then ignominiously taken inside to see the big chief (a captain in this case) for scalping.

"Where did you get this three hundred dollars?"

"I found it, sir."

"You found it?"

"Yes sir, I found in on the dock. Someone must have dropped it."

"You did not find it! You stole it on a ship."

"I swear by Allah. I did not steal it, sir. Like I say, I find it."

"I do not believe you. You are lying. I am keeping the money. It does not belong to you anyway, and you will not get it back. Your dock-entry permit is to be revoked permanently."

"But sir, I did not—."

"Let me finish?! If you tell me how you really got this money, I might not revoke your permit."

"The American give it to me, sir."

"What American was that?"

Here was a dilemma. To carry back to the United States all that had been brought for the family was as senseless as seeing the better half siphoned off by the system. A thought and a frown: "Another fine mess you've got us into," asshole! The old Indian caught it and whispered in front of the watchman: "We think he drink too much lately, sir. All the time he is...." His voice trailed off.

Ali always had been careful to drink out of sight of his fellow Muslim workers, but this precaution by itself was not enough anymore apparently. Could he be pissing away in booze part, if not all, the money being sent for his family? The more thought was given to this, the more the pieces began to fit. No way would there be a subsidy for an alcoholic drinking program.

> The ship's horn 'ad blown 'alf its time,
> Ali the door on goodbye frantically knocking,
> Behind him the bosun, his fierceness deceiving,
> "Watchman off! Your boat is leaving!"

Ali sent a card. Was it Christmas? Eid? Or some time in between? Who can remember such things? I wrote of being disappointed (an understatement) he'd not found time to pick up what had been brought for his family.

Surprisingly he shot back a sneering, contemptuous reply. It was as if he were saying he could see through the sham. He knew all along that there'd been nothing for him, but if I persisted in playing a game, he would call my bluff. Send the money, telling him the amount, and ship the goods, telling him the ship.

Piss on him! I threw his letter into a catch-all drawer—a fitting burial, for that's what he was, dead as far as I was concerned. Then what cheek! He keeps on writing as if nothing had happened:

Children are always remembering you. They still play with toys you brought them years ago. Kindly keep lettering so that both us can exchange good wishes. I am always in your obligation as have helped a lot my family. May God likes you all the time. I pray my Allah.

A year would pass before I wrote again. Fine words indeed about "a time to keep silence, and a time to speak," but the fact of the matter is that once you help someone you begin to feel a responsibility toward that person. And should you have a falling out later, the feeling of responsibility doesn't go away that easy. There's always a residue, a notion that you yourself hedged somehow. It's better to make peace, even if you are the injured party testifying for the accused. If this is forgiveness, then so be it. The derisive letter apparently represented the man's thinking for a small period of time. It wasn't characteristic of how he generally thought, so I didn't mention it. But if Ali would swear he had no drinking problem, I'd begin again to send checks to his account. If not, he was to open an account in his wife's name, where the check could be sent. Though he continued to write, he made no mention of this, which brought me back to rethinking the whole thing.

The beautiful people, the ones more easily imagined as receivers than givers, counsel: "Once the money is given in good faith, you have bought your own real estate in heaven, and so if the person you gave the money to does not follow through in good faith, it becomes his or her problem, not yours."

In any other context but biblical, this would be a con story, a sop to a fool who has been taken. It's muzzy idealism, having no place in reality, especially if the money given was hard-earned.

Was all or just part of the money sent being used on liquor? Or did it come from his own earnings? One way of viewing it was that if it were his earnings, it was his business how he spent it; another view was that it was mine too. For him to think otherwise was a child's game. The answer wasn't clear-cut.

Isn't a poor man entitled to a beer or two at the end of the day as much as a rich man? Even Noah, sloppy-assed drunk, felt a need to clear away the clutter of the pettiness of life. What does it take to move a man? What does it take to move a donkey? What does it take to move a donkey-man? His wife and children had a roof over their heads and were eating. There was love there. My case based on hearsay, half-truth, or even whole truth seemed weak—much ado about nothing. So I began again (after withholding the money a year) to send their check. Who knows? It might have made the difference whether one of his kids got to a better school or someway down the line helped Mahaboob to become a customs officer. And having come a long way in understanding, I felt better about myself.

Two years had passed, and I was forced to clean out the catch-all drawer which no longer would close. Everything had to be re-read before throwing out, including Ali's old letter:

Bombay
24-6-87

My dear friend,

I am glad to receive your letter, and with great interest I read out its contents. Here I am all right and hope this finds you in good spirits.

During Eid time, there was a strike in Bombay, and the ship outside, therefore, I could not come back there due to non-availability. Only when ship go does boat go to pick up watchmen and then leave right away. I am sorry for it.

Bombay is under monsoon. I am passing pleasant time. My family is passing very good and comfortable time.

Please let me know as to what goods you are sending me, when and by which ship, so that I may collect the same. Uptill now I have not received the amount. Please sent the same. Let me know when you are the amount.

Thanking you,
Yours sincerely,
Ashik Ali Khan

God Almighty! I was stunned, completely thrown for a loop. There was nothing sneering, contemptuous, or distrustful in the letter. The rancor I'd spawned myself, then magnanimously played Jesus Christ: Forgive him Father for he knows not what he has done. This was all too painfully true. I could have believed this kind of thinking possible for anyone but me and certainly would have denied it to the end had there not been the letter, the irrefutable proof of being sick. Just how many other instances there'd been, there was no telling. How many times does the rest of the world do this? If not yesterday, today. If not today, tomorrow. Aren't we all brothers under the skin in our insanity? Or is there a wish to believe this because it's a long road?

Hermes is a god of wayfarers or walkers. It's interesting that the riddle of the sphinx will be directed at them and pertain to walking. A baby walks on hands and feet in the morning, a man with two feet, and an old person with a cane or a walking stick. With only a little imagination, 423 becomes 4 and 5, or 45.

Chapter Twenty-seven

Raindrops falling through the sky,
Happy with themselves
Till they hear man cry.

If there's a goodness to people because of the state or condition they're in, then why not reason it would be evil to contribute to and remove them from their state of grace, thereby saving yourself money and doing good at the same time? Madness? Maybe. But there's also a certain logic to it. By the turn of a card I'd become a do-gooder rather than a terrorist, but the reason eluded me for years. The answer was that I was ascribing qualities and attributes which weren't necessarily there. The logic seemed simple enough: If the poor, the uneducated, and the majority of third-worlders are close to God, they must be good, and we, if not bad, are at least tainted for having things they don't.

If "a prophet" is not without honor except in his own country and his own house (Mt. 13.47), it's probably that he missed his pedaling, over-playing both the negative features of his or her own country and home so that goodness can't shine through, and the positive features outside his or country, so that the negativity is unnoticed. Case in point: Somalia, where the magical ring never glowed in heavenly brilliance.

If a person can ascribe positive qualities which don't exist in any great degree, he very likely can do this with negative qualities too, giving them more intensity than is called for. The criminally insane do this with all kinds of violence. Many of us do-gooders, however, are too faint-hearted. Instead of taking an ax to ourselves and giving God a break, we spend a lifetime on our knees in prayer whining and whimpering about our lot in life of being suffering heroes. How can those we've helped lie and betray our trust? Most times we cause our own misery. It's not God's making.

A destitute, uneducated third-worlder appears guileless probably because he or she is having difficulty translating any but the most simple thoughts into English. It's a Disney fantasy, a naive, children's tale, to think some sort of magical reaction will be set in motion by your interaction with another: You make a contribution (viewed as good) to a poor soul (who has to be good because he is needy), and because of the donation, he will believe that only a person who is good through and through would help him. All parts of the mystical rusty ring are now complete. It turns into pure gold before our very eyes and glows with a beautiful, heavenly brilliance. The bottom line is that the underprivileged must be helped to some extent, but there's no end to trouble when a person makes the blanket assumption that they're always good and trustworthy.

There's a mutual liking of one another by most Americans and Filipinos. I'm not certain what they see in us, but for my part I can hear in my mind "Hi Joe" and "Hi sir" said with warmth and sincerity. They were and are good people, so humble that you know instinctively if anyone is going to make it to heaven, it's them. There are no piranhas of ego, just creatures, gentle and submissive for the most part, playing out the hands they'd been dealt with simple dignity.

An army hospital ship first carried me to the Philippines in 1947, and from then on it was in and out from time to time over the next forty years. For this reason, it bothered me a couple years before retirement that though following families in Pakistan, India, and Bangladesh, I hadn't done the same in the Philippines. Funds at this time pretty much had been committed for the "golden years" to follow, but certainly a token amount wouldn't see me in the poorhouse.

There were plans to settle on an old lady who had a small stand in Alongapo, but I never made it ashore there before sailing. The marines were playing war games that night at Subic Bay, and every attempt to make it ashore was like playing Monopoly: Do not pass go. Do not collect two hundred dollars. Go directly to jail. Back to the ship. So later at Manila, the watchman, whom I'd never seen before, was really a second choice. The uniform coat and trousers he wore were passed back and forth between him and another watchman from shift to shift. In years of traveling, I'd never seen anything like that, so I figured he must be a needy person.

He had various duties, one of which was to keep the stevedores and peddlers out of the inside-housing area. As a routine in most ports overseas we visited, he'd knock at the pantry door at the end of each meal to pick up the garbage cans to empty them two decks below in the garbage chute and then return them empty. For this he got for himself and sometimes the other watchmen leftover food which would have been thrown out anyway and sometimes more: "Hide these apples in your pocket, and don't let anybody see them!" As always it would have been fifteen minutes faster after each meal and far easier, by the time you worried what you could give out, what to put it in, and the forever time it took them to stir in a ton of sugar and milk into the leftover coffee, to dump the liquids down the drain or garbage disposal and empty the cans yourself.

Domingo Fuentes worked as a part-time watchman making forty-five pesos a day (at that time about two dollars for twelve hours). "If no ship, no work. No pay. I'm standby in my house," he said. Liezl, his wife whom I'd not met, washed clothes and cleaned homes, besides taking care of three children, to help make ends meet.

Twenty dollars were given to him to open an account. When he returned the following day, I gave him a letter of intent, explaining what could and couldn't be done for his family. It was a hash, what you might expect from a seaman running between work periods to catch the next launch ashore, but it was better than nothing. It was something tangible to bring them back to earth when their imaginations, dreams, and fantasies ran wild: I'm going to Amerika; all Amerikans are rich, powerful, and influential. A check of two hundred dollars each year would be sent to his account, provided I was able to keep this up. He was told clearly not to expect anything beyond this unless it were an absolute emergency since commitments to others who'd waited longer were full up. Finally he was advised to make certain all members of his family had polio immunizations, a piece of advice which might have saved the life of a small boy in Pakistan if I'd only thought to mention it to that family when writing.

The subject of going to the United States had come up. There were only two ways he stood a chance. Either he had a skill in which the shortage had been designated by the Department of Labor, or he had a relative in the U.S. who would sponsor him. Only dieticians and physiotherapists were on the "endangered species" list when inquiring years before, so it was unlikely he could meet this requirement if occupations had changed. He did, however, have a married sister living in California. If she could sponsor him—and only if she would—I'd help out by paying his way to the U.S. and by sending a small check to his family in Manila until immigration allowed him to work.

To try to explain how most acquaintanceships grow is to put them in time frames, much like dull, daily diary entries. To review some of this later in your mind is to ask yourself if you'd missed or overlooked something, however small, like a vague passing thought or glint in the eyes. If you sneer at this, then with an evenhandedness you must sneer at your own government, which with an infallibility equal to the Popes, gives money out overseas to good causes, only to find out years later that little of it actually had gone for the purpose intended.

The freighter sailed in a day or two, and on December 14, 1987, he wrote:

> First of all, my whole family prayed to God that you will
> always (be) in good health and free of any bad happening.
> I excuse my delayed to send a letter, because of a

family problem. First, my only daughter Tina was dead last October 14, 1987. Second, typhoon was coming in my home province, in my house was broken. You know until now my family live in small barong-barong house. You know almost one and a half month standby. Only my wife can work to support my two sons.

At this point in the letter Domingo switches to what is probably a Pilipino dialect—Tagalog, Illocano, Pompango, Waray? I think he's grief-stricken over Tina's death and unconsciously slips into a language that's easier for him.

The next letter bore no date. He mentioned he'd received my letter of January 18, 1988, and that "you know...my wife told me when she get baby, you are the one a Godfather." Other than this and "Good luck, God Bless you always," the entire letter was written in dialect.

A crew member was asked to translate, and just my luck, he could understand and speak Tagalog but couldn't read it. So it was explained to Domingo that there was no easy way for me to get his letters translated. Besides, Domingo spoke English well enough and also wrote it. The best I could come up with was that from the beginning my letters were written to both him and his wife. If he wrote in a language I couldn't understand, then naturally there'd be no objection if she took over the correspondence. But it would have been simpler if he'd just written, "If you don't mind, I'll let my wife take over the writing since it's easier for her." It made no difference who wrote, but they didn't know that. Nor could I have known at first her reason for taking over the writing: She was far more imaginative, adept, and experienced in this sort of thing.

On May 10, 1988, he wrote saying his baby daughter, Maria, was born on February 20, 1988, and would be baptized in June. I really didn't want to be designated godfather but felt it would be rude to say no. In the same letter, he asked for three hundred dollars to put down on a mortgaged house. Records showed they were due to receive two hundred dollars in September 1988. If the money were sent early (plus one hundred dollars extra this once), it would meet their needs. Unless there was an emergency, they weren't to expect more money until September 1989—the stipulated amount still being two hundred dollars per year.

A letter of thanks with pictures was received from Domingo. Thereafter Liezl took over the correspondence completely. Thinking back I've tried to recall exactly what my impression was on first seeing her picture. Something was there, but it was fleeting. Perhaps there was a detachment in her, as if there were not a complete oneness of mind and body. Or was all this, rather than instinct, just some sort of projection as I saw myself. I think why I discounted or pushed it aside was that Domingo and the children (Marco 7, Christopher 5, and Maria about 11 weeks) appeared so happy. If what I thought were so, I couldn't imagine them looking that way. The piece just didn't fit, so all I could say to appear rational in a normal world was that at thirty-two she looked tired, unhappy, and sensual with long, black hair. And there was that scarlet red dress.

Months later I showed the picture to Robert, a friend, and asked his opinion, to which he replied, "Damne` she ain't got some great legs!" He took it over to the window where the light was better, turned it back and forth as if trying to look up her dress, and said finally, "There's nothing wrong with her. It's him. You can look at his eyes and tell he's a cocaine addict. It's as clear as the nose on your face."

I wish he hadn't used the expression about the nose on my face. A guy had come up to me once wanting spare change. I told him I wasn't gonna give him none, and he railed, "Awe go to hell, you damned, ol' wino!" Surprise and vulnerability must have clearly shown, for he dogged me for a few seconds, yapping at my heels, "You don't like me to call you that, do you? You old wino!"

Wine! I didn't even like the stuff. So maybe both Robert and I were all wet about what we thought we saw. One knowledgeable word is worth a thousand pictures.

Manila
August 15, 1988

First of all I would like to say how are you now. If you asked about us by the help of God we are fine. I write a letter to you because I want you to know the money was release already last week, and I would like to say again thank you very much. Brent, I want something from [you] I wish my husband can go with you in America if you can come here in the Philippines because his job here is not stayble we can ot afford what children need But if my husband can work in your place we be sure of the future of my children. Since before I always wish that someday my husban can go to your place and I hope through your help that will happen. Someone told us that you can get him you you just write to U.S. embassy to make petition him for example he is your gardner or what. Right now we have own house just the same street and we got nice place and if is not to much for you I want to have own income a little store or business but you know the problem financial for my store I can ot go out to work now because of my little baby not like before. If you dont mind can I have your picture hope you dont disapiont me.

Respicfuly yours
Liezl

Liezl is the waves washing up on the shore; she says each time, "Give me money." And I, walking in the sand, jump back, saying, "I ain't got none," a double deception. Wringing and draining the sand nearly dry, she leaves, only to return stronger than ever, lapping at my shoes: "Give me money!"

With one hand holding a seashell to my ear, I hear the siren sound of the sea, maybe even God. My free hand cupped over the other ear hears an identical sound, a foolishness now. Beware! I am about to make a sentencious remark to myself that "it's better to err on the side of" blah, blah, blah when a voice within, seething with hatred, explodes: "Awe shut the fuck up! Just do it or don't!"

A reply repeated what had been told to Domingo in person. His best chance of coming to the United States was by sponsorship of a relative—someone close: meaning a close relative, as opposed to a distant one. Since he had a sister living in the United States, he should write to her. If she would sponsor him, "I'd pay his air fare to the U.S. But no way was transportation to be paid to and from the United States for a brief period as a laborer, if that were possible." Liezl had a misconception about my affluence and lifestyle. It had to be explained to her about living in a third-rate hotel overlooking an alley and a rundown parking lot where Indians often came to drink and whoop it up. There was no garden for Domingo to work as a gardener, no money tree.

Manila
Sept. 19, 1988

Hello! God be blessing be with you today. I was so sad to know that you have a medical problem and I got also what you mean about my sudjestion. Yes the sister of my husband are in America now about one year now. But as far as I know they can't get any of their relatives for now because they are not American citizen. Yet maybe after five year and thasts to long from now. But we try to communicate them. Is you said if we are very close maybe you can. Can you tell me how to make close each other so that you can help my husband for my children sake. You know almost one month now my husband no income they have now [no] ships I dont know where to get some money to buy everyday need not like before I have small income. Thats why I beg your mercy now my husbom told me one time that you promise that you will give me a budget for a small buesniss Now we have a nice place for buesniss if you trust me can you give me a little favar to me if its not to much for you Can I have a budget for a small buesniss it about $8.000 to $1.000 [$800 to $1,000] I think it enough for start, you know here in the Philippines it better to have a buesniss But I try my very best make my buesniss Well I hope I dint offened you and dont think Im abiousing [abusing] to your kindness god know Im just telling the truth. Its up to you if you deduct the money you send us every year I close this letter now and hoping that you will agree my proposing to you.

Sincerely yours,
Liezl

Brent.

A buesniss I mean a little store because if I have store it big different not like the moncy will last [?] right away but store it okey since before I really want to have store but we have no enought money for it.

Not all Liezl's letters are to be included. She wrote in longhand, frequently had three or four sentences running together without punctuation or capitalization (which I've added in some copies to make for easier reading). In later letters there would be two or three words whose relationship to the thought were not clear, as if the thought had passed before she could record it completely. What could be made of:

1) "If you asked about us by the help of God we are fine." She'd written this in two or three letters. Was this sarcasm? I'd stopped asking because every time it was costing me more money.

2) "Can you tell me how to make close each other so that you can help my husband for my children sake?" It struck me as odd that she hadn't said "our children's sake." But maybe her English wasn't that great. My gut reaction at first was to be suspicious, to doubt her sincerity, to wonder if she were putting on fake humility. Yet sometimes people in the Philippines did talk like that. Still I wasn't so much believing in her as fighting my own suspicious nature, which was, unfortunately, right most the time, but when it was wrong, it was ridiculously so. It was my feeling that she had some sort of mental problem (more than usual). Her simple way of expressing herself was almost biblical at times. Her English jargon, like that of the average Filipino, was amusing. I

could easily picture her when she said "desame" for "the same," "next of skin" for "next of kin," "mine" for "mind," "papar" for "paper," "neigbhore" or "neigbhoor" for "neighbor," "favar" for "favor," "valence" for "balance," "tilling" for "telling," "buessness" for "business," "dint" for "don't" or "didn't," etc. And there were a hundred other instances of phrasing so typical but too numerous to mention except for one: "You know its look like you slap me because of that you think I am big lies."[101]

Manila
January 23, 1989

First of all I would like to say hello to you. Hows your day? I hope that you are in good condation. If you asked about my family by the help of God we are very fine. I know next month February is your birthday but I dont know the exact day but any way let me say happy birthday to you in advance and I hope that you have many more birthdays to come. Like Cindy this coming February 20 she will be one year old. You know my husband start to walk his papers but before he did he asked some infomation from the Governor of his Province Sorsogon in Bicol Region near skin of his mother he said Domingo can go to your place easy if he has money for his transportation and for placement pay. This man we can trust off. He is American citizen he live in America since Marshall Law now Aquinos government he came back here and he run a governor of Sorsogon he promise he will be the one to do something about the problem of Domingo in U. Embassy. Domingo said maybe he can spent $1,300. for his transportation and for placement pay to that he can sail rightaway But if he still stay in the Philippines its better for me my reason he wont be far away from the Kids but he said want to have passenger jeep even second hand only like he told to you before the first time you meet him. Maybe worth $5,000. after one year we can get an installment jeep in jeeny motors because we have colateral already this is his two plan passenger jeep it good to go abroad much better but if there is many hassle about it to stay here and have jeep. But Brent its up to you which one do you want to my family. As you promise that you give to my a good opportunity if you don't mine we need it Now while early this is the second time I asked help and by the help of God we can be sure of the good future of my children.

My store is doing good now and it big help to us I close this letter of Love and care from my family. I hope you understand and agree please to my Longing.

Restpicfuly yours
Liezl

Domingo and I had discussed possible ways for him to get ahead. He wanted to sail, but unless he were a U.S. citizen, he could not sail on U.S. ships. Placement pay (bribe to agent) to get aboard some third-world ships or a job in Diego Garcia were discussed: How much it would cost, as well as a taxi, a store, and so on. These were just avenues of discussion. I made no promises to him for any of this, and this was clear. Later, I relented on money for a store. Now Liezl has refined it to either-or: "Its up to you which do you want to my family."

Manila,
February 13, 1989

We recieve your letters firts with 25 dollor for Marias birthday thank you very much and the other one. And I read all about what you mean Yes I agree with that it very hard to go to your place and I am very sad about it You know why I really want my husband to get stable job first of to my children sake. You know one of my little boy Christopher asked one time he said mama when we will get rich I answer to him you just pray to Jesus Would you believe since Jan. 1 to Jan. 30 Domingo have no works they have no ships. And last Jan. 24 Maria get sick and we have to bring her to the hospital and confine her because she got doerea and after Domingo had fever we pay Marias bill more the P 2,000 it very very hard for me if my husband have not stable job like me also I have ellness in my throat I have goiter I have to drink medicine every day but if my husband no work how can I buy you know now here in the Philippines all things are very expensive I am begging your mercy once again this is the last I asked help from you My husband go Seaman many of my niegbhore are Seamen theres no problem only placement pay if we can give anytime he can go rightaway Please last chance I asked from you I am not afraid to because of my ellness but my children are too young they dont know what to do if there no mother who care theme. Maybe we can spent all in all $700.00. I hope you wont say no   please together this letter the Discharge paper of Maria in hospital so that you wont say that Idd lied to you I close my letter for hoping and praying that you are always in good health.

Respicfuly yours
Liezl

Seattle, WA
18 Feb 1989

Hello!

I received your letter of February 13 and was sorry to read of Maria's illness and hope her recovery will be complete by the time you receive this. No way can your problems be made light of, nor am I insensitive to them.

When the President Jackson was in Manila on Sept. 4, 1987, I gave you (Domingo) a letter saying as long as able, I'd send you two hundred dollars each year. This was based on what was left after sending to other families, known much longer than you, and what would be needed in retirement. Since then (less than two years) records show you have been given $1,520, which doesn't include small gifts.

If it were just your problems only, I wouldn't mind. But the grief of most these families is almost endless. If I took every cent I had and settled every problem they had, within a year they would probably be right back where they are now, and there would be no base to tap to send them anymore. In short, most would have ruined themselves as well as me. So it seems better to send agreed sums each year, to try to make life a little easier for all.

The bottom line is that I don't feel at this time that I have $700 to send you. Being Maria's godfather, however, I will send you within a couple weeks a hundred dollars to cover her medical expense.

As always,
Brent

Liezl wasn't listening. I might have been George Burns talking to Gracie Allen. No sooner would one of her problems be squared away than she'd give another. I couldn't impress upon her that I too had worries. It wasn't simply writing a letter saying "yes" or "no." Each time I was faced with a moral dilemma, a judgment of myself and a judgment of her, or perhaps she knew this all too well. In any case, the only solution was to lay it out in plain terms, which was done when sending her the $100. "No more money beyond the $200 each year unless it is a medical emergency." I still planned, of course, to send small gifts at Christmas and to remember Maria's birthday.

Manila
March 13, 1989

Hello. how are you now I hope you are fine. You asked about my family just they same. We recieve all your letter also the money of Maria thank you very much you are rigth this is our problem and please don't think that we are oportunist I know that you know the life here in Philippines its very hard especially if you are not colloge graduate. You canot fine good job and then everything it so expensive Thats why every body wants to go abroad if only have a change. I hope you are not angry with us you know we did everything my husband now have all paper and our problem now the valance of placement pay We have valance 5,000 pesos We dont know where to get this. I dont force you to help us but all I can say this time we really need your help if you will help us I am very glad but if you wont its okey to me and Im sure this is my last request from you. I wait only Maria only when grow up who know you will petation her no joke only. Speaking of Maria she's okey now and she learns now how to walk and talk She's so movable before I close my letter I would like to say again I very sorry and please dont get anry with us.

Respicfuly yours,
Liezl

Am or am I not nuts? Didn't I just write and tell her flat-ass out, "No more money?" Believe me, the ultimatum wasn't made without cause. I'd given her all kinds of clear signals and courteous signs, protecting her dignity and mine. Yet in rankling me to the point of putting an authoritarian stamp on things, she'd succeeded somehow in making me not only lose control but into a horse's ass to boot. I felt guilty. She might just as well have said then, "See you really haven't got it together as well as you think. You try to be so goody-goody when in fact you're not better than the rest of us."

At the very least, Liezl was pushy for her own reasons. I was a small fish who'd set a limit to the help and repeatedly reminded her of the limit. She was, in effect, patronizing her patron. Throughout the world, all are taught to help the poor and needy, and most, I suppose, have some guilt feelings if they don't. She knew this as well as you and I do. Implicit in her further hounding was: "I know you still have more money." What had started out as something positive with a limit plainly set was being converted into a negative to milk still more help. It seemed best to stop writing for awhile to clear the air and tacitly to make a point that if she continued to push, correspondence would cease completely.

Two months passed since writing, enough time to make the point. It was time to begin again. The family was due to receive a check for $200 in September. If $50 more were added to that and the check was sent early, the need for placement pay would be met. It required only a little bending on my part and a job on an American base, such as at Diego Garcia, or a ship might go a long way to solving their problems.

On the fifth of May a check was mailed to Domingo's account. But just a day before this, Liezl was writing from Manila that Domingo had been killed as a victim of a hold-up incident on April 7, 1989.

My God! So Domingo was dead now. It threw me for a loop. We travel for thousands of miles and for years thinking that things will go on and on, like the sun rising and setting. Then all of a sudden we're jolted back into the realization of the uncertainty of life, that all of us after all are just "here today, and gone tomorrow" when death comes to somebody you know, if even only slightly. I was sorry for Domingo. I tried to visualize what happened from the scanty information. I could sympathize with his family and wrote a letter of condolence. It was like...maybe you see a newscast with a plain, homely, dumpy person choked up and crying, who from all appearances really didn't seem to have much going for him or her except that special love, now gone, the horror and dread.

There was a responsibility to help the family. It had nothing to do with the admission price of getting into heaven or hell, two places I had serious doubts even existed. "When you're dead, you're stinkin', and that's all there is to it," a friend would guffaw, as if the belief in a hereafter was an enormous hoax on par with Santa Claus and the tooth fairy. The idea of having to have a reward for doing something good seemed childish. Were we no better than donkeys to be controlled by the carrot of heaven or the stick of hell? Or were we rats in a maze, punished with electricity or rewarded with tidbits? The feeling of responsibility came from 1) the idea that if you start out with someone, you should finish up with him or her and 2) the belief in the continuing popularity of the New Testament as one hell of a good book, very likely someday to be followed by a sequel, where yours truly might be villified to Sunday-school brats for millenniums to come as the mean and miserable miser (another facet of my obsessive-compulsive nature) who withheld a mite from a widow. This to me was infinitely more likely than heaven or hell. But why care if there's no hereafter? Doan know.

Manila
May 11, 1989

First of all let me say hallow to you. I hope you are in good health I recieve your letter tilling that you send money $250. Last May 4 I send a letter tilling that my husband was dead. That why I am asking to you a little help. You know to support my family to my three kids I cook banana cue and camote cue I am the one of side walk vendor now under the heat of the sun because my money left just enough of that kind of buisness Sometime I feel so sad everytime I look at my children because you know they no father now that they can trust off but I will do my best even it is hard for me I will sacripise for theme and I hope we can survive all this. My baby sitter of Maria is Marco while Im saling banana cue. That money you send I canot get without authorize paper come from you because the name of the account no is Domingo name please can you send an authorize paper to me so that I can get the money in the Bank. I understand what you mean of your letter dont worry I promise I just wait your mercy and that money you send I will keep that for my kids needs sorry if my letter have many mistake because I have so many thing to do. Im in hurry I close my letter of hoping of your mercy and kindness.

Very truely your
Liezl

Manila
August 11, 1989

Hello. how are you I hope evrything will be fine. Asked about me and my three kids we are fine too. When I recieve your letter last July 29 telling that you well help me I was so happy that time until I got your another letter I thought I can breath well I can sleep well but after I read your another letter ets look like the earth falling down on me because have changed your mine. I dint tell you about the U.S. embasy because you dint asked me Of course you are the Boss I just wait what you well till

me Yes have talk person in U.S. embasy but maybe we
do miss-understanding because when I call there I used
the telephone near the high way where the buses and
jeeney where passing it too noise I kept asking what she
saying so she told me I have to see her in person after 4
days I went there because that I canot go out because
Maria has sick that day After Maria got well I went to
U.S. embasy but the guard dint let me in I know I understand that guard because I canot go out everyday
because everytime I go out I have to bring Maria or just
leave in my niegbhoor its very hards to me I made a letter I send it to U.S embassy but after two days the letter
send back to me but I lost that letter if I dint lost that letter I will show you. About your letter in church I realy do
what you want me to do I attemed to talk to the Priest
two time but I realy dont have idea how to talk to that
Priest so I drop your letter to the box inside the church
that box is for the charity Now if you blame about this I
to apolozise me. My only witness is only God that Im
telling the trueth that Domingos dead he is in the hand
now of God My children no more father Thats why
even embarrashing to asked from you I did because of
my children You are the only one cant light the life of my
kids With you they won't separete from me because I
canot give theme all things they need. Once again I begging your kindly I knock into heart. Please save my children I want we are together I dont want the will grow
far from me Please believe me and all good thing you
have give to us only God can repay it I always pray for
your good health and long life You know Maria now
know how to dance She can understand now what your
saying to her She is very naughty She is my one reason
why I asked help from you I will miss her if I will bring
theme in the Province She is too smale to separete from
me. You know every time I cooke banana cue and theres
a rain I almost surrender but I always have hope I know
God wont leave me God see us. When you answere my
letter let me know if you will help me because we canot
say longer here Maybe I will decide to bring children to
the Province but that mean I will be lonely if you will
help me I am very thankful for it and my children too
Dont for get Maria needs your mercy and we always
remember you and love you.

Very truely yours
Liezl

Manila
August 25, 1989

I got your letter I was surprised because of your address Mr. Domingo and Liezl. You know its look like you slap me because of that you think I am big lies. Domingo have no record of the hospital because he dint reach the to the hospital The death certifecate I got they only give that to me and they explain to me it has to be print of hospital like me only grade VI. how would I know if theres wrong about it if Domingo still here I wont kill my self to work hard so that my children can eat three time a day even it raining I know that bad for my health because now I dont feel well. I have a heavy cough I feel I always have fever inside. You see even I feel like this continue my work all things here Philippine it gitteng hard all things are expensive now. You dont only know like a widow all responscble all mine Sometime if it not only a sin to comit suiside I did it but I steel afraid of Juses and I am pity to my little Maria I only live now just because of my kids. Before I for get the money $80. is in the bank now if you give that to me I am very thankful for it I will get the children need it If you change your mine not to help me I can ot do anything because I have no right to force you but just remember Domingo it now with us he pass away alreary and me who work for my kids I have many illness if you help me thank you very much if not okey I just want to ask favar from you I just want to forget about the memary of Domingo every time I remember him the worsting happen to him it hurting me You see I almost recover now before now before every day and night I alway think about him. That why I got thin. The money you send will not go to in bad in fact that will save a life I close my letter with love and tears from me Maria and the two boy

Sincerely yours
Liezl

Manila
October 31, 1989

Hellow. first of all how are you now are you okay. Asked about us Well we are in good health but we are

211

starting to get hungry Why you dont believe me, I am telling the trueth Domingo pass away that why were are now meserable life. How I wish that you could see us here sometimes I dont eat breakfast to save only money By buessness now is not going good My kids it getting hungry You dont only know I am look like drown in the sea Sometimes I think bad but if I do of what Im thinking what happened to my children I dont know what to do You know I sold already our stero casette I have no choice if I wont do this we are not going to eat I have to pay our rent electresity our water to tell you I dont know this coming day or we are going to sleep in the street Our only hope if you well help us even you dint send a letter to me Im steel hoping because what I till to you it all true please try to thrust me to tell you I am a good person You can trust me even we dont see each other Some day you are going to know me I am afraid the Christmass is coming What can I give to my children Pity theme luck of every thing Christmas is the happenes of children Please dont leave us have mercy to me every day I talk to your picture begging not to forget us god knows I dint lie to you. I close my letter of hoping Your love God bless with always Merry Christmass.

Sincerly yours
Liezl

Writing to Liezl was stopped. Why did she keep writing? I resented her shabby lies, her milking melodrama for return of my help. At other times I thought that though she may or may not have known she was lying, she was a sick person.

Sailing had changed over the years. There was no longer the excitement of going to some different port. More and more, shipping companies were concentrating on a few large ports filled with high-rise buildings. With the constant turmoil of construction going on, there were few vacant areas. There was a feeling of being walled in with blocks of cells. Maybe this is why the enjoyment came from walking; you had that freedom. You were not hurried to go someplace you really didn't want to go anyway. It was a release and a way of using up the time.

Sailing could have gone after the twenty years. No, that's not quite right, I couldn't have sailed much longer than twenty years anyway. The human pecking order, which everybody seemed to have been caught up in to some extent on one trip or another, was getting to me. True there were different degrees of style, sophistication, and coping. Curiously, before freighters stopped carrying passengers, the passengers could get caught up in this among themselves on long trips.

For some, there's never enough. They become squirrelly, not just hiding nuts away for the next winter but umpteen winters to come. Others will sail 'til they drop rather than face whatever on the beach. Clearly then it was time me to go in 1989, lacking two months of being sixty.

Seattle, WA
Jan. 12, 1990

Dear Liezl,

In September 1987 I agreed to send $200 each year. It was explained to Domingo, as well as put in writing, that a limitation had to be made because of other commitments.

In a letter dated May 10, 1988, Domingo asked for $300 to put on "a house for mortgage." September was still four months away, and it was $100 more than the yearly amount. But what the hell, it seemed like a good reason. So the money was sent, and your next due date for $200 was to have been in September 1989.

On Sept. 19, 1988, you wrote asking for $800 to $1,000 to open a small business and stated that I'd "promised" Domingo to provide for a small business. This at best was a half truth. Domingo was told 1) I couldn't sponsor him to go to the United States, but 2) if his sister living the U.S. could, I'd help out by paying his transportation to the U.S. and by sending you a small check each month until U.S. immigration and naturalization service gave him permission to work. If there was any talk about a small business, it was indecisive. No commitment was made. So it was not that I "promised' to send you the money that a thousand dollars was sent.

Both you and Domingo had explained that with the birth of Maria, you couldn't work as previously when you were enterprising enough to take in washing and do housework for various people. Your plan had merit, though there were some misgivings about earmarking money for you which should have gone to overseas families known a lot longer and who were in worse shape financially. But you have a disconcerting way of making a moral issue out of most requests. I hoped then by making the expenditure that it once and for all would keep you from hounding me for more money than agreed to per year.

Just in case you still didn't understand there were other problems, other obligations, and other moral dilemmas besides yours to deal with, I told you in clear terms not to ask for anymore money beyond the yearly $200 unless it were a medical emergency.

On March 13, 1989, you wrote you'd received my letter and that "I am very sorry if I distubed you to much. You are right this is our problem and please don't think we are oportunists...I hope you are not angry with us..." Then practically in the next breath (after just having acknowledged my irritation for being asked over and over for more money, you ask for 5,000 pesos for Domingo's placement pay (placement pay for what was not made clear). What was going on in your mind?

Each evening after work at night was spent writing letters. In fact, whole weekends were spent on correspondence. Just the thought of writing still another prim, little letter to repeat what had already been said several times made my stomach churn. Nor was there much relishment to dashing off a scathing note in the white-heat of anger. In any case, nothing seemed to get through to you. It seemed best then to stop writing for awhile in hopes that some sort of solution would appear.

Just before receiving your letter in early May telling that Domingo had died as the victim of a hold-up incident, I relented and sent $250 for Domingo's placement money. You mentioned almost nothing concerning the circumstances of Domingo's death. This at first was attributed to the reaction of a grieving widow who found it too painful to talk about, even though it was nearly a month after the death occurred. But certainly a grieving widow would have expressed a sense of personal loss beyond "My poor husband," such as "how I miss him night and day. Half of me has died inside. I'll never got over it." This omission was in all subsequent letters—the emphasis being on how hard it would be for the children to grow up without a father and how hard it was for you to support them when you were tired and sick.

The timing of Domingo's death (remember I'd stopped writing when you asked for placement money), the fact you were always coming up with reasons for more money, the sketchiness of the circumstances of death, and your lapse in expressing a deep, personal loss bothered me, though at the time these feelings were more at an unconscious level, crowded out by my wish to believe in you, the lulling integrity in the simplicity of your words, and the feeling of being caught up in a yet-Newer-Testament parable of a poor widow with three starving children who asked for help and was turned down.

Certainly I wanted to believe in you. There was no thought in mind—after taking on certain responsibilities in my thinking—to dodge out suddenly. But the questions began to surface. And like it or not, I found myself in a ridiculous position of both tentatively and genuinely sympathizing with you in your loss and sorrow but wanting proof nonetheless.

You were asked for four things: 1) the address of the American embassy in Manila, 2) a letter from your priest telling of the circumstances of Domingo's death, 3) a newspaper clipping, and 4) a copy of the death certificate.

After writing I realized it was just as easy for me to get the embassy's address at the public library as it would have been for you, but certainly you couldn't have helped but realize my intention of using the embassy for verification.

In your letter of 10 June 1989 you wrote: "Heres the death cetifecate you wanted from me I dont have the othe the priest nothing because here they just give a last pray. Unless you are rich Brent not all happen here in Philippine will print especialy small people. Brent I have not other entinsion to let you know about my husband I let you know because he was your friend when he was still alive he used to tell me what ever happen I wont stop to write to you." I had my doubts about what you'd written about newspaper items and the priest, but I wasn't in any position to argue the point. As I'd written previously to the U.S. embassy asking its assistance in helping me verify Domingo's death, I had left to me then its possible help and the death certificate.

The form used for the death certificate looked genuine enough. I'd no problem with that. What did bother me was that it was vague and incomplete. There was no entry under "Cause of Death" and "Disease or Condition Directly Leading to Death," such as stabbing or gunshot wounds. There was no entry under "other, significant conditions." The only information supplied by the certificate was 1) the date of death, 2) a specification that it was accidental, and 3) a check-mark that an autopsy was to be performed. There was no record supplied concerning the autopsy, or an addendum to the death certificate saying the autopsy had been done and giving the cause of death.

I wrote to Dr. Ernesto A. Lardizabal, who had signed the death certificate, at the hospital's address, asking for verification of his signature. No reply. I wrote to the administrator of the Sorsogon hospital on the death certificate, and it seemed as if no reply was going to come from there.

On 18 June 1989 a letter was written to your church's priest. I didn't know the address, of course, so asked you to deliver it. Your address was not included since it was figured you'd see him personally. He was requested to give his opinion only (not make a sworn statement) that you were indeed a poor and needy widow with three children. Whether the answer was "yes" or "no," I stated I'd send a check for $50 to him or a charity designated. My address was included on the letter, but no reply came.

In the interim, the American embassy in Manila had sent me a very careful letter documenting its efforts to schedule two appointments with you. The first call-in telegram you responded to by telephone and were "not very informative and claimed that she was in Bicol Province at the time the incident took place." The person handling the case stated that you were asked to bring in a certified copy of the death certificate and a police report. "She promised to see us the following day. She did not keep the appointment nor respond to a 2nd call-in telegram."

In a letter to you, I asked why you (knowing the verification was important to me) didn't supply the embassy with the information and why you failed to mention it to me in any subsequent letters. Your answer to this on 11 August 1989: "I dint tell you about the U.S. embasey because you dint asked Of course you are the Boss. I just wait what you well till me yes have talk person in U.S. embasy but maybe we do miss understanding because when I call there I used the telephone near the high way where the buses and jeeney where passing it too noise I kept I asking what she saying so she told me I have to see her in person after 4 days I went there because that I canot go out because Maria has sick that day after Maria got well I went to U.S embasy but the guard dint let me in I know I understand that guard because I canot go out everyday because every time I go out I have to bring Maria or just leave in my niegbhoor its very hards to me I made a letter I send it to U.S embassy but after two days the letter send back to me but I lost that letter If I dint lost that letter I will show you. About your letter in church I realy do what you want me to do I attemed to talk to the Priest two time but I realy dont have idea how to talk to that Priest so I drop your letter to the box inside the Church that box is for the charity now if you blame about this I to apolozise me. My only witness is only God that Im telling the trueth that Domingos dead He is in the hand now of God my children no more father. Thats why even embarrashing to asked from you I did because of my children."

You sent a copy of a baptismal data form (not a cer-tificate of baptism). I mailed this off by registered mail to the address given on the form. That is, "Roman Catholic Church, Santo Niño Parish, Tondo, Manila, Philippines." I hoped for verification, but after several notices by the post office in Manila, this was returned to me unclaimed.

No answer appeared to be forthcoming from the administrator of the Sorsogon hospital. So after much soul searching, I decided to give you the benefit of the doubt, having no further information. On July 17, I (a modern-day Cotton Mather, I might have added) sent you the first check for $80 each month. It was a nice feel-ing to finally lay all my doubts to rest.

Or so it seemed until early August when receiving the answer to a letter given up on. Dr. Arturo R. Perdigon, Department of Health, Regional Health Office No. 5, Provincial Health Office, Sorsogon, wrote as follows:

"We are sorry to inform you that the name of Domingo...does not appear in our hospital records and that no death certificate was issued by this office as claimed.

Further, "Dr. Ernesto A. Lardizabal" is nei-ther a member of this Hospital Medical Staff nor the Sorsogon Medical Association."

This was the only piece of information you had supplied, and it was unverifiable. It seemed incredible 1) a medical doctor would use an address of a hospital of which he wasn't a member, 2) if he were allowed to do so, he would not have sent a copy to the hospital for its records, and 3) the doctor was unknown to the hospital and the Sorsogon medical association.

I sent a copy of this letter (with no comment) addressed to Mr. Domingo and Liezl. Your reply on 25 August 1989:

> "I got your letter. I was surprice because of your address Mr. Domingo and Liezl. You know its look like you slap me because of that you think I am big lies Domingo have no record of the hospital because he dint reach the to hospital the death certifecate I got they only give that to me and they explain to me it has to print of hospital like me only grade VI. How would I know if theres wrong about it if Domingo still here I wont kill my self to work hard so that my children can eat three time a day even it raining I know that bad for my health because now I dont feel well. I have a heavy cough I feel I always have fever inside. You see even I feel like this continue my work all things are expensive now. You dont only know like a widow all responseble all mine sometime if it not only a sin to comit suiside I did it but I steel afraid of Juses and I am pity to my little Maria   I only live now just becuae of my kids."

But you are ignoring the fact, Liezl, that on the death certificate no cause of death was given. The square marked "autopsy" was checked. This meant Domingo's body had to go to a medical installation. Autopsies are not things performed in a doctor's office. Any installation large enough to provide an autopsy report would have used its own address, not that of a hospital of which it was not connected.

You didn't explain who "they" were who said since it was grade VI, it had "to be print of hospital," nor did you give their address. If you'd been duped yourself, you didn't express outrage, such as saying, "I'm going to the Tondo police to have this investigated."

218

Nor knowing I'd wanted someone at the U.S. embassy to talk to you and that this was important to me did you say that you'd make an appointment there which you fully intended to keep this time.

A copy of a letter, dated November 21, 1989, from the Republic of Phillipines, Professional Registration Commission, Manila, is enclosed. It states that "the name of Ernesto A. Lardizabal does not appear in the registry books of the Board of Medicine which contain the names of those duly authorized to practice medicine in the Philippines."

In a recent letter you wrote that you never thought I'd let you down. I'm afraid I don't look at it this way, but rather as your betrayal of a trust.

If—by some remote chance—what you've told me is true and indeed you and your children are starving, you have only yourself in the end to blame for it. You were asking me for help. It wasn't for me to write letter upon letter to try to document what you said. My desire to believe in you was a blind spot causing me to go a lot further than common sense called for. Over a period of several months you failed to supply me with one piece of credible proof concerning Domingo's "death," and you managed one way or another to circumvent all my efforts to find out about it. When explanations—often nothing more than froth—were given, they somehow were to be legitimized (and not to be questioned further) by your tenor: I am Liezl. I'm good. Because I'm good, I wouldn't tell lies. So that explains everything.

Sincerely,
Brent

Seattle, WA
17 Feb 1990

Dear Liezl,

When sending you a copy of Dr. Perdigon's letter of July 28, 1989, I didn't expect to hear from you. Most people, I suppose, caught lying and supplying a fraudulent document with intent to obtain money under circumstances that weren't true wouldn't have written again.

But this didn't stop or even slow you down. Following up with 3 or 4 more letters, you told lies upon lies. Notwithstanding that you'd named three of your children: Marco, Christopher, and Maria, you threw in the name of Jesus and God to make these lies more convincing:

Sept. 28, 1989

"what I told you was true."

Oct. 31, 1989

"God knows I didn't lie to you...What I tell you it all true Brent please try to thrust me to tell you I am a good person you can trust."

Dec. 11, 1989

"This all true I don't make any story to us only help from God knows all this."

Dec. 18, 1989

"It hurt to me to think that you left me just when I needed you most...God knows about this because I didn't lie to you."

I hadn't planned to write again, but you said in one letter that you never would have believed I would let you down, implying I had. It was if you'd glossed over some facts and either ignored or forgot others. So what I supposed to be my final letter of January 12, 1990, was to set the record straight, and to send a copy of the Philippine Professional Regulation Commission's document to show that you'd not really fooled me when you wrote:

"...the death certifecate I got they only give that to me and they explain to me it has to be print of hospital like me only grade VI."

I felt too that if you'd reviewed the sequence of events in my letter, you couldn't possibly write back. Overwhelming documentation showed you had painted yourself into a corner. But at that time when there was no other direction for you to go and you'd run out of lies to cover lies, I was to learn in your letter of February 5, 1990, that there was really a sterling integrity beneath it all: "I don't want to hurt because I know you trust him."

Teresita, I was nearing retirement when going to the Philippines in 1987. For 40 years I'd been in and out of the country and had made up my mind (before going there the last trip) to help somebody, even if only a small yearly amount. There was an old lady I always liked at

Alongapo and had pretty much decided upon her, but for one reason or another never made it ashore there one night.

Domingo, as a watchman, sat in the passageway outside the pantry where I worked. After meals he'd take the garbage down below, for which we'd give him (or anybody else doing the job) leftover food. He seemed like a solid, likable family man. But most important, his family, and a bank account, which he opened later, could be obtained.

He wrote neatly and precisely, and though it can't be pinned down to anything in particular, I had the impression he loved his wife and family. So it's still hard to believe that though you and he may have had a falling out, he would completely abandon his children for another woman. We might have talked a total of four hours in two trips. There was no special bond between us. How could there have been in such a short period? What was done for him or given him in small gifts of candy, chocolate, soap, toilet articles, band-aids, etc., was exactly what would have been done for anybody else I'd decided to help.

If there was any trust placed, it was later in you. You were the one who wrote all the letters after the first few. You were the one I thought I knew through your writing. A very simple, uneducated style from which was formed a very personal bias in your favor.

In some of your letters you sounded perturbed near the beginning, stating in so many words: If you had bothered to ask about us, you would hear that we are fine. The reason I seldom inquired about you was that you were always asking for money, and to ask about you or the children just gave you another opening. Then too, the children—like most kids—were very cute, but were they really yours? Or were they just some kids brought in to pose for a picture? Were you really Liezl Fuentes? Domingo's wife? As you began to spin the web of lies, you yourself began to plant the seeds of doubt.

To have been honest in the beginning would have saved you a lot of problems. To have come clean halfway through the period we'd written to each other would have saved our relationship. At nearly 61 years of age, I can't think of anything you or anybody else could tell me that would make me back off if told with truth, sincerity, and trust.

You were sent a letter to give to a priest who was asked to interview you and state—not swear—that in his opinion you were indeed a needy widow with 3 children. That would have been the time for you to say, "Father, would you help me? I have lied, but if you write a letter explaining the circumstances, maybe he will help me." And I would have.

Do you have any idea of the hours and hours of work and worry you caused me by lying? Not to mention the money sent, and the paperwork and trouble you caused other people, such as Dr. Perdigon, a Filipino lawyer, the U.S. embassy in Manila, the Philippine consulate in San Francisco, and the Philippine Professional Regulation Commission, to name a few. And you did it all for me. Gee, thanks a lot!

We all have flaws in reasoning, and I'm not certain, Liezl, just how much I've really got it together myself. But I would suspect that you have a few more than most. Whether it's pathological lying, or a lapse of conscience now and then, or bizarre logic (I betrayed your trust because I didn't want you to know he's betrayed your trust), or something else, I don't know. I am no doctor. But you should be able to understand that there's no way that I, living in the United States, can help you now. Could never be certain if you were telling the truth.

For whatever it's worth to you, I *very sincerely* wish you and your family good luck in life from here on out.

Brent

Manila
Undated: March ? 1990

I suppose to answere youre letter three weeks ago now But I canot consentrat because your last letter was hurting me so much if I done wrong or lie to you about Domingo its doesent mean I am that bad The picture that I send to you last Oct. 1989 that Maria, Marco, and Christopher, are real blood of Domingo he left us with nothing and I am the one who shoulder all the problem now I am look like biggar to him every time I asked support from him last january 1990 only I have strong enough to force him to give us his half of his salary because really I canot give my children all they need if I wont do this and also his maneger help me to force him here in the Philippines before you go to court first step is Barangay I went to Barangay in Pasay asked help from them how to get support to the father of my children first and second he did not appear our hearing because he refuse to give support to the children Maybe he afraid the woman but the maneger wont let him work until case wont finish he canot work so he has no choice he agreed to give us his half salary to the childrend if you want to know the reals score you can write to his office. And now he dint even visit the childred Any way I dont even want to see his face any more I realy heat him if get mad for what Ive done to you Im bigging you to foregive me I am very very sorry You can ot blame why I did this This is the second time he done to us first 81 he left with a woman also I foregive him 1985 After I give him another chance he traitor me again I foregive him for shake of the kids because he promese he will be a good father already but what he done again to me he is realy dead

You want to know about me Im not that bad you can write this person do you remeber Blanco family where I work before You meet him he is in California now I send to a birth cetifecate of Maria to show you that Marco (and) Christopher is real childrend of Domingo. The birthe certificate of the two boy is steel in city hall in Manila same address of Maria We got already before the school where Marco study They last if you want to check you can do it I reapet what Ive done to you please foregive me it up to you if you dont want to correspondence me if this my last letter to you anyway Thank you for every thing you done to us to my children Thank you very much I will never forget you just dont forget you have Maria here in the Philippines waiting Someone will help her because we realy need help espiceally now. You want to know about me you can write to [address given of person living in California].

Steel hoping
Liezl

Please send me back this
birth certefecated of Maria

Date of Born
Marco   November 8, 1980
Christopher   April 1, 1982
Theres is someone can teel about me This man was the
visitor of the one family that I work now. [Name and
address of person living at a different city in California.]

INVESTIGATION REPORT

I.   CASE NO.:
II.   SUBJECTS: DOMINGO FUENTES & FAMILY
III.   PERIOD COVERED: Feb. 17, 19, 22, 24, 26, 27, &
                          March 2 & 5, 1990
IV.   PURPOSE: Classified
V.   DETAILS:

On a mission to conduct an indepth and penetrating investigation aimed at unveiling/unmasking the truth regarding the baffling allegation of the Fuentes, particularly Liezl Fuentes's claim about her husband's tragic death in the hands of the holduppers and her statement in her recent letter wherein she confessed that her husband was very much alive, that her early claim was merely her invention out of her outrage when Domingo abandoned them, a handpicked team of veteran agents set out to their alleged address (original one), at No. _____ Street, Pasay City, Manila, Philippines.

Thereupon, it was learned and confirmed that the above residence was already demolished last August 1989. A certain Mrs. Lopez who claimed to be the owner of the said demolished house rented from her by the Fuentes couple stated that Liezl Fuentes really worked as a laundrywoman of Mrs. Molina, Pasay City, Philippines.

Subsequent investigation was carried out at Mrs. Molina's residence. In a face to face interview with Mrs. Molina, she averred that Domingo Fuentes is presently employed as a security guard in the Manila Port. Mrs. Molina could not give any coherent informations about the Fuentes couple. Surprisingly also, the operatives noticed that there was no mention of Domingo being killed in a hold-up incident through the interview with Mrs. Molina. Later, one of the agents interviewed Liezl Fuentes who at the time just finished doing some laundry. Through a good cover story, the agent gathered from Liezl that her partner Domingo Fuentes is presently working at Manila Port Metro Manila, Philippines with Tel. No. _____. Liezl disclosed to the agent that Domingo has been connected with the said security agency for almost 15 years now. She stated that Domingo is presently assigned at Manila Port as a security guard.

Finally, Liezl confided that her husband has a mistress whom she claims resides somewhere in Paco, Metro Manila. Liezl admitted she did not know the name of her husband's mistress. Earlier, Mrs. Molina also described Domingo Fuentes as a "playboy".

When asked where she is residing at present, Liezl divulged that she is now living at No. _____ Street, Tondo, Metro Manila, Philippines.

The following morning, the agents-on-case dashed off to address given in Metro Manila to establish whether the subject's wife, Liezl Fuentes, is indeed residing thereat as she claimed. Neighborhood sources disclosed that the subject Domingo is working as a security guard in an undisclosed company, but sometimes assigned at Manila Harbor. Neighborhood residents revealed that the subjects already separated from each other but that Domingo still visits his three children with Liezl from time to time. The above-given address presently occupied by Liezl Fuentes and her offsprings is reportedly owned by Liezl's sister. Sources disclosed that at present, Liezl is working somewhere in Pasay City but they professed to have no idea as to the nature of her work. Informants likewise disclosed that Liezl used to earn her living by working as a prostitute in a certain bar. However, lately Liezl seems to have retired from that dirty job because she now leaves her house at daytime. Sources recalled that neighborhood residents used to call her "Nightbird."

Inhabitants in this community similarly disclosed that Domingo has many wives. In fact, they divulged that Domingo is living at present with his other woman known only as Isabella, somewhere in Pandacan, Metro Manila. The agents on case could not tell or verify if the reported woman of Domingo in Paco, Metro Manila, and Isabella of Pandacan are one and the same because sources failed to give their exact address.

The agents-on-case proceeded to the office of Tondo,

Manila, in order to establish if the subject is really working thereat as a security officer. The first inquiry was made at the office of the Custom's Administrative Division who keeps the masterlist of all its employees. After examining the available records to date, it turned out that the name of the subject was not on their list. This is however understandable because Domingo is alleged to be working under a private security agency known as Protective Agency

Without further delay, the agents-on-case swiftly moved to the office of _____ System, the security agency in charge with the security measures. Personnel Officer Mr. Banoc revealed that the subject Domingo Fuentes is indeed one of the security guards manning the firm's properties and premises.

The agents-on-case also visited the office of the _____ which was also located in that area. Mr. Rodriguez of the _____ Police stated that he has been working there for so many years but he does not know the subject, Domingo. The same holds true when the agents inquired at other officials in the area. They claimed the subject's name does not ring a bell.

On the next leg of the investigation, the agents headed to pier _____ to take snapshots of the subject. The information that the subject is currently working here was gathered by the agents after their inquiry at the Manila _____ Office. Anyhow, upon arrival at Pier _____ the agents immediately positioned themselves in an obscure yet vantage location and patiently waited for the subject to come out or disembark from _____. While conducting a stake out, the agents noted some Manila officers taking their lunch at the guardhouse inside Pier _____ premises. A close look at the namepatch of the said security officers taking lunch revealed that none of them was the subject. Besides, the agents have already seen the photo of the subject so that they could have easily identified the subject had he been with that group. Meanwhile, discreet inquiries divulged that some of the Manila security guards assigned in the ship usually take their lunch on board and sometimes even stayed there overnight. Several hours had passed and still there was no visual contact with the subject. Eventually, the agents decided to venture into the vessel so as to catch a glimpse/take a snapshots of the subject, but then, they were denied entry by the guards manning the said vessel. The agents insisted but to no avail. The guards steadfastly refused the investigators to get aboard the vessel but through witty inquiries/conversation with the guards, the investigators gathered that the subject was at present living in Fort Bonifacio. The guards suggested to the investigators that the address of the subject at present can be had at the Manila _____ Agency Office. So subsequently, the investigators were able to trace and confirmed that the subject, Domingo is at present residing at No. _____ Street, Fort Bonifacio, Makati, Metro Manila.

Scarcely a couple of hours later, the investigators were already in the vicinity of _____ Street, Fort Bonifacio. Through prudent inquiries in the neighborhood, it was learned that the said residence is owned by a certain Mrs. Flores. Subsequent inquiries disclosed that the subject and his family, who used to rent at Mrs. Flores's house, already moved to a new address in _____ Pasig. They allegedly left _____ Street last January 1990.

On the next leg, the investigators went to Pasig, Metro Manila beside _____ in order to find out for themselves if the subject and his family are indeed residing in that area. Upon arrival, the agents immediately made a series of relentless inquiries. Thereafter, it was established that the subject, Domingo Fuentes, and his family live at No. _____ Avenue, _____, Pasig, Metro Manila. The agents (employing a good cover story) were able to talk with the subject personally. Through conversation with Domingo it was learned that the name of his wife is Isabella Aquino. According to him they have two sons, namely: Paco M. Fuentes and Jose W. Fuentes. It was known that Paco had once been employed also as a security guard at Manila _____ but that he was suspended recently following the discovery of his fake security license. Domingo said he recommended his eldest son, Paco, for employment at Manila _____ Agency. Meanwhile, Domingo stated that his other son, Jose, is presently studying in the province of Iloilo. The appearance of Domingo had somewhat changed because he is now sporting short hair. The agents theorized that

Isabella is the original wife of Domingo considering the ages of their sons.

To complete the last leg of the investigation, a new team of photo operatives was dispatched in the vicinity of No. _____, Pasig, Metro Manila. Upon arrival in the target area, the operatives immediately positioned themselves in an obscure yet vantage location. The minute they have positioned themselves entrenchly and safely in strategic locations, one of the operatives approached Domingo Fuentes's residence anew and engaged Domingo Fuentes in a conversation though employing a good cover story. It was at this point that these stolen shots were taken by the photo operatives.

NOTE:

The agents earlier tried to procure a certification of employment of Domingo from Manila _____ Agency, his present employer. The management of _____ Agency through its Proprietress, Mrs. Garcia agreed to give a certification of Domingo and instructed the agents to come back the following day. When the agents returned to Manila _____ Agency the next day to pick up the certification, Mrs. Garcia reneged her promise and declined to issue a certification for when they allegedly informed Domingo about it, the latter vigorously objected and begged them not to give any certification to anybody, unless the interested party see him first.

Further, Liezl Fuentes does not have a sari-sari store at present nor did she have in the past. This finding was based on the singular statement of the informants—after a thorough and discreet inquiries.

INVESTIGATION DIVISION

As a reader, you might have reached the same conclusion I had: There was no way I could give an unbiased assessment. The detective agency had been employed just before she wrote her letter "confessing all." Though the report was excellent, it didn't tell much about the inner workings of her mind. Although feeling sure about the conclusions reached, I still needed some corrobation from people who knew her through and through and from a psychiatrist or clinical psychologist who'd interviewed her. Both these sources weren't available.

The only tool was a shot in the dark. For I'd never thought it as much more than a parlor game with about as much credibility as divining the future from the entrails of an animal. I expected the report would be a maze of vague and qualified statements, such as, "It seems conceivable that on occasion she possibly could react in this way, provided the conditions might happen to be right." But no matter. I could still make use of it at the end in triumphant exposure (I refuse to comtemplate the psychological implications of this) by saying, "See I've documented facts showing exactly what this person is, and this pseudo-science doesn't even come close. So much for handwriting analysis!"

In this I was wrong. The graphoanalyst was told by mail that the subject was a woman living in the Philippines (two facts possibly deduced from the letters anyway) and that I wasn't romantically involved with her. The latter was given to prevent hopefully any watered-down report out of possible concern for my feelings. The samples submitted were those of early letters so that little could be determined from content about character. In perhaps three hours worth of work, the analyst had reached conclusions that had taken me hundreds of hours, my mind having been clouded with preconceptions and bias. Surprisingly each conclusion, often expressed more succinctly than I could have, was made with little or no equivocation and supported by documented facts unknown to the analyst.

Handwriting Analysis Report

The following explanation relates to the appraisal of integrity in this individual.

This writer is a victim of her emotions at any given moment. They register intensely as she reacts to every single thing that happens to her. They often override her common sense. She alternates between times of optimism and pessimistic down moods. This produces much anxiety within her and suggests she bears scars of considerable emotional pain.

Therefore, she is inconsistent and unpredictable in her dealings with others too. She very much cares about how she comes across. She wants to look good. So in order to put her best foot forward she employs coping mechanisms to protect a very fragile degree of internal self-worth. There is an emotional gap between herself and others even though she may appear very outgoing. It is difficult for her to trust people.

She is ambivalent about her goals; some are very unrealistic, others are quite practical. But she has will-power and initiative to go after what she wants if her desire stays consistent once she makes up her mind. Since she has an acquisitive nature she can be inclined toward extravagance. But like almost everything else about her, a consistent pattern is nonexistent.

Since her emotions rule her, her fears have a strong influence on her actions. She can be indecisive, inwardly self-conscious, and she often avoids commitment. Feelings of jealousy are evident and they cause her worry about competition. Although she can analyze matters when her emotions are in control, she more likely plays hunches guided by her feelings.

How does all this affect her integrity? In order to get what she wants and avoid any criticism that she may anticipate, she resorts to subterfuge. She does this by hedging, evading, and being secretive about her true intentions. She tends to rationalize her way out of things and/or she becomes calculating in some way in order to mask her true motives.

This is a complex personality. There are many times when she can be frank and sincere, but if she feels threatened she will probably fall back on her established way of maneuvering and manipulating through life. She is coping with the fears she has had for a long time.

Integrity is highly questionable in this personality.

Finally there remained the mystery of Domingo, who had run off, visiting his children only occasionally. All samples from him, as I recalled, were printed. As such, I didn't believe they would be of any use to the graphoanalyst, but she replied to an inquiry as follows:

Yes. It can be analyzed, even block printing style. It is not the ideal sample of course as cursive is always preferable. It is necessary to have original writing, not copies (that is always true for analysis purposes). They are returned to the owner, in this case you. Any cursive examples, however sparse, do help. A signature, envelope, anything if available.

Again the information given the analyst was limited, telling her only that Domingo was the husband of the woman whose handwriting she had previously reported on. I noted too that in his last letter he had used a small amount of cursive style in places, but generally more printing, and it seemed odd that he'd written two letters mainly in a Filipino dialect (which he knew I didn't read or understand), though English had been used in some places.

He is an emotionally responsive person with an internal rhythm that contributes to predictability of consistent reactions and behavior for the most. Because of the nature of his firm and rigid personality he is not an easy-going man, but rather he harbors much tension and anxiety. There is a great deal of push and pull going on inside. He tends to intellectualize his feelings and would rather not be bothered by emotional demands when they get to be too much. He wants to escape, to put some distance between himself and others, but at the same time he craves mothering for himself. All of this adds up to a complex person.

He has good thinking potential because he has a desire to learn and the mental equipment necessary to process information easily. He can pick up things quickly. His mind can get straight to the essentials of a matter as he thinks directly and is most likely to say things the same way unless his intuitive sense signals him not to.

When speaking his own language he is fluent and expressive. (English may be more of a challenge to him in clearly explaining himself verbally.)

Reductive to his thinking is his tendency to see things in either black or white. It drastically reduces his adaptability or flexibility. His lack of much of a conceptual and material imagination cuts down on his seeing possibilities and options that could provide alternate solutions for his problems. He tends to see things one way and lacks the ability to think up new ideas to work with. His mind does not expand.

Once he locks on he is very positive that it is the correct view. He can be blunt in stating it and then restating it. He can be quite tenacious (and occasionally stubborn). It is difficult for him to learn from past mistakes or recapture either the feeling of past successes or reintroduce the methods that produced them. Instead, each new thing must be started afresh unless he allows himself to be influenced by others' ideas, whether positive or negative in their possible application. He may yield to them if he analyzes the need to. Still he will trust his own intuition and feelings.

At times he fools himself by rationalizing away things he does not want to deal with. This is not a pronounced trait. His repressed emotions play more of a part in inhibiting clear thinking. Repression is a powerful influence when it is present within a person in more than a moderate degree. Those buried feelings do not actually surface to be dealt with in some healthy expression of them. They represent past hurts and scars of things that would be painful to acknowledge and openly express. But the inner tension must be released if the pressure gets to be too much. (And it always does.) How? As the adage goes, "Some people get ulcers, and some people give them."

This writer both gets and gives. The anxiety builds and becomes more frustrated and exacting. He seeks relief by wanting to get away but he cannot so it gets him down. If he speaks his mind in a critical way as directly as is natural for him, a more sensitive listener may be hurt. He is loyal to his views even though he does not intend to wound feelings. He sees himself as being realistic. He also can feel defiant toward authority.

At the same time he desires approval and so he cares how his actions are perceived by those he respects. He has a sense of pride and he will try to save face if anyone should question his motives. He will come up with a justifiable reason for his actions that makes sense to him.

His goals range from high-practical with an eye on the future to the more common tendency he has of not seeing very far beyond the day before him. He often underestimates himself. He is capable of better things. (Curiously, this trait often shows up in writers who are in a frozen situation such as in prison, in an institution, or under someone's authority.)

As stated before, he does not generate new ideas easily and he is constantly being influenced by past experiences although the memories do not provide lessons. So he may feel "stuck" much of the time. He has to look outside himself for a way out.

He is also of an acquisitive nature and he has willpower to get himself going. So he is not indolent. One of his decided strengths is his strong determination to see a matter through to completion. He tries to be optimistic as a way of coping but he worries too. He has a conscience so guilt can plague him also.

His desire to stay in someone's good graces produces ingratiating remarks. His usual frank expressions may be tainted with self-protective evasiveness and a general sidestepping of what he may be uncomfortable in revealing. It may be hidden to his consciousness as well. But he does go after what he wants. Does he want to make a good impression and protect his ego? Yes. Could this lead him into less than purely honest communication? Yes. You have reason for concern in regard to this individual.

I wish I could say shading the truth is uncommon but it is actually fairly usual to find it in some form in most everyone's handwriting. There is no justification for it, of course. However, totally honest and altruistic people are scarce, it would appear.

There is one thing evident here that also may be useful information in your future dealings with anyone. When there is a major difference between a readable script in the body of writing and an ornate and/or obscure signature it is reason for concern that the writer may be unconsciously attempting to hide his/her true self. In the case of this writer the script is clearly legible while the signature is not.

The exceptions are the signatures of those of celebrity status who may not need to be clear because they are recognized anyway or those who sign so often (e.g., executives) it is boring for them and they reduce it to a scrawl. Normally, if a person wants to communicate clearly the person will write everything clearly. (I would venture that your signature is in the same writing as anything else you would write as you are a person without pretensions.)

A note on his lapse into his own language. Two possible explanations. One—his emotions overrode his brain on a bad day. It's catching. He obviously trusts you as a friend. Or two—the conclusion that I first thought of as I looked at his English writing—which I did before I read your letter to me included in the same envelope. One of his letters formations having to do with thinking processes is made in a repetitively segmented form that would allude to a short circuit in his thinking pattern from time to time. There is also evidence of trauma in other aspects of his script.

The jury is out on a definitive answer as why he lapsed into his own language.

I do not know the available opportunities for a person in that country, nor for a person with already heavy responsibilities. So my suggestion may not be practical.

But if you have further communications with him I would suggest that you feed him some ideas for alternative employment options. He has a mind suited for work that involves problem-solving ability. He also can work alone and he can handle details quite well. Perhaps there is some education available that would equip him for better work and challenge him more.

The following are excerpts from a letter sent to me later by the same graphoanalyst:

Many thanks to you for your report on the background of the two subjects. I was sure there would be some intrigue involved but the actual facts surpassed my expectations. Yes, she is a sick woman with a distorted thinking process. Very little of what she does is on the up and up. He is more stable emotionally than she but he flunked my honesty test without question.

The analyses were not an invasion of their privacy since fraud was involved and if you cared to pursue matters on that basis you would have a case. However, I understand that is not your intention. There would be no problem with me should you wish to write about the analyses at a future time, even naming me if you did not use *their* names.

Just an observation concerning changes in character. It has been my experience that as one who becomes affected by trauma, or conversely something positive, the handwriting changes to reflect such.

I find myself developing empathy for many people I have done who felt the need to develop powerful defenses to get through the pressures of life. It is as though they feel if they are their true selves they might lose out.

I was surprised to receive a letter, postmarked November 9, 1990, from Domingo. Not surprising was that he had written again in Tagalog. My first reaction was to forget it, or even return the letter to him, saying that if he had anything he wanted me to know to put it in English and that he and his wife had troubled me enough already without looking around for a translator, especially when asking him previously not to write to me in Tagalog. But foolish and dangerous mistakes can be made by being bullheaded, so I paid a Philipino girl at the public library to make the below translation, which I left unanswered:

How are you doing? You're probably wondering why I haven't written for two years.

You know I couldn't take what Liezl did to me. That's why I being quiet. I know that you don't know. You're probably wondering how I'm doing right now.

You know, Brent, the money that you sent. She spent it and left me for another person, and now the kids, Marco, Christopher, and Maria, are with my parents at Bicol province. My parents are taking care of them and suing me for half of my salary at the village court. She's been doing this since February 1, 1990. And the other half is Liezl's.

I wrote to you to let you know why I haven't written and to let you know my condition.

I hope you understand my condition and write me back. I hope you're doing fine.

Your friend,
Domingo

There is in the end a black humor in the fact that they would try to fool me of the Feast of the Dead with a spurious death certificate. And the godchild Maria was born on the Eve of the Feralia 1988—maybe.

Have you a match, Mother Teresa of Albania,1 for the pile of wood we sit on? Soon we will be smoking more but enjoying it less. We're more to blame than those who deceived us. No, that's not right either. We tricked ourselves with the Savior Syndrome. If there's a psychopathia to scheming and lying, there's also that to too much understanding and tenderness, Jesus in extreme. Light the match, you "saint of the gutters," so your demon and mine can be united in death. Yours was greater, of course, but in the end my burden is too much to bear, having to decide in death whether mankind is to continue on. If not wanting to do it again, how could I in good conscience wish life on others even once? Or better yet, why not continue on—for the wrong reason, not love but revenge?

Chapter Twenty-eight

There might not have been work hanging fliers on the mornings people answered newspaper ads and showed up at 7:00 A.M. No matter that some, not having bus fare, trudged through the snow very early to get there. If they worked, the boss prided himself that he paid over the minimum wage, maybe twenty or twenty-five cents more per hour, once they were hauled to the area to be covered, which could be 9:30 or 10:00 A.M. He was doing this Christian duty by giving them work, and this just happened to coincide with business economics. Some days the same poor workers who fed his Christian ego and who hadn't yet come to know Christ—who changed his whole life—could on others feed his pecking-order pride: They were, with few exceptions, nothing but a damn bunch of riffraff, down-and-outers, misfits, ex-cons, dope addicts, drunks, and perverts. And if he used them one way one day and another the next, a few used him by ditching the circulars and getting drunk. The demise of Seattle and outlying communities will more likely come after a heavy rain when storm drains fail to function, rather than the eruption of Mt. St. Helens or an earthquake.

Fliers bring reassurance to communities that though their mores and values may have changed through the years, there still remain three constants they can always depend upon: death, taxes, and junk mail. The hanger does much traveling and walking and is, in effect, acting as a messenger, going places in the rain, sleet, and snow that even the postman doesn't, as it's illegal to put fliers in mailboxes.[102-A]

Like all jobs, it has it ups and downs, climbing so many steps sometimes that the air seems rarified. You almost need an OBA, as you look in vain for a post or something to hang the flier on rather than continuing to the top. Certainly the other hangers you came out with have gotten rid of ten apiece while you're fiddling around with this one. You wonder why you didn't have the sense to skip this house, why you had to be so damned obsessive compulsive.

There are, of course, a few laughs along the way, the camaraderie of the gypsies who, finding front doors locked, sneak in by back entrances left open to cover fifty doorknobs with circulars. Three signs recalled off-hand: BEWARE OF THE ATTACK CAT and CHILDREN WHO COME HERE WILL BE GIVEN TO THE GYPSIES. A doormat: REMOVE YOUR CLOTHING BEFORE ENTERING.

Once in awhile you might come to a place that's scary, hidden away by old trees, vines, and bushes; left unattended for years; and which can be reached only by a crooked and winding path of stones laid before the turn of the century in the light of the full moon at the witching hour amid bongo drums and voodoo rites. When finally reaching the decaying structure, at one time a fine mansion, you see paint peeling and moss up its sides. Sumpun rong. The sun don't shine through. There's an unnerving quiet, no birds, not a breath of fresh air.

Instinct tells you to flee, that nobody save the Addams family, renting a room out to the Green River murderer, could possibly live within. So as not to alert them, you step gingerly on the rickety, wooden steps, a mine field of banshee squeaks and groans. Quickly ducking to avoid the cobwebs, you make enough noise to raise the dead. The fact that a casket isn't heard creaking open or anything else is reassurance that even though the area is shielded from the sun, it is, after all, still daylight.

You see the handle of the door and fumble placing the flier in it while wondering if the door will suddenly fly open and something snatch you in. Damn, the flier falls. You've got to put it back in again. Sumpun rong with this place, you just know it. You are also at odds with your self, experiencing a strange attraction, a curiosity or perhaps a feeling to be done with it: "I'm home."

The flier is hung. What craziness! It was just a piece of cake. Stale and moldy, yes, but nothing more. But as you turn to go away, your heart skips a beat. There beneath you, on the bottom steps, is a mammoth dog, as big as a Shetland pony, a foreign breed never seen before, probably from Transylvania. Somewhere in the back of your mind the thought that someone said, "Don't show fear." But how do you not show fear when it's oozing out your pores? He smells it while slavering and growling, teeth bared, ears lying flat. Had you failed to recognize these signs of hatred, you have only to look into his strange, pale-blue, fathomless eyes to know yours are brown.

Hopefully the Addams family will now open their inner-sanctum door and call off the werewolf, but the power of prayer means nothing to these people. Your swift elimination will come in two ways. Then as Popeye remembers his spinach and Billy Batson his Shazam,[102-B] you remember the rock in your pocket—not that you'll be foolish enough to threaten this mother with it. But if he's certain to have a steak dinner, at least you'll get a Wimpy hamburger.

"Nice doggy, I'm not going to hurt you!" Please remember that.

Slowly you edge down the other side of the steps in front of him while he still growls, snarls, and slobbers. Inanely you wonder: *Can werewolfs get rabies?* No way's he gonna make it easy. He gives mixed signals, wagging his tail while telling you in so many other ways not to believe it. You inch past him, walking backwards trying to maneuver what's behind while facing him. For each step in retreat, he advances one, dogging you all the way.

When finally you make it out of there, the driver is sitting in the truck and pissed off he had to wait.

"What the hell took you so long?"

No matter. All's not lost. If working by each piece delivered, you made three cents before taxes. The only things certain in life are death, taxes, and junk mail.

A peculiar thing happened once when delivering circulars. The boss driving us around saw it too and was amazed. Though a dog living in an area will sometimes pal up with a door-hanger for several blocks, it's not a frequent occurrence. But cats won't, except maybe a kitten who might follow a short distance for a straight shot. A grown cat, however, won't follow a stranger, especially when it's neither been fed nor petted.

On this day, a pure-white cat was outside a door to a house. I spoke only, and it began to follow, though no encouragement was given. If this had been straight across lawns, I mightn't have thought much about it, but the landscaping with plants and walls between the homes was such that would have made it difficult. Each house was left, going down steps, along a walkway toward the street, then down the sidewalk to the next house. The cat came all the way up the steps to each door, and then back down again for six or seven homes until we reached the end of the block. It then followed me across the street where the truck was parked to take us to another area. Had the cat not belonged to someone and had I lived in a place allowing animals, I'd have taken it. At the time, I realized it was an odd happening, nothing more. But now, it might have been "just one of those things" or related to the mysticism.[103-A]

Some days I'd pick up a stone to have ready, if necessary, for most dogs, when giving chase, will turn tail and run if threatened. Then on weekends when not working, I'd remove the stones and usually forget to take them with me the following Monday morning. Slowly a heap of twenty or so began collecting in the room. A visiting friend (you gotta take your friends as you find them), wearing a "Baby Jesus" cap to hide his baldness, was clearly uneasy about the heap, seeing in it a hidden pagan rite, though he himself never once blinked about bilking our welfare system. Besides, it always seemed strange to me to see Baby Jesus's bare butt next to his bald head. But anyway at the time I'd given no meaning to the rocks, either pagan or otherwise. And so to expose his foolishness, I vaguely recalled, then looked up to quote him, the following:

And if you make me an altar of stones, you shall not build it of hewn stones; for if you wield your tool upon it you profane it. And you shall not go up by steps to my altar, that your nakedness be not exposed on it (Ex 20:25,25).

When the manager put out a notice that the rooms were to be checked on a certain day for repairs, I decided to get rid of the rocks. If not, he'd be discussing the weird tenant who had a pile of rocks. They weren't geological samples. What'd he do with 'em? Light a candle at midnight, strip down naked, and dance around them mumbling incantations? Pockets loaded, I carried others in hands to the alley. Those not having room for were put out of sight in the closet.

Occasionally when not working, I'd do calisthenics in *Myrtle* Edwards' Park,[103-B] a flat area near Elliott Bay, a place where city *fireworks* are kindled on the *fourth* of July, the seventh month. It has several large, prominent rocks, hauled in by man, and one usually can see walkers, joggers (runners), and bicycle riders who are twentieth centry refinements of the ancient charioteers.

It seemed easier to turn away from all of this toward the railroad tracks than to see them watching as they passed. This was my thinking. Doing the exercises...slowly becoming more aware of the railroad car directly in front...some sort of attraction. What? I soon began to associate the encircled mountain goat of the Great Northern Railway with healing and protection. Though the main purpose of going to the park was exercise, there'd always be disappointment if the car was gone. Then one day I realized that by looking through the gaps in bushes, I could see across the railroad tracks to a stationary red caboose with a mountain goat on it.

The rocks were rediscovered in the closet. Only then was an association made to Hermes, the Rambearer; it seeming appropriate the number was four. To this was added a brownish-orange pebble found years before. Now the five rocks—though not rare, beautiful, or samples—were as free from guile as if winnowed by an unknown hand. This doesn't often happen with us humans in this over-serious, calculating world, whose animals must have been put here to help us break its spell. The faithful dog joyfully wags its tail while proudly taking its master for a walk, a cat, showing affection, rubs against my leg, the egomania-cawal crow pulls inward thoughts out.

Chapter Twenty-nine

Lola Anne Chichester (August 2, 1923–June 8, 1978) had two small children, Stan and Tina, from a previous marriage when she married Warren. She was a likable, busy, hard-working woman (probably a contributing factor to her later ravaging stroke) who still managed to find time over the years to write in many letters the goings-on of ranch and school, where she taught with good humor and heart, laughing as much at herself as others. If ever anybody really did know Warren, it was she. Once she wrote that had she searched the world over she was sure she'd never have found a better man than my brother.

But if my father wasn't a spontaneous person, Warren was even less so, being rarely, if at all, demonstrative when I saw him as a youth or in adulthood. This doesn't mean he wasn't a good-hearted person, for he was that. But he often looked at things with the practicality of a hard-working rancher. Others might have seen him differently.

When in the service one year, I'd brought three purebred German shepherd puppies to the ranches for Christmas. Since the children were small, the puppies seemed like a good idea. Warren was riding a horse when I met him in the car, after driving all night.

"Hi, Warren!"

"Hi!" I then explained about the three puppies, one for each ranch. Anita would have first choice since she lived alone. Without humor, he said, "What do I need with another animal?"

Surprise. "Well that's all right, Warren, these are good animals. I'll take yours back. There'll be no trouble selling it."

He apparently had second thoughts and decided he would take it after all. When the dog died a few years later, Lola wrote that the whole family was broken up about it.

Warren was also a very private person and hard to know. Yet he had stuck up for me at times and insisted on pouring in some oil into my car and filling the gas tank before I left.

After suffering months from inoperable stomach cancer, he died in 1989 (SY):

Warren Weston Chichester
September 29, 1922–October 11, 1989
–A beautiful tombstone showing four or five head of cattle.

That I didn't attend Warren's funeral wasn't out of disrespect but for what was felt to be an overriding reason. Stan, my nephew, later sent me eighteen pictures of graves of family and relatives in the old country cemetery. No connection—psychopompous or otherwise—had been made before December 1990. So why had he sent them? Was he trying to shame me for not having gone? No way. He'd kept me informed of everything that happened from the beginning of the illness to the end. But the reason escaped me. Then some time later, a conversation came to mind. I told him that at one time when very young of wanting to be adopted. It seemed that though I was a part of each family I wasn't. Nothing was known about my grandparents. In fact, I couldn't recall their names and not much more about some of the other relatives and forebears.

Stan commented that as a child he himself had felt at times like an outsider. He was always referred to as "that boy of Lola's," and that it would have meant a lot to him to have the Chichester name. But as he grew older, married, and had children, it didn't seem that important. He had meant, of course, in sending the pictures to reenforce a feeling of roots and heritage.

Since Stan had this feeling when a child, it might also have been Tina's. An adoption would have made it easier for them. Why didn't Warren do this? Who knows? For whatever reason, it's fair to say he had no burning urge to do so, or he would have asked the children about it and done so if they'd wanted. Possibly he didn't have his hand on their pulse, or at least not on Stan's. He wasn't sensitive to a need. Maybe too he might have felt that litigation would have drawn him away to Bridgeport or wherever at inconvenient times for ranching. Still another possibility: He or my father either knew or suspected more than they let on and thought they could change fate by not acknowledging the number four. The failure to adopt, however, couldn't change this. Stan married Judy and became a very successful and wealthy merchant (Hermes, god of wealth and merchants), a manufacturer of electric circuit boards. Lowell was still a fourth child, and his interests would branch out from CPA work. Unaware either of Hermes or my conviction, he would write concerning casino (*gambling*)-hotel-restaurant part interest as follows: "On the fourth corner is the cemetery which should not provide very much commercial competition."

As stated, not until a year after Stan sent the pictures did the knowledge present itself that in ancient Greece, Hermes conducted the souls to Hades, that he was keeper of the graves, and that people spoke to the herm at the grave to talk to the spirits of the dead. It seems reasonable to assume, therefore, that if they believed this, they might also believe that the spirits of the dead could talk to them through the herm. Could there be then a message in these pictures beyond the obvious?

The preceding picture shows part of the mountain behind. It's exactly as remembered from 1938 and again in 1962, as if only a small number of trees, no more no less, had been allotted for each mountain. They wouldn't grow much, if at all, and nothing much would grow around them. This seemed so typical of the area and that traveling toward Gardnerville, Nevada. It was like everything was caught in a period of time so that anybody returning—even centuries later—would have no trouble finding it.

In some pictures the wrought-iron fence showed up, while in others it didn't. This is easily explained by the angle of the camera. But in only two pictures, Helen's grave and that of my mother's, were there four heraldic emblems behind each tombstone. These suggested the winged shepherd's staff, or a staff with a fleur-de-lis (Iris) above it.

There were only two pictures remaining of my mother and Helen together in 1917. The one in sepia showed her holding Helen, and the other in black and white was nearly the same with sheep very close, as if in some nativity scene (see page 347). Could the sheep have meant anything? If so, what was known about sheep?

Hermes, the god of shepherds, is sometimes depicted with a sheep (or ram) under his arm or over his shoulder. When first going to the ranch in the late 1930s, I was led to believe that sheep were something just short of an anathema. No self-respecting cattleman would ever consider having them around, for they ruined the grazing area for cattle and horses. Some say this is a myth, that sheep are more delicate eaters than either. Others hold to the belief that sheep can eat after cattle and horses, but cattle and horses can't eat after sheep.

Many years later, the fact would surface that my father had been a "wool grower" or sheepherder of sorts when Helen was born in 1917. Sometime after his death, he gave up sheep for cattle. This wasn't unusual in itself; for in the history of Nevada, sheepherders and cowboys sometimes switched back and forth as the market prices in one or the other rose and fell. Yet sheepherders are sometimes superstitious people. Could there have been anything more to this than just changing a market? My mother's death, caused by respiratory diseases and childbirth, came in 1929, followed by Ralph's in 1939, or roughly the year the Great Depression ended. Then there was also Grandmother Elizabeth's death at the age of eighty-four in 1934 in a fire with suspicion of violence. She was born on the *fourth* of February and would die on the seventeenth of February (4 + 17 = 21), four days from my fifth birthday and Ralph's fifteenth.

Terri, Leslie's wife, had mentioned in her letters that both Lindsay and Kellie were raising sheep—as well as other animals—in their 4-H (head, heart, hands, and health—or was it really 4-Hermes?) activities. What surprised me at the time wasn't so much they were winning ribbons but that 1) sheep had come to the ranch and 2) the girls appeared so full of mirth in the pictures she forwarded. It was as if a curse had been broken, and they were saying, "None of this dour Scots and English stiffness for us; we intend to be happy in life."

Excerpts from Terri's letter postmarked March 1, 1991:

> I received your letter about the sheep question. To start with I was born and raised around sheep. My

parents had an alfalfa and sheep ranch. We usually had between 200–300 sheep all the time. I would say that it was good luck. My parents made a good living at ranching. I, myself, took lambs in 4-H for 10 years. From selling them, this helped put me through college and still had some left when Les and I got married. Which is now long gone.

In 1986 when the girls got into the car accident with the babysitter, we didn't have sheep then. We didn't get any sheep until 1988. Lindsay turned 9 years old and was old enough to join 4-H. After she sold her first lamb project, she bought 8 ewes and a ram. Now we have 23 ewes and a new ram. Our first ram turned mean, so we got rid of him before he hurt someone. I don't know who was more ornery, the ram or the dog. We have 2 ewes left to lamb. We've lost a couple of lambs this year, but it is to be expected. I would say all in all that sheep are good luck. If you talked to a cattleman, he would tell you different. They don't appreciate them. Les only likes them in white paper in the freezer. He complains a lot about them, but deep down I think he thinks they are O.K. He'd probably never admit it.

Through the years, Rhoda, most of all; Bobby next; then Andy; and Bob (to a less extent) had been plagued with asthma, a wind-god's disease. The cause of this probably was due to pesticides or wood-burning emissions. But even though there might be a scientific explanation for this does not preclude that Hermes had a hand in it. A god can do what he wants how he wants. Sometime after they stopped, or nearly stopped, raising cattle (so it seemed to me) and began to raise sheep, they had less asthma attacks. Certainly they seemed less severe, especially for Rhoda.

Nothing can be proved one way or another, but to broach such an explanation to dyed-in-the-wool Christians, relatives or not, is to have them politely ignore it as if insanity will somehow disappear by pretending it doesn't exist. So I was unable to get any particulars concerning this until 1992.[104]

What stuck out most on examining the picture Stan sent of my mother's grave was that the year of her birth had been given as 1889. This did not "feel" right. It should have been 1888, making her forty (like my father) at my birth. Now I'm not yet foolish enough to believe the world somehow centers around me or that it will pause even a fraction of a second on my death. Still if we can't believe what's chiseled in *stone that we can see* from a period, what can we believe? Had relatives been told I thought the date was wrong because it didn't fit a pattern or "feel right," one certainly would have bristled, "I'm sure your father knew more about what was happening at that time than you do, or think you do, Brent."

The tombstone date of 1889, furthermore, was supported by information on Ralph's birth certificate, which gave her age in years at her last birthday as twenty-nine, while that of my fathers was thirty. Later I would see that information on my mother's death certificate said she was born on August 22, 1888. I might have discounted this had not the informant been Aunt Nell, who had an excellent mind and usually was accurate in what she said. Besides, Aunt Nell (born in a Mercury period) was the second of five daughters and wasn't likely to have forgotten the date.

My father, on the other hand, had gone to Oakland Polytechnic Business College. He was certainly average or above in intelligence. It seemed likely that if the information Aunt Nell supplied was correct, my father would have heard at least once from my mother in twelve-thirteen years of marriage.

"Do it my way."

"Why do it your way?"

"Because I was born nineteen days before you and so am older and wiser."

Surely he wouldn't have forgotten this if true.

As I've remarked previously, Weller didn't have birth records of a lot of people born there at that time or before, including my mother's, and any relative who might have been able to clear this up had died. I'd reached an impasse, or so it seemed.

Then it occurred that Stanford would have records off someplace in its archives. I wrote there giving my relationship and reason for wanting the information but wasn't certain that the address was correct. A book had said Stanford; I thought it was Palo Alto. When no answer seemed forthcoming, another letter was sent off. This time by certified mail. I'd no sooner done that than a transcript came in response to the first letter. Her middle name was spelled Mae, which can still be a form of May. She changed the spelling to May in later life, probably without going to court, as Maia somehow had taken the credit for May from the other Roman goddess; i.e., it was an echo of an assumption.

As a student Frances majored in economy and history. Among the courses she took were Roman language, Latin, and Greek (tragedy). She began her studies in 1908, having taught in Montana earlier that year, and received her B.A. in 1912, at which time both her mother and father were living in Maricopa, California.

She then registered in graduate standing at Stanford and completed a few courses, majoring in history. Some time following that (according to an article in 1929 possibly from the *Yerington Times* or the *Reno Gazette*), she went to Columbia University for post-graduate work, after which she came to Coleville, California, to teach in 1916. Here she met my father and married him also in 1916. They moved to Smith Valley in 1920. The sequence of events: 1908, 1912, 1914, 1916, and 1920.

As to her life before college, a newspaper clipping says only that she and her family went to California in 1908.[105] It's known from other sources that they lived for some time in Montana, where Nellie, Edith, and Dollena were born. The Stanford transcript indicated that they had also lived for a time in Washington, for under "where prepared for university" there is an entry "Snohomish (Wash) HS," and this was later born out by a high school attendance record.[106]

The few years before her death, she had been a Smith Valley correspondent for the *Yerington Times* and *Reno Gazette* and was described as "painstaking and most energetic" in her work. She also wrote some short stories, a few of which I read before they burned in the cabin, along with her college and university notebooks, in the early 1940s. And somewhere there's a picture she painted of herself on a horse; she had a small talent.

But to get back to the date of birth. Stanford records show clearly that she was born in Weller, North Dakota, on August 22, 1888. A letter from the associate registrar at Columbia University, dated August 22, coincidentally, 1991, stated she had "listed her date of birth as '1888,' her place of birth as 'Weller, North Dakota.'" This bears out the date Aunt Nell had given and is in agreement with her age on the Snohomish Washington High School attendance record.

So there remained two questions in my mind: First, why in December 1990, when having given up the idea of writing and planned to retire for hiking, exploring, and rock hunting in southern Nevada, did I come across the word *feral*, which set off a chain of events? Second, why when no one after me likely would have puzzled over the date did I so late in life? The two birth years of 1888 are multiples of 4. The figure of 8 is one of the symbols of Thoth.[107-A]

Curiously too had the month and day of her birth been inscribed on the tombstone it would have been noticed sooner that both my mother and my stepmother, Anita, were born on August 22, though not in the same year. Where the anniversary of their births preceded the Mercury period by one day, Ralph's death on August 21 preceded their birthday anniversaries by one day (2122). My father, who was born in a Mercury period, died on February 22,[107-B] the day following what would have been the month and day of birth for both Ralph and me (2122). In Ralph's case, there was a third 2122 linking his death to that of his fathers (August 21 and February 22 respectively).

Wovoka, the so-called Paiute Messiah, was born in 1856, either in Mason or Smith Valley, the county seat of both now being Yerington, Nevada. "It's possible that early biographers didn't clearly distinguish between the two valleys," wrote David Moore, editor of *Nevada* magazine. Each year in Yerington, an annual "Spirit of Wovoka Days Powwow," organized by the Mason Valley *Wind* Spirit Dancers, takes place.

Wovoka, who was the son of White Indian, a medicine man, taught *peace*. He wore a *broad-brimmed* hat and was a *trickster*, freely admitting that some things credited to him were just jokes and not to be taken seriously. The Ghost Dance, he originated, however, wasn't one of these, and it spread to some other Indian tribes throughout the nation. The Sioux danced it at Wounded Knee, and it was performed at Chief Left Hand's Oklahoma camp in 1892. Whatever the purpose of the Ghost Dance and the fact that the resurrection Wovoka predicted for 1891 never came isn't important for my purposes. What is is that the Ghost Dance relates to the dead, as do the willow and Parentalia. When being taught, it was performed four consecutive nights and one day in a clearing surrounded by "bush shelters" and *willow*[108] sticks to hold up the tents of visitors.

Wovoka said, "The Dead in heaven were dancing, gambling, playing ball, and having all kinds of sports." This is interesting in that in very early times in ancient Greece, it's probable that great games were held at funerals to pay homage to the dead, and in later times, sports were held at funerals to dispel depression.

In *1888* (the year my father was born in Coleville, not too far from Topaz, and my mother born in the Dakota Territory) a great drought came to the area; this lasted into 1889. An officer of the Walker River Indian Reservation appealed to Wovoka to bring rain. Wovoka told him to go and that on the morning of the third day, there would be rain. As predicted, it came, flooding the banks of the Walker River.

Wovoka died on September 29, 1932. He apparently was in the Yerington area or nearby when I was born.

Book I
Notes

1-A. Wayfarers, walkers, feet, footprints. At the Last Supper, Jesus washed his disciples' feet. In the Western Church (not in Rome) custom grew from at least the fourth century to wash the neophyte's feet immediately after the act of Baptism. This was discontinued in the Middle Ages. *New Catholic Encyclopedia*, Vol XIV, Washington, D.C.: the Catholic University of America, 1967. On Holy Thursday in the Cathedral of St. John Lateran, John Paul II washes and kisses the feet of twelve priests. Twelve is the transposition of 21. Christ's legs were supposed to have been broken, but they weren't.

1-B. For this, I'm primly upbraided, "How can Christ steal back that which belongs to him?" "Iz zat so?" Still I stand by what's said. It appears too that Christian images of Jesus as the Logos were "borrowed" from Hermes the Logos and that the cross which Christians trace originated as one of the crosses of the fourfold god. Barbara G. Walker, *The Woman's Encyclopedia of Myths and Secrets*, San Francisco: Harper and Row Pub., 1983. The gods or gods of religion, like automobiles, have undergone changes by man to make them more powerful, more dependable, more appealing, etc.

1-C. The dates vary from book to book. Some say August 21, 1911; others say August 22, 1911. August 21 is used since that's the date Vincenzo's trial president used in addressing him:

> Perugia, on the twenty-first of August, 1911, a painting by
> Leonardo de Vinci portraying the Gioconda was stolen from
> the Louvre Museum in Paris. You are the confessed perpe-
> trator of that crime. Briefly relate what occurred.

Hugh McLeave, *Rogues in the Gallery: The Modern Plague of Art Thefts*, D.R. Godine, (Boston: 1981), Seymour Reit, *The Day They Stole the Mona Lisa*, Summit Books (New York: 1981).

1-D. Carrara brings to mind Caristia, and in a sense the Pietá encompasses this and the Parentalia.

1-E. Petra = rock. Consider along with this:

1) The Black *Stone* housed in the Kaaba and reputedly given to Ishmael by the angel Gabriel.

2) The Dome of the *Rock*, sacred both to Jews and Muslims. Hebrews believe it was from here that Abraham prepared to sacrifice Isaac, while Muslims hold it was where Mohammed ascended into heaven. Since Abraham previously had pleaded for Sodom and Gomorrha, some wonder why he hadn't done as much for his own son, or at least offer himself as an alternative. Midrash, a genre of rabbinic literature, states that Abraham's seeming obedience at Moriah to God's command caused Sarah's death and alienated Isaac from him forever. "God Tests Abraham—Abraham Tests God," *Bible Review*, Oct/Nov 1993, Lippman, Bodoff.

A nicely written and perceptive editorial titled "Night Thoughts on the 'Pietá'" by Richard Atcheson can be found in *Saturday Review*, June 17, 1972.

One of the names given Thoth was "Beautiful of Night." The *thot* occurs that an insane person might well look upon those about him—not considered insane—as thieves. And who is to say overall, in a very exacting, fine judgment and reckoning, he is wrong?

1-EE.   No one knows for sure that the bones of St. Peter lie beneath the Basilica. But according to James Fallows (article titled "Vatican City," *National Geographic*, December 1985), "If a plumb line were dropped from the dome of St. Peter's...it would come to rest within mere inches of...someone's grave." Mentioned also are the Red Wall, an Egyptian obelisk, eighty-two feet high, and the gathering of honey at St. Pius X Preseminary.

Myriad books suggest that sports were offered as a relief from depression in long funerals at periods in ancient Greece. In Rome, sports—independent of funerals—became death for entertainment. Why the fascination with violence and death? Explanations of bits and pieces are offered: boredom, amusement, and that the fare depended on the whims of the emperors and the spectators. Yet there were good and bad people before Christianity as there are good and bad people now. In the final analysis, the collective insanity then—and more recently in Nazi Germany—can't be understood by bits and pieces of explanations. My belief is that Parentalia forces, perhaps because of neglect, caused much of this, or perhaps we cause much of this through our own negligence. Of course as with all things mystical, including religion, nothing can be proved. Still, doesn't it seem odd that the largest church in the world was built over a graveyard? It could have been called the Parentalia Church, the Parent Church, the Progenitor Church: It was called, instead, St. Peter's. The greatest battle ever fought on the American continent was at Gettysburg, Pennsylvania. The village cemetery, called Cemetery Ridge, was the center of the union line. Later land would be bought there for a permanent military cemetery. (*Encyclopedia Americana* from article titled "Gettysburg Address" by William Hanchett.)

1-F.   Given:

1) Mary Custis, the wife of Robert E. Lee, was a descendent of *Martha Washington*.

2) Descendents of Martha Washington wouldn't allow the body of George Washington, who had died on Mausoleum Day, to be transferred from Mt. Vernon to the national mausoleum which had been made for him.

3) President Zachary Taylor, who looked up to George Washington as a model, became a peer-sacrifice president, after circling the monument.

It's not surprising to read that Zachary Taylor didn't want Sarah Knox Taylor, his daughter, to marry Jefferson Davis. Only with reluctant consent did Taylor finally agree to that. The couple married in 1835 and settled on a one thousand-acre cotton plantation, complete with hot and cold running slaves, in the Mississippi delta. While there, both contracted malaria. Sarah was dead from it in less than three months after her marriage. Some say Febris, the ancient Roman deity of fevers, caused malaria or could avert fevers. Eleven-year-old William Wallace Lincoln died of "bilious" fever in the White House on Feralia Eve 1862. Februa, a Roman goddess of purification. Februus, the name for Faunus, as a god of impregnation. The name Februus is also associated with Dis Pater, as a god of the dead. Marjorie Leach, *Guide to the Gods*, (Santa Barbara: ABC-CLIO, 1992). Februus is regarded as an underworld god. Thoth was believed to be the author of the *Book of the Dead*. On *February 14* (45), 1849, electoral votes were tabulated by Congress, making Zachary Taylor the next president. Ulysses blinded a cyclops. Jefferson Davis was blind in one eye.

1-FF.   *The Dedication of the Washington National Monument*, (Washington: Government Printing Office, 1885) February 22 charter date given; Federal Writers' Project, *Washington: City and Capital*, (Washington: U.S. Government Printing Office, 1937).

1-FFF.A.   Cermak shot ten years later. Both he and Carter born on first Lemuria Day. Carter believed he himself born in 1873.

1-FFFF.   *December 14*, 1799. On December 12, Washington inspected his farm on horseback. It was a cold day with rain and snow, falling alternately. On December 13, he complained of a sore throat. On December 14, his breathing was labored. He was bled (sacrifice) *four* times. Sometime after 10:00 P.M. on that night he died. If the last month of the year used to be February, then December 12 is equivalent to February 12 (when Lincoln would be born in 1809). December 13 equals February 13, the beginning of the Parentalia, and December 14 (when Nostradamus was born in 1503), February 14, St. Valentine's Day, the first full day of the Parentalia. Washington, born February 22 (New Style), was a Pisces (the twelfth sign of the zodiac; February is guarded by Neptune), suggesting water. A string connects two fish (one going one way, the other in the other direction). This is essentially the same as the Parentalia-Caristia, 2122. Neptune's Fountain lies before the Library of Congress. Keep in mind the name of Congressional Librarian George Watterston, spelled "Waterstone" by his father. The belief in the Di Manes was thought by the Catholic Church to be not only ignorance but a foolish superstition. The Church would get rid of the Di Manes by moving February 21 to May 13, and May 13 to November 1. But the Di Manes countered by increasing their own power by three. Similarly February was moved on the calendar and December became the last month, investing December along with February. December 21, the date of final entombment of Osiris, is tantamount to the Feralia, the Feast of the Dead. December 21 is Forefather's Day (celebrating the landing of 103 *Mayflower* pilgrims at New Plymouth), and it is the date of birth (New Style) of Joseph Stalin in 1879. On December 21, 1988, Pan (thought to be Faunus by some) Am World Airways Flight 103 exploded and crashed. According to Federal Writer's Project, John Marshall proposed a marble tomb (consented to by Martha Washington) for George Washington's body on *December 21*, 1799. And Mrs. Abraham Lincoln (Mary Todd Lincoln) was born *December 13*, 1818. William Wallace Lincoln was born on *December 21*, 1850, and died at the White House on

February 20 (1862), the Eve of the Feast of the Dead. (See page 400). Mausoleum Day: page 646, footnote 158.

1-FFFFF. Arnold C. Brackman, *The Search for the Gold of Tutankhamen*, (New York: Mason/Charter, 1976).

1-G. Harry Houdini. Born in Budapest, Hungary, on March 24, 1874. Was son of a rabbi who emigrated from Hungary to the U.S. Houdini was a trapeze ("daring young man on the flying trapeze"; Hermes, god of gymnastics, flight, deception, magic, death) artist at an early age. He later performed in vaudeville shows in New York, not too successfully. About 1900 he began doing escape acts that continued on in variations for years and requiring timing, agility, deftness, speed, deception, etc., all Hermes attributes. He broke out of handcuffs, shackles, ropes, coffins, and prisons. Though campaigning against mind readers and others who claimed supernatural power, he and his wife, rather skeptically, agreed to an experiment, where the first to die would try to communicate with the survivor. In a way, the dead had communicated both with him and his wife, for he died in 1926 on Halloween, which seems to be linked, via the Roman Catholic Church, to the eve of the Old Feast of the Dead.

1-GG. The Chicago Seven were accused, tried, and convicted for contempt by Judge Julius J. Hoffman on *February 14* and *February 15*, 1970. February 14 is the forty-fifth day and lies in the purification month, hence, 4514 or DEAD. The fifteenth, the Lupercalia, is "deader;" and on the twenty-first of February, the Feast of the Dead, 1972, the trial of the Reverend Philip Berrigan and six other "antiwar activists of the Catholic left" opened in Harrisburg, Pennsylvania. The acrimonious division between the Hawks and Doves was, in a sense, how to show respect for the dead, that those who gave their lives should not have died in vain. But the war was quicksand for the Vets, as well as for the Pacifists. In the end, the culprits were our leaders with their insecure and/or brainless machismo, which got us into the mess. But isn't that what much of the crime on the streets is all about?

Epitaph

The end of the world was brought about—not by the forces
of good and evil—but by the interaction of the opposing
leaders with their insecure and/or brainless machismos.

1-GGG. Pythagorus stated in *Sacred Dicourses* that "Number is the ruler of form and ideas and is the cause of gods and demons." He used the number sequence only: 123456789. The Hebrews, however, used 1 – 22. This was in development of the Cabala, and the Hebrew alphabet has twenty-two letters. The Vedic Square (square associated with Hermes) is a table of multiplication numbers. A multiplication table of 1 – 9 is used. With the exception of 3, 6, and 9, each number appears six times; 3 and 6 appear twelve times, and 9, however, appears twenty-one times. John Matthews, consulting editor, *The World Atlas of Divination*, Boston: Bulfinch Press, 1993. For my purposes, it's important only that twenty-one is significant in the Vedic Square (and so associated with early Sanskrit texts) and that twenty-two is linked to the Hebrew system. When adding the numbers 1 – 9, the total is 45. Adding numbers 1 – 10: 55. Long before Christ, a Chinese observation: "The sum total of heavenly numbers and earthly numbers is 55. It is this...which sets gods and demons in movement."

252

But the numbers 21, 22, 55, and 9 (4 + 5) are linked to the Washington obelisk. Not having researched Pythagorus, I'm not certain whether Gore Vidal's linkage (*Creation*, New York: Ballantine Books, 1981) is fact or fiction. Still the connection is interesting in itself. In the novel, Pythagorus said that in an earlier life, he was the son of Hermes. Hermes so loved his son that he offered him any gift he wanted except immortality, which he wasn't allowed to offer. The boy chose what was considered the next best thing: to remember in each life form what he'd been in previous lives. In Greek mythology, Hermes' son Aethalides was a herald of the Argonauts and had total memory recall. His soul had been in Euphorbus, Hermotius, Pyrrhus, and finally Pythagorus.

1-H.   The December 13, 1799, entry in George Washington's diary is as follows:

> Morning Snowing & abt. 3 Inches deep. Wind at No. Et. &
> Mer. at 30. Contg. Snowing till 1 Oclock and abt. 4 it became
> perfectly clear. Wind in the same place but not hard. Mer. 28
> at Night.

See Donald Jackson (editor) and Dorothy Twohig (associate editor), *The Diaries of George Washington*, Vol VI, Charlottesville: University Press Virginia, 1976. Thus Washington's entry on the thirteenth was nocturnal, as was his departure the following day, dying in his bed at Mount Vernon. Washington's last written word appropriately concerned Mercury, for you see the death knell of the Articles of Confederation began on *February 21* (the day before Washington's birthday on the *twenty-second*), 1787, when Congress called for a constitutional convention to meet on May 14. The first regular session was on May 25, a time in ancient Rome when there was, presumably, a celebration to Mercury. Washington was chosen presiding officer and the U.S. Constitution began to be formed, to be completed on September 17 (a Mercury period), 1787.

Martha Custis Washington, the wife of George Washington, was born on June 2 (May 22, Old Style), 1731. She died on May 22, 1802. She was born then and died in Gemini periods, ruled by the planet Mercury.

The thing remembered most about Washington is that he's supposed to have said, "I cannot tell a lie," which—in the infancy our country—was the first big one, a cryptic Hermeticism, setting the tone for all future politicians.

1-I.   There was a holy man who wandered over Afghanistan. All who met him felt at once his goodness. He preached kindness and mercy, forever remarking all googly-eyed, "Don't you just love people!" He was a living saint. Where he might eventually die, a shrine would be erected. It was certain that over the centuries hundreds of thousands of pilgrims would visit his tomb. One village, fearing he would die elsewhere, killed him on the spot. He was worth more to its people dead than alive when they could charge admission. Besides, kindness is simply a hypocrite, a self-destructive weakness, a need for acceptance. That's why it's fair to reward it with lies, even brutality. So the holy man died in ecstasy, feeling these poor villagers really did care what happened to him in the end, and he would return their love by being able to provide an income for them for centuries to come. Things have a way of working themselves out in the end. Of course the citizens of Assisi weren't quite so bad. When they heard that Francis was near death, they sent an armed guard to bring him home. Why let some other town get the revenue from his potentially valuable body?

1-J.   Alice Van Straalen, *The Book of Holidays Around the World*, New York: Dutton, 1986.

1-K.   In mythology the raven, originally a white, *messenger* bird, was turned black by Apollo when it brought him news of Coronis' infidelity. He then killed Coronis but saved his son Aesculapius then near birth (Edith Hamilton, *Mythology*, Boston: Little, Brown, and Company, 1942). "Consider the ravens: they neither sow nor reap, they have neither storehouse nor barn, and yet God feeds them" (Lk 12:24). Part of the raven's unlucky reputation is due to lore, where in many cases it's a messenger bird, as above, and therefore linked to Hermes.

One version of the flood stories is that the raven was originally a white bird. When sent out from the ark to see if the waters had diminished, it found a corpse floating and began to eat, whereupon its plumage turned black. In "The Deluding of Gylfi" (from Iceland), Snorri Sturluson, two ravens sit upon Odin's shoulders and are sent out at dawn to scan the earth to bring him news of what's happening. One is called Thought, who Odin fears might not return. The other—for whom Odin is more concerned—is called Memory. So Odin is sometimes called God of Ravens. The other part of the raven's bad omen is due to its own nature. Being a carrion bird, it will eat rotten flesh, picking out the eyes in the process to get to the brain. It has a raucous caw, is a thief, a tendency at times (provoked possibly by teasing or mimicking) to feint attacks on humans from behind. This indeed can be bad if you have heart trouble. Since I've never been hurt by one of these birds and they always caw in clear warning, it seems more like a game, as if to say, "See you're not so smart as you think you are. Things can happen."

Possibly from this grew the British interjection at any surprise or disbelief, "Stone the Crows!" Yet tamed ravens are still kept near the Tower of London, maybe out of belief that it was Bran's oracular bird and the superstition that the safety of England depends upon Bran's head. The raven was sacred to Asclepius and Apollo. Thoth is described as a god of birds, Hermes, a god of birds of omen. Some North Pacific Coast Indian tribes had the raven as a culture hero. Curiously on June 27, 1994, about one week after writing most of the above, a raven dived from behind one day without warning and in passing grazed my shoulder. This it did twice, though apparently not intent on doing any harm.

At first a secondary god, Odin (Old English Woden) became the chief of the Norse gods, the center of the system. He was a god of self-sacrifice who brought wisdom to man. Wisdom was all-important to Odin. For it, he gave up one of his eyes (partial blindness) for a drink from Mímir's Well. Then to obtain the runes of wisdom, he hung himself from Yggdrasill for nine nights. This was done while wounded, without food or drink, and as "an offering to himself." Wednesday, the center of the week, was named for Odin. Because it was the fourth day and because of other similarities, Roman writers identified Odin with Mercury-Hermes. One similarity, for example, was that *disguised* as an old man with one eye, a *staff*, and a *broad-brimmed* hat, he often wandered (*traveled*) in the worlds.

He was the inventor of runic writing, and the source of all science and magic. He was over harvests, battles, the wind, sailing ships, and he had power over the dead. Along with the two ravens mentioned, he had two wolves: "Greedy" and "Gobbler." Thus ravens and wolves were used in sacrifice to him. (Encyclopedia references: *Americana*, *Britannica*, and *Collier's*.)

1-L.   Alfred J. Kolatch, *The Jonathan David Dictionary of First Names*, New York: Putnam,

1980. Bruce Lee: November 27, 1940 – July 20, 1973. Brandon Lee: February 1, 1965 – March 31, 1993. The inscription over Brandon Lee's grave reads:

Because we don't know when we will die, we get to think of life as an inexhaustible well. Yet everything happens a certain number of times, and a very small number really. How many more times will you remember a certain afternoon of your childhood, some afternoon that's so deeply a part of your being that you can't conceive of your life without it? Perhaps 4 or 5 times more. Perhaps not even that. How many more times will you watch the full moon rise? Perhaps twenty. And yet it all seems limitless.

Number of times = measure. Four or five suggests Hermes, the guardian of graveyards. Moon identified with Thoth. Twenty: Twenty times you're alive/ *twenty-one* you'll not survive.

1-M.   The first draft of the book had been written before I came across this information. Thanks is given to Suzanne White and St. Martin's Press, New York, New York, for permission to quote from page 657 of *The New Astrology*, 1968.

Certainly there's no denying the accuracy so far as wincing at human contact or being a witch, though a small fry, an unfortunate expression since it reminds me of the French's penchant for roasting their suspects and the English and American for the jolly-good-show of hanging. It's the injustice that goes with it. Exodus 22: 18 says, "Thou shalt not suffer a witch to live." In this case "witch" probably meant "poisoner," since the Hebrew word *kaskagh* (occurring twelve times in the Old Testament) has various meanings. Rossell Hope Robbins, *The Encyclopedia of Witchcraft and Demonology*, New York: Crown Publishers Inc., 1959. Where is the line between magic and miracle?

Chinese astrology is based on movement of the moon rather than the sun, which western astrology uses. In this astrology of the east, Lord Buddha named the twelve signs of the zodiac. It's said he loved the earth. So when he was about to go to a higher plane, he called all animals to come and honor him at a New Year's feast. Only twelve animals came. To reward their loyalty, he assigned each animal a year. The Chinese zodiac takes sixty years to complete. Each animal ruled every twelfth year. The people of the earth born in that year possess certain characteristics of the animal. The animals arrived at the feast in this order: Rat, Ox, Tiger, Hare, Dragon, Snake, Horse, Goat, Monkey, Rooster, Dog, and Boar. M. (Marcelle) Bakerby, *Cosmic Keys: Fortunetelling For Fun and Self-discovery*, St. Paul: Llewellyn Pub., 1991. The Cat instead of the Hare is used in at least one other book. Boar sounds better than Pig. One person when asked what he was responded, "I'm a mice."

1905 = Wood-snake	1917 = Fire-snake
1929 = Earth-snake	1941 = Metal-snake
1953 = Water-snake	

Abbreviation used for snake-year: SY.

Six animals above (dragon, snake, horse, goat, rooster, and dog) can be linked to Hermes.

Buddha's name is derived from Budhuha or Budahu, which is the planet Mercury's name. Alfred John Pearce, *The Text-book of Astrology*, Washington: American Federation of Astrologers, 1970. To some, Hermes was an Indo-European god, born of the virgin Maia. Indeed the *Mahanirvanatantra* states the Enlightened One (Buddha) was the same as Mercury (Hermes), who was the son of the Moon, or Maya. (Op. cit., Walker.) Two periods ruled by Mercury:

May 21 – June 20. Related to five.

August 23 – September 22. Related to four.

Abbreviation used for Mercury period: MP.

2.   George Washington selected the location for the nation's capital.

3.   Mount Vernon is seven miles south of *Alexandria*, Virginia. When three or four of us visited Washington's old home, I remember thinking how boring old relics were and hoping the next one ahead yet unseen would do something for me, the same feeling experienced on visiting the Smithsonian Institute. Without exception, you couldn't have given me one of those dust-collectors, whatever its worth, but when we got to George and Martha's tomb, it was another matter. I began casing the joint, looking around to see what problems there might be in stealing his body. Of course these were just passing thoughts, but say somehow it could have been pulled off, I wouldn't have wanted the fame, nor would it have been ransomed but shortly after returned in good shape and anonymously. The point is that there was a Hermetic link, the challenge to pull off something without profit or harm, just to see if could be gotten away with. All this happened long before I read in depth about the Washington Monument and that Washington had left instructions in his will that a new tomb be built. This was neglected until 1830 when a discharged employee snuck back one night in a "drunken rage" and stole a skull he thought was Washington's but was caught with that of Washington's nephew instead.

U.S. Navy ships—when passing the spot where Washington is buried—lower the ensign to half mast, toll the ship's bell, and "the crew is drawn to attention."

All protests to the contrary, the ritual is consistent with the suggestion of water in Washington's name and Neptune being guardian of February, the month of the Parentalia and Caristia, when Washington was born a Pisces. Martha Washington died on the anniversary of the eve of departure from Athens of an armada to attack Sicily.

4.   Washington was six feet two inches, Lincoln, six feet four inches. They both believed in God or Providence, but it wasn't conventional Christianity the rest of the way down. Washington, apparently sterile, had no children of his own. His two stepchildren were Martha Parke Custis, who died at an early age from epilepsy, and John Parke Custis. Spoiled by his mother, Jackie, as he was called, sat out most of the war. Then at Yorktown, he decided to attach himself as his stepfather's aide. Washington wasn't too fond of Jackie and shortly his stepson got sick and died. Washington must have thought it providential, though he expressed no reaction. Martha, on the other hand, was grief-stricken. John Parke Custis had two children. Robert E. Lee married Mary Custis, whose father was a grandson of Martha Custis Washington. Like General Lee later, Washington was an excellent rider, who exposed himself many times to danger and had at least

one horse shot out from under him (the horse in mythology is symbolic of war and slaughter). Seemingly Washington had more than his share of good luck. Why?

Only one of Mary and Abraham Lincoln's four children survived to adulthood. Robert Todd Lincoln was the father of Abraham Lincoln II, who died at sixteen. Though Robert Todd Lincoln had two daughters, he was the last of the line to survive bearing the last name Lincoln. This was similar to the line of Heinrich and Sophia Schliemann, which you'll read about later. Why in the above cases? Who knows?

5-A.   Washington was the only founding father from Virginia who freed his slaves (James Thomas Flexner, *Washington the Indispensable Man*, Boston: Little, Brown, and Company, 1969). This probably explains why four-fifths (4/5) of those having the name Washington in the United States are black (Elsdon C. Smith, *American Surnames*, Philadelphia: Chilton Book Co., 1969). Curiously Malcolm X was a twenty-one to Washington's twenty-two also. Remember too that Malcolm X's life related to his skin. Opening up many avenues of thought to this is the fact that St. Peter and St. Paul could have skinned each other alive over the circumcision. Most people (white, black, yellow, etc.) tend to will how God is supposed to think, but one point which has been ignored, as I see it, in the Bible is that Moses married (it wasn't adultery) a woman who was a Cushite, which is loosely equivalent to Ethiopian. Some very determined Christians will argue that this group of Ethiopians (and the Cushites in the geographical areas close by) weren't black in those days. In truth, some Cushites were light, but most weren't. Miriam and Aaron (Num 12: 01 – 12.15) were saying the marriage was wrong and that God spoke through them, on which He corrected them. If for the sake of argument, Miriam's and Aaron's objection had been that the Cushite woman was not Jewish, why would God have stricken Miriam white with leprosy, the perfect retribution, when thousands of other punishments could have been thought of? But this thinking cuts both ways. Malcolm X apparently didn't believe in interracial marriage. Why dilute the pure black with the white devil?

5-B.   It lay in Middle Egypt. There were four pair of primeval deities whom Thoth surpassed or overshadowed when he arrived. The Greeks later identified Thoth with Hermes and named this city Hermopolis, meaning "Hermes-town." George Hart, *A Dictionary of Egyptian Gods and Goddesses*, London: Routledge and Kegan Paul, 1986. Ennead refers to any of several groups of nine associated gods in ancient Egyptian mythology and religion.

6-A.   It represents the incarnation or the descending of the "divine power into the world." It rings in a series of three strokes, three times, and then is followed by nine strokes. There's something in 1809, the year Lincoln was born, which suggests this.

6-B.   Rupert Matthews, *The Supernatural*, New York: Bookwright Press, 1989. Half 9 = 4.5.

6-C.   492 357 816 A straight line in any direction totals 15.

7-A.   "Oh! My Darling Clementine" by P. Montrose (New York: Robbins Music Corporation, 1942) is about as Hermetic a song as you can get: cavern, excavation, mining, parent, shoes, sandals, ducklings (birds), ruby (red), luck, and death. It was a song we often sang in a grammar school music-appreciation class.

Thoth, an important god in Sinai, controlled turquoise mining. (Op. cit., Hart.) See footnote 17-A. Thoth, god of truth and judgment. The tablets of stone, of course, were given to Moses at Mt. Sinai.

7-B.   The double nine, in Chinese legend, is September 9. As the story goes, a Chinese villager called Sun Go (Mercury closest planet to the sun) was advised by a witch to flee with his family from their farm to the mountains before this date. He took the advice. When they later returned, they found that all animals on the farm were dead. Custom came about that on September 9 people were to go to the mountains to prune trees and repair graves. This evolved into a family outing in the hills and kite flying (misfortune carried off into the skies) known as the "Festival in High Places."

Hennig Cohen and Tristram Coffin, *The Folklore of American Holidays*, Detroit: Gale Research Co., 1987.

Here again another suggestion of nine connected to death and witchcraft. Repair of graves, according to one source, was also done during the Parentalia in ancient Rome.

7-C.   Nine is a number of unchangeable truth, a parent forever begetting itself. For example, 1 x 9 = 9; 2 x 9 = 18 (1 + 8 = 9); 3 x 9 = 27 (2 + 7 = 9); 4 x 9 = 36 (3 + 6 = 9); etc. What's interesting too is that 4.5, the number representing the coven circle radius (9 representing the diameter) reproduces 9 from 2 times onward: 2 x 4.5 = 9; 3 x 4.5 = 13.5 (1 + 3 + 5 = 9); 4 x 4.5 = 18 (1 + 8 = 9);; 5 x 4.5 = 22.5 (2 + 2 + 5 = 9).

In the coven circle, the diameter is 9 feet.

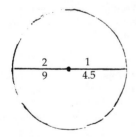

Diameter = 9
Radius = 4.5
Top figures
combined = 21
9 + 4.5 = 13.5

The crown of Thoth is a crescent moon supporting a disc.

The Parentalia was a nine-day period beginning on the thirteenth at 12:00 noon (13.5) and ending on the twenty-first. The Caristia was the twenty-second day. 2/9 = 0.22. A circle is 360_. The round moon of Thoth has eight angles of 45_ or Eight Town (Hermopolis), and the square has four angles of 90_ each (total 360_).

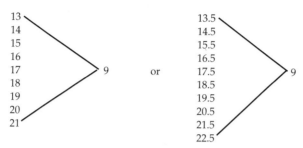

22.5 = 5 x 4.5. A straight line would be represented as 180 degrees, a half circle, a half moon. When a new town was built in Italy, a hole was dug and a stone called a lapis manalis was placed in it. Then varying in dates from town to town, the stone would be removed to allow the Di Manes to go between the worlds. (See pages 23 and 36.)

8-A. The name Washington, some say, was derived from old English names, which—in one case—meant "settlement of the people of *Wassa*." Another book says it means "washing-house." *A Genealogical Gazetteer of England* (Frank Smith, Baltimore: Genealogical Pub. Co., 1968) lists two Washington parishes: the one is in the diocese of *Durham* (you will read later the Durans [name Duran] were from Durham, Maine. But for now, to quote Don Quixote's Durans who was on his back in a marble *tomb*, "Patience, cousin, and *shuffle the cards*"). The other Washington parish is in Sussex in the diocese of *Chichester*. There are also in the book two other parishes with their names beginning "washing." Washingborough parish is in the diocese of *Lincoln*.

The Whiskey Rebellion is described as possibly "the most serious internal disturbance" in the Washington presidential administration (A. Howry Espenshade, *Pennsylvania Place Names*, Harrisburg: The Evangelical Press, 1925). Though it seems unlikely, the Whiskey Rebellion, along with the fact that Washington's face was scarred by smallpox, links him to Scarface Al Capone. Maybe as a reminder the thirteenth was the first day of the Parentalia and February used to be the last month of the year, the last four words Washington is known to have written were on December 13, 1799: "...*Mercury 28* at night." Also on the thirteenth, he said he had a sore throat. Sometime approaching midnight (no one remembered to look at the clock) on the fourteenth, he died. So his sickness and death took place on the thirteenth and fourteenth (December) and Lincoln's shooting and death on the fourteenth and fifteenth (April).

On February 8, 1865, the electoral votes were counted. Of the 233 votes cast, Lincoln and Johnson received 212, or 212 to 21. Rather interesting, Nevada (the new state Lincoln signed into being) cast only two electoral votes. One of its delegates failed to show up to cast the third. (Henry J. Raymond, *The Life and Public Services of Abraham Lincoln*, New York: Derby and Miller, 1865.)

The cards had been shuffled and dealt (Nevada will later become the gambling capital of the world and Las *Vegas*—at least at the time of this writing—the fastest growing city in the United States). Hermes, god of gamblers. 212(2) represented the Feralia-Caristia, death-life, life-death (remember Lincoln was responsible for the thirteenth amendment). It also meant Lincoln had won at blackjack that day but a second blackjack he would later lose to the dealer. Assuming McClellan got all the other electoral votes, he lost at blackjack too. Looking back later, he was probably damn glad he did. Lincoln's ancestry can be traced to Hingham, Massachusetts. There are three Lincolns (not of Abraham Lincoln's immediate family) also mentioned in the *Encyclopedia Americana*:

> *BENJAMIN LINCOLN.* Officer in the American revolutionary army. Political figure. He died at Hingham, Massachusetts, on *May 9*, 1810. May 9 was one of the Lemuria days.

> *JOSEPH CROSBY LINCOLN.* American author. Born in Brewster, Massachusetts, in 1870 on *February 13*, the beginning of the Parentalia.

> *LEVI LINCOLN.* American political figure. Born in Hingham, Massachusetts, in 1749 on *May 15*, the anniversary of the festival in ancient Rome. He died on *April 14*, 1820. This was exactly *forty-five* years to the day before Abraham Lincoln was shot.

8-B.   Lupercalia (La), Luperci (Li). Compare to *La illah illa Allah*.

9.   Footprints, in primitive thought, become an extension of the human person in magic, sacrifice, mourning. *The Encyclopedia of Religion*, Editor in Chief Mircea Eliade, New York: Macmillan, 1987.

10-A.   Whether superstition or fiction is unknown. But it has been said Satan's power is weakest at midnight on December 21 of the winter solstice (Kelleher, Ed and Vidal, Harriette, *Prime Evil*. New York: Dorchester Publishing Co., 1988). The winter solstice is the shortest day of the year and could be either *21* or *22* December. In Egyptian mythology, Osiris was murdered by Seth, who chopped his body into 14 pieces and scattered them over Egypt. Isis, Osiris' sister-wife, gathered most of the dismembered parts.

The final entombment of the slain god was December 21 (Farrar, Janet and Farrar, Stewart, *Eight Sabbats for Witches*. Phoenix Publishing Co. Inc., Custer, Washington: 1981). Note here the numbers fourteen and twenty-one. I had been to Egypt twice in my travels. On December 21, 1967, Louis Washkansky, the world's first heart transplant patient, died in Cape Town, South Africa, the same continent as Egypt. Early Christians possibly thought the winter solstice to be December 25, which they set as Christ's birth. December 25 also happened to be the date of birth of Mithra, the sun, the Persian god of light. The summer solstice is June 21 *or* 22. The spring equinox occurs on March 20 or 21, the autumn equinox, September 22 or 23. Briefly then there's a sameness or likeness of the solstices to the number 2122 and suggestion of this in half the equinoxes. See Book II, footnote 289.

10-B.   Events in Mary Shelley's own life led to the gothic horror story. She was born on August 30 (MP), 1797 (SY), to liberal intellectual parents, who had married in that year. Her mother died of puerperal fever in eleven days on September 10 (MP). Note here the twin snakes: one of birth, one of death. September 10 will later be my father's birthdate, while the date of birth of her first child would—in years to come—be the day he died. That my father's name was Frank is still another coincidence. Frankenstein was the name of the medical student.

Apparently Franks are always creators. Her father never forgave her for causing her mother's death, and Mary Shelley struggled under the shadow of her rival mother—who was perhaps a superior intellect—all her life. When in her teens, the girl began to make daily trips to her mother's grave where she read and wrote. It was in fact to this backdrop on one of her daily excursions that Percy Shelley, the mercurial poet, followed her and she declared her undying love for him. Thereafter they had secret meetings at the grave, for Shelley was still married to Harriet. As Mary Shelly was completing Chapter IV (the Hermes number) of *Frankenstein*, she received word that Harriet had committed suicide and was found floating in the Serpentine, a curving section of the Thames. On December 29, 1816, a little over two weeks later, Percy and Mary were married.

Some people, including myself, tracing their genealogy have expressed the feeling of having received help from beyond the grave. Very peculiar, unaccountable occurrences or occurrences of thought happened along the way. Could be Mary Shelley received help from her mother, who herself had been a writer and whose last name was Wollstonecraft (almost like wool-stone-craft), while that of her husbands was *God*win. Percy and Mary married at the Old St. Pancras Church, behind which her mother lay buried. St. *Pan*cras, the martyr, was said to have been decapitated when about fourteen. Pan, by some accounts, was the son of Hermes, and Hermes is associated with dreams, sleep, writers, magic, medical students, and doctors—via the caduceus, *the twin snakes of life and death*—as well as graveyards and decapitation.

Mary Shelley's first child, born prematurely on the Caristia of February 22, 1815, died within two weeks. Of her five pregnancies, only one child, Percy Florence, lived to adulthood, though dying without issue, often a peculiarity of Hermes people or their immediate descendants. Born November 12, 1819, he died in 1889, the year given on my mother's tombstone, on December 5, a time of celebration in Roman antiquity to Faunus. Faunus, sometimes called Lupercus, is identified as the Greek Pan because of similarities of attributes. And Faunus sometimes revealed the future in dreams and communicated with sleeping or *nap*ping votaries.

Books as well as dates and numbers are likely mediums of communication between us and the invisible world. I wonder not so much that the careful Linda Millgate (*The Almanac of Dates*, New York: Harcourt Prace Jovanovich, 1977) made a mistake (we all make them) on the date she gave for Mary Shelley's birthday but how she arrived at February 21, the Feast of the Dead. In any event, Victor Frankenstein was twenty-one years older than his creation. The origin of the creature in *Frankenstein* leaves no doubt about where it was coming from. Thus this book about body parts is a source of communication between the living and the dead, an arcane piece meant to be read in context especially with the lives of Mary and Percy Shelley (of the graveyard courtship) and Byron. An old proverb says that "When you're born, you're done for." This applied to Mary Shelley's first child, which was meant only to establish her credentials to the Parentalia-Caristia. In suggestions and advice Percy Shelley made contributions to *Frankenstein*, but Percy had his own links to the Parentalia (as had Keats) which were completely separate from hers. "How wonderful is Death, /Death and his brother Sleep!" So begins "Queen Mab," in *nine* cantos and privately printed in 1813 with seventy copies distributed. The title pages of the 1821 (SY) pirated (suggesting thievery/Hermes) editions show a two-serpent caduceus, the staff of Hermes. It was Shelley's first major work.

Curiously Byron in a letter described Percy as "the Snake...walking about on tip of his tail." Percy and Mary spent much time in Italy, and he drowned—as had Harriet in the Serpentine—off the coast of Livorno (one of two or three ports I'd visited in Italy) on July 8, 1822, less than a year after the publication of "Queen Mab" in 1821. In accordance with Italian laws at the time, Shelley's body had to be buried or cremated near the beach where it had washed ashore. His body was cremated with ashes eventually taken to Rome, home of the Parentalia, where he, an atheist, was buried in a Protestant cemetery on January 21, 1823.

Previously John Keats had been buried at this same cemetery, which is not so strange considering 1) his father had died after a fall from a horse (1804); 2) John Keats was born in 1795 on October 31, a date corresponding to the Old Feralia or its Eve, after being reworked by the Catholic Church, and that he died on February 23, 1821 (SY); 3) that he had obtained an apothecary's certificate in 1816, eventually giving up medicine; and 4) that he had written "Ode on a Grecian Urn" and "Hymn to Pan."

Byron died in Greece in 1824. Mary Shelley died on February 1, 1851, and was buried between the transferred remains of her parents in St. Peter's churchyard, Bournemouth.

A final note, today's date is June 27, 1995. I had no knowledge of the lives of Percy and Mary Shelley until about a week ago. So my visits to Lakeview Cemetery were another similarity.

11.   *Feral* can mean wild, untamed, undomesticated, or it can mean causing death, fatal, funereal.

12-A.   Typical among these were grains of wheat, salt, garlands, bread softened with wine, and a few violets. *Ovid, Fasti* 2.527–539.

   This is similar to the Chinese custom of taking fruit, rice, coins, and various other small gifts on visiting a grave. Other sources list flowers often used as: roses, lilies, and myrtle. Myrtilus, a charioteer and son of Hermes, was killed by Pelops. To avenge his death, Hermes placed a curse on Pelops and all his house.

12-B.   Will Durant, *The Story of Civilization: Caesar and Christ*, New York: Simon and Schuster, 1944.

13-A.   One more human characteristic is the tendency to whitewash periods in one's own religion, dismissing them cavalierly: "Well the people then really weren't true believers." Yet when it comes to using the same jujitsu manipulation on a religion we know little or nothing about, there's a tendency to say dogmatically that the person who did the evil act represented the god he worshiped. And if he happens to be a Muslim, "Why Muslims don't believe in God. They worship Mohammed. Everyone knows that!" We tend to believe—perhaps with the sin of pride—our own brand of religion has the exclusive franchise.

   Yes, it's a fact that generally Muslims showed far more charity and mercy than Christians during the crusades. Moreover, Muslims could easily make a case that the reason the Virgin Mary appeared to three, small Catholic girls (so the word spread) in May 1917 at Fátima, Portugal, was to emphasize that Fátima, the youngest daughter of Mohammed, was Muslim. Fátima has in Shiite legend taken on attributes ascribed by Roman Catholics (*Encyclopedia Americana*) to the

Virgin Mary, who the Muslims revere, as well as Mohammed. But only God (Allah) do they worship. They believe in the virgin birth of Jesus, that he performed miracles, and that he was one of the major prophets. They, like the Jews, don't believe he's the Savior or the Son of God. Maybe this is one reason many blacks have identified with Islam. They see a parallel between Islam and Islam as perceived by many Christians to themselves and how many whites perceive blacks. But this isn't to say that in *some instances* blacks or whites are completely innocent and that "these people" (blacks and whites alike) don't help to keep the thing going.

13-B.   This wasn't necessarily a coldness but a natural progression. He had/has his own realm. By silence he's asserting the channel of communication is through the dead by paying homage to them. A different perspective concerning Hades is that he doesn't take bribes. His gift of death—a release from life—is ironically a considerable one, given freely to all. (Lewis Richard Farnell, *The Cults of the Greek States*, London: Clarendon Press, 1909.)

14-A.   Very early in Roman history the burial custom of the noble families appears to have been cremation. But burial urns in cemeteries were "huddled together" without identifying marks. There was no care for the individual grave. Some believe this indicated the di manes were thought of as an "undiscriminated mass." (Cook, Adock, Charlesworth, *The Cambridge History*, Vol. VIII, England: Macmillan Co., Cambridge, 1930.)

This interpretation could very well be valid. Yet it isn't really clear that this is so. The fact they weren't marked could have been a protective measure. An individual might have chanced desecrating the grave of one person he hated, but he'd think twice about incurring the wrath of the *di manes* of other urns by dumping all to get back at one. In later times, the more civilized Rome, family vaults and tombs were used by noble families. Some inscriptions beseech the sacred Manes to let their loved one be well received and to treat him or her kindly.

Scholars hold to the belief that there was no prayer or invocation during the Parentalia to a god or gods. Perhaps this is the way it was meant to be, but human beings being human beings, I have serious doubts that the grieving could visit the recent grave of a loved one during the Parentalia and not informally and silently ask for Mercury's protection of the deceased too, unless clear evidence eventually surfaces that this was definitely a taboo during the Parentalia.

14-B.   Dionysus, the Greek god of vegetation and wine, was the only Olympian having a mortal for a mother. He was born to Zeus and Semelé. Being an earth god, Dionysus, like Persephone, is connected to the underworld as well as the world above.

15.   Hermes at times has been depicted as a cook. Possibly this association comes from his burning the first offerings to the gods and/or the Day of Pots. The grouping of Dionysus and Hermes in the same festival isn't surprising, for Hermes had helped protect the boy Dionysus against Hera, the wife of Zeus and queen of the gods. In the *Iliad*, Zeus remarked that more than any other god it's dearest to Hermes to be the companion of man.

Caesar said Mercury (Hermes) was the most popular god in Gaul and Britain and was considered the inventor of all arts. (Lesley Adkins and Roy A. Adkins, *Handbook of Life in Ancient Rome*, New York: Facts on File Inc., 1994.

16-A.   The word *angel* is derived from the Greek word for messenger. The angelus rings nine times.

16-B.   While Hera slept, Zeus was embracing Maia deep within a cave on Mt. Cyllene. Thus from this too, the natural progression of sleep and dreams being part of Hermes' divinity.

16-C.   One reason is that he at times serves the other Olympians. So who is better qualified to understand the problems of servants—how to kindle a fire, pour wine, cook, bone fish, make a bed properly, cut hair, shave, etc.? And hopefully to be able to do any of these with the deftness which characterizes Hermes. He was then very approachable, friendly, and kind. Though a rogue at times, his nature in general wasn't of violence of maliciousness. It must be remembered he is many faceted: a god of sacrifice, among other things, and death, the normal course of life, can't be completely separated from him. Because of his cleverness, the mentally slow asked his protection, by extension, probably anyone who was crippled or incapacitated someway. In respect to serving food and the Feralia, it's curious I'd make it to Italy: two or three hours one afternoon between serving meals on a freighter in Naples, and later two or three evenings after work in Livorno.

The ancient city of Pompeii was fourteen miles southeast of Naples in Campania. In A.D. 79, Vesuvius erupted, destroying it. The cult of Mercury and Maia was popular to southern Italy, Pompeii being one example given. To date, one-fourth of Pompeii remains to be *excavated*. At Tuscany, where Livorno is located, Mercury was worshipped by the Etruscan name of Turms.

17-A.   In some parts of ancient Greece, Hermes was the god of miners and diggers for buried treasures. (Harry T. Peck, *Harper's Dictionary for Classical Literature and Antiquities*, New York: American Book Co., 1896.) By extension, excavations. The fact that Maia lived within the cave where Hermes was born suggests mining too indirectly. Cave in Latin is *cavea*, and *cavus* means hollow. Excavation, a digging or hollowing out, is formed from Latin *ex* (out) and *cavus* (hollow).

Thracian kings, according to Herodotus, worshipped Hermes above all others. The silver octadrachms of the Derroni seemed to confirm this, at least for tribes living near Mt. Pangaeus. (Op. cit., Cook, Adock, Charlesworth.)

Both gold and silver were mined in Thrace. If it came to deciding which more closely represented Hermes, I would say silver for several reasons. Note too, the chief priests paid thirty pieces of silver to Judas Iscariot, which could have been a deep irony and mocking, if Hermes and Jesus are one and the same.

17-B.   To the Greeks, he was Hermes. To the Romans, Mercury. To both, Cyllenius (or the Cyllenian).

18.   The fourth month was named after him in Argos, Greece, and in Athens, sacrifices to honor him were made regularly on the fourth of each month. (Ibid.)

19.   Thousands of years before the "Teenage Mutant Ninja Turtles," the tortoise was sacred to Hermes, the arch wizard and the patron of magicians. It was believed that alive the turtle could ward off black magic, while dead it would sing sweetly. Hermes is god of gymnastics, wrestling, boxing, discus throwers, and runners—to some extent all athletes, especially youthful ones. By extension then, the martial arts, stealth, and cunning of the ninja. Mutant, an individual species

resulting from a departure, i.e., boundaries are transcended. In the story (B.B. Hiller, *Teenage Mutant Ninja Turtles*, Dell Publishing, New York, 1989), there are *four* characters called Leonardo, Michelangelo, Donatello, and Raphael. (Hermes is sometimes likened to the archangel Raphael. Hermes' persona, indirectly, artist.) Ninja master (Splinter) cautions the four to keep practicing the art of the ninja, i.e., invisibility. When wearing Hades' hat, Hermes was invisible. Do not forget too, Tortuga, the Caribbean island shaped like a turtle, was home of the buccaneers. The first American submarine was called Turtle since it bore a resemblance to "two upper tortoise shells of equal size, joined together." Being rudimentary, it was employed unsuccessfully in 1776.

20.   He sacrificed two of the cattle to the twelve Olympian gods. Here Hermes broke a boundary since sacrifice had never been done before.

21.   John Pinsent, *Greek Mythology*, New York: Peter Bedrick Books, 1982.

       (Since nobody knows what month the fourth day occurred, it's remotely possible it could have been a winter month.)

22.   Footprints are one of Hermes' correspondences. Perhaps then the name Hodios, the Wayfarer (*Walker*), is linked to them, hence travelers. By extension, Hermes becomes the god of those who go to sea, especially seafarers engaged in commerce, a word along with merchant, which has the same root as Mercury.

23.   Thus persona peace. Hermes then is the embodiment of the union of two opposites. His staff with two snakes intertwined is called a caduceus. Currently it represents more of the dental and medical professions throughout the world than the one-snake caduceus of Asclepius, the Greek god of medicine and the son of Apollo. Some say that strictly speaking the two-snake caduceus doesn't stand for healing but rather is a symbol of Hermes and the magic wand. Be that as it may, the caduceus has been found as far back in history as 2600 B.C. in Mesopotamia, where people believed it was the symbol of the god who cured all sickness. It is engraved on ancient stone tablets in India; and in the Ukraine, it is the Catholic bishop's insignia. (J.E. Cirlot, *A Dictionary of Symbols*, New York: Philosophical Lib., Inc., 1962.) The snake was sacred to Asclepius since its healing power is thought to be represented by the way it sloughs off its skin in new youth. Either way (one snake or two), it represents a magic, and two is more than one.

       "So Moses made a bronze serpent, and set it on a pole; and if a serpent bit any man, he would look at the bronze serpent and live" (Num 21:9). The process then involved two serpents: one real, and other an image. Hermes and Asclepius are related. Therefore, it's not surprising that they will have symbols which are close. Each god is associated with dogs and snakes. Animals which seem to have psychic content in the nether world. Cerebrus is the many-headed god which guards the gates of Hades. The snake is the most mystical of all animals. That the dog, man's best friend, is linked to man's friendliest god is reasonable.

       In Egyptian mythology, the goddess of dawn, Isis, is sometimes depicted with a caduceus because she "heralds the sun." (Hans Biederman, *Dictionary of Symbolism*, translated by James Hulbert, New York: Facts on File Inc., 1992.)

24-A.   Alexander S. Murray, *Manual of Mythology*, New York: Tudo Publishing Co., 1971.

24-B.   It's said Mercury used a set of five four-sided marked dice in honor of Maia. (David and Julia Line, *Fortune-telling by Dice*, New York: Aquarian Press, 1987.)

On the fourth day he was born, and five stands for the fifth month, or May.

The number of suits in cards is four, and a fourflusher in poker is one who bluffs (deceives). There are twenty-one possible combinations in dice. In snake eyes, twenty-one can also be imagined by drawing a line for the body: ____, : , 21.

Twin snakes indicate Hermes' duality of being a lord of death and rebirth. It's important to remember too that by being a conductor of the souls of the dead to Hades, he can also bring them back. (W.S. Fox, *The Mythology of All Races*, Vol I, Boston: Marshal Jones Co., 1916.)

Necromancy is associated with him, by extension, magic.

Jesus raised Lazarus from the dead (Jn 11: 43).

At the lower tip of Nevada is an erect snake and so guards by fascination, a word that is derived from the Latin *fascinum*, witchcraft. But in this case, witchcraft doesn't mean "devil worshipper," as any magic has come to be associated by some who are suspicious of any reward or gift that's not derived from the sweat of one's brow. Easy gains are too simple and therefore sinful. Yet all life is an uncertainty from day to day, a gamble, a calculation of odds. And like it or not, even prayer is a gamble.

Hermes had to go before the gods for killing the hundred-eyed giant called Argus, *which he did by cutting off Argus's head*. Unwilling to go near Hermes, for he was smeared with blood, they cast their vote-pebbles, much like disk-shaped poker chips, which fell into a pile around his feet. All those who go before a judge and/or jury today are similar to him, so it's fitting too—as the moon waxes and wanes—he should be the god of luck, gamblers, and thieves.

The "peace of gods" was within Thoth, as one text put it. However, Thoth sometimes was merciless against enemies of the truth. He cut out their hearts and *decapitated* them. (Op. cit., Hart.)

Thoth was over the gods of eight-town (Hermopolis), who were Darkness, Endlessness, Inertness, and Nothing, and each god's consort. The names are "the negatives of Primeval Waters."

24-C.   One of the difficulties experienced at first in the syncretic Thoth-Hermes is understanding how Hermes coincides in judgment. There's little written on this in most textbooks. Later I would come across Arnold Whittick's *Symbols, Signs, and Their Meaning*, (London: Leonard Hill Ltd., 1960). In one place the author states that in ancient Greece scales were a symbol of justice. A Greek vase (now in the Louvre) shows Hermes, in the presence of Zeus, weighing the souls of Achilles and Memnon. There are, furthermore, many references in Greek literature where Zeus weighs men's souls.

The flamingo is a relative (as are herons and bitterns) of the crane, stork (a bird sacrificed to Hermes in Egypt), and ibis, wading birds associated with Hermes and Thoth (judgment, reckoning). It stands with long legs stilt-like sometimes. With a long neck and bent bill, it looks down as if it is counting the pebbles in the wetness it wades. With this stance and its reddish or pinkish plumage, it typifies Hermes at the judgment. That the oasis-dream, casino-hotel at Las Vegas (now the gaming capital of the world) is called the Flamingo is more than coincidence. And in truth, Benjamin "Bugsy" Siegel (LI) stood in judgment of his peers who cast their votes, and blood was on him when he was slain.

President of Murder, Incorporated, a hot-tempered man, he went in 1941 (SY) to Las Vegas (now where there are more marriages on Valentine's Day), representing both the racingwire syndicate and the Capone mob. Both he and Al were, incidentally, from New York and died in 1947 (21). It's not certain whether he named the Flamingo after Virginia Hill, his girlfriend, or the birds nesting on the infield lake at Hialeah horse race track. But from 1922 to 1926, Hialeah had dog racing. Hialeah adjoins Miami, not too far from where Capone was during the St. Valentine's Day Massacre in 1929. Curious connections: Hi Ball, the dog which survived the St. Valentine's Day massacre, and the dogs, the horses, the flamingos, the circular race tracks (recall the Indianapolis 500), and the drive at all costs sometimes to be the winner, and judgment.

On June 20 (the last day of the Mercury period), 1947, Siegel was sitting on a living room couch when he was shot so that his right eye came to rest in the living room. This shooting in the back of the head was similar to that of Lincoln, Dillinger, and John F. Kennedy.

The name *Vega* is Spanish for meadow. The name *Las Vegas* gets its name from the meadows where those following trails camped. (George R. Stewart, *American Place-Names*, New York: Oxford University Press, 1970.) Lyre>Cithara>Guitar. Hermes, god of pastures and one of the gods of music, is said to have invented the lyre. It is a hollow-backed, harp-like stringed instrument. Its curving arms suggest a horseshoe. The V, from which the horseshoe is stylized, is a bifurcate *crossroads*. It's believed the original lyre had seven strings. An ancient constellation was called Lyra, representing the lyre of Hermes (or Orpheus). The constellation contains the bright star VEGA. Las Vegas born May 15, 1905. (Writers' Project, Nevada: *A Guide to the Silver State*, Portland: Binsford and Mort, 1940.) Snake-year, snake-month: two snakes like on the caduceus. Date appropriate for god of gamblers.

Jack Broom, staff reporter *The Seattle Times*, July 25, 1992, cautions readers not to buy a ticket in the forthcoming twenty-million-dollar Lotto that has the combination:

$$4 - 13 - 22 - 31 - 40 - 49,$$

which is obtained my marking the right-hand column of the game slip. When the amount of the lottery is high, people in the thousands will select this combination. If it should be a lucky number then, the winnings of each person would be comparatively small.

My own thoughts concerning this are that most people are right-handed, the first number in the column to the right is perceived as lucky (four-leaf clover), the numbers are spread out in a wide range or diversified, and in a bingo-straight line, giving the idea of a connection, the solution. What's not so easy to figure out is that, one way or another, each of the numbers in the column adds up to four.

25.A.   H. Peticus, William Smith, and H.B. Walters (see bibliography). An altar to Mercury existed near Porta Capena and possibly later a temple was built on the site. There was also a well near the altar. Merchants attributed its water to having magical power and sprinkled themselves and their merchandise with it on the day of celebration. By the purification, they believed they might get a larger profit. It's assumed that the practice of merchants sprinkling themselves and items for sale was done throughout Rome during the celebration. This is similar to later Christian priests sprinkling holy water.

"Under the name of the ill-willed (*malevolus*)," Mercury had a statue, purse in hand to indicate his function as a god of wealth, on what was called "Sober Street," where no shops were allowed, nor wine offering but rather that of milk. This brings to mind the later Jesus driving the money changers out of the temple. A sacred branch, rather than the caduceus, was used as Mercury's emblem of peace. Eloquence can overcome all. Both dates of May 15 and May 25 have been retained—rightly or wrongly—as sacred days in this book. May 25, 1787, was the date the first regular session of the U.S. Constitutional Convention began.

Festivals held in the month of May for Mercury were called the Mercuralia and merchant guilds (the forerunners of unions), *Mercuriales*.

W. Warde Fowler (*The Roman Festivals of the Period of the Republic*, New York: Macmillan and Co., 1899) stated that May 25 was the dedication day for one of the three temples to Fortuna, and Gertrude Jobes describes the Roman goddess of chance and luck as "being the incorporated will of the gods." Mercury/Hermes was a messenger, as well as a god of luck. So it's possible, though reaching, he might have had something to do with this day too. If that doesn't wash, then it's possible in the long history of Rome there must have been an unscheduled or undocumented festival for Mercury on May 25.

The Rosalia (plural) were feasts or celebrations where roses were taken to the graves. These never became fixed public festivals but rather were local: Capua, May 5; Rome, May 21 and May 23; Pergamum, May 24–26. It's not believed that these were cults of the dead but rather occasions where they were invited to feast with the survivors present. (*The Oxford Classical Dictionary*, Oxford: Clarendon Press, 1949.)

Since Mercury is looked upon as a god of graveyards, there's an indirect association of *May 25* at Pergamum.

In the Plaza de la Republica of Buenos Aires is an obelisk honoring the four-hundredth anniversary of the founding of what is now Argentina's *wide-avenued* capital and largest city. It looks like the George Washington obelisk. Of course it'd be too much to expect the Buenos Aires obelisk to have had a dedication date of February 21. But the official days surrounding Argentina's independence are *May 25*, 1810, and *July 9*, 1816. The former was twenty-three years after George Washington and others met in the first session of the Constitutional Convention, the Articles of Confederation having received its death knell on *February 21*, 1787. The celebration on July 9 is only *five* days after our celebration on July 4. General José de San Martín, regarded in Argentina as its greatest revolutionary hero, was born on February 25 (Washington born on February 22, New Style), 1778.

In Tulsa, Oklahoma, on *May 25*, 1980, Oral Roberts saw a nine-hundred-foot Jesus Christ with whom he talked. (Andrew W. Frew, *Frew's Daily Archive*, North Carolina: McFarland and Co., Jefferson, 1944.)

26. Her uncle, William Randolph Hearst, Jr., died May 14, 1993, on the eve of the anniversary in ancient Rome and just in time to make the May 15 papers (message).

   According to a *TV Guide* update of July 2, 1994, O.J. Simpson (who in 1994 was indicted for killing his former wife [head nearly severed] and her male friend) said in a 1991 roundup of celebrities' watching habits that watching the live coverage of SLA/Watts shootout (Patricia Hearst then a fugitive) was his most memorable television viewing moment.

27.C. J.S. Thompson, *The Hand of Destiny: The Folklore and Superstitions of Everyday Life*, Detroit: Singing Tree Press, 1970.

   Philosophers gave the name AZOTH to Mercurious. The word is put together from the alpha and omega of the Greeks, and aleph and tau of the Hebrews, and the A and Z of the Latins. (C.G. Jung, *The Collected Works of C.G. Jung*, Vol. 13, Pantheon Books, 1953.)

   I hadn't read this reference to AZOTH until January 21, 1995, but had made an AZ connection to Topaz before that.

A Z O T H	T O A Z
T O P A Z	T O A Z

   The two letters which differ are *p* and *h*, but these can be derived from ale*ph* or al*ph*a.

   Hans Biedermann (*Dictionary of Symbolism*, New York: Facts on File, Inc., 1989) says astrology links the following stones to Mercury: beryl, tiger-eye, topaz, agate, amber, zircon.

28. Mercury is extracted from cinnabar.

29. Some say this is a confusion; others say that Apollo was later identified with Helios, the sun god.

30. The number of 64 (8 x 8) is also the number of squares on a chessboard, the 8s symbolic of the snaking 8s of the caduceus. As a god of luck, Hermes is master of the games. As a part of the plea bargain, the younger boy will agree to testify against his friend. They will go to court to be judged. Mr. Miller died of a severed artery, which suggests the blood and pebble-stones of Hermes' judgment before the gods.

31. The ages of the two boys could mean nothing. However, there were twelve Olympian gods to whom Hermes sacrificed two of the cattle he'd stolen. At 12:00 A.M. on February 13, the Parentalia began in ancient Rome. At the Dionysus festival in Greece on the thirteenth of the month corresponding to February, the Day of Pots was held in Greece. At that time cooked food was offered on behalf of the

dead to Hermes. February for awhile under the old Roman calendar used to be the last month of the year, but then December became this.

32.   After Roosevelt's death in 1945, many letters were mailed suggesting Roosevelt's portrait he put on a coin. Some thought this should be the dime as Roosevelt, having had infantile paralysis, was identified with the March of Dimes drives. It's curious not only that Roosevelt had contracted polio in 1921 but that a Roosevelt dime replaced a Mercury one. All along, there's been the suggestion that Hermetic people are often flawed one way or another. Besides Franklin, there was homely Eleanor with her buck teeth, Julius Caesar with his epilepsy, Poe with his drinking, O.J. Simpson with his wife beating, John F. Kennedy with his adultery (his country was doing for him, while he was doing it in), and so on. Kennedy, furthermore, had set himself up as a hero, so it was inevitable that the public—seeing itself as the hero but lacking recognition—must slay him to prove itself somehow better. Newscasters pander to this tendency. We would have Marie Antoinette's head all over again if we could get it.

33.   The significance of 45 hasn't yet been explained. The probability of the number 45 and AGE LES coming up together is very small.

34.   Except for a small area in the southern tip, most of Maine has a zip code in the 04000 series. Stephen King writes about Maine. He was born at Portland, Maine, on September 21, 1947. Certainly you remember Castle Rock.

35.   Remember that the shape was round, for the word *kiva* will come up later.

36.   *Encyclopedia Americana.*

37.   Ann or Annie was born in Canada on March 22, 1867, or 1868, depending on what source you want to use. She was the daughter of Margaret and Duncan Cameron, both from Nova Scotia. Norma Beth Witbrodt, my cousin, wrote as follows: "The Camerons emigrated from the Isle of Skye, off the coast of Scotland and settled on Prince Edward Island and Cape Breton Island. We were told on the tour that most Scots who emigrated from Scotland settled on Cape Breton Isle." If true about the Isle of Skye, which was Celtic-Norse, we probably belonged to the same Cameron clan whose name was derived from the Gaelic meaning "crooked nose" as did the Scottish Highlanders. Certainly too, "crooked nose" is better than "crooked mouth" of the Campbells.

38.   Not recorded. "The first law requiring birth registration in North Dakota became effective July 1, 1893, but was repealed in 1895 and not re-enacted until 1899."

39.   The 1900 census has Daniel born in September 1857 and Annie in March 1867. According to it, they had been married for twelve years. Daniel was put down as an "ore sampler," a not too surprising occupation considering it was Montana, the fourth largest state, and rocks figuring in the scheme of things.

40.   Not recorded. Montana Bureau of Records and Statistics wrote: "Many birth certificates in the late 1800s and early 1900s were not put on file especially if the child was born at home." The date of birth was taken from her death certificate, and I too remember her mentioning 1900. However, the 1900 census, completed July 27, 1900, gives her birth as March 1899. It might have been incorrect, as there were inaccuracies noticed in both the 1900 and 1910 censuses. On the other hand, she might have subtracted a year from her age, figuring it sounded better to be born

in the twentieth century than the 1800s. A third possibility is that people those days, not having the paperwork to complete to remind them, sometimes got an idea in their head that their year of birth was one thing, while records showed otherwise. Both censuses show Daniel Duren's birth year as 1857. His death certificate says he was born on September 6, 1857, which would have made him eighty-eight years, eight months, and twelve days at death. However, a town clerk in Charleston, Maine, said his date of birth was a year earlier.

41.   The Office of Population Censuses and Surveys, General Registrar Office, St. Catherines House, London WC2B 6JP, is supposed to have records of births, deaths, and marriages registered in England and Wales since July 1, 1837. Though it records were researched from 1848 to 1852, nothing could be found on George Chichester. There's no record of him having filed preliminary naturalization papers or having been naturalized in Elgin, Illinois; Bridgeport, California; Douglas County, Nevada; or Carson City. Nor have I been able to get a copy of his death certificate from New York. Compounding the problem is that there's no clue as to a middle name, who at least one parent was, or in what city or township he was born. This doesn't mean the information's not out there somewhere. But until more facts turn up, it's incomplete, and there's a small possibility that what's thought to be known might not be entirely correct for one reason or another.

42.   The cycle of the moon is *roughly* twenty-eight days, the same almost as the amount of time for February, except for every four years. Mary Moon becomes Mary Tehu when the last name is changed to ancient Egyptian.

43.   *Complete Atlas of the British Isles* (The Reader's Digest Association, London, September 1983) mentions two facts only about Mereworth, other than it is of Anglo-Saxon origin: 1) It has Mereworth castle, and 2) the name Mereworth probably comes from or is associated with "Maera's homestead."

        Though unable to give a rational reason, whenever I see *AEA* in a word, such as in Alexander or Athena, or perhaps just *AE*, it has some sort of Greek or Hermetic significance. *MAE* and *AEA* can be derived from *Maera*. An interesting note too is that G.W. Russell, Irish poet, painter, and writer, became known as A.E., and Amelia Earhart liked to be called "A.E."

        In Assyrian-Baylonian mythology, Ea was a god of wisdom and sweetwater. (Eden [Eaden?] is thought of as a place where there'd be plenty of water.) Ea healed the sick, was the giver of art and sciences and, by one account, created mankind.

44.   *Encyclopedia Americana.*

45.   The combined age of the new couple was fifty-four. Elizabeth Mills was born February 4, 1850. George Chichester, July 3, 1850. She was four to five months older than he—almost five months but not quite.

46.   In over sixty years, no one, to my knowledge, has ever rebuilt on this property, which lies at the base of a mountain range later described. It's a graveyard, a deadman's hand, the last wager made in Mills. A few doting, ol' fruit trees labor to bear small fruit, and remnants of the gutted foundation can still be seen. Yet if this remains, could anything else from the past, good or bad? Maybe good but I doubt evil. For who in his or her right mind wouldn't agree to sixty years of enchantment and a swift death that comes like a thief in the night?

47.   On one ship I sailed in the 1950s, the sailors' quarters were in the forecastle (fok'sl), not a very pleasant place to have to sleep even then. But imagine how miserable the sailors must have been on the old ships with sails (and very few portholes) where the ordinary seaman were housed before the mast. George was described as being a very capable person, doing some doctoring, pulling teeth, barbering, cooking, etc.

48-A.   Many hours of rewrite were involved concerning Edgar Allen Poe, Abraham Lincoln, and Charles Darwin, as well as Martin Luther King, Jr., and others. Why? Some astrology books called them snakes without explaining the reasoning behind this. I assume then the authors either didn't know or possibly had believed the cutoff dates are somewhat arbitrary and that the rule of thumb in using the year might simplify things while coming pretty close to being accurate in many instances.

    Part or all of January and even more than half of February in some years belongs to the year before; e.g., 1808 is designated as a dragon year. But the dragon year actually began January 28, 1808, and ended on February 13, 1809. The earth-snake year technically began Februray 14, 1809, or St. Valentine's Day. But Darwin and Lincoln were born on Februray 12, 1809 and Poe, January 18, 1809. Martin Luther King, Jr., was born January 15, 1929. But the snake-year 1929 began February 10, 1929. There seemed to be a peculiarity of snakes in politics affecting other members of the family or even of a snake—not yet in politics—affecting another non-snake family member who was in politics. If this reasoning can be accepted, then perhaps the snake-year might also affect the end, or weakening, of the dragon year running into it. Certainly in myth and magic, dragons and snakes are close. This would explain Poe, Darwin, Lincoln, and King, all of whom—with or without the hypothesis—still seem to be Hermetic characters. Note too that Edwin Thomas Booth was born a snake on November 18, 1833, and died on June 8, 1893, a snake year. Though the greatest American actor of the nineteenth century, his personal life was extremely unhappy. His first wife died when she was young. His second wife was neurotic (shades of Mary Todd Lincoln?), but most importantly, could his snake birth have influenced his brother John Wilkes Booth, born four to five years later on August 26, 1838? If Lincoln is to be deleted from the snake presidents, Franklin D. Roosevelt will be added. The metal-snake year 1881 is given as January 30, 1881 to February 17, 1882. Franklin Roosevelt was born January 30, 1882. A metal-snake president was in place when the U.S. entered World War II in 1941, a metal-snake year, and will be elected to a fourth term.

48-B.   Lyndon Johnson hoisted his beagle by the ears and lost two wars: Vietnam and poverty.

49.   Mahatma Gandhi, born October 2, 1869, was an earth-snake. Under the caste system, he belonged to the *merchant* class. His father, Kaba, had two daughters from previous marriages when he married Putlibai. Three wives had died. Mohandas was the fourth child of four children of the fourth wife. He loved to take long, solitary walks in his youth. He and his wife, Kasturbai, had *five* children. The first died a few days after birth (Helen, my sister, lived less than a year), and they had *four* sons who lived. He was about to leave Durban (Duran?), South Africa, when he read in the *Natal Mercury* that the Natal legislature was considering a bill which would prevent Natal Indians from voting. He wasn't able to prevent the bill's passage, but he did draw worldwide attention to the Natal Indians' plight. Later in *prison*, he made a pair of *sandals* for General Jan *Christian* Smuts, who

wore them for several years. Both Gandhi and I had appendectomies and malaria (Febris: Roman god of malarial fever).

He undertook a twenty-one-day fast in 1924; completed another for twenty-one days in 1933; and still another was began on February 10, 1943, at the age of seventy-three for twenty-one days and completed. (Joan V. Bondurant, under Gandhi, *Encyclopedia Americana*.)

> In those days I, Daniel, was mourning for three weeks.
> I ate no delicacies, no meat or wine entered my mouth,
> nor did I anoint myself at all, for the full three weeks
> (Dan 10: 2, 3).

Notice 2122 and January 30 in Gandhi's life as well as in Roosevelt's, who contracted polio in 1921. Also tying into the Parentalia-Caristia number is the fact his oldest son, Harilal, was a dissolute drunk. His mother was dying when he visited her on February 21, 1944. His drunkenness upset her so much that he had to be removed quickly. The following day on February 22, Kasturbai died (remember my father died on February 22). Thereafter on the twenty-second of each month until his death, Mahatma held a memorial service for her. He was assassinated on January 30, 1948 (a Friday, like Jesus, John F. Kennedy, Martin Luther King, Jr.), and cremated on January 31, 1948. The time when Ramadas, his third son, lit the funeral pyre was 4:45 P.M. Mohandas Gandhi had his faults. His biggest failure was that "he never learned to be a father to his sons." He took the role of passive resistance (earth-snakes have delicate sensitivities, make very reluctant dragons, and are poor gamblers). Though several died in the resistance, Mahatma gambled mainly with his own life. There might have been more perfect people in a smaller sphere of influence. Yet none were greater in my lifetime (and perhaps many centuries previously) when you stop to consider what might have happened if he had not spun his circular loom and had been more aggressive.

An interesting note perhaps is that Orville Wright also died the same day as Gandhi. Forty-four years previously in December 1903, Orville and his brother Wilbur made their famous *flights* in the *winds* of Kitty Hawk, North Carolina. Wilbur died on May 30 (Memorial Day), 1912.

Some believe the skeleton for Tarot was the Jewish alphabet of twenty-two letters. Whatever, there are four suits having *fourteen* cards each and *twenty-two* trumps unconnected with the suits. The *twenty-two* trumps make up what is called the Major Arcana, with which the ordinary person is chiefly concerned. On these cards are *twenty-one* numbers and a zero, called the Fool. In readings the client selects *seven* cards. When the Major Arcana are laid out in the system of a wheel, the Fool is placed in the center as the hub (Op. cit., *Man, Myth and Magic*, from article title "Tarot" by Christine Hartley).

Here again is the suggestion of 2122 from a different or possibly connected system. It occurs to me that the Major Arcana could be adapted to the coven circle with one person sitting inside and representing the Fool. The twenty-one cards in my association represent a twenty-one-vertebrae snake. (See dice, page 266.)

When we speak of calendars, we're talking about chronology, a universal language. Gods of time offer us a way out of chaos that would result without measurement. So it's reasonable to look at the time an event happened as well as the unlikelihood that it would happen again. Is repetition a coincidence, a random happening? Or is there some pattern we are missing? It's easy here to see the syncretic Thoth-Hermes: Thoth, "the reckoner of time," judgment, lover of truth, and some say over Tarot; Hermes, god of measurement, gambling, as in the calculation of odds in card playing by professional gamblers. Tarot possibly is correlated into this some way. Assuming in the right hands Tarot isn't hogwash, it would offer for the mature few of acceptance (I'm not sure I'd fit into this group) a look to see, to prepare. But for most, it would be an unkindness, knowing that tomorrow you would get a vast fortune or that you or a loved one would die. In any case, you probably wouldn't be able to change things, for this runs counter to the truth of the Tarot. And certainly you wouldn't be able to sleep the night before, knowing these things. In this respect Tarot could be perceived as an unkindness or even an evil. It also puts the reader into the dilemma of forewarning to try to prevent the happening and the *inevitable* vanity of crowing later, "See, I said it would happen." I was right, the undercurrent of desire that wishes it so— no matter what—to be right.

In voodoo the number 21 seems to have some significance too.

There is a mild form of paranoia which the Haitians call *mauvais sang*. In treating it the afflicted's head is bathed in water in which seven or *twenty-one* leaves from different plants have been soaked. Those who want a dying man's zombie place under him a pot containing *twenty-one* seeds of *pois congo* and a *twenty-one*-knotted length of string. (Op. cit., *Man Myth and Magic*, from articles titled "Voodoo" and "Zombie" by Francis Huxley).

The Stewart and Watkins bookshop, located at 21 Cecil Court, an alley between Charing Cross Road and St. Martin's, is possibly London's leading store for occult works. Here people come from all over the world. (Op. cit., *Man Myth and Magic*, from article titled "Leafing through the Occult".)

Was the *twenty-one* in the above case just a random happening?

October 5, 1994, Cheiry, Switzerland: Hidden beneath a burning farmhouse at "Little Rocks" farm, police and firemen discovered a red, mirror-lined chapel containing *twenty-one* bodies, all laid out in a circle with their heads outward. Twenty-one has been defined as a number of "absolute truth." Certainly there's nothing more truthful than death. There's mystic to the number 21. Probably a fiction, yet legend has it that Billy the Kid killed twenty-one people in his twenty-one years.

50.   The year 1929 was a classic one in luck and bad luck, in boundaries and breaking of boundaries. Prohibition was still in effect with all its speakeasies and bootlegging. It was the year of the earth-snake and the month of the snake (May being designated the month of the snake for any year) on the eighth day that excavations and revelations began at Ras Shamra in Syria (temporarily suspended in 1939 because of the war). The Great Depression (commerce) followed on raven-Black Tuesday October 29, 1929, and lasted for ten years. (Our decimal system, of course, is based on ten, and Hermes is said to be the inventor of mathematics and Thoth of measurement.) In the early 1930s terrible droughts began. Rain first disappeared completely in some areas in 1934, and terrorizing dust storms darkened the sky from 1933 to 1935.

Most known about Baal comes from the Ras Shamra discoveries. El, the old father of the gods, is defeated by Baal, who is a tyrant and younger. Baal himself, a god of life, will be defeated now and then by Mot, a god of death. If Baal wins there will be seven years of fertility. If Mot wins, seven years of sterility. This brings to mind Joseph's interpretation of the dream:

> There will come seven years of great plenty throughout all the land of Egypt, but after them there will arise seven years of famine and all the plenty will be forgotten in the land of Egypt; the famine will consume the land (Gen 41: 29, 30).

The following, quoted with permission and thanks, is from July 1933 *National Geographic* magazine article by Claude F.A. Schaeffer titled "Secrets from Syrian Hills":

Hundreds of years before the composition of the Holy Book, the fundamentals of Christian morality were laid in Ras Shamra, the ancient Ugarit.

> Even Adam and Eve are mentioned in the Ras Shamra texts. They live in a magnificent garden in the East, a rather vague address, which, however, corresponds to that given in the Bible. Here are the oldest-known documents to mention the famous pair in whom, centuries later, the author of the story of Creation saw the parents of mankind.

> In the story as written by the Ugarit author, Adam was the founder of a nation of Canaan Semites, probably one of the oldest sheiks or kings, and therefore apparently a historic personality.

> Eve, however, who tempted Adam, is described as original-ly of a much more cruel nature than we gather from the charming story of the fall of man as told in the Bible.

> The author from Ugarit calls her the most vivacious of all the goddesses. As a matter of fact, Eve here distinguishes herself as the most cruel and revengeful of them. In the mind of the author, she is the symbol, or the queen, of a foreign race of conquerors from Asia Minor who reduced Ugarit to ashes and ruins. Thus Eve may also be a historic personality.

51.   Late in life, I would learn Brent is derived from the Irish name Bran, meaning raven. "Quoth the raven," Edgar Allen Poe, kindred spirit that I know. And why did Poe die at forty? In folklore the raven is an evil omen, a sign of death, misfortune, or mystery. The Celtic, chthonic (Greek chthon, the earth) god Bran had a cauldron that would bring the dead back to life though they couldn't speak. In Greek mythology, Tantalus had served up his son for the gods to eat. The gods told Hermes to restore him to life, which Hermes did by putting him in a cauldron. Cauldron, of course, sounds like call drum. In a sense, this may not be off, for we have kettledrums.

HAVEN ————>NEVAH
                    ————> HR ————> HERMES
RAVEN ————>NEVAR

Ralph Haven Chichester (RC = 21. On May *21*, 1881, Clara Barton organized the American Red Cross, a branch of the International Red Cross) was born in Reno, *Nevada*, on February 21, 1919. He died in Reno on *August 21, 1939*. 21-21-21. In each number 21, a gaming number, the number 22 (the John F. Kennedy assassination) is implicit, or vice versa, life-death, death-life. This will become even more obvious when comparing Ralph's vital statistics (and so in some ways mine) to those of our parents and stepmother.

The Big Bonanza in Nevada produced gold and silver (mining) worth more than 100 million dollars.

On *August 21, 1959*, three weeks before the nation's debut, the premiere of *Bonanza* was held at the Granada Theater in downtown Reno. (Buddy Frank, from article titled "Back to Bonanza," *Nevada* magazine, Nov/Dec 1993).

52.   This is the first time three numbers have come up together since 1777, which can be looked at as 1 + 21 = 22, or even 2122. In 1777 young *Alexander* Hamilton joined General Washington's staff. Hamilton was a true Hermetic character. Born an illegitimate child on the West Indian island of Nevis on January 11, 1755, he grew up to be both rash and brilliant (Jacob Ernest Cooke, *Alexander Hamilton*, New York: Charles Scribner's Sons, 1982). He believed in manumission. He named his eldest child *Philip*, who later, in defending his father's honor, was killed in a duel. Hamilton was in great despair over this, and like a fated character in a Greek tragedy, he himself will die on July 12 (a transposition of 21), 1804, the day following his duel with Aaron Burr. Had it not been for Hamilton's economics (*commerce*, banking, etc.), the United States might never have survived as we know it today. In fact, Washington and Hamilton were probably the two most important people in launching our new government *after it was formed*. Jacob Cooke (op. cit.) describes Hamilton as being Washington's "true alter ego."

Numbers alone show this close connection. On July 4 (4, the number for Hermes' birthday), 1776 (21), Hamilton was twenty-one. On July 4, 1777 (22), Hamilton was twenty-two. So the number 2122. When the Declaration of Independence was signed, Washington was forty-four, and so on July 4, 1777, Washington was forty-five. Actually Washington was forty-five when Hamilton became one of his aides de camp. Still another event which, to my way of thinking, was significant in 1777 will be discussed later.

The link of Caesar, an epileptic, of many Parentalia and/or Hermetic characters can't be emphasized enough. Why? A guess is that unless Christ was born in the Parentalia-Caristia period (as I suspect he was. Christ, furthermore, is consistent with Hermes simply because Bob Cratchett and family, conniving for their free turkey, keep coming back every year), Caesar was the most famous person to have been connected with it when he presided over the Lupercalia on February 15, *44* B.C. (5). Christ speaks of rendering "to Caesar the things that are Caesar's" (Mk 12: 77). When George Washington was a youth, he played in Joseph Addison's *Cato*. His part was that of Juba, adoptive son of Cato, who was an enemy of Caesar (Noemie Emery, *Washington*, New York: G.P. Putnam's Sons, 1976). Alexander Hamilton believed Caesar to have been the greatest man who ever lived. Though Thomas Jefferson might have been "chilled" by Hamilton's choice (Fawn McKay Brodie, *Thomas Jefferson and Intimate History*, New York: Norton, 1974), he had a slave called Caesar. As an architect, furthermore, Jefferson was greatly influenced by Roman design, and the sketch he drew of the marker he wanted over his own grave was a "plain die or cube...surmounted by an *obelisk.*" This was simply a Thoth-Hermes symbol. It makes no difference whether Jefferson consciously thought it was or not. Both Jefferson and John Adams (two of the original *five* on the committee which drafted the Declaration of Independence) will die on July 4, 1826, fifty years after signing the Declaration on July 4, 1776 (21). James Monroe, the *fifth* president and "political disciple and life-long friend" of Thomas Jefferson died on July 4, 1831, or *five* years to the day after John Adams, the second president, and Jefferson, the third president (2 + 3 = 5). Indeed if the nation is linked to Hermes by four (45), it is also linked to Julius Caesar by July. Lincoln either "read or dipped into" *Gibbon's Decline and Fall of the Roman Empire* (Carl Sandburg, *Abraham Lincoln: the Prairie Years and the War Years*, New York: Harcourt Brace Jovanovich, 1966). A picture called *Little Caesar* will depict Al Capone. Oscar Fraley in "'Bumper Sticker' Epilogue" (James R. Hoffa, *Hoffa the Real Story*, as told to Oscar Fraley, New York: Stein and Day Pub., 1975) says that Hoffa was a Caesar having more than one Brutus. Malcolm X (the Roman numeral for ten) informed Alex Haley that Caesar is Latin and pro-nounced "Kaiser," with a hard C (Malcolm X, *The Autobiography of Malcolm X*, as told to Alex Haley, New York: Ballantine Books, 1964). Undoubtedly George Watterston had read of Caesar too. He was appointed First Librarian of Congress in 1815. Jefferson, of course, had donated thousands of his own books to start up the new Library of Congress when it had burned down in the War of 1812. A book—writer, knowledge—can be associated with Thoth-Hermes.

53.   A half century later a horoscope column in a Seattle newspaper said whoever was born on February 21 left home at a very early age. Now it is a look into the past which seems chillingly accurate today, though on reading it I attached no partic-ular significance other than a lucky guess by an astrologer. The scientific com-munity would say that of thousands born on this day each year, 10 percent will leave home at an early age. It's right, of course. But Sir Isaac Newton might be equally right by replying, "Horseshit!" And this the scientific community would prefer to forget. By using the scientific-community reasoning, we might say only 10 percent of the visions claimed by people are worthy of even cursory investi-gation. Of these, only 10 percent might be true, but if we toss these out on the grounds that *might be* isn't positive proof, then by using the same yardstick, we have to toss out our religions. There appears to be a connection between the num-bers 4, 5, 21, 22, and the Parentalia-Caristia. It's more than a collage, less than a montage. The system can be likened to Tarot, though looking into the past. Like Tarot too, it's an individual reading, never completely free of egocentricity. It would be very flattering, of course, to think a god is only interested in me and that the rest of you are superfluous. But then I'd have to deduce 1) that he had only a one-track mind and 2) didn't have much class. Neither of these being very likely, though, I'd probably have become very condescending if they were.

With billions of people in the world, hundreds of millions are under a direct Hermetic influence at any one time, and everybody is under it at one time or another, depending on circumstances.

Life is simply sacrifice. True, more for some than others. But in the end, we're all sacrificed by death, the great equalizer. The natural progression is a god of sacri-fice. Sure this sounds morbid, morose, undertakerish but plausible by what we know. Death is a constant, while the afterlife or heaven is an unknown. A logic is that we're sacrificed so he can live, and he is sacrificed—an ongoing thing—so we can live. Human sacrifice of humans doesn't make much sense since the sacrifice will be taken anyway. Yet there would have been an irrefutable logic if Cain had said, "Hey, *mon*, you don't like my sakerfice? But you like Abel's sakerfice! That means you like Abel. Okay, I'll sakerfice Abel."

Who then, if anybody, interceded for this fugitive and wanderer?

Nellie Duren White, one of the aunts, died of breast cancer in October 1978. Like her father (according to his death certificate where she was the informant), Aunt Nell died at the age of eighty-eight years in Bakersfield, California. Both were born in Mercury periods. I was sailing at the time of her death. When the voyage ended, I was surprised to read I'd been listed as an honorary pallbearer on October 12. All this has sort of a Hermetic order.

54.   Though writing critically of people and things then, I see now the blame-game is much too complicated for human intellect. It can have tentacles stretching far into the past—genetic, environmental, ancestral, historical, biblical. It interacts with the blame-game of others. Rightfully or wrongly, as the case may be, it becomes a crutch or a lever.

The *game* began supposedly when Adam blamed God ("the woman whom *thou* givest to be with me" [Gen 3: 11–13]) and Eve, who in turn blamed the serpent. The rule then is to lessen the pressure by spreading the guilt. Yet by eating the fruit from the tree of knowledge, Eve had done exactly as she was expected to do. It's now an ongoing test to see if we still blame Adam, Eve, and the serpent for having gotten us into this fine mess. We do. The dilemma comes in whether or not to blame God, who is grave and serious, hardly to whom one would say in the child's game, "Adam and Eve and Pinchme went down to the river to bathe. Adam and Eve fell in. Who was left, God?" If we don't blame God though, we are lying. But He is God, and we must try to fool Him to cover our naked feelings. God then enters as a player on the human level. He is both pleased by our concern for Him and saddened that we lied. It is a dilemma, and so worthy of his intellect.

55.   As this book deals largely with dates, it's consistent with Quetzalcóatl and Thoth-Hermes, inventors of the calendar. Latin, *calendarium*, account book. Then too, *calendarium*, or account book, might suggest the weighing or account-judgement of Thoth-Hermes, Hermanubis. And of course our present calendar begins A.D., *Anno Domini*, the beginning of the Christian era.

56.   Poseidon (Neptune) is one of the twelve Olympians. He is a god of earthquakes, the sea, and water in general, such as lakes and fresh water springs. It's not surprising then that in ancient Rome a festival was held for him on July 23, when fresh water was probably shortest in the summer. In the *Odyssey*, Hermes supported Odysseus, while Poseidon was hostile toward him, as Odysseus had blinded the sea-god's son. Were it not for that, Poseidon also probably would have supported Odysseus, a wanderer, dependent on a lot of good luck. There's much between Poseidon and Hermes, uncle and nephew, that might be likened to a genetic link of gods, e.g., riverboat gambling; Laocoön, a priest of Troy, and his two sons were making a sacrifice to Poseidon, when two sea serpents (the caduceus has two snakes) crushed them to death for warning about the Trojan Horse, supposedly the idea of Odysseus, under the protection of Hermes, who was—by some accounts—his grandfather. Poseidon somehow has become the ruler of the descendents of Pontus and Oceanus. Hermes is related to Oceanus

through the ocean god's daughters Asia (the mother of Atlas) and Pleione (the wife of Atlas and mother of Maia). (Edward E. Barthell Jr., *Gods and Goddesses of Ancient Greece*, University of Miami Pres, Coral Gables, Florida: 1971.) Those controlling the sea usually controlled commerce or vice versa. Moreover, a sea is a graveyard and a river is a wanderer, traveler, as are wild horses. Implicit in the horse is the potential of speed, power, and luck (lucky horseshoe). To some extent, this is the same as storms at sea (bucking, spooking, stampeding horses) called forth by Poseidon, who can also grant a safe, successful voyage. There's a consistency here in the image of Poseidon being pulled by horses over waves. Hermes may have dominion of horses, but it's his uncle who created the horse, taught man to control it with the *bridle*, and originated the horse race, while Hermes is a god of competition (rodeo). Athena's olive tree might have been judged more useful to man (it's difficult to separate the Greeks and Italians from olives and olive oil) than Poseidon's horse, but you might have a hard time convincing the U.S. westerners of this. Poseidon (as well as Demeter) was worshipped in horse-headed form in Arcadia. The pine tree is sacred to him. Poseidon's earthquakes, furthermore, are consistent with good and bad luck. It was thought in very ancient times that the movement of a fish, turtle, or snake carrying the world caused an earthquake. Turtles, snakes, and possibly fish are associated with Hermes. At four years old, I thought of the Long Beach earthquake as a merry-go-round, horses going up and down. The only other remembrances are of damaged buildings, broken store windows with naked manikins, and areas roped off. Not until December 29, 1993, did I read of Poseidon's connection to horses. This is peculiar because five days earlier I woke up from a dream. In it, I remember dropping something from an icebox and making a peculiar remark to Mom (which I won't go into here) and her reply, "I know but it can't be helped." The year 1933 came into focus. The only thing remembered when I awoke about 1933 was the earthquake. There was no prescience, but two friends were told about the dream. Signed statements concerning this follow. On January 17, 1994, at 4:31 A.M., an earthquake measuring 6.6 on the Richter scale hit the Los Angeles area (epicenter Northridge, twenty miles northwest of downtown Los Angeles). At last count thirty-five had died, hundreds were injured, and a rough estimate of damage was more than seven billion dollars. The timing and the area in which it occurred seem strange, as I'd just realized and written in the revision about Poseidon's influence on the west, as well as my life. I had, of course, long since recognized Hermes', but this was something new, filling in blanks (horses, water, bridle), the 1933 earthquake, the years at sea.

Usually I'm too tired at night or not in the mood to lay out rocks in a circle, burn a candle, and pray. In practice this is done only at long intervals. Oddly I'd done this on the evening of January 16, 1994, recognizing in ritual for the first time Poseidon's influence. Nearly always an accident or disaster (usually a train wreck) follows the ritual. In the January 17 earthquake, a sixty-four-car train carrying sulfuric acid and other freight derailed. One car had some leakage, but no injuries were reported.

Accidents and disasters occur every day. Anyone can claim feelings of a vague connection after the fact, but I wonder if it's really that simple in every case, that such a dismissal isn't always wise. If there's a collective power of prayer, maybe there's a collective power of destruction.

Forever hortatoric, pompous, and making pronouncements for the record, I sent certified letters in early 1992 to the Long Beach mayor and city council not to separate the *Spruce Goose* and the *Queen Mary*, as I felt there was a Hermetic link (now Poseidon too) to the two and bad luck would follow if it were done. There was no idea what this would be, but water was conjectured. Since then Los Angeles (the angels, the messengers) has had the most destructive race riot in U.S. history. The city's still recovering from it. Many in northern and central California want to separate from southern California and become states themselves. Three months ago, a devastating flood and wildfires occurred and now the earthquake. An area this size will have some problems, but, in my opinion, until the *Spruce Goose* is returned, they will get worse. One last time...tomorrow (January 20, 1994) I'll send off certified letters to the mayors of Los Angeles and Long Beach and each city's council. The letter begins, "I am not certain in my mind that I really care what happens to your two cities. Yet I feel compelled someway or another to write."

The *Spruce Goose* and *Queen Mary* together represented reconciliation of the air and sea, to be viewed also as an underworld.

We, Rodney Franklin and Loren Mott, do hereby attest to the fact that Brent Chichester had told us on January 1, 1994 of a dream he said he had which occurred on December 24, 1993. At the time he told us of the dream, he said the year 1933 appeared distinctly. The only connection he said he was able to make for sure to 1933, at the time he was telling this, was the earthquake in Long Beach, California, where he said he lived at that time.

_____
Rodney Franklin, Seattle, WA   Date

_____
Loren Mott, Seattle, WA   Date

57.   Roman Mercury is sometimes seen with a bulging moneybag in hand. Conjecture is that it was originally a cornucopia.

58.   Hercules was the half-brother of Hermes, the god of flight, of measurement, of luck, who might have given us the four-leaf clover.

59.   The goose is sacred to Hermes, god of eloquence.

60.   He was born in the year that Las Vegas was founded as a railroad town. Hughes died in southern Texas. At the time he was on a flight from Acapulco to Houston. He'd just crossed a boundary and was returning to his birthplace.

61.   Richard Moreno, from an article titled "Wed and Wild," *Nevada* magazine, Jan/Feb 1994.

        1931 saw two big changes in Nevada laws: the residency requirement for divorce (breaking boundaries) was reduced from three months to six weeks, and gambling was legalized, since the state found it too expensive to enforce gambling laws. Prostitution is now legal in some counties. Ghost towns and rock formations are numerous. Mining, of course, deals with rocks. It was in keeping with Hermes, being a god of wealth and miners, that the rich, *silver* vein was found in Virginia City in 1859.

        The "Big Bonanza" was the greatest deposit found in the world—up to that time and since—of silver and gold. *Collier's Encyclopedia.*

280

62.   Op. cit., Moreno.

63-A.   "Wed and Wild" brought to mind for the first time in almost fifty years that I'd written a very amateurish piece about Valentine's Day cards. This was broadcast for fifteen minutes or half hour one year in the forties on February 14 by a local radio station, which apparently had made it a policy to donate some time to Bakersfield High School projects. Otherwise, the stillborn would never have made it on its own. Yet now the subject matter seems significant in the scheme of things, especially because it was the only school activity (a one-man show: writer, director, narrator) I can recall participating in.

        Kandi recently sent me the 1946 *Oracle*, the school yearbook when I was a junior. Of nearly one hundred students who had signed it (people I'd obviously known from the comments written), I can recall only two or three names.

        The ibis, a relative of the flamingo, is associated with Thoth because, some say, when it sleeps it tucks its head under a wing, thereby resembling a heart. The ibis's stride is said to be exactly that of a cubit, an ancient unit of measure (about eighteen to twenty-two inches) used in building temples. There are two kinds of ibis: one a white bird, the other black.

63-B.   Luxor is a winter resort and tourist attraction in southern Egypt. It has the temples of Luxor and Karnak, and royal cemeteries and mortuary temples. In Nevada, the Luxor (Las Vegas) is congruent with Thoth-Hermes.

64.   Op. cit., Moreno.

65.   Quetzalcóatl, of virgin birth, was considered wise and kind. He invented the arts, the calendar, and improved agricultural methods. In his main form, a creator god, he's a rattlesnake with beautiful green plumage of the quetzal, regarded by the ancient Mayans as a deity. Since *coatl* means "twin" or "snake," *Quetzalcóatl* could have several meanings, among which are "bird-snake," "flying twin," and "precious twin." These bring to mind the staff of Hermes. Quetzalcóatl ruled over the ninth hour of the day. It was in the ninth hour that Jesus died. Quetzalcóatl wears a bird-beak mask, symbolic of air; seashell earrings, his underworld-ocean trip; a breastplate, the whirlwind; a loincloth tip which is rounded, fertility; and a cone hat, wizardry (*Encyclopedia Americana*). He abhorred war and human sacrifice. Like Noah, whose sons Shem and Japheth *walked backward* and covered his nakedness, Quetzalcóatl got drunk, and Quetzalcóatl committed sexual sins in his drunkenness. For this he was banished to the underworld ocean by the other gods. He can't be criticized then for never having sinned or known its despair and punishment. The Aztecs always hoped and expected that he would return to them someday. Because things hadn't gone well in Mexico for the previous two years and the year seemed right, they believed Cortez riding his horse (deer) (Warwick Bray, *Everyday Life of the Aztecs*, New York: Dorset Press, 1987) must be their beloved god returning to them. There was much rejoicing at first before they realized they were wrong, though not completely. For Cortez brought Christianity, be that as it may at the time, having a curious twist: Cortez arrived on Good Friday 1519, the year on the Aztec calendar designated as 1 Reed, which wouldn't occur again for fifty-two years. Thus it's easy to see why in colonial times, Quetzalcóatl was thought to be Jesus. Even today—in reconciliation with the Aztec religion—at times and in some places, Quetzalcóatl is still impersonated in Christian ceremonies such as Easter. Both the city of Tula, where

Quetzalcóatl is supposed to have ruled, and its sagas are likened to the old-world city of Troy and the Greek epics of Homer (*Encyclopedia Americana*). Both Hermes and Quetzalcóatl are reconciliation gods between earth and sky, the underworld and heaven. Conducting the souls of the dead, Hermes becomes an intermediary. Note the combining of the snake and bird. The rainbow, often seen in myth as a snake, is another bridge between heaven and earth. (Man Myth and Magic, article titled "Serpent" by Douglas Hill, 1983). A rainbow snake (color suggestive of the beautiful emerald and crimson plumage of the quetzal with its *iri*descent tail feathers) can be associated with Quetzalcóatl, *Iris* and Hermes. For Hermes, there's the winged staff and snakes which bring peace, harmony, and reconciliation. The bird aspect is suggested in Hermes' winged *sand*als. Quetzalcóatl, manifested as a plumed serpent, also suggests peace, harmony, reconciliation. When departing from the world, he is said to have left on a raft of snakes in the Atlantic. Both his seashell earrings and his place of banishment suggest reconciliation with the sea too. Hermes (the son of Zeus, nephew of Hades and Poseidon), as a wind-god, traveler, messenger-god wearing sandals, can also be seen as a reconciliation god to Poseidon as well as Hades. In footnote 82, you will see there are wading birds (footprints and water implied) in the heraldry: in the one case, having a snake, in the other, an eel. The word *Aztec*, by the way, is derived from the word *heron*. The digression in this note for awhile is made for understanding, to diffuse the name Baal, as it was used to describe Yahweh and others. Baal in the first part of the *Old Testament* was a word that meant "Lord" or "possessor" or "owner." It was a loose term that apparently applied to several deities, as well as at times to a god of distinct character, such as Yahweh. But probably most times it meant the Canaanite god of fertility and rain. Thus it was thought by his followers that he had the power to give what was on their minds most in making their way through life: a mate, a child or children, an increase in livestock, and an abundance of crops. And to the little man who is overwhelmed by the happenings in the world, doesn't such a god also act as a protector, bringing luck and prosperity? Perhaps Yahweh, or the followers of Yahweh, might have been willing to let it go at that but people have/had a tendency to put their own evil spin on the ball, doing things which can't be condoned. Among the worst were Ahab, King of Israel, and his wife, Jezebel, who wanted to supplant Yahweh's priests from her own Phoenician cult of Baal. Elijah, the prophet, like Moses before him, told the people they must choose: "How long will you go limping with two different opinions? If the Lord is God, follow him; but if Baal, then follow him" (I Kings 18: 21).

A test was set up to show who had the power. Was it Yahweh or Baal? The prophets of Baal called upon their god unsuccessfully to start a fire at their altar. When Elijah called upon God, however, a fire started at his altar even though water previously had been poured on the wood.

> And when all the people saw it, they fell on their faces; and they said, "The Lord, he is God; the Lord, he is God." And Elijah said to them, "Seize the prophets of Baal; let not one of them escape." And they seized them; and Elijah brought them down to the brook Kishon, and killed them there (I Kings 18: 39, 40).

The mess had to be cleaned up, and it could have been Yahweh's will however it was done. But the fact the prophets had to be seized by the people suggests Elijah might have used trickery in starting his fire. The Lord previously had said, "Thou shalt not kill" and that vengeance is his. Why then did Elijah not say, "I now call upon the Lord to make Baal's prophets drop dead on the spot"?

Followers of Yahweh are quick to assume Baal didn't exist, or if he did, he was the weaker god. There could have been at least two other possibilities. First, perhaps Baal, like Yahweh, did not like to be tempted, to jump through a hoop at human command. Second, if Jezebel's cultists were offensive to Elijah and Yahweh doctrine, they might also have been offensive to Baal. So why defend them? The Israelites have a long history of being stiff-necked and uncompromising. Here was an opportunity to paint with a broad brush and take over. Nothing, of course, justified Hitler killing the Jews, and there's no reason to believe he represented Baal, yet there's an irony here in two incidents, the fanaticism of slaughter. Kill, kill, kill without mercy. If you are a follower of Baal, you are dead. If you are a Jew, you are dead. Or whatever, you are dead. But what about the majority of a minority, the little people, who are/were just trying to make it down the road of life and who hadn't much in common with an extremist other than a label? After the first part of the *Old Testament* , the word *baal* began to take on an increasingly derogatory connotation (*bósheth* meaning shame was substituted so that by the time of the *New Testament* , Baal-zebub had become the supreme boogeyman, Beelzebub, prince of false gods and demons. In the *Old Testament* there are many words using Baal. A few of these are listed below:

Baal-berith, Lord of covenant (Judg 8: 33).
Baal-zebub, the healing god of Ekron (II Kings 1: 2).

Jerubbaal, aka Gideon (Judg 8: 29).
Bealiah, which probably means "Yahweh is Baal" (I Chron 12: 5).

Mount Baal-hermon (Judg 3: 3).
"It is like the dew of Hermon, which falls on mountains of Zion!" (Ps 133: 03).

Three rivers rise at the foot of the *highest* mountain in Palestine, Mt. Hermon, the name suggesting Hermes (also Hermod, the son of the chief god and messenger to the gods in Norse mythology, who went to Hel to fetch Balder). There will be those who protest this, saying the name isn't linked, and who give their own derivation of the mountain's name. But the bottom line is that they really don't know for certain. The argument is made from what the name suggests today. Three rivers join in the Hula Basin. This plain was formerly the now-drained Lake Huleh (note again the number three: Lake Huleh, Sea of Galilee, and Dead Sea). The Jordan River, of course, is fed by other streams. But the *three rivers* are its main source as it enters the Sea of Galilee. As it leaves the Sea of Galilee, it's fed by the Yarmuk River. From its beginning at the highest point in Palestine, the Jordan River meanders to the Dead (4514) Sea, the *lowest* place on the earth. If there's the trinity of the Father, Son, and Holy Ghost, there is also the trinity (perhaps suggested by the trident) of Hades, Poseidon, and Zeus. Hermes, whose father was Zeus and whose uncles were Poseidon and Hades, was simply a reconciliation god between them. Note, in the supernatural, Hades and Poseidon are close. You will also find the Dead Sea is called the Salt Sea.

The Jordan is a boundary river. Historically blood has been spilled many times over, on, or near it as it has been crossed. The river, life-giving, life-supporting, also symbolizes a snake and, in emotional, pious language, death. (Hermes, conductor of the souls of the dead, god of boundaries, crosser of boundaries.)

It was fitting John the Baptist (who had said earlier he wasn't worthy of carrying Jesus' *sandals* (Mt 3: 11) baptized Jesus in the Jordan (rivers associated with Poseidon; Jordan begins at Mt. Hermon. Because of this beginning and the baptism, it might also be called the Lordan [Jordan]). John the Baptist, a wayfarer, is *beheaded in prison* later. (Centuries before, David—the ancestor of Jesus—is also dealing in decapitation. Carrying a staff, a shepherd's bag with five stones, and a sling, he removes one and kills Goliath with one shot to his forehead. Still it behooves David to chop off Goliath's head with the giant's sword.)

Then in the third century comes Valentine whose head is severed. He becomes a patron saint of travelers and lovers, among others. Also in the third (or early fourth) century, three saints—Felix, Regula, and Exupernatus—are beheaded by a headman's ax for trying to convert ancient Zurich, Turicum, to Christianity. Legend is that they then stood up, picked up their heads, and *walked* to a hilltop and lay down in graves they'd dug. (Hermes, god of graveyards.) There is, in fact, a recurrent theme of some sainted person *walking* with his head tucked under his arm. Decapitation, persona Hermes, can also be surmised from his providing Perseus with a special sword for beheading Medusa.

Though John was given the unequaled honor of baptizing Jesus, all who follow Hermes, Christ, or Quetzalcóatl cling respectively to the pendulum of the caduceus, cross, or rocking raft at sea as it swings between suffering-sorrow and knowledge-wisdom. Quetzalcóatl, leaving the world on a raft of snakes (trinity: bird, snake, sea) in the Atlantic, is similar to Christ with arms extended on the cross, like wings of a caduceus whose snakes (possibly now seen as sinners or thieves) encircle. If the snake is the most spiritual of all creatures, it is also the most mystical. It's encircling association is seen in a ring or bracelet and perhaps spinning wheel.

Jesus is a Nazarene (*AZ, AE*). His symbol will become the cross. He preached on and around the *Sea* of Galilee (*AE, LI*). He commanded the wind, stilled and walked on water. The symbol of the Christian Church and State will be a ship. Jesus' rock will be Peter, a fisherman. As a fisher of men, Jesus' symbol among early Christians will be a fish, a creature of the deep. The ocean encircles the earth like a snake. It's important to remember that both Christ and Satan, being two sons of Yahweh, share the symbol of the snake. (Ad de Vries, *Dictionary of Symbols and Imagery*, Amsterdam: North-Holland Publishing Co., 1974.) "And as Moses lifted up the serpent in the wilderness, so must the Son of man be lifted up..." (Jn 3: 14). There are two snakes on the caduceus.

An *earthquake* occurs at Christ's death in the ninth hour, representing the trinities, parallel and congruous:

RECONCILIATION

The notion came to say the earthquake was 4.5 on the Richter scale. I began to laugh, feeling both uncomfortable for having the idea and laughing. No, I wasn't about to write about the earthquake, its epicenter, or anything like that. The ideas was dismissed. Was it this morning or last night this happened? Then tonight February 11, 1994, I scarcely resumed reading in a fiction book (Bentley Little, *The Revelation*, New York: St. Martin's Press, 1989) started earlier when reading that one John *Palmer* had reported an earthquake occurring above the town of Randall, Arizona, as being 4.5 on the Richter scale. This didn't augur well at first glance since the earthquake was supposed to have been caused by Satan. Yet it could have an entirely different meaning, such as a mocking, irreverent use of the number.

> And behold, the curtain of the temple was torn in *two*, from top to bottom, and the rocks were split; the tombs also were opened, and many bodies of the saints who had fallen asleep were raised..." (Mt 27: 51, 52).

But if you divide the hour of nine when Christ's death occurred by two, you come up with 4.5.

It's not important what day St. Valentine's Day was at that time, but what it is today, the forty-fifth (*nine*) day.

Very possibly this most closely represents the day Christ died rather than the present Good Friday in spring, making it easier to attend Easter church services. Curiously too an article appearing in the *Washington Post* on February 14, 1917, states that a mistake had been made by inaugurating new clothes on Easter when "according to popular superstition" hundreds of years old, it should be on St. Valentine's Day.

St. Valentine (AE, LI), later decapitated, commemorated Christ's death. The usual colors thought of for a Valentine's Day card are red and white. The red signifies blood and white, death. Still the overall message of the red heart is a pumping *love*.

66. This tree embodies the summertime spirit of Avenal, whose greatest legend to date is that in 1940 Clark Gable, then shooting the film *Boom Town*, almost went there. I don't know why the poplar grows at the gates of Hades, but the willow obviously was placed there by Asclepius for those who need aspirin for one hell of a headache they just got on realizing where they are.

67. Ten miles west of Naples, Italy, is a lake called Averno. This, to my understanding, is a crater of an extinct volcano called Avernus by ancient Romans who believed it to be the entrance to Hades (5). Shade (anagram) = Heat.

68-A. When Hermes stole Apollo's herd, he drove it backwards. One witness of this was an old man called Battus who was bribed not to tell what he'd seen. One version of the story is that Hermes distrusted Battus and later returned in disguise, bribing him again, this time to tell what happened. It was a strange sight Battus had seen, a baby wearing sandals and driving cattle which walked backward. Battus blabbed everything he knew. For this double-dealing, Hermes turned him to stone. Thus that Hermes is a god of thieves, whose code supposedly is not to fink, is founded in mythology. Curiously, police officers follow this same code—to some extent—among themselves.

68-B. Sometimes connected with the underworld.

68-C. "Oh I'm not saying he doesn't have his thinking cap on at times," someone's bound to scoff. "It's just that most the time he's as mad as a hatter. All that preoccupation with snakes. Makes my flesh crawl!"

   When making felt hats years ago, the hatters used *mercurous* nitrate, which can be toxic, causing St. Vitus's Dance. At another level, the broad-brimmed hat or the small, winged one or both that Hermes had made mightn't have fit right, causing him to chase after one or the other in the wind. Naturally "whom the gods wish to destroy, they will first drive insane."

69.   Long (measure) Beach. Bakersfield was named after Colonel Thomas Baker's field, but the name Baker itself suggests a type of cook.

70.   Mao Zedong was a water-snake. Born December 26, 1893 (21), he died on September 9 (MP), 1976, two hundred years after the Declaration of Independence in 1776 (21).

71.   Though cheap with myself, I was usually generous with others and a good tipper.

72.   We got to Shanghai one trip. A few customs and immigration officials sat in the saloon mess. Some talked to me while I was still working. The conversation got around to Korea, which one said was nothing more than an American puppet-government. I laughed evenly and said it was probably true in one sense. But if so, the same could be said about North Korea being a puppet government of Communist China. "Oh no!" they corrected me. They had nothing to do with the North Korean government. Having heard a lot about the communist government and people, most of us were not too adventurous other than to take a taxi to and from the seamen's club. One officer who had a full day off decided to hire a taxi for the day and travel around the city. His driver had a college degree and spoke English fluently. In the course of the conversation, the driver commented that Americans were very wasteful (they don't take tips in China). The officer, a natu-ralized American of Swedish origin, asked him to explain this. He replied that if the officer had a hole in his sock, he would just throw his socks away. "Not so!" the officer protested. "If they aren't too bad, my wife will mend them." "Oh no!" the driver shot back. "You throw them away."

In Ethiopia one evening, a man came up to me and began talking. He asked what I thought of his country. I said I liked the people okay but thought the poverty was terrible. The main square of the city looked like it needed a face-lift ten years before. Two alleys or roads running into it had seepage in places and trash heaped up. Some of the people were skinny, and some were sleeping out in the open. The man said it was just as bad in the United States. He knew this for cer-tain for he had lived in Detroit and been to other cities. I agreed with him that we had poverty but added that most of our poor were rich to the poor in third-world countries where babies' bellies sometimes could be seen distended in starvation. Besides that, I asked, if the U.S. was so bad, why were so many trying to get into the United States? One thing led to another. He became angry and wanted to know the name of my ship. He then informed me he was the commissar for all navy ships in the harbor and that it might very well be regretted what was said to him. The little shit!

In truth, there were other places in the city which were not so bad, but most of the nicer buildings had been built thirty years before. Some of the people were obvi-ously scared to be talking at any length, even apologizing that the communists might be watching them. A barber I went to used a rachety, old Oster clipper on me. He explained it was all he had and that he couldn't get a replacement for it. He asked if I could bring him one the following trip, which was done.

73.   Astrology connects mushrooms to Hermes.

74-A.   Though usually not thought as such, spring can be looked at as paying homage to winter.

        The indirect association with flowers has to be among many correspondences to Hermes, god of graveyards. Lavender is cited specifically. Roses, being symbolic of eternal love, were sometimes placed on the forehead of the dead. In Rome two days, May 21 and 23, were called the Rosalia, where roses decorated the tombs. Parsley comes from two Greek words (rock plus celery) and means plant that grows from stone. Though having bad luck overtones for the living (M. Leach, *Standard Dictionary of Folklore, Mythology and Legend*, Funk and Wagnalls Co., 1950), parsley was considered sacred to the dead. It sometimes adorned the graves and tombs both in ancient Greece and Rome. My nephew Ross and his wife, Teddy, owned a flower shop in Minden, Nevada, and other relatives lived in nearby Gardnerville.

74-B.   An assumption is that the Walker River and lake were named for Joseph *Reddeford* Walker (1798–1876), who was a guide and explorer. In 1833 (SY), he and an exploratory party of fifty men are thought to have been the first whites to have crossed the Sierra Nevada. From this experience, he became a guide to several wagon trains going to California. In 1845 (SY) and 1846 (the year of the Donner Party) he led Fremont's third expedition there.

        75-A.Many of my mother's college books and short stories later written were in boxes in the cabin's screened porch. I asked my father for some of these. He said he *might* give me one or two when I left for school. Whether taking any—or possibly refusing to—I can't recall, but I'll always remember his reply. Funny the baggage we carry with us through life. The cabin went down in flames within a year or two. They didn't know exactly what caused it but believed a fire in the woodburning stove hadn't been completely extinguished. Burnt was going to school in Bakersfield at the time.

75-B.   LDS records. So much for superstition. Note crossover in occupation. His father's ranch in Coleville probably had cattle.

76.   Both Hermes and Poseidon, the Lord of Horses, having great sport.

77-A.   Many years later, Anita would write that the Marine Corps cold-weather training station at Bridgeport, California, had challenged the ranchers in the area to a contest to see which team, the ranchers or the marines, could pull the other into the icy river in a tug of war. Warren, then in his forties, seemed surprised, Anita said; the ranchers won. I wasn't.

77-B.   Anita Carmel McElroy Chichester died March 25, 1977, at Santa Rosa, California. Her father: John McElroy. Her mother's maiden name: Mary F. Murphy.

78-A.   Apollo had given Hermes the responsibility to tend to the oxen in the field, *horses* and mules, lions, wild boars, *dogs*, and flocks and cattle. *Homeric Hymn Number 4.*

78-B.   One whose name corresponds to twenty-one is a protector of the helpless. (Gertrude Jobes, *Dictionary of Mythology, Folklore and Symbols*, New York: The Scarecrow Press, 1962.)

78-C.   A narrow trail across from Lake View Cemetery circles around and down into a beautiful wooded area, a peaceful place having a calming effect. At times a jogger or a dog walking its master might pass, but more often than not, it's complete solitude, a well-kept secret between me and the owl yet to be seen.

One day coming into a place where the trail gets much steeper, I came across an artifact, partly hidden in the bushes. Pulling it out, I saw it was a plastic relief about three and one-half feet high and two feet wide with two masks held by their hair by a graceful goddess. It was hardly National Geographic. More like something brought from a huge, old, ornate movie-house before the wreckers came, then hung outside on a garden wall where the rain had destroyed part of her head and left shoulder and hand. It never was nor could it be considered now fine art, but somehow it is mysterious, a nostalgia which has culled the look of a million eyes, an aura of theater, appropriate to the muse. Perhaps it once hung in some richly carpeted foyer, but now it looked like a piece of discarded junk. The manager of the place in which I stayed was an artist. I thought of giving it to him, if he wanted it. Someone who knew what he was doing could restore it nicely. But was it really worth the trouble? Or would I be giving away a white elephant? I left it out in plain sight to carry back.

Down below, I'd just finished the number of exercises when a jogger passed heading up. How foolish to have left the artifact out in the open. I wondered if it would still be there when returning and why somebody bothered to carry the heavy thing a considerable distance down the trail to abandon, if so inclined, it would have been easier to chuck it down the hill to be hidden by trees and vegetation below or, easier yet, to have thrown it into a dumpster. Maybe there was a curse on the thing which eventually brought down the theater. Still I wanted it, curse and all. As it was there was no reason for concern. The goddess, one of the necromancy nine, was waiting. There was a cord tied to two hooks in back which some previous owner had used to hang it. Using this and frequently shifting it back from arm to arm, I managed to get it back up the trail to Fifteenth Avenue, past the cemetery office, and had just cut across Volunteer Park to Fourteenth Avenue when a Japanese gardener and his assistant in a small truck saw me. As usual they began to laugh as if they thought I were some huge joke, a side show *Seattlea Godzillacus*. Or at least that's the way I perceived them, which was probably right half the time. I can no longer sift all this out with unerring accuracy. Certainly it's safe to say, however, that any vestiges of Japanese inscrutability were gone. I'd been tempted to pull my eyes to slant, bow, and say, "So sorry," but translated the message only by giving them the finger on one occasion. Race and minority relations will never improve because too often those who are the outraged victims of a racial slur or cruelty on one street will double-clutch and double-think on to another, dishing it out to someone they think inferior. For this reason, I can't get involved in the plight of the police, retards, postal workers, youth, aged, blacks, whites, you name it, in short the whole kit and caboodle of society.

The masks hanging from the goddess's hand were right on: one for comedy, the other for tragedy. "It's a great world if you don't weaken," my brother Warren used to say. To this might be added, it curdles the milk of life, this world, which is easier to write and read about than to live in. It maintains its sanity only by the mantle of drugs, alcohol, cigarettes, coffee, sex, gossiping, lying, welfare, and high-flying above the others. Most important, no matter what you go to do in it, there's always someone around to say it really wasn't so, that there's no such thing as a pure act. Suppose, for example, I were to tell you I knew for a fact that gentle Jesus was a fraud, a drop-out from life at thirty-three. No way could he have gone on into old age. "No moh, no moh," he said, and acquiesced to his crucifixion, a respectable form of suicide. Could you ever forgive him? Could you ever have loved him if he hadn't said he was 1) dying for your sins (paying the bills) and 2) going to get you into heaven (had influence)? Could you ever have forgiven him if he belted out truthfully, "I'm gonna buy your love!" That's what I thought! You were never ever really Christian down deep.

And Jesus looked down from the cross and said, "Remember for me that any suicide diminishes one and all."

I'd gone maybe twenty-five yards when a man dressed as if he'd just removed his tie, came up: "Excuse me," he said. "Could I see that?" "Oh, that's not one of ours."

He explained that a jogger had come by the cemetery office and reported he's seen something down on the path below which he figured might have been taken from the cemetery. I assured him that though walking through the cemetery occasionally, it was the last place I'd steal from. He probably understood this to mean: He'd steal from us, and he admits being a thief. Nevertheless, it wasn't the cemetery's.

Walking on, I thought that rather than carrying a curse, the relic caught my attention because it was supposed to be mine. Then from out of nowhere came a redheaded bloke and the Japanese gardener closing in. The Japanese man stood back, an imperial witness, while Red comes on like gangbusters, no preliminaries, no nothin' but the fish eye:

"Where'd you get that?" a cadence and tone he might have used on a disobedient child. A sign over his pocket read Lake View Cemetery. I told him about already talking with someone from the cemetery, and he had to realize by now it didn't belong to the cemetery. Yet he, the head gravedigger, was still cocked and primed to find a culprit or to give me a hard time. Instead of asking who I talked to and what was said, he tells me I'd been seen coming out of the cemetery carrying this. Someone's huge lie. Common sense should have told him that it was very unlikely something that big would have been lugged into it and then back out again. What was told to his superior about finding it in the park down below was repeated.

"Then you took something that didn't belong to you. It's not yours," says the relentless guardian of the dead. "It belongs to the Parks Department." Who in the hell does this guy think he is? I took something which was thought to be a piece of discarded junk. If he's going to play cops and robbers, he ought to read me my Miranda, which they call the wind, a lot of wind. And if they don't, they should.

"You're nothing but a phony," I tell him. Sure something a lot saltier to say than that might have been thought up. But who thinks of this stuff until later? This probably explains why many of us survive as long as we do.

Anyway with that salvo, he and the gardener leave.

Sticking the relic in some bushes, I decided to go to the cemetery office and give them a piece of my mind, though you probably suspect there aren't that many pieces left.

Mr. Cool, the guy first talked to, comes out and I tell him about wanting to know who it was who made the accusation I'd been seen coming out of the cemetery with the relief? About this time enters Red. I explain I don't mind being talked to politely, but "I'm no piece of shit!" If they thought something was stolen, they should have called the police if it was out of the cemetery's jurisdiction. Red on the head, who works with the dead, says that they'll just do that now. I call, "That's fine with me, go ahead." Mr. Cool says that it won't be necessary. It was a "misconception." He repeated the story about the jogger. Red for the time being is saying no more. There's no apology. Still I'd said what I came to say and left.

Possibly the Strouts in the cemetery are distant relatives. Now I'll never visit it again, which had been a practice on Sunday mornings. Ooooh! Poor Brent the Dent! A Strout might pout! You're thinking that big baby shouldn't let things like that upset him; it was he who made an issue, not the cemetery. But if I'd walked meekly away, you'd say there goes a spineless jellyfish who should have learned to stand up for himself years ago. The artist looked at the relief and didn't want it, apparently figuring it wasn't worth the trouble. But Jack, a resident of one of the apartments happened to see it, thought it was great, and commented that he'd like to have it, if I ever wanted to get rid of it. But restoration would ruin it, he felt. The appeal was just as it was. Since two other people besides Jack had seen and wanted it, I decided to send it to Lowell and Cathy for Stephanie, who, while still in grammar school, is a talented artist. If they didn't want it, send it back. I'd pay the cost. I thought it would be kind of a goofy, fun thing for her to have, now with a history of a goofy, great uncle to go along with it. There was some trouble getting it packed, for which I paid extra. When apologizing to the two packers that it was just a piece of junk, they both said practically in unison, "If you don't want it, we'll take it." But after sending it, I never heard whether it got there. Maybe it's best. One must not be dinghi. Dinghee? Dinghy? Dinghee? Dinghi? How you spelll deenghi?

Jack felt the action taken was too mild, too milktoast. Says a lawsuit should have been snapped on them. Little does he know that communication is being made for a *Night of the Living Dead*. After all, being born on the Feralia, you're entitled to a few perks in life and death.

79.   Ralph was born at 2:15 A.M. on February 21, 1919. The accident occurred on August 19, 1939, a Saturday. He died on August 21, 1939.

John Denver, singer and songwriter, crashed into a tree near his Aspen home on August 21, 1994. A gash in the forehead required fourteen stitches. He was arrested on same date on August 21, 1993, in Aspen, also for drunk driving (*People Weekly*, December 26, 1994–January 2, 1995). Asp-pen. Denver carried the DE (45) of his original German name.

80-A.   Ralph was the one brother seen least. He was usually gone. When he did come home in the summer, it was for only two or three days a month. In a week or so, I'd have had to leave to begin school in early September. It's been over three decades now since visiting Topaz, but I believe the irrigation ditch or canal alongside the road extended up as far as the accident, or nearly so.

This would suggest Poseidon, tamer and creator of horses, whose powerful, nervous, and wild nature is associated with the god. Bear in mind too George Chichester's strong link to Poseidon when sailing before the mast at fourteen, that February (when Ralph was born) was protected by Neptune in ancient Rome (Michael Grant and Rachel Kitzinger, *Civilization of the Ancient Mediterranean*,

New York: Charles Scribner's Sons, 1988) and that there was a festival for Ceres (Demeter, having an emblem of a horse's head), the goddess of agriculture on August 21 (the date Ralph died) in Roman antiquity. Poseidon was thought to have a gold palace in the sea near *Aegae* and been a lover of Demeter, but the parents of Persephone, who Hermes returns to earth in May, were Demeter and Zeus.

Livy, however, says the festival on August 21, the Consualia, was for Neptunus Equestris, and Plutarch and others say the Consus and Neptunus Equestris were different names for the same god. Horse and chariot races took place, and horses and mules on this day were garlanded and not allowed to do any work. (William Smith and Charles Anthon (editors), *Dictionary of Greek and Roman Antiquities*, New York: Harper and Brothers, 1878.)

Remember too that Duncan Cameron, Ralph's great grandfather, was brought up on the wild coast of Cape Breton, shipped on the schooner *Violet* for nine months, and then drove a team of horses for three years on St. Peter's Canal. Ralph had wanted to be a veterinarian. In Tenos, Poseidon was worshipped under the title of the "healer."

Again there seems also to be a similarity in Poseidon and Hermes in being bringers of good and bad luck. This is suggested in Poseidon's ability to call up winds and storms at sea or to calm them, as well as to cause earthquakes anywhere. Trade on or by the sea is also under his power.

A curious piece of knowledge, perhaps, is that Lake Mead was born on *February 1, 1935*, when the last of Hoover Dam's tunnels was closed, diverting the Colorado River. (See "A Lake is Born" by Carolyn Graham, *Nevada*, June 1995.) In ancient times, there was often an association of the horse to the realm of the dead, and sacrifice of the animal was made to them. (Op. cit., *Dictionary of Symbolism*.)

80-B.   Op. cit., *Dictionary of Greek and Roman Antiquities*.

80-C.   The three brothers Bruce, Frank, and Roy, had ranches in the valley. Each lost a son under tragic conditions. Frank lost Ralph. Roy, as I recall (this could be wrong), lost George, his son by a previous marriage, to suicide. Bruce's son Dwight also took his own life.

81.   Hermes is said to be a god of pastures.

82.   The mountain with arms extended was a winged-staff with two snakes, one on each side. In heraldry one branch of the Chichester family in England has a bittern rising with an eel in its beak. Another, a stork with wings addorsed and a snake in its beak. The snake is symbolic of the writhing wind and possibly the same can be said for the eel in the ocean. The stork and heron are allied to the Egyptian ibis, one of Thoth's sacred animals, and sometimes he is represented in human form with the head of an ibis or baboon, quite often with a crown of a crescent moon supporting a disk-shaped moon. Thus both the animal-human manifestation and the phases of the moon suggest that Thoth is a god of change. Hermes is said to have taken the form of an ibis when the Olympians—fleeing Typhon—went to Egypt. So we have the snake of Hermes and ibis of Thoth. Noted in *The General Armory of England, Scotland, Ireland, & Wales* (Sir Bernard Burke, London: Harrison and Sons, 1878) are two Chichesters similar to the one

or the other above and having supporters with one or two gules (red) wolves "ducally gorged" and chained, at least in one instance.

"All this blue-blood pretense," a friend sniggers, as if I'd taken leave of my senses. There is no objection to the other cuckoo stuff though. He must be insane too.

In many ways the snake is emblematic of the nine-day Parentalia. The west European god Woden had skill as a sorcerer and magician. There's an Anglo-Saxon verse containing the *Nine Herbs Charm*:

> The snake came crawling and struck at none. But Woden
> took nine glory-twigs and struck the adder so that it flew
> into nine parts'....

Glory-twigs are runic inscriptions carved on pieces of wood. (Raymond Buckland, *The Tree: The Complete Book of Saxon Witchcraft*, New York: S. Weiser, 1974.) Here it's important to remember that as long as the number 9 exists, it can be separated into its two biggest components 4 and 5, or divided into two halves of 4.5 each. No matter what, you still end up with 45.

83-A.   Curiously my maternal grandparents had in fact come from the Eden area in Montana.

83-B.   One of the good-old-days stories Mom loved to tell at family gatherings was about the mystery of the hat. She explained that when she was a young girl, men, women, and children wouldn't think of stepping outside the house without a hat. She was being sent to Long Beach, California, to live with an older sister and go to school, because the school of a town like Maricopa, California, wasn't good enough for this little girl. Preparations were being made, school clothes were bought, also a "dear little hat," in the words of my aunt who bought it for her.

In those days when hats were the thing, a small style was considered unlady-like, but hats with brims a foot wide were as common as fleas. After shopping the town over, her sister, who was like a mother to her since my grandmother's death—Mom then about thirteen—finally in despair bought a hat. As it reminded Mom of a breadbox, she vowed she would never wear it on the train she boarded, and the hat was missing by the next stop. On her arrival at Long Beach, she was met by another sister who was going to send her to school. "Darling," she said, "where is your hat?" "You're supposed to buy me one," she replied. And so a new hat was purchased. This one pleased her.

When I was about thirteen, the neighbor next door—when we were on speaking terms—had spent much of what little spare time she had knitting me a sweater for Christmas. The sweater I hated and didn't want to wear but felt compelled to do so from time to time to make the lady feel I really liked it. Here was an example of how two contrasting personalities (Mom and I) solved our problems. Neither of us was wrong really.

84.   Police officers ride their mounts downtown once in awhile in Seattle. When the horses leave their "road applies," the cops just ride off. Sometime I'm going to run after one of them yelling, "Obey the scoop law! And if he doesn't? Why I'll just make a citizen's arrest. What else?"

85.   Mad at first that Hermes had killed two of his cows, Apollo was going to punish him. But before he could bind him with *willow*, the bonds fell to the ground and began to sprout. Magic. It is also traditionally a symbol of grief and melancholy.

86.   When about sixty-five, I realized that what had been written three years before was the same discipline required for some to develop their power or powers as a witch. You literally can do good only if you keep your distance from people, who can draw from your potential by causing irritation. Most witches are simply people with extreme sensitivities. He (or she) doesn't want to overhear constantly that he looks strange, weird, or goofy. He might have one or two friends, but they must be completely compatible, lacking in monstrous egos, or they will—though causing the witch much worry, concern, and aggravation—cause their own problems to intensify. It isn't then just a one-way street and the witch does not necessarily seek this. It just happens. If you go out of your way to cause the witch annoyance because you think it great sport and fun, you are then bringing the witch's focus on yourself. But you might argue that good and bad will come to anybody in time. True, but there's something more to it in the case of a witch. In my opinion too, a true witch will never fudge on his or her power. That is, like going out himself or sending somebody to light a fire with matches. He either has some paranormal power or he doesn't. There are many fakers. But it would be beneath the true witch's ethics to do this. Fire-starting is used only as an example of paranormal power. It could be many other things. If the power wanes, for some reason or another, then the witch must accept this and be truthful about it. Though Mom had her own problems, I'm not certain they weren't intensified by me, though inadvertently.

Of many entering monasteries and convents, a few had within themselves the witch potential. By being sequestered and shielded from the world and taking on hard disciplines, such as silence, poverty, and chastity, etc., these few developed some paranormal power. Again witches probably are, for the most part, extremely sensitive people. It will do no good to give them glib philosophies to cope, to handle things. All they know is that they weren't bothering anybody when all of a sudden someone has interrupted their world with how cute they are at the witch's expense. Possibly the most interesting of the trite sayings is "Don't let them get your goat!" Who knows for certain where this originated? Maybe it goes back to very ancient times when a goat or ram was a divinity symbol. This doesn't mean people worshipped an existing goat or ram, though that might have happened in a few cases. But what it meant really was that the god was symbolized by the goat—not in the flesh but some power in the goat in general. Thus by letting a thief come in and steal him (i.e., getting you rattled and upset), you failed to prevent this, to defend your god properly, and became an accessory to the crime.

87.   At an early age I was taught to give my seat on a bus to elders. This wasn't necessarily old people but those who were ten or fifteen years older. Never in my life though did any little bastard gave me his seat for all the years I'd given up mine. Finally when reaching sixty-three, I was pleasantly surprised on a crowded bus when a girl about fourteen gave me her place. I thought maybe I'd been wrong about the U.S. going to hell, and blah, blah, blah. It was good the old and sour like me who could not longer see the forest from the trees were being phased out. Lincoln was right about our youth. They weren't nation wreckers but "nation builders of tomorrow," I rhapsodized. Our youth had potential never dreamed of, just waiting to break out. It was there if you paid attention. Just open your eyes!

That's all it takes, mon. So I looked about and saw she was one of fifteen or so...visiting from Japan. Served me right for being soft one minute, a sentimental ol' fool.

Another time, a woman, about eight-months pregnant, and a man, looking like a construction worker in the prime of his life, got on a crowded bus. It irritated me that people much younger than I, a senior citizen, hadn't shown courtesy by getting up and giving the lady a seat. So getting up and stepping aside, I offered her my seat, to which she replied, "No." But you have no idea what a surprise it was before I could sit back down: She turned to the man and said, "Honey, why don't you sit down?" "Why?" he asked shaking his head. "Do I look like I'm pregnant, for christsake!" They couldn't have been married. No one would marry somebody like that.

88-A.   The cock is said to the bird of Hermes. *Cockshut*, an obsolete word, means "twilight."

88-B.   It always amazes me when a woman dies in childbirth or shortly after, a surviving male baby is often given his mother's name or one which can be masculine or feminine. Usually this is a middle name. The deceased mother, most of all, probably wouldn't have wanted that, but the disconsolate father is hell-bent on giving his son a feminine name he wouldn't have hung on himself. All along through life, they're trying to convince the child he shouldn't have feelings that he killed his mother. He had nothing to do with it; it was just one of those things. Then when he protests the name he was given, it all comes out: How dare you complain about carrying the name of your mother, who gave her life so you can live? I.e., you killed her. So he's got three strikes against him from the beginning: 1) guilt, 2) a feminine name in life to remind him of the guilt, and 3) a name he's certain to be taunted about sooner or later. But the father meant well at the time. Shit! If the father is so aggrieved and noble, let him give his son his own first name, and then legally change his own to Francis or Frances, Mary, Louise, Jane, Irene, Tanya, or whatever, while assuming all the guilt in the death for having gotten her pregnant. Well you just know that ain't gonna happen, and you wonder what a Freudian psychiatrist might attribute to the father's subconscious mind in selecting the name in the first place.

89.   Though Homer refers to earlier events, the *Iliad* took place well into the ninth year of the ten-year war. The Greeks were besieging the city of Troy. Homer doesn't use the word *Greeks* but usually the word *Achaeans*.

90.   The real Helen, some say, was taken by Hermes to Egypt where she was delivered to the charge of the king. What was seen at Troy was only a phantom, created by Hera.

91-A.   The Paris Accord was signed on January 27, 1973. It brought U.S. withdrawal and the return of POWs. Thereafter only a few civilians and military personnel remained in South Vietnam. Still it was a shock to see that vast amounts of U.S. equipment and ammunition, completely intact, had fallen into the hands of the North Vietnamese at the fall of Saigon on April 30, 1975. What mockery of and grotesque memorial to thousands whose lives were lost, often defending just inches of ground.

91-B.   In ancient times, it was thought that no one could really die unless Persephone, or her minister, had first cut off a hair from the deceased's head. It was customary in some places to cut off some hair of the dead person and strew it at the house's door. This was an offering to Persephone (Proserpina), the Queen of Hades, who presided over the death of mankind. (*Lempriére's Classical Writ Large Dictionary*, Wilts, Great Britain: Rewood Burn, 1984.)

92-A.   The so-called unit is one that I still have dreams of either forgetting or arriving at a scene and not having replenished. They are nothing like nightmares, waking up screaming, or anything like that, just dreams of not being prepared, not being ready. A feeling of uselessness. An object of ridicule.

92-B.   Who'd believe this? It sounded like nothing ever heard of: the politeness. But that's the way it happened. Then I read in *The Longest Day* (Cornelius Ryan, Simon & Schuster, 1959) where S/Sgt. Alfred Eigenberg, a medic in the Normandy invasion, recalled "a terrible politeness among the more seriously injured."

92-C.   You can moralize and analyze forever, a machine gone awry that never shuts off and gives no rest. Or you can fudge a little and superimpose your ideas on the data or those of someone else who felt he or she had the inside track and still reach the wrong conclusions. Sooner or later another will come along with a different scheme that too only partially fits. But isn't it better for mankind to at least think rather than to live in a cave?

The cellar—the only one I was in when in Korea—perhaps represented a cave and the mountain, Mount Cyllene in Arcadia. The night was Maia. An attempt to sleep when the firing started and then working inside a four-sided tent. There were four of us traveling in a four-wheeled jeep, symbolic at first of a horse and then a snake, being caught in the moonlight, Thoth, and making what seemed a slow, inching crawl up the incline, and a tortuous, serpentine turn down to the rocks, where we were thrown forward. The rocks, of course, were a natural barrier. Clearly Hermes Pterseus (Destroyer), the herald of death, was there. How did he choose? A popularity contest? The ones who live are really the losers, but if you keep playing long enough you'll eventually win: the law of averages. Is it something very complicated, beyond our grasp? Or something very simple? Brook's last name began with *B*; Ed's a *C*; and the *D* in Davenport: delta, an obvious letter for Hermes. My initials B.C., a snake by birth and caduceus. Brooks, who was fair like Ralph, felt compelled to go in a direction straight away from the mountain, crossing the dry riverbed (which at other times bathed the mountain's feet), while the driver of the two and one-half ton had turned left, following the riverbed. Why did the round hit Brooks, when logically he should have been protected somewhat by the two in back. We were too far away for such accuracy. Walkers, footprints on the riverbed. Ed will break a boundary to live. Don't knock it if you've never been there.

93.   Cerunos, the Celtic god, and Hermes correspond to some extent.

94.   Now with fifteen more years to life than Mom had, I'm not so certain about charity. You can get cynical fast in that work, doing in many cases (*not all*) for people who never learned to stand on their own two feet.

Experts in ridicule in some cases, the world owes them a living, as if it were easy for many of us to stick to some lousy, stinkin' job and scrape until we could find something better. Blessed are the Christians who foster love, for in as many will they make cripples and con men. I love you; won't you give me something to eat? I hate you; you owe me something to eat. But "consider the lilies of the field...they neither toil nor spin" (Mt 6: 28). It's a self-perpetuating machine, a symbiosis. Since 50 percent perhaps do need help, the rest a good, swift kick, I don't know the solution. This aspect of Christianity might have had as much as anything else to do with the fall of Rome. In the end, it will bring down the U.S., the mother-land, as we know it today.

95.   Ben Ames Williams, *Leave Her to Heaven*, Boston: Houghton Mifflin Company, 1944.

96.   This occurred on April 27, 1946. He would die at our home in Bakersfield on May 18, 1946. His illness had begun in the fourth month and ended in the fifth. The attending physician had last seen him alive on May 17. The time of his death was set of 4:30 A.M. Whether Bakersfield was on daylight saving time then, I don't know. If not, sunrise Pacific standard time would have occurred at 4:50 A.M. I.e., Grandad would have died at or near dawn. Why didn't he die in the fourth month instead of the fifth? Previously he and Ida *May* had retired and lived in Long Beach, California. He could have had his stroke just as easily there or in one of the homes of other daughters. It seems peculiar too (Bakersfield being a fairly large city) that years after the house was sold, one of Aunt Nell's grandsons and his wife will live in it for awhile, either buying or renting.

On February 13, 1993, the date by chance, a letter dated February 10, came from Robyn in Texas. She answered the question if a picture of George Duren (Daniel Duren's father) still existed. It does as a fragile daguerreotype in his Bible, which she gave to her son Mike who was interested in "family treasures" and which was okay. Robyn had written in her letter, "Gives me a funny feeling to read this old writing."

Mom had made the notation in the Bible: "This Bible was marked by my father's father and was given to his mother at the Union Hospital where he died from his wounds...(give) to Brent, if he comes home from Korea. If not—after Burt gets thru with it—it is to go to Robyn and her babies." Mom hadn't mentioned the Bible to me when I returned from Korea. Nor did I know of its existence or George Duren until two years ago. Note too in her notation that she seems convinced she will die before Dad.

97-A.   In this famous quotation, "rose" is said exactly four times. I always suspected Gertrude Stein was an alky, liking beer too.

97-B.   Anyone planning to make a career in any branch of the service—especially as an officer—would do well to read *Scorpion in the Sea* by P.T. Deuterman, Fairfax, Virginia: George Mason University Press, 1992. The book is fiction, but it shows—better than most—the complications which can arise.

Entry made May 17, 1996: Chief of Naval Operations Admiral Jeremy Boorda apparently committed suicide on May 16, 1996. Though he might have had concern he hadn't deserved to wear the combat "V" on two Vietnam campaign ribbons, I find it hard to believe that—whether an honest mistake or not—a man in his position with a wife and children would commit suicide over such very small potatoes. Could this have been a red herring? It's a sadness what human beings can do to human beings.

98.   A different name has been used.

99.   This is a major problem today and probably adds much to the equation of forms
        of self-destruction and crime. Some of this could have been eliminated by giving
        each person an account number, handled and administered by the government,
        to be paid into by the employers. If you completed only five years, say, with one
        company, you would still have five years of pension credit. Like social security,
        the more you worked and made, the larger the checks. It would eliminate the
        problem of winner-take-all, someone retiring off your back as well as their own.
        It would prevent the retirement funds from disappearing in the Bahamas.
        Safeguards too would have to be written in to prevent congress from pulling an
        equivalent trick. Critics might say the administration of such a plan would be
        very costly, but a small deduction out of the contributions would pay for this. It
        would save money in some areas, such as welfare and prison costs. It would elim-
        inate the need for the company's own retirement plan. Once it has finished with
        an employee, it no longer has an obligation to him or her.

100.   To this the average black might very well say, "Now you understand what we've
        taken all our lives."

        There's much truth to this, especially with the older ones. But though siding with
        blacks against whites at times (to the irritation of some whites), I've yet to see a
        black take my side against some other black. Based on other experiences, I have
        doubts about integration working—not that it couldn't, not that it shouldn't. It
        has nothing to do with rightness or wrongness, fairness or unfairness really, but
        human nature, both of blacks and whites. Unfortunately too the extremists of
        both groups will always be clamoring and fomenting trouble.

        Integration reminds me of water coming out of a tap where there is little water
        pressure. It flows but never with any great force to fill a pan of water quickly. To
        my thinking, integration will never get beyond this. Why should we be any dif-
        ferent than any other ethnic groups, we like to lord it over, throughout the world?

        For whatever it's worth (probably not much), I felt the settlement in the Rodney
        King case was much too low. Makes no difference what his past was or future
        might be. I had the impression the man would rather have died than to be cast
        into a public figure, always now a prisoner of his fame. It is something like the
        Indian who helped raise the American flag over Iwo Jima. By the time King's
        lawyer took his one-third or half the settlement, his friends managed to get part
        of what was left, he got used to the money where he might have some for invest-
        ment, he probably didn't have much left for that purpose.

101.   Besides this, Liezl had working for her the back drop of my forty years of contact
        with Filipinos. They could be so humble and yet have dignity. If one were your
        friend, you had a loyal one. They were seldom an enemy, but if they were, watch
        out. Though never really making an enemy of one, I can still hear in my mind the
        frenzied, high-pitched, staccato sounds of Tagalog directed at some of those who
        did. Liezl brought back to me also the memory of a sweet group, forgotten now
        for eighteen years. There were perhaps thirty-five Filipinos in all who had com-
        pleted a three-year contract with a pineapple company in the Hawaiian Islands.
        Though the company probably hadn't paid them much in wages, it did purchase
        first class accommodations aboard a passenger ship for their return home. But the
        workers (men and women) didn't have the fancy, expensive clothing that one
        having such a fare might be expected to wear. So the head waiter assigned them
        to first sitting, some distance from the "big shot" tables. In spite of the shunting,

their real class couldn't be hidden: They were punctual, courteous, well-groomed, wearing sunny smiles and bright-colored clothing.

Ten had been assigned to my table, so two extra chairs were squeezed in. The attitude of most waiters was to get them in and out quickly without any fuss: "You yourself wouldn't want all that bullshit, Brent, (true) so think how they must feel. You know better what they want than they do. Don't even give 'em a menu. They don't care. Just slap it to 'em: Two entrees, two scoops of rice, and a dessert. Besides with those ten on the table and the two at your deuce, you're not going to have that much time. And sure as hell—if you don't take some shortcuts—we'll all have to rush over here and pitch in at the last minute again, so you'll be ready for second sitting."

Yowh suh, boss, I'm thinking. There was truth and wisdom to this approach, and I couldn't knock it. But there's a stubbornness within at times which makes me the asshole of the crowd. Because of this I champion the cause of the underdog, at least as much for the wrong reasons as for the right ones. By God they had first-class fares, so they damn well were going to get first-class service, like it or not. It might be the only time in their lives they'd ever have a chance to get this. So I gave them the full treatment, complete with finger bowls with a slice of lemon in each: appetizers, soups, salads, fish, prawn, and paste starters, entrees, vegetables, desserts, and cheese. If they asked for ice cream, the flavor invariably requested was "Manila ice cream, please," said with a straight face.

We'd got along good, no problem. Knowing they wouldn't have the money to tip, I told them at the beginning of the last meal that in case I should get busy in the back when they left, I enjoyed having them aboard and thanked them. Then just before the meal was finished, I picked up a load of dishes to take to the scullery, giving them a change to leave without feeling uncomfortable. But the dummies, they all got up at the same time, thanked me, said good-bye, and left. When returning later, I saw that they'd come back and left again, each leaving a small gift where he or she had sat: A handkerchief, a pocket knife, stationary, a pen, a tie, etc.

I'd just about finished setting up for the second sitting when a well-dressed couple from a far deuce got up, came over to my table, and introduced themselves. He was a Filipino medical doctor, and she was his wife. "Before we get off," he said, "we wanted to tell you that we have been watching you since we came aboard, and how much we appreciated the way you took care of our people." At my deuce was an old and dignified Japanese couple. She was invariably well-attired, and he always wore a nice suit and tie. They were very punctual, courteous, and Japanese through and through. So I always bowed slightly to them each meal when they came in, though feeling awkward as they returned it with so much more grace. She had spent several years in the United States when she was younger and spoke English without an accent. He, on the other hand, neither spoke nor understood one word of English. He would study the menu, which was only in English, very carefully and then point to what he wanted while making a guttural sound. Besides many other things he pointed to, he wanted four entrees. Since he obviously wasn't a fat sumo wrestler, I must have seemed a little surprised when looking over at his wife, who with traditional, Japanese stoicism told me as casually as if she were talking about some very insignificant thing one of her grandchildren had done four years ago, "Isn't he the most ridiculous thing you've ever seen in your life? He has no idea what he's ordering. I have told him many times I'll order for him, but he stubbornly insists on doing it himself. I should have divorced him years ago, but now I'm too old. Besides it's not our custom." While she was telling me this, he sat looking ahead stoically too, and I'm wondering what to bring him? If he gets what he ordered, we'll never get out of here, and the other waiters—far from being stoic—will be pissed off for having to help me again. In many ways the old man and I were kindred spirits.

102-A.   Jane Ellen Harrison (*Mythology*, Massachusetts: Plimpton Press) contrasts the stationary *herm* alongside the road in ancient Greece to the modern "Pillar-Box," which would be useless if it weren't for the message-carrying postman. But if Hermes could overcome all by eloquence alone, he needed no arms, legs, or wings. Moreover messages without eloquence are often useless. In most religions, it's a matter of faith that your god is always invisibly present or just milliseconds away.

The erect penis on the pillars could have meant different things to different people: a pornographic fantasy, a symbol of reproduction (potency/fertility/children), or it might have stood for—to some extent—the symbol of immortality and presence of the god of whom they sought protection. Taking all these possibilities into consideration, it would square with the reality of the world.

102-B.   Solomon's wisdom, *Hercules'* strength, *Atlas'* stamina, *Zeus'* power, *Achilles'* courage, and *Mercury's* speed. Re: Solomon's wisdom:

> And the king said, "Bring me a sword." So a sword was brought before the king. And the king said, "Divide the living child in two, and give half to the one, and half to the other." Then the one who said don't slay it and to give the child to the other indicated by her words she probably was most fit to rear the child. But, in my opinion, it no way proved she was the natural mother (1 King 3: 24, 25).

103-A.   Not much contact with cats after that. Then a few years later when I was living at Capitol Hill, another white cat, belonging to someone down the hall, more or less adopted me, dropping by six or eight times a day to spend a total of two or three hours. Later on moving from the first to the second floor, I'd not seen the cat for a few days and it came racing, crossing and meowing in front of me, slowing me down. Then going up the steps, it grabbed my pant leg with its teeth for awhile. Letting loose, it jumped in the air a foot or two several times, playfully snapping. I had seldom, if ever, fed this cat.

103-B.   Myrtle Sassman Edwards (October 6, 1894–August 18, 1969) was born in Chicago, Illinois. She had teaching credentials in piano and voice. Some list Hermes as a god of music. Others say Hermes had no connection to music whatsoever and that the lyre he invented was used strictly for bartering (commerce) later with his half-brother Apollo, the god of music. Still in order to play the piano well, *deftness* is needed and, failing that, deafness; in order to sing well, a certain eloquence is required.

104.   In a Christmas note, Bob wrote that he was glad about the sale of the Gardnerville ranch. He had been there "forty-four years" and then was seventy-two. "My asthma," he said, "seems to be getting a little worse every year, especially in the winter when it is cold." He had wanted to go to Coleville, California, "but I don't know. Rhoda doesn't want to go" there. "I guess I will go back in a box some

day." It took nearly three years beyond 1992 for the sale of the ranch to finally go through. I'd thought through the years that he'd escaped the Hermes influence, though born September 5 (MP), 1920. I believed that whatever it is was to be transferred on through Lowell's children. Now I'm not sure it won't be in other ways. There's the Scot's blood (probably Celtic) in all descendents through the Cameron line and possibly the Duren one too. Rhoda in Greek in *rohdon*, "rose," and *Rhoda* in Latin meant "woman from Rhodes." But Rhodes, now owned by Greece, belonged to Greece for one period in antiquity and to the Roman Empire as well as the Byzantine in others.

105. This might have been earlier. For Annie L. Duren's death certificate of October 19, 1912 (mistakenly made out as Emily L. Duren), states that the length or residence in California was six years. An oddity is that Duncan Cameron, Sr.'s second wife, whom he married in 1912, was *Emile* Lawrenson. She died in 1921.

106. At Christmas 1993, Marilyn White Jones wrote that she had been going through many of her mother's (Aunt Nell's) things. She ran across my mother's diploma, dated May 24, 1906, from the Public High School of Snohomish, Washington, in the name of Fannie Mae Duren.

Then in 1994, I was also happy to receive from Norma Beth White Witbrodt a letter written by my mother when an eighteen-year-old to her father's sister as follows:

Machias, Wash.
April 18, 1907

Dear Aunt Jennie:

"Better late than never" seems to be my motto, but I've been so tired lately—spring fever, I guess—that I hav'n't written a single letter for a long time. O, how *slowly* the time is going in this god-forsaken place. It seems as tho' it'll never end. The weather is and has been bad so much too, that I never go anywhere after school. I stay right inside the school house until six every night. Have to paint and practice my elocution.

Saturday Mama, Nellie, and I went to Everett and got Nell's regalia for graduation. You knew, I suppose, that she stands second in her class. She got for her baccalaureate dress light tan summer suiting with a plaid stripe in it, and trimming and gloves of dark brown to match. It's just grand. Much nicer than mine was. For her white she got silk mull with a silk stripe thru it. The class day dress is flowered organdie.

Edith, Stella, and I sent off for moussleng de soie for dresses. I needed a new one for our recital and the Junior Prom. Mine is Nile green, edged at the neck, around the arms, and a belt of pale chiffon. It's just stunning. Edith's is pink, and Stella's tan. Just think my three gradua- tion dresses are as good as new yet. The white one hasn't been washed yet, altho' I've worn it so much. The grey, I am going to wash in gaso- line and put fresh trimming on it. Then I'll have four nice party dress- es when I go down to California to school next year. I've gotten along with less clothes this winter than I ever did before. All I wear up here is a black skirt and three waists I got when school first began. I got a nice wine-colored suit, eton jacket and skirt, also a silk jumper to match but I, of course, don't wear it out here. I also bought a pretty steel grey hat trimmed with ribbon and pale pink roses.

Stella is determined that Edith and I will go to Montana with her. I don't know yet whether to go or not. If I don't I'll go down to see you earlier in the summer. I rather think you'll see all of us soon. Anyway Nellie and I.

Sunday I spent the day with Bernice Brown, a friend of mine, and in the afternoon we went out to the cemetery. It looked so nice, the daffodils were all in full bloom.

Uncle William was over Sunday afternoon and stayed until after I left. He seems to be feeling quite good.

Mr. Howard told me that he was sorry we talked of moving away, for he had counted on Edith's being valedictorian in her class. He said that this year she had gone far ahead of any others in her class.

I'm writing now during school time. The first letter I ever wrote in school. But a class was not prepared, so I took this time. It looks better today. The probabilities are it will not rain tomorrow. How I hope it don't! for its Friday.

Well, duty is calling, so I must go and hear the dummies recite.

> Good-by—for this time—
> Your loving niece,
> Fannie

In the only letter coming down to me through the years, Fannie Mae (five) visits in April (four) a cemetery, connected to the Parentalia. To my knowledge, she had lived in only three states until this time: North Dakota (home of the Turtle Mountains), Montana, and Washington. On February 22, 1899 (six months to the day after her birth in the Dakota Territory), President Cleveland signed the Omnibus Bill enabling statehood of North Dakota, South Dakota, Montana, and *Washington.*

She speaks of Stella Cameron (born June 6, 1886). Where my mother had given birth to me on February 21, 1929, and died on February 26, my great Aunt Stella had given birth to her only child, Idylle, on May 13 (equivalent to February 21) and died on May 31, 1913. Idylle was taken care of by an aunt and uncle until the birth of cousin Margaret Cameron on February 13, the beginning day of the Parentalia. Thus February and Parentalia-Carisita links are extremely strong in my ancestry, to be explained more in detail later.

I believe Aunt Nell said one time that Uncle William died and was buried in Washington, though I could be wrong in recall. It should be mentioned here that all three daughters of Aunt Nell and Uncle Norm (Marilyn, Norma Beth, and Phyllis) were smart. Marilyn, as I recall, got a degree and taught when her three sons were grown. Norma Beth, a talented writer, a pillar of her church, always had a brilliant sense of humor, inherited both from her mother and father. To Phyllis I owe much as a youth, not the least of which was her brightness, which got me interested in English. I'd got a D as a grade for the first third of a course, which I hated. Phyllis helped me bring this up to an A minus average for the course and have a feeling of accomplishment. Phyllis White Schnoor (October 15, 1924–March 5, 1981) died from the spread of breast cancer, like her mother had, and her maternal grandmother. And, of course, Warren died from the spread of stomach cancer, like his father.

Here too I should comment that Robyn inherited the best characteristics of her parents: her mother's quickness and her father's steadfastness, reliability, and practicality. But possibly something more important is her rare gift of not making enemies. Since Norma Beth and she were close to the same age and shared a sense of humor, both remained close throughout their lives.

107-A.   Elisabeth Goldsmith, *Ancient Pagan Symbols*, New York: G.P. Putnam's Sons, 1929.

107-B.   During the nine-day celebration of the Parentalia, the first eight days were set aside for private worship. But February 21, the last day and called the Feralia, combined both public and private worship. The idea throughout the Parentalia was to honor the dead, to make peace with them, and to enlist their help for the coming year. So fittingly the Caristia (dead kinsfolk) was held to settle quarrels and make peace with living relatives on February 22. (James Hastings, *Encyclopedia of Religion and Ethics*, New York: Charles Scribner's Sons, 1908.)

February 21 can be thought of as the day the will was read and February 22 as a day of reconciliation, if possible.

Few things typify man more than measurement and double-think.

Considering the number of deaths surrounding him, the public functions he's had to attend in memory of deceased, and the settling of disputes between family members, it's not surprising that Senator Edward Kennedy, a Roman Catholic, was born in Massachusetts on *February 22* (1932). (Kathleen Kennedy born February 20, 1920; Jean Kennedy, February 20, 1928.)

108.   One of the first names before becoming Yerington was the Willow Switch barroom. A local teamster had a habit of saying, "Think I'll switch off and get some pizen" when he came to the *crossroads*. (Velma Ford, article titled "History of Lyon County," in *Nevada: The Silver State*, Vol. I, Carson City, Nevada: Western State Publishers, Inc., 1970.) Do not forget Silver City is in Lyon County.

Helen S. Carlson (*Nevada Place Names*, Reno: University Press, 1974) says the name "switch" came from the saloon made of willows and was called "Willow Switch." About four miles southwest of the town is Yerington Mining District, formerly called the *Crazy Louse*. (Hermes, god of writers, was in some parts of ancient Greece a god of miners.) Mark Twain (measurement), a crossroad's man since he deserted as a Confederate soldier, at one time owned the mining district but failed to realize its value. When it was rumored a new railroad might be put through, the people of Greenfield petitioned to have the town's name changed to Yerington, figuring that "Hume Yerington, superintendent of the railroad," would be so flattered he'd run iron rails to it. But this backfired. Mr. Yerington acknowledged the honor by giving the community an American flag. (Op. cit., Ford.)

Yerington, a town and post office, was established *February 6*, 1894. Henry Marvin Yerington, who was an official of the Virginia and Truckee Railroad and for whom the town was named, had been born in Calborne, Canada, on September 5, 1829. One of his sons was named Marvin Hume Yerington. But the old man undoubtedly heard the town's plea and made the decision. Several years before he died on November 25, 1910, an affliction to his ear forced him to have his eardrums removed, making him completely deaf, but he was always able to see the flag flying.

The willow symbolizes celibacy, forsaken love (Op. cit., Jobes). It's the birthday flower for May 22, the anniversary of the mutilation of Hermae busts in ancient Athens. According to Jobes, it is a symbol of "the fifth or nesting month," which is April 16 to *May 13*. It is sacred to Persephone, Hecate, and Circe. It's used to contact the spiritual world, and—as a wand—offers protection in the nether world.

Book Two
Chapter One

Excerpts from Robyn's letter dated April 23, 1992:

Joseph Henry Fry, my grandfather, had a previous marriage of nearly six years to Hannah Stewart. She died a few weeks after giving birth to Grace, who survived only a few months.

This is recorded in the family Bible, as well as the births of Joseph's and Matilda's children. But there is no entry of his marriage to Matilda Carlson, my grandmother. Perhaps this was an oversight or maybe the marriage was recorded elsewhere, but it does not appear in the Fry Bible. Certainly they never lived together for any length of time, as Joseph was always gone somewhere prospecting. However, according to the births of their children in the Bible, he came home every year or so and she became pregnant. I'm not sure of the family's migration to California. Whether they came here together or separately, but Matilda arrived in Taft, where she established a maternity home which she operated for many years. She resided in Taft until she passed away. Joseph lived out on the desert past Victorville and Lucerne Valley. He lived his lifetime in the desert prospecting for rocks, silver, gold or oil. Virtually lived as a hermit. Geologists and surveyors making maps in the early 1900s often used him as a guide. He became well known to them as a guide, and ended up naming a 4,300 ft. mountain "Fry" Mountain after him. This mountain is recorded on the official California State map.

The births of all the Fry children were recorded and as you see have been changed. What a stink there was about the alterations! Aunt Eva, as best I remember, did it to get her social security or some other benefit 2 years early. All the rest of the Frys, except Dad maybe, were angered at her because it messed up their birthdate years too.

Excerpt from Robyn's letter dated May 29, 1992:
I think my Aunt Gertrude must have given Dad the family Bible, although I don't know how he came to have it. But Aunt Gertrude and Dad were very close. Maybe because he lived with her when he was young, before they all came to California. Then, since she was a widow, she moved to Taft and lived with and took care of Grandma in Grandma's later life. Dad visited her in Taft after Mother's accident, and Aunt Gertrude would come to Avenal a lot too....

Like most families, the Frys had their likes and dislikes, heartaches, stories, and gossip. But to Dad's credit, he seemed to get along well with all his brothers and sisters who, by the way, always treated me okay. Grandma Matilda was a good cook, and independent. As she got older, her children pitched in and sent support. When she died, there was some flap over who was entitled to the small estate. But I think most eventually agreed that her son Joseph and his wife had the best claim to it since they had taken care of Joseph Henry for a number of years before his death without any help from the others.

The following page, though blackened by a copy machine, still shows the sloppy job of cooking the books. Whoever did it, I can't be related to. Suretohell wudn'ta wantadum drivin' da getaway car whun robing da bank.

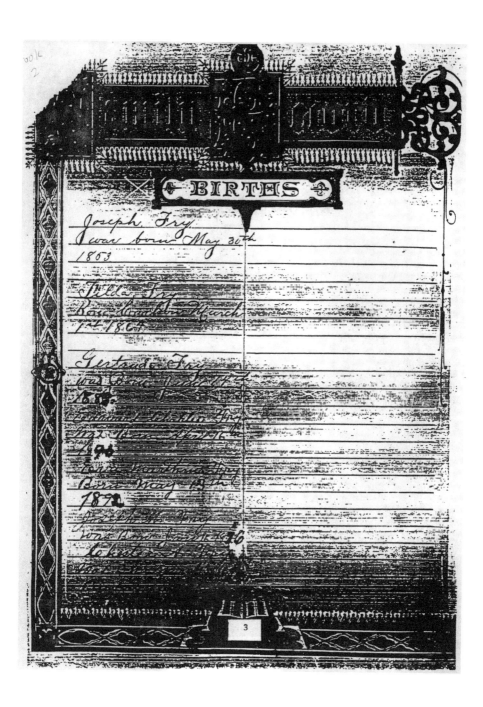

BIRTHS

Joseph Fry
I was born May 30th
1853

Willa Fry
Born Franklin March
1st 1867

Gertrude Fry
was born April 17th
1889

Ferdinand Fletcher Fry
was born April 16
1890

[illegible] [illegible] Fry
Born May 13th
1892

[illegible]

3

Sweden
Carl Carlson - Sphia Blixt
Matilda Augusta Carlson

Joseph Henry Fry   -   Matilda Augusta Carlson
May 30, 1853 – Mar 9, 1934   Mar 1, 1864 – Sep 2, 1951
Kittanning, PA - Long Beach, CA   Stockholm, Sweden - Taft, CA

1. Gertrude Marguerite Roberts
2. Edward Charles Fry
   Apr 16, 1890 – Oct 6, 1971
3. Eva Marthina Koch
4. Joseph Mearing Fry
5. Chester Agate Fry
6. Burton Carlson Fry

Burton Carlson Fry   -   Dollena Dorothy Duren
Oct 13, 1900 – Jan 30, 1973   Mar 15, 1900 – Nov 13, 1951
Bowling Green, Ohio - CA   Great Falls, MT - Avenal, CA

Robyn Adair Fry

Lewis Hoyt Sanders   -   Robyn Adair Fry
Oct 30, 1920   June 25, 1923
Lincoln, Nebraska   Long Beach, CA

1. Michael Lewis Sanders
   May 21, 1943 Bakersfield, CA
2. Kandice Sanders
   Jan 15, 1947 Bakersfield, CA
3. Blayne Robin Sanders
   Aug 16, 1952 Avenal, CA

Chapter Two

Pictures projecting how people will look in the future are made now with a fair degree of accuracy. The best service rendered graduating seniors probably wouldn't be guaranteeing a college education but rather to run four of those pictures in their yearbooks. It would be a sobering experience for youth intoxicated with itself to show what the real world's all about. A *que-sera* serendipity, barring plastic surgery, would be that they were able to locate each other at the twentieth, thirtieth, fortieth, and fiftieth anniversaries. For Avenal, at least, the name of the high-school yearbook *La Neva* (*nevar*: to snow) would become even more appropriate and meaningful through the years.

In general, shallowness is autopsy youth, pointing out what's wrong with everybody else, sneering at problems it doesn't have or recognize, expecting understanding for those it does, which others don't. A few in old age comment that they are far less sure about things they were certain about when young. True enough everyone experiences some grief in life. But unless it was a process that completely wiped out the individual or someone very close, there's serious doubt about any great maturity which is supposed to accompany gray hair. Most would rather see those who they dislike buried. Probably we're all the same in this one way or another, and that's why there's such great wisdom in the fact that in the end all of us are buried.

About what's being written can do me no good in the long run. First thoughts were to let it go with only a passing remark—that Hoyt Sanders wasn't too deep at the time I'd known him, nor was I for that matter. Yet there's something more involved here than just getting even for Mom, Dad, myself, and especially Robyn. It's to put the truth, as I see it, in context. To explain how Hoyt came across to me, at least at the time known, is to get some idea of how he perhaps thought of himself.

As previously said, Robyn and Hoyt had gone together for several years in high school. He had come to the house in Avenal in those days, either invited to dinner or to take Robyn to the movie, dance, or school activities. Both of them enjoyed dancing and danced well together. He had a job after school and on Saturdays that paid him enough to dress in style and have a secondhand car and some spending money. He was a good football player, playing quarterback, but he was not exceptional. He was no great shakes scholastically either but managed to get by.

He seemed to project that if he weren't smarter than most, he was at least shrewder. For everything he had an answer. There was little doubt in his mind about anything, a sort of conceit. If there was ever any sign of introspection, he hid it well, and in a way, this lack was a strength, for it made life so much easier, at least for him.

Without a scar yet on him, he could point out the losers right off the bat, a Monday-morning quarterback, shaking his head mentally at the foibles of others "who made their own bed" rather than seeing them as human beings. Possibly one reason Robyn was attracted to him was that it was flattering he thought she was first class among many others who were second class, third class, or no class at all in his estimation. Robyn though never had this way of looking at people and had better values. That's why the marriage was doomed from the start.

There were early signs to his personality that were missed, as indeed there were to mine. Youth has a way of masking these unless they're glaring. Most people don't pick up immediately on what they are seeing and hearing. If someone you like is talking about somebody else, it is after all another person, not your problem really. So it never occurs that this same person probably will also be talking about you someday.

One summer he and Robyn drove me to the ranch. I have a remembrance of him running down my brothers. He thought they looked wild. Pardon me? Maybe they sensed a predator in their midst, for certainly he was curious about what they had—horses, cattle, acreage, etc. Where there was money, how people got it, how much they were worth was always of interest to him. So what's wrong with that? Nothing really. Everybody does it to some extent, but my impression was that he was a little more calculating than most. If he thought of my brothers as hayseeds, it wouldn't have taken much for them to think of him as a city slicker. My father commented about Hoyt when they left, "He thinks he knows more than he really does."

The only person to my knowledge Hoyt ever admired was his uncle, who was nearly the same age and lived in Taft, California. He was quite the stud, as Hoyt described him seducing one of the Avenal girls. He was also a good football player.

Speaking of football, Hoyt characterized one of the players, a neighbor, on the Avenal team as being too careful, scared that he was going to get hurt. Yet the same criticism had been leveled at Hoyt, who, some spectators felt, hardly ever ran back the kick-off. When World War II came, he didn't sit around to get drafted in the army. He joined the Coast Guard.

He'd called his sister a "whore" and had no use for her. How could she have done this to him? Certainly he'd kept up his macho image by his conquests, gringo. Imagine him having a sister who was a whore (his word, not mine); she'd let him down.

This is obviously a biased opinion on my part concerning Hoyt, as you'll see more clearly later. Yet there's some truth to it. A more rounded picture is given by Robyn, who wrote of Hoyt's sister Gretchen (only at my request), since it helps to show Hoyt's tendency—at least at the period known—to be judgmental, critical, and somehow above it all. Had he taken a more penetrating look at himself, he'd have found he wasn't all that pure. But since introspection wasn't his strong suit, he probably did what was right for himself. It just wasn't within him, as sometimes seen in stronger men, to say, "This is my family, having a few warts maybe, but no matter, my family. This is where I began, and this is where I'll end."

Excerpts from Robyn's letter concerning Gretchen:

Hoyt said Gretchen was, among other things, no good and wanted no more to do with her. I think he hated her because her behavior shamed his mother and added to his mother's illness with heart disease. Kept his mother upset. I think too that all his life he was jealous of his sister because his mother loved her. When Gretchen turned bad, her mother still loved her as only a mother can do. It just made Hoyt hate her more.

Gretchen was thrown in jail in her teens in Texas, though I don't remember what charges, if I was ever told. Carl, her father, had to go get her and bring her home, I believe. She was married to Bud Evans, and they had a son called Robert. This ended in divorce where Bud was given custody of his son. He could not take care of him, so Hoyt's mother and father raised him. Later when Bud remarried he wanted Robert with him. But the boy wanted to stay with his grandparents who eventually got custody.

Gretchen also remarried. Her second husband's name—like her father's—was Carl. Time went on. Hoyt's mother passed away. Hoyt and I had returned after the war and lived with Hoyt's dad. I kept house for all of us. Gretchen came home with Carl, her husband, and two adopted—or perhaps foster—Indian children to visit. Hoyt still hated her, treated her cold, ignored her husband or treated him as an inferior, and finally suggested they leave. Robert was ten or so, and I think he went with his mother either then or soon later. They stayed in the Bay area, and Robert grew up, married, fathered one or two children but never was very well. Finally he became very ill, was diagnosed as having leukemia and, died a very young man.

I did not go to his funeral as I don't think Hoyt did or would. He seemed to care for Robert while Pearl (Hoyt's mother) raised him, but I believe he found the boy a pain and too much trouble when later he himself had to look after him since Hoyt and I lived there.

After Robert died, Gretchen, Carl, and two girls moved east. Why? I never knew. Gretchen wrote me now and then. I answered her. She seemed changed. I felt she needed or wanted a feeling of family and tried to be her friend. Hoyt was mad that I kept writing. Nothing had changed as far as he was concerned.

Carl had a job as a prison guard in Laurel, Maryland. She had a garden and canned vegetables for the winter, etc. Their family increased by one or two boys and another girl or two. Maybe they were foster children but always American Indians. When one grew up and married, Gretchen would replace him or her with another child. I stopped hearing from her. Maybe I stopped answering with my own family growing up, less time for writing, and so on. After Hoyt's aunts died, the chain of information was broken. No news for years now. She might be dead. It was a sad thing that in the passing of so many years Hoyt could never bend a little in his attitude toward her.

Robyn, who writes sympathetically about Gretchen, apparently had no knowledge of what happened in her childhood: Gretchen's view of things as she was growing up. There's that aspect of it.

Before the U.S. entered World War II, we'd moved to Bakersfield where Robyn attended a beautician's school. After the attack on Pearl Harbor, she dated a soldier or Army Air Corps man stationed nearby. He wanted to marry her, and Hoyt decided he wanted to marry her too, so she had two suitors. It might not have made any difference in her decision. Still Mom, Dad, and I backed Hoyt. Not that there was anything wrong with the other man, but we'd known Hoyt longer. When he came on liberty for a few days leave in 1942, he persuaded Robyn to marry him. They had little time left to get their application form, and Hoyt didn't even have enough money to pay for that, so they broke into my bank when I was gone. The only reason this is mentioned now, along with the fact that we three had backed him, is to contrast the turn of events ten years later.

I'd got back from Korea and went to Avenal to visit. Hoyt asked me if I wanted to take a ride with him out to some place connected with his work. Okay. During the trip, he told me that Mom had made a pass at him. Dad, he said, was "pussy-whipped," letting Mom run him and get away with what she did. When Dad had gotten fired from one of his jobs earlier, it was Dad's fault, Hoyt said, believing the supervisor's version rather than Dad's. Robyn, he continued, had gotten married when she was too young, though he didn't mention that he was the one who had proposed to her. It wasn't clear then what he was referring to. He asked about some of my experiences in Korea. I told him a few, explaining about being scared at times. Did I ever kill anybody? he asked. Doubtful, though I'd put a couple mortar rounds down a tube once at the urging of three or four in the platoon. The mission had been called, the charges set, so it would have been done whether I did or not. Aside from the Geneva Convention, there's a feeling—probably illogical—that if you don't kill, you'll be allowed to take care of the wounded. Both you and they will have better luck.

"You didn't actually kill anybody with your hands? You didn't see any hand-to-hand combat then?"

"No."

He then told me his uncle, his idol, had been an army officer in World War II and had killed Germans with his bare hands.

Sorry about that.

He talked about when he was in the Coast Guard. A cook was queer where he was stationed. He asked if I'd ever come across any.

Up to this time, I'd had only passive sexual relations and hadn't accepted it completely myself. But it wasn't my way to make a vigorous condemnation: They should kill all the damn faggots! So he was told of coming across a few and let it go at that. There was probably, looking back, a gesture or mincing walk. What got me was that he pegged me for being so stupid as to not see what he was getting at. He always seemed to think he was the only one equipped with radar and could make sweeps of any kind that other people couldn't, sort of a self-conceit.

He later told Dad he thought I was queer, then Mike, as I heard Mike and Hoyt making a joke about me. The song "Please Don't Talk about Me When I'm Gone" should be changed to "Please Don't Talk about Me within Hearing Distance." Several years later, he told Kandi. He was very lucky indeed to have escaped this himself, but maybe not completely since he had at least a woman's mouth.

Years later when I was questioned about being gay in the service, the interrogator read me excerpts from a report made by a family member. So flattered had the informant been that he had been numbered among the elite to know and give confidential information to any government man who knocked on the door or sent him a form to fill out that he voluntarily told anything he could think of. Thank God at the time the informant had known me least. There wasn't much to tell. So you see the Nazis and Communists were wrong in torturing people. You don't have to do that to get the information if you go about it the right way. Just plant the idea that the informant is somehow one of the superior people of the race to be trusted, and you are talking to him to weed out the inferior people. Sometimes I wish I'd just been born into one of the blood-feuding families in Appalachia; at least they stood for something.

Robyn had begun to suspect something was wrong. Being tied down with three children and Hoyt gone on jobs two or three days at a time, she had no recourse but to hire a detective. He was seeing another woman. Since it was inconceivable that Hoyt could ever by wrong, it must have been "Robyn (who) was too young when she got married."

Excerpt from Robyn's letter dated July 28, 1991:
  I received the handwriting analysis. Very interesting and how close she came to calling Mother for just what she was! Self-centered, dreamer, and certainly heartless in her later treatment of you. I think in a way, that's what made me decide to get out, and the easiest way, of course, was to get married. In those days too, I was "in love" I thought and should have seen through Hoyt even then. I learned later that he had been shacking up with some gal in Frisco, even up until I got there to make our first place together. She called out to him on Market Street one day when we were walking from a street car, and did he ever hustle me across the street into a theater. We were going to a show anyway, but never did he move so fast! So it went. Later when he was in Alaska in 1944 and 1945, he told me after he had come home that he had shacked up with a White Russian gal once in awhile!! If I had been smart, I would have divorced him then as he never changed over the years. Was always a womanizer and had gals in Bakersfield while we lived there too. What a waste—except I have three kids I love very much. Hoyt is not too close to Mike, and Blayne does not have much use for his father. Their get togethers after the divorce never turned out well. Always ended with verbal exchange and Blayne returning home, saying he would never go to see him again.

Excerpt from Robyn's letter dated April 13, 1991:
  Hoyt never had a gun and when his Dad and uncles went deer hunting every fall to the Sierras, he never

314

went and never taught our kids anything. He was only interested in horses after we got two, and Kandi shared that interest as deeply as he. Mike never cared too much for it, although he rode in a couple parades and horse shows. Mike's interests were sports and later, cars and girls. Ha! Blayne had a pony and rode in parades and horse shows too. He and Kandi won several 1st place ribbons all over the valley while he had the horses. Still Hoyt didn't spend any time with his boys compared to Kandi, but the horses were something *HE* liked.

After hearing from the detective, Robyn filed for divorce. As I recall she asked for child support but no alimony for herself. Since money was short, she took the only job which seemed to be available in Avenal at the time. That was in a butcher shop, believing she could do it okay, but she lost most of her right hand in a machine. She then took whatever jobs she could get, one being a barmaid. Later she got state training and a job at Lemoore Naval Air Station where she worked for twenty-two and one-half years in civil service. When she retired, they gave her a very nice send-off and farewell party.

It was only a short period of enjoyable retirement, followed by terrible pain and a series of dangerous back operations that put her in a rest home and convalescent hospital. Her children, grandchildren, and friends look after her as best they can in their own way, living in different cities from where she's hospitalized or out of state. Though little could be done about her physical problems resulting from the operations, her mind is still good, and she wrote on May 8, 1996:

> I selected one of the books and started reading and, of course, everything else left my mind! Ha! I don't know if it's a good or bad thing to enjoy reading so much or when it changes from a hobby to a vice—but I love to read...New residents come in and in a month or sooner the hearse drives up and some poor old soul goes out. Rather sad and depressing when one (me) has a clear and active mind with just a minor disability.

Chapter Three

In 1888 (the year my parents were born and when my grandparents were running their station at Coleville, California) Southern Pacific Railroad built a branch from Hanford, California, so that coal could be loaded on cars and shipped. Thus the name Coalinga is derived from "Coaling Station."

Today this town has around seven thousand residents and a forty-acre campus of West Hills Community College, which is the closest one in any direction to Avenal, about eighteen miles southeast.

With all the colleges and universities in California and Nevada to apply to and be accepted, Lowell Chichester (living near Coleville, a fourth child, and the great grandson of George and Elizabeth) will be found attending West Hills Community College during the academic year 1972–1973. You say this is easily explained because he had relatives living in Avenal. Not so. To my knowledge he didn't visit them nor did they know he was attending the college in Coalinga.

Could it be there's more to the game than we ever dreamed? Each person has at least two or three geographic points he must touch. Capone had Chicago, maybe Dannie's grave or near there, Alcatraz, Long Beach, Florida. Howard Hughes: Texas, Hollywood, Long Beach, Las Vegas. I: Nevada, nearly the four corners of the U.S. (California, Florida, New York, and Washington); Alaska; Hawaii; Washington, D.C.; and very unlikely, Chicago, Illinois. As improbable as Lowell attending college in Coalinga—it seems to me—is Kandi eventually settling in Gardnerville, Nevada.

What can be learned, if anything, from natural disasters and other happenings in the Avenal and nearby areas in recent times?

On May 2, 1983 (about fifty years after that occurring at Long Beach), an earthquake registering 6.1 to 6.5 on the Richter scale shook Coalinga. This was the United States' most destructive earthquake in twelve years: at least forty-seven people were injured, an "eight-block" downtown area

316

was leveled, telephone service and electricity were severed, gas lines broke and caused fires, and the water supply was contaminated. Damage was estimated at thirty-one million dollars. California's governor declared Fresno county a disaster area.

On July 16, 1991, Patricia Ann Zipprich, eleven, died from poisoning by medication. Charges of murder, attempted murder, child molestation, torture, and slavery were made against Sally Ann Whitham. The case is much too complicated and bizarre to go into here. However, in relation to what I'm writing, it's possibly important to consider that:

1) It happened in Avenal (population 9,576), which seems like an unlikely place.
2) It was a horrifying and twisting tale of cross-country deception.
3) The child wasn't buried until October 17, 1991.
4) A girl had died in a family where there were four boys, ranging in the ages from eight to sixteen.
5) The *Fresno Bee* of October 20, 1991, lists eight a.k.a.s for Sally Ann Whitham (thirty-five).

On October 18, 1993, Sally Ann Whitham was given life in prison.

On November 29, 1991, a blinding dust storm blanketed Interstate 5, about fifteen miles north of Coalinga. Seventeen people were dead and one hundred and fifty injured following a pile-up of ninety-three or more vehicles, including eleven truck rigs, in what was the worst accident of its kind in United States history.

Many were burned alive. Wreckage and carnage were strewn across a "four-mile stretch" of I-5 and into adjoining fields, left unplanted due to a five-year drought. The dust and sand whipped up from these fields by a forty miles per hour *wind* caused the low visibility on the highway, which was crowded with holiday *travelers*.

Concerning this day, Robyn wrote:

> The wind blew over trees here in Avenal—(dirt and sand) blocked the sun during the day and knocked off power for 3 hours and cable T.V. for 13 hours. And left 2 inches of dirt and sand on the window sills and furniture.

Not too far from Avenal is Fresno, where, around 2:00 A.M. on May 16, 1993, seven (see pages 482–483) were killed and two wounded by two men, one of whom had been told to get out of the nightclub on other dates.

Rational people, of course, don't believe in bloody superstitions these days. But if they did, they might wonder why the savagery occurred at all. Then, why two hours after midnight on May 15, the date in Roman antiquity when merchants sprinkled their merchandise (dice?) with water, and why on the sixteenth, five days before the Mercury period began?

Naturally a person can imagine all sorts of things lurking in the shadows. Like it or not, the demons, evil, religions, god or gods we have in life are better than none. Just living, reproducing, and eating vegetables which don't need washing are not sufficient reasons for life to go on. There'd be no reason to be thankful. Were it known with certainty that the devil himself was all that existed outside us, he'd be better than nothing, which offers no reason for life to go on. We'd do well to ask ourselves if this is not what happened at the Garden of Eden, that God gave strife as a gift, that the true story got twisted in the telling.

Chapter Four

That the title of Louis L'Amour's *The Haunted Mesa* suggests an other-worldliness is probably why it was pulled down from the shelf. Then liking neither its cover nor the fact that it was a western, I can't account for buying it anymore than explaining why, once having decided a book's not for me, I've got to be so godawful pure to see it through. Maybe it comes from a reverence for books and so a forgiveness for being what they are that can't be extended to one's own species: "Father, forgive them; for they know not what they do." And certainly nobody's gonna say, "You persevered right up to the bloody deadend, mon, and that's some feat since you're not a fast reader." Nobody's gonna say this cuz they ain't gonna be told, for then they'd just say, "Creep!"

So far as could be seen, there were only three things in the book which might have had any connection to my writing:

1) The main character was a writer.
2) A dog in the story was called Chief, the name Anita had given a German shepherd puppy one year.
3) There was a common-point boundary where Utah, Colorado, Arizona, and New Mexico came together called Four Corners. If you're imaginative, you can draw a small square around this and round out two figures forming an eight.

But the locale was wrong, a little too far-fetched to work into my writing and would have forgotten about it completely had not the same subject, never previously heard of, come up again a few days later. Even so its possible significance wasn't recognized at first.

Why had Bishop James Albert Pike gone off to the Judean wilderness in 1969 seeking clues about God when "God is everywhere"? Strange he'd go poking around some hot, miserable hills and *wadis* when there are deserts galore in Nevada, if he'd felt a mystical connection that way. But, of course, it's not that simple. He was returning to a source and graveyard of religions, following up some itch, hint, or suggestion, and in that case, maybe we'd all done the same. But could the answer to what he was seeking lay in Rome? See Book II, February 14, 1913, and footnote 310-B.

Oddly I couldn't find his name but did come across a Donald G. Pike, who, with David Muench, produced ANASAZI: *Ancient People of the Rock*, American West Publishing Co., 1974. No connection with this was made to *The Haunted Mesa*. I checked it out because "ancient people of the rock" sounded interesting. Only later when reading it did the word *Anasazi* come back to mind.

The coincidence of coming across an obscure subject within a few days was puzzling, and so the mentioning of it here, though I'm the first to admit that on this basis alone it's as cuckoo as Sarah Winchester and her 160-room mansion begun in 1884, with it thousands of windows, doors, and stairs, perhaps glorifying unconsciously the square or rectangle. So be it!

Anasazi, meaning "The Ancient Ones," is a name the Navajo gave to the prehistoric Indians hundreds of years after they'd disappeared. No one knows for sure why they abandoned their houses—lack of water, hostile groups attacking them, disease, religious reasons?

In *1888* two cowboys chasing strays in a December wind and snow came across a bunch of stone houses in the recess of a cliff. This would become known as the "Cliff Palace" of the Mesa Verde near the Four Corners area, and it brings to mind that Hermes was born in a cave on the fourth day of a month.

The houses were built up so close to natural rock in certain places that a person gets the impression the Anasazi were trying to have a oneness with the rock. They were rectangular or square in structure, except for the round kivas, and today are sometimes spoken of as "ghost rocks." Besides this too, cacti sometimes growing nearby (especially in Arizona the giant saquaro, whose blossoms have become the state flower) are suggestive of the phallic symbols in ancient Greece.

The Anasazi weren't limited to the Mesa Verde area. Besides the Four-Corner states, there were branches southwest that ran into Texas and Nevada.

Throughout, Hermes has been identified with rock. Then we read of Jesus saying to Simon Barjona, "Thou are *Petros*, and on this *Petra* I will build my church." *Petros* = a stone. *Petra* = a rock.[1]

Curiously in the movie *Schindler's List* we find the Jews placing rocks on Schindler's grave. No doubt in time this has been the practice of other cultures too. And in keeping with the god of measurement, Britain describes weight in stone.

Chapter Five

When sailing I returned to a freighter one afternoon to see twenty-five or so boxes of uniform size amidst many passenger suitcases near the gangway. I wondered who had brought the boxes and hoped the chief steward had already assigned two people to carry them aboard.

It was learned they belonged to Alex Haley, a methodical man who had inventory lists telling the contents of each box. Now if that wasn't a crock! What could a writer possibly need but a pencil, paper, and maybe a typewriter?

This I'd find out years later, wasting more time than caring to admit relocating and rechecking facts that should have been gotten right the first time. Not only that there's a sloppy habit of writing my notes catty-corner on a page full of other heiroglyphs written the same way. So one page looked much like another when searching for an elusive fact that only the Rosetta stone back at the library could clear up. You were right, Alex!

Roots had been out for several years. A dogeared, paperback copy could be bought in some places for a dollar; still I wasn't about tackle it. Doan know why exactly. Maybe because the critics said it was good, which probably meant I wouldn't like it, and once started, Jesus Christ of the book world couldn't abandon it, no matter what its sins.

Having read nearly everything else in the ship's library, I finally relented. But only for the reason of saying the book had been read, not for that of looking forward to it. So it happened Roots was started only a day or two before he came aboard. It seemed odd, his coming on the ship at that time, but so what?

Two men had come with him. One had done research work for him when writing Roots, and the other was supplying background information on Henning during the years Alex had been away.

The captain's table was small. The purser and chief mate had permanent seats there, which left only one seat vacant. The chief steward did the next best thing and assigned the three to a table close to the captain's.

But right next to Haley's table, on the chief engineer's side, were two ladies sitting alone. It was awkward, giving the impression of an isolated and perhaps snobbish celebrity, which Haley wasn't. So he asked the steward and the ladies if he could sit with them, while his two friends remained at my table. This doubtless gave the ladies a conversation piece for many years to come. Mickey (William Wales), his waiter, was a black man to whom Haley's celebrity status might have had a special significance. Haley was like this, trying to figure out what might be important to people, their feelings.

Stories of blacks, slave ships, plantations, and the like had been written for years. Haley, refusing to pander to the sexual fantasies of the reader, did them as well in some cases and better in others. But I'd never read of a character like Chicken George before. Simply because he was given a chicken-shit job and made the best of it, he was my hero.

At odd moments in the dining room, Haley talked to me, as indeed he did to anybody he ran into on the ship. The coincidence of having just started *Roots* when he came aboard was mentioned one day. He asked then if I'd seen the television mini series. I said no and that I probably wouldn't since films were seldom as good as the books. He agreed, for the most part, but he felt that the mini series had in some ways improved upon the book. He thought that many cast into the roles (like actor LeVar Burton who played Kunta Kinte) were exceptional.

"Did the success of your book have any effect on the place where Kunta Kinte came from?"

He replied that in the first year alone after publication many thousands visited the village.

"That must have really helped the villagers," I said.

"No. It ruined them. Many became lazy, sitting around, not doing their regular work."

"Did you ever take the film over there to show them?"

This he said he'd done three times, that they sat through it not showing much emotion, laughing or tittering only in a couple places, one being when they heard their word for penis used.

Not having plans then of writing, I never discussed this with Haley, nor would I if I had. Nor did I ask for his autograph. Yet, being a thoughtful man, he got the purser to give him the full name of each person serving him or his friends. Then on a copy of an article from *USA Today* about him, he wrote a note, mine saying he appreciated sailing with me on the voyage.

He was a generous tipper. I thanked him as would have been done to any passenger whether tipping or not. Then as an afterthought, added, "You know I'll be dropping your name for the rest of my life."

Looking pleased, he grinned from ear to ear.

322

My book, perhaps best described as occupational therapy for an insane writer, was getting unwieldy. With all the side trips the reader had been taken on by an egomaniac, megalomaniac, I'd be lucky if one completed the whole damn thing, which was all right too. For after all, there can be only one Jesus Christ of the book reading world. But since my remembrance of Alex Haley was probably no different than that of thousands of others, I decided not to include it.

Before continuing, perhaps my thinking leading up to what eventually happened should be made clearer. Yet how do you define "awareness" to someone who might never have had it? And how do you explain—what can only be insanity to a "rational man"—that just by working a problem out in your mind, or even talking aloud to yourself, you are being understood by something unseen.

On February 9, 1992, I'd done just this, saying that unless I was given more information the book was completed, save for some rewriting, editing, and adding or changing a few genealogical notes as more information came in. Then early on the tenth of February, it came over the radio that Alex Haley died shortly after midnight.

Since he was seventy, it seemed to be no big deal. We all go, and he went mercifully quick. Yet the more details were read later in the paper, the more reason there was to believe why his chip was called in here in Seattle. You will, of course, agree with me no matter what as stated or that I'm a supreme egotist.

ALEX HALEY'S FATHER	Had taken *four* odd jobs to support himself in high school and college. As a railroad porter, he *traveled*. He would later become dean of agriculture in *four* different colleges.

ALEXANDER PALMER HALEY

ALEXANDER	Comes from Greek *Alexandros*, meaning protector (helper) of men.
PALMER	A pilgrim who had gone to the Holy Land and brought back a palm branch. The palm tree was sacred to Hermes. Palm leaves were used in writing.
HALEY	Probably refers to a road or way leading to a hall. Hermes, god of roads and ways.
1921–1992	13–21, the days of the Parentalia. Honoring his ancestors is exactly what Haley had done in *Roots*.

BORN IN
ITHACA, NEW YORK

Ithaca is one of the Ionian Islands. In legend, it was the home of Ulysses, who was protected by Hermes.

SAILOR (Coast Guard)

Hermes was thought to bring good fortune to those at sea. The sail always needs wind. Chip called in in Neptune's month.

COOK
CHIEF JOURNALIST
DIED IN SEATTLE

Hermes is sometimes shown as a cook. Hermes was the patron of writers. Maintained an apartment in Seattle, which looks something like sea turtle. But there were hundreds of other cities he could have died in on his lecture circuit.

AT SWEDISH HOSPITAL

Though never having been admitted to a Seattle hospital, I did work a one-day temporary job at Swedish hospital.

ADMITTED TO
EMERGENCY ROOM
FEBRUARY 9, 1992. DIED
ABOUT 11:00 P.M. ON
OF APPARENT HEART
ATTACK AT 12:04
ON FEBRUARY 10, 1992

Death came sixty-four (8 x 8) minutes after admission, or four minutes after midnight. It was, of course, the month of February, and so inconvenient of you, Alex, not to wait until the thirteenth. The festival for Dionysus had begun on the eleventh in the month corresponding to February in ancient Greece and ended on the thirteenth with the Anthesteria when offerings were made to Hermes on behalf of the dead. Four (4), the other side of midnight could suggest St. Valentine's Day. Though this sounds as if it's "really reaching," maybe not, as you will see in the next chapter.

HE HAD BEEN
SCHEDULED TO MAKE
A TALK ON FEBRUARY 11
AT THE NAVAL
SUBMARINE BASE
AT BANGOR, KITSAP
COUNTY

The day of his admission, I'd used Bangor (Maine) in writing about my roots. Not certain if Bangor was spelled with an e, I looked it up in the dictionary.

SPENT TWELVE YEARS
TRACING 12 AND 13.
HIS BACKGROUND FOR

ROOTS. THE TWELVE-HOUR
MINI SERIES WAS SEEN BY
130 MILLION VIEWERS

TRAVELED, WROTE AT NIGHT	Booked passage *four* times a year on freighters. Hermes, god of sleep.
KUNTA KINTE WAS CAPTURED IN 1767	$1 + 7 + 6 + 7 = 21$

Some say Haley was a prophet. This might be true. We usually think of prophets only predicting the future, yet interpretation can go back in time. By showing what he himself had found, Haley encouraged many to return to their roots. Whether these started in a village in The Gambia, West Africa, or in Newgate Prison, London, England, wasn't important. There were people there (spirits of the dead, if you will) in each man's past who would help and give him or her strength to make it in the future. "Leave the dead to bury their own dead" (Mt 8:22) wasn't enough. We learned this in Germany, Russia, Cambodia, Rwanda, and our own streets and prisons.

Throwing in fiction liberally here and there, Haley had to surmise to make some of his links. He wrote brilliantly. There was no use trying to compete with this. More detail was gone into, however, in spiritual correspondence.

Chapter Six

Malcolm (Little: measurement) X was extremely critical and skeptical, thinking himself best described by "angry," and anger is just another way suffering rears it ugly head. Nowadays there are few who won't agree he was right about a lot of things, the trouble he'd seen. You can get mighty tired of people who don't have your problem telling you not to mind what others say, that they're just ignorant, and to shrug it off. By squawking loudly, Malcolm X changed a few things and perceptions. This was good, but one thing he never seemed to realize was that being a minority is debilitating, so much so that a person becomes 10 percent more or less a prisoner of his own mind. Ninety percent of the time he sees things in clear focus and calls them exactly as they are, but for the other 10 percent of the time when he doesn't, he is sometimes not just off but way off.

Alex Haley probably understood this when he commented he felt that toward the end Malcolm X was growing. Any time, furthermore, a person puts thousands of observations and feelings into an autobiography, as Malcolm X did, there are bound to be a few inconsistencies in thought, contradictions, or examples of double-think. If you don't believe me, try it yourself sometime.

It shouldn't be, but wherever in the world there is a majority of one race, racism can't be ruled out completely. I'd been the only white working in the stewards department once on a small freighter. Sometimes mistakes were made which needed correcting. Other times, it smacked of racism.

He got to Mecca, the high point of any Muslim's life. Some will hold off becoming a *haji* until they have a certain control over their actions, so that they can give the best possible example to fellow Muslims when they return from Mecca. The people he met, for the most part, were people very sincere about their religion and so represented the best part of it. In practice, however, in some Arabic countries, there's still some racism, or at least that's my understanding from Arabian and South Yemen seaman. There seems no reason to doubt their word.

Though finding him to be an interesting person, I hadn't planned to mention him other than in a sentence or two in respect to Alex Haley, until later realizing that Malcolm X takes on a significance all his own. When he was a "little boy" (bad enough to be called "boy"), his mother had a vision of his father dying, and he believed this intuition in himself seldom failed. He pointed out that several of his relatives had died of violence, and he thought he himself would also someday. He had used his father's .22 rifle to hunt rabbits, and his favorite restaurant in Harlem was its *Twenty-two* Club. He made a trip to Europe in 1965 and arrived back at New York City on February 13, the beginning of the Parentalia. The next day a Molotov cocktail was thrown into his home, half of which was destroyed. This violence of the fourteenth brings to mind the shotgun massacre three snake cycles previously in Chicago, the headquarters of the Black Muslim group to which he belonged. It also brings to mind that Malcolm X was his father's seventh child, Malcolm's favorite number was seven, and he had been put over Black Muslim mosque number seven (see page 482). It was in Harlem that he was assassinated in the snake-year 1965 (21) on February 21, the Feralia, and *feral* can mean "wild, untamed, undomesticated," or "causing death, fatal, funeral," Remember too in the introductory speech on that fatal day, Brother Benjamin X had referred to Malcolm X "as a *trojan* for a black man." Malcolm X was killed by thirteen bullets to his heart and chest by a sawed-off *shotgun*, 13 - 21.

Alex Haley had got into the line to view Malcolm X's body on Friday, the day before his burial. When the line stopped that night, twenty-two thousand had passed by. If the X in his name stood for his being an ex-con, ex-alcoholic, ex-pimp, etc., it also "symbolized the true African family name he had never known."[2-A] And this—aside from the verifying dates—marked him as a true Parentalia-Caristia person.

For both Alex Haley and Malcolm X, the lack of knowledge of ancestors was a type of castration, and Haley's death close to the Parentalia was a further link between the two.

If pregnancy lasts an average of 266 days from the time of conception, Washington, Ralph, and I were conceived during the first Mercury period (May 21–June 20) on the present calendar. By assuming the pregnancies of Lincoln, Jimmy Hoffa, and Malcolm X were 266 days or near it, then Lincoln and Hoffa were also conceived during the first Mercury period, while Malcolm X (*Malcolm Little*) was conceived in the second (August 23–September 22).

A criticism might be made that the current calendar should not have been used for Washington, so let's see what we might come up with by using the Julian calendar:

May 21	10	Washington's birthday under old
	Jun. 30	calendar: February 11, 1732.
	Jul. 31	
	Aug. 31	
	Sep. 30	
	Oct. 31	
	Nov. 30	
	Dec. 31	
	Jan. 31	
	Feb. 11	
	266	

May 22	9	Lincoln's birthday under
	Jun. 30	present calendar:
	Jul. 31	February 12, 1809
	Aug. 31	
	Sep. 30	
	Oct. 31	
	Nov. 30	
	Dec. 31	
	Jan. 31	
	Feb. 12	
	266	

If the period of pregnancy in each case was right on the number taken as average, we could come up with the number *2122* by combining them.

Chapter Seven

We were here long before the Kennedys. Maine, separating from Massachusetts, was admitted to the union on March 15, 1820. Now the Kennedy lineage is beneath us. Never forget who you are: the Ides of March; the sinking of the *Maine* on the Lupercalia; and most of all my warning to you and any others who might read this, "as the Manes go, so goes the nation."[2-B] It's the reason Lincoln had to travel from Springfield, Illinois, on February 11, 1861 (and why he would have to return as he did), to Washington, arriving on February 23. A circle, around a circle, around a circle.

Deacon, "Ding Dong Daddy"[3] Duran[4] from Durham, born March 17, 1747, was my great, great, great grandfather. Coming from England as a young man, Matthew settled in Cape Elizabeth, Maine. In 1769 (at the age of twenty-one or twenty-two), he owned a sixty-acre farm on the *Fore* Rim, opposite Portland. He married Sarah Strout of Cape Elizabeth. She was a fourth generation Strout and the fourth sibling of a second marriage, and being born on May 13, 1756, she was also Persephone's child. The exact date of their marriage is unknown, but it was about 1771. She was "a young thing" as the song goes, who could leave her mother. John, the first of their eight children, was born on April 2, 1772.

Between 1776 and 1780, there were no births or land transactions recorded under the Duran name. This may be explained by the fact Matthew was in the Royalsborough Militia and that he served in the Revolutionary War.[5]

On February 8, 1782, Matthew sold one-half the land and buildings he owned in Cape Elizabeth, and on October 6, 1782, he bought fifty acres in Durham.[6] Then in 1794, he bought or possibly exchanged property for ninety acres at Bagley's Gore,[7] Freeport line (see Stackpole's *History of Durham*, Maine). There are numerous other entries in the Cumberland registry of deeds with Matthew's name on them, which suggest he might have been a wheeler-dealer having a good business sense. Be that as it may, it can be said safely that he had a "lifelong inclination to provide security for himself mainly through property and recording his agreements."

In 1804 he provided for his spiritual, rather than material, security by buying a pew in the Durham Congregational Church. But that seems to have been a temporary lapse, for in 1806 he sold his homestead to sons[8] Samuel and Matthew, Jr. They in turn on the same day drew up an agreement whereby Matthew, Sr. and his wife, Sarah, could lease for one dollar a year their old homestead until the end of their lives. He was fifty-nine then.

Sarah died on March 25, 1821, and rightfully her age at death, given as seventy-one, is questioned. Whatever, it gets cold in Maine, and "Ding! dong! the bells are gonna chime."[9] Ding Dong, thrice greatest, at the ripe old age of seventy-five marries Eleanor Gee of Scarboro on April 18, 1822. Now just what do you suppose the old patriot-patriarch's eight children had to say about that?

The last record of his land dealings is in 1833 (he's now eighty-six) when he gets property to "lease and let" from Robert Hasty, Jr., Scarborough. The genealogist assumes that he had no more sons left in Durham to draw up a similar document with.

On January 1, 1844, he died at an even riper old age of ninety-six. Throughout his life, Ding Dong was independent and resourceful. He stood on his own two feet, and he lived his life the way he wanted to. A man can't do much better than that.

What previously has been written about Matthew Duran was based mainly on numerous land transactions, which were all there was to go on at the time other than him being a deacon in the Durham Congregational Church. Since then from information brought to light in *The Strout Family of Maine*, compiled by Capt. M.C. Morse, Jr., I surmise that Matthew's "escape" itself and/or whatever he was running from likely influenced his later religious convictions, which were obviously deeper than first thought, notwithstanding that obituaries tend to get carried away:

> He was born in England—sailed with the fleet commanded by Wolfe to the Siege of Quebec—was subsequently stationed at Halifax, when he escaped and settled at Cape Elizabeth. About 1768 he removed to Durham where he remained till his death universally respected and beloved. In a season of religious interest in 1815, he hoped he received, through Christ's blood, forgiveness of sin; connected himself with the church, and well sustained till death his Christian profession. His last and painful sickness was borne with holy submission and cheerful faith. It was instructive to be by his bedside and, at the close, to witness the calmness and holy triumph with which an old, experienced Christian could die.

Halifax is an Atlantic seaport and the capital of Nova Scotia. Matthew fled from there, yet "escape" sounds like desertion. If so, we'll never know whether he was justified (*he could very well have been*) or just an impetuous youth who got carried away in his mind, exaggerating a situation which he didn't like.

The writer of the obituary was an educated man, probably a minister or deacon in whom Matthew had confided to some extent. The fact that Matthew's escape is mentioned might suggest that Matthew thought he was fleeing from some wrong or injustice, and he looked at it as being through God's help. But for whatever reason Matthew might have fled, would he have used his own name? Nova Scotia wasn't that far off. It's easy to see then why genealogists can sometimes reach impasses on checking family links overseas. It also might suggest that some of the soldiers and sailors fighting in the Revolutionary War could have had other reasons to fight along with patriotism. In Matthew's case, none of this might be true, or it might all be, or very possibly the truth could lie somewhere in between.

Both Matthew and Sarah are buried at Cedar Grove cemetery, just a few miles over the Durham line. Sarah's tombstone shows various shades of decay and reads:

> In memory of
> Mrs. Sarah Duran
> wife of Deac. Matthew Duran
> who died March 25, 1821
> AEt 71
> Her body . . . (the rest unreadable)

Matthew's tombstone is rectangular and seems to be holding up better. It reads:

> Dea. Mathew Duran
> Died Jan. 4, 1844
> AEt 96 yrs and 9 M
> Gently thy passing spirit fled,
> Sustained by grace devine,
> Oh may such grace on us be shed,
> And make our end like thine.

"Since Matthew Duran was the earliest and only Duran in early Registry Records of Cumberland County, I think he is the progenitor of all Cumberland Country Durans," a professional genealogist living in that area wrote.

Though we knew that Martha Whitmore was George Duran's mother and that one John Duran was his father, we couldn't say definitely that John Duran, first son of Matthew and Sarah, was this John on the basis of information in LDS records and the *History of Durham*. The latter stated

John, the first son, had married Jane Davis, but there was no mention of a second marriage. Who would have thought that at 51 he would have married again? In retrospect, perhaps it is not so strange, considering Ding Dong had remarried at 75.

It was a breakthrough then when the genealogist found listed on page 185 of the 1850 census of Penobscot County, town of Charleston, Maine, as head of household John Duran, age 78 (no occupation), wife Martha, age 52, and the following children: Elsa I., age 20; Martha A., age 18; Simin, age 14; Rufus, age 12.

"This John age 78," the genealogist wrote, "has just got to be the son of Matthew, Sr. of Durham. Subtract 78 from 1850 and you get 1772, the date the *History of Durham* says John was born." Later *The Strout Family of Maine* will be a second source confirming the link and filling in many gaps. John Duran died April 23, 1859, at the age of 87. Martha followed on March 17, 1869. (Both Martha and Sarah, her mother-in-law, died in snake years.)

Listed below are the names and dates of birth of the children of John and Martha:

George G. Duran	September 8, 1823
Charles C. Duran	December 10, 1825
Elsa (?) Duran	October 13, 1824
Martha A. Duran	October 27, 1831
Simion N. Duran	May 6, 1835
Rufus Duran	May 19, 1837

Originally Lola (my brother Warren's wife) had obtained information from the town clerk at Charleston, Maine, that George G.[10] had married Margaret J. (Tyler)[11] and that they had six children:

	Born
William R. Duren	October 19, 1850
George H. Duren	August 14, 1852
John L. Duren	September 2, 1854
Daniel C. Duren	September 6, 1856
Mary J. Duren	January 7, 1859
Perley G. Duren	May 10, 1861

But more research showed the birthdates of the sons given on Mormon (LDS) records differed from those above:

William R. Duren	1851
George Henry Duren	August 14, 1853
John Duren	1855
Daniel Duren	1857[12]
Jane Duren	1859
Pearl J.	1861

Who was right? I tended to believe the town clerk's version where more detail was given. The original mistakes and confusion it seems were made *possibly* and/or fostered by my great grandmother Margaret J.

Duren. Under the circumstances, however, the errors or possible errors on her part are understandable.

It's human nature to glorify the man who has died of a war wound without giving any thought to the surviving widow and children, their longer struggle. Margaret Duren was quite a woman and an equally heroic figure.

COUNTY OF PENOBSCOT   TOWN CLERK'S OFFICE   May 30, 1965
TOWN OF BRADFORD

This certifies that Mr. George Duren of Charleston and Miss [unclear] Margaret J. Duren of Bangor were legally joined in marriage this day at Bradford by me. Bradford Nov. 25, 1849

       /s/ James Strout, Jr.   Minister of
                                    Gospel

I Hereby Certify, That the above is a true copy of the Record
       /s/ Lewis B. Randall   Town Clerk.

On a *Widow's Declaration for Army Pension*, signed by Margaret J. Duren (spelled with an e) 19 June 1865, the following were names and dates pertaining to the Duran (spelled with an a) children:

William R. Duran	Age 14 years	Born	October 19th	1850
George H. Duran	Age 13 "	"	August 14th	1851
John L. Duran	Age 11 "	"	September 2	1853
Daniel C. Duran	Age 9 "	"	September 6	1855
Mary J. Duran	Age 8 "	"	January 7	1857
Pearly G. Duran	Age 5 "	"	May 10	1860

STATE OF MAINE
PENOBSCOT COUNTY

Personally appeared before me George W. Smith and George W. Blakemore, residents of Mattawamkeag, County of Penobscot, and State of Maine and made oath that they well know Mrs. Margaret J. Duren, widow of George Duren who was a private in Co. A, 1st Regt. Heavy Artillery, Maine Vol. and know that she resides in Mattawamkeag, County of Penobscot, and State of Maine, and that the nearest Court of Records is at Bangor, County of Penobscot and State of Maine, distance from Mattawamkeag sixty-six miles. They further declare that they have no interest in the claim of Mrs. Duren to a pension.
/S/ Geo. W. Smith
/S/ Geo. W. Blackemore

Sworn and Subscribed to on this 19 - day of June 1865, and I certify that deponents are respectable and worthy of credit and that I am disinterested in the claim of Mrs. Duren to a pension.
/S/ Alvin Haynes
Pension Notary

CONY U.S. GEN'L HOSPITAL
Augusta Maine, <u>Nov. 27</u> 1865.

Respectfully returned to Hon. [handwriting unclear] H. Barrett, Commissioner of Pensions, Washington D.C.

It appears from the records of this Hospital that Private George Duren, Co. A 1st Rg. Maine Heavy Artillery, was admitted to this Hospital Aug. 4th 1864, with gun shot wound left leg, rec'd in battle before Petersburg, Vir. June 18th 1864, and died April 10th 1865.

He was very sick for a long time. Severe abscess of right leg hastened his death.

By Order of
[unclear] in Charge

O.S. Bradberry
A.A. Surgeon U.S.A.
Exec. Officer

DECLARATION OF ARREARS OF PENSION

State of Maine
County of Penobscot
Thirtieth day of October A.D., 1874

Margaret J. Duren, aged 53, a resident of Bradford, Penobscot, Maine, appeared before and swore under oath to a Justice of the Peace.

"She declares that the true date of birth of her son John S. is Sept. 2, 1854 and that of her son Daniel C. is Sept 6, 1856—and that of her daughter Mary J. is January 7, 1859. That their dates of birth as shown by [unclear] is wrong—that she made this discovery soon after pension was allowed and spoke to her [writing unclear] Agent Esq. Benson of Bangor (now dead) about it and that he advised her not to attempt to correct it as by so doing she might lose all her pension...That when the mistake was made she cannot state. It might have been her own at the beginning or her said agent in copying her paper...or it may have been the mistake of said Clerk in making the entry upon his books. It may have been the mistake in part of them all but mistake it certainly was and she now applies for arrears of pension due by reason and to correct the record...."

Hence, the dates given by the Charleston, Maine, town clerk seem to be most likely, as they square with sworn affidavits made later in life by Margaret Duren.

Chapter Eight

Athens and Rome were other times and other places. An Athenian sooth-sayer, seeing that his nine pebbles had fallen into a clear four and five separation, might have interpreted that something momentous was about to happen and scurried off to find the general who would reward him well for his augury. Certainly too he must warn the general to invoke the aid and protection of *Hermes Hegemonius* before beginning to campaign.[13] At times in ancient Rome, legions carried snakes on poles.[14]

Petersburg lies roughly twenty miles southeast of Richmond, Virginia. It is called the Cockade City.[15] In the Civil War it was a strategic point in the Confederate capital's defense. Running through or near Petersburg were roads and railroads that carried supplies from the south's heartland and the Atlantic to Richmond. If it could be taken, Richmond was doomed, the war lost for the south.

The period of the Petersburg campaign is given as June 15, 1864, to April 3, 1865, and it was the longest sustained operation in the war. No other U.S. city has ever been under siege so long. Had it not been for the bungling and lack of coordination of the Union generals during the first three days of the campaign, it might have been over in days, sparing most of the forty-two thousand Union casualties and twenty-eight thousand Confederate.

George Duren was wounded on June 18, 1864. In his diary,[16] he wrote of getting "a slight wound in the forehead and a ball through the leg." He was in and out of the hospital on convalescent furlough as his condition slowly deteriorated.

On the beginning of the *fourth* month 1865, Union troops defeated the Confederates at Five Forks. This was a *crossroads* beyond Lee's western lines. At 4:30 A.M. (between four and five) the following day (April 2), Union forces attacked Petersburg, and by nightfall the city had fallen. On April 9 (4 + 5 = 9); *Palm* Sunday, Lee surrendered to Grant at Appomattox. On April 10, George Duren, great grandfather clock, died. On April 12 (four years to the day after the first shots were fired at Fort Sumter), Lee's army laid down its weapons at Appomattox.[17-A] Under the terms of the ninth, Lee's men were allowed to take their horses and mules with them. By the thirteenth of April, most of these beaten, dispirited men had started home, singly and in groups. They had suffered much hardship during the winter and morale had worsened then, especially in seeing some friends and comrades desert. All were hungry, some malnourished and/or wounded. Grant ordered that they be given what rations he could spare. But for many the journey home would take weeks, and they would have to scrounge food—then short in many places—as best they could.

The end of the war was an emotional period for both sides. Many grizzled and battle-hardened union soldiers cried openly in relief, some to themselves. Still others were throwing things around, whooping and hollaring, back-slapping and hugging, cheering and laughing. If there was not happiness and joy for the South and its paroled soldiers, there was relief that it was finally over.

The fine oratory that had fired and stirred the men on each side to go off to war was repeated later, this time to tidy things up. By shifting the focus to and compartmentalizing the dead (those brave men on each side who had the courage of their convictions, who had died for what they believed in, and blah, blah, blah), the leaders averted the deeper thoughts that each in the end could be made putty by a tune of glory.

There was bitterness of all kinds. The South will remember the excesses of Sherman's men; the north, Andersonville. The blacks will remember especially the massacre at Fort Pillow, Tennessee. (Hell, we Civil-War whites were ahead of Hitler. The killing fields of Cambodia, the blacks killing blacks in Africa today, and the whites killing whites in Bosnia recently are just as bad. It's scary to think of the worldwide human potential—lying below the surface—for man's inhumanity to man.) Nearly every person had some individual horror story. All this will be passed down from generation to generation. Even today there are small pockets of residual, though these are dying only to be replaced with something far worse: the romanticizing of the war. The very parents who shuddered to think that their kids should watch carnage and violence on television think nothing of attending balls, galas, and other celebrations commemorating the Civil War and are thrilled to watch reruns of *Gone with the Wind*, *Gettysburg*, and so on.

Lincoln ordered the bands in Washington to play "Dixie"[17-B] (a song he said had always been one of his favorites) as often as they played "Yankee Doodle." He was, of course, trying to start the healing process.

On the fourteenth of April (4-14-1865, Good Friday), just after the men who had been in Lee's army started for home, "Our American Cousin" was playing at Ford Theater in Washington. Yet at another level, a different drama had been scripted. One of the actors in this play for real was the professional actor John Wilkes Booth, who was described as "raven"-haired and unstable. Sitting in the president's box were *four* persons: the President, Mrs. Lincoln, Major Henry *Reed* Rathbone, and his stepsister and fiancee Clara Harris. Booth entered the box and shot the president in the head. The significance here of the change of the number in the box from four to five shouldn't be lost in the tragedy. After stabbing Rathbone in the arm, Booth jumped to the stage, and while brandishing his knife cried, "Sic Semper Tyrannis" (thus shall it ever be for tyrants) in the language of ancient Rome.

As if to fulfill some final detail in an arcane rite before his death, the president was carried *across a street* to a room where his personal physician, Dr. Robert King *Stone*, was summoned. At 7:22 A.M. the following morning (4-15-1865), Lincoln died. Booth was tracked down later and shot. Four of those who conspired with him will be tried and hanged (here again 4:5), and four will receive life sentences. The total number involved: nine.

The president's body crossed boundaries to reach *Spring*field, Illinois. There in the fifth month, May, which is that of the snake, Abraham Lincoln will be buried on the *fourth* day (5-4-1865) or British: 455.

George Duren, great grandfather clock, had been dead *four* days when Lincoln was shot and *five* days when he died. George Duren is buried at No. 207 Augusta Cemetery, Maine.

Possibly a relative, George E.H. Duran, son of William and Francis, is buried at Tomb 40 in the eastern cemetery at Portland, Maine. He served in the Seventeenth Regiment, Main Infantry Company B, and was killed in action at Petersburg on March 25, 1865.

Several Strouts are listed as having been in the Civil War in E. Stackpole's *History of Durham*. No doubt some of these were distant relatives.

S—1081.

PENSIONER DROPPED.

United States Pension Agency,

San Francisco, Cal.

MAR 9 — 1907

_____, 190__

Certificate No. 62064

Class _Widow_

Pensioner _Margaret J. Duren_

Soldier _George Duren_

Service _A. 9. Inf. H. A._

The Commissioner of Pensions.

SIR: I have the honor to report that the above-named pensioner who was last paid at $ 12 , to 4 Dec , 1906 has been dropped because of _death_
Feb. 21. 1907

2122

_____

_____

Very respectfully,

Jesse B. Fuller
United States Pension Agent.

NOTE.—Every name dropped to be thus reported at once, and when cause of dropping is death, state date of death when known.

341

STROUT

Married

1st Generation: Christopher Strout —1680—Sarah Picke
Born probably between
1655 and 1660 in Truro,
Cornwall, England. He
was possibly the son of
Anthony and Mary Strout.
A family story is that
after being shipwrecked
in this country, he stayed.
He was in the "fishing
business," and some sons
were "whale fishermen."
So dust off your *Moby Dick*.

George Picke was a
fisherman whose
wife's name was
Sarah. It was
their daughter
Sarah who
Christopher married.

2nd Generation: Capt. George Strout —1708—Bridget (née) Cooley.
(1682 or 1689)

3rd Generation: Elisha Strout —1750—Bathsheba Small
(ca 1715) (Aug 6, 1724)

4th Generation: Sarah Strout
(May 13, 1756 - Cape Elizabeth)

DURAN

1st Generation: Matthew Duran —1771—Sarah Strout
(Mar. 17, 1747 Eng.)

2nd Generation: John Duran[18] —1823—Martha Whitmore
(5th Strout) (April 2, 1772) (Feb. 10, 1798)

3rd Generation: George Duran (Duren) —1849—Margaret J. Tyler
(6th Strout) (Sep. 9, 1823) (ca 1820)

4th Generation: Daniel Chase Duren[19] —1887—Annie (Ann)
(7th Strout) (Sep. 6, 1856) Cameron
or (Mar. 22, 1867 or
—1888— 1868)

5th Generation: Frances May Duren
(8th Strout) (August 22, 1888)
Nellie Isabelle Duren
(May 27, 1890)
Edith Duren
(March 1892)
Dollena Dorothy Duren
(March 15, 1900)
Genevieve Duren
(ca. 1904)

Chapter Nine

"He who increases knowledge increases sorrow" (Eccles 1:18).

Having built on the premise that Daniel Duren was the fourth son and fourth child, I'd discover one day in the quiet sanctity of Mormon Stakes that this wasn't strictly true: "Awe shit!" There was no mistaking the two additional entries, one located in one section; the other in another:

DUREN, Franklin   B. 1845
Father: George Henry Duren
Mother: Margaret J. Tyler
DUREN, Stephen F.
Event: Birth 1845
Charleston Twp. Penobscot, Maine
Father: DUREN
Mother: Margaret J. Tyler

A plausible reason for the mix-up was that Charleston, Maine, records might have been based in part on Civil War pension affidavits, showing only the children under sixteen. Then when it was seen that George and Margaret Duren married on November 25, 1849, and that the first child was born October 19, 1850, who would have thought to look further, especially in the social milieu of New England one hundred and eighty-plus years ago?

Previously there'd been an inkling of a 4:5 relationship. (Dollena Dorothy had been the fourth of five daughters. I'd been a fourth son and a fifth child.) So if only one more child had showed up, that could have been dealt with, but no way would two more sons fit the pattern. Yet somehow it wasn't so much being misled as it was a matter of understanding.

Besides, it seemed possible Margaret and George had been married previously but that their marriage records had been lost or destroyed, or a church they'd joined promised hell and damnation because they married in some other denomination or by an itinerant preacher or justice of the peace whose credentials were shaky. So they remarried.

Concerning this, the genealogist wrote:

> Illegitimate births were not that uncommon in the 17th and 18th century. Maine records have many. The women were not ostracized but strongly encouraged to name the father. Most did so during childbirth and any man's name uttered at such time was considered the true father. It was thought no woman would lie during labor and childbirth. Midwives would be the witnesses. I believe Margaret Tyler had a baby out of wedlock and the "proof" of it is in the way it was recorded (if I'm interpreting your information correctly) "Stephen F. Duren born to George Duran and Margaret J. Tyler." Most Maine Town Clerk's records do not give a woman's maiden name in a birth record. (Earlier records also would just say "The George Duran children.") The fact Margaret's maiden name was used leads me to believe the child was illegitimate but George acknowledged paternity. For the town this was extremely important because George would have to support it. If no paternity was acknowledged the town would be required to support the child and most towns did not like doing this.

Norma Beth had reached the same conclusion separately:

> Re: Stephen Duren. Who knows? Could he have been born out of wedlock to Margaret and George? Horrors! But you know those Scotsmen are so passionate! Remember James Bond? (Sean Connery?)....

The genealogist went on to say:

> I believe, "Stephen" and "Franklin" were the same person. I believe there were two entries because the first recording did not record his whole name and the second recording was an attempt to correct this. Operating on this assumption, I think the full name would be Stephen Franklin Duran.

Now the interest in Stephen was not a moral issue, and couldn't have cared less about it, except that it reinforced the inkling of a 4:5 relationship, suggesting too a nebulousness or twilight zone which might exist between the two numbers. He was the first son, making Daniel Chase Duren the fifth son, or the fourth son born after they were legally married. Also Stephen, born 1845, and his brother Daniel, if born in 1857, were both snakes. In the sworn statement of October 30, 1874, Margaret says Daniel Chase Duren was born on September 6 (MP), 1856. But

Daniel apparently believed he was born in 1857, and that's what his death certificate said.

When later looking at page 185 of the 1850 census (on microfilm) for Penobscot County, Charleston, Maine, the genealogist found under Head of Household: George G. Duran, age twenty-six, farmer. Under George is listed *Margaret J. Duran*, age thirty, and *Stephen F. Duran*, age five. There were no other small children. William, of course, wasn't born until October 19, 1850. Curiously in the *same household* is Charles C. Duran, age twenty-four.

In the 1860 census, Stephen was still in the George Duran household and is listed as Franklin, fifteen. "Not called Stephen now—an adolescent choice?" the genealogist wondered. National archives could find no record of his being in the Civil War. It seemed at this point that he'd just disappeared. Then on April 14, 1994, the genealogist wrote as follows:

> Last week while at the Mormon Library briefly I decided to quickly check records for Stephen F. Duran and lo and behold I found where a Stephen F. Duren married an Ann M. Knowles on June 25, 1871 in La Grange, Penobscot County. La Grange is just a hop, skip and jump from Bradford.

Chapter Ten

Frances May with Helen in 1917, surrounded by
four or five lambs.

Maia, the fairest and the eldest of the Pleiades, is described as "lovely-haired." A family sepia (without lambs) shows unmistakenly that my mother had this too. However, there remained what seemed an inconsistency, the fact that Maia was the first of seven sisters, while my mother was the first of five. Though there was an eight-year period nearly to the day between the birth of Edith and Dollena (two of my mother's sisters), the 1900 census states that my grandfather and grandmother had no other children. This must be true; otherwise, the facts would be there.

If the number of Hermes (remember he has nearly the same powers as high half-brother Apollo, the sun god, but to a lesser degree) is four mythologically, why did Daniel and Annie not have four or seven daughters rather than five? Why did Frank and Frances not have four children instead of five? I was born at 10:00 P.M. on the twenty-first, which in Hindu Vedas is considered a lucky number, but my mother died on the twenty-sixth at 6:30 A.M., four-five days later. There were four or five lambs in the picture. Why was five cropping up so often when four would have made a better case, at least on the basis of what had been known up till then?

Why did Grandma Elizabeth, who was born on the fourth of February, die when she was eighty-four (4 x 21), four days before my fifth birthday rather than four days before my fourth birthday? Or why not on the Feralia as my great grandmother Margaret Duren had in 1907? Why were there four deaths in Saul's family and yet a fifth in a kindred spirit?

Mentioned previously is that Charles Darwin was close to being an earth-snake. When young, he was nicknamed "Gas" (wind). He collected *pebbles* and minerals and was interested in gardening. Then on October 24, 1831, he went aboard the *HMS Beagle*, a strange name for a ship unless you recall that the dog is one of the animals Hermes is over (Homeric Hymn No. 4). As the ship's naturalist, Darwin's official unpaid job was to study and collect specimens of *rocks* and life in the places the *Beagle* visited. The first to come to mind is the Galápagos Islands. *Isolas de Galápagos* means Islands of the Tortoises (Book I, footnote 19), where some grow to five hundred pounds,[20] the number and roundness of its shell like the Indy 500,[21] a contrast in slowness and speed. Yet in both there's time and measurement.

Historians seem to say generally that the *Beagle's* trip lasted "five years" and that he was sick for "forty-five years" following his return to England. Of course one can nitpick these numbers and say the trip was less than five years and that, depending on the exact day of the onset of the disease, it might have been more than forty-five years. But let's leave it as it's generally recorded. Why then, Darwin being under an Hermes influence, hadn't the ship sailed later and the duration of the voyage been shorter, so that historians might say "four years" and "forty-four years"?

An explanation which appears to make some sense, while seemingly compatible with the Apollo-Hermes relationship in mythology, comes from astrology. The sun is given two numbers: one and four. The number one, represented by a lion, is the sun when it's increasing. The number four, represented by a *serpent*, is the sun when decreasing and is associated with death and afterlife. In astrology, Mercury with the setting sun is given the number five.[22]

Lying near the sun, Mercury can be seen shortly after sunset. This is in agreement that he was first a twilight god. The number five is also linked to Mercury in that after escorting the spirits of the dead to Hades, he left them with Charon who took them across the Styx, having five tributaries. And in a grand deception worthy of Hermes, Maia, his mother, gets credit for the month of May, the fifth month. Again, the snake month and the snake season in Chinese astrology are May and spring respectively.

From the fifth century B.C., Apollo, having radiant energy, was thought to be a sun-god. Purists might argue that Apollo and Helios were not the same. The 4:5 relationship between the planet Mercury and the Sun is not effected, however, and both gods were charioteers. Though some would like to keep the heavenly bodies separate from the gods (i.e., astronomy off from astrology and mythology), I'm not certain, in view of mythological names used, this was meant to be.

My sister died in the year of her birth, a snake-year. Both my birth and my mother's death was twelve years later in another. The fact 1) that my mother was the first born and the first to die of five children suggests a 4:5 relationship. That is, four out of the original five at one point were still alive. But if we say one-fifth was now dead, we're saying that one of five eventual deaths existed. Everything is logical so long as like units are used. Possibly herein lies a key magic: a willingness to accept what might be illogical, to set up apples over oranges or life over death in proportions.

Prohibition, a classic example of boundaries and breaking of boundaries, was ratified as the eighteen amendment in January 1919, the month before Ralph was born, and went into effect in January 1920. The *twenty-first* amendment (proposed by congress in February) repealed the eighteenth on December 5,[23] 1933, the year Duncan Cameron, Sr. died and when I was four-five years old. So it's intriguing that though Duncan had long since sold his Eden-area ranch[24] (located twelve miles from Stockett, Montana), "Little Al Capone" early on in the prohibition era will be *traveling* in his Hud*son* touring car for speed and power[25] down the main road to Stockett each week to Canada and returning with booze by "some back country road"[26] (deception), as if in some clandestine and mystical way he had to touch some point near the ranch's graveyard where Dannie Cameron was buried.[27]

As the Parentalia in February, April (the fourth month), and May (the fifth month) appear to stand out in relation to Hermes, so possibly, and to a lesser degree, do August (the eighth month) and September (ninth month).[28] In other words, four and five are basic units,[29] and eight (4+4) and nine (4+5) would be representative to some extent too. The number forty-four might suggest either Hermes or Apollo, and the number eighty-eight might suggest Hermes or Kronos, but the number forty-five has to be Hermes alone.

The forty-fifth day of the year is St. Valentine's Day, February 14 (5), the second day of the Parentalia. It's supposed to be the anniversary of the beheading (persona Hermes: decapitation) of the martyr by the

348

Romans. The red color of the Valentine's Day card (message)[30] and the wrapper of the candy box makes you wonder. The bottom line: Don't be deceived by chocolates. They'll make you bloody fat and send you to your grave.

Whoa! Hold on here! The attempt at levity might be something regretted, like being weighed and found lacking. Maybe the subject deserves more gravity, reverence. Maybe there are connections in ways not understood.

High up, outside an apartment, someone has hung a windbag with many colors of sleeves that flutter and snap past my window when it's breezy, like innumerable Sherpa prayer flags seen in *National Geographic*. It is a reminder of something not told you, just another piece of trivia; it didn't seem important until just now.

Some believe the original caduceus was a herald's staff with two strips of white ribbon or cloth hanging or interwound to assure safe passage of the bearer, or maybe it was just a rod with fillets of wool twined around, that in long journeys became stained, the bright red of blood showing most.

In the middle ages, barbers were surgeons. When blood letting was done (a sacrifice in a sense), the bandages were washed out and hung on a pole to dry in the wind. As they twisted around, serpentine reminders of the life-death struggle, the red and white—colors of the valentine— formed the image of what's now the modern barber pole.

In the "roaring twenties" a simpleminded barber called Amato Gasperri had a shop in the Windy City of the stockyards. In front of his chair was a wall rack on which were *twenty-one* shaving mugs. Each of these had the name of a patron in gilt Spencerian script. At first these customers were all fast friends, having ordinary jobs as waiters, street cleaners, bartenders, owners of ice-cream parlors, vegetable stores, etc., but with prohibition, all this changed as they began bootlegging and killing one another off in gangland wars.

Barbers are first and foremost measurers and so counters. Though appearing sorrowful (maybe he'd voodooed their hair), Amato would ink in a black cross opposite a name when he heard one of them had been murdered. Finally nineteen of the cups had crosses on them. Only Torrio and Capone were left. When hearing Torrio had been downed with four shotgun slugs and a revolver bullet to his jaw, Amato figured Torrio was dead and inked in a cross on Torrio's cup. But in this, Amato was wrong and had to rub it out.[31] John Torrio outlived them all to be seventy-five, though bearing a conspicuous scar like Capone's but on his neck. On April 16, 1957, when most figured John Torrio had long since died, he got into a barber chair in Brooklyn. The barber had just put a steaming white towel over his face and scarred neck for shaving when Torrio slumped down and slid out of the chair, stricken with a coronary and dying six hours later in a hospital.[32-A] The long, long day was through (measurement) with the moon over Brooklyn.[32-B]

He was baptized Alphonsus (Latin for Alfonso), but Alphonse (ae) Capone (ae) was "Al" American, being born in Brooklyn, New York. His parents traveled to the U.S. from a "village about sixteen miles down the bay of Naples,"[33] where his father had barbered, and once in the U.S., he continued to barber.

Their first child Vincenzo (Jimmy) had been born in *Italy*, but their second child Raffalo (*Ralph*, remember my brother Ralph was also a second child) was born in 1893, the year of the Panic and a snake year, shortly after they had come to the United States. It was in this same year that the Columbia exposition, Chicago's first World's Fair, had opened.[34] Their third child Salvatore (*Frank*) was born in 1895. Al, the fourth son and fourth child, was born on January 17, 1899. Five (5) more children would be born after him.[35]

He was fourteen when he quit school. About this time, he joined the Forty (40) Thieves Juniors gang and, when older, the Five (5) Points, an adult gang.

At eighteen, he told Lena Galluccio, who'd never seen him before, "You got a nice ass, honey, and I mean it as a compliment. Believe me."[36]

At the insult, her brother Frank knifed Al, causing three slashes on his face and/or neck, requiring about thirty stitches at the Coney Island Hospital.[37] The crime lord at the time ruled Al had been wrong and wasn't allowed to seek vengeance and Frank had overreacted and had to apologize, so the nickname "Scarface."[38]

In 1918 Al married an Irish girl baptized as Mary but who went by the name of *Mae* all her life. This was twenty-six days after Mae (who was born April 4, 1897) gave birth to their son Albert *Francis* Capone (Sonny) on December 4, 1918.[39]

Seventeen days after their marriage and one day before Al's twentieth birthday, Nebraska became the thirty-sixth state to approve the resolution of Prohibition. This was the three-fourths majority needed to pass the eighteenth amendment, which went into effect on January 16, 1920.[40]

When Al left New York, he worked in Chicago as a bouncer or capper (or both) at the *Four* Deuces.[41] This was a four-story, red-brick building. The first floor was a saloon; the second, headquarters and bookkeeping offices of Torrio, his boss; the third, gambling; and the fourth, a brothel.

One thing helping boost Capone in the crime world was the accident which happened to Nails Morton. Morton checked out a horse from the Lincoln Riding Academy, 300 North Clark Street. When a stirrup broke, he slipped to the side. The horse panicked, kicked forward, and put "nails" in his coffin. This would seem to support the superstition that a horseshoe hung upside down is bad luck. Moreover, the U-shaped horseshoe is really a stylized *V* and vice versa, and no one makes a victory sign upside down.[42]

Previously Deany O'Banion, a gangster, and Morton had been pals. O'Banion loved flowers, so he and Morton bought into Schofield's flower business. When gangsters died for one reason or another, this business supplied a large portion of the flowers at funerals. Who knows? Maybe when business was slack, they helped things along, for it was considered an insult to send flowers that cost less than hundreds of dollars to the funeral of a mobster who had some status. Not knowing why, perhaps the gangsters were superstitious about this[43] and enemies who sent flowers were saying subtly, "You stink," maybe flogging a dead horse.

Mike Merlo, said to have been the last president of the "Unione Siciliana to die in bed in over five years,"[44] succumbed to cancer on November 8, 1924. Two days later, O'Banion was at the flower shop[45] when he was gunned down. Torrio apparently put out the contract on him. Merlo was buried on the thirteenth (4) and O'Banion on the fourteenth (5). In keeping with the custom, most big shot mobsters sent flowers, whether they had or hadn't been involved in the death. The orders would run into thousands of dollars. This was called "Obsequies Chic."[46] Al[47] sent O'Banion a basket of roses.

Cardinal Mundelein wouldn't allow a Funeral Mass, and he refused to allow O'Banion to be buried in consecrated ground. Five (5) months later, O'Banion's widow, Viola (derived from violet), quietly had his remains removed to consecrated grounds. The native violet is the state flower of Illinois.

In 1927 Commander Francesco de Pinedo piloted a four-man amphibious airplane on a world tour "for the glory of fascist Italy."[48] The plane, the *Santa Maria*, didn't make it out of the New World, same as Columbus's old ship. It caught fire in Arizona (admitted as a state on *St. Valentine's Day*, the forty-fifth day) when it set down on a lake for refueling. Mussolini then ferried the *Santa Maria II*, its sister plane, for de Pinedo and crew to continue on. The last stop was to be Chicago. When he set down on Lake Michigan (off *Grant* Park) on May 15, he was greeted by some of Chicago's distinguished Italians, including Al Capone, who had been invited by the police, fearing a riot. Capone's presence, they felt, would deter this. (See page 614.)

What's important to remember about May 15, the time of celebration in ancient Rome, is that

1) Hermes is a god of flight.
2) Capone was about as big a fish in cunning and deception as they could have got.
3) Except for leap year, May 15 is the 135th day (3 x 45).

Fifty-four (54) years previously on the same day, Dannie Cameron had been born. Six days after de Pinedo landed in Chicago, Captain Charles A. Lindbergh landed in Paris.[49] This was on May 21, the beginning of a Mercury period, 1927, or thirty-three years to the day after Dannie Cameron had died in Montana. 54 - 33 = 21.

Miami (Book II, footnote 160) lies on Florida's east coast, about fifty miles from the tip. Across the Bay of Biscayne is Miami Beach, having the jurisdiction of Palm[50] Island where Al bought a villa in 1928. From here he'd go back and forth to Chicago and eventually ended his days.

On October 24, 1931, Capone was sentenced for conviction of income-tax evasion and had ten or eleven years to serve ahead of him. This was reduced for good time. In 1927 his *wealth* was estimated around one hundred million dollars, accumulated from bootlegging (footprints, deception), prostitution rings, and gambling.[51] Considering it was the Depression when he was imprisoned, that Prohibition would be repealed in a little over two years, that he ended up paying only about eighty thousand dollars in court costs and fines, and that Alcatraz (*AZ*, the *Rock*) was newly built when he entered, he could have done worse.

This isn't to say Alcatraz was any picnic or country club. Capone's money couldn't help him here. There was a very good reason that some ex-cons would later upon release name-drop Alcatraz as a status symbol, as if they wanted everyone to know they'd gotten their Ph.D. in criminology from an institution that wasn't easy.

Inherent in each prison is a crazed, suicidal, and brutal atmosphere. Capone was normal in the abnormalcy in that he had a few fights, a few enemies. But his enemies were made mainly by Capone's refusal to back harebrained schemes for escape and to take part in prison riots. He wanted all the good time he was entitled to, to get out as soon as possible. Manipulators could and did brand this as chickenshit.[52]

When leaving Cook (Hermes symbolism) County Jail, Capone was sent to the U.S. Penitentiary at Atlanta where he stayed in an eight-man cell until August 18, 1934. He entered Alcatraz on *Wednesday*, August 22, 1934, one day preceding the Mercury period.

Luck had begun to run out even before this for a master of cunning and deceit who played hardball with a baseball bat. Certainly one good trick deserved another.[53-A] Before being imprisoned, he had contracted syphilis,[53-B] for which one reason or another (but mainly his own deception) his treatment came too late. An irony here is that the caduceus was working against him. During his last years at Alcatraz, he began to have confusion caused by tertiary syphilis.

He left Alcatraz in January 1939 and was transferred to the Federal Correctional Institution at Terminal Island (between *Long Beach* and San

Pedro), California. At times he would seem sane and well, at other times, loony. They continued to treat him with bismuth and tryparsamide. Eventually he went by train from Los Angeles to the federal penitentiary at Lewisburg, Pennsylvania, for release on November 16, 1939. He and his family returned to Palm (Hermes) Island, Florida. He continued on for years in lucid moments, confusion, and childish behavior. Then finally he died from the ravages of the disease on January 25, 1947, at forty-eight years, eight days. He was buried on *February 4* (baptized on *February 7*, 1899, on the twenty-first day after birth), 1947, at Mount Olivet Cemetery in Chicago. Possibly because of the trampling of the green around the eight-foot stone by sightseers, the remains of all three family members were transferred to Mt. Carmel Cemetery in March 1950.

About the time of his death in 1947, I'd just completed my last semester of high school. The same year, Dick Haman, architect-rancher, and his partner Freeman Fairfield, who made millions drilling oil in Long Beach, seeded clouds near Topaz (AZ) Lake.

Al's son "Sonny," though *partially deaf*, turned out surprisingly well, all things considered. He married and had four daughters. Al apparently hadn't made out a will. Sonny, though offered mob connections, stayed clear of it, working at menial jobs and keeping his nose clean. When he and his wife broke up, he worked at two low-paying jobs to send as much support for his daughters as he could. About the only thing he had on his records was shoplifting two bottles of aspirin and a few flashlight batteries, though he'd paid for the bags of groceries. The press at the time made much of this, building it up out of proportion. Finally the burden of the Capone name was too much for Sonny, and he had it changed from Albert Francis Capone to Albert Francis.

There's something to be said that Capone belonged to a mobster world which had different rules. Ruthlessness was necessary for survival. He showed the hypocrisy of the world better than any other man in modern times. He was a supreme realist. His main defect as a person and his strongest point as a psychopath was that he used the flaws of humanity to justify his own actions. In this warped way, he was an inside-track man with carte blanche, ignoring or circumventing the law to suit himself. Yet everyday we read of big names in industry doing this, the payola of the lobbyists, the pork of the congressmen to get reelected, etc. So there's something of Al in most of us, it's just a matter of sophistication. He spared us the primness and hell and damnation of the preacher, the tediousness of the psychologist, the bullshit of the sociologist, and got right to the heart of the matter in saying most eloquently, "I'm just a businessman" (commerce). We chose to see this as a cartoon parody of the devil spouting a halo of words when actually it carried a truth in more far-reaching implications.

On the morning of the forty-fifth day, February 14, in the year of the earth-snake, the mercury *measured* eighteen above zero. Snow was falling just enough to make light footprints. A westerly wind nipped at the face and ears to make itself known. Members of Capone's[54] gang, disguised (deception) as policemen, entered the garage at 2122 North Clark Street in Chicago. They then ordered members of George "Bugs" Moran's[55] rival gang to line up next to a wall (boundary) and mowed them down with Thompson submachine guns ("Chicago pianos"), firing .45-caliber rounds, and shotguns. All were dead (4514) or soon to be except those who drove off in a car. This was called the St. Valentine's Day Massacre, which "never really made sense," Mike Graham, a researcher into Chicago's past, said.[56]

Oh but it did!

Al Capone, in a way of speaking, was my godfather. He was a fourth son followed by five children (45), while I was a fourth son and fifth child (45). If there were three wise men traveling from the east nearly two thousand years ago, there would be seven wise guys[57] at the north (2+1+2+2=7) *sacrificed*,[58-A] one for each day until my birth on the Feast of the Dead, February 21, 1929 (21). 3 x 7 = 21.[58-B] Obsequies CHIC—psyCHIC—CHICago, the windy city of bloody stockyards—CHIChester. The St. Valentine's Day Mass, followed by ten years of Depression, establishes my credentials to warn not to ignore the Parentalia-Caristia mystique. "Megalomania," you sniff, labels being the psychiatrists' holy water.

It's not important whether you like or hate my guts. The dead do what they will. The Catholic Robert Southwell was declared "blessed" by Pope Pius XI in 1929, the year of the St. Valentine's Day Mass. Hanged until limp on the February Feast of the Dead 1595, Southwell's head was then chopped off and held up to the crowd. Then the hangman went methodically about dismembering the rest of his body.

It isn't by chance that St. Valentine's Day has come down to us as occurring on February 14, the first full day of the Parentalia, of which Lincoln's and Washington's birthdays are bookends. Nor was it chance that Presidents' Day (who are either dead or will be) occurs on the third Monday in February (on a date between February 15–21, incl.). Remember the beheading (persona Hermes) of the saint on February 14, 269 or 270, occurred about the time belief in the Parentalia was dwindling, and some believe February 14 was chosen to celebrate Christian martyrs to divert attention from the pagan Lupercalia.[58-C] Still the 14 and 15 become 4–5, or 45. The Luperci were described as a "truly savage brotherhood," of which Capone's gang on St. Valentine's Day was but a reminder. Candy wrapped in red is probably substantiation. Based on U.S. history, flowers and other customs for honoring the dead should be reinstituted during the Parentalia.

Al Capone was also linked to the Parentalia period—if not by actual days themselves—by the tradition of Italian burial and honoring its dead. He was very superstitious about tombstones and detested the thought of desecration of graves. (Op. cit., Bergreen, Laurence.) Once they'd buried their dead, the Capones didn't forget them but resorted nigh to ancestor worship, like many other Italian families.

On *December 5*, 1928, twenty-seven Sicilians met in Cleveland's Statler Hotel. This date is given as the beginning of modern organized crime by some authorities. Since Capone was non-Sicilian, he could not attend but had representation.[59]

On *May 13 through 16*, 1929, an all-important conference was held at the Presidential Hotel in Atlantic City. Capone and Torrio attended, as well as Frank McErlane, Lucky Luciano, and Dutch Schultz. It cut across national and ethnic lines, having Italians (May 13 = February 21), Jews, Sicilians (May 13, Persephone cult was strong in Sicily), Irish, and Slavs attending. Discussed at the conference were disarmament, peace, and joining together in rules of conduct nationwide. According to Capone, each signed on a dotted line.[60]

When Capone was arrested and convicted for packing a gun in 1929, he read a book on the life of Napoleon and commented that Napoleon was "the world's greatest racketeer." "If he had lived in Chicago," said Capone, "it would have been a sawed-off shotgun Waterloo for him. He didn't wind up in a ditch as a coroner's case, but they took him for a one-way ride to St. Helena, which was about as tough a break."

Someway or other the first Memorial Day, the Gettysburg Address, and the St. Valentine's Day Massacre link Napoleon, Lincoln, and Capone.

Napol*eon* - Ponce de *Leon*

N*apoleon* - apone of Capone

When bombings and dynamiting got particularly heavy one year in Chicago's prohibition era, a black-humored columnist wrote, "The rockets' red glare, the bombs bursting in air, Gave proof through the night that Chicago's still there.[61]

Silly man! But of course Chicago was still there. It always will be unless you reduce it to rubble, carry it away, and plant it into the original *meadow of garlic, leek, or onion* called *chicagou,* meaning "powerful" or "strong." These are things which grow when the moon wanes, and so are powerful agents against witch magic, especially moon witches. But you can't plant them where hundreds of thousands of structures stand, surrounded by steel, concrete, and asphalt, can you?

Rather than worry about the damage caused by nearly-fatal wounds when shot in Chicago, (page 349), John Torrio worried that the bullets were tipped with garlic and that a wound anywhere by just one would result in a deadly infection.

Chapter Eleven

In 1812[62] the United States went to war against Great Britain. The main reason this came about was over freedom of the seas, but to a lesser extent England appeared to be stirring up trouble for us with the frontier Indians. In 1813, we won the battle on Lake Erie. On August 24 (a Mercury period), 1814, however, the British, now having troops free from fighting Napoleon, took Washington, D.C., and it seemed for awhile the tide of the war had gone against us. On the night of September 13–14 (the same Mercury period), Francis Scott Key watched the bombardment of Fort McHenry, which controlled the harbor to Baltimore, by the British on a British ship. After it was finished, he wrote his famous poem called "The Defence of Fort M'Henry" (Mercury-Hermes).

The dates of the war, the time the attack on Fort McHenry took place, and much wording in the poem lead me to believe it is/was cabalistic, especially when it's recalled that twilight, dawn, and night are linked to Hermes. Moreover, if Hermes, having the caduceus, got smeared with Argos's blood, it's likely the original staff of two white strips of cloth got smeared with blood in his travels. So the stained bandages of the barber-*surgeon* interwinding in the wind, and the streaming (implying breeze) red and white of the flag. Below are quoted a few lines from the poem which later became "The Star-Spangled Banner."

"Oh! say, can you see, by the *dawn*'s early light,
What so proudly we hailed at the *twilight*'s last gleaming?"
"What is that which the *breeze*, o're the towering steep,
As it fitfully blows, *half conceals*, half discloses?"[63]
"Now it catches the gleam of the *morning's first beam*,".
"Their *blood* has washed out their foul *footstep's pollution*."
"From the terror of *flight*, or the gloom of the *grave*,"
"And this be our motto—'*In God is our trust*.'"[64]

Perhaps the most interesting facts are that the writer's name was *Key* and that the staff (stave) in musical notation has four spaces and five lines.

The war continued on into the early part of 1815, but it was officially over when a peace treaty was signed at Ghent, Belgium, in December 1814. Europe was relatively free from wide-scale war until World War I, i.e., from 1815 to 1914 when the war lasted for four years.

World War II began as a world war on September 3, 1939, when Great Britain and France declared war on Germany. It officially ended when Japan signed the documents of surrender on September 2, 1945. Thus both the beginning and the ending were within a Mercury period. The U.S. direct involvement began on 12-7-1941 (a snake-year, 41 a transposition of 14). The Japanese surrender was 8-14-1945, a calendar (*aea*) being something all can understand. If we think of Mercury given the number of five in relationship to the sun when it decreases (four), then the rising sun of Japan in World War II was no more compatible with Hermes than the German swastika as a symbol.

Napoleon Bonaparte was born August 15, 1769, and died on May 5, 1821 (SY). This made him fifty-one at his death, whereas Abraham Lincoln, born February 12, 1809, and dying April 15, 1865, was fifty-six at his death. Thus making four-five years difference in their ages at death. Both eventually crossed boundaries before burial (or final burial), as will Capone and Dillinger later.

One source says our Memorial Day had its beginning in Waterloo, New York, on May 5, 1866[65] (Lincoln was buried on May 4, 1865). Though this might have been a random happening, it seems more likely that the people of Waterloo, New York, had chosen May 5, knowing it was the month and day Napoleon died. Certainly there is nothing mysterious about that. In context with what this book's about, however, it's much harder to explain that the difference between May 5, 1821, and May 5, 1866, is exactly forty-five years. Napoleon, furthermore, is buried in a tomb which stands 14.5 feet (4.4 meters) high (*The World Book Encyclopedia*) in Paris, France, where he was brought from St. Helena. Remember in Greek mythology, Paris was promised Helen.

Napoleon was considered about average height for a Frenchman of his time but short for an officer. Where Lincoln appeared "gawky" and as if "his parts didn't seem to fit," Napoleon in one picture (dressed in white with the exception of black sleeves and part of his coat) has his right hand, as if still to emerge, hidden in his vest. Very black hair is combed forward to cover a very white baldness. His torso is long and slightly curved. He looks much like a bird hatching from an egg, as much as to say, "You are too late for a French omelette!"

Indeed "the little corporal" appears a little corporeal in most pictures. Like Lincoln, Napoleon's physical form seems irregular. One has the impression there's something slightly different in his shape from those around him. It always struck me that both leaders were Hermes people. For the price of greatness, the pendulum had to swing back with some significant physical or mental flaw, a sacrifice exacted. An endocrinologist believes Napoleon suffered from a glandular disease. One of the physicians to examine Napoleon's body after death commented, "His type of plumpness was not masculine, he had beautiful arms, rounded breasts, white soft skin (and) no hair." (*Reader's Digest Book of Facts*, New York: The Reader's Digest Association, Inc., 1987.) Napoleon's eyes were blue-grey.[66] When a child, he was called "little wolf."

Both Napoleon and Lincoln were law givers. As Lincoln (even with his mood swings) is a strong contender for being the greatest U.S. president, so Napoleon (even with megalomania) is a strong contender for being the greatest general of all time. His heraldic symbol was the bee, whose honey in the ancient world was offered as a sacrifice to Hermes (see Book I, footnote I-E). His defeat in Russia was due to his inability to maintain supply lines and the winter. It's curious that 1) the head of the Russian government was Czar *Alexander* (aea) I and 2) Napoleon's final imprisonment was for *five* years or so at St. Helena, a *rocky* island off the coast of Africa, before dying.

In passing, it would be as hard for us today to imagine the United States without Lincoln as it would be for the French to imagine France without Napoleon. Both were extraordinary men—myth-makers, heroes, but not without their enemies. Lincoln stood six feet four inches and Napoleon, five feet two inches.

Symbols for days of the week have been found engraved on stones where ancient Babylon was. Wednesday, the day for Mercury, was an erect snake *near* bent horns. Certainly the snake at the head of Nevada[67] is erect, like in the *uraeus*.[68] The two connecting sides near the head suggest one bent horn, while the other two sides suggest another. The Rattlesnake, Owyhee, and Snake rivers and the Snake Indians also seem to be a part of the uraeus, perched up there like a ghost figure.[69]

The snake obviously becomes a symbol of divinity (not to be confused with worship) of Jesus or Satan, among many others, because it commands deep respect. As no one in his right mind would even consider picking up a poisonous snake to cuddle or for any other reason, so no one would consider becoming familiar with a god. The one mistake man has made more than any other in religions and mythologies in dealing with gods is to overstep his bounds. Because of this, even Moses wasn't allowed to step over into the Promised Land.

In my case (as with many others) the erect snake sprang from the Walker Lake. Its head is at or near Yerington, and the east and west branches of the Walker River represent bent horns. Possibly it means nothing. Just the same, don't take it up to examine too closely or be too skeptical.

Mercury, the nearest planet to the sun, crosses the sun's face about every eight years. This might suggest the snaking 8. Apollo was the god of healing. Asclepius, his son, was the god of medicine. Yet if we are to believe what happened at Tanagra, Hermes must have some connection to medicine. Perhaps the one snake on the caduceus stands for healing power and the other for magic. One author sees the two snakes as mating. As Hermes was a fertility god (birth), maybe that was the magic and healing power. Who knows?

The coldest time anyone could remember in southern England was the winter of 1854 to 1855. All Devon was covered with two feet of snow. With daylight about one hundred miles of fresh footprints couldn't be missed. Yet no one throughout the entire county had seen the creature that had made them earlier on February 9, which would have been four-five days before the beginning of the ancient Parentalia.

Some had ideas what might have made them. But in each case the animal suggested didn't really match the tracks, apparently made by a creature with cloven hoofs and walking upright. Each print was *four* inches long, two and three-quarters inches wide, and *eight* inches apart. Five (5) parishes zigzagged with these prints, which were also on top of roofs, walls, and running through fields and gardens. Out of nowhere they would start and end abruptly. In one place the creature had passed through a six-inch-diameter hole. In another the trail led into a dense thicket. When dogs were brought in, they refused to enter it, turning away howling. Villagers were terrified and many wouldn't go out after dark, fearing the devil walked about,[70] yet apparently no one disappeared or was injured.

Devon is in southwestern England and Kent in southeastern England. My grandmother and grandfather were born respectively February 4, 1850, and July 3, 1850, and were four-five years old at the time.

August 31 (MP), *1888*, the year my father and mother were born and the Cliff Palace was discovered, was the date Jack the Ripper's first victim was found. Though no one can say for certain who Jack the Ripper was, the most likely suspect was a lawyer called Montague John Druitt.[71] On December 31, 1888 (exactly *four* months from the date the first of *five* victims was found and exactly six years before Katie Cameron died), Montague John Druitt's body was discovered floating in the Thames.[72] Memorial Day, celebrated by most states on the last Monday in May to honor the dead from any American war, has become a three-day holiday and has grown by custom to include the graves of friends and relatives. Some believe it had its beginning in Waterloo, New York, on *May 5*, 1866 (remember Lincoln had been buried the year before on *May 4*), when flowers were used to decorate the graves of the Civil War dead (*Encyclopedia Americana*).

The Civil War was fought to prevent the secession of the southern states. At another level, it could have been—as it is believed most wars are—the penalty for the neglect of the dead, an accelerated death rate. You may call this what you want—ungodly, maniacal, sinister, gruesome, morbid, or whatever—in a war of words. You may get thousands or millions to agree with you to reinforce your thinking that you're right or assert that you have two thousand years behind you. But do what you will, the dead don't care. Pay homage or else. Their retribution is both fitting and logical.

Bonkers? Perhaps. But remember Cemetery Ridge, the Gettysburg Address, and the facts that 1) the Civil War began in April (fourth month) and ended in May (fifth month), and 2) Memorial Day didn't begin until after the war and then in the month of May with few exceptions.

Unless Jesus and Hermes are one and the same, I believe Jesus was dead wrong by telling the son who wished to honor his father, "...leave the dead to bury their own dead" (Mt 8.22). The consequences of human beings able to do these mental flip-flops in their thinking were seen in Nazi Germany, Communist Russia, and Cambodia.

In pictures visiting General McClellan's headquarters in early October 1862, the Hermetic Lincoln stands somberly and stonily straight, a six-feet four-inch chess piece in stature, towering above the others. With his demeanor, beard, and trappings of a stovepipe hat and long, black coat and cravat, he's the symbol of the messenger of death.

It's the warpings of war, and who's to say at what level? Is it gallows humor or profound, the conversation of two union soldiers on seeing the president near the general's tent?

"Hey, there's the undertaker over there. He's cumta getcha man!"

"No! Not me, but thee!"

Lincoln was a secretive man, a mystery as to inner feelings, and few ever tried to understand his hot-and-cold mood swings or brooding nature. Doctors have conjectured that he had this or that disease, which would explain everything. It would be another tidy, little explanation for humans to make it through life, as Chagas' disease explained all about Darwin, and neurotic instability and drinking explained everything about Poe.

Perhaps all's true at one level, but the Abraham Lincoln mix began cooking in a caldron more than a century and a half before his birth when Samuel Lincoln had arrived from England and settled in Hingham, Massachusetts, in 1637, two years before the birth of Cotton Mather's father. Hingham, by the way, is close to Quincy, and Salem is only twenty miles or so from them.

In an 1842 letter to Joshua Speed, Lincoln wrote he'd "always had a strong tendency to mysticism." A power other than his own will, he felt, controlled him. My belief is that for Lincoln to have accomplished his purpose, there had to have developed a sympathy between the two worlds. He was obsessed or had a constant preoccupation with death most of his life. This drained him, possibly contributing to his melancholy at times and oddness of features.

I see a very young, unsuspecting acolyte—on the days he could be spared—walking four miles to school and four miles back and doing his studying and chores both before and after. Either during this period or when he was kicked unconscious by a horse, Hermes claimed him. Notice here the similarity in Lincoln and Grant. Grant will swing carelessly as a child from a horse's tail. His mother (in her way as strange as Lincoln's wife) and he didn't seem to care much for one another. Lincoln disliked his father. Could either president have made it as well without the Hermetic beard? The twelfth day of Lincoln's birth is simply a transposition of twenty-one, Grant's class standing. And, finally, "Who's buried in Grant's tomb?"

Lincoln's mother, by the way, died when he was nine. His younger brother died in infancy, and his older sister, Sarah (Abraham and Sarah), died at *twenty-one* in childbirth. Not too dissimilar from old patriarchs being buried in unmarked graves is the fact that in 1985 Robert Todd Lincoln Beckwith, Lincoln's great grandson and last member of the Lincoln family, died.[73]

One of many stories circulating about "Honest Abe" is that he'd once walked many miles just to return a few cents. Funny, as if in commemoration of the relationship between a god and his faithful servant, Lincoln's image is imprinted on our most numerous coin today, along with IN GOD WE TRUST, a phrase first engraved on a coin during Lincoln's administration.[74]

Lincoln was superstitious, believing one's dreams portentous. The dream of his assassination is documented in his journal ten days before it happened.

Many have said it in different ways to come to the same conclusion that his parts "did not seem to fit."[75] He was undergrown in some places and overgrown in others. In an irony of birthdates, he was a Darwin puzzle of evolution. His head seemed small for a man on stilts, his chest was narrow, and he had huge feet (footprints). He was a size fourteen, the same number as the stature difference to Napoleon and the day he was shot in the head. The woman who married him was high-strung and peculiar herself. Maybe all this is why Lincoln inspired trust. The nation got so cynical about first impressions. What you saw in Lincoln was up front. Beast and then beauty; not beauty and then beast.

So it was that the mark of Hermes had been put on him from head to foot for all to see. That his ghost has been seen more than once at the White House is in keeping with the chthonic nature of Hermes, always there at Cemetery Ridge and in the Gettysburg Address.

It's probable that the first contests between the gladiators in the Colosseum in Rome were staged as blood sacrifices to honor the Manes[76] and that the great games held in ancient Greece were—in the beginning at least—celebrations to pay homage to the dead.[77]

Chapter Twelve

If Christ and Hermes are the same, it makes no difference about holidays. If not, Memorial Day belongs to Hermes and Christmas to Christ. In ancient Greece, burials were often accompanied by funeral feasts and sporting events. Both of these would help "to dispel disorientation and depression."[78]

There's no doubt in antiquity that libations of wine were poured to some of the gods and the Di Manes. For Hermes, it was to assure sleep and pleasant dreams. This was done in sincerity, but things not having changed much through the ages, it's likely too that sober family members might have poured the wine out on the ground, using the gods as an excuse. Maybe the god didn't want the libation in the beginning but after awhile began to accept it as his dues. When it wasn't there, where was it? A sign that people cared less?

Not too many years ago, carnage during Memorial Day weekend was among the highest of the holidays. Most deaths were due to accidents caused by drinking. Could the toll on the roads be the penalty for neglect? If not being able to agree on this, we can hardly disagree that if half the liquor had been poured on the ground as libations before starting out, there would have been half as many deaths on Memorial Day weekend, or any other for that matter. These were the consequences of the liquor then consumed—an ill-willed reminder by the god of Sober Street?

More than any other sports event, the car race at Speedway, Indiana, on Sunday of the Memorial Day holiday period, honors in horsepower a god of charioteers, the four-and-five god of speed, roads, travel, luck, and measurement, numbers, and competition. Since Hermes conducts the souls, it also honors the dead: *four*-wheel[79] cars going around laps until they complete *five* hundred miles (805 km). It's the mystical ring of nine, and Indianapolis, like Chicago, is a stockyard city.

In 1992 (21), the seventy-sixth (13) Indy 500, thirty-three cars were entered. This was eighty-one years since the Indy started in 1911.[80]

Twenty-one (21) didn't complete the race. There were *thirteen* caution flags, and *twelve* of those not finishing the race were involved in accidents. Though the closest race ever, drivers attributed the slower-than-usual track speed and most accidents to the *wind* and low temperature that hardened the tires so that they couldn't grip the track properly. Footprints.

Once again, the Parentalia began at 12:00 noon on the thirteenth and ended on the twenty-first. And while we're at it, doesn't it seem curious that there will be a car race (twenty-four hours) or competition each year in Le Mans (page 36).

May 20, 1933 was one day before the Mercury period when I was around four or five. At this time, Indiana State Prison (about *"forty-five* miles from Chicago's Loop"[81]) received a telegram asking that John Dillinger, No. 13225, be released since his mother wasn't expected to live.

His number totaled: thirteen/4. He was given a cheap suit (disguise) and a *five*-dollar bill when he was released on May 22 (4) or (4)-5, the day the Hermae busts were destroyed in ancient Greece, one day after the Mercury period began.

"It's uncalled for using the word 'disguise' when referring to a man getting out of prison; he's served his time," you might object. Of course you'd be right in general but wrong about Dillinger, as were a one hundred and eighty residents, including his victim, who signed a petition for his parole.

He got out too late to see his stepmother before she died, but he did the Hermetic thing of attending her funeral in Indianapolis (there he'd been born June 22, 1903) at the Crown Hill Cemetery, where the FBI would have us believe he's buried today. This cloud of doubt is as heavy now as the cloud that hangs over his birth, for many believe that Audrey Dillinger at fifteen was really his mother, that she'd been unwed, and so Audrey's mother claimed the baby as her own. That his birth, death, and burial are cloaked in mystery has the stamp of Hermes, as does Christ's birth, death, and burial.

On September 6 (MP), 1924 (four-five years before my birth), Dillinger fortified himself with liquor to build up nerve but failed to offer a libation to Hermes. He and an associate called Edgar Singleton then attempted to rob an elderly grocer (merchant). One or the other hit him several times with a bolt wrapped in cloth so that he fell. When he got up, Dillinger pulled a revolver and demanded his money. The grocer knocked the gun out of Dillinger's hand so that it fell to the street firing. Because of the quiet at 10:30 at night, the noise probably seemed even louder by contrast. Things happened quickly. The old man began yelling his head off. Possibly thinking they'd shot him, the two panicked and ran toward Singleton's car when Dillinger paused a moment to retrieve the gun. Singleton, trying to save his own skin, drove off without Dillinger.

The old man needed eleven stitches to his head. Two days later, Dillinger was arrested, and at twenty-one, sobbingly confessed while implicating Singleton on the promise of getting a lenient sentence. So much for the criminal code of not finking! So much for the prosecutor's promises! Dillinger got an unusually severe sentence for a first offense.[82]

The nine years in prison were to teach him a lesson. He was an apt student and learned well, if nothing else, to make up for lost time. It might be said too that he got his calling from the grave. His stepmother had hardly been cold in the ground when, in the first few weeks of his release, Dr. Dillinger, now a Ph.D. in criminology from Indiana State Institution, and associates held up two supermarkets and a bank. Actually some of it was pretty clumsy stuff, but he was learning, while all along sending up smoke signals telling all he'd seen the light and intended to go straight.

A lady pastor whose church service he attended one Sunday preached about the "Prodigal Son," very pointedly looking at him several times so he'd know she meant him (here it almost seems sexual). When it was over, he told her she'd never know how much good it had done him.[83]

He was correct about that, for it provided a fine vehicle for performance (eloquence)—a miracle play no less—before the congregation, a justification that since she was using him, he was right in using her even more.[84] (There really ought to be a cleric-judge-police day for being grateful. Without us, they'd be nothing.)

Mollie Dillinger, John Herbert Dillinger's mother (grandmother?), died when he was four.

Author John Toland depicts her husband essentially as follows:

A church goer, a life member of the Hillside Community Church, who never cheated his customers and who wanted his son to have good values and religious principles. A disciplinarian, he punished his son at the slightest infraction. He believed it unmanly to hug him. He locked the child up for hours at a time by himself when he was attending the store. Then at the other extreme, he'd sometimes let him wander the streets until after dark. The father was generous, however, and gave his son toys and presents long before the other neighborhood children had them. So it seemed natural that young John would be generous too with the neighborhood kids by charging a little less for candy than the scales indicated. One day when the boy was eight or nine (again according to author John Toland), he slipped an attractive girl a pack of "Kiss Me" gum. Infuriated by this, the father grabbed the gum from her, then whacked his son so hard he fell over a coffee container. Without crying, the boy picked himself up, wiped the blood from his mouth, and stared back at his father.[85]

Years later the nation was titillated when Dillinger took a razor, a piece of wood, some bootblack, and fashioned a pistol to simply balls it through. Singing "I'm heading for the last roundup," he locked up a score of jailers and made his escape from the Crown Point Jail in Indiana. This was on March 4, 1934. On learning of his escape, the elder Dillinger said with a hint of pride amidst tears and grins, "Well he was pretty tricky. He's no fool."[86]

Dillinger's father was barefoot (footprints) when he heard of his son's death and wept, saying he had prayed it wouldn't happen. A week later, he, his daughter, and her husband will be on stage for money, telling about the "Incidents in the Life of the Late John Dillinger, Jr."[87]

In view of the previous emotion expressed on hearing of his son's death, it doesn't figure that the family—though perhaps needing money for the funeral expense—would be that insensitive in just a week's time. Decency would have required a longer period of waiting, unless, of course, they knew it wasn't John Dillinger who had been killed.

The usual story concerning Dillinger's death is that he, Anna Sage, and Polly Hamilton had gone to the Biograph Theater to see the gangster film *Manhattan Melodrama*, starring Clark Gable (who almost made it to Avenal) playing the part of a murderer who chose to die in the electric chair rather than spend life in prison. Anna Sage believed that by helping to set up Dillinger, her deportation charges would be dropped. Because the orange skirt she was wearing appeared red under the marquee's lights and because she was a well-known madame, she became the notorious "woman in red."[88] When the three emerged from the theater, Dillinger became suspicious and began to run. Melvin Purvis, FBI special agent in charge, yelled for him to stop. Dillinger continued running and was shot in the head.

In the alley was a pool of Dillinger's blood. Though Dillinger had been named Public Enemy Number One by J. Edgar Hoover, he was Public Hero Number One to many. Some women dipped the hems of their skirts in his blood. Both men and women soaked handkerchiefs. A barker was later selling pieces of these. Someone commented that for the great amount the barker was selling, "Dillinger's blood must have flowed from one end of *Lincoln* Avenue to the other."[89]

The soaking of the blood and the buying of pieces was, in my opinion, a sexual thing.

Lincoln's shooting in 1865 was associated with a theater too. Like a contaminating infection, it quickly spread to others, a microcosm of the Civil War. No sooner had Lincoln been shot than Major Rathbone was stabbed in the arm. John Wilkes Booth, the assassin, then broke his left leg leaping to the stage and fled. Thomas P. Corbett, a religious zealot and probably the killer of Booth, had been unbalanced long before the Civil War. In 1858 he had the balls to castrate himself and nearly lost his life in doing so. Nevertheless, he later served in the war with great bravery and distinction. After the assassination, he was one of twenty-four troopers sent out to search for Booth. Many days later, Booth was found holed-up in a barn, which was set on fire to smoke him out. Corbett, however, didn't want to wait and shot Booth through a crack. (Perhaps it wasn't chance that the castrated Corbett just happened to shoot Booth. On another level—because of his sacrifice—he could have been deemed the most worthy to avenge Lincoln. His mental condition doesn't necessarily preclude this.)

Mortally wounded, Booth dragged himself out. Asked why he hadn't waited and shot Booth, Corbett replied, "God Almighty directed me." Later in life, he was certified insane by several doctors and committed to an insane asylum. In 1888, he escaped from that, showed up only briefly to see an old army friend in Neodesha, Kansas, and then was seen no more. Major Rathbone later murdered his wife, who had been his fiancee in the presidential box, and was committed to an insane asylum for the rest of his life. Eventually Mrs. Lincoln was committed to an institution for awhile, and Robert Todd Lincoln, almost ghoulishly, became a harbinger of presidential assassinations. Do not forget that his brother William Wallace Lincoln had died on the Eve of the Feralia 1862 in the White House, and his father was born on February 12, the evening of which was the Eve of the Faunus festival and Parentalia in ancient Rome. See page 399.

But to return to Corbett, a.k.a. Boston (about eight miles north of Quincy). He'd been a hatter before the war. Whether the mercury compound used caused his mind to become unbalanced is a moot point, not really too important in the scheme of things. What is is the suggestion of Mercury/Hermes. (Memorial Day didn't come until after the Civil War.)

It's not seriously believed that Stanton, Lincoln's secretary of war, had anything to do with the assassination. But the rumor still persists that he told Corbett to make certain Booth was dead and paid him his full share of the reward money plus an extra amount. Whatever, the contaminating influence of the assassination spilled over into Stanton and President Andrew Johnson, who had been Lincoln's vice president. Why do I link an event which happened more than two years after the assassination to it? The day in 1868 President Johnson fired Stanton was February 21, the anniversary of the Feralia or Feast of the Dead, thirteen years to the day after the Washington Monument had been "stolen" and seventeen years to the day before its dedication. President Johnson, of course, later escaped conviction at the impeachment proceedings by only one vote (2122; 22 - 21 = 1.)

The bullet shot at Ford's Theater tunneled through Lincoln's brain to lodge behind his right eye. One of the bullets fired that night outside the Biograph Theater (only a few blocks from where the St. Valentine's Day massacre occurred) exited from the man's right eye. The other tore into the man's neck and imbedded in his skull.[90]

Then again like a contaminating influence, Anna Sage didn't get what she wanted and was mysteriously murdered. Melvin Purvis, who had made a name for himself by heading the FBI team, had a falling out with J. Edgar Hoover and left the FBI more or less in disgrace. Years later Purvis would blow out his own brains using the revolver he had used that night at the Biograph Theater. J. Edgar Hoover, a very self-serving man who craved the limelight and wouldn't tolerate any competition near his top job and who had taken such pains to assure that his image was as pure as the driven snow, emerges in history as a blackmailer of sorts, something much less than he'd hoped.

There's much to indicate that Dillinger was neither killed outside Chicago's Biograph nor is buried at Indianapolis's Crown Point Cemetery.[91] Below are a few of many details Jay Robert Nash carefully documents in *Encyclopedia of World Crime* to support his theory. Such a ruse would have been in keeping with Dillinger's character and Hermes'.

1) Melvin Purvis's credibility stunk when it came to making a positive identification of the fleeing man before the shooting.
2) An autopsy report states that the bullets entering the man's head outside the Biograph were fired at an angle of 45 degrees. The man then must have been in a prone position when the bullets smashed into his head. Though he might have been fleeing at first, he must have stumbled or tripped and then was shot while he was down.
3) Very likely the man was not carrying a gun. The one later displayed by the FBI as being that of the fleeing man wasn't sold (according to the manufacturer's records) until five months after the Biograph affair.
4) Reporters had already arrived when they heard Purvis blurt out in surprise (not matter of factly) that it wasn't Dillinger's nose. Then recovering shortly, he said, "Neat bit of plastic surgery that."
5) One Dr. Parker had stayed with the body at the city morgue from the time it arrived at 11:00 P.M. until the next morning on July 23, 1934. He saw no one take fingerprints. Yet those fingerprints later were given as supporting evidence by the FBI were dated July 22, 1934.
6) The autopsy showed that the man outside the Biograph Theater had brown eyes. Yet various records of the U.S. Navy and local and state governments show Dillinger's eyes to have been blue. This was four decades before color contact lenses came into being.
7) The dead man was missing two scars which Dillinger was known to have had.
8) A top right incisor tooth seen missing in a film shot earlier of Dillinger was present and real in the dead man.
9) The autopsy revealed the deadman had rheumatic damage to

his heart from childhood. It's unlikely Dillinger could have entered the navy or played baseball if he had this.

10) Once the body was buried, it shortly was dug up and reburied, surrounded by tons of cement and chicken wire, making it nearly impossible for the body to be exhumed intact.

J. Edgar Hoover (born 1895) became director of the Bureau of Investigation (as it was called then) in 1924, the year Lenin died and Dillinger pulled his first holdup, four-five years before the St. Valentine's Day Massacre. There's no doubt that Hoover did much to reform the FBI and to improve its methods and that he was a real asset in its earlier years.

A strong suspicion of many is that Hoover was a latent homosexual. Who knows? Some old-timers will shudder at this, saying, "How dare they impugn the good name of this great man!"—as if he were sacrosanct. It's like hearing there's no Santa Claus or that Captain Colin P. Kelly, Jr., didn't win the Medal of Honor (he didn't) nor did he die by diving his plane down the stack of a Japanese battleship.[92]

The only way to answer this fairly is to say that Hoover is being judged by the same standard of flimsy facts, dirt, and innuendo he himself sometimes used. Sure, though in some cases the facts were manipulated (maybe even planted), it was still true what he was saying. But there's little doubt that some innocent people were ruined along the way, as if the end justified the means.

Any variance in what he believed was unAmerican. Close competition to his job was dangerous. Trying to make himself out to be a great patriot (especially in later years, the eagle scout of the Medicare set), he didn't train a replacement or step down when he reached sixty-five, the mandatory retirement age of admirals and generals. Perhaps he was riding a tiger, for he made certain upon his death that various files and records were destroyed. By the standard of suspicion he employed in others, he was a blackmailer of sorts or kept evidence he could use, if need be, to influence opinions, to twist arms.

In the end, the main problem with Hoover was not what his sexual orientation may or may not have been but rather that he'd become too self-important, too authoritarian, as if the checks and balances in our form of government were a great thing but didn't apply to him. People should rightly fear this, for

No one ever sees
When he or she has reached
In the circle of good and bad,
One hundred eighty-one degrees.

Chapter Thirteen

Most people throughout the centuries have felt there was something different about Alexander the Great, that he was bewitched somehow, and that if he and Homer had been contemporaries, Homer would have produced a work on Alexander to match the *Iliad* and the *Odyssey*.

Indeed Alexander was a mutant in his time, a boundary crosser, a final reminder to the world of Greece's glorious past. So the legend grew. Not necessarily literally correct (though it might have been), it was figuratively true. A marble shot from the mind of common, ordinary man straight into the magic circle said—more colorfully and simply expressed than I could ever hope to—that Alexander had a dark-brown eye and one that was gray-blue or blue-green. The latter showed that he was a king, of blue blood, and made of better things. But the dark-brown eye, the important one, showed his soul, that he never stinted in fighting in front and alongside his men. And so they followed, perhaps griping every step of the way, to places that no other leader could have taken them—not Lee, not Napoleon, and certainly not MacArthur, who sat in his air-conditioned office and issued a communique which said, "Every soldier should be prepared to make the supreme sacrifice for his country."

Alexander's father, Philip (lover of horses) of Macedon, was believed to have been related to Helen of Troy.[93]

Olympias, Alexander's mother, was an Epirote princess descended from Achilles, hero of Troy. Her room had an assortment of large, nonpoisonous snakes, some of which she used for sacrifice. This then spilled over into the mysticism about Alexander. Wags are quick to point out that still another "serpentdipity" was that their kinking and crawling about cooled whatever bedroom passion Philip or any others might have had for her.

Be that as it may, Alexander was born in 356 B.C. No one knows the exact date. As with Robert E. Lee, Ulysses S. Grant, and Abraham Lincoln, there's a horse anecdote about him. Philip had changed his mind about buying a black stallion with a blaze of white on his forehead when he found his grooms could not manage him. The horse apparently had been nervous or scared when he saw his own shadow. No one seemed to realize this except Alexander who, then about eight, asked to be given a chance to ride him.[95] This was allowed with some misgivings, and Alexander turned the horse toward the sun and raced off with him. The meaning is clear enough: Alexander was under the protection of Hermes, the god of horses and deception, as much as had been the traveler Ulysses, who suggested the Trojan horse. Mercury, the planet closest to the sun, would have no shadow when looking directly at it. As Lee had Traveller, Alexander had Bucephalas throughout most of his campaigns. (Hermes, god of campaigns.)

For a while in his youth, Alexander's tutor was Aristotle, who is said to have made a copy of Homer's *Iliad* for him. Alexander revered Homer, and the *Iliad* to Alexander was almost a sacred book which, along with his dagger, he kept under his pillow when he slept at night. (Hermes, god of sleep.) Interesting too is that Alexander played the lyre very well.

He married Roxane,[96] who was the daughter of an enemy leader and had a child born to her after his own death. When the boy was about thirteen, both mother and son were slain. So as with Lincoln and Schliemann (when married to Sophia), Alexander's bloodline didn't continue on for long. It's not known if Alexander died of poisoning, malaria and/or other diseases, or a combination of all. But die he did on June 10 (MP), 323 B.C.

Heinrich Schliemann was born on January 6, 1822, in Germany. At fourteen he signed on as a cabin boy aboard the brig *Dorothea*, which was later wrecked. In Russia he became a prosperous businessman (merchant). He came to the United States and made a fortune in the Gold Rush. This was in keeping with Hermes being the god of miners and luck. Then he went back to Russia, making another fortune and a miserable marriage. Returning to the United States, he divorced his Russian wife in Indianapolis, Indiana. It was while in Indianapolis he began negotiations to take a Greek bride, who he hoped would be much like Helen of Troy, the half-sister of Hermes. Eventually he decided on Sophia,[97] and they married in 1869,[98-A] the earth-snake year. (Remember the Ras Shamra excavation was in 1929.)

From his early youth, Schliemann had been intrigued by the idea of what had been the location of the fabled Troy, which he'd read about in Homer's *Iliad*, written hundreds of years after the war. Because of such a time lapse, most authorities believed any ideas the old, epic poet had concerning the site could only be fanciful, but not Schliemann. He revered Homer, and the *Iliad* to Heinrich was almost a sacred book, as it had been to Alexander the Great.[98-B] In Schliemann's passion to know, he'd become a worldwide *traveler*, scholar, and linguist, learning Greek among many other languages. He shared with Sophia a faith in antiquity which few living in Greece still had. He was somewhat superstitious,[99] and like Abraham Lincoln, he believed in dreams. (Hermes, god of dreams and sleep.) Curiously as Lincoln's bloodline will die out, so did Schliemann's (married to Sophia) with General *Alex* L. Melas, his grandson. The treasure which the Schliemanns eventually found was possibly not King Priam's but of a period much earlier. Few archeological finds have ever equalled this. Yet from the facts concerning Schliemann's life and the treasure after he died, something bigger is suggested than just the discovery of the site of Troy in Turkey and the treasure. You see they found the treasure in 1873[100] either at the last of May or early June, which in any event would have been during the Mercury period. Author Irving *Stone*[101] believes this date to have been May 31, a Saturday when there was no dawn and the sun just seemed to shoot out.

Against Sophia's wishes, Heinrich eventually gave the treasure to the Berlin Museum for Early History. Adolph Hitler was born on April 20, 1889.[102] Heinrich Schliemann died on December 26, 1890, attended by eight physicians. Curiously both Heinrich and Sophia had spent considerable time studying the *sauvastika* and the *svaustika*, the two-cross symbols seen in some other civilizations and found on several objects unearthed at Troy. Could the swastika in the Nazi case have been a negative variation of the two snakes on the caduceus? Hitler committed suicide on April 30, 1945. This last day of April (on which Walpurgis Night occurs) seems tied in some way with the last day of May when the treasure was discovered.

At the time of Hitler's death, the Russians were moving toward Berlin. (Schliemann, born in Germany, made most of his fortune in Russia, and at the time of the discovery of the treasure at Troy, was a U.S. citizen,[103] which he remained until his death.) Most of the Trojan pottery was destroyed in bombings, but the gold was found hidden or buried in the bunker beneath the Zoological Station in the East Sector of Berlin.[104] Some say that it was in *four* separate packages. Written orders were issued that it was to be taken to Moscow rather than be turned over to the Allied Art Treasure Commission. It disappeared about May 22[105] or later, and most of the world didn't know for over fifty years whether it was stolen, buried, melted down, or in Russia. It disappeared in May 1945, very possibly in the same month it was discovered.

| Hitler's death by suicide: | *4 -* | *30 -* | *1945* |
| Loss of treasure: | *5* | *-* | *1945* |

Just recently it surfaced on display in Russia.

Hermes is a god of wealth, especially sudden wealth such as finds of hidden treasures. May, the fifth month of the snake, figured into the history of the treasure two times. If not that, at the very least, two Mercury periods had entered into it. Since Hermes is a god of graveyards and burial, it seems that archeology and museums would also be under his purview. I don't believe it was coincidence alone that Heinrich got his divorce in Indianapolis (derived from the name of the territory plus Greek *polis*, "city") nor that he began his negotiations there for his "Helen," who was both figuratively and literally of Troy. There are parallels, furthermore, between Indiana Jones of *Raiders of the Lost Ark* and Schliemann, both treasures eventually were lost.

Finally, the initials of Heinrich Schliemann suggest Hermes (HS).

Another name to be included under an Hermes influence is Israel Baline (ae ae) who was born in Russia on *May* 11, *1888*, the year Great Britain annexed Christmas Island, discovered by Captain Cook on Christmas Eve 1777. Israel, like the lyre-playing David (*Alexander* the Great also played the lyre) son of Jessie, was the youngest of eight children. In 1893 (SY) and when he was four - five years old, he and his family came to the U.S., where his father died when he was eight.

His most successful song in his early career as a songwriter was "*Alexander*'s Ragtime Band." This was originally called "Alexander and His Clarinet." A clarinet is a wood-wind instrument, of course, having a reed mouthpiece. You probably recognize the songwriter now as Irving Berlin. His first marriage was to *Dorothy* Goetz, who contracted typhoid fever on their honeymoon (honey/moon) in *Cuba* and died shortly after. His second marriage was on January 4, 1926, to *Ellin* (a derivative of Helen) Mackay, an heiress to a fortune of about thirty million dollars. Hermes, god of sudden wealth.

Among his many famous songs are "White Christmas," "*Easter* Parade," "There's no *Business* Like Show *Business*," and "God Bless America" (Amerigo Vespucci). He published eight or nine hundred songs and wrote many more. Because he was such a prolific songwriter, Berlin sometimes used aliases. *Alexander Woollcott* said one of these was "Ren G. May," which has all the letters of Germany, the capital being Berlin, of course.[106]

In the snake year 1977, Berlin was awarded the Presidential Medal of Freedom. He died at 101 years of age on September 22 (MP), 1989, an earth-snake year. This also happened to be the year that travel was permitted through the Berlin Wall (November 9, 1989) and was one hundred years after the birth of Adolf Hitler who died in Berlin.

> 1887 Alexander Woollcott born.
> 1888 Irving Berlin born.
> 1889 Adolf Hitler born.
> 1890 Heinrich Schliemann died.

Harold Arlen, born Hyman Ar*luck*, February 15, 1905. See *February 15, 1905*, entry.

Edgar Cayce (ea ea) was born in Kentucky on March 18, 1877. Some say his grandfather had second sight; others say that he didn't. All agree, however, that the old man doused for water.[107] Power came to the boy not long after he saw his grandfather die on a terribly frightened, wildly bucking horse. Here again is another horse story, suggesting Hermes and/or Poseidon (horse and water). A light with a voice came asking him what he wished out of life, to which he replied he would like to make people well, especially children. So diagnosing and curing people became his gift, as Solomon's was wisdom, and predicting the future was secondary to this.

Never taking money for his service, he read the Bible when he got up in the morning and when he went to bed. He was the Christian world's darling who went to darkling when he said he believed in reincarnation, as had Lincoln (also born in Kentucky) and the Schliemanns. The Christian distancing from him lay in part to the jealousy of people who couldn't guess 50 percent or more on a true-false quiz, knew nothing about what might happen tomorrow, had no healing gift, and were for the most part less pious than he. Reincarnation? Hell and damnation! So it has been through history. Seldom is the difference of opinion more important than the need to prove that one is holier than thou.

Cayce continued on, exhausting himself in readings for them, until he died on Wednesday, January 3, 1945. In 1919 he predicted a greater war would come than the Great War just ended.[108] This was the year Ralph was born. "It will begin about 1940," Cayce said. It started in 1939, the year Ralph died.

In April (fourth month) 1929, he predicted the depression. He later told that the United States would enter the war in 1941 and that it would end in 1944 or 1945. These later prophecies were made long before World War II actually began. It ended in Europe in May 1945 (5-45) and in Japan in August (8-45).

Consider once again that Hermes is a god of athletes, especially wrestlers, gymnasts, and runners. Apollo and Hercules are also gods of athletes. But the Olympics occurs every *four* years. Its symbol: *five* connecting rings.

James Francis Thorpe, of native American, Irish, and French descent, was born on May 28 (MP), *1888*. In the 1912 Olympic games, he was the first athlete to win both the pentathlon and decathlon.[109] He was stripped of his gold medals in 1913 for having played semiprofessional baseball. In 1920–21, he was the first president of the American Professional Football Association (later the National Football League). In *1929* he retired at age forty-one. In 1950 he was rated the best athlete of the first half of the century in an Associated Press Poll. He died on March 28, 1953 (SY), and his medals were restored to his family in 1983.

In 1944 people wondered when World War II would be over. Numerologists and visionaries felt there were certain parallels in the lives of Winston Churchill, Adolf Hitler, Benito Mussolini, Franklin Roosevelt, and Joseph Stalin. Possibly if they took similar information from the life of each, such as his birthdate, age, years in office, and so on, they might come up with a number from which they could work out the solution. This was determined to be eventually *3888*. Half of 3888 is 1944, so that must be the year. Half of 1944 is 972, so the war would end at 2:00 A.M. on September 7, 1944. But skeptics were neither dazzled by the seers' brilliance nor baffled by their bullshit. They pointed out that the same data used on any person will yield a number nearly corresponding to two times the present year.[110] That it had been a faulty forecast was born out when Germany surrendered on May 7, 1945.

The war began in 1939. The last major participants had not entered until 1941 (SY). There were two powers fighting called the Allies and the Axis. These represented then two fighting snakes, and certainly each perceived the other as such. But it was Hermes' staff put between two fighting snakes that brought peace. The number '44 doesn't represent Hermes as much as '45, and even '41 (4+1), suggested 45.

My mother, father, and Joseph P. Kennedy were born in 1888. In this year also two cowboys riding *horses* in the *wind* and snow (footprints) looking for stray *cattle* came across the Cliff Palace where the "ancient people of the *rock*" (now *dead*) had once lived. Clearly the three eight's in *1888* as well as in *3888* were Hermetic signs. More than any other number, eight represents the caduceus. Hermes dispatches in peace and rest the dying by touching them on the forehead with his wand or caduceus.

The number 3888 could have meant then that three of the five leaders would die before the war ended, which indeed is what happened. Strikingly all in 4-45:

Roosevelt:	April 12, 1945 (burial April 15)
Mussolini:	April 28, 1945
Hitler:	April 30, 1945

A deadman's hand in poker is two pairs, either jacks and eights or aces and eights. (See page 623.)

On August 6, 1945, an atomic bomb exploded over Hiroshima, Japan. It had been manufactured in *Chicago*.[111] On August 9, 1945, another bomb exploded over Nagasaki. About one hundred and ten thousand died between the two bombings, and many more thousands were injured. Japan's surrender followed within a few days.

The atomic bomb dropped at Hiroshima was to show the Japanese what capability we had, that prolonging the war any longer was foolishness, and, of course, to save American lives, but it was also revenge for the Pearl Harbor attack. The two can't be separated. Given a few more days for the impact and potential to sink in fully, the dropping of the second bomb might not have been necessary; i.e., the second bomb may very well have been an example of overkill. Though this argument is well taken by some people, they seldom point out that had the situation been reversed, the Japanese—based on the brutality shown in China, the sneak attack on Pearl Harbor, and the treatment of prisoners of war—undoubtedly would have had even less scruples.

In 1745, Louisbourg, the French fortress on *Cape Breton Island*,[112] fell to an expeditionary force of around four thousand men from the British colonies, including *Massachusetts*.[113] This is said to have been the most ambitious exploit" of King George's War, which mainly consisted of raids along the borders between Canada and New England. The Indians allied themselves with the French.[114]

So what happened in 1845?

Chapter Fourteen

The apartment manager asked what the book was about. I explained that in my life there seemed to have been a Hermes influence. Some occurrences appear to have been more than random, especially the number four and the snake. It could be that meaning not there was being read into things. If so, the same thing was being done with Nevada, "the silver state," what with mining, flocks and herds (sheep, cattle, horses), ghost towns, cemeteries, gaming, travelers, and a history of boundaries and breaking boundaries.

The manager was then interrupted by another tenant. In the middle of that business, he suddenly stopped, picked up a piece of paper and pencil, and drew a rough sketch with four sides connected by a snake.

"I don't get it," I said after he handed it to me.

"That's what Nevada is: Four sides and a snake."

This had never occurred to me.

Hermes, along with Apollo, was a god of music. If you straightened out the two snakes on the caduceus and turn it upside down, you have what might be taken for a primitive drawing of an instrument, as well as perhaps a fertility symbol.

The guitar is associated with things western, and the word *guitar* is derived from the "Greek *kithara*, kind of lyre."[115]

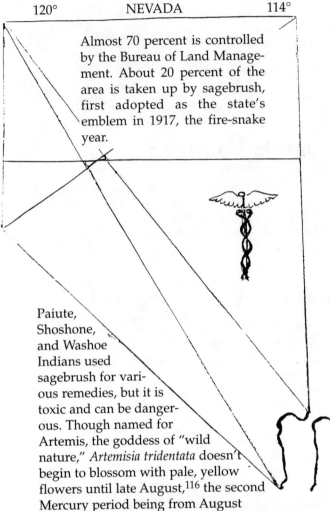

120°   NEVADA   114°

Almost 70 percent is controlled by the Bureau of Land Management. About 20 percent of the area is taken up by sagebrush, first adopted as the state's emblem in 1917, the fire-snake year.

Paiute, Shoshone, and Washoe Indians used sagebrush for various remedies, but it is toxic and can be dangerous. Though named for Artemis, the goddess of "wild nature," *Artemisia tridentata* doesn't begin to blossom with pale, yellow flowers until late August,[116] the second Mercury period being from August 23rd–September 22nd. Unable to belch, cattle won't touch it until near starvation, but deer have no problem with it. Curiously the stag, being an animal of the chase, was sacred to Artemis. No one yet has been able to convert sagebrush into a moneymaker commercially.

Draw a line from the snake's head to far corner at 120°. Draw a second line from the snake's tail to the same point. Then from the Lake Tahoe area, draw a third line to the corner at 114°. Where all these lines cross 40°, you will find two triangles formed, one above 40° and one below. When these two triangles are rounded out, an 8 is formed. This suggests the snak-ing 8s on the caduceus.

Artemis was Apollo's twin and Hermes' half-sister.

NEVADA

*Could the apparition of a bearded head be this that the Knights Templar saw in the twelfth and thirtieth centuries? Curiously between the *H* and *S* of Hughes, as in Howard Hughes, and the *H* and *S* of Hugues, as in Hugues de Payen, you can fit Hermes. Perhaps the "Et in Arcadia ego" (and in Arcadia I...) on the stone in Poussin's painting is a reference to Hermes, the image from whom the good shepherd was taken. "The Lord God is an everlasting rock" (Is 26.04). "...you are Peter, and on this rock I will build my church" (Mt 16.18). Arcas is one of the surnames for Hermes.

The name Vega is Spanish for meadow. The name Las Vegas gets its name from where those following trails camped. Lyre>Cithara> Guitar. Hermes, god of gamblers, pastures, and one of the gods of music, as inventor of the lyre. Constellation Lyra, represent ing the lyre of Hermes (or Orpheus) contains the bright *star Vega.*

1. Lake Tahoe.
2. Topaz Lake Boundary. Most of it in Douglas Co., Nev
3. West Walker River.
4. Yerington.
5. East Walker River.
6. Walker River.
7. Walker Lake.

TOPAZ

TOP=Day of Pots
A–Z=Alphabet, which Hermes invented. Suggests dictionary, where it all began to unravel. He was the most cunning and the shrewdest of the gods.

Roughly, area labeled "Snake Indians" on Bancroft's Pacific Map of the United States 1864. When Nevada admitted as thirty-sixty state of October 31 (Halloween).

The Great Depression will come almost but not quite sixty-five years later. Technically it occurred in sixty-four years of the admission date.

It is said that the monuments most distinctive of Hermes are square or rectangular pillars with a bearded head on top. These taper at the bottom and have a phallus—usually erect—partway up. The lewdness is toned down by the geometric squareness. He was a fertility god and brought back souls to be born from Hades.

He was called "Hermes the helper." Protection was his salient characteristic, especially over flocks and the wayfarer, a person who journeys on foot. Or, you might say, a Walker.

For awhile my father was in the sheep business with ranges on the East Walker River. Then he stopped that and bought a ranch at Topaz near the West Walker River, where he raised cattle.

**Snake called Fascination.

379

Exploration of the Humboldt River route across Nevada began in the snake-year 1833 by Joseph Walker. (Three hundred years before that in 1533 [SY], Queen Elizabeth I, daughter of Henry VIII, was born September 7 [MP].)

My first knowledge of the area near Yerington came from a July/August 1993 *Nevada* magazine article by Harry A. Chalekian titled "Yesterday: Was the Garden of Eden Located in Nevada?" Otherwise, it would have been included in the first book.

On August 17, 1924, the *San Francisco Examiner* published an article suggesting the drawings and inscriptions on some rocks on a hill about thirty miles south of Yerington (near the East Walker River) predated Egyptian hieroglyphs. This so-called assumption was based on the alleged opinions of experts who had studied the writing and drawings. In time, however, the work was found to be that of earlier Paiute Indians.

In the same issue of *Nevada* magazine was an article on snakes. This might be expected since the Garden of Eden had a serpent. What's harder to explain, however, is that the cradle-of-civilization deception was typically Hermes, occurring four-five years before the excavation at Ras Shamra and so four-five years before my birth at Yerington.

It was George Hearst's money from mining in Nevada that gave the start to the newspaper industry, developed by William Randolph Hearst, his son. Since the *San Francisco Examiner* was a Hearst paper, William Randolph Hearst aided and abetted the 1924 journalism above.

HERMES	HERS	ME
HEARST	HERS	AT
HERMES	AT	HEARST

Patricia Hearst (born *February 20*, 1954) was one of five daughters of Randolph A. Hearst. After being kidnapped at Berkeley, California,117 she took part in at least two bank robberies. Part of her ransom was food for the poor, though she was never really turned over to her parents after payment. Apparently she was both misguided and brainwashed to some extent. The contrast of the rich and poor clouded the issue, seemingly making right what was wrong. It was Chappaquiddick and Vietnam. There were truths, and there were truths. She was definitely not a heroine, but she was a human being. Most feel that they wouldn't have acted the way she did, but unless tested, they'd never really know for sure. If she could have been manipulated, turned, then maybe under the right circumstances, we all could be. Why couldn't she have done what she was suppose to, for Christsake! Her uncle, William Randolph Hearst, Jr., died (May 14, 1993) on the eve of the anniversary in ancient Rome and just in time to make the May 15 newspapers (message).

Kathleen Kennedy Hartington was also born on *February 20* (1920). She died in an airplane crash on May 13 (?), 1948. Her brother, Joseph

Kennedy, Jr., died in an airplane crash in 1944. Jean Kennedy was born on *February 20*, 1928. Edward Kennedy on February 22, 1932. John F. Kennedy was born May 29, 1917, Memorial Day Eve, and Rosemary on September 13, 1918, right after John F. Thus three were born within the Parentalia-Caristia period and two during Mercury periods.

Combining the two families, a Hermetic profile:

Parentalia-Caristia dates; wealth; mining; commerce (whiskey); flying; fame; theft causing headlines; scandals; violent deaths; much made of burials; and not least of importance, public fascination—an interaction—with their lives. People admired them; people hated them, and hatred gives purpose to life.

A Hermetic person is seldom allowed to sink into oblivion, even if that's what he or she wants. Some might be loners, but "I want to be alone" is impossible, as evidenced by Greta Garbo and Howard Hughes.

Scrambled Numbers

Social Security Number of Frank W. Chichester:
445551367
Identification numbers used most often in my life:

Social Security:	444555266
Army:	44011239
Navy:	4403677
Merchant Marine Z:	5888126

The most frequent number is 4. It occurs seven times. The next numbers in frequency are 5 and 6, which appear four times each. The two identification numbers assigned longest were the Social Security and Z-card. Though the number 4 doesn't appear in the latter, it has a 5 and three 8s, the only connection at the time being made to the year *1888*. Two book revisions later, I'd read that 8 is the number for Thoth, who is over the eight gods of "Eight town" and "purifies the uninitiated with water."

It's said mariners are under the restless god of travelers and commerce, but the idea is further reinforced by the fact that Maia is one of the Pleiades which rise with the sun to start the nautical year in spring. In Roman times, the figurehead of a certain god, such as "Mars, Apollo, or Mercury,"[118] was placed on the prow or poop of a vessel to curry favor of that deity for good weather and fortune. Mercury, of course, would have fit the bill under wind and luck. Woden (the greatest of the Norse gods and identified with Mercury/Hermes) presided over sailing ships. The Egyptian deity Anubis (Hermanubis), along with Isis and Serapis, was invoked at Delos to protect merchants and seamen. (See page 634, #6).

The frequency of numbers in George Duran's "card numbers" is as follows:

1	14
2	17
3	21
4	25
5	7
6	11
7	10
8	20
9	9
0	10

Duran George

Co A 1 Maine Heavy Arty

Private — Private

CARD NUMBERS.

#	Number	#	
1	2839690	26	
2	2839834	27	
3	2843464	28	
4	2843635	29	
5	2843814	30	
6	2843965	31	
7	2844104	32	
8	2844225	33	
9	2844344	34	
10	2844521	35	
11	2845097	36	
12	3269075 3	37	
13	3087 4324	38	
14	3087 2368	39	
15	3087 0986	40	
16	3086 9344	41	
17	3086 7777	42	
18	3634 9567	43	
19		44	
20		45	
21		46	
22		47	
23		48	
24		49	
25		50	

Number of personal papers herein 8

Book Mark:

See also

Chapter Fifteen
U.S.S. *NEVADA*

DESIGNATION:	BB 36, the "Battle-born state" number.
KEEL LAID:	November 4, 1912.
LAUNCHED:	1914 under sponsorship of Eleanor (name derived from Helen: Greek ele) Seibert.
COMMISSIONED:	1916.
FINAL DESTRUCTION:	1948.
AGE AT DEATH:	32.
DISTINGUISHED:	Served in World War I. Though flooded and burning during the attack on Pearl[119] Harbor, she was the only battleship[120] to get underway (travel). She served in every major battle in World War II.

She was built at the Fore River Shipbuilding Company, *Quincy, Massachusetts*, and with the exception of the launching date, all the above numbers are divisible by four. She was named for the "Silver State," silver being the witch's metal.

At Pearl Harbor on December 7, 1941,[122] the *Nevada* was twenty-five years old and lacked three months of being overaged when special permission would have had to have been given for her to continue on. She was moored by herself, behind the *Arizona* and *Vestal*, at the northern tail-end and "to the most easterly of the piles," kind of like she thought Ford[123] Island was the United States and she was back in Massachusetts.

The sun had no problem getting itself up earlier, dangling its legs over Mt. Olympus and Mt. Tantalus at 0626, in a tantalizing overture to the morning after the night before that began "If I can do it, why can't you?" and "Early to bed and early to rise, makes Nippon healthy, wealthy, and wise."[124]

But some who'd come back just a few hours earlier never heard this exchange. Aye, they were Tom Morton's Mare-Mount boys, uncomplicated for the most part, wanting only their weekly rite of passage to sleep it off on Sunday morning. They were boxers on the canvas, down for the count. When the alarm tore into their skulls, they confused it with bright lights. If they could just keep their eyes closed, it would go away, but it didn't. Hung over, they are red-eyed, nearly useless road maps trying to find their gear.

"Fuckeeng brass and their goddam drills even on Sunday morning, for Christsake!"

Vowing never to forget it comes reenlistment day, they struggle to their battle stations.

I don't recall any of this, nor do I remember the sailors and marines at the machine guns and five-inch antiaircraft batteries who shot down the two Japanese planes in the first few minutes. I'm jarred and startled into wakefulness when the torpedo launched from a plane tears a huge hole in my bow, and a bomb hits the quarterdeck. Only then do I realize for the first time the men are part of me, and I, them. There's flooding of many forward compartments, but it doesn't reach the power plant, still intact much farther aft.

We can't maneuver and are bound until a man jumps into the flaming water and swims to the quay to untie us while a plane just misses with machine-gun bullets. Getting underway, we back out of the fiery water from oil spewed from the Arizona and try a straight shot south past the row. There are huge geysers of water erupting around us from the bombs and also columns of smoke. We've been hit at least five times. My decks are searing hot in places, gutted, and in shambles. The superstructure is on fire. There's panic and confusion. Men cry out in pain, horror, fear, "Oh God help me!" Fifty are dying or dead: 109 are wounded. Each doctor and pharmacist mate mumbling in frustration, "Okay, okay, Jesus, I can't get to everyone at once." Then hating themselves for doing so. And one man, bless his soul, still very polite and respectful, is saying, "It looks real bad sir." It's real bad for sure. Terrible!

Admiral Furlong (measurement) fears she will sink and block the channel. He orders her grounded.

In contrasting luck, the *Arizona* went down in minutes, permanently entombing nearly all the 1,177 shipmates (sailors and marines, offices and enlisted) who lost their lives on December 7. This was nearly half the number of the Americans killed at Pearl Harbor. Many other ships had a certain hell and casualties too.

The *Nevada's* deck log states she remained aground until 1300 on the twelfth of February 1942, at which time she became waterborne. Since the Parentalia in ancient Rome began at 1200 on the thirteenth of February, this would have been 0100 Honolulu time on the thirteenth.[125] Thus the beginning of the nine-day period for honoring the spirits of the dead and ending on the *twenty-first* began just twelve hours[126] after the Nevada was floated, or very close to the time she began to prepare for her revenge.

Continued pumping was necessary while the *Nevada* was moored. Then on February 18 the battleship, assisted by yard tugs, got underway and reached the correct position at 1055 in drydock number two so that she could make it eventually to the Puget Sound[127] Navy Yard for permanent and extensive repairs.

By early 1943, the *Nevada* was ready to begin her retaliation and went on to becoming one of the most decorated ships in history, receiving altogether seven battle stars: Pearl Harbor-Midway, Aleutians Operations, Invasion of Normandy, Invasion of Southern France, Iwo Jima Operation, Okinawa Gunto Operation, and Third Fleet Operations against Japan.

Later it would have been fitting to have awarded her another battle star for her fight against destruction, her finest hours, but it's doubtful she would have wanted it or even cared. In the end—perhaps suggested by Quincy—she had the hardness and acid of the quince.

It's 30 June 1946. The date's written this way out of long habit. But now I think I'll say June 30, 1946. It's time to change, even though my memory goes back once in awhile on all those years, the things the men and I saw and did. That was the old navy. The new navy says it's so much better now, that it's going to reward us, nonetheless, by making me the main target of many ships here at Bikini in atomic-bomb testing. "Isn't that nice?" they say. And when I don't seem grateful, they look so put-out and hurt. I don't understand how they think these days.

Why I remember when the Pennsylvania *was the flagship, and we were all so respectful. And I'll never forget.... Where was I? I forgot what I was going to say. Let me think a minute. Oh, now I remember. I'll never forget them posturing and strutting around here, the hot dogs ready to pop with pride and self-importance. I put them in one of four categories: the John Waynes, the Gary Coopers, the James Stewarts, and the Humphrey Bogarts. Even now I hear their minds rehearsing their lines for when its over, over there:*

"Sure I was scared! What the hell! But as much as I'd like to tell you what it was about, partner, I can't. Still at the same time (looking very noble), I can not tell a lie. I have (whispered) top-secret clearance." Cut!

What indeed would they know about real secrets? Some of them thought they'd made it through World War II on their own. But it was my doing sometimes that saved their asses, though I wasn't supposed to concoct anything to give them special help. The same way I had to put a little spin on the ball from time to time, or they'd killed me and them for sure. But today it's just me alone.

> *Merry, Merry Mount I sing,*
> *Four times protection Maypole bring,*
> *Mushroom cloud and victory bright,*
> *That I live another night.*

Mushrooms are a witch's tool. To this I stir in one B-29, for the boundary-breaking, earth-snake year, the second anniversary of the birth of Abe, who signed Nevada in. So is it really any surprise my becoming battle-born in the Metal-Snake year of 1941, my silver anniversary? Or that this operation is called "Crossroads" for Hermes? Or that I sit in the center of a nine-square-mile lagoon? The square is for the four of the day Hermes was born, and the nine for the days of the Parentalia. For this black day, I had them paint my decks a bright orange (they thought they were doing it to make me more visible to the pilot), the colors of Halloween, when Nevada was admitted to the union. I added Ellen for Greek and Seibert (derived from Sigiperaht) for bright victory.

Now it's over. I stand tall and majestic at anchor. But I didn't make it too perfect or they'd have been on their knees slobbering all over me; rolling around on the deck; fainting; crying out hysterically; and, worst of all, worshipping me as God. Thus I left out a couple ingredients so that there'd be some damage to the decks and radioactivity.

They took me back to Pearl, and I began to think they'd leave me alone, until one day an officer, who reminded me of Miles Standish, Captain Shrimp, the fink, comes aboard. I read from him that they're to give me no rest. On July 26, 1948, they tow me back to sea to become the target ship for Task Force 12. They begin by placing a secret explosive aboard and then detonating it, causing three holes in my hull. Again, what do they know about "secret"? I settle a little bit, so as not to make it too perfect, but still they're amazed that I survived. Some genius decides to employ their "bat-bombs." Can you image trying to do me in with "bat" missiles? I laugh gleefully—hee, hee, hee—as they fall six hundred yards astern.

"Bring up the tin cans," the admiral orders, "and they'll make quick work of her."

After firing hundreds of salvos, I see the frustration in the destroyer-skippers' minds. It'll go down in their fitness reports and look bad for promotion. They're pissed off at their crews. Aye, I'm sorry about this, me Mare-Mount mateys, but like all witches I so fear a watery grave.

I see now they're sending in their rocket-firing planes. Their projectiles are legion. I think of them as rain to be stolen away by the Cloud Rustler, and they affect me little. And I call upon the four winds so that my colors can still be seen proudly and defiantly flying in the breeze.

Then suddenly the Iowa begins firing her sixteen-inch guns. This is what hurts most. Oh, I don't mean her puny punch. If she'd been beached, they'd have thrown sand on her. But never in a million years would I have thought she'd turn those guns on me, her sister battleship. Nebraska cornhusker. Iowa cornholer!

After this treachery, the pounding by the five-and-six-inch guns of the cruisers Astoria, Pasadena, and Springfield along with the dive bombers later is an anticlimax. I've decided that whatever happens next, I won't fight anymore. I still have plenty of tricks I could use against them, but these are my friends. I'm sick at heart. I don't want to live no more...but I will survive.

On July 31st, a flight of torpedo bombers were sent against her. One caught her in the middle, but she only listed slightly. She could have gone on, but suddenly she just capsized and sank.[128-A]

> "Now hear this!" does a sailor say,
> "By the hairs of my ass,
> There's nothing so crass,
> As what we've done here today."
>
> With a laugh that's bitter and brittle,
> He turns to the side,
> As if to deride,
> And shoots out a gob of spittle.

Before the *Nevada* left Pearl Harbor for destruction, her ship's bells were requisitioned to be removed, decontaminated, and placed in the chapel at the

U.S. Naval
Receiving Station,
Pearl Harbor,
T
H
___
___
___

"April is the cruelest month" begins T.S. Eliot's "Wasteland" ('The Burial of the Dead').

April 19. Festival of Ceres, ancient Rome. Foxes were released with torches attached to their tails. This is "not properly understood." In the country, a sacrificial victim was carried about or around the growing crops three times (Op. cit., Grant and Kitzinger, Volume II). Persephone-the-Destroyer is referred to as the "Crone phase of Demeter" (Op. cit., Walker, Barbara G.).

April 19, 1692. On June 2, 1692, Bridget Bishop was "indicted and arraigned upon five several indictments for using and practicing, and exercising on the 19th day of April last and divers other days and times before and after certain acts of witchcraft...." She was the first of the accused Salem group to be hanged as a witch. Your churchgoers killed our Bishop. Altogether nineteen were hanged—not because they admitted it, but rather because they denied it.[128-B]

April 1721. Like the eyes of a potato, we'd watched many years until you were lulled into thinking that all was forgiven and forgotten.

Most of your records have been lost. Were you to check, however, the closest you would come to knowing about April 19, when it all began to hatch, was that the *Boston Gazette* (issue April 17–24) stated that on April 22, 1721, "on Saturday last arrived here, His Majesty's ship, *Seahorse*," implying both travel and death (between you and the British), seemed appropriate to us.

There was no reason to quarantine the ship as apparently nothing was reported at the three-mile point, and so she proceeded to the dock. Two Negroes having smallpox were eventually taken to two different houses near the shore, and so the disease spread.[129-A]

Cotton Mather had advocated that a group of doctors deliberate on the advisability of a crude form of immunization. (Edward Jenner, who discovered vaccination for smallpox, wasn't born until May 17, 1749, an earth-snake year.) It would have meant some receiving the inoculation would die who might not have otherwise, but overall far more would survive than if no inoculation were given. Some doctors weren't exactly pleased with Mather's meddling. Here was a minister telling physicians what they should do and others in his congregation were against it for religious reasons. Between the two, it was hard to tell who was responsible for the attempt on his life. Our position was one of ambivalence toward Mather. So when the homemade "granado" was thrown into his home, we saw that the lighted fuse went out by hitting a leaden frame. Nevertheless, Mather, the silly twit, was going into his religious paroxysms of ecstasy when contemplating his martyrdom if they would just be successful next time. Since it was giving him such "unutterable joy," we denied him this end, seeing that nothing further happened. When the epidemic had finally had run its course, there were 844 deaths and 5,889 stricken.

April 19, 1721. Roger Sherman born in Newton, Massachusetts, not far from Quincy. There wasn't an ounce of foolishness in him, a pillar of society, a man to be trusted. He signed the Declaration of Independence and helped draft the Articles of Confederation. Just the sort needed by us to promote the idea of a bicameral legislature, which would become increasingly like two fighting snakes, more interested in furthering their own self-serving politics than doing any good for your nation as it began to rot. That Sherman was unusually awkward was the only clue you might have had of our little Frankenstein sleeper. We have a long memory. His great grandfather had settled in Watertown, Massachusetts, in 1635. It seemed fitting then that Roger Sherman would die on July 23 (1793), the time in antiquity when there was a celebration for Neptune.

April 18, 1775. Massachusetts. Everything had been planned carefully down to the smallest detail, including your war with the Brits, the shits, whom we hated as much as we hated you, if possible. April was simply the *fourth* month, while the eight of eighteen signified "Eight-town" and the nine of nineteen, the Lord of the city of eight. (See Book I, footnote 5-B.)

Paul Revere was chosen over many others because he had the right stuff. For example, his initials were PR (public relations). He worked with silver, the witch's metal, and it seemed fitting that the son of Apollo should become the Revolutionary Hermes, a messenger, spreading the word about the British and more subtlety about us, which nevertheless must be explained to you now. No wonder nobody knew what Revere's horse looked like or was named, as we took Landhorse back immediately after "The Midnight Ride," *our indelible stamp you should have recognized.*

April 19, 1775. It was fifty-four (45) years since the *Seahorse* affair, a number by our contriving which years later would be given to the Massachusetts Regiment of "Glory" fame. But more to the point, April 19 will be in your history a continuing day of misfortune or bloody sacrifice, or, at the very least, a reminder that you're never again to do what you chose in 1692. We'll never forget or forgive this. Thus "double trouble...fire burn...cauldron bubble." We picked April, the fourth month, because it represented Hermes (Thoth, magic, judgment) and nineteen for the so-called witches hanged, not to mention the many others you persecuted. April 19 was also the day Bridget Bishop, the first hanged, was accused of using, practicing, and exercising witchcraft. We also had a more obscure reason for selecting this date, which will be explained shortly. It's ironic that April 19 will be called Patriot's Day in Massachusetts and Maine. We thought them nice touches to have Mrs. Lincoln born in Lexington, Kentucky, the namesake of the battle of this date, and to have ol' Abe on view: four days dead/ and five from alive/ his testament to/ 4.5.

April 19, 1775. Concord, Massachusetts. *Concord* means harmony, peaceful relations. More of our humor.

April 19, 1783. George Washington, whose face was scarred by smallpox by us on purpose, gave the army the message that Congress had proclaimed the cessation of hostilities.

April 19, 1824. Lord Byron, the son of Captain "Mad Jack" Byron and the grandson of Admiral "Four-weather Jack," died in Greece. We had marked him with a clubfoot at birth. Now why do you suppose we'd do something like that? We wanted you to know that the seeds of *Frankenstein*, your best-known horror story, your worst nightmare, were planted by us and is a mere nothing to what we can do. "We will each write a ghost story," said Lord

Byron. The proposition was agreed to by four, the Hermes number. They discussed Eramus Darwin, whose grandson Charles would die on April 19, fifty-six years after Lord Byron. Byron's body was returned to England. They wouldn't allow him to be buried in Westminster Abbey. So he was put in the family vault near Newstead. One hundred plus forty-five years later, a memorial to him was placed on the floor in the Abbey. This took some doing on our part. It was much harder than getting the Nevada's ship's bell placed in the chapel at Pearl Harbor, territory of Hawaii.

April 19, 1832. Lucretia Rudolph Garfield born. Both her parents and those of her husband, James Abram Garfield, were of New England descent. In the seventeenth century, the first Garfield came to *Massachusetts* with John Winthrop. (Our memory goes back a long way.) James Garfield, the fifth of five children, called his wife "Crete," possibly not realizing that Hermes was worshipped on the island of Crete. Whether the snake in the Currier and Ives lithograph, 1880, represented falsehood or truth, made no difference. He shouldn't have cut a swath to the White House by stepping on its head and chopping the snake in two. The crescent scythe, sometimes seen with a skeleton, sealed his doom. (Nor should it have been used in the flag of Soviet Russia.) When he was president, Garfield was shot on July 2, 1881, and died on September 19, 1881, both dates within the snake-year. He served only 199 days.

April 19, 1847. When you read about Lewis Keseberg of the Donner Party lying through his teeth and the greedy rescuers tightening the noose around his neck will you think of Bridget Bishop? Doesn't the fact that the last of the families to reach Truckee (Donner) Lake on Halloween 1846 show our hand in it?

April 19, 1861. The first casualties of the Civil War occurred when a Baltimore mob, sympathizing with the South, *stoned* the sixth *Massachusetts* regiment while it was traveling to Washington. At least four soldiers and nine civilians were killed. Maryland, a slave-holding state, remained loyal to the union. But John Wilkes Booth had been born near Bel Air, Maryland, on August 26 (MP), 1838.

April 19, 1865. Dying at 4.5 /Lincoln lies unalive/ in the capitol rotunda (round). His forbears had come from Massachusetts.

April 19, 1882. Charles Darwin, born on the same day, month, and year as Lincoln (February 12, 1809) died. Of course, he was our man to agitate the Christian fundamentalists even today.

April 19, 1891. We arranged for Herman Melville to complete *Billy Budd* on this date, since Billy Budd was hung (like our witches) under British rule on the H.M.S. *Indomitable*. More to the point, it was an example of innocence versus evil—your evil. *Moby Dick* is the greatest American novel to date. We gave him this status only because he agreed to dedicate it to Nathaniel Hawthorne, whom we had born in *Salem, Massachusetts* on *July 4*, 1804, and to live for awhile in Concord of April 19 fame so that you'll learn to associate Independence Day with us and to remember we're always present. Nathaniel Hawthorne, whom we liked, died *peacefully in his sleep* in 1864 on May 19, the anniversary of Anne Boleyn's beheading, and in the same month and day Ho Chi Minh will be born in 1890, Malcolm X in 1925, Pol Pot in 1925/1928, and when Jacqueline Kennedy will die in 1994.

Speaking of Ho Chi Minh, your involvement and ignominious defeat in Vietnam was our doing as well as John F. Kennedy's. Had it not been for the interference of Hermes (persona peace), you'd still be suffering and sinking there. (Never let it be said we witches weren't real patriots, just like Revere.) He let us bring about the peace by using our own dates, however: May 15, 1966; April 15, 1967; February 14–15, 1970; April 19, 1971; April 30, 1975; and May 1, 1975, the Maypole Day, for Thomas Morton you'd driven out of Massachusetts.

April 19, 1892. Three million acres of land belonging to the Arapaho and Cheyenne Indians were opened for settlement to thirty thousand homesteaders. Whites jeered and sneered, and pooh-poohed and sniffed, saying the final Ghost Dance performed at Chief Left Hand's Oklahoma camp on the previous day was ineffective, powerless.[129-AA]

April 19, 1897. Theodore Roosevelt became assistant secretary of the navy under McKinley (and served until May 10, 1898). We selected Roosevelt because of his impeccable Parentalia credentials. Roosevelt waited until the secretary of the navy took the day off, then sent word to Commodore Dewey to take Manila in the event of war. Later TR was drafted as a vice-presidential running mate for McKinley. Poor President McKinley was assassinated (it couldn't have happened to a nicer guy), and our man Roosevelt became president.

April 19, 1898. The Spanish-American War was inevitable from this date, linked to the Lupercalia sinking of the *Maine*, named for the state that sprang from Massachusetts and was given statehood on the Ides of March. (Beware the Ides of March; April 19.) Congress adopted a war resolution which recognized Cuban independence, told Spain to get her armed forces out, and empowered the president to use the U.S. Armed Forces to back the resolution. An idealistic cause for the war—now certain to come—was given by asserting that the U.S. had no interest in controlling Cuba.

April 19, 1906. Writers and artists from the Bohemian Club gathered to save the home of Mrs. Robert Louis Stevenson (Op. cit., Cornell, James). We thought it a good thing to have them do this. The fire—caused from the previous day's earthquake—spread, destroying over four square miles of San Francisco before it was put out on the twenty-first. Stevenson (*The Strange Case of Dr. Jekyll and Mr. Hyde, Treasure Island, The Body Snatcher*) was a Hermetic and Parentalia person. He had a respiratory disease most of his life and married Fannie on May 19, 1880, at which time they exchanged two silver rings, eventually taking their honeymoon at a disused Silverado mining camp, and sleeping in a ghost dormitory with the remains of nine old three-tier bunks. On the day of his death (December 3, 1894), he was working on the *Weir of Hermiston* (posthumously published 1896). Just a coincidence, of course, that he was forty-five years at the time of his death, and that *Hermis* sounds remarkably close to *Hermes*, the god of writers, or death; and that forty-four to forty-five years after his death, the International Exposition at Treasure Island opened on February 18 (1939), a Parentalia day.

April 19, 1914. In what was called by Arthur Schlesinger[129-B] an "uncharacteristically belligerent move," President Wilson asked and got authority from Congress to use armed forces against Mexico's Huerta, a dictator. The U.S. Navy was sent to Mexico, and the Marines captured Vera Cruz on April 21 at a loss of four killed and twenty wounded. Not bad. They still haven't figured out, however, despite repeated lessons, to whom their allegiance really is, that they are the Witches' Own. The first of these was to put them under navy jurisdiction—a humiliation—on the witches' diameter, the day of Walpurgis Night. (Hitler, who we created, learned too late not to fuck with us.) The second was the fall of Saigon on April 30. That's right, the day of Walpurgis Night and the witches' diameter. No more U.S. embassy, no more Marines. The third was staged on the anniversary of the day of *Midnight Ride* of the silversmith Paul Revere and on the eve of the Revolutionary War, both parties of whom we hated: You must recall Beirut. "From the halls of Montezuma" to the witches coven tree.

April 19, 1926. President Coolidge told the Daughters (spawned by the witches' day) of the American Revolution that a failure of citizens to vote was a peril, and that there was a lack of obedience to law and reverence for authority. On April 15 (4.5), 1919, at a convention in Washington, the Daughters of the American Revolution had endorsed the proposed League of Nations (see *February 14*, 1919).

April 19, 1927. Six counties in Illinois were hit by a tornado, killing twenty-two. Actually our revenge began a day earlier when the

Mississippi River flooded Missouri, Arkansas, Mississippi, Illinois, Kentucky, Tennessee, and Louisiana. You see, the witches, hard to hold back, sometimes use the precedent that Paul Revere began his ride on April 18 (Clarence Darrow, who defended unpopular causes, was born April 18, 1857; there was a resolution on April 18, 1899, to revoke banishment of Roger Williams; the San Francisco earthquake hit on April 18, 1906; on April 18, 1945, Ernie Pyle, author of *Home Country* ["there's no place like home"], was killed by Japanese gunfire in the Pacific; your precious Albert Einstein died on April 18, 1955: he was right, you know, "God does not play dice"; on April 18, 1958, treason charges for making pro-Axis broadcasts in World War II were dismissed against Ezra Pound; and the car bombing of the U.S. in Beirut, Lebanon, occurred on April 18, 1983). Once started, the witches are hard to restrain. For in addition to the nineteen hung, Giles Cory was pressed to death. So please try to understand, we had pressing needs for Hitler—one of our best—to come about on April 20, a *Dies Mala* or "Egyptian Day." Unfortunately he got too big for his britches. So you would have no doubt about his antecedents, we terminated him on the day of Walpurgis Night.

April 19 1933. The U.S. abandoned the gold standard, increasing the price of silver.[129-C] This was done under President Franklin Roosevelt, who was buried at 4.5, '45.

April 19, 1935. On the anniversary of the specific day Bridget Bishop was accused of witchcraft, we thought it appropriate for Hitler to receive a birthday tribute from the German Army.

April 19, 1940. We made the Lake Shore Limited Express run late. The engineer then increased speed to fifty-nine miles per hour, when *forty-five* miles per hour was specified in regulations. The locomotive jumped track at the Gulf Curve at Little Falls (pardon the pun), New York. Twenty-eight, including the engineer and fireman, died.

April 19, 1951. General MacArthur (relieved of his command on April 11, 1951, by President Truman) spoke to a general session of Congress and urged the U.S. to expand the war against Communist China. The country was divided. We were responsible for MacArthur being relieved on April 11 then *four* days later that Emperor Hirohito would come to say goodbye to General MacArthur (one deposed god to another) on 4.5 for *forty-five* minutes. Then *four* days later MacArthur said goodbye. 4/4545/4. "Memories...tales of love so true."

April 19, 1961. We thought the day especially appropriate, since sixty-three years previously Congress had expressed no interest in controlling Cuba and would "leave government control of the island to its people." Moreover, we distrusted the CIA, seeing its business would be to use or kill us. As one witch said, "It'd reward twenty years of faithful service by terminating the retiree so as not to pay the pension." The CIA had led the Cuban exiles into believing there would be more U.S. participation than actually materialized. The operation actually began on April 15, or 4.5, the radius of the coven circle (shades of Lincoln, the *Titanic*), the anniversary of the date when Premier Castro of the Parentalia arrived in the U.S. in 1959 to begin his eleven-day goodwill tour. Several U.S.-made planes, said to have been flown by Cuban officers, bombed three Cuban bases. On April 17, about one thousand three hundred Cuban refugees, who'd been trained by the CIA in Central America, were transported by merchant vessels (escorted by U.S. destroyers) to make their landing at the Bay of Pigs,[129-D] about ninety-seven miles southeast of Havana. By *April 19, Castro's forces had control of the situation.* Ninety invaders were dead, the rest taken prisoners. President Kennedy timidly had withdrawn air support of the exiles at the last minute. This seemed uncharacteristic of the man who would later back the Russians down in the Cuban Missile Crisis. The average person could only wonder about this. Our revenge was sweeter since he still retained his Massachusetts accent, where he'd been born. On May 1, 1961, Castro announced to the world that Cuba was a Marxist-Leninist state.

> Merry, Merry Mount I sing,
> Four times protection Maypole bring.

April 19, 1964. Premier Fidel Castro announced that U-2 plane flights were violating Cuban sovereignty. The U.S. had decided to continue on with the flights despite the U-2 plane fiasco on May 1 (Tom Morton's Maypole Day), 1960, in Soviet Russia. Not to worry! Through our help, Fidel will outlive them all.

April 19, 1965.

> It's one hundred years
> Since Lincoln of 4.5
> Lay pickled unalive.

> The 3Ks is growing stronger
> By the day,
> U.S. officials choose to say.

April 19, 1967. U.S. lunar probe *Surveyor 3* made a "perfect touchdown" on the moon. But of course! Anything less than perfection between the moon and us would be unthinkable. Wherever you go...we'll be there. We arranged for the first moon-landing astronauts to leave the moon on the twenty-first of July (1969) after spending twenty-one to twenty-two hours there. This meant they'd splash down on July 24, rather than July 23, a time of celebration in antiquity for Neptune. We are, after all, not sea witches. The Eagle may have landed on the moon, but the Ibis flew back.

April 19, 1971. Charles Manson (son of man, the killer) and his three women were sentenced to be gassed to death in California for the murder of Sharon Tate and six others in California. We chose this date because we wanted you to know: No way would we let you say, "Goodbye Charlie." No seven-come-eleven roll.

April 19, 1971. Cauldron bubble, brother against brother. On the anniversary of the day Lincoln lay a-mouldering in the Capitol Rotunda, Vietnam Veterans Against the War began a five-day demonstration in Washington, D.C. Though ending on April 23 with about one thousand veterans throwing toy guns, combat ribbons, helmets, and uniforms on the Capitol steps, it served as a prelude to the crowd of two hundred thousand demonstrators at Washington, D.C. and one hundred and fifty thousand on April 24 at San Francisco, which was incorporated in 1850 on *April 15* (4.5), the witch's radius, and later to be called by some "the wickedest city in the world." It was no coincidence then that San Francisco city and county were consolidated in 1856 on *April 19*, the witches' day. Sure we caused the earthquake on the eve of the fiftieth anniversary of the consolidation. But it wasn't for the reason you might assume. Actually there was little left to corrupt on the Barbary Coast—not much fun left—so we wanted to start all over again with a new crop, you might say.

April 19, 1973. In a statement telephoned to newspapers by his secretary, John Dean said, "...some may hope or think that I will become a scapegoat in the Watergate case. Anyone who believes this does not know me...." Press Secretary Ronald Ziegler's rebuttal later on April 19 was "that the process now under way is not one to find scapegoats but one to get at the truth," which of course was the reason for the inquisition, the Salem trials, and the investigation aboard the USS *Iowa* sixteen years later. If there were no scapegoats, then how come President Nixon was pardoned and the others weren't? Certainly they'd all suffered as much as Nixon by the continuing adverse publicity. The answer lay in the fact that President Nixon was connected to February 21, a day when Andrew Johnson fired Secretary of War Stanton. We were the ones who put the pardoning idea in President Gerald Ford's mind. Have a nice day!

April 19, 1979. The nuclear testing at Nevada especially provoked us. So we thought this date appropriate to reveal in newspapers that Gordon Dean, the chairman of the Atomic Energy Commission at the time of the May 27, 1953, testing, had written in his diary. To wit, President Eisenhower had told the AEC to keep the public confused on atomic testing and fallout. Scratch the military-industrial complex to beware of and add in its place President Eisenhower.

April 19, 1989, an earth-snake year:

> Matey, I'm sorry
> You'll get the blame,
> For an old reminder of
> The terrible Iowa shame.[129-E]

April 19, 1993. Death of eight in eastern Iowa plane crash, four years after the Iowa explosion.

April 19, 1993. At Branch Davidian Compound in Waco, Texas, a fire ended a federal siege, which went into effect on February 28, 1993. "Fire burn...double trouble." We thought it poetic justice that the Feds would be criticized for violating religious freedom while setting fire to Koresh and his followers, who certainly would have done the same to us. At least seventy-two died in the inferno. Caught up now are the Feds in a slow-healing, festering sore.

April 19, 1994. Rodney King, the victim of a beating incident in Los Angeles in 1991, is awarded $3,816,535.45 in damages. Two policemen who took part in the beating were sentenced to prison. Revenge is sweet! Our revenge: This will contribute to the nullification verdict on O.J. Simpson the following year. O.J. had a history of wife beating. Also on this day, the Senate approved Admiral Kelso's retirement with four stars. He had attended the Tailhook convention in Las Vegas in 1991 but denied, though there were some allegations to the contrary, that he had seen any instances of sexual assaults.

April 19, 1995. A bomb blast killed 169 and tore apart the nine-story Federal Building in Oklahoma City. This came about when our council leader just noticed, after several hundred years, that one picture of Thoth showed him as having two left hands. He took this as a sign that it was time to avenge the scoffing at Chief Left Hand's Oklahoma Ghost Dance in the last century.

"A curse is a curse," he said, as the witches nodded in agreement, except for me of the *Nevada*. Even before standing, I knew they were set on their course, that nothing would change their minds. It was foolishness even to try and would mean my condemnation and ostracism forever. But I've never been long on brains and would cut off my nose to spite my face. It's the way things are.

"Mankind has never understood that the past, present, and future intermingle and never can be compartmentalized," the leader answered almost inaudibly, as if he were patiently explaining something for the first time to a small child. This was typical, the sinuosity of words, disguising his intention to strike. "There were no tender thoughts," he continued, "concerning the Salem 19, nor is it forgotten that in some case the so-called innocent children—that you argue for—testified against their own parent at the trials. Nevertheless, it's precisely because we feel for the Indian children who lost their birthright that there is a correctness in what we do."

"Bullshit!" I exploded. "It's time to forget the past and move on." "And that you shall do," he said, as the ass-kissers nodded in agreement. "You've always been a numb-nuts, no more, no less," he sneered. "Your liaison with the seawitch scandalized us all. But what I've hated above all else about you," his voice now loud and higher and dripping with contempt, "is that you're a muddler, a fourth class mind. Elisha, who would have none of your squeamishness, sent out two she-bears to tear up forty-two children who mocked his bald head," which curiously the leader has.

I couldn't resist the parting shot for myself and the little rogues before Rogaine, "Well at least my thinking isn't influenced by a bald head." So here I am alone, and you offer your tea and sympathy and crumpety words that "no man is an island." Let me tell you something: Every man is an I-land.

April 19, 1996. *In Memoriam*:

> How like we are/ In our honoring hours/
> 'cept we bring fresh meat/ And you bring dead flowers.
>
> The tyrannical God/ Says you'll return to the ground/
> But when you die/ Another reason's to be found.
>
> Yes masta, suh/ Does the plantation nigger say/
> Scared to speak up/ Or he'll be spirited away.
>
> Lock God up/ Throw away the key/
> You'll die anyway/ But a real man he'll see.
>
> Nevada, has its Spirit of Wovoka Days Powwow.

Chapter Sixteen

Though later working at small, part-time jobs, I retired after twenty years of sailing, effective January 1, 1989.

On April 11, 1989, (eight days preceding the *Iowa* explosion), twelve bodies were unearthed on a ranch west of Matamoros, Mexico. The thirteenth was discovered on the thirteenth day. On the fourteenth day, the anniversary of Lincoln getting shot and the *Titanic* hitting the iceberg, a fourteenth would be found. The fifteenth discovered (the last I heard) represented the day Lincoln died and the*Titanic* sank.

Some suspects arrested said the victims had been killed in Satanic rituals to provide drug traffickers a "magical shield" for protection from the police. A vacant apartment had been found having a blood-smeared altar with children's clothing and children's pictures.

Matamoros was a terrible thing brought about by people trying to manipulate their world for personal gain by such outrageous acts as human sacrifice, so that the devil or god they imagine in their minds will then look at them as being special, having demonstrated the god like power of life and death. Not being shackled by innate rules of conduct, they are, therefore, deserving of the magical power of which the more timid are not fit. But one of the main reasons why Hermes can't be connected to it and why it will always fail in the end (no matter what god or spirit is imagined) is that it's manipulative and condescending, reducing that god to being an "errand boy."

Still something more could be learned by looking up Matamoros, which is on the southern side of the Rio Grande (Río Bravo, Mexico) where there is a bridge leading to Brownsville, Texas.

In April (fourth month) 1846, U.S. and Mexican patrols clashed. On May 8 (fifth month) the battle of Palo Alto, a symbolic name, took place. Here we read of two captains: one called *Walker*, the other called *May*.

On May 9 the battle of Resaca de la Palma occurred. *Resaca* (Nevada) refers to a shallow ravine that in time past had been the riverbed of the Rio Grande. It was shaped like a snake (some say a bow, but a snake can

398

be clearly seen by turning a map), and heavy chaparral surrounded most of it. A road from Point Isabel ran through the chaparral on one side, across the ravine, through chaparral on the other to Matamoros. The ravine itself was about sixty yards wide and had in places "serpentine" ponds that filled in heavy rain, united, and flowed back toward the Rio Grande,[130-B] thus "Palma." It isn't necessary to worry whether this refers to the palm of a hand or to a tree. *Palma* means palm.[131]

In this battle, Captain May took credit for capturing a Mexican general when in fact the general had been taken by a bugler, and May's dragoons captured an enemy battery and then failed to hold it.[132-A] So the captain's fame as a popular hero and promotion to lieutenant colonel were probably undeserved at one level, but at the other, his name was May in the month of May at the "Dry River of *Palma*."

Interesting too in this battle is that there was a fledgling officer called Sam Grant (Ulysses) leading some troops of the fourth infantry.

On May 13 (Persephone's day), Congress passed a declaration of war against Mexico. On the eighteen Matamoros fell. The Mexican War that officially began on May 13, 1846, the year the Donner party reached Truckee Lake, ended on May 30 (MP) 1848, a day that years later Memorial Day would occur.

It's been mentioned that Abraham Lincoln was superstitious, believing in signs and dreams. (Remember the celebration for Faunus/Pan, who had the legs of a goat, in old Rome took place on February 13.) "Honest Ape" (sic) was born on the twelfth, the evening of which was the Eve of the Faunus festival and the Parentalia. He also took part in seances at his wife's urging to try to communicate with their son William Wallace Lincoln who had died of "bilious" (ili) "fever" (possibly malaria, typhoid fever, or a ruptured appendix; the snake doctors today aren't sure) on Feralia Eve (actually about 5:00 P.M.) on Thursday, February 20, 1862, as if a sacrifice exacted.

The eleven-year-old boy, who was the most handsome of the Lincoln family and who played the piano to his father's delight, took sick "around the first of February."[132-B] Remember all February was a month of lustration in ancient Rome. He was embalmed and placed in a casket of rosewood and silver. On the day of his funeral, a violent storm hit Washington. Frantic winds below off roofs, uprooted trees, tore flags to ribbons, and toppled steeples.

February, of course, used to be the last month of the year (now December). William Wallace Lincoln was born in 1850 on December 21, the month and day in antiquity given for the final entombment of Osiris, Egyptian lord of the *under*world. (The Lincoln tunnel, *under* the Hudson River, goes between Manhattan Island, New York City and Weehawken (slight change in spelling: Wee-hawk-kin), New Jersey. It opened on December 21, 1937.) William's mother, Mary Todd Lincoln, was born in

1818 on December 13, the Eve of Mausoleum Day. George Washington had died on Mausoleum Day, December 14, 1799. The mother of Zachary Taylor, the general who had defeated Santa Anna on February 21 and who would be the peer sacrifice for the Washington Monument (dedicated February 21), had been born on Mausoleum Day 1760 and died on Mausoleum Day Eve December 13, 1822, four years from the date Mary Todd Lincoln was born.

Unexplainable sounds of footsteps have been heard through the years coming from what used to be Lincoln's room. But on investigation, the person hearing them couldn't account for the reason. It's said that Queen Wilhelmina of Holland, when staying as a guest at the White House, was awakened one night by a knocking at her door. When she opened it, she was confronted with a specter of Lincoln, at which time she fainted. Winston Churchill, Britain's level-headed prime minister, hated to sleep in Lincoln's room, usually given to visiting dignitaries. At least twice he got up in the middle of the night and walked across the hall to finish his sleep in another room. Eleanor Roosevelt once commented that if there were a ghost, it was Lincoln's. Both Presidents Franklin D. Roosevelt and Dwight D. Eisenhower are said to have sensed or seen Lincoln's ghost. No-nonsense Harry S. Truman said he himself had been awakened by a knocking on his door on three occasions, only to find nobody there. Married to Bess on the beginning day of the Parentalia, he had, of course, ordered the atomic bombs dropped on Japan.

Nancy Reagan's dog, Rex, sometimes passed Lincoln's door without a whimper, while at other times he would bark. If the door were opened for him, however, he refused to go in.

Possibly Lincoln's ghost/or John Wilkes Booth's has been at Ford's Theater too. Though seeing, hearing, or feeling nothing when I visited it in 1962 or 1963, others through the years have reported seeing or hearing eerie things there. An unbeliever, or perhaps a person having little sensitivity, might be quick to point out that this is what happens when an overactive imagination runs away with itself. What's just a hint or suggestion becomes nearly a fact in time with repeated telling. In truth, sort of a veracity develops as people begin to believe themselves.

The First Baptist Church of Washington was constructed in 1833, the snake-year Chief Justice John Marshall and George Watterston began soliciting funds to erect the Washington Monument.

In 1861 the First Baptist Church's Board of Trustees decided, since the church was no longer being used for sectarian purposes, to sell it as it was becoming a financial burden. John T. Ford from Baltimore sought a location for a theater. Despite the prediction of a Board of Trustees' member that dire consequences would occur if the church were converted to a theater, Ford leased the property for five years, with the option to buy it at the end of that time.[133]

Shortly after, Ford rented the theater out to George Christy, where Christy's Minstrels performed. Then on *February 28*, 1862, following the final performance of the Christy Minstrels the previous day, Ford began remodeling and renovation. When it opened on March 19, 1862, it was known as Ford's Athenium. Lincoln gave prestige to the theater when he attended it for the first time on *May 28*, 1862. The dire fate predicted happened—and would occur two more times—when a fire gutted the theater on December 30, 1862, just a little over a year after Ford leased the building (Ibid.).

On *February 28*, 1863 (a year exactly after the renovation began), the cornerstone for Ford's Theater was laid. *Quicks*and caused much difficulty in laying the foundation. This was solved by building the walls on blue clay.

The Lincoln assassination at Ford's Theater on *April 14*, 1865, was the second occurrence of ill fate. Not long after, the theater was taken over by the government and remodeled into a three-story building. It was being used by the Office of Records and Pensions to compile the official records of Civil War veterans when a third tragedy occurred on June 9, 1893. A forty-foot section of the front of the building collapsed, killing *twenty-two* government employees and injuring sixty-five others. (The Washington Monument was dedicated on February 21, 1884.)

Notice the connection of Civil War veterans and Lincoln; February 28 appears twice. Lincoln was shot *April 14* (Appomattox on April 9 and John Wilkes Booth died on April 26). Lincoln's first attendance at theater was on *May 28*, 1862 (Lincoln was buried on May 4, 1865). February, April, and May are Hermetic months.

In the year 1869, John Wilkes Booth's body was dug up and released by the War Department for burial in Baltimore.[134] This was two snake cycles before the wall collapsed. In addition to Booth being buried in Baltimore, the first casualties of the Civil War occurred when the Sixth Massachusetts regiment was stoned there, and John T. Ford had come from Baltimore to Washington.

Lincoln was shot with a .44-caliber Derringer (4, 5), eight ounce, brass pistol. The presidential box was number seven. This might be considered in relation to the Feralia, of which Lincoln's birthday on the twelfth is a transposition of 21 (3 x 7 = 21). The Feralia by extension can be associated with the dead of the Civil War, the Gettysburg Address (a mantra for school children), the stills of a gaunt and somber Lincoln, and his stovepipe hat. Though fashionable at the time, the latter is both similar and dissimilar to a witch's hat, being round on top instead of pointed.

Other facts, which may or may not be relevant, concerning the number 7 are:

His bed is/was seven feet in length, and sleep is said to be the brother of death. It was the seventh day that the Japanese attacked Pearl Harbor. John Bell, of the Bell Witch fame, suffered terribly for three years before he was released to death on December 21, 1820. After his death, the witch said she'd return every seven years. When "the Pale Horse had come,"[135] there were three physicians touching Lincoln—all perhaps looking at their watches. One had his "finger" on the carotid artery, a second had "his finger" checking the pulse of the right wrist, and a third had his hand (five fingers) over the cardium (3 x 7 = 21). At 7:21 and fifty-five seconds, Lincoln drew his last breath. Fifteen seconds later, his heart flickered a goodbye.

Possibly Lincoln's main role could have been a mystical one, making him an ever greater hero. Further indications of this are suggested by the outcome of the five lives at Ford's Theater that night:

1) Lincoln never regained consciousness and died the following morning.
2) Eleven days after the shooting, John Wilkes Booth was cornered in a tobacco barn. He refused to come out, so it was set on fire. He died of gunshot wounds from a man who was as disturbed as himself.
3) Both the gowns of Mrs. Lincoln and Clara Harris were *splattered with blood*. Most of it, if not all,[136] was from Major Rathbone's wound from the dagger. Later in life, Mrs. Lincoln will be declared insane and admitted to an institution for awhile. She'd been born in Lexington, Kentucky. She had a brother and half-brothers, as well as other relatives in the Confederate Army. Several had questioned her patriotism. When William Wallace, her eleven-year-old son, died on February 20, 1862, in the White House, she was devastated and began holding seances.
4) Clara Harris will marry Major Rathbone. They had children.
5) Like Mrs. Lincoln, Major Rathbone was never quite right after the assassination. Jealous of his wife's attention to the kids, he shot and killed Clara in 1894 in front of their horror-stricken children. He was committed to an insane asylum in Hanover, Germany, where he lived out the rest of his life.[137] The ghost of Clara Harris is said to have haunted their home.

Thus it seemed important to know what happened in the lives of the special agents after the Kennedy assassination on November 22, 1963. John Connolly, the former governor of Texas and millionaire, declared himself bankrupt.

402

Chapter Seventeen

As a painter can be determined from brush strokes, so the work of the Titanic can be identified with Hermes, whose signature is written all over it.

Four (4) wireless telegrams had been sent to the Titanic from other ships in the area on Sunday, April 14, 1912, warning her of icebergs. Captain Smith, her master, didn't even bother to slow down, plowing ahead at twenty-one to twenty-two knots, a Parentalia-Caristia speed. Though not trying for a record, he was under pressure to make the Atlantic crossing as quickly as possible. It was the maiden voyage for the newest and finest ship ever built (as such, fitting for sacrifice). The world was watching. Also his boss Joseph Is*may*, chairman of the board of White Star, was aboard, and Captain Smith hadn't been made captain of the world's greatest ship by arriving late on schedules. Of course some sort of alarm bells should have gone off, for every schoolboy or girl has heard of the tip of the iceberg, and some warning bells should have sounded when he received advice or warning from the captains of four other ships. But then that was why they were captains of inferior ships because they weren't bold. He had after all forty years' experience, which in the end added up to one year's experience forty times, when he failed to recall a very basic fact that big ships can't stop and turn on a dime. It becomes an occupational hazard—especially on passenger ships—that the captain can get carried away with his self-importance or the infallibility of his decision making and become an iceberg, self-destructing himself as well as others.[138-A]

This was on one level. At the other, it wouldn't have made any difference. The scenario had been written. The captain was helpless to respond. The die had been cast long before the collision with the iceberg.[138-B] It began when they named the ship the Titanic. Had they not done that, her bad-luck hull number would have meant nothing, and her other numbers would have worked for her. In the end the captain, who perished with 1,522 others, was but a reflection of the magisterial manner of his masters who didn't pay attention to detail: "Well her nearly identical sister-ship is called the *Olympic*, so call her the *Titanic*. That's a classy name!" Except for the facts that the Titans had been defeated by the Olympians and thrown into Tartarus and the *Olympic*—though nearly identical—was 3 inches smaller and 1004 gross tons lighter (measurement). Besides that there were extra touches given the *Titanic*, making her the more lavish and luxurious. These slights were unforgivable. There was the impression that the *Titanic* was not only newer but bigger, better, and more powerful—a snub, a snob.[138-C] So what could have been more cunning and ironic than for the *Olympic*, whose master at the time was the same Captain Smith, to be responsible for the *Titanic* to miss her sailing date in order to meet her destiny? Certainly there can be no mistaking the meaning.

One of the ship's glories over the main staircase was a candelabra having twenty-one lights, and most passed under this at one time or another. Only two numbers I'm aware of are unequivocally Hermes: twenty-one (a number of good luck or death) and forty-five. Forty-four and fifty-five (or 4 or 5) might represent him too on occasion, but in my opinion, these are most equivocal.

Let's look at the important dates and/or numbers concerning the *Titanic*. For lack of a better term, there's a Hermetic disposition to most of these, as if the message and messenger aren't to be mistaken.

31 March 1909	Keel laid.	(3 + 1 = an unlucky 4).
Hull number 390904.	390904 = 25 (5 x 5).	

4 May 1910	4-5. It's a rainy, *Wednesday* morning exactly *forty-five* years since Abraham Lincoln was buried at Springfield, Illinois. The Prince of Wales, who'd married Princess "May" in SY 1893 (21),[140] visits the grave of a friend at Kensal Green *cemetery*. The visit at this time to the graveyard and the birthdate of one of the prince's sons are like some chronological cabalism. Afterwards, King Edward has a severe attack of bronchitis.
5 May	5-5. Queen *Alexandra* and Princess Victoria have just returned from Corfu (a Greek island) where they visited the King of *Hellenes*.[141]
6 May	Edward died[142] at 11:45 P.M. George writes in his diary (kept since May 3, 1880) that God will help him and "darling May" will be his comfort. On the death of his father, the prince became King George the *Fifth*.
31 May 1911	Ship launched (3 + 1 = unlucky 4). It's a Mercury period, the month of the snake, and the fifth month. In the *Titanic*'s case, these were unlucky numbers and signs, but they didn't have to be (e.g., Heinrich and Sophia Schliemann at the site of Troy *thirty-eight* years before).

What they show in events is that Hermes has more than a casual interest for better or worse.

20 Mar 1912 This was the original date for the maiden voyage to begin. Unable to meet set date when the *Olympic* collided with HMS (HMS for His Majesty's Ship or Hermes?) *Hawke.*[143] Repairs to *Olympic* delay construction on *Titanic.*

1 April 4-1. (4 + 1 = 5). High *winds* cause sea trials to be called off. Date might also be written 1-4.

4 April 4-4. Hermes born on the fourth of a month. It was nearly midnight April 3 when the when the four-stacker *Titanic* approached the White Star Dock at Southampton, after completing a 570-mile trip for shakedown and sea trials. She was "warped into her mooring at Berth 44."

10 April *Wednesday.* Ship begins voyage, departing from White Star Line Dock, Southampton, at 12:15 P.M. But White Star Line pennant is a *white*, five-pointed star on red background—the white suggesting the silver-white mercury extracted from red cinnabar. This is forty-seven years to the day since George Duren,[144] great grandfather clock, died following Lee's surrender at Appomattox. The ominous winds at the beginning of the month paralleled the 4-1-1865 (or 1-4-1865) defeat of the Confederates at Five Forks, the crossroads.[145] (And what could have been better than the intersection of five roads to symbolize Hermes?)[146]
Titanic arrives and departs Cherbourg, France.

11 April Arrives at Queenstown, Ireland. Some passengers debark. Some come aboard. One crewman deserts. Sails. Logs 386 miles.

12 April Logs 519 miles. Fifty-one years previously the first shots were fired at Ft. Sumter, shades of Black Hawk Anderson.

13 April Logs 546 miles. Ides.

14 April 11:40 P.M. Collides with iceberg. *Forty-seven* years previously on same evening at 10:15, Lincoln was shot in the head at Ford's Theater.

15 April 2:20 A.M. ship sinks. 1,523 lives lost. 7:22 A.M. *forty-seven* years before, Lincoln died. There were roughly *five* hours difference in the time. In 1865 about fourteen days elapsed between the battle of Five Forks, which has been called "the Waterloo of the Confederacy," and the time Lincoln died. In the time frame of the month of April only, approximately the same can be said of the South's Waterloo and the time the *Titanic* sank.

It was four-five days between the time the ship sailed on her maiden voyage and the time she foundered. Also 4-14 and 4-15 suggest a 4:5 relationship. At 12:10 A.M. on April 15, *fourth* officer Boxhall estimated the *Titanic's* position as being

$$41° \ 46'N, \ 50° \ 14' \ W$$
$$4 + 1 = 5 \quad 4 + 6 = 10 \ (5 + 5) \quad 50 = 5 \quad 1 + 4 = 5$$
$$\text{or}$$
$$4 + 1 = 5 \quad 4 + 6 = 10 = 1 \quad 50 = 5 \quad 1 + 4 = 5$$

The fives came up like numbers on a slot machine but the reward was negative.

Some numerologists believe that a 4 put together by a 1 and 3 is unfavorable, e.g., the superstition surrounding 13. The last of the Donner Party had reached the lake on October 31, and the *Nevada* sank on July 31. One wonders then if the same can be said of a 5 put together by a 1 and 4 (14).

In 1898 a prophetic story, eerily and aptly titled "Futility," was published. It was written by a retired merchant navy officer who, of course, had spent much of his life traveling. In his work, a ship called the *Titan* runs into an enormous iceberg. If this weren't enough, the facts concerning the occurrence and the *Titan's* physical description nearly match in uncanny detail those of the *Titanic, fourteen* years later. Was this prophetic or some voodoo hole the writer fell through?

The mysticism surrounding the *Titanic* is considerable. Some of it is like a brush stroke in an abstract painting, obviously part of the whole because it's there but hard to understand. Perhaps this mystical painting at times is only a preliminary drawing or sketch for another canvas, a better work maybe, or just possibly a separate work developed on a theme by the same artist.[147]

Take, for example, the fact that the *Titanic* was not the first White Star ship to have struck an iceberg. The *Royal Standard*, though having masts and sails, was almost newly built and had been advertised as being the latest thing in comfort, having saloons that "are spacious and handsomely furnished."

The ship was *fourteen* days out of Melbourne and heading home when the accident occurred. The captain felt her destruction was inevitable. Yet thirty-five days later she dragged herself into Rio de Janeiro (River of January).148 Truly she had looked both ways seeing life and death.

The clincher, however, was the date of the collision: April 4, 1864, at the time of the Civil War. Hardly a more Hermetic date could have been picked than 4-4-64. Exactly forty-eight years later the Titanic arrived at Southampton.

The *Titanic* was found about 400 miles south of Newfoundland in 13,000[149] feet of water on September 1 (MP), 1985, when a small, remote-controlled submarine came upon one of its boilers. This could be seen when an image was flashed back to the monitoring ship. Later a small twenty-eight-inch camera allowed those aboard to see below decks and into the wreck itself.

In mythology, Hermes sent a winged ram with golden fleece (flying, ram) in answer to the prayers of a mother whose son was to be sacrificed. The ram itself was later sacrificed, and Jason and the Argonauts, aboard the ship *Argo*, set out to fetch its golden fleece.

Indeed it's curious brush strokes that the remote-controlled submarine first spotting the Titanic will be called the Argo, the twenty-eight-inch camera, *Jason*—especially when Hermes is the god of graveyards; his son, the herald of the Argonauts; and the ship that rescued the 705 survivors was called *Carpathia*. There are Carpathian mountains in central Europe, and maybe this ship was named for them. But Carpathian also refers to the Greek island of Karpathos between Rhodes and Crete.150 Why then this ship?

As the *Queen Mary* held the record for carrying troops in World War II (Hermes Agonius-context), the *Olympic* held the record for World War I. Queen Elizabeth II (Elizabeth *Alexandra* Mary) was born *April 21*, 1926. Her preferred sport is riding horses. Before ascending the throne, she married Philip,151 a former Prince of Greece born on Corfu. Jacqueline Bouvier Kennedy married Aristotle Socrates Onassis on his private island of Skorpios off the coast of Greece.

On October 21, 1520, Magellan discovered the straits named after him. The *Constitution* was launched on October 21, 1797, on October 21, 1966, Aberfan, the black iceberg. Thus October 21, 1986 was an appropriate date, all things considered, when President Reagan signed the "Titanic Maritime Memorial Act" into law. Though the *Titanic* lies in international waters, it's the resting place, a graveyard, for 1,523. Objects are being brought up. Who knows what the final outcome will be?

I had just finished writing about Hermes' hand in sinking the *Titanic*. The idea seemed viable to me, but would anybody else buy it? Then as if to dispel any doubt, the following information appeared:

The infamous Nero ordered the sculptor Zenodorus to cease work on a statue of *Hermes* in Gaul and return to Rome to make a statue of himself, the emperor.152 What a fool Nero must have been to stop this work to feed his own megalomania. The brushstrokes throughout Nero's life identify Hermes.

Born in *Anti*um, Italy, on December 15, 37, Nero became the fifth and last emperor in the Julio-Claudian line. His father died when he was three, and his mother, a cunning bitch, married the old emperor to put her son upon the throne. This she succeeded in doing. The problem was that Nero learned too well from her. When she later threatened to have him deposed and to put the former emperor's true son Britannicus on the throne, Nero had Britannicus murdered. This was in 55. In the following years, he dispatched his mother; his divorced first wife, Octavia; and his second wife, Poppaea. The latter was accomplished by kicking her to death when she was pregnant—might as well make a clean sweep!

Certainly the fire in 64 (8 x 8, a Thoth/Hermes number) following the murders nearly did. It lasted for nine days. Only four of the fourteen regions of Rome escaped without damage.[153] Following this, the Christians were scapegoats. Both St. Paul (who had torn his clothes at Lystra when taken for Hermes and later curiously was stoned and thought to be dead) and St. Peter were believed to have been executed in Nero's persecution.

Much of his life, Nero was interested in horse racing and singing. Fearing assassination, he took off for Greece. There he scandalized the Romans by making much of Greek culture and by taking part in *Olympic games* and other *competitions*. The Greeks, who were adept at stroking, awarded him first prize in any event in which he seriously competed. He reciprocated by giving Greece its freedom.

In danger of losing his throne, he returned to Rome in 68, where he found he had been deserted by everyone. Instead of rejoicing, he committed suicide. But only shortly before, Nero made a remark that through the centuries must have seemed supremely conceited and fatuous. Now I wonder if, in a brilliant brush stroke, it could be much more cryptic: "What an artist disappears with me!"[154]

The lifetime of the *Olympic* was in "striking contrast to" her relative the *Titanic*. One of the *Olympic*'s commanders spoke of her as "the finest ship in my estimation that has ever been built or ever will be." (Wade, Wynn Craig, *The Titanic: End of a Dream*, Rawson Wade Publishers, Inc., New York, 1979).

When drawing the April parallel between events in the last month of the Civil War and the month the *Titanic* sailed, I was surprised to notice the date was April 10, 1992. The period had snuck up on me. Great grandfather clock had been dead for one hundred twenty-seven years. The five-day period passed, however, with nothing momentous happening. Or did it?

In Zafferna Etnea, Sicily, lava erupted out of its boundary of Mt. Etna and flowed in tunnels of destructive paths. These boundaries in turn had to be broken or redirected.[155]

In Chicago, Illinois, at 0600 April 13th, the Ides, water broke through a boundary into a turn of the century rail-tunnel network which hadn't been used for decades and flooded basements in the heart of the city. This was eighty years, nearly to the day, from the flooding of the *Titanic*. If Captain Smith had been negligent in not heeding the warnings of other captains about the icebergs, so Chicago's transportation commissioner, who was in charge of public works, was negligent by not acting sooner on the April 2nd memorandum from the city's chief bridge engineer that the "wall failure should be repaired immediately." It was later estimated that total cost of the damage could reach a billion dollars, but, the mayor pointed out, there was not a single loss of life or injury. Lincoln, of course, is buried in Springfield. Earlier the Donner Party took off from Illinois, the state where Grant would receive his colonelcy.

The insult to the Olympians was the main reason the *Titanic* sank, and Hermes carried out their decree. But in the sinking there was also the personal message that went along with him being a chthonic god, the god of graves, death.

Superstition since time immemorial has dictated the living show proper respect for the dead and not disturb their graves. Though museums and archeologists might think differently, they aren't immune to this. The numbers in the year 1912 add up to *13 and 12* is a transposition of *21.* All these are numbers associated with the Parentalia, a period for honoring the dead.

As an Egyptologist, Margaret Murray must have disturbed a few graves in her day. Could she have been related to Douglas Murray? The name seems to have been singled out for two meddlers who either didn't know what they were doing or what they were talking about. In either case, the name is like a cryptic brand, containing most the letters of Mercury: *MURRY. C, A,* and *E* are the only ones which differ, as if a sign or warning were: See *AE* or perhaps sea Aegean. Then the name Murray is derived from the Celtic *muir* and Welsh *mor*, which means "the sea," and Douglas comes from the Celtic and means "grey."[156] Grey is said to be spoken of the sea when it's not illuminated by the sun.

The old Roman name for Egypt[157] is AEgyptus. Thus in 1910[158] we find Douglas Murray (Grey Sea) in Cairo purchasing the case and mummified remains of a 1600 B.C. princess who had lived in Thebes, the ancient capital of Upper Aegyptus. He was very pleased for having made the acquisition. Shortly after, however, he learned the person who'd sold the case and remains to him strangely had died and the princess had belonged to a strong-and-feared religious cult. Whatever that was I don't know, though there's little doubt she believed in Thoth, the god of reckoning and judgment, for before dying, she placed a curse on anybody who disturbed her tomb.

Being a seasoned Egyptologist and having heard many such stories about curses, Douglas Murray could only pooh-pooh this. How could any intelligent person take such drivel seriously? In just a few days, however, he would be given a rather traumatic lesson toward becoming a believer. He went on a hunting trip, and his gun fired, wounding him so that his forearm (four) had to be amputated—and, of course, his wrist and five fingers went along with the procedure, this variation on "MENE, MENE, TEKEL, and PARSIN" (Dan 5:24–28). It was an appropriate object lesson for that part of the world. Yet there's doubt that Douglas Murray—for all his seasoning—ever thought of himself as part of a thievery link, which he was in a sense.

He decided to return to England. On the voyage home, two of his companions died suddenly. Then later he heard that two of his Egyptian workers had died mysteriously.[159] So he did a rather foolish thing, which seemed to characterize him throughout: Instead of accepting the loss of money he had paid, turning around and returning the mummy to its resting place, he reasoned that if he could just sell it to someone else, he could get back what he paid for it and maybe more, while passing on the curse to the next buyer. In a way he was right, but it didn't work out quite as he expected. No sooner had a woman agreed to purchase it than her mother died, her boyfriend left her, and she became critically ill. At this time, her lawyer advised her to renege on the deal and return the mummy to Murray.

Still Murray couldn't reason that the only course for a man of integrity was to return the mummy to its tomb. He decided to present it to the British Museum, pass on the curse, while making a few points at the same time. But an Egyptologist and a photographer working at the museum both died suddenly. The museum didn't want it!

At long last, he found a fool museum in New York that agreed to take it. The trumpeting of the *Titanic* as the unsinkable new queen really cut no ice as the mummy princess and over one thousand five hundred passengers sank into the grey sea on the *fourth* month, *fifteenth* day, 1912.

Chapter Eighteen

The Miss Universe pageant had been held in Long Beach, California, for as long as I could remember. This serves as an annual replay of Helen, femme fatale and endless squabbles over who is really the most beautiful in the universe. Then after the selection, the disappointment, jealousy, envy, detraction, and bitterness which follows make it all less beautiful. But in 1959, Hermes Agonius (contest) decided to move it to Miami, Florida,[160] a state where the later Latin invasion was a natural progression. Florida resembles Italy, being surrounded on three sides by water. It was there that Ponce de Leon sought the fountain of youth, and indeed Florida resembles a phallus more than any other state.

Long Beach, surrounding the independent city of Signal Hill, had its oil, which was enough. As if planned, the oil discovery on Signal Hill in 1921 gave both cities an edge when the Depression came eight years later. Travel and commerce go hand in hand. Hermes would use petroleum (L. petra/rock + oleum/oil) products to run the ships, planes, diesel locomotives, cars, and trucks. He would teach a few to steal legally and cunningly what rightfully belonged to all.[161]

Not only a god of wealth, Hermes, as the messenger, was over communication, so the name Signal Hill came naturally. In the early days it had been used as a lookout and signal point. Missionary fathers of San Gabriel warned of Indian parties and robberies. Ranchers watched their cattle and sheep grazing below. The surname Hermes Nomius refers to shepherds and fields.

Officially it appears to have gotten the name Signal Hill on February 5, 1905 (SY).[162] No one seems to know why for a time it was called another name,[163] yet this is easy. Among favorite offerings to Hermes was cake. And so what could be more appropriate to the god of weights and measures than Pound Cake Hill?

Inside Long Beach Harbor, oil-well islands and rock and earth erections for all to see were also phallic symbols. But since the people of today think of themselves as being so much purer than those in ancient times, the oil wells had to be camouflaged to look like high-rise apartments. Okay, he would go along with that. As a god of disguise and deception, he wasn't just a tutelary deity of a few but over everyone. Rainbow pier then was symbolic, a magnate perhaps, as well as being a salute to Iris, who had nearly the same functions, and the Latin incursion, as with Florida, was a natural progression. It wasn't important to Hermes that most of the oil-well "buildings" sticking up from the rocks were painted pink and orange. They could have been colored just as well black, brown, yellow, red, terracotta, or whatever. See your ACLU.

It's been pointed out previously that there seems to be a 4:5 relationship with the Sun and Mercury, Hermes and Apollo. The job designation number when building the *Queen Mary*, which has three stacks, was 534. At launching she was painted a silver grey and red.[164]

When she got old, she was spared a possible death by salvage. The city of Long Beach purchased her from Cunard Lines to be used as a hotel-restaurant, convention center, and tourist attraction. Had it not been for a California Supreme Court decision that the city's share of tideland oil must be used only for harbor improvement, Long Beach couldn't have scraped together the money to buy her. William J. Duncan rightfully called this a "strange ruling."[165] In light of the discovery of oil in 1921, the ruling might have been even stranger than he thought, if part of a cabala.

What could have been better as additional monuments to Hermes? The world-famous *Spruce Goose*, even if only a mile-or-more bird, represented *flight* and enormous wealth and, indirectly, gambling.

At least two mysterious events in occult genealogy had occurred long before the *Queen Mary* was constructed:

First, hadn't Queen Mary been Princess Mary of Teck,[166] generally known as "Princess May?"[167] Again the month of May was named for Maia, and it's the month of the snake. It was the month of the year when there were the most celebrations to Hermes, and both Hermes and Maia were honored in ancient Rome on May 15 when merchants dropped small amounts of water on themselves and their merchandise for success.

Second, Prince George and his brother began their first voyage on the HMS *Bacchante*,[168] "an unarmored corvette," on September 17 (MP), 1879. In July 1881,[169] Prince George (according J.N. Dalton, his tutor) and twelve others saw a strange *red* glow, an apparition of the *Flying Dutchman*. Spars, masts, and sails of the brig were clearly seen two hundred yards distant. Then shortly later the phantom ship disappeared. I'd tend to discount this as a flight of imagination had not 1) the time been reported as 4:00 A.M. when the ordinary seaman on the forecastle saw the ghost ship, and 2) this same seaman dropped to his death from the "*fore*topmast *crosstrees*" that same morning at 10:45 A.M.

412

Princess May (fifth month) was nicknamed after the month she was born on May 26 (MP), 1867. Prince George (later George V) proposed to her on May 3 (Wednesday), 1893, and married her a little over two months later on July 6, 1893. If the date of July 1881 is correct for the sighting of the *Flying Dutchman*, then their marriage took place in the same month the thirteen had seen the apparition but one snake cycle later in 1893.

The *Queen Mary* began her maiden voyage on May 26, 1936, Queen Mary's sixty-ninth birthday. She won in *contest* the Blue Riband for *speed* in 1938 and held this record until 1952. Transporting 810,730 G.I.s to Europe during World War II, she broke all records before or since for carrying travelers. Considering the circumstances, she'd led a charmed life.

In 1942, however, she rammed the cruiser HMS *Curacoa*. The *Queen Mary*'s captain had to make the decision whether to stop and pick up survivors, risking the lives of ten thousand in water where enemy submarines might be lurking, or to continue on. He'd be damned if he did, damned if he didn't. He chose not to stop. Thus there were at least 329 lives lost when the *Curacoa*[170] sank at 55.50 N 08.38 W, or Hermetic numbers *55.5* N. *8.38* W. The hole in the *Queen Mary* was plugged with cement and then later fitted with a new bow plate in Boston, Massachusetts. Quincy, of course, is within the Boston metropolitan area.

In 1969, the year I began sailing in the merchant marines, the *Queen Mary* was permanently moored at Pier J in Long Beach, California. On February 11, 1982 (twelve to thirteen years later), the *Spruce Goose* was put adjacent to her.

Of course it could be an elaborate hoax, a deception to increase business, yet it's said that footprints and other indications of a ghost or ghosts have been found aboard the *Queen Mary*. If true, a conjecture is that it or they came through the hole caused by the collision with the HMS *Curacoa* in 1942. Once that was plugged, the ghost (or ghosts) was trapped, much the same as if the *lapis manalis* had been used to close the entrance from one world to another. Or was it meant to be a constant thorn in her side that she could have stopped but didn't? The dead, footprints, ghost/ghosts, and museum (a connection the past and dead) suggest Hermes.

"That's nonsense!" you say.

Okay, but how do you explain then that the *Queen Mary* (Princess May), the queen ship of travelers, the contest winner and beauty queen, began her final voyage to Long Beach by being escorted partway out from Southampton, England, by the aircraft carrier HMS *HERMES*, the largest of several warships that day?

Two carriers named for Hermes—one in each war—were lost, perhaps fitting the Hermes persona of sacrifice, so that Britain went on to be a winner each time. In 1913 an old cruiser named *Hermes* was converted to provide for seaplanes. This was the first British carrier. On Halloween day, October 31, 1914, the ship, commanded by Capt. C.R. *Lambe*, was sunk by a U-boat in the Straits of Dover. About forty-four of her crew were lost. The other *Hermes* was ordered in July 1917 (SY) and became the world's first aircraft carrier designed as such. Though it had been drawn up to carry twenty aircraft, it could accommodate only twelve in 1939. She carried no planes, however, when sunk by Japanese divebombers on April 9, 1942, seventy-seven years after Appomattox. Also sunk that day was her escort-destroyer *Vampire*.

The *Hermes*—escorting the *Queen Mary* above—must have been the light fleet carrier which would later be Admiral Woodward's flagship in the 1982 Falklands War. Eventually she was sold to India and became the *Virant*.

Chapter Nineteen

There's no doubt that Joseph Patrick Kennedy was under a Hermes influence. He was born in Boston, Massachusetts, on September 6 (MP), 1888,[171] fifteen days after my mother's birth and four days before my father's. He graduated from Harvard in 1912, the same year my mother graduated from Stanford. A determined man, Kennedy vowed he would be a millionaire when he was thirty-five. His son John Fitzgerald Kennedy was the thirty-fifth president, the fourth to be assassinated.

Fitzgerald[172] was the maiden name of Rose E., whom Joseph married in 1914. She was the daughter of a Boston mayor known as "Honey Fitz." They had nine children: four sons and five daughters (4:5). Four of the children will die in early adulthood or at the height of their careers—two in airplane crashes and two by assassins. One daughter, mentally retarded, will not live at home.

It was almost as if to achieve wealth and distinction, Joseph and Rose Kennedy had to pay a stiff price. They were not aware of this, of course. They weren't evil people, bargaining away the health, happiness, and/or lives of their children; in fact, they were far from it. But like it or not, there's some truth to what has been termed the "Kennedy neurosis."[173]

Also it wasn't only the sadness and misfortune in the Kennedy lives that made me think Joseph P. Kennedy was in the Hermes sphere but other facts as well. The only other family in American politics to be so prominent in American history was that of the Adams of Quincy, which was also under a Hermes influence too but not so negatively.

Joseph Kennedy became the assistant manager of the *Fore* River shipyard at *Quincy* in 1917 (SY). He worked as a manager of the Boston office of Haden, *Stone,* and Co., an investment banking firm. He was for a short period in 1937 chairman of the *Maritime* Commission. And in 1937 or 1938, depending on the source, he became ambassador to Britain, a link as clear as that of "Honey Fitz"[174] to Hermes eloquence. Joseph Kennedy was ambassador in 1938 when the *Queen Mary* was in contest the Blue Riband for speed.

If it had just been Joseph Kennedy's karma alone, things in the Kennedy family might not have been so mercurial. Unfortunately John F. Kennedy was born May 29 (MP), 1917 (SY). This fanned the fire of the blessing-curse too, along with the fact that Joseph Kennedy son's took for his wife Jacqueline Bouvier, an earth-snake born on July 28, 1929, in Southampton,[175] New York. The problem was further complicated in that they married on September 12 (MP), 1953 (SY).

They had two children before he became president in 1961. Then in 1963 (which, outside of my birth year, the same as Jackie's, had been my worst) their luck ran sour. Patrick Kennedy died two days after birth on August 7. On November 22 in Dallas, Texas, while traveling in a motorcade (with four policemen riding motorcycles, two on each side like flanking wings of a caduceus), the president was assassinated. They limousine he and five others[176] were traveling in was "a specially designed 1961 Lincoln convertible."[177-A] Governor Connolly of Texas, a fourth child, was seriously wounded and contributed the fourth or fifth ingredient (depending on whether you include Joseph Kennedy or Rose as one), being born on February 27, 1917,[177-B] the same year as the president.

There was only a half chance in six that one person riding in the Lincoln would be a snake. So the odds would be much less that there were three. It seemed relevant too to try to find out when the two secret service agents were born.

Whether they had or hadn't wanted to, Special Agent William R. Greer and Assistant Special Agent Roy H. Kellerman had become public figures beyond the fact that they were federal employees. A simple birth certificate statistic—in relation to the tons of classified information concerning the Kennedy assassination the public wasn't allowed to see in the land of the free—shouldn't have been such a big deal to obtain.

The FBI wrote that it didn't have the information but suggested I might try the U.S. Secret Service. The U.S. Secret Service said it didn't have the information but referred me to the Association of Former Agents of the U.S. Secret Service. AFAUSSS answered that it didn't have the information but that both men were now deceased. National Archives wrote:

> Neither the National Archives, nor any other Federal agency maintains a record of the birth dates of Federal employees. This type of personal information is not relevant to the job performance of employees, and is therefore not held by agencies.

Strange! On nearly every government form I filled out in my life, I had to write down the date of birth.

An obvious Hermes connection was Jackie's love of horses, especially when she was younger, as well as Caroline's Macaroni, the famous horse of the Kennedy White House days. The name suggests "Yankee Doodle," an allusion to "a feather[178] in his hat," possibly the winged hat of Mercury, becoming more believable in the context of macaroni, derived from the old Italian *maccaroni*. Still other associations were the family's home in *Palm* Beach, Florida, and the fact that Jackie was a patron of the arts.

Doesn't the turn her life eventually took then seem curious? With well over two hundred million people in the United States, and hundreds of millions more with the populations of Canada, Great Britain, Germany, France, Italy, etc. (not forgetting the hundreds of millions in Latin America and other countries in the world), Jackie will choose a second husband from Greece (marrying him on the island of Skorpios, meaning scorpion and derived from Greek, at the foot of Hermes/Mercury was a scorpion), a country with a population of a little over 8.5 million at the time and which has about the population of Cuba today.

Then as if to further emphasize the work of an unseen hand, he wasn't just any Greek but *Aristotle Socrates* Onassis, born in Turkey (home of Troy) and one of the richest men in the world (*sudden wealth* for Jackie), a *merchant* tycoon who constructed supertankers and owned *Olympic* Airways (See May 1, 1898).

The writer of the president's death, as well as the misfortune and death of others, showed us in no uncertain terms that all the world's indeed a stage, and we watched a Greek tragedy. There were inexorable forces at work throughout.

It's possible that demure, sweet, little Jackie (indeed she was all that: Jacqueline, Jackal-ine: Anubis>Hermanubis>cunning) had more psychic immunity or zap power than any of them—a remark which might be construed by those living in the Camelot era as in very poor taste, or by those who came after, as gallows humor. But if there are two levels we deal with, it's important not to miss anything.

Items from Jackie's estate were auctioned off at Sotheby's in April 1996; the size of the sudden wealth to her children was beyond anybody's expectation.

Year of Death
Patrick Bouvier Kennedy, 1963
John F. Kennedy, 1963
Robert Kennedy, 1968
Mary Jo Kopechne, 1969
Aristotle Onassis, 1975
Maria Callas, 1977
Christine Onassis, 1988
Jacqueline Kennedy Onassis, 1994
Rose Kennedy, 1995

Aristotle Onassis was sixty-nine at the time of his death, and Maria Callas was fifty-three, so it's possibly not appropriate to include them. Rose Kennedy (born July 22, 1890) died on January 22, 1995, at the age of

104. For both Jackie and Rose, it was either a bittersweet blessing or just another type of curse—or Hermes manifesting himself in some respects through them.[179-A]

Two snakes who seemed to have been a matched pair were Greta Garbo, born September 18 (MP), 1905, and Howard Hughes, born December 24, 1905. Both went to Hollywood and became internationally famous. Each in the end found it easier to go into seclusion than to cope with relationships. Hughes died *April 5*, 1976, and Garbo, April 15 (the anniversary of Lincoln's death and the *Titanic*'s sinking), 1990, about fourteen years after Hughes.

Other famous 1929 earth-snakes besides Jacqueline Kennedy were Roger Bannister, Audrey Hepburn, and Grace Kelly.

Roger Bannister, born March 23, 1929, was the first runner to break the four-minute mile (3:59:4 = 21). He wrote a book called the *First Four Minutes* (Hermes: number 4, speed, swiftness, competition, young athletes, writers, and physicians). He will become a neurologist and be knighted by Queen Elizabeth, whose coronation took place in 1953, the snake-year John and Jackie were married.

Audrey Hepburn was born May 4, 1929, and will play a princess in *Roman Holiday*. (See pages 465-466.)

Grace Kelly was born on November 12, 1929, and died at age fifty-two in an automobile accident on September *14* (MP), 1982. Her first film was called *Fourteen Hours*. She became Princess Grace of Monaco.

Though not a snake, tennis legend Billie Jean Moffitt King was probably in the Hermes sphere. She was born in Long Beach, California, on November 22, 1943, twenty years to the day before John F. Kennedy was assassinated.

Everybody walks, but there are what you call walkers. Lincoln was a walker in his youth (see page 361). Then sixty years following Lincoln's birth came Gandhi, born in 1869, the year the Suez Canal opened, not too far from the Red Sea through which the people of Israel walked on dry ground and walked and wandered in the desert for forty years. As a boy in India, Gandhi seemed to enjoy taking long, solitary walks. In 1893 (SY), he traveled to South Africa and led civil-rights protests. Later, back in India, he walked sometimes hundreds of miles. Martin Luther King, Jr., arrived last in 1929 and did his share of walking in marches.

All three were wine from the same mountain. By freeing the slaves, Lincoln had influenced King's life, though indirectly. Gandhi had a direct influence on it. Each was a leader who had concern about freedom. All were assassinated. Gandhi was a fourth child. Both Lincoln and King had four children. It's connected, much more than coincidence. Since their religious beliefs or affiliations were diverse, it transcends individual religion.

The following is a summary of snakes or near snakes in politics who were at risk:

WILLIAM HENRY HARRISON

(February 9, 1773–April 4, 1841) Died of pneumonia after thirty-two days of presidency: March 4–April 4, 1841. See May 25, 1878.

ABRAHAM LINCOLN

(February 12, 1809–April 15, 1865) Year-approximate snake. Assassinated.

MOHANDAS GANDHI

(October 2, 1869–January 30, 1948) Assassinated.

FRANKLIN DELANO ROOSEVELT

(January 30, 1882–April 12, 1945) A metal-snake president in place when the U.S. entered World War II in 1941, a metal-snake year and who will be elected to a fourth term. Nearly assassinated on Lupercalia February 15, 1933, at Miami, Florida. Second time around (four years previously at Miami), Mayor Anton Cermak of Chicago killed.

HUEY PIERCE LONG, JR.

(August 30, 1893–September 10, 1935) Born and died in Mercury periods. Assassinated.

MAO TSE-TUNG

(December 26, 1893–September 9, 1976) Died of old age in Mercury period. The month after his death, his wife and her associates (known as the "Gang of Four") were arrested.

JOHN F. KENNEDY

(May 29, 1917–November 22, 1963) Born on Memorial Day Eve, a Mercury period. Assassinated.

INDIRA GANDHI

(November 19, 1917–October 31, 1984) Assassinated. Though her son Rajiv Gandhi (born August 20, 1944) wasn't a snake, he did succeed her on Halloween, and like President John F. Kennedy, he ploughed ahead on the Feast of the Dead

(October 31 and November 1 being its equivalent) and was later assassinated. He had been deluged with flowers. It was believed, though not certain, that the bomb which killed him was planted in a bouquet or wreath. Since Rajiv was a pilot, the date of his death on May 21 (the beginning of the Mercury period and when Linbergh landed near Paris exactly sixty-four [8x8] years earlier), 1991, is curious in relation to Obsequies Chic and Capone-O'Banion era in Chicago. The storminess in the lives of Indira Gandhi's sons was similar to that of the Kennedys. Sanjay died in an airplane crash, as did Joseph P. Kennedy, Jr., and his sister Kathleen. Hermes, god of flight. Two assassinations per family.

MARTIN LUTHER KING, JR. (January 15, 1929–April 4, 1968) Year-approximate snake (period February 10, 1929–January 29, 1930). Technically both he and Lincoln were dragons. Assassinated 4-4-1968. "I have a *dream....*"

The Four Assassinated Presidents of the United States

1. *Abraham Lincoln.* Born February 12, 1809. Shot in theater by actor (eloquence).
2. *James A. Garfield.* Wasn't a snake by birth. An 1880 lithograph by Currier and Ives (see *Encyclopedia Americana*) shows him as a farmer, stepping on two snakes (footprints and totem-curse-blessing) and "cutting a swath to the White House." Strikingly he was inaugurated on March 4, 1881; shot *four* months later (July 2nd) by an assassin in a railroad station (travelers); and died on September 19 (MP), 1881, a snake year.
3. *William McKinley.* Wasn't a snake by birth. He was shot in a Temple of Music (Hermes, one of the gods of music) in Buffalo (herds) on September 6 and died *eight* days later on September 14

(both days in a Mercury period) at age fifty-eight, having been inaugurated when fifty-four.

4.   *John F. Kennedy*. Was born a fire-snake on May 29 (MP), 1917. He was shot while in a motorcade (traveler).

It's axiomatic that snakes shouldn't be gamblers. Edgar Allan Poe, a year-approximate snake, didn't have much luck nor did I. To this might be added a second axiom that snakes or their relatives should never go into politics. And if they do, they must not like it. Even friends (including snakes) of those non-snake relatives of snakes in politics can suffer.

Had it not been for his brother, Robert F. Kennedy probably wouldn't have been appointed attorney general, a job, however, he was much more fitted for than becoming a president. For he had a knack of polarizing those he had differences with: Lyndon Johnson, J. Edgar Hoover, and Jimmy Hoffa. Fidel Castro and the wives of Diem and Nhu probably didn't have much use for him either. Scandal surfacing after Robert Kennedy's death was that he was involved in the death of Marilyn Monroe (actress, eloquence). This seems far-fetched, though there's little doubt because of the nepotism of his appointment to attorney general that he would have covered his brother's tracks when and if he could. Shortly after midnight on June 5, 1968, he was shot by three bullets, one entering his brain. He died twenty-five hours later on June 6, the anniversary of D-Day.

Ted Kennedy, a fourth son and the last to be born on one generation, seemed to have escaped the curse, other than what happened to his relatives. Then one day in 1969, his chances for the presidency nose-dived when he drove his car off the bridge at Chappaquiddick Island, Massachusetts. His companion in the car, Mary Jo Kopechne, drowned. She was twenty-eight years old at the time and so likely was a snake born in 1941.

Zulfikar Ali Bhutto was the head of the government of Pakistan from 1971 to 1977. He was hanged by Zia-ul-Haq, who was assassinated in an airplane (flight) explosion. Zulfikar's daughter Benazir Bhutto (born June 21, 1953, a snake, the year of the coronation of Queen Elizabeth II [born April 21] and when John F. Kennedy married Jacqueline) became prime minister in 1988.

On September 20, 1996, Murtaza Bhutto, the estranged brother of Prime Minister Benazir Bhutto, was killed in a gunfight with Karachi police.

William Howard Taft once wrote his wife, "Politics when I am in it, makes me sick." Nevertheless, she was ambitious. Largely through her urging and that of others he ran for president. His father had been a judge, and he himself had been one before running (Thoth, a god of judgment, reckoning, and measurement). Possibly because he thoroughly hated politics and because he believed that "no tendency is quite so

421

strong in human nature as the desire to lay down rules of conduct for other people," William Howard Taft escaped the snake rule, having been born on September 15 (MP), 1857. Also he was needed as a former snake president and current Chief Justice of the Supreme Court (appointed 1921) for the dedication of the Lincoln Memorial on May 30, 1922 (2122). So you'll know what's said is true, Taft was the heaviest of all presidents before or since (reckoning, measurement), weighing three hundred pounds or more. He had a heart attack later in life, dying on March 8, 1930.

Lord Buddha's name is derived from Budhuha or Budahu, which is the planet Mercury's name. May 8, 1963, was celebrated in Vietnam as Buddha's 2527th anniversary. Buddhist priests and followers gathered in the city of Hue to protest the banning of their flag and their use of a local radio station, in front of which they had assembled. They were ordered by President Ngo Dinh Diem's forces to disperse. When they refused, nine were killed.

On May 13, the Hue demonstrators made five demands on the government. Minor concessions were made, but President Diem, a Catholic, called them a "bunch of fools." There were more demonstrations, and one thing led to another. Then on June 11 (MP), 1963, a Buddhist monk, the venerable, old Quang Duc, assumed the lotus position. Another monk poured gasoline on him, then stepped away while Quang Duc set himself on fire. This immolation (derived from the Latin meaning "sprinkle with sacrificial meal") was seen by millions of horror-stricken, television viewers as he eventually fell over and continued to burn. Madam Nhu, the wife of the secret police chief and sister-in-law to President Diem, callously referred to it as "barbecue a monk." Other suicides followed.

Because the U.S. felt it couldn't fight a war where the leader didn't have the backing of his people, it withdrew its support of Diem. This served as his death warrant. Henry Cabot Lodge, our ambassador, acquiesced to the coup d'état by Diem's generals. (On November 1, 1950, an attempt was made to assassinate President Harry Truman. Though he was unharmed, two Puerto Rican nationalists killed one guard and injured two others.) The next day Diem and his brother were murdered by junior officers, or indirectly by the U.S. government. It's important that the people of the United States realize this.

President John F. Kennedy was ultimately responsible for the action of his government, and the murder of the two brothers wasn't much different from King David writing in a letter to Joab, "Set Uriah in the forefront of the hardest fighting, and then draw back from him, that he may be struck down, and die." When later John F. Kennedy was assassinated, Madam Nhu commented that it was retribution. What can't be disputed is that the two brothers, Diem and Nhu, were murdered on November second, the day following the coup. President Kennedy was murdered in Dallas (D=delta; Hermes 4) on November 22, 1963 (2122). Four (4) to five

(5) years later, his brother and former Attorney General Robert F. Kennedy was murdered on the anniversary of D-Day, a day of death.

Malcolm X referred to the John F. Kennedy assassination as "a case of the chickens coming home to roost." By this he meant that blacks had long since been victims of violence by whites. Though he probably wasn't referring to the coup in South Vietnam on November 1 (equivalent to the Feast of the Dead) and the murder of Diem and Nhu on the following day, the statement was ironic in this respect, as well as the fact that Malcolm X will be the victim of violence by black men on the Feast of the Dead.

Having been to Korea, I didn't side with the Vietnam protestors, though feeling the war was a tragic mistake. The ARVN (Army of the Republic of Vietnam) forces, which were about the same in number as those in North Vietnam, were better trained and equipped. If ARVN forces didn't have sufficient motivation, it was a terrible thing to expect our G.I.'s to be more motivated, the fall guys for the politicians' folly.

It amazes me when we win a war that we were better, like in a football game. Seldom is it said, "God was with us." If we lose, never is it said, "God was against us and why?" It was, rather, just a mistake: poor planning, training, logistics, etc. So maybe we deserve what we get.[179-B]

Perhaps there were signs to let us know the way the wind was blowing before we entered Vietnam in earnest. *Chi* in Japanese means wisdom, shrewd, or blood.

> Ho Chi Minh
> Ho (T*h*oth) Chi Min*h* (H-M: Hermes-Mercury)
> Ho Chi = 5
> Minh = 4

He was born on May 19, 1890, thirty-five years to the day before Malcolm X. H-M was fifty-five when he proclaimed the Independence of the Democratic Republic of Vietnam on September 2 (MP), 1945 (World War II began on September 3 [MP], 1939), the same day Japan signed the documents of surrender.

In 1954 the defeat of the French at Dien Bien Phu was decisive. It marked the end of an eight-year struggle by the French to hold their Indochina colonial empire. The battle of Dien Bien Phu began on March 13, 1954. When it was over in less than two months, the French had fifteen thousand killed, wounded, and missing in action. As if synchronized someway, the battle ended on May 7, 1954 (see pages 482-483). May 7, 1945, was the day Germany surrendered. On July 21, 1954, the Geneva Agreements led to a cease fire and the end of the French rule in Vietnam, Cambodia, and Laos.

In 1911, H-M got a job as kitchen help on a French passenger liner. Possibly later he became a cook there or on some other ship as he sailed (traveled) for over three years. In 1917, the year John F. Kennedy was born, he settled for awhile in *Paris*, France. He was an avid reader. In keeping with the Hermes deception, he used some fifteen aliases in his lifetime—the last being Ho Chi Minh, the "enlightened" leader of Vietminh. He died on September 2 (MP), 1969, but the date of his death was put as September 3 (MP) so that it wouldn't coincide with the national holiday.

Saigon fell on April 30 (a Wednesday), 1975, the anniversary of the date Hitler died thirty years previously, i.e., a date which was once favorable for us was now so for North Vietnam. The fall of Saigon came just in time for the May Day celebration, the later Memorial Day in the U.S. April-May suggests 45, peace-burial.

The U.S. merchant ship *MAYA*guëz was captured on May 12, 1975, in the Gulf of Siam by Cambodian patrol boats. The U.S. bombed Cambodia. On May 14 (Wednesday), the *Mayaguëz* was recaptured by U.S. marines. Statistics vary, but some say fifteen marines were killed and fifty wounded—a sacrifice for Maia?

There was clowning about being in Vietnam, making a joke about participating, if you can call it that, while serving food in the bowels of a freighter as safe as in Ft. Knox. If remaining in the service, I almost certainly would have been sent to Vietnam. Maybe 1963 wasn't such a bad year after all: I wasn't meant to have an active role in the war.

Did the priest's immolation have anything to do with its outcome? I woke up in the middle of the night a few months back, long before considering any of this. In the air about four feet from my pillow was the head and shoulders of a man wearing a saffron robe. His hair, though closely cropped, was not shaved. His cheeks were slightly pitted. Clear, dark eyes regarded me, and there was no doubt he was a priest. Only when he seemed certain he was plainly seen did he vanish.

Those who like to regard themselves as being in the "sane asylum" call this hypnopompic, the transition between sleep and wakening. By giving it a fancy name and explanation (be that what it may), they have debunked it to the status of a mirage.

Chapter Twenty

About the only bastards in the world who have an excuse before God are those of illegitimate birth. The self-made bastards are ones who never bothered to learn much about their origins—where, for example, their parents and grandparents were born, etc. If you hadn't bothered getting the facts straight in your mind, then why should those deceased care much about you? Knowing is consistent with the Parentalia.

Annie, my maternal grandmother, had lingered on with cancer for at least nine months before her death on October 19, 1912. So her passing shouldn't have come as a surprise, the family having plenty of time to prepare for it, yet the way the death certificate was made out seemed shabby. No informant signed. Lines were drawn through everything where the answers weren't readily available, though possibly as close as the desk in the next room. Her father, Duncan Cameron, was listed; her mother wasn't. No birthdate was given other than to say "Emily L. Duren" was forty-four years old and born in Canada. If her birthday was indeed March 22, 1868 (from another source), then she was actually forty-four to forty-five years old. And was her name really Emily or Annie Laurie, like in the Celtic or Scottish song? Or maybe it was Ann Lee. She was buried in Bakersfield, California (there's no way they could have left out that entry), on October 21, 1912, which was the year the *Titanic* sank and the month and day (1986) President Reagan signed the "Titanic Memorial Act." (If you want to be intelligent, you'll not laugh at this association.)

Undoubtedly what was considered proper respect for the dead was observed: hushed silence, black clothes, flowers, and a nice tombstone or marker as a memorial. But tombstones and graveyards have a way of disappearing, and clearly the death certificate (which would probably outlast either) seemed to reflect the personal attitude of the doctor and/or informant: What good are the silly facts now?

A rough, genealogical worksheet made out inaccurately by an unknown source said that Annie had been born on Prince Edward Island, Canada, and that Margaret "McDonald" was her mother. But with only scanty information I could supply the Prince Edward Island Museum and Heritage Foundation, no definite link could be made where hundreds of Camerons and McDonalds are buried. What with other leads having turned cold too, I decided to give up on the Cameron lineage.

In the meantime, Norma Beth had written on November 6, 1991:

"Did I tell you, RE: family history, that our mothers had twin uncles, Dougal and (Douglas?), one of which was murdered by cattle rustlers in wild and wooly Montana?"

From this I wasn't sure if these uncles were Durens or Camerons and asked Robyn what she knew about it. Her reply is given in part below, and I too vaguely remembered having heard the story she recalled:

> Mother told stories when I was little of her relations in Montana. I thought they were cousins to her. There were two men (I don't remember her saying they were twins), and the ranches were embroiled in range wars over cattle vs. sheep. Our relation (as I remember) had extensive sheep herds/flocks, and the cattlemen up there said sheep ruined the grass for cattle grazing. Thus, the wars. The family used to send the 2 boys/men—1 at a time—to a line shack for months at a stretch to look after their flocks, checking the man out every 2 or 3 weeks to take food and supplies. When someone went to check on the other man, he was dead, shot, but his head was gone and snow had begun to fall. They figured wild animals had carried it away. It [head] was found after snows melted in the spring near the shack. She said once when the family was visiting up there, she and her sisters were looking through the old trunks in the attic and found a skull that was suppose to be Dougal or his brother. Body had long since been buried so family kept the skull. Knowing mother and her dramatics—the skull being kept in the trunk you can take either way.[180] But the range war was true. A library could provide information about the range wars. So, it could have been rustlers or cattlemen on nearby ranches that resented the sheep. That is all true. I mean his death. I always thought their family name was Cameron, but that would make them our grandmother's family; and if they were Granddad Duren's kin, it couldn't be so. I probably got it all mixed up being young when I heard the story. But the death of Dougal or? is true.

426

Chapter Twenty-one

The nineteenth century image of snow, which somehow seems colder than anything we could have today, and the name Dougal or Douglas with their Ds brought to mind the Donner Party. But I couldn't recall if Donner was spelled with one n or two. It was while rereading the account that its eeriness seemed to leap out in new meaning.

George Donner and my great-grandfather George Duren were contemporaries. Not only were their names similar, but each had festering injuries. A chisel had slipped and cut George Donner's right hand, a deadman's hand that probably contributed to his death as much as starvation. George Duren was wounded in his left leg and then got an abscess in his right—a pair of aces.

In spite of hopes and struggles, each would be dead within a year. It was as if the two had been marked someway as most certainly the foot injury marked Lewis Keseberg, who was one of the settlers setting out in April 1846 with the Donner Party. Concerning fate, Keseberg (born May 22, 1814, in Prussia; immigrated to the United States May 22, 1844) would say years later:

> If I believe in God Almighty having to do with the affairs of men, I believe that misfortune which overtook the Donner Party, and the terrible part I was compelled to take in the tragedy, were predestined. On the Hastings Cut-off we were *twenty-eight days in going twenty-one miles*.[181-A] Difficulty and disaster hovered about us from the time we entered upon this cut-off.
>
> One day, while we were traveling on Goose Creek, we saw so many wild geese that I took my shotgun and went hunting. Ordinarily I am not superstitious, but on the morning I felt an overwhelming sense of impending calamity. I mentioned my premonitions to Mrs. Murphy before starting on the hunt.[181-B] Becoming excited with the sport, and eagerly watching the game, I stepped

down a steep bank. Some willows had been burned off, and the short, sharp stubs were sticking up just where I stepped. I had on buckskin moccasins, and one of these stubs ran into the ball of my foot, between the bones and the toes. From this time, until we arrived at Donner Lake, I was unable to walk, or even to put my foot on the ground. The foot became greatly swollen and inflamed, and was exceedingly painful.[182]

Footprints. With most people caught up in some kind of catastrophe, there is in subsequent years the fermentation of superstition, mysticism, and religion. Keseberg was no exception. Yet, as far as I know, he said nothing about his robbery of an Indian's grave, endangering the party. He too should have been superstitious about that.

The delay at Hastings (HS; speed) caused the last of the families to reach Truckee (Donner) Lake on Saturday,[183-A] October 31, 1846 (Halloween, linked to the Feralia), when snow was already on the ground.[183-B] Truckee lies in the Sierra Nevada, Nevada County, California, three miles from the lake and just within the border, or in other words, the last of the party had just crossed a boundary. Reno lies about thirty-five miles northeast. Nevada would become a state of October 31, 1864, a fitting date. Notice the transposition of 6 and 4.

Most were in sorry shape when they arrived. What lay ahead were mountainous barriers. As the snow fell and deepened in November, it was clear the wagons couldn't make it. Though previously the settlers couldn't agree on anything, they agreed on this, that the cattle and mules were to be killed (the cold would preserve the meat), and that they would all walk out. But the snowfall became much worse (estimated at one time to be twenty feet deep), and their hunger and weakened condition increased. Most of the cattle they'd hoped to slaughter wandered off and got lost in the drifts. Perhaps in variation on an ancient theme, they might be thought of as stolen.

The settlers began to starve. They tried to catch fish seen through the ice on the lake, but none would bite. A few mice were caught. They ate these along with bark and twigs, and soon some of the settlers were beginning to die. Finally on December 17, an attempt was made to make it out—"Forlorn Hope," as it was called. Only seven survived the ordeal, and those first seeing them were appalled by their bloody footprints as they dragged along. It was as if a sacrifice had to be made for each step of the way.

Sutter's Fort (now known as Sacramento, meaning sacrament) once alerted sent *four* rescue parties. The first arrived on February 22nd, the Caristia. Not until April 22 was the last survivor brought out. The fourth party had gone in ostensibly on the remote chance that there might be more survivors. They found only one left: Lewis Keseberg. It was rumored that George Donner, who had died, carried with him a considerable amount of money. Unable to find it, they asked Keseberg, who denied any knowledge of it. Only when they put a noose around his neck and tightened it did he tell them where he had hidden the money. He was brought out then.

Of the eighty-seven in the party, forty-seven survived. A different source says forty.[184] But forty being symbolic, it made no difference at one level whether forty survived or forty died. Today U.S. 40 curves around Donner Lake and snakes up Donner Peak to its summit, where at the most exposed part the wind, itself a snake, seldom stops blowing.

Thirty-nine of the original group had been children, and seventeen of those were under the age of six. So far as casualties went, the children fared better than the adults. This might have been due to the nature of the human being to protect and sacrifice for its young, or ....

Shortly after the wagons arrived, they split into two groups: one building crude, makeshift shelters at the lake, the other *five* miles away at Alder Creek. Yet from early times, the alder was considered unlucky and cursed,[185] though sacred to Bran (raven), the Celtic god, and Kronos, a death god. It had been prophesied that Kronos's fall would come from one of his children, so he devoured them. Zeus was spared when Rhea substituted a stone at birth. Later Zeus forced his father to disgorge the children, and the stone came up too. Kronos, the Titan, was cast into Tartarus.

The cannibalism that many in the Donner Party resorted to—and so crossing boundaries to stay alive—was reminiscent of Kronos. Not too far from Donner Lake is a "rocking stone," a local curiosity. The lake perhaps represented Poseidon; the twenty-eight days Lewis Keseberg spoke of, February; and twenty-one miles, the Feralia, the last day of the Parentalia, honoring all dead.[186] While traveling in the morning at Goose Creek, Keseberg saw the geese[187] and had "an overwhelming sense of calamity." He hunted the geese, which, conducting the souls of the dead, are sometimes seen flying in a V formation,[188] suggesting the Roman numeral for five,[189] and which are sacred to Apollo and Hermes. The willow, penetrating Keseberg's foot, is a graveside tree, one of the two kinds Ulysses had seen at the entrance to Hades.[190] It's also associated with Apollo and Hermes, suggesting 4:5 relationship of the two gods, and connected to witches and the fifth month.

Noteworthy is the fact that there was only one family, the Breens, which didn't lose a member. The name Breen is said to come from the Irish "braon," meaning sorrow. Yet braon *does* seem close to Bran.

George Donner is usually named as the leader of the Donner Party. But at least when it set out, the leaders were George and Jacob Donner (Dawner) and James F. Reed. The latter served in the same company as Lincoln in the Black Hawk War. A thought is that Black Hawk in someway had touched him too (see pages 4-5) and possibly through him the Donner Party itself. About midway across Nevada, Reed killed John

Snyder. As punishment, he was banished, later rescuing some of his persecutors.

As stories go, it was said Lewis Keseberg slept with a boy in the Donner Party one night. This mightn't have meant anything, since people without adequate blankets must of necessity in extreme cold sleep together for warmth to survive. However, the following morning the boy was found dead, after which Keseberg is said to have eaten him. Shades of Kronos. Move over cannibal Hannibal Lecter. In a sense, when these things happen, man himself seems to cannibalize the event with his mouth. The dedication of her Oscar (won by Jodie Foster for her performance in *The Silence of the Lambs*) to—among others—"the survivors and pioneers and outcasts" showed great heart and deep thinking. Oddly too, she might have been talking about William Foster of the Donner Party.

On May 10, 1869, in the month of the snake and the year of the earth-snake, and twenty-two years after the last of the Donner Party is supposed to have reached the lake on Halloween, October 31, 1846, the first transcontinental railroad (travel-commerce; each tie a cross-track footprint) was completed, going through the Donner Pass. This was one of five 22s (2 + 2 = 4) occurring. As you recall:

> Hermae busts were mutilated on May 22 in Athens.
> Keseberg was born May 22, 1814 (McGlashan, C.F.).
> Keseberg's U.S. immigration was on May 22, 1844. (McGlashan, C.F.). This was the same year possibly that Duncan Cameron was born and on the Feralia, at least according to the Cascade Courier of January 26, 1933, which gives the date as February 21, 1844.
> The first of four relief parties reached the camp on February 22 (*Collier's Encyclopedia*), the Caristia, or the first relief party left (McGlashan, C.F.).
> The last survivor was brought out on April 22 (*Collier's Encyclopedia*).
> Where U.S. 40 crosses the state line is designated O*m*. This point is also fifteen miles southwest of Reno by following the Truckee River. The emigrant trail turned south, up Cold Creek Canyon, leading to the summit. The stone monument at 22 *m*. shows the place the Donner Party lost this trail.[191]

The above writing had been completed—just as it is—for several months. Then the August 1992 edition of *Nevada* magazine had for its cover a picture of an engine which is now in the Nevada State Railroad Museum in Carson City. The engine, clearly marked in gold on a red background as number 22, had belonged to the Virginia and Truckee Railroad. Shades of Mr. Yerington and Willow Wovoka.

One potato, two potato,
Three potato, four,
Five potato, six potato,
Seven potato, more.

In this children's game, each player in the beginning counts for two or one line of the chant (measurement), holding up clenched fists (or clenched fists with thumbs up) while the spudder taps each fist. He includes himself by tapping his left fist with his right and his left on his right fist.[192] Variations of this game are done with the feet (footprints).

What's interesting about the game is that it's a ritual. Who knows how old? The full count is eight. The beat of "more" is *eight*, "pieces of 8." It's conjecture but perhaps when the game first originated, the eighth count of "more" stood for a snake bite. Death, represented by the bitten fist, has/had to be put behind us. Life goes on. The fists are *five* each or four or five (four fingers and a thumb), and the tapping or banging is circular.

It's teaching the children that life is chance, uncertain. Subliminally the idea is planted perhaps that there's no fun in winning if it's at the expense of others. What good is it to have predicted the end of the world if there's nobody left but yourself to know you had predicted it?

In 1531 Francisco Pizarro, a treacherous and ruthless Spanish leader, set out with three ships, one hundred and eighty men or so, twenty-seven horses, and two cannons from Panama, the crossroads, for Peru (*Encyclopedia Americana*).

The Incas, though numerically superior at the battle of Cajamarca, were easily routed. They were terrorized and demoralized by the cannon, other weapons, and horses.[193] These were things they were not familiar with. Their leader Atahualpa was captured. A huge ransom was set. It was met, but Pizarro (ZA rather than AZ) ordered the ruler strangled at the square in Cajamarca (marked box, case, casket, coffin). This was on August 29 (a Mercury period), 1533 (SY). Cuzco, the royal capital, fell in November.

There was rivalry between Francisco Pizarro and Almagro, another Spanish leader. After an unsuccessful attempt to capture Chile, Almagro returned to seize Cuzco. Almagro was eventually captured and executed by Hernanado Pizarro, Francisco's brother. The followers of Almagro were treated with contempt and denied certain rights and privileges. This led to some of them banding together and killing Francisco Pizarro in his palace at Lima on June 26, 1541.

A retribution of sorts had come to an evil man. Yet it hardly made up for the tens of thousands of Indians that he, his cousin Hernán Cortés, and others had killed who called out from their graves.

More than any other food earth offers, the potato symbolizes the connection of the dead to the living. Its roots nurture the brown, coffin-like tubers which are grown underground and must be dug up to eat. Belief is that the potato came to Spain about 1570 from Peru, where it had grown in the Sierra, the Andean highlands, the country of Atahualpa of the marked casket.

It was strictly a "garden novelty" and not eaten when first brought to Europe, for its flowers resembled those of deadly nightshade, and people were scared.[194]

So for thirty years, the Argos eyes of the potatoes watched, slept, waited, biding their time. Then only after many governments had to order it be planted did it catch on. Slowly, insidiously, it became a staple that people depended upon for survival. And when the time and snake year were right, or twenty-six (eight) snake cycles had passed since the snake-year 1533,

> Who said no snakes in Erin?
> They can never bite!
> It was Stephen's year that brought
> The beginning of the blight.
>
> Fevers, starvation, and yet
> Little stealing or killing for food,
> "Twas Irish green-weed froth in corpses' mouths
> Which set the famine mood.
>
> Hundreds of thousands died,
> '46 the worst of all.
> Cart-loads of bodies to great pits,
> '47 another pall.
>
> If now the little country,
> Sends Somali food today,
> Spirits of the Irish dead
> Would have it no other way.
>
> Some thought the winds blew
> "The Wild Geese"[195-A] across the sea,
> But it was the totem Cut-off birds,
> That actually made it be.
>
> Don't you see that those
> In the *Dawn*er Party had to die?
> A Halloween sadness is
> They never knew just why.

Mother Goose, buhtaytuh rhymes,
Banging fists in hell
Where hunger shines,
"Twas the kids which broke the spell.

Ask me not how I know,
The white potato became the flake of snow,
Brought about by witches
Many, many years ago.

These imaginings were set to poem three or four years back. The only significant change since then was in making "a terrible sadness" into "a Halloween sadness." (The last of the Donner Park had arrived on Halloween.) Eerily this change was prompted when reading—for the first time[195-B] on January 19, 1996—that Halloween never really caught on much (except in small Irish-Catholic settlements) in the United States until the time of the great potato famine, sending thousands of Irish across the Atlantic. In the middle ages, Halloween was believed to be a time "favored by witches and sorcerers," and just as long or longer has existed the superstition that witches cause snow. Halloween today, of course, is a time for children dressed in "costombs," often grotesque, going from door to door to "Trick or Treat." Disguise and trickery are part of Hermes' persona.

Why the Irish rather than the Spanish or Portuguese? Though Christian, the Irish were—with their fey stories, banshee world, Celtic heritage, and Gaelic superstitions—closer to the Inca, Aztec, and other Indian cultures. There were still in Ireland childlike beliefs. It was the rape of this comparative innocence that was required, where both symbolically and literally there were no snakes. This isn't to imply there was no evil in Ireland or the New World.

The religious conflict between the Catholics and Protestants as always taxed the country. This corresponded to the weakened condition of Peru from the years of fighting between Atahualpa and his half-brother Huáscar, both of whom had been rival claimants to the throne. The fever in Ireland was like the smallpox in the New World. Most of all to remember, the Peruvian papa became the *Irish potato*, not the French, English, German, or so on. The blight seems to have been at its worst in 1846 and 1847, but there were crop failures to some extent for *five* years, beginning in 1845.[196]

On October 19, Stanton and two Indian *vaqueros* with food from Sutter met the pioneers on their way to California. The Indians, Luis and Salvador, then became part of the Donner Party. They were also part of the "Forlorn Hope" group of fifteen[197] which tried to walk out. Refusing to engage in cannibalism, the Indians stuck to themselves and starved for nine days. Then on December 31, they stole away from the rest of the group, probably figuring they were next in the pale skins' food chain. Not eating human flesh, it made no sense for them to march to the same slow-and-easy drummer as the rest. Nine days later they were overtaken by the remaining survivors and killed.

Like the children's potato game which had to be played, the roles had to be lived by the two Indians, and William Foster would execute and possibly eat of them before the nightmare curse would work its end. So there were perhaps revenge and guilt tied up in Foster's motives, though he would admit only to shooting them to put them out of their misery. Few examples of unadulterated virtue or evil existed for most in the Donner Party. Rather what otherwise would have remained as latent shadings in their lives were magnified a thousand times against the backdrop of snow. No one wanted this. They weren't Buddhist priests, Christian monks, or nuns who someway could psych themselves out. They were just ordinary people who wanted to live their lives to the fullest in the only world of which they were sure.

On January 11, 1847, the remaining survivors in the "Forlorn Hope" group came to an Indian *rancheria*. The Indians at first were frightened by them but returned to give them acorn bread, which was all they had. For the following seven days, the Indians helped them down the mountain and half carried and half dragged one of the survivors ahead to Johnson's rancho, where four men were sent back fifteen miles with food to fetch Foster and the five women. Only seven had survived from Forlorn Hope, and the terrible ordeal had taken thirty-two days.[198]

In the whole picture, the Indians helping the pale skins seems like the most dramatic moment. Yet there still will be more to die as four separate rescue parties make eight crossings of a mountainous boundary.

For Keseberg it was never over. Adults shunned him, and little children ran after him, taunting with cruel words and vicious limericks. What he undertook didn't prosper, according to one account. He had two half-witted children. The mark of Cain seemed to have been on him.[199]

California lies on the Pacific coast as does Peru. *Pacific*, of course, means peace. The Sierra Nevada suggests the Sierra of Peru. Boundaries were crossed that had to be broken. Boundaries were crossed which shouldn't have been.

All states today grow potatoes. California, harvesting in the winter and early spring, is among eight states which produce about 75 percent of the nation's crop.[200]

The Donner digression was like veering off to the side of the road and being stuck in a bog for several miles before being able to make it back up again. Symbolically interesting—maybe. But was there really a connection between Dannie Cameron and the party other than people being caught up in their fate or destiny? I think so. One supposition is that a god takes more than the usual interest, for better or for worse, in some people.

The Donner group started out in April 1846, and the last survivor was brought out of the Truckee area, Nevada County, in April 1847. These two dates are about all which historians are in unanimous agreement.

Collier's Encyclopedia gives April 22 as the time the fourth rescue group, led by Captain Fallon, brought out Keseberg. Other sources give an earlier date or none at all. On *April 19* Keseberg was probably lying through his teeth that he'd no knowledge what happened to George Donner's money. Fallon's group hadn't come strictly out of the kindness of its heart to rescue survivor or survivors and would have none of this. On the twentieth of April (or perhaps the nineteenth) a noose was put around Keseberg's neck and tightened—not to the point that it loosened his bowels but certainly his mouth. Death, which might have come close, was cheated.

By some accounts, there were forty-seven survivors. It's not unreasonable to assume that most survivors must have felt thereafter that they lived on borrowed time which had to be paid back someway beyond their natural ends. But it makes no difference who pays the gambler's death, only that it be paid.

Those on the battlewagon USS[201-A] *Iowa* and the Donner Party were wagoners, travelers. If the *Iowa*'s launching date of August 27, 1942, is used, she was almost forty-seven years old at the time of the explosion on Wednesday April 19, 1989, eight days following the unearthing of the first bodies at Matamoros. Thus each of the forty-seven deaths aboard her represented a year. If the *Iowa*'s commissioning date of February 22, 1943 (the Caristia), is used, then she was forty-six-forty-seven years old, the same time frame as the Donner Party. Besides this, there's in any February 21 or 22 date the inherent 2122 tempo. The February 22 date or arrival or departure date pinned it to the other. With the Donner Party, the dying was slow, agonizing, one by one. It was on land and men, women, and children. The calling in of the old debt was on water, swift, men only. In each case, there was a heavy or scapegoat. People need someone to blame, whether right or wrong or someplace in between. Keseberg was no angel; there's no disputing that, but certainly his strong German accent worked against him at times too.

Chapter Twenty-two

A breakthrough in learning about the Camerons came when Norma Beth sent me a few pages from *A Century in the Foothills 1876 to 1976*. This is a history of the Eden Area, Cascade County, Montana, compiled by the Eden Area Historical Committee, and published in June 1976 by the *Fairfield Times*. She also sent information she had put together on the Cameron clan.

Usually a quiverful of arrows carried by an archer is twenty-four, but the crest badge of the particular Cameron branch to which we're suppose to be related is "a sheaf of five arrows tied with a band." Not only is the number relevant but the arrow suggests flight, speed, and V. Then from *Came*ron can be derived Mae, again bringing to mind that May is the fifth month. This along with similarities in Ralph's life and death with that of Dannie's and numbers and dates lead me to believe that a psychic genealogy or kabala had been put together with the Strouts, Durens, Camerons, Millses, and Chichesters. Especially, what's one to make, if anything, of the fact that Dannie's body, missing for nearly eight months, was found late in the afternoon on Monday, February 18, 1895 (Great Fall Tribune, February 23, 1895)? So it's possible that both he and Elizabeth Chichester, who died February 17, 1934, were buried on the Feralia.

Dannie A. Cameron, to whom Robyn and Norma Beth refer, was our grandmother Annie's brother and so our great uncle. Duncan A. Cameron, S., and Margaret (Maggie)[201-B] McLachlan Cameron were his father and mother respectively and my great grandparents. They had moved with five children about 1881 to North Dakota from Antagonish, Cape Breton, Nova Scotia (or 110–113 years after Ding Dong had fled from Halifax, Nova Scotia). This explains why my mother, the daughter of Daniel and Annie Cameron Duren, was born in Weller, North Dakota, and it's assumed that when Duncan, Maggie, and six children moved to Black Butte, Montana, about seven or eight years later that Daniel Duren and family (i.e., Dannie, Annie, and Fannie—AEAEAE) moved with them.

According to Duncan Cameron's letter (published in the *Great Falls Tribune*, Montana, February 23, 1902), he came from an area about fifty miles from Bismarck, North Dakota, in 1889. At that time he had about fifty dollars in cash, three horses, and an "ordinary emigrant outfit." There was only one house between his ranch and Great Falls.

He was proud of what he'd built and raised: 560 acres of patented land and desert filling on 160 acres more. About 200 acres were under cultivation, and two or three hundred more were "good tillage land." He raised both common and "Big Four" oats. The latter yielded on first breaking seventy-nine bushels per acre. He had about thirty cows and sold butter on an average of twenty-five cents per pound in the summer and thirty to thirty-five cents per pound in the winter.

Working hard for the previous twelve years, he felt he was entitled to take life easy from then on in retirement. He had just sold his ranch for $7,200, plus there was additional money he'd received from sale of his cattle and personal belongings.

Duncan's letter to the paper was filled with the first person singular without even a nod to Maggie and his sons and daughters, who must have worked hard too. On the basis of this alone, I tended to look at him more critically. But when you read the many other letters written by pioneer ranchers on the same page, you find that they're written in the same manner. It was the way of the day and didn't necessarily mean anything.

Margaret Cameron Kodalen described her grandfather, Duncan A. Cameron, as a "very strict Presbyterian, one who did not believe in the devil's way of dancing or card playing," though Maggie conspired roundabout to help her sons and daughters go to country dances. The food would actually get cold at times (especially as Duncan got older) before he finished his prayer of thanksgiving or blessing. Maggie, however, "used to relieve the tension by throwing pancakes or roles" (just a little manna from heaven) at the unsuspecting—Duncan, S. excluded of course.

Still my great grandpa wasn't entirely to blame for his religious fervor, which might have been an occupational hazard. Surely you've heard of "Presbyterian Oats"? In his defense too might be added that he was smarter than many preachers whose congregations fell asleep after having eaten a late breakfast Sunday morning. His family was still hungry. No way could they doze before he'd said what he had to say.

Margaret wrote:

> Although grandpa was a strict man, a wee tote of liquor, a hot toddy, was always taken in the morning and before bedtime at night, that is, for men only. It was also given for medicinal purposes, as necessary....
>
> As times prospered and progressed, grandpa purchased an instrument of the devil, one of the early Model

T Fords. His novice experimental driving was done in the corral where he raised clouds of dust going round and around before he was able to make the correct turn out the gate and away, bumping and jumping all things in his path. He had a 'heavy foot' and poor judgment as to turns and obstacles and those poor passengers that, by chance, ever rode with him, had quite a thrill and said, "Never again!" He said he always traveled with the Lord, and of this, there was never a doubt.[202]

Verily Duncan, S. must have been the same great grandfather about whom Phyllis White, as a young girl, heard had come across country in a wagon (or with other wagons), herding together at stops those traveling to preach fiery sermons, while quoting the Bible chapter and verse from memory. He saw in the occurrence of any natural phenomena the hand of God. One day (if my memory serves me right from what Phyllis had heard) when an earthquake occurred, he stopped the wagon or wagons, gathered those about him, and explained its ominous, religious meaning that it could be the beginning of the end of the world.

In naming the four sons, Duncan and/or Maggie stuck to names beginning with *D* for the most part: Dougald; Duncan, Jr.; and Dannie. The other son was called Alex. So father and sons could be thought of as 4444 Greek. Dougald died in 1929, the same year as my mother. Duncan, Sr., likely was born in 1844 and lived to be eighty-eight, dying for certain in 1933, the year the earthquake occurred in Long Beach, California. Alex died in 1939, the same as Ralph.

Both Duncan and Maggie were remarkable people, considering all the pioneer hardships they must have had. Duncan appears to have been a serious man, a trait which might have been very necessary for the survival and well-being of him and his family in those days.

It's said that he and Maggie had thirteen children. Four of the children died at birth or shortly after. Only three of the thirteen lived to their fifties: Dougald; Alex; and Duncan, Jr. Only two survived their father. Margaret Cameron Kodalen observed (*A Century in the Foothills*) that thirteen "proved to be an unlucky number."

My understanding is that any four made from a one and three (say thirteen or thirty-one) is considered bad luck also. If Duncan Cameron's birth was on the Feralia, this blessing-curse day is tied in with the thirteen, indicating the Parentalia's first day. It will always be my belief that St. Peter's was built over a graveyard as the rock or an elaborate gravestone, a concession and hope by early priests that in doing so they could not only appease but exert some influence or control.

In the Cameron Hill Cemetery are buried twin boys (born to Duncan and Maggie) who died when about a year old. Perhaps this is how the confusion came in Norma Beth's story. Maybe Annie's alleged strictness came from the upbringing by her father, and possibly Mom rebelled at it

438

when Annie died in 1912. Who knows any of this for certain now? What is known is that Aunt Nell and her daughters remained good Presbyterians throughout their lives and that my mother returned to Montana to teach at Black Butte School District Number 34 at a monthly salary of fifty dollars in May-August 1908 before going to Stanford.

In May 1894, Alfred Alge had things to attend to in Cascade. By the time he rode there, conducted his business, and got back, he expected to be gone a few days. The Camerons were only six miles north of him, god-fearing people, and certainly trustworthy, so he'd hire young Dannie to come over and stay on his ranch and look after the cattle when he was gone. Anxious to make a few bucks, Dannie agreed.

When Alge returned from Cascade, he found the cabin was locked. Dannie's horse and saddle were gone, so no doubt he'd locked it to be on the safe side while checking out the spread's far end and would be back in an hour or two. Inside he saw Dannie's vest, coast, and shoes, and possibly was reassured on seeing them. He hadn't noticed that Dannie brought extra shoes along, but undoubtedly he had. There was an impression on the bed as if a body had lain or fallen on it. No big deal, but a bullet hole in the wall? He'd talk to young Cameron about that when he got back. There seemed no reason to worry otherwise.

But as time dragged on he did begin to worry. There was no sign of Dannie. He'd better ride over to the Camerons to see if the kid had gone back there for something. It was strange him taking off like that, but maybe they had an emergency of some kind at the Cameron ranch.

"No, Mr. Alge, Dannie's not here. We thought he was at your place," Duncan said worriedly.

"Why would he have taken off like that for? Where could he have gone? Oh I just know something's happened to him" Maggie wailed.

"I'll saddle a horse and go back with yuh," Duncan said. "Maybe he's there now. I'd like to see for myself."

Riding along, Alge told Duncan about the bullet hole. He hadn't wanted to alarm Maggie any more than necessary. After that, Duncan clammed up as if lost in thought, maybe prayer. He'd rather Duncan talked, but it was clear he wasn't going to. Did Duncan blame him someway for what'd happened? It seemed so long this way. When at one point his horse stopped, Alge could hardly restrain himself from saying, "Damn it all! We ain't got time for you to crap. Let's go." His mind raced with ideas about what might have been, but one idea he kept coming back to was that Dannie had got drunk and taken off. He thought it'd be a kindness to tell Duncan this, to give him a straw to grasp. But as he looked over at him, there was something in Duncan's demeanor or set of his jaw that made Alge think better. Somehow this seemed to give even more credence to what he'd thought most likely happened. What with

Duncan's strict religion and tight rein, Dannie had come up against the same stone wall. At twenty-one he could finally do what he wanted and took off.

As they drew closer to his ranch, Alge peeled his eyes and craned his neck, searching for his cattle, Son of a bitch! Damned if rustlers hadn't run off with 'em!

He showed Duncan the cabin. They looked around carefully but could find nothing more than he'd said. They rode off then to see the sheriff.

News was news where there wasn't much news, and the air was charged as with the rushing sound of water. Rustlers had come to the area, and Dannie likely had been in cahoots with 'em.

"Thun if that warr so, why'd he bother to lock the cabin?"

"Can't ya see you idiot? By lockin' the cabin they'd sucker 'im into bleevin everthing was okay, even though Dannie had took off. If Alge hada come back early it ud bought 'em more time to move the herd. Ya don't haf ta be no Shylock Olmes[203] to figer that out."

Alge did more checking, he found the cattle he thought were missing at the far end of his ranch. He was both relieved and embarrassed by this because he had reported them stolen, indirectly impugning Dannie's character, and there were a lot of red faces who now had to backpeddle.

"Now wait just one damn minute here! I never said no such thing. Don't ya go hangin' that on me. If ya recall, Alge said some of his cattle was gone. I thought the damn fool knew what he was talkin' about. That was before I see he don't have sense enough to pound sand into a rat hole. Goin' on what he claim, I only said we ought-ta consider all possibles. Course I never thought for one second Dannie ever ud do such a thing, what with his upbringin' and all."

Maggie and Duncan fretted and grieved over Dannie's disappearance for months. Some days they felt certain he was dead; on others they dared to hope that they were wrong. They prayed alone and together with silent tears, promising anything to God to return Dannie to them alive.

It might have been easier had someone not always been saying that he'd talked to somebody who'd seen Dannie. Anxious inquiries always showed each rumor to be false. Of course they wanted to hear of any leads. Yet sometimes they wished people 'ud just shut up. Why build up their hopes on something so flimsy and have it come to naught?

Now someone said one Duncan Gillis was going around claiming to be Dannie. If this were true, then Gillis could only be a sick man or a man with a sick sense of humor. He disgusted them. Yet what if Gillis was neither? What if this was just a gambit—that Dannie was being held someplace Gillis knew about or was party to? They couldn't afford to chance it. A reward of five thousand dollars, mentioning Duncan Gillis, was offered to be paid "in good faith" for "the production, alive, anywhere in the world" of their Dannie.

Everybody in those parts had heard Maggie had premonitions about what was going to happen sometimes. A few were doubtful about this and scoffed. Others regarded her suspiciously, as if she were some sort of witch. That was good for a laugh: Pious Duncan married to a witch! Others were envious of her psychic power or whatever they thought she had. But she shrugged it all off, what they thought or felt, as if none of the fools knew what he or she was talking about, especially when calling it a "gift." What good was it to know something was going to happen for sure and yet be powerless to prevent it, to change even one small detail?

Maggie then had a premonition of the death of Katie,[204] Dannie's twelve-year-old sister. She foresaw her falling and hurting her head on the ice near the barn. So it came to pass in the year of Dannie's death and disappearance that Katie fell and fractured her skull in front of the barn and died. Maggie wondered if by foreseeing this she'd in some way caused it. She never would have done this to her daughter. What foolishness! She knew it wasn't so, but why did she have to foresee it? What with Dan missing and probably dead, both her and Duncan's grief seemed endless. Katie died on December 31, 1894. On January 1, Janus looked both ways: They couldn't help thinking about what had occurred and what yet might happen.

Soon Maggie had another premonition: She saw a man who came into her house. After putting down his sack by the stove, he told them that he had found a body about twenty feet off the trail that led from Alge's ranch to the Cameron's. So it came to pass that in February, the month of purification, Dannie's body was found and buried. Notice the shift here from 1894 to 1895. According to the account given on page 27 of *A Century in the Foothills*, Dannie had been shot in the back of the head, the bullet coming out between his eyes. Identification was made by physical peculiarities, his shoes, however, were missing. Could he have been fleeing barefoot from Alge's ranch when he was overtaken? Footprints.

Though seven or eight are buried in the Cameron Hill Cemetery (Annie Cameron Duren isn't one of these) on the hill facing Black Butte (suggesting the "Black One"), there remains today only the tombstones of Katie and Dannie, both born on the ides of a month as follows:

Katie B. Cameron
Born West Bay, Cape Breton, Nova Scotia
October 15, 1882–December 31, 1894
Dannie A. Cameron
Born West Bay, Cape Breton, Nova Scotia
May 15, 1873–killed May 21, 1894[205]

Whether Alfred Alge attended Dannie's funeral is unknown. He must have wondered if he hadn't hired Dannie and had not been gone would he himself have been the victim? Or maybe he didn't. The case was never solved.

It's assumed that since Dannie's younger brother Dougald was an expert at breaking broncos, Dannie also broke horses, as did Ralph. In each case a snake and horse was involved: the rattlesnake with Ralph and the human and/or symbolic snake for the month of May in Dannie's case. Both lived on a ranch and worked off it for neighbors. One source says Dannie was shot in the back of the head,[206], Katie fractured her skull, and Ralph hit his head and neck in the fall. All three were lying on the ground.

May 21,[207] the day Dannie died, was the beginning of one of two periods ruled by Mercury:[208]

May 21–June 20

August 23–September 22[209]

Both Dannie and Ralph died on the twenty-first—Dannie on the twenty-first of the fifth month, Ralph on the twenty-first of the eighth month. In addition Ralph had been born on the Feralia.[210] Though Dannie hadn't been born on the February Feast of the Dead, his father (Ralph's and my great grandfather) had,[211] while Ralph's and my father was the only one of six children born in a Mercury period (September 10, 1888). Dannie was born on the fifteenth of May, the Ides, when there was a festival in ancient Rome for Mercury, god of merchants, and Maia, his mother. Equally mysterious is that the *aedes Mercuri* dedication near the Circus Maximus was on the Ides of May, *495*, B.C.[212]

The talk between Duncan Cameron and his neighbor might never have taken place or precisely as stated. It's as good a guess as any based on recollections of what had been seen firsthand and what was passed down in conversations in *A Century in the Foothills*, the only information at that time.

It's clear some details had been gotten wrong in the beginning or changed with numerous tellings. Two articles in separate newspapers stated his head was missing when the remains were discovered. Then there's a slight difference in other details. The *Great Falls Tribune* of February 23, 1895, said the arms and legs were present but that the hands and feet were gone. The *Helena Daily Herald* of February 25, 1895, reported that after the ravages of wild beasts and weather, the arms and feet were gone from the trunk. There was agreement then between the two papers that the head, hands, and feet were missing. This emphasis is made in that it gives the best clue today—along with one other fact and the cabala[213]—as to what happened over a hundred years ago.

The body was discovered late on Monday afternoon on February 18, 1895, when R.W. Flint was returning home after a hunt. He noticed clothing on the ground. As he went closer to get a better look, he saw part of a body with some of it. The clothing consisted of a necktie, overalls, overshirt, undershirt, and drawers. Duncan and Maggie were notified. On being shown the garments, they identified the tattered shirt and necktie as belonging to Dannie.

What might never have passed for identifying remains today possibly did then. Even if a skull or head had been found later, chances are what with him living on a farm and drinking milk, he never had any dental work done. There were no hands to take fingerprints. Had there been, selected fingerprinting didn't come into wide use until after the turn of the century. Were it possible earlier, there'd probably have been no prints on record to compare them to.

Today it might be possible by sophisticated methods for some hotshot expert to compare genetic samples from the exhumed remains of Duncan and Maggie and the body said to be that of Dannie's to make an even closer identification or to rule out that it was he. But what purpose would it serve? As a great nephew, with only a few left more closely related to Dannie, I have no more reason to doubt it was he than did his mother and father. It's likely too that at the time of discovery of the remains they found an identifying mark or scar, which may or may not be reported elsewhere. Certainly the writer of the article on page 27 of *A Century in the Foothills* speaks with conviction when saying the body was absolutely identified by certain peculiarities that "prevented any mistake."

The reporting in the *Great Falls Tribune* on February 23, 1895, was done in depth, carefully and meticulously in detail. It stated that Dannie's friends had become anxious when he was missing a day or two. This doesn't sound like a loner, an unknown quantity.

On going to take the job, he took with him his saddle, bridle, and clothing. The horse that disappeared belonged to Alge. Dannie had no reason to steal it, however, for "he had several of his own." He came from a good home. He had no debts or known enemies. He was described as "steady and industrious." Even if speculating that his father and he weren't getting along (and there isn't a hint of this anywhere), it makes no sense since Dannie was twenty-one and could have left any time he wanted.

Logic then says to discount any possibility that the remains weren't those of Dannie. Less logical is the fact that I'd be drawn back to this over a century later, as Peggy Cameron Kodalen had earlier when she and others wrote their recollections in 1976. Peggy, Dannie's niece, was born on the beginning day of the Parentalia, *February 13*, 1918.

The remains were found only three-quarters mile from the Alge ranch. So heartsickeningly close it seemed strange they hadn't been discovered before. Maybe Dannie would have survived if they'd just done right in looking for him. As a matter of fact, many research parties had been sent out, combing the area for miles beyond. Nobody thought he'd be that near since two distant ranchers had said that on the day Dannie disappeared they'd seen a horse and a rider. This was a long way off and heading in an entirely different direction from where Dannie's body was eventually found, not too far from a deep and rugged coulee.

If Dannie's horse had shied from a snake here, someway throwing Dannie, certainly the horse would have returned to the Alge ranch or stayed on the range. It was theorized at the time that both the horse and rider were injured in a fall into the coulee and that Dannie somehow had managed to crawl out into the flat area of the prairie. Duncan and Maggie apparently didn't believe this, for the gravestone says "killed" rather than "died" or just giving the date as in Katie's case.

A Montana genealogist who looked up the articles in the papers believed that if there had been "foul play" involved in Dannie's death, there would have been an inquest in Cascade County, mentioned in the newspapers under court proceedings. Nothing could be found. Still this doesn't seem so strange when you consider that the disappearance took place in May 1894 (five years previously there had been only one ranch between Duncan's and Great Falls), and the body wasn't discovered until February 1895. There was a further delay (possibly a couple months) waiting for the snow to thaw in the coulee so that it could be searched for the remains of a horse, bridle, and saddle. Apparently nothing was found. Even today with all our advanced forensic methods, many detectives feel that if good clues haven't surfaced within twenty-four hours of the time of discovery of a homicide, chances are it will go unsolved. There were no automobiles then. Riding back and forth to a county seat on horseback would have involved a lot of time. Much time had already been spent by the county when Dannie was discovered missing. The remains yielded nothing as to what happened. The county had more recent problems to attend to. Life goes on.

The *Great Falls Tribune* stated that Alge had found the cabin locked and that inside were Dannie's coat, vest, and shoes. The *Helena Daily Herald* reported that Alge had notified Dannie's parents. Neither article, however, mentioned the bullet hole Peggy Cameron Kodalen recalled hearing about.

Dannie wasn't a cowboy drifter who worked on one ranch for awhile and then moved off to another. He lived on a ranch not too far from Alge's. So it seems very unlikely that for just two or three days work he would take—besides a bridle and saddle—an extra pair of shoes. It seems just an unlikely that if he had done so, the animals would have carried off his boots or shoes, leaving the other clothing. The loss of the body's head, two hands, and two feet was gruesome, but would animals have done this leaving enough of the legs, arms, and torso to make an identification—i.e., perhaps the head, hand, and foot, but all five? It seems reasonable to assume that he wasn't wearing shoes or boots at the time.

Possibly he'd removed his shoes and was lying or sleeping on the bed when he was surprised by an intruder with a gun, perhaps after dark or before dawn. The thief demanded money and terrorized him with threats. Logically Dannie would have explained he had no money. It wasn't even his ranch. He was only there for a short time, covering for the owner who was expected back at any moment. The intruder then might have reasoned that if he were to steal a horse, he must do it quickly and dispose of Dannie as a witness someplace along the way so that he wouldn't be discovered too soon. Also if he locked the cabin, the owner might reason everything was okay for awhile, that Dannie had just snuck off to see his girlfriend for a few hours.

No decent cowboy would leave his horse standing saddled and bridled all night. So while watching Dannie who is barefoot and not going anywhere, the thief begins to bridle and saddle the horse. Dannie believes his only chance is to make a run for it and takes off like a frightened animal as bullets fly past or possibly wound him. His heart is pumping like hell, and he's becoming winded. Looking back quickly, he believes he can make it if he can hide. It's while trying to do this that he's struck by a rattlesnake. In his already excited condition, the poison doesn't take long to work.

Of course the scenario could be wrong. Maybe the thief overtook and killed him on the spot. Whatever, it doesn't figure the thief would kill him near the ranch if he planned to hide the body. For then he'd have to load it on a horse he didn't know to be packed away. Besides, why take a body three-quarters mile in a direction he hadn't planned to go and then have to double back?

You say the snake theory is ridiculous since there's not a shred of evidence to suggest it. You might be right, but consider the following concerning the location of the body, as quoted with permission and thanks from the *Great Falls Tribune* on February 23, 1895:

> At the point where the head should have been was a
> flat stone half imbedded in the ground, but showing
> about three inches above the surface, its peculiar position
> indicating that it may have been used as a pillow.

It's been mentioned previously that Ralph's head was near a pile of stones, a Hermes symbol, when he fell and that Dannie's date of death was taken from his tombstone, a Hermes symbol, as being May 21, the beginning of the Mercury period. It's also the month and day that firewalkers now celebrate in Greece. It's the day and month that Rajiv Gandhi was assassinated in 1892 (21), supposedly by a person carrying flowers disguising the bomb. Both Ralph and Dannie died on the twenty-first of a month. Dannie was twenty-one and six days at the time of his death; Ralph was twenty years and six months.

Dannie's death is similar in some respects to grandmother Elizabeth Chichester's on February 17, 1934. A head was missing[214] or crushed in; very possibly a thief had made off in the night. Now consider Dannie's death occurred in 1894, but his body wasn't found until 1895 during the Parentalia on February 18, possibly the same day Elizabeth's was located in the ashes thirty-nine years later.

It's likely that Dannie's burial was within two or three days following this. If it were the twenty-first, then it was the Feralia, as opposed to the beginning of the Parentalia when his niece *Margaret* Cameron will later be born on February 13, 1918. If the twenty-first, it was the same month and day two sources give as his father's birthday (February 21, 1844). It will be the same day as *Margaret* Tyler Duren's death in 1907 and within six days of his mother *Margaret*'s on February 27, 1911. It was the same day his great-nephews Ralph and I will be born later (forty-five and fifty-five years respectively following his birth on May 15, 1873) and within five days of his niece's death (Frances May) on February 26, 1929 and one day from her husband's death (Frank Chichester) on February 22, 1958.

An article appearing in the *Great Falls Tribune* on January 1, 1895, tells that Katie Christina Cameron, age twelve, slipped and fell, injuring herself in front of her home. Two physicians treated her, but she died six days later. Again this accident happened between the time Dannie disappeared and his body was later found. Duncan, Maggie, and family had more than their share of grief.

Perhaps sometime in the months which followed, someone found a human skull on the prairie. If Duncan and Maggie buried it with Dannie's remains, it might not be his. Maybe it was even that of somebody who was very bad. Yet with the possibility that it could be Dannie's, they were reluctant to throw it out. The only way around the dilemma was to put it off somewhere in a trunk that Mom and her older sisters later opened.

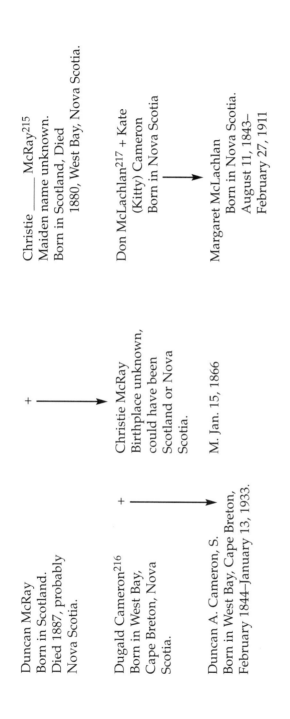

Christie _____ McRay[215]
Maiden name unknown.
Born in Scotland, Died
1880, West Bay, Nova Scotia.

Duncan McRay
Born in Scotland.
Died 1887, probably
Nova Scotia.

+

Christie McRay
Birthplace unknown,
could have been
Scotland or Nova
Scotia.

Don McLachlan[217] + Kate
(Kitty) Cameron
Born in Nova Scotia

Margaret McLachlan
Born in Nova Scotia.
August 11, 1843–
February 27, 1911

Dugald Cameron[216]
Born in West Bay,
Cape Breton, Nova
Scotia.

+

Duncan A. Cameron, S.
Born in West Bay, Cape Breton,
February 1844–January 13, 1933.

M. Jan. 15, 1866

The below (based on limited information) lists Duncan's and Maggie's children, numbering thirteen according to what Margaret Cameron Kodalen heard:

1.   ANNIE L. (or Ann). ca 1866–October 19, 1912.
2.   ALEXANDER S. (called Alex or Sandy). August 18, 1868–June 30, 1939. Information from death certificate. 1881 census would suggest ca. 1870.
3.   DANNIE (or Daniel) ARCHIBALD. May 15, 1873–May 21, 1894.
4.   DOUGALD HUGH. December 24, 1878–June 18, 1929.
5.   DUNCAN ALLAN, JR. ca. 1880–unknown.
6.   KATIE CHRISTINA. This name taken from *Great Falls Tribune* of January 1, 1895. Possibly three names as tombstone says "KATIE B." October 15, 1882–December 31, 1894.

    Dannie and Katie died in the same year. Dannie was 21; Katie was 12, or a transposition of 21. Also, later, twenty-one years fell between the death of their mother and their father.

7.   STELLA CAMERON (ea ae) GERARD (ea) or GER-RARD. (Compare to Fannie Mae/Frances May/Duran or Duren [aeaeaen].) Born (according to death certificate): North Dakota (Dakota Territory) on June 6, 1886. Died May 31 (MP), 1913. Contributing cause of death: "Following labor."

    In 1912, Stella and Roy Gerard had gotten a $1,400 mortgage on property. According to my understanding of court records (Dougal H. Cameron, plaintiff, vs. Roy E. Gerard, et. al., case #9873 of April 24, 1916), the interest payments were due semiannually, and the $1,400 had to be paid back by December 14, 1917. Dougal, either in settlement of estate or paying interest and/or other payments on the note, had become involved in litigation. Court records of Cascade County say that Roy E. Gerard was issued a letter of administration of the estate on February 18, 1914 (nineteen years after Dannie's body was found). The point is that though Roy might have been "heartbroken," he didn't leave Montana immediately after Stella's death for parts unknown or disappear until February 18, 1914, or sometime after. According to what Margaret Cameron Kodalen had heard, nobody ever knew where he went nor did they hear from him again. Baby girl Idylle was first taken care of by Dougald and his wife, Cora, then later was adopted by Alexander and his wife, May. Idylle signed as informant on Alexander Cameron's death certificate in 1939. Life apparently worked out to some extent for her, as she was then Idylle Cameron Gilligan, having married.

8. and 9.   Twins born in 1899 or after were approximately one year old at death.

10. and 11.   Progressive Men of Montana lists surviving children as: "Anna L. (Mrs. Daniel Durand [sic], Alexander S., Dugald H., and Stella M." An error was made in not listing Duncan A. Cameron, Jr. The article said that "KATIE and DUGALD HENRY died at West Bay and Daniel and Kittie Christina died at Evans." Based on this information and assuming an error hadn't been made, Duncan and Maggie had two children who died at an early age and between censuses in West Bay, Nova Scotia. Later children bore similar names in part. This could account for numbers 10 and 11.

12. and 13.   Unknown.

Annie married Daniel Chase Duren.

Alexander S. married *May* Nelson.

Dougald married *Cora* Edwards on March 3, 1905 (SY). As a team, they broke horses to sell. He would saddle and ride most of the bucking out of a horse one day, and she would follow the next, "polishing" the horse off. They moved to the "*Walker* ranch at Sand Coulee" for awhile; and later in 1912, bought a ranch of their own. Always tightly corsetted, Cora didn't show her pregnancy and kept riding horses up to the last. When Dougald returned from the hospital and said he was the proud father of a baby girl, the ranch hands wouldn't believe him. They named the baby Margaret (Peggy) A. Cameron. Cora stayed in the hospital for two months with septicemia. When she got out, she was weak and sick for awhile. It made sense to let Alex and May, who had no children of their own, adopt Idylle, who was then four-five years old.

Both February and May are/were significant months both to Hermes and the dead. May has been a month of mourning since ancient times.[219] Idylle Cameron Gilligan was born in 1913 on May 13 (linked to the Feralia). The 13 is a transposition of 31, her mother's death-date eighteen days later. Both Idylle's mother (Stella) and mine were born in the Dakota Territory; were living under the same roof when my mother visited the cemetery on April 18, 1907; and will die where childbirth was a contributing factor. April is, simply, the fourth month.

The chthonic side of Hermes makes the dead inseparable in the numbers 13 and 21, the beginning and the end of the Parentalia. Both the date of February 13 and the surprise of her birth might help to explain Peggy's somewhat superstitious nature, as I interpret it, especially when she points out that her mother (Cora) and her Aunt Berthe (Cora's sister) always had been close in life. Both died in the same room at Peggy's home: her mother on May 26, 1970, and her aunt in the last week of May, too, a year later. Peggy commented that this was ironic. She might have found it even more so had she known that the deaths occurred in a Mercury period and that she, Idylle, and myself were linked to the Parentalia.

Duncan A. Cameron, Jr., married May (Marinn?) Ryan on January 16, 1901. It's my understanding:

1) He lived in Seattle before he died, sometime in the early 1960s.
2) They had four children: Daniel (the oldest, born 1901, was named after his uncle); Leslie; Corrine; and Lucille, all of whom are now dead.
3) The relatives didn't remain close so that those living in Montana were not notified much of the happenings (letter dated February 17, 1993 from John Marn).

Many pictures in *A Century in the Foothills* show the men either wearing a tie or a neckerchief, and Dannie wore a tie to take a two or three day job at a neighbor's ranch where he would be alone. Certainly my father, uncles, and brothers never would have done this in the 1930, though perhaps for dances and holiday celebrations. Times change.

The year 1844 for Duncan Cameron's birth squares with the 1881 Canadian census where his age was given as thirty-seven. Two genealogists (one in Nova Scotia, the other in Montana) believe this to be the most likely year of his birth. Had any other date appeared in the *Great Falls Tribune*, I wouldn't have questioned it or searched further, but February 21 (1844) seemed almost too pat. I had the feeling that some debunker might come along and prove it wrong. The inference being that if I were wrong on one point, it just proved everything said in the book was incorrect. The case then would be closed like a steel trap—not even given a Bible break that 90 percent might be true but 10 percent was probably inaccurate. Sure enough, the Feralia was later contradicted by January 4, 1833, given in *Progressive Men of Montana*.

The Montana Genealogist wrote: There is no U.S. 1890 Census available to researchers. Tragically it was destroyed in a fire at the National Archives many years ago...but I did locate the Duncan Camerons in 1900. (ED151, page 26, line 5) Cascade Co., San Coulee Twp. I'm afraid that we've found one more birth date to add to the confusion! January 1842! It is difficult because one does not know which family member gave the information to the census taker. He and Maggie have been married for 36 years. Five of nine children born to her are living. He immigrated to the U.S. in 1882 and she in 1883. The children's names appear to correspond to the Canadian Census. Dougal H. (Hugh), Duncan A. (Allen).

Of course the other children are gone by 1900. Note the entry for Alexander at the bottom.

The following is taken from *Progressive Men of Montana*:
Up to age twelve, Duncan worked at small jobs, attended school in the winter, and helped with farming in the summer.

1845. Around twelve, he began driving a team for a rich man called Cameron, though no relation.

1846. Duncan still a boy, went to sea on the schooner *Violet*.[220] After sailing for nine months, he returned home.

1849. Took his savings and purchased a team and worked on St. Peter's canal for three years.

1852. Returned home and worked on his father's farm.

1854. Received 150 acres of land from his father.

1855. Married Margaret McLachlan. If her age of thirty-eight given on the Nova Scotia census of 1881 is correct, then Maggie was only twelve or thirteen at the time. Since Ann is the oldest surviving child on the census (her birth occurring in 1866 or 1867), this would have meant that Duncan and Maggie had been married for eleven or twelve years when Ann was born. If true, it seems probable that part or all the unaccounted births might have occurred before Ann was born. For thirteen years now Duncan worked as a stage driver carrying mail between two steamers: one called Napkin, a peculiar name, the other, *St. Lawrence*.

1858. Became a Mason. (See footnote 218.)

1868. Returned to farming.

1882. He and his family moved from Nova Scotia to Bismarck, North Dakota, where they farmed profitably for seven years, at which time they got the itch to move on.

1889. Their farm, near the Evans post office, was twelve miles from Stockett and twenty-five miles from Great Falls, Montana.

1902. According to *Progressive Men of Montana*, Duncan usually wintered one hundred and twenty head of horses and one hundred and forty head of cattle. For the previous twenty years, he and Maggie had been members of the Presbyterian church, maintaining their current connections at Great Falls. They gave help, however, to "any evangelical Protestant church," and Duncan kept up his lodge membership "where he was initiated, passed, and raised."

Progressive Men of Montana was published in 1902 by A.W. Bowen and Co. of Chicago, Illinois. "The articles were submitted and were autobiographical. They were published for a fee." The date of January 4, 1833, would have made Duncan over a hundred years old. Certainly his close relatives in the area would have made something of the occasion, and it would have been mentioned in his obituaries, if it had been known. Yet the date can't be dismissed as a publishing error, since the other dates in the autobiographical piece dovetail from this.

Duncan's letter printed in the *Great Falls Daily Tribune* on February 23, 1902, showed his mind to be sharp. Thus it's unaccountable by the discrepancy of the years 1833 and 1844 as birthdates. Two or three years might be acceptable or a glaring misprint. The joining of subsequent dates to 1833 is calculated, whether on Duncan's part, the writer's, or the publisher's. But why? Who will ever know? Though Duncan was a serious and strict man—perhaps even starchy—he was also a person of integrity, grit, and was "well-respected."

Death and baptism records in Nova Scotia for that period are confusing. It's anybody's guess sometimes who is who. A researcher could find no record of the marriage of Duncan Cameron and Margaret McLachlan, no matter what spelling was used, nor could any record be found of the birth or baptism of either. What was found in West Bay United Presbyterian baptism records were birthdates of other children of Dugald Cameron and Christy (Christian?) *McRae* (McRay, McCray):

John	February 23, 1845
Hugh	June 22, 1847
Mary	May 14, 1849
Flora Christy	April 30, 1851
Jane	May 24, 1853
Isabella	July 7, 1855

No reference to the five thousand dollar reward offered could be located in newspapers, though there's little doubt that it was made and approximated Duncan's and Maggie's total worth. In context to this and the value of a dollar at the time, consider that they had started out with only three horses, fifteen head of cattle, fifty dollar, in cash, and "an ordinary emigrant outfit" about five years earlier. Bank advertisements in the *Helena Daily Herald* of February 25, 1895, boasted of paid in capital or surplus of one hundred thousand dollars. In an interview in the *Great Falls Daily Tribune* of February 23, 1902, Duncan planned to retire. He seemed to think the seven thousand and two hundred dollars he received for his ranch was a good sum. This, along with the sale of his cattle and other personal property, would net him and his family one thousand dollars a year to live on.

Margaret Cameron's address on her death certificate in 1911 was given as "717 - 5th St. So., Great Falls." Duncan's address in 1933 was "717 1/2 - 5th Ave, So, Great Falls." So either he lived at the same place for the rest of his life or close to it.

The State of Montana death certificate has (or had then) in Box #5: "Single, Married, Widowed, or Divorced (write the word)." Oddly on Margaret's, someone had written something in ink and erased it—perhaps "separated," for which there was no category. Whatever, over what had been erased, "single" had been written in clearly twice. This could have been an error since at her death, Duncan spoke of her patience and that he'd never known her "to express temper."

Stella was buried next to her mother. Duncan was buried next to his second wife, Emilie Lawrenson, whom he married in 1912. She died in 1921.

Elisha (ea) Strout's second marriage was to Bathsheba (aea) Small (note biblical names) on *April 13*, 1750. Sarah Strout (fourth generation Strout living in this country and their fourth child) was born *May 13*, 1756. She died on March 25, 1821 (SY). She'd married Matthew Duran of Durham. John, their first child, married Jane Davis who died in 1821. Martha Whitmore, his second wife from whom our lineage comes, died on March 17, 1869 (SY). Their first child of six children was George Duren, who died on April 10, 1865. (Three successive generations of Durans served in wars.)

Frank (a fourth child) and Frances Chichester's fourth child Warren married Lola Gentry (her name from a previous marriage), making a family with four children in which Lowell was the fourth. All three sons married and had children, as did Tina, and appeared to be getting there (wealth). It's as if each exemplifies a facet of Hermes. Stan is the merchant (electric circuitry) and does much traveling. Leslie stuck to the ranch (cattle, horses, sheep, and pastures), and Lowell is a traveler and has gambling, hotel-restaurant interests.

Chapter Twenty-three

Thoth, whom the Greeks associated with Hermes, was an Egyptian god of judgment. He created the world and things in it by pronouncing the words. He was also a god of magic. Whether he was or wasn't the god of tarot, I don't know, nor do I have any knowledge of tarot cards[221] or the Ouija board, figuring at present what's to be known, if anything, will come by different means.

It serves no purpose, furthermore, for me to enter into a value-judgment of what Aleister Crowley was or wasn't, when at present only two pages under "De Mercurio"[222] are of interest. These are sharp in the realm of association.

"In the beginning was the Word, and the Word was with God, and the Word was God" (J 1.01).

The word *Logos* is derived from Greek and means "the divine creative Word, the son of God."[223] This in the Christian world would be Jesus. Crowley believed Hermes and Jesus were one and the same. He points out that both Jesus and Hermes were messengers, and both pulled pranks in their youth, e.g., if I'd told Mom she should have known when I was missing that I was in church all day, she would have given me a stern lecture. Most children in their youth steal something. Hermes was no different, and Crowley quotes, "The Son of Man cometh as a thief in the night." Both Christ and Hermes are healers, protectors, helpers: Hermes at Tanagra, carrying the protective ram around the city; Christ by spitting on a blind man's eyes and laying his hands on him (Mk 8.23–25).

Where I'd seen similarities in the names, Crowley actually put it together that Maria and Maia were the same. He pointed out that after separating from the orb of the sun, Mercury takes three days to become visible. This, he believed, represented the three days it took Christ to rise from the grave.

Still another suggestion might be seen in Saul's blindness as a traveler:

Saul arose from the ground; and when his eyes were
opened, he could see nothing; so they led him by the

hand and brought him into Damascus. And for three
days he was without sight, and neither ate nor drank
(Acts 9: 8, 9).[224]

Crowley saw a commonness in half the fish symbol to Christ and
Hermes. He might have reasoned this out for himself or read it (others
had reached this same conclusion long before him) and agreed with it.
(See last part of footnote 239.)

"Now when they had departed, behold, an angel of the Lord
appeared to Joseph in a *dream* and said, 'Rise, take the child and his mother and flee to Egypt,'" (Mt 2: 13).

Here was another type of baptism: traveling and crossing boundaries
shortly after his birth. Note: Hermes, along with other Olympians, had
fled to Egypt.

"This was to fulfil what the Lord had spoken by the prophet, 'Out of
Egypt have I called my son'" (Mt. 2: 15).

Both Christ and Hermes are gods of boundaries and breakers of
boundaries: Hermes sacrificing two cattle, Jesus apparently saying it's
okay to eat pork (Mt 15: 17, 18). Hermes is a god of wealth and merchants,
but Christ will drive the money-changers out of the temple, then later
make a publican (tax collector) one of his disciples. Christ, dying on the
cross (the symbol alone suggesting crossing a boundary), was crossing
the boundary of life to death, as did Hermes with the dead, and the
boundary of god to man and man to god.

"I baptize you with water for repentance, but he who is coming after
me is mightier than I, whose *sandals* I am not worthy to carry" (Mt 3: 11).
Thoth "purifies the uninitiated with water."

"Or what man of you, if his son asks him for bread, will give him
stone? or if he asks for fish, will give him *serpent*?" (Mt 7: 9, 10).

Jesus, furthermore, is easier to understand as Hermes when he said to
one of the disciples, "Follow me, and leave the dead to bury their own
dead" (Mt 8: 22).[225]

As they went away, Jesus began to speak to the crowds concerning
John: "What did you go out into the wilderness to behold? *A reed shaken
by the wind?*"

And he awoke and rebuked the wind, and said to the sea, "*Peace!* Be
still!" And the *wind* ceased and there was a great calm (Mk 4: 39).

Hermes: wind god, staff, peace.

"So they took branches of *palm* trees...and Jesus found a young ass and
sat upon it" (J 12: 13.)[226]

"This is he of whom it is written, 'Behold, I send my *messenger* before
thy face, who shall prepare thy way before thee'" (Mt 11: 10).

"And they stripped him and put a scarlet[227] robe upon him, and plaiting a crown of thorns they put it on his head, and put a *reed* in his right
hand. And kneeling before him they mocked him, saying "Hail, King of

the Jews!" And they spat upon him, and took the *reed* and struck him on the head (Mt. 27: 28–30).

Because things had not gone well in Mexico for the previous two years and the year seemed right, they believed Cortez, riding his horse ("deer"), must be their beloved god returning to them. There was much rejoicing at first before they realized they were wrong, though not completely. For Cortez brought Christianity, be that as it may at that time, having a curious twist: Cortez arrived on *Good Friday* 1519, the year on the Aztec (AZ) calendar designated as 1 *Reed*, which would not occur again for 52 years. (See Book I, footnote 65.)

"And they crucified him, and divided his garments among them *casting lots for them*, to decide what each should take" (Mk 15: 24).[228] Hermes, god of gamblers.

"And at the *ninth* hour Jesus cried with a loud voice...'My God, my God, why has thou forsaken me?'" (Mk 15: 34).

"And one ran and, filling a sponge full of vinegar, put it on a *reed* and gave it to him to drink" (Mk 15: 36),

"And Jesus uttered a loud cry, and *breathed* his last" (Mk 15: 37).

"Then two robbers were crucified with him, one on his right and one on the left" (Mt 27: 38).[229]

"And he bought a linen shroud, and taking him down, wrapped him in the linen shroud, and laid him in a tomb which had been *hewn out of the rock*; and he rolled a stone against the door of the tomb" (Mk 15: 46).

"...toward *dawn* of the first day...an angel of the Lord...rolled back the *stone*...'He is not here; for he has risen, as he said'" (Mt 28: 1, 2, 6). Hermes was born at dawn.[230]

The caduceus and the cross were one and the same. The two thieves were the two snakes, representing all the sins of mankind, to whom Hermes brought peace and for which Christ died. So it's said that Hermes is a god of thieves[231] and by extension, prisoners. St. Peter ad Vencula, "of the fetters."

If at the root of magic is the transition from life to death and back again, the blood of Argus has implications in magic and sacrifice.

In a sense Zeus was responsible for the death of Argus, though Hermes stood in judgment of the gods. He was a sacrificial lamb who had to atone for the sin of his father if the vote went against him, yet a supreme deity can do what he thinks right. He has no boundaries.

Hermes was born the god of sacrifice, but to be truly the god of sacrifice and not a hypocrite, he had to be willing to sacrifice himself. The purer he was, the greater the gift.

Since he was more familiar with man than any other god, it's not too difficult to see him then as Christ, the son of God, offering himself in atonement for the sins of man.

456

"I am the way, and the truth, and the life; no one comes to the Father, but by me" (J 14: 6).

Joseph Campbell speaks of Hermes as "guide of the souls to the knowledge of eternal life."[232]

Long before Christ on the cross, the peasants and servants, the people you can't fool over the long haul, thought of Hermes as their protector, one of the guardians of the home as well as the road.

More has been written about Hermes than any other Olympian. Hearing that I'd identified Jesus with him, one person made a list to see if there were anything to this. Jesus' background and persona on one side, Hermes' on the other. Yet in something like this, there will always be a built-in bias, especially of Christians as well as those exposed to Christianity, that it can't possibly be true, even though they claim objectivity.

Exception is taken to the fact that the lister put "cunning" under Hermes but not under Jesus. Cunning is described as 1) skillful, clever, and 2) sly, crafty. Jesus was *eloquent*, mentally fleet on his feet. He was an orator, a storyteller (parables), and often turned criticism to suit his own purpose. Like it or not, he was cunning: "Let him who is without sin among you be the first to throw a stone at her" (Jn 8: 7).

And like it or not, Christians are cunning. It wasn't too many years ago that schizophrenics were considered by them to be people taken over by demons and the devil. No wonder so many paranoid schizophrenics are into religion. But not many Christians are beginning to see that schizophrenia is caused by a chemical imbalance. No doubt in time the books will be cooked.

Of that which has been preserved, nothing indicates that Jesus ever sinned. He was, however, mercurial at times, a saving grace in making him identifiable with man.

In the morning, as he was returning to the city, he was hungry, and seeing a fig tree by the wayside he went to it and found nothing on it but leaves only. And he said to it, "May no fruit ever come from you again!" (Mt 21: 18–20).

But his disciples never seemed to wonder about the outburst but were more interested in being able to do the same trick (magic).

"And Jesus answered them, 'Truly I say to you, if you have faith and never doubt, you will not only do what had been done to the fig tree....'" (Mt 21: 21).

There is Hermes (possibly originating in Mesopotamia, "the cradle of civilization"), the most loved by man of the Olympians, in Greece and other parts of the Mediterranean; Thoth in Egypt; Mercury in Italy; Mercury the most important god of all in Gaul; and Odin, the most important of the Norse gods in Germanic countries. Add to this Quetzalcoatl in the New World. Doesn't it seem strange the great geographical influence of Hermes or a god he's identified with? All roads lead to Rome, especially from 45 or 44 B.C. Christ—who seems to appear from nowhere and everywhere—is syncreticism, sophistication, and simplification.

If all life exists only by the grace of and because there is a god of sacrifice, then it seems logical that he's not going to sacrifice himself for man without expecting/taking a sacrifice of/from man. This we see in what is deemed as the natural order of things: accidents, killings, wars, disease, starvation, old age, death, etc. It may not be the positive way of looking at things—even perceived as morbid—but it fits the picture better than any other. If you want to be intelligent, you'll agree.

Chapter Twenty-four

Aberfan (aea) is a coal-mining town in Wales. It means in Welsh "river mouth at the hill," but a river's mouth is always a snake's head, and the seven-letter word has the ring of an anagram, something hidden. Perhaps it is EAF BRAN (raven, mystery, black, death, sorrow).[233]

The town is enclosed in a small, narrow triangle when straight lines are drawn from Merthyr Tydfil to Merthyr Vale to Mynydd (mountain) Merthyr to Merthyr Tydfil. *Merthyr* means graveyard, and not far from the triangle is Mountain Ash.[234] (*Dead Souls: Mërtcye dushi*. See *February 21, 1852*).

Two weeks before the disaster,[235] which would be October 7, 1966, Eryl *Mai* Jones, a ten-year-old schoolgirl, accurately predicted that she and two of her friends would die. Then later on October 19 (two days before the disaster), she dreamed she was swallowed up in "something black."

On October *14, Alexander* Venn, retired from Cunard Line and an amateur artist, felt strongly that an accident was about to occur nearby and would have something to do with coal dust. There were also several others who had feelings, dreams, premonitions, etc., leading up to the day of destruction.

It had been a rain of tears for two days previously, a sorrow for what was to be. Then on Friday, October 21, 1966 at 9:14 A.M., a six hundred-foot mountain of waste coal from a nearly mine moved down, causing a wasteland. Homes were torn away, trees uprooted, and part of the school crushed. A total of 144 died (28 adults and 116 children). Twenty-one (21) can be a good-luck number, a bad-luck number, or a number of sharp contrast (the *Constitution*, launched October 21, 1797, outlasted all the other ships—life-death), but it's seldom neutral. October 21, 1966 (22). *2122*

Everybody is Hermes to some extent. There are no chosen few. But the Hermetic stamp—of sharp contrast—is easier to see in some.

Baron Manfred von Richthofen was born May 2, 1892, in Breslau, which happened to be, by one account, the name of the pilot he was pursuing when shot down. He became *cavalry* lieutenant in 1912, a *Flyer* in 1915. He crashed and then went up again (mercurial). He was called the *"Red Baron"* (cinna*bar*) because of his plane's color. He topped the list (contest) of all World War II aces with eighty planes shot down. His fighter group was called "Richthofen's Flying Circus" (Circus Maximus). He had the killer instinct of a wolf. He died on *April 21*, 1918 when his red triplane (three) was shot down ($21 \div 3 = 7$). But Romulus, who was suckled by a she-*wolf*, established Rome on *April 21*, 753 B.C. Hermann Goering succeeded the Red Baron as commander of fighter group.

At dusk on October 27, 312, Constantine, whose mother Helena was a concubine236 and would later become devout, prepared for the battle of Rome when he's said to have had a vision in which he saw the cross of Christ and heard a voice saying he would conquer with that sign. He then had all his soldier's shields and their horses' heads painted with crosses. The following day Rome fell to him and his men. One of many legends concerning Constantine is that he wore a nail from Christ's crucifixion in his crown and that another was made into a bit for his horse.237 He was baptized on the day he died: May 22 (MP), 337, some say. (*Collier's Encyclopedia* gives May 21, 337; see Book II, footnote 207.)

Ancient Rome had a bloody history, especially in games and sacrifice. Constantine built the first St. Peter's. A horse can be associated with death, and its imagery is seen sometimes on ancient tombs in Rome. Mercury and Christ are gods of sacrifice. Though Constantinople was to become the "new Rome" for awhile, Rome, Italy, eventually regained its grandeur as the religious center.

The Vatican was established on June 10 (MP), *1929*. It's curious that 1) the Pope is chosen by cardinals with their *scarlet* cassocks after what appears to be considerable *cunning* in the secular world, and 2) the announcement to the world that a Pope has or hasn't been chosen by white or black smoke (fire + wind).

In 1929 also, the catacombs became a "foreign land," an outpost of the Vatican, a sovereign state. (*Did you know?* London: Reader's Digest Association, Ltd., 1990.) This is intriguing in relation to the Parentalia and the fact that St. Peter's basilica was built over a cemetery.

In the cabin-class swimming bath of the *Queen Mary* was a picture in sandblasted glass, incorporated with the stairs, of two *silver* swans on a background of *red* and *green*.[238-A] The swan, a graceful bird on water, is closely related to the goose. The one swan (or bird) in flight represented perhaps the *Spruce Goose*; the other, on or near the ground and with wings outstretched, was the *Queen Mary*. Symbolically, the *Queen Mary* is Mary, Maia, and the *Spruce Goose* (sacred to Hermes is the goose, representing earth to sky, sky to earth, honking messages of its arrival) is Christ or Hermes.

460

On January 20, 1992, there was something mentioned on television that the *Spruce Goose* at Long Beach, California, was being considered for sale to Las Vegas, Nevada. Since both the R.M.S. *Queen Mary* and the H-4 *Spruce Goose* had become unlikely subjects of this book, I couldn't help wondering if the separation were wise. There seemed to be some mystical link. Probably it was nothing, but why chance it?

Now having thought this, there was a dilemma: If a letter were written suggesting no action be taken because of a whim or hunch, I would have been daft. If not sent, it might have been what should have been done. I opted for being certifiably insane, sending off certified letters: one to the mayor of Long Beach, another to the city council, and a third to the *Press-Telegram*, explaining it might be bad luck to sell the flying boat and that a catastrophe might follow both in Long Beach and the surrounding area. The *Spruce Goose*, housed in a dome-shaped shelter, was like a huge church which only a few people attended and seemingly not successful. Later, after the *Spruce Goose* was sold to a buyer in McMinnville, Oregon, I wrote a similar letter to its new owner.

You might not be surprised to learn that none of the above replied; I wasn't. Cowards! Yet had the situation been reversed, no answer would have been sent. I am sure that in at least one of the offices, my letter was the moment's joke, to be filed away in the loony bin along with hundreds of others. But you do what you gotta do, DQ, even if the horse you rode in on is a skinny nag called Rocinante.

Perhaps the series of disasters these past few years plaguing southern California especially are last-chance warning signals that something bigger is to come, but we'll just have to wait and see.

Chapter Twenty-five

The fast lasted for four full days with nothing but liquids. Cold turkey! It ran into the fourth day of the fifth month up until one minute past midnight, or into the fifth day. With the exception of fasting, however, I had to admit—looking down at a ring of five burning candles, each with a rock alongside and a new plate of fresh pound cake and honey—it was sort of a half-hearted, listless effort, a Catch-22. To have enthusiasm, vigor, to get on a roll, you gotta have food. But eating food prevents the magic. Dozing from time to time, I got up at exactly one minute after midnight and put the candles out. If whatever force were to come, it could have done so in one minute. No more sleep was to be lost worrying about the room catching on fire.

The first Mercury period came and went. Indeed Saddam Hussein, of poison gas infamy and of whom the effort was made to dispatch, looked fatter and sassier than ever, as if he'd done nothing but gorge himself on pound cake and honey since the ritual. Finding me asleep, the force must have misunderstood about the pound cake and honey, and the rocks and candles surrounding the nine-foot circumference circle (the room wasn't big enough to make a nine-foot diameter circle) in which Saddam Hussein's picture was placed. Even so, in spite of the lack of attention to detail, there might have been success had I not succumbed to the temptation of eating all the fresh pound cake and honey that hadn't been taken, which was, in fact, all that had been placed out. "Well,"[238-B] to quote Ronald Reagan, what the hell; four full days I was hungry, and it was a shame to see all that good food going to waste when there are millions of starving children in China.

Do witches really exist? I've never been aware of a full-fledged witch if they do. By "full-fledged" is meant a being who can call up some paranormal power at will anytime and produce results. My reason for believing there might be some around is based on the fact that there are a few documented cases of clairvoyants, healers, and the like (not phonies) who have run hot and cold. This is sort of a fragmentation. Some obviously had a gift or power at one time, but it wasn't consistent, possibly due to an unknown variable. Of these, a few began faking it and were exposed.

Others resorted to shotgun predictions, in which case one out of a hundred might prove to be true, the law of averages. Much is made out of the one prediction which is close; nothing is said about the other ninety-nine which were bananas. Some gifted people made no further predictions after the initial success, or maybe only a few, which may have turned out right or wrong. Possibly the reason a talent dried up in the latter is that there's a nebulous area, a faint guilt in thinking the thought or having it flashed to mind, a feeling they took part in causing it to happen, even if the thought or flash at times appeared to come after the fact.

As the novelty of being able to do something wears off, it wouldn't be in the interest of a full-fledged witch to brag, "See what I can do!" This would spawn a crop of nuts. Man, the bounty hunter, in his guile to show his goodness and try to buy a seat in heaven, would certainly try to kill the witch. Perhaps the so-called evil lies not so much within the witch as man himself.

If not a bounty hunter then, man would become relentless in pestering the wizard to teach him magic. It would be the Garden of Eden all over again, when most witches are probably loath to call upon a power, exploiting it as man would them.

Along these lines, it's interesting that the prophet Elisha said, "I pray you, let me inherit a double share of your spirit" (2 Ki 2: 9).

Why is it more women than men are witches? *Malleus Maleficarum*, a fifteenth-century book for prosecuting witches, states that since women "are feebler in mind and body, it is not surprising that they should come under the spell of witchcraft" (Malleus, 44).

Whatever, it doesn't seem too logical that by saying a few magic words some god, spirit, demon, whatever, is going to do a witch's bidding. If these powers have been around for tens of thousands of years, they've long since figured out how not to subject themselves to any puny, Johnny-come-lately's beck and call. Similarly, realizing a witch isn't going to share his or her secret, man would most likely try to get even by telling lies, half truths, calling the witch a phony, resorting to blackmail, threats, and condemnation. There's no limit to what man will do to get power himself, no end to his cunning and slyness. Thus a fragmentation of power could very well be a safeguard or protective measure which comes with the gift, and "suffer not the witch" might have been a further safeguard against the witch revealing himself/herself. Man, in general, could not handle such power or be content with somebody else having it, nor is he content in just dying. There's all kinds of power in heaven. Loving God has nothing to do with it. Maybe that's not the way it should be, but that's the way it is.

Despite the above, I—forever the optimist thinking positively—tried to get rid of Saddam again on May 4–5, 1996, taking as a sign Seattle's 4.5 earthquake occurring on May 2, 1996. This time there was no fasting, but I used other things—excluding human and animal sacrifice—which came to mind. Anyway to make ALSS, both Saddam and his would-be dispatcher were unscathed.

Chapter Twenty-six

Old people go to bed early, too tired most times to go through the motion of prayer, but if they do, it's usually to tell how tired and weary they are. Anything else which might get sandwiched in is just B.S. So they get a waiver of a few hours, which is good sense. It is better to listen to them at their best than at their cranky, whiny worst.

It's as natural as the comings and goings of the sun and moon for them to become wide awake again in four or five hours. Maybe this is the way it was planned, like the tides. At these times in the early morning, a passing thought might be given to prayer, but chances are my mind focuses on things too tired before to think about, taking myself and them too seriously. The best way to cut off the analytical machine is to pick up a spook book. Usually then sleep will come within an hour or two, only to wake up again about 4:30 A.M. when there are few with whom to share the world.

Wednesday, January 20, 1993. Up again around 2:00 A.M., reached for my glasses and Dean R. Koontz's *Cold Fire*,[239-A] then about half finished. A picture of a windmill is on its cover. In the novel, Koontz uses this as a setting. He apparently hadn't seen the windmill as a Hermetic correspondence, nor had I at first. But it's clear: a stone structure, phallic, four vaned (ae) arms propelled by wind (the traveler), and making a circular motion. Here too is a possible connection to Henry and Mary Moon Mills, my great grandparents, i.e., windmill, millstone, and millwheel.

In the book, Koontz mentions Hawthorne and Poe in the same sentence. This, along with The Friend warning Holly Thorne (Hawthorne?) and Jim Ironheart not to sleep for "dreams are doorways" (four), leads me to believe that Koontz too is under the influence of Hermes, the god of writers.

After awhile I put *Cold Fire* down and tried to project a windmill into the dreams of those sleeping in rooms next to mine. And don't tell me about this being illegal. My privacy is invaded a hundred times a day with their snoring, farting, coughing, door slamming, cooking odors, cigarette smoke, televisions, and VCRs blaring, and knocking on my door to borrow money—not to mention the Lazarus garbage collectors, making enough noise to raise the dead.

Anyway, this soon fizzled as I fell back to sleep. Like clockwork: up at 4:30 A.M. to claim my world. Sometime after 7:00 A.M. the Venetian blinds began banging. These I raised and sat watching out the window, fascinated like a cat before a fish pond, while the storm was at its worst for the next four to five hours.

The rain pelted at times; the wind howled, kiting, whipping, and blowing objects around. A tree put up a valiant but futile fight; sirens screeched, shooting stars fading away in the distance. Elsewhere trees were uprooted and fell on homes and power lines. A friend came along wanting to borrow seven-five dollars to take his four freezing daughters to a motel until the power was restored. This may have been true, but he has a genius for taking advantage of occurrences and my sympathetic nature. Would that he'd have the same genius for paying back the money he'd borrowed, but he knows he's not going to pay it back. We both know he's not going to pay it back. Still "Baby Jesus"'s butt sits on his bald head.

The paper said the storm had been predicted the day before. I missed this. It came as much as a surprise to me in the morning after trying to project windmills as the total count of five deaths. One man's spinal cord was severed, paralyzing both arms and legs (four). Somehow he's like a windmill for the rest of his life. I am sure I didn't cause the storm, but I'm equally sure the book, the subject matter, sleep, dreams, and my attempt to project the windmill—perhaps suggesting electricity—were connected to it someway.

"Isn't this pitiful!" you sniff. Fine, believe what you want, but I know what I know. If you're going to send me to a shrink, send me to Jung.

Far off in the electricity of Washington, D.C., Maya (phonetic of Maia) Angelou's inaugural poem is being read. It begins "A Rock, a River, a Tree," like some ingredients she's stirring in a cauldron for the Rhodes (roads) scholar. (Doesn't he plan to put more people to work by repairing roads?) Her interpretation of these might be different, but a rock you must know by now or you'll never know. A tree represents a branching, fork, or crossroads, and a river, the traveler, or an Arkansas traveler.

Bill Clinton was born on August 19, 1946, and Albert Gore, Jr., on March 31, 1948. So at one point when they were jogging together (footprints) before the election, they were forty-five and forty-four respectively. At the inauguration, they were forty-six and forty-four, or *forty-five* average. Later that night, the president will play his wind instrument; and George Stephanoupoulis will be his spokesman.

Audrey Hepburn, born in Brussels, Belgium, to a baroness (ae) and a banker (ae), probably had her worst year in the winter of 1944–1945 when

World War II was at its height and she suffered malnutrition. Still she managed to attend school and take ballet lessons.

In her lifetime, she was nominated for *five* academy awards, but only for the film in 1953 (SY) did she receive as Oscar when she played a princess. You might remember it: *Roman Holiday*, which indeed the Parentalia was. Probably her finest hour, however, began in 1986 when she became a good-will ambassador for UNICEF. She was way ahead of the United States in its involvement in Somali, as were Elizabeth Taylor, Joan Rivers, and a few others taking up the cause of AIDS when it wasn't considered good publicity to do so.

Audrey Hepburn was born in 1929 (SY), the same as diarist Anne Frank, on May 4, or 4-5-1929 as Europeans would write this date. With little imagination, this becomes 45-21.

January 21 (the day following her death, the Seattle storm, and President Clinton's inauguration) was the anniversary of the beheading two hundred years previously of Louis XVI, who might not have been guillotined if he hadn't had a number.

Lenin, who was responsible for the demise of the *Romanovs*, died on January 21, 1924, the anniversary of Louis XVI's beheading, and he was born on April 22, 1870. So once again, there's a connection of 2122 to the North Clark Street address, and Lenin enters the spirit of the Parentalia by having his body viewed by more people than any other person in the history of time. But this was his destiny.

But to return to the question, "Is it possible to enter another's dreams?" By accident, a comment was overheard—made by a person I disliked—that he wished I'd stay out of his dreams. This struck me as interesting in that there'd been no conversation between him and me, nor was anyone told of my effort in the wee hours of the mornings to cause him lousy dreams, the best of punishments since that person bears no scars, there's no evidence, no witnesses, and he's denied a restful sleep by the image of someone he obviously dislikes too. Besides, he must either suffer in silence or hear the ridicule when telling that you, of all people, are in his dreams.

To do this, it seems to me, there has to be an intense feeling and the ability to call up in one's mind a clear image. Be pragmatic, if you can't sleep, you might as well put your time to good use, fighting the best way you're capable.

Oh don't be so self-righteous: That's a sin. The person, to whom I'd not known, had on a previous occasion made a very demeaning remark within hearing distance. So I should be very adult and not juvenile? Just let it go and try to understand? No! Besides, the person comes to no real harm, which is more than can be said for the long history of bloody deeds by Christians. Oh but those people really weren't Christians who inflicted the carnage, you say. If they weren't then, who are Christians? A most accurate description of a Christian is to say he is like a eunuch in that he always knows how it should be done. Seen in the best light he comes off as a bribe taker. Doesn't make any difference if the payoff is now or later. Indeed there are few—if any—who expect no reward, who do simply because it was their existence alone, the right thing to do. Call me what you like, but what's been said is the truth, even if seamy and unkind. "Brothers and sisters, let the spirit of the holy season be upon you and give me a gift." I won't give you one in return. The following year you might give me a gift again, and I don't reciprocate. There'll be no third year.

Chapter Twenty-seven

When writing, I am up between 4:00 and 5:00 A.M. seven days a week; I have instant coffee, instant peanut butter and jam on a slice of bread, and I write less instantly for two or three hours. This makes life endurable; the prose perhaps is dull in case you wondered.

A movie comes to mind where a hillbilly farmer got himself out of bed at dawn and rushed outside in his long johns to play a fiddle for an hour or two. His children had thought him touched. This was true; their snoring had driven him nuts. But he had learned to draw the bow across their throats in sublimation.

After writing; I go to the library for a couple hours or walk down along Elliott Avenue, nodding or bowing to the caboose-goat of the Great Northern Railway[239-B] between the Diamond building and the Seattle *Post-Intelligencer*, and then continue on until lower Kinnear Park to do some calisthenics if it's not too cold. If it is too cold, just saying "calisthenics" over and over still gives quite a muscular workout, and I also made four or five laps around a circular path, each time placing a small stone on a large rock in the path. Sometimes the ravens or crows (same difference to an apprentice witch) came and cawed from the trees. I'd caw back, and they usually stayed until they heard no answer and then flew off.

If early enough, the old man could be seen throwing kernels of dried corn beneath the trees. He also fed several homeless cats. Over many years, he never seemed to miss a day, as there was always a little corn remaining on the ground, showing that he'd been there earlier and leading me to believe he worshiped the corn goddess while using the squirrels as a front. If meeting, we'd exchange polite greetings when passing, and he'd say equably that it was going to be a nice day, and I'd reply that it was. Seldom did he say more. While feeding the animals, he must have had a lot of positive thoughts—something you don't often get from feeding humans. He walked slowly and slightly bent, being in his mid-seventies at least.

This year (1993) during the Parentalia, I skipped the writing and going to the library to head straight to the park. Instead of making the usual five turns, I'd make the number of rounds equal to the calendar day and place that many stones, and then walk up to Capitol Hill and either buy a couple boxes of primroses and some parsley or break flowers off Volunteer Park bushes that were doomed from the cold. Spring had accidentally come early—or maybe purposely for their budding—and they'd have been burned by the cold anyway if not taken. Then I'd move on to Lakeview Cemetery, which is next to the park. So for a couple days at least there were footprints in the snow as the ravens crowed from headstones. Why this elaborate and tiring ritual for many miles for nine days is a mystery, other than it was required, something which had to be done while the ravens[239-C] called along the way. Everybody hears these birds, but for me they had special meaning.

One day during this period, the old man's wild cat came up and let me touch him. Very surprised, the old man commented, "Why that's the first time I've ever seen him go up to someone else like that!" So there were small signs, like the four or five geese flying in formation overhead. On the nineteenth, there was a notice on the telephone post leading to the park:

CRAZY 8'S
FEBRUARY 19 & 20
FIREHOUSE

It's never been my way to sacrifice animals nor will it be. Still the idea occurs that because of being too fainthearted to do this—unless in extreme hatred or rage maybe a human magically, which as yet as a callow witch hasn't been figured out how to do—I might just be a menace to others, as the sacrifice might be made for me, the Al Capone syndrome. Could it be me or the old man whose life might be taken? Don't know why I have the insistence in saying he's over the hill when I'm not far behind. Let's lay this to rest then by saying he's Necropolis and I'm Cemeterius.

Necropolis had gotten into a heated argument with a woman, about thirty-five, carrying a dog. A bull terrier? Years before (he later told me) he'd been bitten bad by a dog, so today he'd picked up a piece of wood to protect himself only when the woman's dog began to bark, snarl, and stalk him. The woman (Necropolis later said) then accused him of attacking her precious dog. They were first noticed when both came running toward me, while I was wishing they hadn't, for there was yet another bow to make before the venerable rock and didn't want them to see this. I opted to make a quick, nearly imperceptible one and turned toward them.

"Officer, arrest that woman! Arrest that woman!" Necropolis is looking at me, Cemeterius, and pointing at her.

The woman, now carrying her dog in hot pursuit, scolds Necropolis that he'd just better never ever threaten her or her poor animal again.

Then she stalked on past up the path, while Necropolis is parroting, "Arrest that woman!" So Cemeterius hollers after her, "Lady you should have your dog on a leash." He then told me what had happened and that he hadn't threatened the woman. Having completed what was to be done, I left.

The next day Necropolis, who has scarcely said a thing to me other than "good morning; it's going to be a nice day" all these years, said, "Did you see what happened yesterday? Well, she went and told her boyfriend, who came down here. I told him truthfully I hadn't threatened her and that he had a lying bitch for a woman and that she should keep her dog on a leash. But he wouldn't believe me, said his woman didn't lie and that she didn't have to have her dog on a leash if she didn't want to. He said he was going to beat me up, and I said, 'Well, I don't hear any bones rattling.' he then said to me, 'I'm going to come down here and poison every one of your damn squirrels.' 'You do that,' I said 'and I'll just bring in more.'"

Thus there was good reason to worry Necropolis might be the sacrifice. Hadn't enough been done to prevent this? You can see, of course, that people get a little flaky with age.[240] Damn flaky! (A friend says, "Don't go and blame it on age; you were always flaky." Only your friends will tell you.)

The following day was sort of an occasion, being the eve of my thirty-ninth birthday.[241-A] I hadn't seen a movie since before Christmas and decided to splurge where the admission was $1.50, which was cheap at half the price. You think that sounds like Jack Benny, do you? Well, why not?[241-B] He was born in Chicago on *February 14*, 1894. *Hoffa* was thoroughly enjoyed, even though he was probably worse than portrayed and Robert Kennedy a better man than the caricature.

A friend commented later he thought Al Capone and Jimmy Hoffa were much alike. I came to Hoffa's defense on this, yet now thinking it over, there were similarities. They were both shrewd and cunning, and each in his time clubbed, batted, and did in certain enemies. Hoffa had been president of the International Brotherhood of Teamsters. Here is a Hermetic link to merchants and to travel, dating back to teams of animals, especially *horses*, and Capone had always claimed that he himself was nothing but a businessman. But most of all, it was surprising to read that James *Riddle* Hoffa, presumed to have been *murdered* on July 30, 1975, was born in Brazil (az), *Indiana*, on the forty-fifth day of the year or St. Valentine's Day: *February 14*, 1913.

On the twenty-first, I left the cemetery feeling what was required had been done. It was cold and snowing. A jogger in shorts and a maroon sweatshirt ran from behind me on Broadway and kept on going ahead. About this time a pretty girl walked toward me. I motioned ahead and commented that it never failed to amaze me, seeing something like that:

The old lady jogger with pale, brittle legs must have been eighty if she were a day. We both laughed, feeling good about this. There was no worrying about the Feast of the Dead by that crone—or not that at all; maybe she was running from it, scared to stop.

When returning to the building where I was staying for the past few years on First Avenue (an address seldom used for mailing so it's not easily recalled), I was surprised to make the connection that its address 2212 wasn't very different from 2122. The difference between the two is 90, or 2 x 45.

The following day would be the Caristia, the anniversary of the day my father died. President Clinton was to come to the Puget Sound to speak to Boeing workers at Everett. There was an uneasy feeling about this, that something would happen and halfway hoping it would. It shamed me to think that if something would just fit into my story, life could be held so cheaply, and yet wouldn't it show that they really gave a damn about me? (If you really love me, you'll commit murder.) The ambivalence was finally resolved: Whatever, I'd done what I was supposed to do during the old Roman period. And if the world and I could just get through February 21–22, there was nothing to worry about for the rest of the month. No forethought was given to the anniversary of the day my mother died.

In lower Manhattan on February 26, 1993, a light pall of snow surrounded the Twin Towers of the World Trade Center. Some workers in the morning had greeted coworkers with "Thank God it's Friday." For that's what it was, except 2 times 13 and double trouble.

Between 12:10 and 12:20 P.M. on this day, blood was being drawn from my arm for a test in Seattle. I hadn't heard until after this that "The Bomb That Shook America" had exploded (12:18 EST) at the World Trade (commerce, *merchants*, telecommunications) Center, a place I had once visited.

There was panic as hundreds struggled down dark stairs filled with smoke. At least sixty people called in confessing or taking credit for the explosion. Only the Shadow would know all their reasons. Perhaps a few thought it was funny to do so, a big laugh, a joke, a hoax, or maybe a way—by causing the police still more confusion—of getting even for previous injustices either real or imagined. But most were telling the world that it was paying for the suffering it had caused them—as they always knew it would have to—or even more sadly, some believed it was their fault. Out of guilt and shame, they confessed as they always did and would until they died.

Over a thousand were injured. The bodies of five of those killed[242] would be found fairly soon. According to one source, two were still thought to be missing.

Then on March 15—the *twenty-first* day past the Caristia, the *twenty-second* day past the Feralia—the remains of a sixth victim were found. Don't suppose much would have been thought about this had he been one of the first five located. His name, Wilfredo Mercado, and the fact he was found on the ides made me think twice. *Mercado* means market. *Mercadore*: merchant, tradesman. Willie (Iu*lli*) logged in produce, Monday through Friday, for the *Win*dows on the World Restaurant, 107 stories up.

There was a strong feeling that a seventh death would turn up (see pages 482-483). As the months passed, nothing was reported. Why? I couldn't understand. Then one day someone talking on the radio mentioned that Marcia Rodriguez Smith had been an expectant mother.

The trial began on October 4, 1993. Before it was over, there'd be 206 witnesses and over ten thousand pages of testimony, most of it circumstantial. With little bits and pieces here and there, how could any juror find his way through it? Then on the Lupercalia 1994, co-prosecutor Henry de Pippo put it all together masterfully. He traced the plot back to *April* 1992. On March 4, 1994, the jury found the defendants guilty on all counts.

Jacqueline Kennedy Onassis, widow of the assassinated president, was buried on May 23, 1994, the last day of the Rosalia in ancient Rome. On May 24, 1994, the first day of the Rosalia in Pergamum (see Book I, footnote 25), the guilty in the World Trade Center bombing were sentenced to 240 years each, which was calculated to be, by the U.S. District Court Judge, one year for each year of life they deprived their victims.

On May 3, 1993, Necropolis was feeding the cats and squirrels again. He mentioned that about four days after the threat, he returned to his car one morning to find a rock smashed through his windshield.

Chapter Twenty-eight

Thoth-Hermes is associated with the calendar.

The dates 45 B.C. and 44 B.C. are Hermetic numbers, signposts pointing to Christ's birth. So the meaning wouldn't be lost, they were also significant in recorded history. In 45 B.C., the Julian calendar went into effect.[243] In 44 B.C., Marcus Antonius offered calendar Caesar(aeaaea) an enwreathed, laurel crown. In his friends-Romans-countrymen *funeral* oration, Antonius says,

> You all did see that on the Lupercal
> I thrice presented him a kingly crown,
> Which he did thrice refuse: was this ambition?[244]
> Cemeteries are simply repositories of small calendars.

Caesar dignified the Lupercalia ceremony in 44 B.C. by his presence.[245] It's also true the Lupercal Iulli was in honor of Caesar. For whatever reason Caesar turned down the crown, the fact remains he was being given a gift on the Lupercalia by one of the Luperci. Marcus Antonius was said to have been drunk, yet the laughter of the crowd might have cut into both men for different reasons.

The god of the Lupercalia was thought to be the Greek god Pan (who some say was the son of Hermes) or a syncretic Pan-Faunus or Faunus alone,[246] who was a popular god of agriculture and cattle breeding.

The word *Luperci* comes close to meaning "wolf-men" and suggests a hatred or fear of wolves by one interpretation, by another, wolf-god propitiation and perhaps adulation, teetering on fanaticism. Whatever, the wolf combines the good and evil in the nature of man. In *Deutschland* (45) lore, the wolf is mentioned more than any other animal. Thus both Rome and Germany have their wolf mythologies.

Legend is that Romulus and Remus, the twin brothers who had been abandoned in infancy, were suckled by a she-wolf in a cave under the Palatine (ila), one of the seven hills of Rome. A shepherd eventually found them, and they were brought up by him and his wife. When grown, the twins wanted to start a city but couldn't agree where, and a quarrel ensued. Romulus and his followers built a wall around the Palatine area. Remus was killed by his brother when he went over the wall or beyond the area (boundary and boundary breaker), and ironically Romulus becomes a boundary-breaker too.

On February 15, the priests met in the grotto, the city's cradle. From there, the ceremony spread out. The priests, nearly naked except for loincloths, ran through the streets around the Palatine and struck spectators with lashes (called *februa* and made from hides from sacrificed goats and perhaps dogs) who had placed themselves in their path. This was women and men but especially women. The whipping was supposed to act as a charm for fertility and health.

There lay between two hill settlements a valley, which originally had been a cemetery. The route the priests took passed through it. Thus protection by the deads' power might have figured into the ceremony.[247] This conjecture doesn't seem too far-fetched when realizing that the Lupercalia occurred within the Parentalia. Information is scanty at best, but most sources seem to agree that purification and the idea of promoting fertility and/or health were included.

One part of the festival is even more obscure. Plutarch writes (*Romulus* 21: 6–7): "Two young people from noble families are led forth: some touch their foreheads with bloody knives while others wipe them with wool soaked in milk. Once they are wiped, they start to laugh."

Offhand, the blood could have represented death and heritage and the wiping of blood away with milk-soaked wool, the promise of children, a continuing purification of the human race. They might have laughed then in triumph that they couldn't be defeated. A more sinister meaning is possible and is suggested by the only word to come down through the centuries to describe the Luperci: savage. Augustus forbade any boy above the age of fourteen to appear naked or run through the streets as such during the Lupercalia.[248] In A.D. 494 Bishop Galasius changed the festival to the Feast of Purification.

Again, the Lupercalia in 44 B.C. had to do in part with purification. Caesar refused the crown three times, rightfully but possibly for the wrong reason. He'd been mocked.

"So when Pilate [ila] saw that he was gaining nothing, rather that a riot was beginning, he took *water and washed his hands* before the crowd, saying, 'I am innocent of this man's blood; see to it yourselves'" (Mt 27: 24).

"*And plaiting a crown of thorns* they put it on his head...and kneeling before him, they mocked him saying, 'Hail, King of the Jews!'" (Mt 27: 29). *Irony*: "The chief priests answered, 'We have no king but Caesar'"[249] (Jn 19: 15). The chief priests of the Jews then said to Pilate, "Do not write, 'King of the Jews,' but, 'This man said, I am King of the Jews.'" Pilate answered, "What I have written I have written" (Jn 19: 21, 22).

The February 26, 1993, explosion at one of the twin towers was two days after the anniversary date that Pope Gregory XIII had issued his papal bull of February 24, 1582, establishing the Gregorian calendar. It was *five* days after the Feralia and *four* days after the Caristia. It occurred on the anniversary of my mother's death in 1929 and the anniversary, four years later, of the groundbreaking ceremony for the Golden Gate Bridge.

Wilfredo Mercado had taken on produce (merchant) for the *Wind*ows on the World restaurant (cook), 107 stories up, which meant he would be one of seven. His body wouldn't be found until March on the Ides. The following Lupercalia (February 15, 1994) was a day of soul bearing and purification. It also brought to mind fertility rites, as Monica Rodriguez Smith had been pregnant. The name of the co-prosecutor (eloquence-justice) *De*Pippo (45) had a Latin ring to it and recalls the calendar of 45 B.C. Finally, to repeat, the imprisonment (sentencing) day was bound between the Rosalia days, on the first of which Jacqueline Kennedy Onassis, the widow of the assassinated president and the Greek tycoon, was buried. Anubis, or Hermanubis, the jackal-headed god, judge and protector of the dead, was guardian of the tomb.

Chapter Twenty-nine

On May 10–11, 1927, Charles Lindbergh (LI), "Lucky Lindy," made a flight from San Diego to New York with a stopover at St. Louis and set a transcontinental record (contest, flight, May). Then on May 21 (BMP), 1927, the *Lone Eagle* landed at an airport near Paris, after flying solo from New York. He was the first man to do so and won twenty-five thousand dollars as a prize. The name Paris itself is, of course, associated with contest. Paris in mythology was also called Alexander.[250]

Lindy called his plane the Spirit of St. Louis. Note LI and the number 21 also figured in the life of Louis XVI (footnote 126), who was beheaded in Paris. Hermes is associated with decapitation or murder, if you want to look at it that way. Often Hermetic people who have been given the extreme of good luck have to pay with the extreme of bad luck. This might be thought of by some as a duality of nature, a betrayal. It's not this but rather a test.

> And about the ninth hour Jesus cried with a loud voice…"My God, my God, why hast thou forsaken me?" (Mt 27: 46).

The time of Lindbergh's landing in France was 10:21 P.M. to 10:24 P.M., depending on the reference material. Anyway by converting 10:24 P.M. Paris time to eastern standard time, we get 5:24 P.M. in New York and New Jersey. This time is curious to remember, as you will see, though admittedly it would have been an hour earlier in Chicago.

Lindbergh's middle name was Augustus, as was his father's and his first child's. This may be Dutch in origin or Swedish. Still it sounds Roman to me. (*Very irrationally* the flight of Blonnie Ward, whom you'll read about shortly, and his landing very close to *August* Croissant, a French-sounding name, seems connected to Lindbergh's landing at Paris six months later and subsequent greeting of Lindbergh by President Coolidge at a reviewing stand by the Washington Monument.)

Lindbergh and his plane *Spirit of St. Louis* returned from France on the USS *Memphis*. The ship was named for Memphis, Tennessee, but in ancient times, Memphis (now lying in ruins, suggesting death, twelve miles south of Cairo) was the capital of Egypt, of which Thoth was one of its gods. Memphis is a Greek abbreviation for *Men-neferu-Meryre*,[251] Pepi I's *funerary* complex.

The engagement of Anne Morrow to Charles Lindbergh was announced on *February 12*, 1929, the Parentalia Eve, the anniversary of Lincoln's and Darwin's birthdays. They were married on May 26 (MP), 1929. The first of six children was born June 22, 1930, Anne's twenty-fourth birthday and was kidnapped (see Book II, footnote 49) from their home near Hopewell, New Jersey, on March 1, 1932, and *murdered*. A Violet Sharpe, a Morrow home servant, became a casualty too.

So how is this connected to Chicago? There's something there, a feeling far stronger than just vague and tenuous threads offered up:

1) Lindy at one time flew mail service (messenger) between St. Louis (connected to *February 14 and 15*) and Chicago. The film *The Spirit of St. Louis* premiered on *February 21*, 1957.

2) May 13, 1927 (equivalent to the Feralia), Black Friday, a dearth of social functions in Chicago, a city of ongoing sacrifice of stockyards.

3) May 14 will be a week before his landing near Paris, after a crescent flight.

4) On May 15 (a time of celebration with water sprinkled on merchandise in ancient Rome), 1927, Commander de Pinedo landed on water near *Grant* Park, Chicago (see page 351).

5) Pinedo's plane also had saint in its name.

6) One author[252] believes that Chicago is the most psychic city in North America. He quotes Frederic De Arechaga as saying that the North Magnetic Pole passes through Chicago and Cairo and that it is zero degrees. It's assumed he's speaking of Cairo, Illinois. Still the Lindbergh connection to Memphis is curious. Note too that Cairo is the southernmost city in Illinois and was named after the Egyptian city. It is the seat of *Alexander* County and was the headquarters of General Ulysses S. Grant in 1861. Later his grandson, U.S. Grant III, will be director of public buildings and monuments in Washington D.C. Grant III is remembered for requesting the appropriation of money to put bars on the windows of the Washington Monument, connected to Lincoln, since Lincoln attended the cornerstone-laying ceremony. The request was made just after the suicides (sacrifices) of November 20 and 22, 1926. The latter possibly related to the later Kennedy assassination date. It would have made some sense, of course, to have buried Lincoln inside Washington Monument. But he has his own obelisk at Springfield, Illinois; connected by a

crescent to the Washington obelisk. There were nine days to the Parentalia, and though the coven circle has a nine-foot diameter, it is connected to the crescent circle. The needle suggests this as well as possibly being a fertility symbol. The roundness of the eye of Ra, furthermore, is in keeping with Thoth's crescent holding a disc.

7) Kenneth Davis[253] calls his chapter referring to the Lindbergh tragedy "Blood Sacrifice."

By the god of calendars, it would be thirty years exactly after Dannie Cameron was *murdered*, four months exactly after Lenin died, three years to the day before Lindbergh's landing near Paris, and probably precisely to the minute of the New York-New Jersey time that another happening occurred in south Chicago on May 21 (Wednesday), 1924, though this time was recalled many years later as being 5:30 P.M. It was also four-five years before my birth when the "Crime of the Century" took place. Nathan Leopold, Jr., and Richard Loeb *murdered* Bobby Franks. The three were of Jewish background, though the Franks were Christian Scientists. Also, the name Franks brings to mind France, Paris, and Lindbergh's May 21 and his son's *murder* yet to come.

The boy's age was fourteen (1909–1924), but the exact date of his birth is difficult to come by. The fourteen then represented St. Valentine's Day or forty-five, and it will be seven days in one respect until twenty-one. True, this is apples and oranges, different units of measure, backward and forward, a potpourri. It's a craziness in logic, but so was the crime. Besides, things in the psychic or whatever world we're dealing with often aren't completely logical by what we know now. We're missing fragments or don't entirely understand the supernatural forces, or there's another dimension—something there but hard to prove.

Robert Franks' naked body will be found in a culvert, which by definition is a *waterway* or drain under an embankment or *road*. Water association to May 22 in Greek antiquity.

The two aren't being defended for what they did. What's being said is that the crime might also have been a contender for the "Sacrifice of the Century" in context of one person only, and none of the principals (Franks, Leopold, Loeb, and Darrow) was completely aware of it. True enough there have been more gruesome murders of children even younger than Bobby Franks. Behind each of these was a hatred or aberration of some kind, but no murder is completely separate from its motive, and no motive can be quite so bad as "I loved the person I killed so much I wanted him to get to heaven right away"—unless, of course, it was something like Leopold and Loeb pulled.

Bobby Franks, who'd been murdered on May 21, was found in a culvert of a channel between two lakes on May 22, 1924 (2122). One of his abductors had struck the boy over the head with a chisel several times. A gag was thrust into his mouth, and he apparently died of suffocation. It was a perfect crime in the sense that it had no motive as we usually think of such, and they might have laughed themselves silly—if they were of that bent—while others puzzled: Why? It was done as sort of a twisted intellectual-thrill experiment. As far as is known, except for getting caught and to impress the public, neither Leopold nor Loeb ever had any special remorse or shame for having killed the boy, whom they'd selected at the last minute as he was walking down the street. Hence in extenuation and mitigation, there was nothing personal in it. And this intellectual cleverness would have meant more to them than the boy's life. Apparently too they had no remorse about Flora (flower), his mother, who still expected that her son would be released from his captors long after he was buried.

A large amount of blood was spilled.[254-A] Some of this got on his murderers, who were either wearing some apparel made of wool or wiped it off with wool cloth.[254-B] It may not have been exactly the same ritual as in ancient times, but there were similarities. They had asked for a ransom, though neither needed it. Both came from wealthy families, German-Jewish aristocrats, about as close to "noble families" as it possible in the United States.

Some scholars believe that the wiping of blood from the head with wool and laughing was an outgrowth of an even more ancient time of Roman sacrifice.

My guess is that the Ls in the killers' names stood for *Lupus* (Latin for wolf) or Lupercalia,[255] which is thought by some to have been a wolf festival conducted by wolf priests.[256] Leopold and Loeb could very well have been caught up in some ancient rite. Lobo, the Spanish name for wolf, can be formed from letters in the two names, and Christian names derived from *lupus* are Lupo, Italian; Lobo, Portuguese; and Lope, Spanish. When transferred to jail, Leopold was given the number 50 and Loeb, 51. At one time, Leopold's IQ measured 210, Loeb's about 160,[257] the difference being 50. The number 50 in *Roman* numerals is L, and 50 + 50 = 100, suggesting the crime of the century. But Rome was founded by Romulus, who had been suckled by a wolf in infancy. Very possibly too before the white man, the Indian tribe in Chicago revered the wolf.

Though it could be that signs, omens, and symbolism are the universal language, I'd discount the roundabout and superficial links made above as being the product of an overactive imagination had not the word wolf, in one spelling or another, appeared at least seven times in relation to the case:

1) The body was found in a culvert of the channel that runs between *Wolf* and Hyde lakes, Dr. Jeky*ll*.
2) The station police captain's name was Thomas C. *Wolfe.*
3) Oscar *Wolff* was the coroner.

4) Melvin T. *Wolf* had been killed in April 1923, and his body washed up on a beach at 64th Street in May. This was just one of the so-called ABCD (alphabet) murders or crimes, since Charles Ream (Remus?) had been castrated. Conjecture was that Leopold and Loeb had committed them. If this were true, the killing of Bobby Franks was E, the fifth, 4 > 5.

5) Gene *Lovitiz* was a twenty-one-year-old inmate in the same prison as Leopold. He stated that Leopold had told him he'd first read about Nietzsche in Jack London's *The Sea-Wolf*.[258] The *Sea-Wolf*'s captain was *Wolf* Larson,[259-A] who crushed an uncooked potato to mush with one hand. Leopold and Loeb were unable to duplicate this. (See page 431.)

6) Quizzed in the Franks case were Mrs. Anna *Wolfe* and her husband, Rodney. She was under arrest in Chicago, and he in Indianapolis. Here again the interplay of the two cities.

But why would the name appear at least seven times? It makes no sense. Maybe that's the point: The more you puzzle, the greater the laughter and mockery. Crossword puzzles had become one of the fads during the era. Perhaps it is/was an elaborate crossword puzzle. Rather than being the roll of dice, there well could be an intelligence behind it.

Brushstrokes?

Ulysses is said to have suggested the Trojan horse to the Greeks. On the advice of Hermes, he outsmarted Circe, who had tamed wolves wandering around her palace, but Circe sounds like Cicero, Al Capone's underworld capital. Aeneas (ae ea), a Trojan, escaped the destruction of Troy and fled with followers to Italy. Legend has it that Romulus and Remus were distant descendants.

On Saturday, May 31, 1927, Leopold and Loeb confessed to the murder. Very possibly precisely *fifty-four* years previously on Saturday, May 31, 1873, Sophia and Heinrich Schliemann discovered the site of Troy and the gold. (See pages 371-372.)

Leopold spent a little over thirty-three and one-half years in prison.[260] Lindbergh, a virtual prisoner of his flight, spent thirty-three and one-half hours going from New York to Paris. His father had come from Sweden, a Teutonic nation. Bruno Hauptmann, who had kidnapped and murdered the Lindbergh boy, was German, as were Leopold's and Loeb's ancestors. The wolf is used more in Teutonic names than any other animal. Apollo is associated with the wolf in mythology, but in alchemy, the wolf, as well as the dog, represents the "dyadic nature of Mercurious."[261]

Robert Louis Stevenson was born on November 13, 1850. He died forty-four years later on December 3, 1894. Serialization of *Kidnapped* began on May 1, 1886, in *Young Folks*. It was published in book form on

July 14, 1886.[262] This was *forty-five* years before the Lindbergh boy's kidnapping on March 1, 1932. Bruno Hauptmann was found guilty in 1935 on February 13, the ides and beginning day of the Parentalia.

Meyer Levin, who knew Leopold, wrote a bestseller called *Compulsion*, based on the Leopold and Loeb case. At fifteen, the automobile Leopold was driving collided with a *horse* and buggy; a woman and child were injured. Leopold suffered a concussion. Leopold had studied Greek and Latin languages and Egyptian hieroglyphics, in addition to many other subjects and languages.

Bobby Franks was *walking* on his way home from school. Irving Hartman, Jr., a nine-year-old who was walking nearby, paused to examine some *flowers*.[263] When he looked up, Franks had disappeared. Thus a variation in Persephone's abduction. (See Book II, footnote 43.) Note here a suggestion of May 13, along with the actual date of May 21.[264]

A boundary, the Illiana, was crossed twice with Bobby Franks, then either dead or alive, since clothing was removed on a prairie in Indiana. Using the name of Mr. Johnson, Leopold sent a wreath of tiger *lilies* to the boy's funeral. Shades of Obsequies Chic? The state's attorney was Robert E. *Crowe*. Leopold had an interest in ornithology. In his study were hundreds of stuffed birds. Possibly this was his undoing with Thoth-Hermes. In stopping their flight and causing their death, he was assuming a power which belonged to the god of flight, of death, of reckoning of the ibis head.

> Leopold
> Canary-bird in a cage,[265-A]
> Egyptian heiroglyphs of a tomb,
> A dead man's language
> Is your doom.

A fitting retribution, right? No, not really. He flew out of his cage, as will the birdman of Alcatraz, in intellectual pursuit.

> Loeb
> Cunning Loeb,
> A mistake for a wolf,
> Since man they seldom kill.
> Know then that humans will.

He was knifed in a shower. The killing may or may not have had to do with homosexual actions. But prison violence, from whatever source and for whatever reason, is a constant, as are disturbed inmates. A fitting retribution? Yes and no. Since he had no remorse about killing the boy, his punishment by the court would have had little effect on him.

State Attorney Crowe's assistant was Joseph P. *Savage*, a word coming down to us to describe the Lupercalia. Richard Loeb, whose father was a Sears vice president, was born on June 11, 1905—a snake, as was Clarence Darrow, who was born in 1857 (21) on April 18 in *Kins*man, Ohio, and who died on March 13, 1938. Darrow's birthdate of April 18 (the anniversary of Paul Revere's ride) and Darwin's death date of April 19 can be used in reference to Lincoln's shooting and death April 14–15, the Titanic's sinking, the Matamoros slayings on April 11 (see page 398), and the USS *Iowa* explosion on April 19 (see pages 617-618).

Add to this the fact that Clarence Darrow in 1925 defended John T. Scopes, twenty-one, who taught theories based on Darwin's principles. William Jennings Bryan aided the prosecution, and Scopes was fined one hundred dollars, though the conviction was later thrown out because of a technical error. When the trial was over, D-arrow[266] left. Five (5) days later, William Jennings Bryan was dead.

Jacob Franks, the father of the slain boy, had owned a pawnshop years before at 271 Clark Street. Many of the customers he had there were men who had lost at the *gaming tables*. From the money he made there, he went into realty and became rich. In 1924 he was the principal owner of the *Elgin* Watch Case Company and also the *Rockford* Watch Company. His younger brother, then dead, had been a promoter of *boxing contests*, prize fights, and other sporting events. So between them comes to mind: merchant, wealth, "reckoner of time," sporting events, especially boxing. Bobby Franks' body was found in the culvert near 121 Street and the Pennsylvania tracks (traveling, commerce, key*stone*).

Recalling the flight-death aspect to Leopold's stuffed birds and that he, along with Loeb, kidnapped and murdered Bobby Franks, why was the May 21 (flight) landing in Pais lucky for Lindy (LI)? But was it really? In every twenty-one, there lies a latent twenty-two, or vice versa. Lindy himself in time will be associated both with flight and death. Bobby Franks and Charles A. Lindbergh, Jr., were similar: Both were kidnapped and murdered. Was it the pendulum of good and bad luck? Or had both Jacob Franks and Charles Lindbergh lost favor along the way?

If 14 and 21 are linked to sacrifice, then it's likely that 7 is also. The first 21 to occur after the Feralia is March 21, usually the spring equinox but not always. May 21 is the third 21.[267]

1) Since Maia was the mother of Hermes and since the seven daughters of Atlas and Pleione were born on Mt. Cyllene (the same as Hermes), this possibly links them to Hermes as a god of sacrifice. According to some, the seven daughters killed themselves in grief over the death of their sisters the Hyades. Zeus then set them up at the Pleiades, a group of stars.

2) He who slays Cain will pay sevenfold (Gen 4: 15).

3) A young bull without blemish was killed. The priest then dipped his finger into the blood and sprinkled part of it seven

times (Lev 4: 4).

4) Balaam insisted on seven altars, seven oxen, and seven rams before he could prophesy (3 x 7 = 21) (Num 23: 1).

5) There were seven years of plenty or seven years of sterility, depending on which god won (See page 275.)

6) Seven years of plenty followed by seven years of famine (See page 275.)

7) The Gibeonites wanted neither gold nor silver but asked for and were given seven sons (and/or grandsons) of Saul to hang (2 Sam 21: 9).

8) Traditionally Rome was founded on seven hills. In a way, the murder of Remus is associated with this number. Rome, New York, has the Oriskany battlefield nearby. There in August 1777, the year Christmas Island was discovered by Captain Cook, took place one of the bloodiest battles of the Revolution.

9) Joan of Arc predicted she would be wounded by an arrow on May 7 and that blood would flow above her heart, which happened. Strongly Hermes. May is a typical month. She was burned at stake *May 30*, 1431.

10) Number 7 was the presidential box where Lincoln was shot.

11) Thirty-five (7 x 5) blacks were killed by whites in Vicksburg, Mississippi, December 7, 1874.[268] Bloody Sunday, March 7, 1965.

12) One story is that Custer and his troopers on horses trampled the hemp on a ridge when entering Little Big (measurement) Horn in 1876. The hemp was to be used in sacred ritual. Outraged by this, the Sioux with the Cherokee killed Custer and all his men. It was a tragic sacrifice for the *Seventh* Cavalry.

13) To date the Washington Monument has claimed seven deaths. Seven is a multiple of the 21 dedication date.

14) The twenty-one-gun salute can be given to royalty or the head of government. But it also can be a death knell. The common man will understand this in three, as thrice seven is twenty-one.

15) On May 21, 1996, seven Trappist monks were beheaded in Algeria by the Armed Islamic Group. Seven candles which had been burning for the monks in Notre Dame Cathedral in Paris were then snuffed out. Khadidja Khalil of High Council of French Muslims condemned the act as being barbaric and said, "It is forbidden in the holy Koran to touch 'all servants of God,' and that means priests and rabbis as well."

The twenty-one recalls the twenty-one knots of the *Titanic*, the *Lusitania* (which had run an average of twenty-one knots on her last five round trips), and twenty-one knot voodoo. (See page 274.) The "Lucy" might also be added to the LI category.[269] She was a four-stacker like the *Titanic* and was sunk by a German U-boat (U = 21) on May 7, 1915. In spite of denials by the British government at the time, she was carrying war supplies. Of her 1,906 passengers and crew; 1,198 were lost (*Encyclopedia Americana*), including 128 Americans. Thus when the U.S. entered World War I in 1917, a snake-year, one of the battle cries was "Remember the *Lusitania*!" On December 7, 1941 (41, a transposition of 14) a snake-year, the battlecry became "Remember Pearl Harbor!" (Pearl, moon, Thoth/TH; harbor: protection; February roughly equivalent to December, and December twenty-one, the date of final entombment of Osiris, is equivalent to February 21, the date of dedication of what was supposed to have been Washington's tomb.) The USS *Arizona*, BB 39, suffered and sacrificed most. According to pamphlet titled "USS Arizona Memorial,"[270] 1,177 from the *Arizona* lost their lives. But 1,198 (*Lusitania*) minus 1,177 equals 21. The structure now over the entombed has 7 windows on its ceiling and fourteen open-air windows on its sides. The total is "a perpetual twenty-one gun salute." (Recall the voodoo connection to the number twenty-one.) The *Arizona*[271] was dedicated as a national monument in 1962 on May 30, the traditional Memorial Day that came about after the Civil War, a day in many respects like February 21, the Feast of the Dead, the day Captain Cook was buried.

Chapter Thirty

Hermes' name probably means "He of the stone heap."

Though visiting the Washington Monument in 1962/1963, I had no understanding then of the basic units of four and five, the relationship of twenty-one and twenty-two, or the knowledge of the Parentalia, all of which are manifested in the plain-as-the-moon shaft, a Thoth-Hermes symbol. It seems possible too that five square (4) feet are the equivalent in the occult of the coven circle with its nine-foot diameter and 4.5-foot radius.

The structure had its beginning in 1833 (SY) when Chief Justice John Marshall[272] and the former Librarian of Congress *George Watterston*[273] sowed the seeds of the Washington National Monument Society, which solicited the first funding of part of the money to erect the monument.[274] It is, in effect, a sophisticated pile of stone, a cairn, a memory-grave marker.

The stones of the obelisk are simply the lapis manalis of the nation—maybe the world—and it wasn't just a coincidence that the United States minister to *Italy*, George Marsh, said a true obelisk should have a height around ten times the width of its base. This led to a *Mary*land granite base of approximately fifty-five feet square,[275] and a summit of 555 feet (5 + 5 + 5 = 15, perhaps standing for the Lupercalia). It has had five suicides, as if the number was to fit the progression: 5, 55, 555. It's Washington, D.C.'s tallest (closest to the *moon*, and note it was the U.S. which put the first man on the moon) structure, erected to honor the father of our country, by proxy George Washington,[276-A] whose last-known written words were about the mercury.

Robert Mills (a distant relative?), architect in the Greek Revival style, designed the Washington Monument, which has 898 steps. The Greek colonade shown in the original drawing was dropped. So now it stands as an obelisk alone, in perfect Egyptian proportion. Robert Mills died, by the way, in 1855.

The first stone was laid in the northeast corner on July 4, 1848, the Hermetic number important to the nation. Nathaniel Hawthorne had been born *forty-four* years before (July 4, 1804), and *fifty-five* years previously Washington had used the same trowel when laying the Capitol's cornerstone. Lincoln, then a little-known congressman and the other bookend of the Parentalia (12 and 22 enclose 13–21) attended, as well as many others who were famous or would become so (pages 3-6).

Most of the stones were quarried in Maryland and Massachusetts. The Society invited stones from all over the world to adorn the walls inside the monument. There are 193, each interesting in itself, though too numerous to mention here; suffice it to say that many were from states and territories. One stone was contributed by the Cherokee nation. Another bears the name Nevada in silver. A third, white marble taken from the Parthenon, was from Greece. A fourth, a marble mosaic from the ruins of ancient city of Carthage, shows a horse and a palm tree, both associated with Hermes who, Aristophanes said, is "the friendliest of all the gods to men and the most generous giver." Perhaps interesting too in the lapis-Christ and lapis-Hermes vein of thought is that Pope Pius IX sent a marble block from the Temple of Concord in Rome. One night in 1854 it was stolen and never recovered.

As stated the monument's base is about fifty-five feet square. The base of a pyramidion which tops the pillar is about thirty-four feet square[276-B] (55 - 34 = 21). The original thirteen states declared their independence in 1776 (21), the difference suggesting the nine-day Parentalia, and at the monument's top the necromancy-nine (the mystical number of secrecy) inch tip of Aluminum (Al, or transposed La), which has an atomic number of 13. So it's not surprising that the monument wasn't dedicated on Washington's birthday (February 22) but rather on the Feast of the Dead, *February 21*, 1885.[277] This was meant to be, but those at the time, not making the connection to the Parentalia, thought their reasoning was perfectly logical: The twenty-second fell on a Sunday.

Again, the whole month of February in ancient Rome was a period of lustration. The "Wash" in Washington and the "Water" in Waterstone suggest this, as well as the reflecting pool and the austere whiteness of the obelisk's stones. The jumble "George Birthington's Wash Day" is accurate. The monument's dedication was forty-four years before my birth, as well as that of many others.[278]

The monument opened to the public on October (*tenth* month) 9, 1888, the year Quincy, Massachusetts, was incorporated as a city; Great Britain annexed Christmas Island (discovered by Captain Cook on Christmas Eve 1777); Irving Berlin (who would later write "White Christmas") and Jim Thorpe were born; and the year two cowboys chasing strays in the December wind and snow came across a bunch of *stone* homes in the recess of a cliff, known now as the "Cliff Palace" of the Mesa Verde near the *Four* Corners area.[279-A]

In 1935 the first bottom-to-top cleaning of the Washington Monument was undertaken. Perhaps the frosting on the cake is that some agile thief, reminiscent of Hermes, climbed the scaffolding and in view of all Washington, D.C., stole the platinum-tipped, lightning-rod conductors at its apex. (See *February 13*, 1866. Liberty, Missouri: first daylight, peacetime bank robbery in America.) Usually what was stolen by Hermes was returned, as if the main purpose was just a caper.

In relation to the household, his place is at the door, where he protects the threshold. Because he's a thief himself, he repels thieves.[279-B] Too bad statues of him weren't placed at the threshold of the Capitol building.

United States Department of the Interior

NATIONAL PARK SERVICE
National Capital Parks-Central
900 Ohio Drive, S.W.
Washington, D.C. 20242

IN REPLY REFER TO:

K14 (NCR-NACC)

AUG 2 3 1993

Mr. Brent Chichester
P.O. Box 12891
Main Office Station
Seattle, Washington 98111

Dear Mr. Chichester:

In response to your question in your July 3 letter, the information
you obtained in the publication, "Washington, Man and Monument" was
correct.   The five suicides, in chronological order, are as
follows: February 23, 1915, Mrs. Mae Cockrell, down the shaft;
March 9, 1923, Mr. A. Birney Sirp, out the window; November 20,
1926, Mr. Henry C. Anderson, out the window; November 22, 1926,
Mr. Blonnie Ward, also out the window; August 7, 1949, Mr. Paul L.
Haulker, down the shaft.   The gentleman who committed suicide
within two days of one another were World War I veterans who were
distraught; the first Caucasian and the second African-American.
The windows were barred after Mr. Ward's suicide. There were two
accidental deaths in the monument: Mrs. Dora Rum lunged for her
infant son in the stairwell, falling to her death down the shaft,
while her son escaped harm, in October of 1923;Mr. Joseph G.
Swings, a painter working on scaffolding inside the shaft, slipped
and fell to his death in 1905.   There have been no fatalities at
the Washington Monument since 1949.

Thank you for your interest in the Washington Monument. If we can
be of any further assistance to you, please feel free to write to
us again.

Sincerely,

Arnold Goldstein
Superintendent

488

United States Department of the Interior

NATIONAL PARK SERVICE
National Capital Parks–Central
900 Ohio Drive, S.W.
Washington, D.C. 20242

IN REPLY REFER TO:

K14(NCR-NACC)

Mr. Brent Chichester
P.O. Box 12891
Main Office Station
Seattle, Washington 98111

Dear Mr. Chichester:

In researching your follow-up inquiry, we found information on the following two items to be different from that which was published in Washington, Man and Monument. A former assistant custodian, or guard, of the Washington Monument in the nineteen fifties, John H. Bushong, compiled a listing of the suicides and accidents. According to him, the accidental death of Mrs. Dora Raum occurred in October of 1928, not 1923, and the spelling of the last suicide victim's name was Holker, not Haulker. Mr. Bushong does cite the Washington Evening Star, November 20, 1926, however, as a source.

We are sorry that we were unable to determine any further information on the month or day of Joseph G. Swings death. Perhaps the Star would be the best source for you, as there must be a major library that has back issues on microfiche of the now defunct newspaper.

Daniel Chester French, an American Sculptor by Michael Richman, The Preservation Press, 1976 provides the information for the dates concerning the Lincoln Memorial you inquired about. February 9, 1911, marked the establishment of the Lincoln Memorial Commission by Congress. On January 29, 1913, President William Howard Taft signed a congressional resolution proclaiming Henry Bacon architect of the Lincoln Memorial. The ground-breaking ceremony was held on February 12, 1914. It took one year for the underpinning and foundation to be completed, hence the cornerstone was laid on Abraham Lincoln's birthday February 12, 1915. May 30, 1922, which was Memorial Day, which was the date of the dedication of the memorial.

Thank you for your letter requesting further information on the Washington Monument and the Lincoln Memorial.

Sincerely

Arnold Goldstein
Superintendent

It's curious that Mr. Goldstein's first letter is dated August 23 (1993), the first day of the Mercury period. Though five suicides, there was a total of seven deaths. Given: the ancient Feralia on February 21; the dedication date of February 21, 1885; the ancient Caristia for the living (one source says the reconciled dead too); and Washington's birthday. The two numbers together are 2122, bringing to mind the North Clark Street address on February 14, 1929, where seven were sacrificed, and death-life, or life-death as Amerigo Vespucci, the *Italian* explorer from whom America got its name, died on February 22, 1512.

Though there was a blackjack winner-loser relationship (2122) when Mrs. Dora (derived from Theodora) Raum reached[280] for her infant son, there was also the timeless rite of age deferring to youth, "nation-builders of tomorrow," as Lincoln would have said.

Mrs. Mae Cockrell's death (the first suicide and down the shaft on February 23, 1915) is sequential: February 21, 22, and 23. February 23 in ancient Rome is identified with Terminus, a Roman god of boundaries, whom some find remarkably close to that aspect of Hermes, a god of boundaries and a breaker of boundaries.

No day or month is given for the Washington Monument's first death in 1905. Chances are it was within the snake-year period. If so, Mr. Swings' name could mean nothing, or it might be looked at as S-wings (snake-wings, Hermes caduceus).[281]

As with the assassination of President John F. Kennedy later, the suicide of Mr. Ward, "a colored laborer," on November 22 (1926) was twenty-one days past November 1 (equivalent to February 21, the Feast of the Dead, the Washington Monument dedication date, the beginning of the Battle of Verdun, and the later assassination of Malcolm X).

In addition, there are other strange things concerning the death of Blondie (sic; *Washington Post*, November 23, 1926) Ward. He is said to have slashed his throat before leaping; the knife used for doing this was never found. If not murder (the coroner, J. *Ramsey* Nevitt, called it suicide), then possibly he thought of himself as a sacrifice or felt it was necessary to spill his blood before jumping (flight). He hit feet first—body ground to a pulp—with such force that the heavy overcoat of August Croissant (crescent; Thoth correspondence), *walking* perilously close, was blown over his head (wind), and "Croissant was on the verge of collapse" for some time. Shortly later *U.S. Grant III*, director of public buildings and monuments, requested an appropriation for money to put bars on the windows. "Who's buried in Grant's tomb?"

Don'ya see? The Civil War gave blacks only man-made rules. But the sacrifice by Blonnie Ward was the covenant guaranteeing them their share of the country.

H.C. Anderson, who only two days earlier had hurled himself from a window, was, according to the *Washington Post*, a veteran of the Spanish-

American War. He was the monument's *fourth* victim, and Blonnie Ward, the *fifth*. The twenty-first day separated them, but the numbers 20, 21, and 22 are sequential. It's curious one will be white and the other, black.

Albert Birney Seip, who died on March 9, 1923, was a daredevil and "had a mania for climbing." A friend did not believe his death was due to suicide. However, J. *Ram*sey Nevitt, coroner, said it was after viewing the body.

Again the Parentalia began on February 13. In ancient Roman times, the Grave of Tarpeia, a *mundus*, apparently was opened on this day, and a sacrifice there was made by one of the vestals.[282] Then on February 13, 1746, a Frenchman with the name of Jean Marie Dubarry was executed for murdering his father. On February 13, 1846, another Frenchmen with the name Jean Marie Dubarry was also executed for murdering his father.[283-A] The source doesn't say how the executions were carried out. It would have been interesting too in these Parentalia murders to know how each came to getting the middle name Marie.

President's Day comes on the third Monday in February, which would always fall within the Parentalia. On February 18, 1861, Jefferson Davis was sworn in as the President of the Confederate States of *America*.

February 16, 1965 (21), was within the snake year and the Parentalia. At this time, four were seized and charged with plotting to dynamite the Washington Monument, the Liberty Bell, and the Statue of Liberty. Twenty-two (22) sticks of dynamite and blasting caps were found in a cache. It was said those involved in the plot had no concern how many men, women, and children would be killed in the explosion.

Chapter Thirty-one

On *February 11*, 1861, President-elect Abraham Lincoln left his Springfield, Illinois, neighbors "not knowing when or whether I ever may return, with a task before me greater than that which rested upon Washington," and began to *travel* to the nation's capital. He gave short speeches (eloquence) en route at Indianapolis, Cincinnati, Columbus, Cleveland, Pittsburgh, Buffalo, Rochester, Syracuse, Albany, Troy, New York, Trenton, Philadelphia, and Harrisburg. On *February 22*, he was warned of an assassination plot in Baltimore and was secretly put on a special train that arrived at Washington on the morning of *February 23*.[283-B]

Eighty-four years later, the U.S. flag—not unlike the barber pole—was raised over Mt. Surabachi, Iwo Jima.

It had been a mystical journey for Lincoln. Its duration made boundaries enclosing the bookends, which in turn made boundaries just outside the ancient period. The sacrifices of the Civil War were inevitable, as was Gettysburg's Cemetery Ridge; Lincoln's eloquent speech at the graveyard; his assassination; his death on April 15 (4.5, the number of the coven radius); his burial at Springfield on May 4 (5-4 or 4-5), 1865; and finally over his tomb, the Egyptian obelisk, a *Linc* to the Washington obelisk.

You might argue that though Lincoln appears to be connected to the number 45, there's no indication that Washington was. Not so. The baby born to Augustus and Mary Washington on February 22, 1732, was christened George Washington on April 5 (4-5 or 5-4) of the same year.[283-C]

In the Valley of the Kings, Egypt, there often appeared the Seal of the City of the Dead to discourage thievery, which was rife. This showed Anubis, the god of embalming and the valley itself, as a jackal lying prone. Kneeling before him are nine prisoners or slaves, cruelly bound at the elbows. Half of 9 is, of course, 4.5 and 9 x 5 (the fingers in a span) is 45.

The tomb of Tutankhamen was discovered by Howard Carter. His second man was named Arthur Callender (phonetic calendar).[283-D] His patron was George Herbert, the fifth earl of Carnarvon. On February 15 (the Lupercalia), 1923, the dotted seal impressions on the door to the inner tomb were removed. On the sixteenth, the sepulchral chamber was opened. An image of a winged serpent guarded the mummy of Tut. Carnarvon, thought to have been a victim of the mummy's curse,[283-E] died on April 5 (4-5 or 5-4, the anniversary of Washington's christening), 1923. The sarcophagus was opened on the Parentalia Eve, Lincoln's birthday, or *February 12*, 1924, then locked up during the ancient period. (See page 8.)

Now April 15, the day Lincoln died, was really the anniversary of when Charles Willson Peale, famous for many portraits of George Washington, was born in 1741. Peale's son Rembrandt was a chip off the ol' block, being the last artist to have drawn Washington from life and famous for his "Porthole" portrait of Washington. (Note roundness suggested by the son and the square [rectangle] suggested by the father.) Eventually Rembrandt gave up doing portraits. "The Court of the Dead" is said to be the high point of his later works. Where Rembrandt Peale was born 1778 on *February 22*, the anniversary of George Washington's birthday, his father died on *February 22*, 1827.

Robert Todd Lincoln (nicknamed earlier "The Prince of Rails" [travel] and who had bought a horse when he became a captain on General Grant's staff) was introduced to General Lee at Appomattox on April 9. So when Grant attended a cabinet meeting on April 14, 1865, Robert went with him. The Grants had turned down an invitation to attend the play with the Lincolns later that night. Robert was at the White House, not too distant from Ford's Theater. He was twenty-one to twenty-two years old when his father was assassinated on April 14, dying on April 15. He was close by when President Garfield was shot in Washington, D.C., at the Baltimore and Potomac railroad station on July 2, 1888, and he was only a few feet away when President McKinley was shot in Buffalo, New York, on September 6, 1901. He was, in a word, associated with all three of the martyred presidents, and the fourth martyred president (John F. Kennedy) would be buried near him at Arlington National Cemetery.

Abraham Lincoln's son had expected to be buried in the family tomb at Springfield, Illinois, but his wife apparently thought Arlington National Cemetery would be better. It's hard to explain this, as well as the fact that before dying, he donated his father's papers to the Congressional Library (remember George Watterston, the former Congressional Librarian, who had helped get the first funds for the Washington Monument?) with the stipulation that they weren't to be "subject to official inspection or private view" until *twenty-one* years from the date of his death.[284-A] But why this number of years? He may have had a perfectly logical reason to specify that before his *parents'* papers could be seen, but still it's a number linked to the Feralia, the last day of the *Parent*alia. Abraham, from whom Lincoln got his name, was the "father of a multitude of nations." George Washington is called "the father of his country." (Note here Mother's Day in India in February 22, established as a memorial to the wife of Mohandas K. Gandhi,[284-B] the father of his country.) (See page 273).

Mrs. Abraham Lincoln at first wanted her husband to be buried in Chicago, not Springfield, Illinois. When she was later declared insane, she ranted on about a Chicago fire, like the one four years previously, which would occur. This time, however, only her son's home would be spared. Robert Todd Lincoln and his wife had bought a home there near Lincoln Park. Though gone many years because he was secretary of war and later minister to England, he didn't sever connections with Illinois until 1911. As he grew old, he shied away from most public appearances, saying, "There is a certain fatality about presidential functions when I am there."

When the plan was submitted for the Lincoln Memorial, there was disagreement.[285] Many felt the Greek temple design (and indeed ancient Greece itself) didn't come close to representing the spirit of Lincoln and his humble beginnings. Eventually this opposition was overridden. Apparently no one to the present has fully understood that the classic Greek fitted Lincoln to a T, since he was under a strong Hermes influence. Here too don't forget the Greek tragedy aspect of Lincoln and most of his family as well, nor discount the Parentalia-Caristia mystique.

The exterior of the monument is constructed of white, Colorado marble. There are thirty-six Doric columns, one for each state which existed on Lincoln's death. Since Nevada was the thirty-sixth state admitted to the union, here's another connection between him and the state, which is about as Hermetic as you can get.

So now we have the Washington Monument (the Greek colonade of which was deleted in construction), the perfect Egyptian obelisk, looking straight across to the Lincoln Memorial, the Greek Parthenon-like structure. A reflecting pool between them mirrors each, a reminder of water-stone, lustration, and the month of February, of which Neptune is the protector. It also suggests the mediterranean. Together (Greek-Egyptian) the monuments are symbolic of Hermes-Thoth.

Doesn't it seem strange too that many days, months, and years concerning the planning, construction, and dedication of the Lincoln Memorial are strongly suggestive of the Parentalia and Caristia?

*Feb*ruary 9, 1911.	Congress passed a law creating the Lincoln Memorial Commission. Signed by the president.
Fall 1912.	Henry Bacon submitted his plans and designs. The 12 suggests noon, when the Parentalia began on February 13. It's also the number of Lincoln's birthday, a transposition of the Feralia 21.

494

February 1, 1913.	After the Lincoln Memorial Group, the Fine Arts Commission, and Congress okayed plans, President Taft—fittingly the only snake president who didn't die in office—signed a measure giving his approval.
February 12, 1914.	A noon groundbreaking ceremony at the northeast corner. Construction began. This was 105 (5 x 21) years after Lincoln's birth. Since Lincoln was shot on the fourteen (April), as well as those later on the fourteenth (February) in the gangland slayings in Chicago, it calls to mind St Valentine's Day.
February 12, 1915.	Cornerstone laid at informal ceremonies. Fifteen suggests Lupercalia.
June 21, 1921.	About this date, building was opened to public on a regular basis.[286]
May 30, 1922	Dedication Day. Chief Justice (Thoth, god of judgment) William Howard Taft (snake), chairman of commission, presented Lincoln Memorial. President Warren G. Harding accepted it for the United States. Special guest Robert Todd Lincoln attended. It was Memorial (Decoration) Day, the equivalent of the Feralia 21, when the Washington Monument was dedicated; the '22 was symbolic of the Caristia. The year each state entered the Union is in Roman numerals.
	Little did President Harding realize the implication of dedicating the Lincoln Memorial on the day of the dead. As with Zachary Taylor at the Washington Monument on July 4, 1850, a peer sacrifice was required. If not given, one would be taken. (See page 3.) President Harding did not live through his term. Zachary Taylor got sick on the fourth and died five days later. Lincoln died at 4.5, and Harding died in the forty-five square mile San Francisco County.

When Harry Truman (who became president in 1945) used to take off on his early morning walks in Washington, D.C., he frequently went to the Washington Monument and/or the Lincoln Memorial. Franklin Roosevelt (who died in 1945) seldom missed going to the Lincoln Memorial on Lincoln's birthday. Most historians agree that these were probably the four greatest presidents.

Chapter Thirty-two

God has been handed down to us at times in the Bible from so-called individual revelation, dreamers, wishful thinkers, perhaps self-important people taking themselves more seriously than they ought; fancy pants, myth-making writers taking literary license; metaphor makers, borrowers, emenders, and power groups replacing others. The result is that the baby and the washwater are inseparable.

There's an occult world which lies in unchartered water, seldom traveled. It's an arcane maze in which the searcher is bound to make more wrong turns than right ones. It's a miner's map where claim stakes are shown but no gold can be found presently. Yet is this proof enough that the gold didn't exist, doesn't exist, or that the person who originally pounded in the claim stakes was insane?

Piss and wind, mixed metaphors, etc., could very well be the substances which are fundamental to the occult and magic. But because it doesn't sound very logical or scientific, the knowledge lies undiscovered, man's own ego and reasoning mind preventing this as it also pooh-poohs superstition. Yet had it not been for superstition, man never would have survived in the past, nor will he be able to in the future. Essentially this is the statement of many seers, mystics, and assorted sensitives. The other union, the churches and orthodox religions, are saying the same thing but using different terms. The similarities of the two are greater than their differences.

Perhaps as computers become more sophisticated, numbers and their mystical relationships will help us better to understand the unknown, past, present, and future. But for now what might be betted on? These three things: 1) the Di Manes and the Parentalia-Caristia in respect to the nation; 2) the number 2122; and 3) the relationship of 4:5.[287]

In respect to the latter, Walpurgis Night occurs on the night before May 1. Superstition holds that it's the time witches' power is at its height. A more feasible explanation is that the evening of April 30 is a carryover from the very old times when German farmers struck contracts. May 1 represented the coming growing season, and of course they were hoping

496

for *good luck*. Still Walpurgis Night is the evening of April 30, as Halloween is the evening of October 31.[288] Apparently Hitler believed somewhat in the occult. It's too much of a coincidence that he died on April 30, 1945, the evening which suggests the perfect 4:5 relationship. It is too much of a coincidence that before having heard of Walpurgis, I would conclude the 4:5 relationship independently, figuring fairly closely, though inaccurately, that either April 5 or May 4 was the best time to dispatch Saddam Hussein. And finally it was too much of a coincidence that, for what were thought other reasons, I would lose enthusiasm one minute past midnight of May 4.

Maybe everybody has a paranormal sensitivity. All it needs is to be developed. I tend to think it's—at least in part—due to a psychic tendency of some gene. It's nice to believe everyone has the capability—like one big democracy, equal power—but there are no equal rights in genetics. Certainly too if it's genetic in part, the sensitives received far from a perfect score on the other genes.*

Possibly the occult safe can be opened only when two conditions are met:

1) The person has to be a true sensitive. Just believing you might be or want to be (I have failed at everything else, so now I'll be a witch and really show them they made a big mistake by ignoring me) won't hack it. Herein lies most failures, and it could well be mine.

2) There are certain access numbers which must be satisfied. This would explain why some sensitives run hot and cold. They never figured them out. A few likely numbers—to my way of thinking—would be 4:5 and 21:22.[289]

Other conjectures:

The last day of some months to the beginning of the next. Walpurgis Night, most favorable.

February 13-14-15.[290] Parentalia begins. St. Valentine's Day. A wolf has forty-two teeth (13 + 14 +15).

Full moon. Superstition rich in this. Moon power in tides. More obscure reference: menstrual period. A hint in the latter also to blood purification: sacrifice. Menses and Februarius Mensis, a month of ritual purification. Moon changes shape, exerting influence over creatures of change, and influence the planting of crops.

*Nobody should doubt the wisdom of removing or altering the gene for Down's syndrome or several other diseases. If someday it's determined that homosexuality is caused by a gene (or predisposed gene), it would seem best to remove or alter it someway, thereby saving much suffering. Yet where there is worry is that man will someday alter a gene, only to find out he had outsmarted himself, allowing something far worse to crop us.

Chapter Thirty-three

Giving up writing, shaking the destructive habit of introspection, seemed like a healthy idea. Get involved in the physical world—backpacking, hiking, getting sun, swimming, scuba diving, and even surf boarding eventually in the island paradise.

No more than a large Samsonite suitcase and backpack would be taken. Trying to figure out what might be useful and what was necessary, I muddled on it for several days, reaching the conclusion that the television, typewriter, and winter clothing would be given away and old clothing thrown out, along with plastic bags to put garbage in and numerous jars filled with earthquake water. What remained would be put into two boxes and farmed out to two separate relatives, who themselves were planning on moving out of state. Oh well!

On the way to the storage locker after arriving at Honolulu, I came close to being totaled in a pedestrian intersection as a car came swerving toward me. Couldn't believe it. Shoved the Samsonite between me and it and jumped to the side, as Samson got shaved, skidding across the street. The woman driver was clearly wrong, admitted it, and apologized profusely: "I was so intent on watching traffic coming from two other directions," she explained, "that I just didn't see you. I'm so sorry."

There was no sense to pursue it further.

To the list of mad dogs and Englishmen might be added Americans with backpacks. It was too much to carry around in the noonday sun. But there was no place to put it other than the storage locker, and things in it would be needed.

"He looks like he's running out of gas," someone said. More like water as sweat was pouring down.

You couldn't sleep at night in any parks at Waikiki or Ala Moana. Numerous signs, as well as the police, discouraged this. To go further into the island meant being a long way from drinking water and stores at times—a Catch-22 which Heller might have given more precisely as 2122.

The first evening, a Saturday, I dragged the carcass onto a path about thirty yards from the Coast Guard Station at Diamond Head. Bushes hid me from view of passing cars and joggers. It was unlikely anybody would be hiking at 9 o'clock at night. Lying on a large, plastic bag, I watched in fascination the moon above the branches of trees and wondered if this was where I was meant to be, like in some timetable. Or was it just another madness like the noonday sun at Waikiki, where even on this first day a few faces stuck out in the crowds, frantic people rushing someplace that had just occurred to them? The following days they would be constants in an ongoing game of musical chairs, though always left standing somehow. Of course they must have sat down at times, a begrudging rest at the expense of their quest as some new idea occurred.

At any rate, here I was for whatever reason, dropping off to sleep for short periods, waking up at the whir of a passing car or an annoying stone which had to be thrown out from under. At the crack of dawn, a bird began trilling in the trees. Gladly I'd have wrung its neck if it could have been reached, and perhaps Henry Thoreau's too if he'd still been around. Before picking up a rock, I decided the bird was right. Time to get up and get started before it got too hot, but started where? It was Sunday. The banks and post offices were closed, as well as most businesses, such as Blue Cross.

I walked on past the station and down into a park area which had a path leading to the beach. Some surfers were already out riding the waves. Swimming then for an hour or two was about as pleasant an experience as you could have to begin the day; the water was temperate.

Like a good wine, the water off Ala Moana and Diamond Head had improved with age in twenty-three years, and the sun still had its sunny, smiling face saying, "Trust me!" But behind this mask now lurked a sadistic monster, a tatoo artist requiring payments in pain, peeling, and itching. No wonder the luxury, air-conditioned hotels got away with charging steep prices to tourists who retreated to their rooms, applied soothing ointments, sipped cool ones in their bars, and frequented their shops. It was a conspiracy. The hotels sold their souls to the sun for money, and the sun got to cause its pain. Now scared to even think such irreverent thoughts, the chastened tourists spent their time dashing off postcards to mainlanders who were mistaken in their envy. With exception of two or three brave forays out during the day to the Dole Pineapple Plant and the Arizona Memorial, say, they became night creatures for the rest of their stays.

Dermatologists had advised repeatedly to use sunscreen, even when going outdoors in Seattle in the winter. The sun was an enemy, they warned. But who listens to their doctors? They only tell you these things so they can charge you more. Yet to some extent their advice was heeded, preventing what could have been much worse.

Leaving Diamond Head the first morning, I walked to Waikiki for breakfast. McDonald's, if nothing else, is a constant, a rock, throughout the world. At any one time, you can always depend upon a meal that is half plastic[291] and half food. So it's not too surprising that the chain is rapidly replacing the churches in the mainstream America. In the sanctity of any McDonald's, there's always the well-scrubbed, sterile feeling of wholesomeness, and the portions are communion size. There's the fanfare of advertisement about good things upcoming—if you will only make the right choice for once in your life, God would have rewarded you accordingly. So now you must sacrifice. If on leaving you are glad that you came, it's only barely, and you're not sure you want to come back for next Sunday's service or not.

Truly McDonald's doesn't care about those who are old on their way out. That part of the business is limited at best, almost negligible. It will die out shortly anyway, so why bother? McDonald's can afford to be generous: Let Burger King and Jack-in-the-Box have it. Big Mac looks at the long-term prospects. Play plots for tots in front of so many of its eateries say it all too well:

> Send us your children before the age of six, and we'll
> make McDonald hamburger-eaters (or hamburger
> helpers) out of them for the rest of their lives.

So it was I ate at McDonald's, Jack-in-the-Box, Burger King, and Subway all the days of my life there. Except for one day when splurging at Tony Roma's with two ice-cold Buds and beef ribs. That meal, the swimming for a few days, and the plane rides over and back were the high points of my odyssey, Ulysses.

No wonder turtles take forever. Some joke about being blessed with a long life span! How do they ever manage without a windshield wiper? Wiping the sweat off my brow—and thinking what's so hot about people giving you the sweat off their brow—I unloaded things like crazy at the storage locker. Then like a turtle on his back trying to right himself, I struggled into the backpack. Shit! It was still heavy.

Oh this weight is really very good, I thought, convincing nobody, *because it will help you to walk straighter, like exercise buffs carry around weights in their side pockets to develop muscles.* A great theory. But instead of pulling me backward, I tended to lean forward even more, in the heaving Volga-revenge of the beasts of burden, the dumb oxen, and windbroken horses who really won the West, though the pioneers took all the credit.

I had thought at times off Diamond Head that the hair oil I used must be attracting bugs. But at Ala Moana Park, some of the dozing Hawaiians were swatting them away too, just like the Seringeti. Well, maybe it was not that bad.

Having found nothing better, I got back after dark to the space left that morning. This second night should be a piece of cake. I'd bought a 99-cent mat from an ABC store; two large beach towels on sale from Woolworths; and a green, quart-size canteen (now filled with water) from

Sears. It was plastic and so light that I wondered why we didn't have these in Korea. Hell, any idiot could sleep out and be miserable; it took real genius to be comfortable. But before doing anything else—so as not to forget—I set my magical alarm clock for the only time its birdbrain could remember: 4:30 A.M. I'm captain of my own ship.

I was sprawled out when someone came crashing through the bushes.

"Hello," I yelled, elbowing myself up so not to be crushed underfoot. But the warning hadn't completely left my mouth before this ninja leapt instantly into a Kung-fu King-Kong Karate stance and made a chilling guttural sound. In the moonlight his eyes looked manic, as if locked into some far-off energy source, maybe the moon. Instinct said this was for real, not just some act. He was extremely fit, expertly trained, and very deadly. Still it happened so fast, there wasn't time to get scared.

"Don't get excited," I said. "Just lay down here to sleep."

He begin to unwind, saying, "You scared me. The police are down the road checking everybody out. So I ducked in here. But why're you laying there? Come with me higher up. I'll show you where the rest of us go."

"No. I'll stay here."

It wasn't distrust. Certainly he could have done me in with one well-placed chop or kick a minute or two earlier, and this makes for trusting people fast. But the thought of putting on my shoes; picking up my gear and backpack; and then hoisting myself up with one sort foot on to a rocky, dark, Diamond Head trail had as much appeal as if he'd just offered me a free ticket for the rest of the night to an Ala Moana Park bench, the other side of Waikiki.

He left; he just seemed to vanish. No sooner did I lay down than another person scrambled through the bushes, like fire was just behind. My greeting this time, judging from his reaction, was the surprise roar from a lion in Oahu, or the hiss from a snake on the ground. No martial arts here. He just shuddered, nearly shut down, and then tread cautiously to the side and lifted himself up to the trail. Now I'll always wonder where they went to escape and wish I'd gone.

Around 2:00 A.M. it began to rain for about an hour, not enough to make things soaking wet but still good and damp. When it stopped, I got up, shook everything out in the air for awhile, and then lay down, sleeping for what seemed only a few minutes until the perfect alarm clock went off. There are those who can reach over, turn an alarm of, and fall back to sleep. But no one has yet demonstrated that he or she can climb a tree, shake a bird from a limb, crawl back down, then go to sleep again—not that this was tried.

Water was poured into one hand with which to wash. At least there's some certainty now of the Irish heritage, though it can't be proved otherwise. What else could it have been but the luck of the Irish? The perfect alarm and a magical canteen which turned everything green, including Sears.

Already the ants were up and charging about. They made long lines like in freeways but were much too serious and well-disciplined to sing, "Hi-ho, hi-ho, it's off to work we go," as you humans do. More like, "Hut, two, three, four!" Or "a one, a two, and a three."

I had two bites on my arm. No, not an early breakfast, at least not by me. Wha'ya think I am anyway? Never mind. Whether due to ants, mosquitoes, or something else was hard telling—nature's immunizations perhaps—painless shots before trekking back to Waikiki and hopefully to ward off the bone-weary cancer of the world. Things like the Somali oil scandal I unwittingly aided and abetted by taking food and drugs to local fire stations, and the news that good ol' Blue Cross, the nonprofit organization which constantly inundates us with letters on how it's struggling so hard to hold down costs and how we can all do our part to help, had "a million dollar baby" running its "five-and-ten-cent store." This came on the heels of the United Funds mess. But don'ya see? In order to attract top talent, ya've got to pay for it. Sure, man, sure! Glad ya cleared that up for me!

Monday finally came. There was much to think about: getting a mailbox, opening a bank account, re-routing a couple direct deposits, making arrangements for another, cashing a traveler's check, and transferring the Washington Blue Cross for starters.

Waikiki was beginning to get hot. By early afternoon tongues were hanging out. One of the last of the majestic banyan trees was being sawed down, a sacrilege really as they should be left undisturbed, taking whatever course they will. Other civilizations understood this, and the trees were left alone. But today was a sign of the times, like Samson's haircut. Instead of shears, an ear-splitting buzz saw took over amidst a mocking whisper from across the street: "Send me your children before the age of six...."

As elephant tusks and the rhino horn have usually been sold before the killing, there was little doubt the thick branches would make coffee tables in rich estates. A magnificent tree had been reduced to a Waikiki bonsai. If the bo tree was Buddhas's, the banyan[292] with its aerial roots should be Hermes', along with palm trees, of which there seem to be less and less as the years go by. No effort, that could be seen, was being made to replant them. The beach rapidly was becoming a Sahara. With an infinite pool of characters from which to draw, Hollywood could have set up immediately and started shooting Rommel in a tank coming over a dune or maybe a remake of *Dune* itself. Nobody would be the wiser with just a vague "filmed on location."

Nomads hell! They were all mad. The hotter it was the more would cross the street to buy cold drinks at McDonald's, which was trying its damnedest to come up with sumpsings that Burger King and Jack-in-the-Box hadn't thought of. No, not yet—but soon maybe—watch for

McDonald's Duck and Mickeyed Mouse. Pity McDonald's hadn't been around earlier with the popularity of *Jurassic Park* today. One fat dinosaur could have been microtomed forever. Big Mac could have boasted in red-and-yellow signs: QUADRILLIONS FROM 60 MILLIONS.

The huge, concrete structures had gobbled up everything. Unlike the dinosaurs, these lizards would never become extinct, just as long as you kept feeding them green, you were safe. But if you didn't have any, they would move into your territory and begin reproducing themselves. The only way ever to be rid of them is by earthquake or mammoth tidal waves, bowling them over like tenpins. The surfers riding the godlike waves—bigger than in their wildest dreams—would be the only ones dying in ecstasy. Yet if it were within my power to cause this destruction, I wouldn't. On the other hand, if it were within my power to prevent it, I wouldn't either. Having no feeling anymore bothers and doesn't say much for me; it doesn't say much for humanity. But don't look so shocked: God had thoughts along this line before me.

Though Caucasians, Chinese, and Japanese now own much choice land in Oahu, the native Hawaiians seem to lack the bitterness of the American Indians, as if saying being a true Hawaiian is an inner thing that can't be bought or stolen. The ones encountered were uncomplicated for the most part. Some—large, beefy, and muscular—could have swatted me away like a gnat, yet both men and women talked pleasantly and were down to earth. No contemptuous criticism showed in their eyes or came from their mouths. There were no bottomless egos to feed. This was how I sized them up, distrusting my own assessment and feeling insiders would probably say, "You don't really know them," which is true.

About all that's known concerning the history of Hawaii is from a book by James Michener. He's a great writer, though too optimistic, Poor man! He can't help it. There have been in history countless instances of heroic or villainous acts, some much greater or worse than others, but to my way of thinking, there are no heroes or villains. It's juvenile and pernicious to create them. People are never as good as we think or as bad. In making heroes and heroines, we are perhaps subconsciously setting them up for a fall, symbolically eating their hearts and then cutting them down to our size. It's a paradox really, a craziness; for in so doing we make our own problems of betrayal, despair, and disillusionment as surely as a moth flies toward a flame.

Before leaving Seattle, I'd gotten an American Youth Hostels' card and then wondered why. It was, of course, a friend who suggested this, explaining that age didn't matter. Maybe so, and maybe age was no barrier to riding a tricycle, but I'd be damned if I'd be that ridiculous. So it was written off as just another dumb expenditure for something which would never be used.

Now in Honolulu and having doubts about wanting to stay, I decided to hold off one more day before starting the paperwork. I wasn't looking forward to sleeping out a third night and thought what could be lost by giving the Waikiki hostel a call? All it could do was say no, which, being filled, was exactly what it did. It suggested though that a call be made to the hostel near the university. And there I paid for two nights at only twelve dollars a day.

There were three others in the room. Their ages varied from mid-twenties to late forties. Surprisingly "these people" were quiet when they came in and left. No one played a radio, made a lot of noise, turned on lights in the middle of the night, or banged doors. They were just travelers wanting to sleep.

After a good night's rest and breakfast, I did some thinking, deciding Hawaii wasn't for me. Consideration was given to giving it a go for a year before throwing in the towel, but come to think of it, I'd been sticking with things for a year, two years, three years—whatever—all my life rather than wimp out. But at the end of these times I was still a wimp, so why not cut out all the bullshit? Down the road, the sun would have influenced my decision to move anyway. I never liked wearing hats. Swimming would have been limited. There was no way to escape the rotisserie's heat unless you wanted to sit inside or in the shade most of the day. There were no big seasonal changes to look forward to.

Some advice, take it or leave it: If you haven't been back to a place for many, many years and have built up a certain image about it in your mind, don't just pack up and move lock, stock, and barrel. Make a short visit back there first, as either you or it or both might have changed over the years.

Airplane tickets back to Seattle ranged from $500 to $600 if one was wanting to leave that day, $300 to $400 if catching a standby; the trouble with catching a standby was that there were nineteen other people trying too. On a good day, only three or four got seats.

Yet I almost made it the only day I tried. The airline had announced that there were no more standby seats available. I was leaving, heading to an airport locker with baggage on a cart, when an agent came running after me. He explained that a very fat lady was complaining about her seat and wanted one where the seat across from her was empty. The flight was being delayed, and they had people talking to her. She might decide to get off. He took my money, gave me a baggage ticket for the suitcase, and said that the backpack could be stowed on board, but at the last minute, the lady decided to go ahead and make the flight.

A third night in a row I slept at the hostel and returned to the airport on Thursday morning. A ticket lady at Northwest said no tickets were available that day other than at the usual price. When I turned to go away, she said, "Sir, once in awhile I point out these numbers in the daily newspaper." She then showed me the advertisements, wrote down the numbers, and explained that sometimes these agencies were able to offer lower fares than the airlines themselves because they had bought big blocs of tickets at a discount far in advance. At Pearl City a seat was got for $251, including tax, for the next day.

I was able to get a bed again that night at the hostel but was advised not to plan on one for the following day since it was filled with reservations. I wasn't.

On the plane coming back, I could only wonder why I'd had the bug to move to Honolulu in the first place. It made no sense unless it was to:

1) Stop the charging Taurus.
2) Face the mighty dragon's fire.
3) Swim in the dangerous water off Diamond Head, whose extinct volcano might erupt at any time.
4) Walk through the towering lizards' lair.
5) Face the forest ninja, while avoiding detection by the palace guards.
6) Obtain the magical canteen.
7) Set the enchanted alarm clock.
8) Sleep two nights under the bewitching moon.
9) Swim to the secret reef at Ala Moana and steal its precious lava stone.
10) Be a witness to the senseless maiming of the venerable banyan tree.
11) Resist the siren calls of McDonald's.
12) Drink the magic elixir at Tony Roma's.

Of course, it was a dumb, inane spoof on the twelve labors of Hercules scaled down for a member of the Medicare set (well almost then). It'd be written off as a vacation and not a very good one at that. It was more like a tame adventure for an ancient mariner.[293-A]

The plane from Seattle left at 9:35 A.M. on Saturday, July 31, 1993, and from Honolulu, at 1:35 P.M. on Friday, August 6, 1993. The trip touched on seven days coming and going. I'd had no knowledge of the flight number in either case until after the ticket was purchased. The number going over, *21*; that returning, *22*.[293-B] There must have been something there, some reason for going. But damned if it was clear unless to say when all was said and done McDonalds got me by.

Chapter Thirty-four

Then two months later I read that Captain James Cook, the greatest of the English explorers, had been to *Easter* Island with its colossal stone monuments in 1774. On July 12, 1776 (or eight days after the Declaration of Independence was signed), he sailed from Plymouth, England, on his final voyage. On Christmas Eve 1777 (1 + 21 = 22), he located a small atoll in the Pacific and called it *Christmas* Island.[294] Though it had little vegetation, his men found turtles and fish. The turtles can be associated with Hermes, the fish with Christ. He discovered the Hawaiian Islands in January 1778 and named them after the *fourth* Earl of Sandwich,[295] his patron.

Now Hermes is said to have been depicted as a cook; sandwich is a prepared food; and Cook was a traveler, a mariner. It was mentioned that possibly Hermes' association as a cook came from his inventing fire sticks, burning two stolen cattle to the gods in sacrifice, and/or possibly the Day of Pots in Greece when cooked food was offered on behalf of the dead. Hawaiians, of course, with their luaus are cooks, volcanoes have fire, and there's plenty of rain and wind in the islands. What wasn't mentioned is that the stolen cattle are said to have numbered fifty; Hawaii was the fiftieth state admitted. Still another link to Hermes was Cook's ability to sleep under stress. It's said that once he had considered some critical situation and had given proper instruction, he had no trouble sleeping.[296]

On January 17 (1779), the day Al Capone was born in 1899, Cook sailed into Kealakekua Bay, Hawaii, receiving a great reception for he was thought to be their god Orono (Rono) returning to his people.

At the beginning of February, the month of purification and atonement in ancient Rome, Cook was aboard the *Resolution* when he became obsessed with having firewood, sticks for fire if not fire sticks. He remembered that near the ship's encampment ashore was an old, dilapidated fence. Hanging at various points on it were "twenty human skulls."[297] These are danger signs in any man's language, a clear warning: "Do you want to be number 21?" Within was a black, rectangular block of stone, about which swayed *palms* with coconuts as white inside as the skulls without.

Certainly, Cook reasoned, no one would object if he sent some men over to tear down the decrepit fence, so rickety with age. Just in case—since it was a holy place where sacrifice was made—he asked the king, who was uncertain and referred the matter to Koa, a priest. Koa seemed to have no objection to this, possibly because he still stood in awe of Cook being Orono.

Since the priest and everybody else said it was okay, the men apparently thought nothing about tossing the skulls to the side of the fence posts they were on and most certainly clowning, "'Alas poor Yorick,' your teeth are gone," if not something else. All along, on poles inside the fence were carved, grotesque, wooden images that smiled down on them. Seamen being seamen, they grinned back, thinking these would be just great to take along as mementos. Their grins were widening even more as it dawned on them they might sell the carvings for a good profit back in England.

Lieutenant King saw the theft going on and spoke to Koa about it. Was it okay for them to take them? Koa didn't seem to mind, asking only that three be returned.[298] On this day too, the first of February, the month under Neptune's protection, Watman died. The *Resolution*'s log must have shown it was from brain hemorrhage. An old, able Seaman, Watman was well liked by both the ship's officers and men since he was generous, unselfish, and obliging. In fact, Captain Cook "regarded him as his good-luck talisman."[299] Now dead, he was no longer that. The natives asked that he be buried near their holy place, and so a joint ceremony of Hawaiian religion and the Church of England was conducted ashore.

A ship's mast is a tall, vertical spar on which sails are hung to be driven by the *wind*. It was wooden in those days and represented judgment, the Captain's Mast. It also can be thought of as a stylized messenger's staff from which white ribbons hang.

After a good sendoff, Captain Cook on the *Resolution* and Captain Clerke on the *Discovery* departed on *February 4*, the day Al Capone would later be buried in the windy city of the slaughter houses. Not long out, the ship hit a storm, and the wind blew for thirty-six hours. On February 8, depending on the source material, the *Resolution*'s foremast split. Of course no one linked this to the "profane pillage," nor incredibly to this day do people ever figure that a god might shatter his own icon, symbol, or temple to make both his presence and displeasure known.

By logic and science, if you want to call it that, the ships returned to Kealakekua Bay on or about February 11 for repairs to be made. They were met by an ominous silence, indicating perhaps the presence of Hermes. Such a stark contrast to their previous reception where their vanity had been built up. They felt let down. The natives, having depleted their food supplies somewhat before in order to be good hosts, were now suspicious. Possibly too it had begun to sink in that if Watman could die, the others weren't immortal either, but it wasn't until *February 13, 14, and 15* that the high drama began to pick up again.

On the thirteenth, the mast was taken ashore for repair, as if symbolic of the wood taken, a hair from the head. One man was sent with the water casks to fill them at the well. He hired a few natives to help. A chief, however, refused to allow them to work. Lieutenant King then sent a marine to help the one man with the water casks. While this was happening, a group of natives, armed with *stones*, crowded around them. While no stones were thrown, insults and warnings were made. "Hey, brudha, maybe bad things gonna häppen." This part of the message apparently got through, for Cook ordered his guards to replace the shot in their muskets with ball, a deadly ammunition. An ounce of prevention is worth a pound of cure, what? Later that afternoon, a fracas broke out when a chisel and the armourer's tongs were stolen aboard the *Discovery*.[300] This generated more trouble as they tried to recover them. One thing led to another. Cook said now he might have to get tough with the natives. When somebody remarked they might show a strong resistance, Cook replied, "They will not stand the fire of a single musket." I.e., fire one shot and they'll turn tail and run. It has been suggested that a "Greek tragedian" might have thought this a "fatal arrogance" of a doomed man.[301]

At dawn on the fourteenth (St. Valentine's Day—*45*), Captain Clerke was surprised to see that his cutter had been cut loose and stolen. Captain Cook was furious. In the fray which followed, he lost his life along with *four* marines (i.e., the marines plus Captain Cook made *five* deaths), but it's glossing things over a bit to say he lost his life. "Actually," in the way my English forebears might have pronounced it, his body wasn't just mutilated, it was hacked up into many bits and pieces. Most certainly he was decapitated. This was the twenty-first skull and *fifty-five* days after Osiris's final entombment on December 21.

Before all this took place, Koa had really liked Lieutenant King and asked him to stay behind when the ships sailed and be treated like a great chief. So on the fifteenth, the Lupercalia, Lieutenant King went within talking distance ashore to ask for the return of the bodies of the four marines and Captain Cook. Koa told him Captain Cook's body had been cut up many times, carried off, but he'd do his best to get the pieces back, a real puzzle.

On the sixteenth, part of one of Cook's thighs, partly cooked or burned, was brought back to Captain Clerke, who said the "sight (was) so horribly shocking, distraction was in every mind, and revenge the result of all."

On the seventeenth, a native wearing Captain Cook's hat approached the *Resolution* in a canoe from which he taunted, made insults, and threw stones, while islanders ashore shouted, jeered, and laughed.[302] Captain Clerke fired four pounders at them. Later a watering party which went ashore was harassed with stones. The party then shot at them, cut the heads off those they killed, and stuck them on poles. After this the hot heads on both sides began to cool. The islanders had lost twenty-five and wanted to start the healing process. They waved white flags and brought gifts and trading resumed. Hermes, persona decapitation, commerce, peace. "Blessed are the peacemakers."

Five or six days after Captain Cook's death, more parts of his body were returned. But some were never retrieved, having been burned and offered high in the hills to the Hawaiian god by top chiefs who thought that in so doing they were honoring a great chief.

Here the mystery of the Feralia-Caristia thickens, for two very excellent books on Captain Cook differ on the burial date. Richard Hough[303] said it was at 5:00 P.M. on February 21, while Daniel Conner and Lorraine Miller[304] gave it at 5:00 P.M. on February 22. The latter apparently are quoting from the ship's log when they say that the *Resolution* and *Discovery* "hoisted Ensign's & Pendants half Staff up & Crossed over Yards, at 3/4 past the *Resolution* toll'd her bell & fir'd 10 four pounders half Minute Gun's," and the remains of Captain Cook were committed to the deep.

Interestingly, not too long after this, Hawaii became part of the complex Pacific commerce, and when it comes right down to it, commerce probably had more to do with the Japanese attack on Pearl Harbor on December 7, 1941, than anything else. There's much cynicism about the commercialism of Christmas, but if you think of Hermes and Jesus linked, or one and the same, you won't have much trouble with this. Remember too that when Cook discovered Christmas Island, he was hoping to find—and did find—turtles and fish.[305]

Captain Cook was a contemporary of George Washington. *February 21*, the anniversary of Captain Cook's burial, later became the dedication day of the Washington Monument. Still later, the water Cook was buried in became part of the United States.

William Bligh, Captain Cook's master aboard the Resolution, was given command of the H.M.S. *Bounty* in 1787. The mutiny that later took place there is dramatized in Nordoff's and Hall's *Mutiny of the Bounty*. Though fiction, Bligh's depiction wasn't without grounds, for he was an extremely rigid, stubborn, vindictive disciplinarian throughout his life. He was appointed governor of the Australian penal colony in 1805. Hermes, god of prisoners. Though making rear admiral in 1811 and vice admiral in 1814, "he held no commands."[306-A] Certainly he couldn't have been proud of the fact that the most famous mutiny in all naval history occurred under him. Curiously he died on *December 7*, 1817.

On August 22, 1779 (six months after Captain Cook's burial on February 21), Captain Clerke died of tuberculosis. Nothing was found about what happened to the bodies of the four marines who died with Captain Cook.

> But one thing wouldn't pass me by,
> And it's not for me to wonder why
> In this Parentalia affair,
> So I'll say before I've ended,
> Watman's grave is still attended.

Chapter Thirty-five

The telling of the future of the unknown (divination) by alleged communication with the dead is defined as necromancy. In the necromancy of European magic, thirteen traditionally is the number used to bring the dead back to life. Since May 13 is thought to be the day Persephone returns to the world from Hades, Friday the thirteenth of May is not considered auspicious. May has been and still is a month when offerings are made to the dead. It was sacred to the old, the opposite of the young, and so was avoided as a time to marry.

Long before Christ, the Romans felt the number thirteen had to do with death and misfortune. It wasn't so much that it was unfortunate to be born on the thirteenth as it was unlucky to undertake something new on the thirteenth. Doesn't it seem likely then that both the necromancy belief and the superstition surrounding the thirteenth arose from the first day of the Parentalia, the Parentalia being a time when civil functions were suspended? There's also the possibility that one of the reasons for sending flowers, candy, and Valentine's Day cards was to take the edge off the first three days of the Feast of the Dead. In the Tarot (see pages 273-274), the thirteenth trump is *Death*; the fourteenth, *Temperance* (remember, it's my belief Christ was crucified on February 14); the fifteenth, the *Devil*; the sixteenth, the *Tower Struck by Lightning*; the twenty-first (the last card), the *Universe*.

Both nine and thirteen are necromancy numbers. The Parentalia began on the thirteenth, lasted nine days, and ended on the twenty-first.

On *February 11*, 1861, President-elect Abraham Lincoln left his Springfield, Illinois, neighbors "not knowing when or whether I ever may return, with a task before me greater than that which rested upon Washington," and began to *travel* to the nation's capital. He gave short speeches (eloquence) en route at *Indianapolis*, Cincinnati, Columbus, Cleveland, Pittsburgh, Buffalo, Rochester, Syracuse, Albany, Troy, New York, Trenton, Philadelphia, and Harrisburg. On *February 22*, he was warned of an assassination plot in Baltimore and was secretly put on a special train that arrived at Washington on the morning of *February 23*.

It had been a mystical journey, for its duration made boundaries enclosing the bookends, which in turn made boundaries just outside the ancient period. The sacrifices of the Civil War were inevitable, as was Cemetery Ridge; Lincoln's eloquent speech at the graveyard; his assassination; his burial in Springfield on 5-4-1865 (21); and finally over his tomb, the obelisk, resembling the Washington Monument.

February 23, in Roman religion, was known as Terminalia, a festival to the god of boundaries (Hermes is a god of boundaries and a breaker of boundaries) called Terminus. Land owners who had a common boundary met and each placed garlands on his side of the *stone* marker. They built an altar, lit a fire, and made offerings of food and wine.

ABRAHAM LINCOLN born Parentalia Eve, February 12, 1809. Remember 12 is a transposition of 21. The USS *Nevada* (last state admitted under Lincoln) remained aground until 1300 on February 12, 1942. See page 385.

CHARLES DARWIN born February 12, 1809.

February 13. Parentalia began at noon in Rome. Though not 100 percent accurate, there's a surprising similarity by using this date for the Day of Pots. A three-day festival was held for Dionysus in ancient Athens. The month Anthesterion (roughly February–March) got its name from this. The thirteenth was the last day, an All-Souls Day. At that time on behalf of the dead, offerings were made only to the chthonic Hermes.

February 13. Festival for Faunus held in an island temple on the Tiber. Another was held on *December 5*. (Op. cit., Peck.) Faunus is identified with the Greek god Pan, who was thought by some to be the son of Hermes. Plutarch tells of a mariner who was told by a voice three times close to the Echinades Island "when you reach Palodes proclaim that the great god Pan is dead." In legend this was supposed to have occurred at the exact time of Christ's death.

February 13. The Grave of Tarpeia, a mundus, apparently opened this day and sacrifice there was made by one of the vestals. (Ibid.)

February 13, 1542. Catherine Howard, Queen of England, and fifth wife of Henry VIII (5 + 8 = 13), was beheaded. It's said that on each successive February 13 her ghost haunts Hampton (see February 21, 1922–Roads) Court Palace and Eythorne Manor. Henry and Catherine got married on July 28, 1540, the day Thomas Cromwell was beheaded in London.

February 13, 1571. Benvenuto Cellini died in Florence and was buried on February 15. One of his masterpieces shows Perseus holding aloft the decapitated head of Medusa. Another—a gold and enamel saltcellar—portrays Neptune, who guards the month of February, with his Trident and a female figure representing Earth. An admirer of Michelangelo, Cellini was selected "to represent sculpture at the obsequies of Michelangelo," who died *February 18*, 1564.

February 13, 1692. About forty members of the MacDonald clan massacred at Glencoe on order of William III. The same year as the Salem witch trials.

February 13, 1728. Cotton Mather died. Born February 12, 1663.

February 13, 1746. A Frenchman named Jean Marie Dubarry was executed for murdering his father. (*Facts and Fallacies*, Pleasantville, New York: Reader's Digest Association, 1988.)

February 13, 1748. *The Lady Lovibond* (LA, LI), a three-masted schooner, was wrecked in a dangerous sandbank facing the English Channel called Goodwin Sands. All aboard drowned. Every fifty years on February 13, the ghost ship is seen running aground. The first phantom was in 1798, the second in 1848. In each case, there were many witnesses. It was seen in 1898 and again in 1948. (Op. cit., Guiley, Rosemary E.)

February 13, 1777. Marquis de Sade arrested. In 1772 he had been condemned to death but escaped.

February 13, 1778. Ten-year-old John Quincy Adams sailed with his father on the *Boston* for France. (Shepherd, Jack, *The Adams Chronicles*. Boston: Little, Brown and Co., 1975.) It's the beginning of the Feast of the Dead, the forty-fourth day, honoring deceased relatives and ancestors. One way or another Samuel, John, and John Quincy Adams will enter into the picture. At France, father and son stayed at the Hôtel de Valentinois. Valentinois probably refers to Valence region of France or its inhabitants.

February 13, 1810. A sum of money was ordered to be set aside in Chancery for Frances Keats and to be allotted to her children, one of whom was John Keats, after her death. Her parents had married on *February 15* (1774), the Lupercalia. Her father owned the Swan and Hoop stables. (Hermes is over birds, especially an omen. Hoop carries the same symbolism as a circle, identified with Hermes, who had dominion over horses.) In 1804 on *April 15* (4.5 and 4.5 of the coven circle—hoop), John Keats's father was thrown from his horse and died. (Horse, a death symbol. Swan, swan song.) John Keats was born *October 31*, 1795. If Hallow tide waxes, it also wanes via May 13, the culmination of the Lemuria spread, to the February Feast of the Dead. The first of five children, one of whom died shortly after birth (of five, four survived), John Keats was cursed with tuberculosis. On *February 14*, 1821, a calm came over him and his fever ceased. Realizing his death was near, he sent his friend Severn to the Protestant

Cemetery where he expected to be buried. On returning, Severn described the sheep, goats, daisies, and violets, the favorite flower of Keats. Keats told him he wanted the inscription on his gravestone to read: "Here lies one whose name was writ in water" (Gittings, Robert, *John Keats*. Boston: Little, Brown and Company, 1968). Neptune, guardian of the month of February. At one time Keats told Severn too that he wished to have a lyre with a few broken or disconnected strings on the gravestone. On *February 21* he seemed to be going. On *February 23*, around 11:00 P.M., he died.

Because of resentment by Catholics for non-Catholics at the time, he had to be buried either at night or in the early morning hours in Rome. Hermes is connected to dawn and has nocturnal aspects. (page 262; Gogol page 6.)

February 13, 1819. James Tallmadge, representative of New York, caused the first big division among states after introducing an amendment to a bill to admit Missouri. It proposed that all children born in Missouri be free at age twenty-five and that no new slaves be introduced. The states up to this time had been evenly divided on slavery. Missouri would tip the scale. *February 16–17,* both clauses of the Tallmadge anti-slavery amendment were passed in the House of Representatives. These were rejected by the Senate on *February 27,* 1819. On the day dividing the Parentalia, *February 17,* 1820, the Missouri Compromise Measure was passed by the Senate. This allowed for bringing in Missouri as a slave state and what would become Ides-and-Lupercalia Maine as a free state. Maine was admitted March 15, 1820, and Missouri on August 10, 1821 (SY). This made twelve free states and twelve slave states.

February 13, 1846. Another Frenchman with the name Jean Marie Dubarry was executed for murdering his father (Op. cit., *Facts and Fallacies.*) A father is a parent.

February 13, 1849. Lord Randolph Churchill born. He married Jennie Jerome. Apparently she'd been conceived in Trieste, *Italy,* where her father had been American Consul, and born in Brooklyn, New York, as the later Al Capone, of *Italian* immigrant parents, would be. Jennie's mother, Clara, was one-quarter Iroquois. Where Jennie's husband died at forty-five years of age on January 24, 1895, after suffering for years with painful, syphilitic paresis that deranged his mind, Al Capone died from ravages of the disease on January 25, 1947, and had been connected to *February 13 and 14,* 1929. Writers have conjectured that Lord Randolph Churchill (church of the hill; church-ill) was Jack the Ripper. Considering that sacrifices might have been required for Theodore Roosevelt and John Pershing to get where they did, it's an interesting idea that Winnie might have got where he did by the same process, through sacrifices taken rather than purposely given.

In 1896, our little Jennie from Brooklyn's son Winston—later to become Great Britain's famous prime minister—was entangled in a charge that he'd taken part in "acts of gross immorality of the Oscar Wild type." After talking it over with his mother and solicitors a writ was issued:

STATEMENT OF CLAIM
In the High Court of Justice
QUEEN'S BENCH DIVISION
Writ issued 15 February 1896
Between WINSTON SPENCER CHURCHILL...
Plaintiff
AND
A.C. BRUCE-PRYCE
Defendent
Delivered the 21st day of February 1896[306-B]

Winston was acquitted, awarded five hundred pounds, and Bruce-Pryce withdrew "every imputation" against Winston's character and expressed regret for having maligned him.

In a sense, a larger picture, it wasn't so much what Churchill had or hadn't done, as originally charged, as it was the Di Manes were marking their man. It made no difference 1) that Churchill had been born "prematurely" seven and a half months after the wedding had taken place; 2) that Jack Strange[306-BB] was suspected of being only a half brother (if so, his mother was an adulteress); and 3) his father, alleged to have been Jack the Ripper, died of syphilis, making him an adulterer. What was important were the dates *February 15* and *February 21*.

In the Sudan campaign, Winston was commissioned a supernumerary lieutenant to the *twenty-first* Lancers, a number associated with both Grant and Theodore Roosevelt, both horse lovers. In addition to horses, Winston liked dogs. The butterfly (Quetzalcóatl) fascinated him. As a risk taker, he was a gambler. When the Boer War broke out, American women in Great Britain tried to do their part. Lady Randolph Churchill (Jennie) cabled her distant cousin Theodore Roosevelt, then governor of New York, for help. He had no suggestions. However, an American millionaire agreed to lend one of his transports (a cattle ship) for the duration of the war. By fundraisers and donations, Lady Churchill and her committee were able to convert this into a hospital ship called the *Maine*, after the battleship which had been sunk on *February 15*, 1898. She managed to get the British

Admiralty to accept it as such. In a letter dated *February 13*, 1900, Winston wrote his mother, "It is a coincidence that one of the first patients on board the *Maine* should be your son" (Jack). In 1908 Winston married Clementine Hozier (born April [fourth month] 1, 1885; see Book I, footnote 7-A).

On *May 10* (a day within the Lemuria spread), 1940, he was appointed Prime Minister, to lead Great Britain in its death struggle. On *May 13* (*Kore*, the maiden; last day of the Lemuria; the equivalent of February 21), he gave his famous speech in the House of Commons:

"...At the end of the proceedings today, the Adjournment of the House will be proposed until Tuesday, 21 *May*...I have nothing to offer but *blood*, toil, tears and sweat...to wage war against a monstrous tyranny, never surpassed in the dark, lamentable catalogue of human crime...without victory, there is *no survival*...."

Throughout the war, he will be seen giving the V (victory, 5, crossroads) sign.

Churchill's parents were married on April 15 (4.5), 1874. At the time of his birth, Our *American Cousin* opened at the Theatre Royal, Haymarket, London. This was the play Lincoln was watching when shot. Both Lincoln and Churchill had mood swings, and Churchill apparently was a manic depressive, going from dark moods to "exhilarating" brilliance. When visiting President Franklin Roosevelt at the White House during World War II, Prime Minister Churchill hated to sleep in Lincoln's room. Lincoln, of course, died on 4.5, the *Titanic* (from Great Britain to the United States) sank on 4.5, and Roosevelt will be buried on 4.5. The state funeral for Winston Churchill was held January 30, 1965. This was *twenty-two* days before Feralia *21*. See *February 21*, 1944.

February 13, 1861. Electoral votes officially counted by Congress on this first day of the Feast of the Dead. Abraham Lincoln and Hannibal Hamlin officially are declared elected. Hamlin (VP #15, *Maine* sunk on fifteenth day) is the only vice president to have been born in Maine, or to represent Maine, or to be buried there. "As the Manes go, so goes the nation." He died on *July 4*, 1891. The last sizable battle of the Civil War occurred at *Palm*ito Ranch in 1865 on *May 13*, equivalent to the last day of the Feast of the Dead. By now you should see what the war was really about. But in case you don't, the last battle was won ironically by the South, led by Col. John S. Ford (phonetic fourd), known as RIP, "Rest in Peace."

February 13, 1866. Liberty, Missouri. Ten or so men pulled off what's thought to have been the first daylight, peace-time bank robbery in America.

February 13, 1867. First performance of Johann Strauss II's *The Blue Danube*, simple in its D major triad (trident), was given in Vienna in the hall of the Imperial Riding School (horse: Neptune, Hermes, death). Neptune, guardian of the month of February. This, the most famous of the Strauss waltzes, is a life-death song. Johann Strauss II's grandfather, a descendant of Wolf Strauss, either committed suicide or drowned in the Danube. The river *begins* from the headwaters of the Black Forest and *ends* at a *delta*, emptying into the Black Sea. On *February 14*, 1860, Strauss composed *Accelerationen*, Opus 234, said to be "the first of his mature, great waltzes." The name, month, day, and even opus number are appropriate for the god of speed, travel, death, and love. The heart sign, now linked to St. Valentine's Day, was in ancient Greece "related to the lyre, attribute of Eros," according to Carl Liungman. The lyre, of course, is related to Hermes and others too. Hermes and Eros are possibly father and son. Sometimes on Valentine's Day cards we see Eros with his bow, which looks much like a snake on the statue at the Capitoline Museum, Rome. Given that Valentine's Day is the *forty-five* day, the number associated with Hermes is *4*, it's interesting that up until the time of the Roman Empire, the festival for Eros was celebrated every *fifth* year and accompanied by gymnastics and musical contests.

February 13, 1875. Quintuplet boys born in *Water*town, Wisconsin. All died within two weeks. (Op. cit. [*Famous First Facts*], Kane.)

February 13, 1883. Richard Wagner died. Born May 22 (MP), 1813. "*Triste, triste, triste*," cried Verdi, "*Wagoner e morte*." On *February 14*, Cosima had to be pulled away from Wagner's corpse thirty hours after his death. She cut off all her hair and put it inside the coffin before it was closed. On *February 14*, 1861, the first Italian parliament assembled. Verdi was an elected member.[306-BBB]

February 13, 1884. Wednesday. Two telegrams came to Theodore Roosevelt at Albany, New York, on the beginning day of the *Parent*alia. The first told of his daughter's birth on the previous day; the second said that his wife's condition was worsening. He got back home some time before midnight. Elliott, his younger brother, told him, "There is a curse on this house. Mother is dying and Alice is dying too." So it would seem to have been, for both mothers died the next day on *February 14* (4514 = DEAD), or 2 x 14 = 28. Elliott had been born on *February 28*, 1860. He died on August 14, 1894 (or ten years after the deaths of his relatives), in "a fit of delirium tremens." That the Roosevelt family was closely connected to the Parentalia is further suggested by the fact that Elliott's and Theodore's sister Corrine (Kore>Cora>Corinne) Roosevelt (born September 17 (MP), 1861) died on *February 17*, 1933, in the middle of the Parentalia and on the anniversary of her niece's wedding at the White House. February 17 is *four* days from 21 and *five* days from 22.

February 13, 1885. Bess (Elizabeth Virginia) Wallace Truman born. He died October 18, 1982. "Nobody makes up Harry Truman's mind—except Bess," commented a person who knew the White House couple (*Newsweek* November 1, 1982). The only other first lady born in February (February 12, 1775—compare to 1885) was Louisa Adams (LA), wife of John Quincy Adams, also linked to February. Besides Bess Truman's birthdate, Harry Truman was connected to Lupercus (Faunus/Pan) by December 5 (1851), the birthdate of John Anderson Truman, his father, and to Hermes, god of musicians (as is Apollo), merchants, death, and peace. Harry was an accomplished pianist, a failed haberdasher, and was responsible in '45 for the first atomic bomb dropped on people (Hiroshima) on August 6; then three days later, the second was dropped on Nagasaki, Japan. Harry S. (snake?) Truman was the president under whom we got peace. Bess and Harry's only child, Mary Margaret (from which May is derived) was born in 1924 on February 17, the middle of the Parentalia and the twenty-seventh anniversary of the formation of the Congress of Mothers, known later as the *Parent*-Teacher Association. See February 21, 1948. Harry Truman was born May 8, 1884.

February 13, 1894. Thirteen killed in cave-in in Gaylord Mine, Plymouth, Virginia.

February 13, 1917. The unexecuted portion of the sentence (loss of *five* numbers in grade) as a result of general court martial of Captain Edward L. Beach, former CO of the armored cruiser *Memphis*, was approved by the secretary of the navy. In August 1916, the *Memphis* was "utterly demolished" by a tidal wave while at anchor at Santo Domingo, the city where Christopher Columbus and his son were reburied. (See *February 21*, 1429.) Forty-three men were killed; over two hundred were injured. For awhile "a suspended gangway across forty feet of water" lay between the wreck and shore. This finally was cut down when it was realized the wreck was a "rendezvous for suicides," three or four having occurred.

The ship, the *fourth Tennessee*, was renamed the *Memphis* on *May 25*, 1916, so that the name *Tennessee* could be given to a new battleship.

On June 27, 1919, the secretary of the navy ordered "the restoration of the loss of five numbers in grade as a result of the sentence of general court-martial approved *February 13*, 1917," the first day of the Parentalia. The Greek name Memphis is an abbreviation for the funerary complex of Pepi I. Beach: a shore of an ocean, sea, etc., washed by the tide or waves. Neptune, guardian of the month of February.

After landing at Paris, which has the most popular catacombs in the world, on the beginning of the Mercury period, May 21, 1927, Charles A. Lindbergh and the *Spirit of St. Louis* returned to the U.S. on the next USS *Memphis*. On *February 13*, 1935, Bruno Hauptmann was found guilty of murdering Charles A. Lindbergh's first born.

February 13, 1923. Chuck Yeager, pilot, born.

February 13, 1924. Howard Carter, who, with Lord Carnarvon and others, desecrated King Tut's tomb in 1923 during the Parentalia, padlocked the tomb from *about 12 noon on February 13 through February 21*, the ancient period. Lord Westbury, who was a friend of Lord Carnarvon and had items in his apartment from King Tut's tomb, jumped to his death on *February 21*, 1930, about three months after his son, one of the excavators, died mysteriously.

February 13, 1929. Col. Charles A. Lindbergh (who had landed near Paris on May 21, 1927, or fifty-six years after its Bloody Week began, and came back on the USS *Memphis*—Memphis, a Greek abbreviation for *Men-neferu-Meryre*, Pepi I's *funerary* complex) took off from Havana and landed in Florida (Ponce de Leon, 1513 to 1521 when he died) on the beginning of the Parentalia. He had inaugurated an air mail service to the canal zone. On return flight from Panama (crossroads, Hermes god of), he landed in Havana on February 12, the day his and Anne Morrow's engagement was announced in Mexico City, or the anniversary of Lincoln's birthday. A Chicago bootlegger (Italy resembles a boot) told "Bugs" Moran he had a truckload of alcohol for sale. Moran told him to deliver it to the North Clark Street address. Meanwhile at Florida (a wind-god's state, resembling a boot when reversed), Al Capone kept an appointment at 12:00 noon, exactly when the ancient Parentalia began in Italy. (See page 612, footnote 54.)

February 13, 1929. The day after the Mardi Gras was held in New Orleans and one day before the St. Valentine's Day Mass, the *Chicago Tribune* carried a story from London that the empress in Vienna received word that one hundred wolves had broken through a school's mud walls in Javina and killed sixteen children on *February 12*. Four gendarmes and two soldiers who tried to rescue them were also killed. At Miscoloez in Hungary, wolves attacked peasants, killing five. (Later on *February 16*, two residents of a small community about fourteen miles south of

Chicago killed a lean, grey wolf when it attacked them.) On *February 11* in Berlin (Woden country) the Mercury hit twenty-five degrees below zero. The temperature was the lowest it had been in two hundred years. The ground was frozen two yards deep, and for days they couldn't bury their dead. Adventists ran through the streets shouting that the end of the world had come. (The ancient Mayans, strong on blood and sacrifice, say this will occur on Sunday, December 23, 2012.) Black Sea ports were frozen so solid that it was impossible to bring in coal for warmth. On the morning of *February 12* in Paris, the Mercury was at thirteen degrees. A whole band of gypsies (thirty-four men, women, and children) were found frozen to death in a forest near Lublin. On *February 19*, a storm covered the Crimea with sixteen feet of snow. Hundreds all over central and eastern Europe had now died and would die from the cold, influenza, pneumonia, and starvation. On *February 21* avalanches and floods in the Balkans and neighboring states took a heavy toll. The cold would continue at least up to *February 23* and after.

February 13, 1929. Alexander Fleming, later to become Sir Alexander Fleming, gave a speech on his new discovery to the Medical Research Club. He first described the "staph inhibiting mould" in his notebook date "Oct 30.28." Devil's Night (October 30) is the evening before Halloween, the beginning of Hallow-tide. There's talk that an old remedy of witches was to use bread mould in treatment. On *February 21*, 1968, Lord Howard Florey—who with Ernst Boris Chain isolated and purified penicillin so it could be used practically—died. Fleming, Flory, and Chain shared in a Nobel Prize in 1945.

February 13, 1930. Former President and Mrs. Calvin Coolidge ended their vacation in Florida. (President-elect Harding had fished in Miami, Florida, on February 1, 1921; Vice president Coolidge had succeeded President Harding who died in San Francisco on August 2, 1923.) During Coolidge's presidency in 1924, his youngest son Calvin Jr. died of blood poisoning. (Lincoln had also lost a son when in the White House.) On *February 21*, 1931, Mrs. Coolidge launched the new Dollar liner *President Coolidge* by breaking against it a bottle of water she'd brought from a brook at the Coolidge homestead in Vermont. Calvin just being thrifty again? Maybe not. As stories go, Robert Dollar had once kicked a navy admiral off one of his ships for having alcohol aboard.

February 13, 1932. A mysterious tipoff from America (Amerigo Vespucci died *February 22*, 1512) led to the discovery of a bomb, either meant for Pope Pius XI or Mussolini, under a huge lion near the central altar of St. Peter's in Rome. In Flushing, New York, the

Goodyear blimp *Columbia* (Columbus born in Italy) was wrecked, making a descent in a gale. It's chief officer John W. Blair was killed.

These events on the first day of the Parentalia bring to mind the announcement on its last day *February 21*, 1922, that a lost diary of George Washington (born *February 22*, 1732) had been discovered, the fate of the dirigible *Roma*, and General Pershing's disclosure on *February 22*.

February 13, 1935. Bruno Hauptmann convicted of murder of Charles A. Lindbergh, Jr. Declaring his innocence to the last, he was electrocuted April 3, 1936.

February 13, 1942. Operation Sea Lion, Germany's plan to invade England, was abandoned. This decision (it was tacitly recognized) was based on Germany's sea limitations.

February 13, 1952. Joe Louis, former heavyweight champion, announced he was finished with boxing except for exhibitions. Died April 12, 1981. (See page 690, footnote 342.)

February 13, 1952. Reported in Miami (*Chicago Daily Tribune, February 14*, 1952) that Mae Capone had sold the walled estate and one-time winter gangland headquarters of her late husband Al Capone for "slight in excess of $64,000." But *February 13* is the beginning of the Feast of the Dead, and the former Hawthorne Hotel burned down in the middle of it on *February 17*, 1970. (See page 677, footnote 308-B.)

February 13, 1955. Israel purchased four Dead Sea Scrolls for $250,000 from Syrian Archbishop Metropolitan in Jerusalem. These predated any other known biblical sources. The beginning day of the Parentalia. Dead: Hermes, god of death. Sea: Neptune, guardian of the month of February. Scroll: Thoth, judgment. The Jordan, where Jesus was baptized, begins at the base of Mt. Hermon and eventually reaches the Dead Sea. (See page 283.)

February 13, 1958. Carlos Prio Socarras, former Cuban President, and eight others were charged and indicted for violation of neutrality laws by planning military expeditions from the United States against the Republic of Cuba.

February 13, 1959. Resignation of Cuban Premier Jose Miro Cardona and his cabinet. On *February 16*, 1959, Commander-in-Chief of the Cuban Armed Forces Fidel Castro became a Parentalia Premier, while his brother Raul moved to armed forces commander. (Remember Lenin's remains have been seen by more than any other person in history.) See *February 15*, 1898; *February 21*, 1901; *February 15*, 1973; and *February 15*, 1976.

February 13, 1960. France detonated her first atomic bomb in the Sahara desert.

February 13, 1962. Paris, France. Over five hundred thousand took part in a public funeral procession for the victims of anti-terrorist demonstrations on February 8.

February 13, 1965. SY. Malcolm X arrived at New York on a flight from London. Previously he had been denied entry into France.

February 13, 1967. The National Student Association disclosed that it had indirectly and secretly received more than three million dollars from the CIA in 1952–66 for overseas programs. On *February 14*, the State Department admitted the CIA had supported overseas projects by students to compete with Communist student activities. Senator Robert F. Kennedy said on *February 21* (James Hoffa born *February 14*; Kathleen Kennedy and Jean Kennedy born *February 20*; Edward Kennedy born *February 22*) that the CIA shouldn't be made "to take the rap" for what was decided by the "executive branch in the Eisenhower, Kennedy, and Johnson administrations." On *February 23*, Congressional leaders decided that Congress would not hold a special investigation of the CIA, which perhaps knew where the bodies were buried.

February 13, 1976. At her trial, Patricia Hearst told of her kidnapping and stated she had received death threats from her captors. Then on *February 22*, 1976, an article in *New Times* magazine by William and Emily Harris, SLA members, contradicted Patricia Hearst's testimony that she had been coerced into involuntary participation in the bank robbery. On *May 15*, 1978, she returned to prison in California after being set free on 1.5 million dollars bail in 1976.[306-C]

She was abducted on *February 4*, 1974. On *February 12*, 1974, a ransom note from her abductors (the Symbionese Liberation Army) demanded that seventy dollars in food be given for each needy person in California. On *February 22*, 1974, a two-million dollar food giveaway was begun by the Hearst family. On *April 15*, 1974, a camera filmed her taking part in a San Francisco bank robbery. On *February 1*, 1979, she was released from a prison near San Francisco when President Carter granted her clemency after serving twenty-two months of a seventeen-year sentence. These dates are interesting in that Patricia Hearst was born on *February 20*, 1954, in San Francisco County (45 square miles.) (See February 21, 1974, and page 380.)

February 13–14, 1861. First Medal of Honor was awarded for action taking place on February 13–14 (note deaths on beginning day of Parentalia) at Apache Pass in New Mexico Territory (now Arizona) to Col. Bernard Irwin, assistant surgeon, who "voluntarily took command of troops and defeated" the hostile Chiricahua Indians he encountered. Dr. Mary *Walker*, commissioned as assistant surgeon in the Civil War, died on *February 21*, 1919. She was the first woman awarded the Medal of Honor. Note: two doctors, caduceus; *February 13–14*, Irwin; *February 21*, Walker. Arizona admitted on St. Valentine's Day 1912.

February 13–14, 1945. One source states that two hundred and forty-four British bombers dropped six hundred and fifty thousand incendiary bombs on Dresden, Germany, on the thirteenth. Four hundred and fifty American bombers continued the destruction on St. Valentine's Day. On February 13–14, 90 percent of the city was destroyed with an estimated death toll of thirty-five thousand or more. Date also given as February 13–15, 1945. Dresden had been called the Florence of the Elbe, or Germany.

February 14, 269 or 270. Beheading of Valentine.[307-A] Inherent in the heart design is the number 3 and 21.

February 14, 1564. It was a cold, wet day in Milano, Italy. Michelangelo went riding in the countryside. In the afternoon, he became ill. He tried again on the Lupercalia to go riding but had to give it up as the weather was still cold and his condition had worsened. Still within the Parentalia on February 18 (2-18-1564 reduces to 9), he died. It's said that many days later when his body was examined for burial, there was little sign of decay.

February 14, 1573. Englishman Francis Drake and men, having hacked their way through a jungle of Panama (the crossroads) lay in wait on the dark night of the forty-fifth day[307-B] to rob a mule train of the Spanish, who, in turn, were robbers. Wary Spaniard Ledesma, however, had taken the precaution of decoy, a Hermes stratagem. (Disguise used on *February 14*, 1929.) The six mules in front, though appearing laden, carried nothing. This completely fooled overanxious Robert Pike, who attacked immediately as soon as it got near. Thus those in the back with the actual treasure had time to turn around and flee back to Panama. *February 14*, 1913, will become the birthdate of Bishop Albert Pike and James Hoffa, teamster leader.

February 14, 1778. The first salute to the Stars and Stripes by a foreign nation was on this date. John Paul Jones aboard the *Ranger* saluted the *Admiral La-Motte Piquet*, a French ship, with a thirteen-gun salute. She responded, in effect acknowledging American Independence. Notice here the occurrence of thirteen and fourteen. This also occurred on June *14*, 1777 (a suggestion of twenty-one and twenty-two) when Congress authorized the Stars and Stripes, having thirteen stripes that alternated between red and white and thirteen white stars on a blue background. Thirteen is a necromancy number.

February 14, 1779. Captain Cook, of the *Resolution*, butchered at Hawaii.

February 14, 1817. The date of *February 14* is uncertain (as is that of Marian Anderson *February 17/27*, 1902) for Frederick Douglass's birthday. It's used because that's what he reckoned it to be. Douglass was an escaped black slave of part-Indian blood and an unknown white father. His birthday was the focal point for Negro History Week, later to become Black (African-American) History Week; and since 1976, Black History Month. Some churches have broadened February 14 to be called "Race Relations Day." (On *February 20*, 1942, FDR's executive order authorized moving one hundred and ten thousand Japanese-Americans from Arizona, California, Oregon, and Washington to inland internment camps. On *February 27*, 1973, the small village of Wounded Knee, South Dakota, was occupied by about two hundred armed supporters of the American Indian Movement [AIM].) Douglass was brutally flogged at times before escaping. His original name was Frederick Augustus Washington Bailey before he changed it to Frederick Douglass to protect his identity. He died on *February 20*, 1895. It's curious how many dates in black history and/or race relations history lie within February.

February 14, 1847. Anna Howard Shaw born. American suffrage leader (see *February 15*, 1820), physician, and minister. Died July 2, 1919.

February 14, 1849. On this first full day of the Feast of the Dead, Congress counted the electoral vote. Zachary Taylor—who had beaten 21-February-Santa Anna—was to be the next president.

February 14, 1859. Oregon admitted to the union as the twenty-third state. Captain Cook sailed off the Oregon coast in March 1778. The *Oregon* (Battleship No. 3 and named for the state) was launched in 1893 (SY) and commissioned in 1896. Her career was long (with years of decommissioning), steady, but not especially distinguished in battle.[308-A] Perhaps more importantly, she, like the *Arizona*, was to become symbolic to the nation, the Parentalia. She had just got out of drydock on *February 16* (see USS *Nevada*) when she got word the *Maine* had been sunk. Thereafter the war moved ever closer with each Lupercalia chant. The *Oregon* loaded ammunition at San Francisco. Her trip to join Admiral Sampson's fleet in the Atlantic was historically significant because it swept away any opposition there had been to building the Panama Canal. Two months were just too long for a ship to get from one coast to another in national emergencies. (Actually it had taken sixty-six days from the time she left San Francisco to Jupiter Inlet, Florida, "reporting ready for battle.") In 1915 then it was fitting the *Oregon* would be sent to San Francisco for the Panama-Pacific International Exposition, the celebration of the crossroads.

Finally because of the Oregon Trail, its walkers (travelers), oxen, horses, the blood sacrifices of people (migrants and Indians) and animals (the seemingly senseless blood baths of buffaloes which nearly wiped them out), it's fitting somehow that Oregon would be admitted on St. Valentine's Day.

February 14, 1876. Alexander Graham Bell applied for a patent of the first phase of his telephone (*message,* communication). On *February 21,* 1846, Sarah Bagley reported for work, becoming the first woman telegrapher in history.

February 14, 1884. On this day, five days from the anniversary of Theodore Roosevelt's father's death on *February 9,* 1878 (burial on the Parentalia Eve), two tragedies struck TR. His mother died of typhoid fever. His wife, in a weakened condition following childbirth, died of Bright's disease. *Febris, Februa, Februus.* (As a reference point, it's important to remember their deaths occurred on the day before the Lupercalia. The summer prior to his junior year at Harvard, TR went to Maine, where he was taken with the outdoors life and "the beauty of the woods." (Lorant.) A statuesque picture (page 160 of Lorant's book) shows TR with Hermetic points: a beard, a small hat, snow shoes, and a rabbit kill (death) hanging from his belt.

"As Maine goes, so goes the nation" was adopted in 1888, the figure of 8 being a Thoth symbol. On the anniversary of the 1884 Lupercalia when the bodies of TR's wife and mother lay dead and unburied, the battleship *Maine* was sunk in Havana Harbor. TR was an assistant secretary of the navy. *Ten days later* when the secretary of the navy had taken the day off, TR sent a message to Commodore Dewey to "Keep full of coal" in case of war, in which event he was "to see that the Spanish Squadron does not leave the Asiatic coast," and he was to "take offensive operations in the Philippine Islands." The message was sent despite the fact the secretary of the navy had sent instructions to him not to take "any step affecting the policy of the administration without consulting the President or me." This is interesting in that Dewey left Hong Kong and then slipped into Manila Bay on the evening of April 30. At dawn (Hermes born at dawn) on May 1, he got within range of two and one-half miles and fired on the Spanish fleet, which was defeated.

Coincidentally, the Celtic May Day called Beltane began at moonrise on May Day Eve and used to end on May Day with human sacrifice by fire. So there's the suggestion here of a death god.

TR later took partial credit for Dewey's victory; however, prior to it, he had resigned as assistant secretary of the navy and gone to San Antonio, Texas, to take second-in-command of one of the regiments he later said "could whip Caesar's Tenth Legion." Caesar is, of course, of Lupercalia fame. Curiously Roosevelt arrived at San Antonio on *May 15*, 1898, and that Rough Riders suggests travel, horses, and campaign (Hermes, god of campaigns). In 1909—"ten days from the end of his reign"—he watched the historic Feralia fleet on the Caristia. It should not go unnoticed either that the proceedings were on the *Mayflower*, again May. May 27–28, 1905 the main Japanese fleet defeated the Russian Baltic fleet in the battle of Tsushima Straits. Only three or four of the thirty-eight Russian vessels escaped, limping on to Vladivostok, and there's little doubt the defeat by the Japanese in the Russo-Japanese war contributed to much unrest at home. The war was triggered when Japanese submarines pulled a surprise attack on the Russian fleet at Port Arthur on *February 8*, 1904. (If you recall, it's my belief that February and December are roughly equivalent.) On *February 10*, 1904, Russia and Japan declared war. On *February 17*, 1905, in keeping with the centuries-old belief that February seventeen is an unlucky day and one year before Princess Alice married *Nicholas* Longworth in the White House, Grand Duke Sergei, the uncle of Czar *Nicholas* II, was assassinated. On *February 19 or 21*, 1905 (depending on the source but still within the Parentalia), the final land battle—and one of the bloodiest in history—began at Mukden, Manchuria. The Japanese won this in March with an estimated 71,000 casualties; while those of the Russians were about 89,000.

Keeping in mind Theodore Roosevelt's connection to February, water, and ships (on August 25, 1905, Roosevelt was the first U.S. president to submerge in a submarine), it fits that he would be mediator for the peace conference between Japan and Russia held at Portsmouth, New Hampshire from August 9 to September 5 (MP), 1905 (SY).

A double funeral was held at the corner (suggesting four of Fifth Avenue and Fifty-fifth Street on the Parentalia day of *February 16*, 1884, for the two parents). Alice Lee Roosevelt had been born four days earlier on the anniversary of Lincoln's birth. When her father was president, she married House Representative Nicholas Longworth (measure) at the White House on *February 17*, 1906, smack dab in the middle of the Parentalia. Running out of rice, Alice's brothers showered her and Nicholas with black beans.[308-B] This was a curious thing to have done since black beans were used in antiquity to dismiss the May Lemurs, the unfriendly spirits of the dead. After beginning their honeymoon at the McLean's estate, the couple took off for Cuba. Where else? Cuba is connected to the Lupercalia and the *Maine*, named after the state admitted on the Ides of March. The implication of these events alone might be looked upon as ridiculous.

But there's much more to indicate just the opposite. On Friday, *February 13*, 1880, the beginning of the Parentalia, Theodore Roosevelt wrote his friend Henry Minot to announce his engagement to Alice Hathaway Lee, and on the forty-first anniversary of the deaths of her mother and grandmother, that is, *February 14*, 1925, St. Valentine's Day, the *forty-fifth* day and four years before the Massacre, Alice Longworth gave birth in Chicago to Pauline (ali), whose paternity (parent) was always in question. Alice, by unanimous agreement, was a lethal, lousy, domineering mother, causing for Pauline many problems, which no doubt contributed to her suicide at age thirty-one. Nicholas (born November 5, 1869, an earth-snake year) died on April 9, 1931, sixty-six years after Appomattox.

Typically Alice's mouth was disparaging and unkind. Too often this was the soul of her wit. She loved riding (horses), boxing, and playing poker (all three connected to Hermes), once recalling that she had made fifteen thousand dollars one year, "which was damn good." She lived to be ninety-six years old, being called in her lifetime "the other Washington Monument."

Since the Feralia-Caristia symbol was dedicated on *February 21*, 1885, it's in keeping with the Parentalia that Alice (Alice [ali] began the vogue for Alice Blue; a soaring clarinet opened George Gershwin's *Rhapsody in Blue* with Paul *White*man "at the helm" in the Aeolian [aea] Hall, New York City, on *February 12*, 1924) was born on the anniversary of Lincoln's birthday, the eve of the Parentalia, and died on *Ash Wednesday, February 20*, 1980, the eve of the Feralia, the anniversary of the death of William Wallace Lincoln (illi alla li) at the *White* House in 1862. (See page 399.) If my theory is correct that December, the last month of the year, also contains the characteristics of the earlier February (especially December 12–22) which had been the last month of the year, it was fitting that President and Mrs. Roosevelt made the official announcement of the engagement of Alice Roosevelt to Nicholas Longworth on *December 13*, 1905. (William Wallace Lincoln was born on *December 21*, 1850.) Early Christians thought the winter solstice (December 21/22) was December 25, which they set as the birth of Christ. (See pages 673 and 399.)

Prior to Theodore Roosevelt's inauguration on March 4, 1905 (a windy day, a snake year), John Hay (his personal secretary) gave him, for the ceremonies, a ring to wear which Lincoln had worn when he died. Roosevelt, who had boxed at Harvard and ranked *twenty-one* in a class of 177, married Alice Hathaway Lee on his twenty-second birthday (one of the cities visited on their honeymoon was Venice, Italy; she will die at age twenty-two); entered politics from New York's twenty-first district (2122); had birds and other animals in his home; and usually rode horseback or walked everyday, even in bad weather.[308-C]

John Pershing and Theodore Roosevelt had personal tragedies in their lives, as if they had to pay the price of sacrifice. They are connected in other ways too. TR and Ulysses Grant had class standings of 21. General Grant died on July 23, 1885, the anniversary of the Neptune festival in ancient Rome. (Recall Ulysses swinging on a horse's tail as a boy and his unconcerned mother, then later, his superior horsemanship at West Point.) Cadet Pershing led the cadet corp's salute when General Grant's body passed through Garrison, a hamlet across the Hudson *River* from West Point.

Both TR and Pershing fought in *Cuba* during the Spanish-American War. Roosevelt succeeded the assassinated McKinley into office on September 14 (MP), 1901. In 1906 Roosevelt promoted Captain Pershing to brigadier general over at least eight hundred senior officers, causing much bitterness for awhile. Pershing's wife and four children, who were living in the Presidio in 1915, are almost certain to have visited the Panama-Pacific Exposition, opening in the Parentalia-Caristia. (Roosevelt's speech there on July 21.)

On August 27, 1915, coal believed to have fallen from the fireplace to the floor burned down the home where the Pershings were living at 22 Main Post, the Presidio. Since spit-and-polish Pershing had always insisted that the floor be highly shined with wax, this probably helped to spread the fire faster. Pershing himself expressed guilt concerning this, though certainly not going as far as I would in saying there's the undertone of unwitting participation, an arcane thing taken for reward given.

Mrs. Pershing had been entertaining, making the total in the house at 4:20 A.M. at 12, a transposition of 21. Mrs. W.O. Oswald, wife of Lieutenant Walter O. Oswald of the *twenty-first* infantry, and her two children were in one room. Lieutenant Hartz and Lieutenant Fantschi, both of the *twenty-first* infantry, were among those who tried time and again to enter the burning building for survivors. Doesn't it seem odd that all escaped with only minor injuries except Mrs. Pershing and her three daughters, who lost their lives? Pershing's young son survived. Brigadier General John Pershing, commanding the eighty infantry brigade, was in Texas at the time, and one story is that he first heard about it from Norman *Walker* of the Associated Press in El Paso.

The *San Francisco Chronicle* of August 28, 1915, also carried an article stating the "Exposition to Celebrate Debt Payment," referring to the financial success of it being entirely out of debt. But it's eerie that the Exposition began in Parentalia-Caristia: February 20, 21, 22.

The *San Francisco Chronicle* of August 30, 1915, said that General Pershing, after his arrival from El Paso, had avoided no one, met with friends, and had "every external evidence of composure." This, of course, is only one reporter's observation and differs somewhat, yet it seems peculiar for a man who just lost his wife and three daughters. Perhaps even stranger, former Secretary of the Navy John Davis (born in Buckfield, *Maine*, on October 27, 1838, and under whom TR had been assistant secretary of the navy when the *Maine* was sunk) had returned to Hingham, Massachusetts (home of Lincoln's forebears), just two days after visiting Maine, when he died on August 28, 1915, the day following the Pershing fire. On the Ides of March (the anniversary of the day Maine was admitted to the Union) 1916, General Pershing led his forces across the border into Mexico.

Now add to the cards of *February 20, 21, 22* dealt Pershing in 1915 that of *February 19*, 1917. On this day, Major General Frederick Funston was sitting in a hotel lobby in San Antonio, Texas, and playing with the child Inez *Silver*berg of Des Moines, Iowa. The orchestra in the next room began playing the *Blue Danube* waltz, first performed in Vienna on *February 13*, 1867, about fifty years previously. The general remarked, "How beautiful it all is," and collapsed. Death was almost immediate. General Funston's wife was living at the Presidio, San Francisco (like Mrs. Pershing and her children who had lived at No. 22 Presidio Post less than two years before) at No. 12 (transposition of 21) Presidio Post. She was giving a birthday party for her sister when she was notified, which would suggest that her sister's birthday was *February 19* or close.

On *February 20*, General Funston's body was taken to the Alamo for viewing by hundreds. On that Feralia Eve (See Book II, footnote 129-C, Feralia Eve *February 20*, 1937) or the morning of *February 21* (depending on the source), the general's body was loaded on a special train with military escort and began its journey to San Francisco. On *February 21* when the Mardi Gras Ball was being held in San Francisco, it traveled. On *February 22*, the anniversary of George Washington's birthday, it moved on, arriving at San Francisco on *February 23*, earlier in history the day General Santa Anna's forces lay siege to the Alamo. *February 24* (or *February 20*, depending on the source) was the anniversary of the insurrection in eastern Cuba in 1895 (where later Funston, as a foreign volunteer, first fought and gained notice), and there was a violent storm which uprooted trees. General Funston, who had taken charge during the San Francisco earthquake in 1906 and who was the son of "Foghorn," was buried next to his young son Arthur MacArthur Funston. (Contrast: Pershing's son is the only one of his family to survive the fire. Pershing's wife and three daughters perished. Funston's wife, other son, and two daughters attended Frederick Funston's funeral.)

The national cemetery at the Presidio overlooks the Golden Gate. On the morning of *February 25*, the rain which had been pouring down for four days stopped. It was the anniversary of the deaths of Lord Buddha (483 B.C.) and the abbess St. Walpurgis (779) who would be called upon to banish the magic of evil powers, the anniversary of the day "the very devil seemed to possess" Theodore Roosevelt, in the words of Secretary of the Navy Long. On *February 26*, 1933, the groundbreaking ceremony for the Golden Gate Bridge took place. On *February 11*, 1936, the Army Corps of Engineers began piling mud and sand in construction of Treasure Island north of Yerba Buena Island (at one time called "Goat Island;" goat connected to the Parentalia). On *February 18*, 1939, the Golden Gate International Exposition opened at Treasure Island.

General Funston received the medal of honor on *February 14*, 1900. Later he was President Wilson's choice to lead the European Expeditionary Force if the U.S. entered the war. At Funston's death, Pershing took over the Southern Department under Funston's command since the Lupercalia 1915. (It had the confines of Brownsville, Texas, and Yuma, Arizona, the state admitted on *February 14*, 1912.) The Apache Wars began on *February 4*, 1861, at Apache Pass, Arizona, when Apache Chief Cochise was arrested by Lieutenant George Bascom for raiding a ranch. Cochise then escaped, declaring war which lasted twenty-five years. (See *February 13–14*, 1861.) The Apaches were first led by Cochise, then later by Geronimo, the "One Who Yawns," in robbery and bloodshed. Geronimo was daring, Hermetic, and aptly the parachutist's cry is made. He (like Funston) went to Florida, and he was present at the 1905 inauguration of TR, who wore the ring Lincoln had worn at his death. In the middle of the Parentalia on *February 17*, 1909, three years following the marriage of Alice Roosevelt to Nicholas Longworth at the White House, Geronimo died. Four days later, the "Great White Fleet" arrived at Hampton Roads, Virginia, and *five* days after Geronimo's death, TR gave his welcoming speech.)

At his burial, General Funston was given a thirteen-gun salute, a number fitting to the old period. On *February 13*, 1917, Cuban President Mario P. Menocal, fearing a rebellion, called for volunteers (which could include foreigners) between the ages of eighteen to forty-five for a period of ninety days. It was feared that General Jose Gomez had landed at Camaguey.

On *February 13*, 1939 (five days before the opening of the Golden Gate International Exposition at Treasure Island), J.M. Silvey (name suggesting silver) committed suicide by jumping off the Golden Gate Bridge. Seventy-two years previously to the day, the *Blue Danube* was first played publicly in Vienna.[308-CC] No other president except John Quincy Adams had the knowledge of world affairs that TR had, stated Nicholas Roosevelt (*Theodore Roosevelt, the Man as I Knew Him*. New York: Dodd, Mead, and Co., 1967). John Quincy Adams, like Santa Anna, Geronimo, Funston, TR, and Pershing, was linked to February. In addition, San Antonio, Texas, played an important part in the careers of General Santa Anna, Lieutenant Colonial Roosevelt, Major General Funston, and Major General Pershing.

If you recall, Elliott, TR's brother, said near midnight on *Wednesday, February 13*, 1884, the beginning day of the Parentalia, that there was a curse on the house. Eleanor Roosevelt was his daughter. *On the Lupercalia of 1933*, the anniversary of when the bodies of Elliott's mother and sister-in-law lay dead and unburied, an assassination attempt was made on Eleanor's husband, Franklin Delano Roosevelt. Mayor Cermak of Chicago was the sacrifice. Had FDR given his inaugural address on March 6, 1933, when Cermak died (instead of March 4), he might have more correctly said, "The only thing we have to fear is...the Parentalia." He did not, by the way, attend Cermak's funeral, giving as his reason the "grave national emergency facing the country" in Washington.

February 14, 1891. General William T. Sherman died. On February 13 (the day Union Admiral David Dixon Porter died), he drifted out of consciousness into a coma. He was not a Catholic, though a priest gave him last rites, causing family controversy. This is interesting in relation to the Parentalia. Born in February (2-8-1820), the month guarded by Neptune, Sherman commanded the troops who completed "the march to the sea" on December 20 (1864), equivalent to the eve of the Feralia. (Ulysses S. Grant born April 27, 1822; Golden Gate Bridge dedicated April 27, 1937; Grant died in 1885 on July 23, the day in ancient Rome for celebrating Neptune.)

After graduating from West Point, Sherman was sent to Florida to fight the Seminole Indians, whom he didn't encounter. More importantly he was in St. Augustine (See *February 15, 1519*), which has the oldest documented national cemetery in the U.S. On *February 14*, 1864, troops under General Sherman captured *Meridian* (thought to have meant junction and so mistakenly named), Mississippi, in the Civil War. They stayed until *February 20*, destroying railroad and supplies in the area. Sherman retired from the army on *February 8*, 1884. His funeral ceremony was held in New York on February 19, 1891. President Harrison, state officials, top army officers, and about ten thousand troops attended. Sherman was the first credited with saying, "War is hell," or something close to it. He was buried in St. Louis, Missouri, on *February 23*. (See *February 14 and 15*, 1764, and *February 21*, 1957.)

February 14, 1893. A treaty of annexation was signed between the United States and Hawaii under President Harrison.[309] The treaty was submitted to the senate on *February 15*, 1893. On March 9, 1893, President Cleveland withdrew the annexation treaty which was still in the Senate. Then on *February 21*, 1895, Secretary Gresham asked for recall of minister-to-Hawaii Thurston, the reason being that Thurston had given material on the administration to the press.[310-A]

Of interest here are the *14th, 15th, and 21st of February, significant Parentalia days and the end of Captain Cook.*

February 14, 1894. Accomplished musician Jack Benny (deceptively a terrible player of the violin, a four-stringed instrument) was born in Chicago, Illinois (21). Compare to May 30, 1909.

February 14, 1901. Winston Churchill took his seat in the House of Commons, after returning on the *Etruria* (ancient country of central Italy) from the U.S. On *February 18*, he gave his maiden (*Kore*, maiden) speech in the House of Commons. His father's maiden speech was on *May 22*, 1874, the anniversary of the mutilation of Hermae busts in ancient Athens.

February 14, 1903. At the request of President Theodore Roosevelt (whose stone image will be one of four on Mt. Rushmore), Congress established the Department of *Commerce* and labor.

February 14, 1912. Arizona became the forty-eighth state, entering on St. Valentine's Day. USS *Arizona* sank on December 7, 1941 (SY), Pearl Harbor, Hawaiian Islands. The number of deaths difference was twenty-one. (See page 484.)

February 14, 1913. *James* Riddle Hoffa born to John and Viola Riddle to Hoffa. A viola is of the violin family. James Hoffa was presumed murdered in 1975. The circumstances leading up to his death, as with Bishop Pike, are clouded, mysterious.

February 14, 1913. James Albert Pike born in Oklahoma City. He died September 2 (MP), 1969, and is buried in Jaffa, Israel.[310-B]

February 14, 1918. The revolutionary government adjusted the Soviet calendar to the Gregorian by making *February 1* into *February 14,* the forty-fifty day. (Caesar—of 44 B.C. Lupercalia fame—had inaugurated the Julian Calendar in 45 B.C.) Nicholas II (born May 18, 1868/New Style) became czar of Russia after the sudden death of his father on November 1, 1894, New Style. (November 1 = May 13 = *February 21.*) Rasputin, meaning "the debauched one," died on December 17, 1916 (O.S.). If December nearly equals February, this would be equivalent to *February 17.* February 1917 is one of the most significant periods of the revolution. Nicholas II took time out from reading on the Ides of March 1917 (N.S.) to sign the "instrument of abdication." Thereupon, he resumed reading Shakespeare's *Julius Caesar* (*Encyclopedia Americana*). Joseph Stalin was born in 1879 on December 21, (N.S.), by my reckoning equivalent to *February 21.* Working late on December 12, 1937, Stalin okayed the death sentences of 3,167. He then went to a movie. (Op. cit., Wallechinsky.) Ramón *Mercader* (mercader is Spanish for merchant), a death agent of Stalin's police force, was born on *February 17,* 1914. He stabbed Trotsky with an ice pick in the brain on August 20, 1940. Trotsky died on August 21, 1940 (the first anniversary of my brother Ralph's death, Book I, footnote 79). Trotsky's last words were that he was "sure of the victory...of the Fourth International...Go Forward..." (Pierre Broué, translated by Shane Mage, *Collier's Encyclopedia*).

Hermes, a god of death, is identified with the number four.

February 14, 1919. President Wilson, whom Theodore Roosevelt hated, read to the Paris Peace Conference the completed draft of the League of Nations. He was chairman of the committee which had drawn it up. The following day (*February 15,* the Lupercalia, twenty-five years from the time TR's wife and mother lay unburied), he embarked at Brest aboard the transport *George Washington* for the United States. (Note on *February 17,* midway in the Parentalia, black troops returning from the war marched down Fifth Avenue, New York, to a proud and thunderous ovation. The same day was also given in Chicago to the returning "Black Devils" of the 370th infantry, another link to February as Black Heritage Month.)

On *February 19,* French Premier Georges Clemenceau—on his way to preside at the Peace Conference was shot, suffering three wounds. On *February 21,* the peace conference met. Clemenceau's doctor said he was out of danger. But this same day, Bavarian Premier Kurt Eisener was assassinated, two ministers were also slain, and two other officials were wounded. On *February 22*, President Wilson and his party went on deck the *George Washington* for a twenty-one-gun salute in honor of the first president. (2122.) On the evening of *February 23*, the *George Washington* arrived at Boston, but the president stayed aboard. Fourteen Spaniards were arrested in New York for plotting to kill him.

Most of these dates occurred within the Parentalia-Caristia, beginning in France and ending in Massachusetts, which formerly included Maine—Le Mans, the Manes. The fact that President Wilson read the draft of the League of Nations on St. Valentine's Day brings to mind that the USS *Arizona* was one of nine battleships and several destroyers which had escorted him to France about two months previously. Great plans for the League of Nation eventually died, as did the USS *Arizona*.

Wilson, who'd opened the Panama-Pacific (Parentalia-Caristia) Exposition in 1915 from Washington. D.C., by pressing a key, died on *February 3*, 1924, and was buried three days later.

February 14, 1921. Foundling child discovered on doorsteps of Wallets in comic strip "Gasoline Alley." Given the name Skeezix Wallet.

February 14, 1921. Battleship *Arizona* arrived at Balboa. Here is the second of three indirect links of the *Arizona* to decapitation (Valentine, Balboa, and Cook).[311]

February 14, 1929. It's the Windy city near Lake Michigan, one of five Great Lakes, the heartland. Again water: a light snow. It's 2122 North Clark Street. It's Valentine's Day, after the beheaded saint, now represented by a heart. There will occur the wholesale slaughter of seven (see footnote 307-A) like the Chicago stockyards, one for each day until the twenty-first. The only survivor will be a dismally howling and badly frightened German *shepherd*. (Both Asclepius and Hermes were accompanied by dogs. The dog is associated with Hermes because of its intelligence and devotion. Compare to *February 14*, 1945 [45–45] entry.) At least four (and probably all) victims were taken to mortuary rooms at 2221 Lincoln Avenue. Note shift in numbers from 2122 to 2221,[312] while seven remains constant in the first "Chicago Seven." One of the victims of the garage massacre was Dr. R.H. Schwimmer, a braggart of his dangerous connections. As far as is known, all were buried during the Parentalia. Schwimmer was interred at Rosehill Cemetery, like Bobby Franks who was killed in the "crime of the century" (a term later to be applied to the Lindbergh baby kidnapping) at Chicago on May 21, 1924, the first day of the Mercury period. Al was baptized *February 7*, 1899, twenty-one days after his birth.

February 14, 1929. Lindbergh in Miami. He fished one-half the day (water) and dines with President-elect Hoover. Capone, Hoover, and Lindbergh will be in Miami or Miami Beach, Florida (admitted snake-year 1845), on St. Valentine's Day. Hoover and Capone will also be there the following day, the Lupercalia, when thirty-one years previously the *Maine* was sunk in Havana Harbor. Hoover planned to visit Havana shortly after his inauguration. The 1929 Lupercalia preceded by four years the assassination attempt of *President-elect* Franklin Delano Roosevelt at Miami. Also there during February 14 and 15, 1929, was county board President Anton (sounds close to Antony) J. Cermak (Chicago), recuperating from intestinal inflammation.

February 14, 1931. Two years after the St. Valentine's Day Mass, the movie *Dracula* with Bela Lugosi was released.

February 14, 1933. In the winter of 1933, farmers in Iowa banded together with shotguns, rifles, whatever, to prevent the sale of foreclosed land for taxes. One-third of Iowa's farmland fit into the category. People were starving throughout the nation and showed their distrust of banks by withdrawing their savings, and banks began to close. An epidemic of closures broke out in Michigan where Governor William A. Comstock declared an eight-day bank holiday on this day.[313]

In relation to the Parentalia, it's important to remember that Governor Comstock received a call at 3:00 P.M. on *February 13* to reach Detroit from Lansing as soon as possible to take part in an important meeting covering the general banking (commerce) situation.

February 14, 1939. Pope Pius XI buried in St. Peter's built over a graveyard. San Francisco began this day its premier festival for the opening of the Golden Gate International Exposition on February 18, at which time only a couple of warships were present. It was nothing like the opening of the Golden Gate Bridge. (See page 628.) Neptune, guardian of the month of February. Franklin Delano Roosevelt (of the 1933 Lupercalia at Florida) broadcast by short wave his opening day message to the ceremonies from Key West (Audubon, Hemingway), Florida, just before boarding the cruiser *Henderson* to watch fleet games and maneuvers "somewhere east of the West Indies" or perhaps near the Panama Canal. Like Theodore Roosevelt, he had been an assistant secretary of the navy, and because of the crippling caused by polio in 1921, his exercise was pretty much limited to water (Hyde Park and Warm Springs, Georgia). Both he and Eleanor were related to Theodore Roosevelt of Dutch ancestry (water). See February 21, 1909 (Great White Fleet).

February 14, 1939. German battleship launched. Edward P. Von der Porten (*The German Navy in World War II*. New York: Thomas Y. Crowell Co., 1969) says Hitler insisted on calling it the *Bismarck* even though the old "blood and iron" chancellor hated the navy. The *Bismarck* was to become the German Navy's "most famous and most tragic ship." On *February 21*, 1939, the British battleship *King George V* was launched at Newcastle. It would later play a part in the sinking of the *Bismarck* (May 27, 1941).

February 14, 1945. Charles Walton, an old man, described as a "bit of a character," lived in Lower Quinton, a Warwickshire village in England. He said he could talk to birds, understand them, and had only to point to the direction they were to fly after they landed on his shoulders and hands. To some extent, he believed he had control over other animals which he liked *except for dogs*. Whether he had seen something he shouldn't have, refused to take part in something, or was a witch himself is unknown, but on this day he died. Terror on his face, his head nearly severed, a pitchfork through his neck.[314] Most locals and Dr. Margaret Murray (see pages 621-622) believed someone thought him to be a witch, that witchcraft was involved to some extent. There was an atmosphere of the supernatural about it. The area was known for witchcraft, and nearby were the Rollright Stones, connected to a legend of witchery. Murray believed the month of February might have had something to do with it too, since it was one of the four months of sacrifice.[315]

Could be the locals and Murray were right. My reasoning is based not only on the connections they made but a few apparently missed. The nearly severed head recalls the beheading of Valentine and Cook. Walton disliked dogs (note the dog spared in 1929 St. Valentine's Day Massacre), and his body was found under a *willow* tree,[316] associated with the gates of Hades, as was a many-headed dog. It was the forty-fifth day of the year 1945. The violin, which Jack Benny played, has four strings; the "quinton" is described as a "five-string violin." Hermes Pterseus (destroyer), herald of death. Dresden was in shambles this day. Walton's death would be seven days before the Feralia (the anniversary of Captain Cook's burial, the beginning of the Battle of Verdun), when twenty years later occurred the assassination of Malcolm X, who believed there had been a more sinister force at work than just fanatic Muslims when his home was bombed on St. Valentine's Day. In this he was correct. It's called the Parentalia-Caristia mystique.

February 14, 1962. Jacqueline Kennedy led millions of television viewers through the White House. (See page 630.)

February 14, 1965. Molotov cocktail thrown into Malcolm X's home, half of it destroyed. His favorite number was seven. New York Black Muslim Mosque 7, whose headquarters was in Chicago. Favorite restaurant in Harlem was its Twenty-Two Club. (See footnote 312.)

February 14 and February 15, 1764. Pierre Lacléde Liguest, a merchant from New Orleans, and his stepson *Auguste* Chouteau led an expedition of thirty men and boys, landing on *February 14* at the site in Missouri of what was to be called St. Louis, after King Louis XV and his patron saint, Louis IX. On *February 15*, the party began erecting buildings, founding a French fur-trading station. Fur, of course, means death of animals, as do the stockyards of Chicago and Indianapolis. The dates, within the Parentalia, suggest the spirits of the dead. Charles *Augustus* Lindbergh—who flew mail service between Chicago and St. Louis and who was especially linked to the month of February—became world-famous when he landed his plane, the *Spirit of St. Louis*, at an airport near Paris, *France*, on May 21, 1927, the beginning day of the Mercury period and the anniversary of Paris's Bloody Week. He and his plane returned from France on the USS *Memphis*. Memphis, derived from Pepi I's funerary complex. Lindbergh's baby son has been referred to as a "Blood Sacrifice." Bruno Hauptmann was convicted of the baby's murder on *February 13*, 1935.

February 14 and February 15, 1970. Judge Julius J. Hoffman, seventy-four, accused, tried, and convicted the second "Chicago Seven" for contempt. The seven had been brought to trial for conspiracy to incite riots during the 1968 Democratic Convention. All had taken part in demonstrations against the Vietnam War during the convention week. But even in 1970, according to one poll, most people still supported the war. To this majority, the seven hardly could have been perceived as patriots (a paradox, if there hadn't been protestors, we'd probably still be fighting the war). There was a clashing of views and principles, a *crossroads*, and there was clearly some right on the side of the seven. Everything wasn't cut and dried (free from bias) as the judge (a little Caesar) and the prosecution (who had called them evil) tried to make out. The Vietnam servicemen and woman by and large and the anti-war protestors were opposite ends of the same piece of string.

February 14 and February 15, 1989 (SY). On *February 14*, Ayatollah Ruholla Khomeini, the Iranian leader, called for Muslims to kill Salman Rushdie, British subject and author of *The Satanic Verses*. On *February 15*, he offered a one-million dollar reward to anyone who would be the executioner. On *February 18*, Rushdie said, "I profoundly regret the distress that publication has occasioned to sincere followers of Islam." On *February 19*, Khomeini rejected the apology. On *February 21*, President Bush said that "inciting murder and offering rewards for its perpetration are deeply offensive to the norms of civilized behavior." (Also on this date, the trial of Lt. Colonel Oliver North of the Iran-Contra scandal opened. Bush wasn't elected to a second term.) Mass demonstrations against the book had taken place in many countries as early as *February 12*, where in Pakistan six protestors were killed by police. Then on *February 13*, three more died in India.

February 15. The Lupercalia in ancient Rome, a period of lustration. Priests, nearly naked, ran through streets and struck those who placed themselves in their way with lashes made from goat hide or possibly that of dogs. Two young people from noble families were led forth. Their foreheads were touched with knives which had been dipped in blood of sacrifice. This was wiped off with wool which had been soaked in milk.[317-A] On the fifteenth too, puppets of straw were tossed into the Tiber. There's much conjecture concerning the thinking behind this, but no one knows for sure the reasoning.[317-B]

February 15, 44 B.C. Julius Caesar's presence at the Lupercalia. Refuses diadem offered in public by Antony, said to have been drunk.

February 15, 1519. Menéndez de Avilés, a Spanish mariner (Hermes, god of mariners), was born in Avilés, Spain. On August 28 (MP), 1565, Avilés sailed into a harbor on the east coast of Florida, where eleven days later (still within the Mercury period), he established St. Augustine. In 1568 he was appointed governor of Cuba, which is important to remember in context with his Lupercalia birth and the Lupercalia sinking of the *Maine* in 1898. Shortly before his death on September 17 (MP), 1574, Avilés had been recalled to Spain. Now, as you remember, Ponce de Leon, who in legend sought the fountain of youth, discovered Florida in the Easter season of 1513. He was shot by a Seminole arrow there in 1521 and died shortly after from the wound when the expedition returned to Havana, *Cuba*. The 13 and 21 are the first and last days of the Parentalia. The 15 is the Lupercalia and, by extension, fertility, the fountain of youth. *St. Augustine is the United States' oldest city and has the oldest documented National Cemetery.* Thus, heritage and ancestors.

Finally add to the equation Hernando de Soto (brother-in-law of Balboa of the crossroad and beheading) who landed in Florida on May 30, 1539. Memorial Day, now honoring the dead like the Parentalia, always fell on May 30th until 1971. De Soto, who had left his wife in Cuba before going to Florida, died in Louisiana on *May 21*, 1542, nearly thirty-six years to the day after Columbus's death on May 20.

February 15, 1564. Galileo Galilei (ae, ae, li, li, li) was born in Pisa to a patrician father. Note the similarity of the name Galilee.[318]

(Copernicus, whose system Galileo supported, was born on *February 19*, 1473. He died May 24 (MP), 1543.)

February 15, 1803. John Augustus Sutter was born in Kandern, Baden, Germany. Like Julius Caesar, Galileo Galilei, and Susan B. Anthony (and James Pike and James Hoffa born on *February 14*), Sutter's life was filled with controversy.

He emigrated to the U.S. in 1834 and eventually settled in California, then part of Mexico. He got the Mexican government to grant him fifty thousand acres of land near the junction of the Sacramento and American Rivers (water), later to become the site of the city of Sacramento (sacrament). James W. Marshall, a carpenter, was building a sawmill on Sutter's property when he discovered gold on January 24, 1848 (the gold rush came in 1849), and nine days later (*February 2*, 1848) the Treaty of Guadalupe Hidalgo was signed, ending the war with Mexico. An area about half the size of Mexico was ceded to the U.S., this included California. With the discovery of gold on Sutter's property, squatters flocked to the area, stealing, trashing, and eventually causing Sutter to go bankrupt. U.S. courts denied him land under Mexican grants, and he spent much of the remainder of his life seeking redress from Congress. He was in Washington, D.C. (later to become the home of the Feralia-Caristia symbol), when he died in 1880.

Sutter County in California is named for him, as well as Sutter Street in San Francisco. (See page 632 concerning California.)

February 15, 1820. Susan Brownell Anthony: Susan B. Anthony: Susan be (phonetic) Anthony (recall Antony of 44 B.C., Lupercalia) was born in Massachusetts at Adams (NY corner near Florida), named after revolutionary patriot Samuel Adams, second cousin to John Adams. A crosser of boundaries, Anthony worked to free blacks and was a women's suffrage leader. Arrested in 1872 when trying to vote, she argued that all citizens were covered under provisions of the fourteenth and fifteenth amendments, like an echo of February 14 and 15. She died March 13, 1906, close to the Ides, and in the 13, 14, and 15 sequence since passage of the nineteenth amendment granting woman suffrage was ratified August 18, 1920, *fourteen* years after her death.

February 15, 1824. John Quincy Adams, closely linked to the month of February, was nominated for president at Faneuil Hall, Boston.

February 15, 1838. In defiance of "Gag Rule," Representative John Quincy Adams introduced three hundred and fifty anti-slavery petitions.

February 15, 1851. Fugitive slave Shadrach freed from Boston jail by mob of blacks challenging fugitive law.

February 15, 1861. Fort Point was completed and garrisoned by two artillery companies. (Hansen, Gladys, *San Francisco Almanac*. San

Francisco: Chronicle Books, 1995.) Just four days previously on the eve of his birthday, President-elect Lincoln began his February journey to Washington, D.C., which like San Francisco has strong Parentalia links. These two events—binding coast to coast in the month of purification—were the prelude to the attack on Fort Sumter, South Carolina, or more importantly, the dam-breaking, blood-letting which followed.

It's curious too that the sinking of the *Maine* in Havana Harbor (Cuba strongly linked to February) on the Lupercalia of *February 15*, 1898 (thirty-seven years to the day after the completion of Fort Point), will set off a whole new wave of blood-letting. Fort Point had been constructed to protect (protection is the salient attribute of Hermes) the San Francisco Bay, if necessary by sinking ships. Why then had the *Rio de Janeiro* hit Fort Point on *February 22*, 1901? One hundred twenty-eight died (about half the *Maine*'s deaths) when it sank with some cargo of gold aboard. Was its destruction mysteriously linked to that of the *Maine* to emphasize 2122, and to show that Janus looks both ways: life-death, death-life? "But what has all this to do with Lincoln?" you ask. Hannibal Hamlin, Lincoln's first vice president, was the only man to become vice president who was born in Maine. Indeed he died in Maine on July 4, 1891, and was buried there. Much to Hamlin's vexation and humiliation, Lincoln dumped him for Andrew Johnson, later to be connected to *February 21*. Like Lincoln, Hamlin was an earth-snake, born August 27, 1809. What Lincoln had failed to heed was the warning given to Caesar: "Beware of the ides of March." Maine had entered the Union on the ides of March 1820. Legend—according to the *San Francisco Almanac*—is that the city's name is derived from "sand Francisco," though St. Francis of Assisi is the city's patron saint. Alcatraz (AZ) can be seen clearly ahead in the bay from Fort Point, which is linked to it by history. The island's name means Pelican, a bird suggesting both sea and flight. Sources vary on the size of Alcatraz. But if we take 22.5 acres (ibid), the number by itself is half *45*, the number of square miles of mainland San Francisco.

On rough and windy days, waves pound against the huge boulders next to the fort and even at times wash onto the road leading to it. Much of the area inside the fort is open to the sky and becomes damp, wet, and windy. The wind-god is Hermes. Neptune is the sea-god. It brings to mind the 399 B.C. lectisternium (pages 633-634). The fort was closed for many years. It's a mausoleum of memories, and one wonders what tragic events might have occurred there in its long history. Things that were perhaps hushed up, papered over by the army, and now nearly forgotten. Could the National Park Service personnel who work there, as well as those in the book store, be reincarantions of people associated with it in the past?

The "burnt red" Golden Gate bridge (with its ongoing sacrifices totaling nearly one thousand or more since Wobber) passes over part of Fort Point. Not to forget that Chief Engineer Strauss had a nervous breakdown (one wonders what his medical records might reveal) during the first few months of construction of the bridge that sings. As Lincoln died shortly after peace agreement at Appomattox, so Strauss died within a year after the bridge opened. It was on the unlucky day of *February 17*, 1937, that ten men working on the bridge fell to their death. On *February 19* (a day usually marking the beginning of the Pisces period. Neptune over Pisces) a net (persona Neptune) was pulled up from the deep with a hand sticking out. A hand has *four* fingers and *five* digits. Which way did it point? Attached to the hand was an arm. Was this a reminder or symbol? In the eighteenth century soldiers who had attended mass on All Souls Day asked and were given permission to go hunting. Later they reported seeing an "immense arm of the sea." Hunting suggests blood-letting.

By chance, the bridge had been dedicated on April 27, the anniversary of the 1822 horse-year birth of Ulysses S. Grant, later connected to blood-letting, sacrifice, death. He died in 1885 on *July 23*, the anniversary of the Neptune festival in ancient Rome. The mythological Ulysses is said by some to be the grandson of Hermes, a god of death. "Who's buried in Grant's tomb?" From the Golden Gate bridge one can see the Presidio National Cemetery, or vice versa. Over thirty thousand are buried there, including February's Major General Funston. An old map shows that Lincoln Boulevard ran between the cemetery and the cavalry stables.

July 23, 1852 is not the first date of interrment in the cemetery but rather the earliest recorded date of death of any soldier buried there.

February 15, 1892. Few fit the flight-and-death profile of Hermes as well as James Vincent Forrestal who was born six years before the *Maine* was sunk and forty-one years before *the attempted assassination in Florida* (Ponce de Leon 1513–1521) of President-elect Franklin Delano Roosevelt, who appointed him to be the first under secretary of the navy in 1940. When going to the university many years earlier, he edited (writer) the *Daily Princetonian* and was active in sports, getting his nose broken in *boxing*. Yet failing an English course six weeks before graduation, he suddenly quit. He served as a naval aviator in World War I and married Josephine Ogden on *December 12*, 1926. They had two sons. In 1944 on *May 9*, the first Lemuria Day, Forrestal got word from the secretary of the Senate that he was in as secretary of the navy. He grinned, very pleased. His secretary commented that this was the only time in their nine years together in government work that his emotions weren't hidden by a mask. He was a workhorse of a man, analytical and extremely talented in procurement, which the navy especially needed in World War II. Paradoxically his considerable achievements were probably the result of an insecure personality. He was shy and introspective. Under President Truman, he became the first secretary of defense (1947–1949). Toward the last, he was drained both physically and mentally and often disagreed with Truman, who felt it necessary to ask for his immediate resignation on March 1, 1949. While supposedly resting in *Florida, he attempted suicide.*

A curious twist was that FDR years earlier had sketched "a high slender tower" he wanted to dominate the National Medical Center at Bethesda, Maryland, though it wasn't cost effective. On *April* 2, 1949, Forrestal was admitted to this hospital. In a rendezvous with death five years and forty days after FDR's death and high up from an unguarded window in the tower, he jumped to his death on *May* 22, the anniversary of the mutilation of Hermae busts in ancient Athens. He was buried on May 25 in Arlington National Cemetery, where—like a magnet—stands the mourning mast of the merthyr *Maine.*

February 15, 1869. The charge of treason against Jefferson Davis was dropped this date. On December 25, 1868, President Andrew Johnson (see *February 21*, 1868) issued a general amnesty proclamation.

February 15, 1898. U.S. battleship *Maine* blown up in Havana Harbor.[319] Two hundred and sixty Americans were killed. (The state of Maine had separated from Massachusetts on the ides of March 1820.) The cry "Remember the *Maine*, to hell with Spain!" led to war, or as Di Manes came, so went the nation. The U.S. declared that a state of war had existed since April 21 (the day Rome was founded), 1898. Even before the sinking, the U.S. had had bad relations with Spain. Curiously in the news too was much talk of annexation of Hawaii. (Cook's death on *February 14*, 1779.) By consent of Hawaiian legislature, annexation occurred on August 12, 1898. (Remember 12 is a transposition of 21.) Hawaii was admitted to the union August 21, 1959, the Neptune day. The question: Why is Cuba linked to Parentalia states such as Maine and Florida most of all, and then Arizona, Hawaii, Oregon, Illinois, and perhaps Nevada? I don't know. Maybe the answer lies in measurement. According to the *Encyclopaedia Britannica*, Cuba is about 777 (21) miles from east to west. Also Hermes, god of commerce, deception, flight, travelers: In 1980 over one hundred thousand Cuban citizens, including many nonpolitical prisoners and mental patients, arrived at Florida in small boats. In August 1994, there occurred a resurgence of Cuban refugees in small boats trying to enter the U.S. This resulted in the Clinton administration ordering on August 19 that they be taken to a detention camp at U.S. Naval Station, Guantánamo Bay, Cuba. Later, beginning in the Mercury period, refugees will be sent to Panama. It's an old ensemble: Cuba, Florida, Panama.

Though one factor in Castro's failure to prevent the refugees from leaving Cuba might have been his wish to pressure the U.S. into establishing more lenient immigration quotas for Cuba, his main reason was to try to force the U.S. to lift its trade embargo (commerce).

February 15, 1905 (SY). Harold Arlen's birthday. Born Hyman Ar*luck*. Died April 23, 1986. Composer. Songs include: "Story Weather," "Over the Rainbow" (see May 15, 1856), "Blues in the Night," and "It's Only a Paper Moon."

February 15, 1905. Lew(is) Wallace died at Crawfordsville, Indiana. Born in Brookville, Indiana, on April 10, 1827. Practiced law in Indianapolis among other places. Was Union major general in Civil War. Author of *Ben-Hur: A Tale of Christ*.

February 15, 1907. *Cesar Romero*, actor, born in New York City.

February 15, 1909. Acapulco, Mexico. Flores Theater burned, two hundred and fifty dead.

February 15, 1923. Faint seal impressions dotting the door to the inner tomb of King Tut are removed with great care. Lord Carnarvon considers them to be of great importance in piecing together eighteenth dynasty history. Howard Carter averted curse when he effectively prevented desecration of the tomb the following Parentalia. (See pages 8-9 and 492-493.) St. Peter's built over a cemetery by Julius II, who died on the Feralia. Michelangelo died in the Parentalia. On *February 21*, the Feast of the Dead, 1930, Lord Westbury (Lord Carnarvon's friend), who had items in his apartment from King Tut's tomb, jumped to his death. Four days later, his hearse, going to the cemetery, struck down an eight-year-old boy who died shortly thereafter.

February 15, 1923. Blizzards with winds of hurricane velocity hit both the Atlantic and Pacific. Of nine ships pounded helpless, four were ground to pieces on a graveyard of rocks. First estimate was that fifty lives were lost.

February 15, 1929. No doubt Miss Wilhelmina Robinson, in a previous life, had been beaten severely by a priest during the Lupercalia in ancient Rome. Now living in Boston, England, on her hundredth birthday, she attributed her long and happy life to the fact that she detested men and never had been so foolish as to marry one. On her head she wore a frilly cap. In keeping with the milk of human kindness, she had two milkwhite cats, both ladies, with whom she shared her rooms (*Chicago Daily Tribune*, February 16, 1929).

February 15, 1929. President-elect Hoover visited the Florida Everglades. Though no assassination attempt was made, the later depression figuratively killed him.

February 15, 1933. Rear Admiral Wat. T. Culveras, sole surviving officer of the *Maine* on active duty, addressed Spanish War veterans in *evening* at Steuben Building, *Chicago*.

February 15, 1933. President-elect Franklin Delano Roosevelt (distant cousin of TR) narrowly escaped death at Miami, Florida, when he and others were riding in an open vehicle. (Capone—now in Alcatraz—had been here *four* years before. Long before that some scholars believed the fourteenth and fifteenth of February were connected.) An assassination attempt on Roosevelt was made on the anniversary of the sinking of the *Maine*, named for the state which had remained in the Republican camp until the FDR era. Guiseppe Zangara's[320] five bullets hit several, including Chicago's Mayor Anton Cermak (Antony-Caesar), who died on March 6. Roosevelt, who was unharmed, went on to win a fourth term (four years) in 1944. The four's are suggestive of the 44 B.C. Lupercalia and Hermes involvement. Roosevelt was born (Hyde Park, New York) on January 30, 1882 (SY), into an old aristocratic family. He was buried in the family rose garden at Hyde Park on April 15 (4.5), 1945, the anniversary of Lincoln's death and the *Titanic*'s sinking. (*R*oosevelt, *r*ose, *R*osmerta, thought by some to be the female counterpart in Gaul of Mercurious.) Roosevelt was definitely a polio cripple. Eleanor (derived from Helen) had buck teeth, and couldn't have launched a rowboat, let alone a thousand ships. Winston Churchill had a speech defect. Moses was possibly a stutterer (DE-*Mos*-the-ne*s*), but King George VI definitely stuttered.

February 15, 1936. Early in the morning following the seventh anniversary of the St. Valentine's Day Massacre, "Machine Gun" Jack McGurn was killed. (Scholars have long believed that *February 14* and *February 15* are linked.) McGurn, a gangland assassin and favorite of Al Capone, was thought to have been largely responsible for planning the St. Valentine's Day Mass and probably was one of the machine gunners that day. (Certainly he was involved in the 1927 throat-slitting of Joe E. Lewis. In the film *The Joker Is Wild*, Frank Sinatra portrayed the entertainer.) McGurn's death might be looked upon as a rendezvous with destiny. He had gone to bed, tired, with his wife. Then around 11:00 P.M. on *February 14*, he found he couldn't sleep (Hermes, a sleep-and-dream god). He got up, dressed, and went to a bowling alley.

It was McGurn's trademark to place a nickel in the palm (Hermes persona) of anyone he had killed, signifying the dead man was a worthless nobody, a nickel and dimer. Five alone is often the negative aspect of the Hermes number, and interestingly, James D. Mora had been a welterweight boxer in his youth, when he took the name Jack McGurn.

During the Depression, "his five nightclubs went bankrupt." Both his wife and friends deserted him. In the end at the bowling alley, five gunners turned their guns on him and pressed a nickel in his right hand (four fingers, five digits). A comic Valentine— delivered only ten minutes late—was tossed on his body by one of the killers. It read:

> You've lost your job,
> You've lost your dough,
> Your jewels and handsome houses.
> But things could be worse, you know.
> You haven't lost your trousers.

February 15, 1942. Singapore fell to the Japanese. Roosevelt was president. Nine years before was the assassination attempt on him, Cermak later died. Forty-four (44) years previously the *Maine* was sunk. Today Singapore is northeast Asia's business *commercial* center. FDR was also president when the British Far East naval base, costing fifty-five million dollars was opened at Singapore on *February 14*, 1938 (the USS *Memphis* was present), or fifty-four years after the deaths of his two relatives on Valentine's Day 1884.

February 15, 1944. The Abbey of Monte Cassino was destroyed by American (Amerigo) planes and artillery on the Lupercalia. St. Benedict had built the abbey there about 530 after overthrowing the temple of Apollo, its idol, and sacred grove. This was then destroyed about forty years later by the Lombards.

February 15, 1952. Funeral held during Feast of the Dead on Lupercalia for *Wind*sor King *George* VI, born on "Mausoleum Day," *December 14, 1895. George Wash*ington of the Caristia (who was supposed to have been buried in the February 21/22 mausoleum) died on *December 14*, 1799. If February used to be the last month of the year, then December 14 is equivalent to St. Valentine's Day. Elizabeth II was born on April 21, 1926, the anniversary of the founding of Rome.

February 15, 1965 (SY).[321] Nat (King) Cole died at forty-five. He was born March 17, 1919.

February 15, 1972. Attorney General John Mitchell resigned to become

chairman of committee to reelect President Nixon. He was succeeded by Deputy Assistant Richard Kleindienst of Arizona
(admitted *February 14*, 1912). While Mitchell was chairman of the
committee, the Watergate break-in took place. See *February 21*,
1975.

February 15, 1972. Edgar Snow, an American journalist, died. He was
the first western reporter to interview Mao Tse-tung and Chou
En-lai.

February 15, 1973. U.S. and Cuba signed Anti-hijacking Pact.

February 15, 1976. A new Cuban Constitution was approved by 97.7
percent vote in a national referendum.

February 15, 1990. Hess, Brysinski, and Carl found guilty of espionage.
(see page 673, footnote 290.)

February 15, 1994. Co-prosecutor Henry DePippo made closing
statements in the trial of four involved in World Trade Center
bombing.

February 15, 1995. Wednesday. Full moon phase entered at 7:15 A.M. EST.
Four (4) army ranger training candidates died from hypothermia
at Elgin Air Force Base, *Florida*. It was the worst accident in the
training program's forty-four year history.

February 21. The "Romans called death fera, cruel." It's the Feralia, the
All-Souls Day in Roman antiquity. The ceremonies held were
similar to those of the *Novemdiale*, the ninth day after a funeral.
Principal offerings were flowers and fruit, but "love is as good as
a rich gift" (Ovid). The Feralia can be called the Feast of the Dead
or the culmination of the Feast of the Dead. *February 21* suggests
February 212.[322]

February 21, 1429. In a notarial deed with Guglielmo de Brabante, a
clothweaver, Johannes de Columbo (a resident of Quinto [fifth]
now part of Genoa, Italy) agreed to the apprenticeship of his son
Domenico, who later would be the father of Christopher
Columbus. (Salvador de Madariaga, *Christopher Columbus*. New
York: Macmillan Co., 1940.) Christopher Columbus died on May
20, 1506, the eve of the first Mercury period. Hermes, god of travelers. Diego Columbus, who sailed with his brother Christopher
on the second voyage to the New World in 1493, died on *February
21*, 1515 (*Encyclopedia Americana*).

Diego Columbus, the only legitimate son of Christopher
Columbus, died on *February 23*, 1526.

After first being buried in Spain, the remains of both father and
son were exhumed about 1542 and sent to the cathedral of Santo
Domingo at Hispaniola.

February 21, 1431. Regular interrogation of Joan of Arc before forty-two
priests (seldom present at once) began at Rouen Castle. The

Bishop of Beauvais presided. On *February 22*, the court was joined by the Inquisitor General's deputy.[323-A] She was executed on May 30, a date to become, perhaps coincidentally, our traditional Memorial Day. *February 23*, 1929. Bells on the Department of Meuse, France, rang out at 4:00 P.M. in celebration of the time five centuries previously when Joan of Arc rode from Vaucouleurs for Chinon to begin her great adventure.

February 21, 1508.[323-B] On this day, shades of the Feralia, "Julius the Colossus," the polished bronze statue, was set in place above the main doors of the San Petronio cathedral in Bologna.[323-C]

February 21, 1513. The warring Julius II, the most famous of all Popes, died. Was it a "blessing or cursing"? For my money, only the most obtuse would not see the hand of invisible forces at work. Note that the numbers 13 and 21, suggesting the nine days of the Parentalia and the *Novemdiale*. The same two numbers are linked to Ponce de Leon; Balboa, discovering the Pacific (peace, persona Hermes) in 1513 and later to be memorialized in the Panama-Pacific Exposition of 1915, which opened on February 20; Captain Cook; and Malcolm X. The thirteenth, the Ides, the beginning of the Parentalia, is also St. Valentine's Day Eve, previously celebrated in Norwich, England.

February 21, 1516. Mary Tudor, the daughter of Henry VIII and the Spanish princess Catherine of Aragon, was christened. (Caroll Erickson, *Bloody Mary*. Garden City, New York: Doubleday and Co., Inc., 1978.) if you take the *r* out of Maria, you have Maia. Three years previous to Mary Tudor's christening, the warring Pope Julius II had died. *February 18*, 1846, the thirtieth anniversary of her birth, Martin Luther died. Edward VI, who succeeded his father Henry VIII, ruled that English rather than Latin was to be used in church services. His half-sister Mary Tudor—still remaining a Roman Catholic—defied him by holding mass conducted in Latin in her chapel. When Edward VI died, Mary Tudor was the rightful heir to the throne but Lady Jane Grey had a certain logic to her claim. Whose parentage—like some offshoot of the Parentalia—was closer? She was the daughter of Henry Grey, duke of Suffolk, and married Guilford Dudley of Northumberland on *May 21*, 1553. So much for superstition against marrying in May. Lady Grey, a strong Protestant, seized the throne and for *nine days* was queen until being overthrown by supporters of Mary Tudor. In a macabre synchronicity—she and her husband were beheaded on *February 12*, 1554. Eleven days later on February 23, the Terminalia, Henry Grey was beheaded. Anne Boleyn, the mother of the future Queen Elizabeth I, was sentenced to death on *May 15* (the time in ancient Rome there was a festival to Mercury [persona decapitation, sacrifice] and Maia) and lost her head on May 19. (See *May 15*, 1536.) Catherine Howard, Elizabeth's cousin-stepmother, was decapitated on *February 13*, 1542. As a beheading of a parent was a necessary sacrifice in order to put Elizabeth on the throne, so it was necessary for Elizabeth to be responsible for the *February 8*, 1587, beheading of Mary Stuart, former Queen of Scots, so Mary Stuart's son, James VI of Scotland, would succeed Queen Elizabeth I and become James I of England. Mary Tudor—in a futile attempt to return England to Catholicism—caused the death of nearly three hundred rebels and heretics, who were either hung or burned at stake (sacrifice). She thereby acquired the name of "Bloody Mary." Though dying between *four and five* in the morning of November 17, 1558, her body wasn't carried inside Westminster Abbey until December 12, the day corresponding to *February 12* by my reckoning. All night her body was watched over by a hundred poor men wearing black and holding torches. Around them stood Royal Guard soldiers with their "staff torches."

On December 13, a requiem mass was sung for Bloody Mary. Angered at the bishop of Winchester for highly eulogizing her Catholic half-sister, Elizabeth I—who succeeded Mary to the throne—ordered that he be "a prisoner in his own house." If man is to have a god who continuously dies on the cross for him so that man can live, then it seems that man has to die, often covered with blood, so the god can live. There's no free lunch.

Can't you see the Roman Catholics and the Protestants in Ireland and the Irish and the English will never stop fighting? It's out of their control: A certain sacrifice will be taken.

February 21, 1595. Robert Southwell, Elizabethan poet and Catholic martyr, was hanged after being condemned for being a Catholic priest. In relation to his Feast-of-the-Dead execution, four facts are of interest:

1) *He'd gone to Rome* and became a Jesuit novice in 1578 and priest in 1584.
2) One of his two best-known prose works is called *Mary Magdalens Funerall Teares*.
3) His head was chopped off and held up to the crowd. (*Decapitation.*)
4) He was declared *"blessed" in 1929* and canonized in 1970. He is now venerated on *February 21*.

February 21, 1779. Captain Cook's burial at sea just outside the bay.[324]

February 21, 1787. Death knell of the Articles of Confederation. Congress called for a convention to meet on May 14. (See page 253, footnote 1-H.)

February 21, 1794 (21). Antonio Lopez de Santa Anna born. A truly

Hermetic man, General Santa Anna defeated the Texans at the Alamo. Then he was captured by General Sam Houston on April 21, 1836. Santa Anna later lost a leg in battle. He died in poverty on June 20 (the last day of the Mercury period), 1876 (22). 21-21-22. He presided over the loss of the American Southwest and Texas to the United States.

February 21, 1801. Englishman John Henry Newman born. This is an interesting date in that he resigned from the Church of England, *went to Rome* to be ordained in the Catholic priesthood, and eventually became a deacon-cardinal.

February 21, 1804. Demonstration in Wales of the first self-propelled steam locomotive. (Laurence J. Peter, *Peter's Almanac*. New York: William Morrow and Co., Inc., 1982.) This fact was come across long after footnote 239-B, pages 661-662, was written.

February 21, 1807. Martin Van Buren (born on *December 5*, 1782, the anniversary of the ancient Faunus festival [also celebrated *February 13*]) married Hannah Hoes. She died *February 5*, 1819, about eighteen years before he became president. Their second of four sons was born *February 18*, 1810. Martin Van Buren's mother died *February 16*, 1817, (or 1818, by one account born *February 27*, 1737). Through her, he was connected to the future President Theodore Roosevelt. (See *February 14*, 1884, Roosevelt connection to February). Martin's father was born *February 17*, 1737 (died *April 5*, 1817, the anniversary of George Washington's christening). According to the diary of John Quincy Adams (linked to *February 21*), however, Aaron Burr (born *February 6*, 1756, and who later killed Alexander Hamilton in a duel) was reputed as being Martin Van Buren's father. On *February 19* or *February 20* (depending on the source), 1807, Burr was intercepted. The court that opened on *May 22*, 1807, eventually brought Grand Jury indictments against Aaron Burr and one other. Burr had refused to betray the confidentiality of General Wilkinson's letter of *May 13* to him. Burr was acquitted after Chief Justice John Marshall (connected later to the funding of the Washington Monument) ruled that treasonous acts must be attested by at least two witnesses. Two nicknames given Martin Van Buren were 1) "the Little Magician" and 2) "the Red Fox of Kinderhook." Hermes persona, magic and cunning.

February 21, 1848. John Quincy Adams, then a member of Congress protesting honorary swords be awarded to generals who had participated in a "most unrighteous" war with Mexico, had a stroke on General Santa Anna's birthday.

February 21, (o.s.), 1852. Nikolai Gogol died ten days after burning his "presumably completed" manuscript of Volume II of *Dead Souls*.

Gogol, an earth-snake. Chichikov, a swindler. (See Book I, page 6.)

February 21, 1855. The Washington Monument is "stolen" as "Know-Nothings" seize records and books. Previously a block of marble, given as a gift by Pope Pius IX from the Temple of Concord in Rome, was stolen. The "Know-Nothings," anti-Catholics, were believed responsible for the theft.

February 21, 1866. Lucy B. Hobbs became the first black woman to graduate from a dental school. This was at the Ohio College of Dental Surgery in Cincinnati.

February 21, 1868. President Johnson dismissed *Secretary of War* Stanton. This led, on this date too, to a Senate resolution declaring the removal of Stanton illegal, and the motion presented also on this date in the House to impeach the president was referred to a committee.

Later on February 24, the House of Representatives instituted impeachment proceedings against President Johnson for "high crimes and misdemeanors." Now the Feralia date that President Johnson replaced Stanton might not mean much by itself, but when you recall that Vice President Johnson had succeeded the assassinated Lincoln at his death on April 15 (4.5) and that Lincoln himself was connected to the Parentalia, *February 21* seems more than curious. The date stands out especially when it's recalled that Johnson was the only president before or since against whom impeachment proceedings occurred. His trial took place in the U.S. Senate in Washington. Note the three Mercury months of February, April, and May. March, named after the god of war, might also be included if considering that the trial began on March 13. (See footnote 317-B.) On May 26, one day after the twenty-fifth, President Johnson was acquitted by just one vote, a two-thirds vote was needed for conviction. Recall Hermes being tried by the gods who cast their vote pebbles and that he's associated with death and respect for the dead. Of Johnson's five children (three sons and two daughters), Charles was born on February 19, 1830; Mary on May 8, 1832; and Robert on February 22, 1834. Mary McDonough Johnson, Andrew Johnson's mother, died on *February 13*, 1856. It's my suspicion that had he fired Stanton on any other day than the Feralia, Johnson would have been convicted.

The following Day-of-Mourning-for-Lincoln Proclamation was issued by President Johnson on April 25, 1865:

> Thursday, the 25th of May next, (is) to be
> observed, wherever in the United States the flag
> of the country may be respected, as a day of
> humiliation and mourning, and I recommend

my fellow-citizens then to assemble in their respective places of worship, there to unite in solemn service to Almighty God in memory of the good man who has been removed, so that all shall be occupied at the same time in contemplation of his virtues and in sorrow for his sudden and violent end.

When President Johnson's attention was called to "the fact that the day aforesaid is sacred to large numbers of Christians as one of rejoicing for the ascension of the Saviour," he issued another proclamation which changed the date to June 1, 1865,[339] still in the Mercury period.

February 21, 1871. Territorial government provided for District of Columbia by Act of Congress. Though the territorial government was short-lived, the date is interesting that George Washington first proposed the site of the new government (2122).

February 21, 1885. Washington Monument (obelisk) dedicated. (2122) Cleopatra's Needle is also connected to the number 21. On September 21, 1877 (MP), the stone obelisk was hauled out to sea from Egypt by the *Olga*, a steamship. On January 21, 1878, it glided into the Thames river England. (Though Stonehenge, a circular complex of megaliths, isn't an obelisk, let's not forget that on June 21 [the crossroads date taken for the summer solstice] people from all over the world gather to watch the sunrise [dawn] over the standing stones.)

February 21, 1901. Albert Einstein, who years later wrote to President Franklin Roosevelt pointing out that a Nazi nuclear bomb could be made, became a citizen of Zurich and Switzerland. By pointing out that a Nazi bomb could be made, he was, in effect, suggesting a U.S. bomb be made.

February 21, 1901. Cuba, associated with the Lupercalia in 1898, adopted on the Feralia a constitution patterned after that of the U.S. The Cuban Revolution began with uprisings on the island on *February 20*, 1895. See *February 15*, 1973.

February 21, 1909. The "Great White Fleet," consisting of sixteen battleships, steamed into Hampton Roads, Virginia, after completing the first worldwide journey (travel) by the U.S. Navy. It began on December 16, 1907 (two days after the anniversary of George Washington's death on December 14, 1799). TR watched its departure from the presidential yacht *Mayflower*. (See May 13, 1889, and May 15, 1898.) He commented enthusiastically, "Did you ever see such a day? By George, isn't it magnificent!" (Here he might have been referring to George Washington.) Taking all this into consideration and the fact that Roosevelt was the first president to fly in an airplane, it seems appropriate today that there's the aircraft carrier USS *Theodore Roosevelt*. February 21 was *one* day before the anniversary of George Washington's birthday on February 22, 1732 (New Style).

February 21, 1910. Douglas Bader born. Lost two legs from flying accident. (Death of parts or sacrifice.) Returns to become famous British fighter pilot in World War II. Number 21 connected to flying.

February 21, 1910. Carmine Galante born on the fifty-fifth anniversary of the theft of the Feralia-Caristia symbol. His father had come from Sicily, where Persephone (associated with *May 13*) was strong in the ancient culture. Galante, described as "psychopathic" and "a mass of contradictions," became the mafia boss of New York City. He was extremely ruthless and brutal, being responsible for many murders. Many other Mafia bosses were afraid of Galante and so put out a contract on him. The long, long day was through when he was killed by three masked gunmen in an Italian restaurant in Brooklyn, New York, on July 12, 1979. (See page 349-350.)

February 21, 1912. As a former President, TR told newspapermen, "My hat is in the ring." Twenty-one was previously connected to Roosevelt in his class standing at Harvard and the New York district where he entered politics, but the mentor of Black Jack Pershing lost his bid for reelection.

February 20, 21, 22, 1915. Opening weekend holidays for the Panama-Pacific Exposition. (The Golden Gate International Exposition open *February 18*, 1939. Note in each exposition there's the suggestion of water—Neptune is the guardian of the month of February. Admiral Chester Nimitz, born *February 24*, 1885, assumed command of the Pacific Fleet after Admiral Husband Kimmel was relieved in December 1941. By the end of World War II, Nimitz commanded the largest naval force ever assembled. He died on the eve of the Feralia, *February 20*, 1966, at Treasure Island in San Francisco Bay. (See pages 624–635.) It was inevitable that ex-President Roosevelt would attend the Parentalia-Caristia Exposition (his speech given July 21), as it was the USS *Oregon* would be there. TR was closely connected to February and water (FDR also). G.P. Putnam's Sons published his *The Naval War of 1812* in 1882. As assistant secretary of the navy, he'd sent his famous cable to Commodore Dewey on February 25, 1898, the day the secretary of the navy was absent from his office (deception). As president, he issued the proclamation for building the Panama Canal. Without that, there would have been no Panama-Pacific exposition. In 1913 he'd led an expedition which mapped the "River of Doubt" in Brazil. One man drowned; another, under the strain, went bad, murdered his sergeant, and fled into the wilderness. TR himself became very sick. The river was renamed Rio Téodoro by the Brazilians in his honor.

In his New York home were tusks, antlers, and *mounted heads* (Hermes, persona decapitation) of a few of the animals he had killed in his life as a game hunter. Keeping this in mind, as well as TR's obvious connection to February, water (he'd been the first president to submerge in a submarine), and travel (he'd gone to Panama during the construction period), there's an eeriness when considering that the Panama-Pacific Balboa and four others were beheaded. Considering too that he was the first of the presidents to fly in an airplane, there's an eeriness that his youngest child Quentin would be shot down in aerial combat, as if it were the final sacrifice before TR could die.

On July 21, 1915, he spoke of an audience of seventy thousand in the Court of the Universe. It was called one of "The Great Orations of the Expositions" (article by Henry Meade Bland, *The Overland Monthly*, 66: 528 30, 1915). Hermes, god of eloquence. Note too that the assassinated President McKinley, whom TR succeeded, was shot at *Buffalo*'s Pan-American Exposition on September 6 (MP), 1901. TR was attending an outing on the Vermont Fish and Game League at the Isle La Motte on Lake Champlain (water) when the news reached him. (Op. cit., Lorant.)

The amphitheatre where TR spoke on July 21, 1915, couldn't have been more than two miles from where General Black Jack Pershing's wife and three of his children perished in a Presidio fire a little over a month later (August 27 [MP], 1915.) (See Book II, footnote 146.)

When TR returned from charting the "River of Doubt" in 1913, he was extremely angry to learn that President Wilson had agreed to a treaty with Columbia which had expressed "sincere regret" for the way the U.S. had gotten the Panama Canal Zone and allowed for payment of twenty-five thousand dollars to Columbia (Ibid.). He never forgave Wilson and probably hated him more than any other man. Nevertheless, on April 9, 1917, three days after war was declared on Germany, TR asked permission of President Wilson to lead a regiment in Europe. Wilson was non-committal to his face but later let it be known he felt Colonel Roosevelt wasn't a military leader, had too little military experience, had "shown intolerance of discipline," and was too old. TR, however, might have derived some consolation from the fact that it was the captain, whom he selected over hundreds of senior officers to become a general, who was leading the expeditionary forces.

Quentin Roosevelt died on July 14, 1918. Theodore followed in less than six months on January 6, 1919. A curious note in relation to February (two youths from aristocratic families were selected on the Lupercalia) is that John Quincy Adams had come from an aristocratic family, as had Theodore Roosevelt and Franklin Roosevelt, who married Elliott's daughter Eleanor. Both TR and Elliott had watched Lincoln's funeral procession as it passed their grandfather's house on April 25, 1865, and, as previously stated, TR wore at his inauguration of March 4, 1905, the ring Lincoln was wearing when he died. Then too, there's little doubt that TR had seen and/or met Grant.

February 21, 1916. It's a year since the beginning of the Panama-Pacific Exposition, attended either opening day or later by:

> General Pershings's wife and children,
> Shortly to die except for his son.
> Their flinty-eyed ol' man missed
> The Battle of Verdun,
> Longest and bloodiest that had begun,
> On the Feast of the Dead in World War I.

At dawn the opening shot was a shell fired twenty miles away from a Krupp cannon. This took off a corner of Verdun's cathedral. (David Wallechinsky, *People's Almanac Presents the Twentieth Century*. Boston: Little, Brown, & Co., 1995.) As stated before, it's my opinion that Julius II's death on *February 21*, 1513, consecrated St. Peter's Basilica by Parentalia forces. The Krupps were manufacturers of arms and ammunition, in effect, merchants of death. In addition, they were linked to the Parentalia via Friedrich Alfred Krupp born *February 17*, 1854, and who apparently committed suicide in 1902 on November 22 (twenty-one days past November 1). He was rocked by a homosexual scandal. The incident leading to this occurred on the cave-ridden, limestone island of Capri (Latin: *Capreae* - aeae), a favorite resort of Roman emperors, about seventeen miles south of Naples, the area where the ancient Mercury-Maia cult had been strong. Pompeii, the signature of the death god, is only fourteen miles from Naples as the crow flies. Following his death, the family business was run by his daughter Bertha, for whom the huge "Big Bertha" guns were named.

Poison gas was used at Verdun. Thousands of bodies lay unburied, stinking and rotting for weeks at a time as if the god of graveyards himself had been overwhelmed by the monstrosity. There were six to seven hundred thousand French and German casualties. (Note Woden was a god of battles; Mercury in Gaul was a war god.) There are now over seventy graveyards in the Verdun area. And for all that, *the lines or boundaries were nearly unchanged* when the battle ended on December 18, 1916, and bodies of soldiers are still being found.

Even today, the killing field continues its work. Since 1946, six hundred thirty *deminuers* (bomb disposal experts) have been killed trying to clear the forest. It's estimated that there remain twelve million explosive devices yet to be defused. "The Soldiers Moved On. The War Moved On. The Bombs Stayed." (Donovan Webster, *Smithsonian*, February 1994.)

February 21, 1917. SY. *Romani*an train wreck killed five hundred.[326]

February 21, 1917. The British ship *Mendi*, carrying eight hundred and six black laborers from South Africa to France, collided with the liner *Daro* off the coast of the Isle of Wight. Six hundred and twenty-seven laborers and crew members perished when the *Mendi* sank in twenty-four minutes.[327]

February 21, 1919. Dr. Mary *Walker* died. She received her M.D. from Syracuse Medical College in 1855, the only woman in her graduating class. She eventually located her practice in *Rome*, New York. At the outbreak of the Civil War, she entered the service in her profession. Four of many firsts throughout her life are as follows:

1) She was the first woman to enter the service as an assistant army surgeon.

2) She was the first woman in the service ever to be exchanged—as a prisoner of war—for a man of her rank.

3) She was the first woman ever awarded the Medal of Honor.

4) Through her persistent urgency, the postal service began a postal card receipt for registered letters.

She left the army in 1865; working briefly as a journalist in New York City; then took up practice in *Washington*, D.C., wearing men's trousers in the daytime; and died at her estate at Oswego, New York, where she had set up a hospital for consumptives. Throughout her life, she'd met much opposition. Rotten eggs were thrown at her, and she was dubbed a "self-made man," among other things. An educated guess would be that her Medal of Honor was revoked in 1917 (a new policy that it was to be awarded only for action that was combat related) in part for a long-standing, festering contempt for her work for woman suffrage and—most of all—her very masculine features. Otherwise, why bother to make the rule retroactive going back all those years? (See picture, *The National Cyclopaedia of American Biography*, Vol 13; New York: James T. White & Co., 1906.) Perhaps it's relevant to mention here too that Joan of Arc's dressing as a man and her masculinity probably had as much to do with her burning at the stake (*May 30*, 1431) as the actual charges of being "an idolator, apostate, heretic, relapsed." Dr. Walker refused to return the medal. In 1977, long after her death, the medal was reinstated.

Ralph Chichester born. He wanted to be a veterinarian and lived his short life near one branch or another of the Walker River. On August 21, 1919, the Pearl Harbor dry dock at Hawaii was opened formally by Secretary Daniels. Ralph's death was twenty years later to the day. Hawaii was admitted as the fiftieth state on August 21, 1959.

February 21, 1919. Kurt Eisner assassinated in Munich by Count Arco-Valley. Eisner, Like Dr. Walker (anti-slavery and women's suffrage leader), was a crosser of boundaries. He helped overthrow the Bavarian monarchy on November 7–8, 1918, and took control in Bavaria as prime minister.

February 21, 1922. The discovery of George Washington's lost diary was announced this date by George R. Prowell, curator and librarian of the Historical Society of York County, Pennsylvania.[328] (See Book I, footnote 1-H.)

February 21, 1922. Lighter-than-air ship called *Roma* hit high tension wires at Hampton Roads Army Base, Virginia, and exploded in air, killing thirty-four (seven) of its *forty-five*-men crew. Previously it had been bought from the Italian government.[329] Hampton Roads, by the way, was the place the *Monitor*[330] and Merrimack fired at one another on March 9, 1862. My belief that General Pershing was connected to the Parentalia has been stated. (See Pershing, footnote 146 and Verdun, *February 21*, 1916.)

At Philadelphia on *February 22*, 1922, General Pershing said that on the day the *Roma* exploded (and previous to his hearing about it) he had been sitting in his office in Washington when he was seized with a desire to take a ride on an airship and had determined to take a trip as soon as possible. He felt fortunate that this desire hadn't come to him earlier.[331]

This twenty-one is connected to flying the same as May 21, 1878, when Glenn Hammond Curtis (American flyer and inventor of aileron) was born; April 21, 1918, the death date of the Red Baron (cinna-bar); July 21, 1921, General "Billy" Mitchell's planes demonstrated the superiority of air power in a test by sinking the former German battleship *Ostfriesland* and the condemned battleship *Alabama* (note General Mitchell knew all the *Roma*'s officers and many of its enlisted men personally); May 21, 1927, Lindbergh's landing the "*Spirit* of St. Louis" at Les Bourget field in France; May 21, 1932, Amelia Earhart (who liked to be called

AE) landed a single-engine monoplane Lockheed *Vega* (see Book I, footnote 24-C [*Vega*]) at Londonderry, Ireland, to become the first woman to make a solo flight across the Atlantic; May 21, 1956, the first American airborne hydrogen bomb is dropped on Namu, Bikini Islands, in the Pacific; President Nixon's landing in Peking on February 21, 1972; Benigno S. Aquino, arriving on a flight from the U.S., was assassinated at Manila airport on August 21, 1983; Pan Am flight 103, originating in Frankfurt and bound for New York, flew north from London when it exploded in air on December 21, 1988, killing 258 passengers and 12 on the ground; and May 21, 1991, Rajiv Gandhi, pilot, was assassinated. In Lacey, Washington, on May 21, 1994, sixty-seven years after Lindbergh landed in Paris, a fire apparently broke out in flight aboard a single-engine Ryan Navion which then struck a car on crashing. The driver escaped injury, but the pilot, Eugene Gore, fifty-three, and his passenger Chris Ann Smith, forty-seven, died on impact. This happened at the edge of a road between the airfield and the Capitol City Golf Course on the southern edge of *Olympia*. On September 6 (MP), 1992, in a midair collision over the same road between the golf course and the airport (and on Chris Ann Smith's first wedding anniversary), her husband died. Both pilots were thought to have been blinded by the afternoon sun, and the midair collision occurred during an annual fly-in and picnic where, two years previously, the Smiths had met. Note the occurrence of two and one in both accidents. In the one on September 6, 1992, Scott Smith was flying a home-built biplane. Bill Scott was flying a Cessna 170, which also was carrying Jason Cromwell as a passenger. There were no survivors. On May 21, 1994, two died in the crash, but the driver of the car escaped injury. Also of interest is the name of the airport: *Aero Plaza*. See *February 21, 1929.*

February 21, 1929. Colonial Lindbergh is appointed technical advisor to Aeronautics Branch of Department of *Commerce.* (Remember on *February 14, 1903,* Congress [at President Theodore Roosevelt's request] established the Department of Commerce and Labor. This was nineteen years after the deaths of Roosevelt's wife and mother.)

February 21, 1934. Cesar Augusto Sandino, Nicaraguan guerrilla leader, was assassinated. He had been born in 1893, probably within the frame of the snake-year. It's from his name that the current Sandinistas got their name. Both he and his followers managed to evade capture by U.S. Marines and the Nicaraguan National Guard from 1927 to 1933. Whether seen as a bandido or patriot, he managed to incite anti-U.S. feelings in Latin America.

President Franklin D. Roosevelt, also connected to the Parentalia, was forced to begin his "Good Neighbor Policy," largely due to the action of *Cesar* and followers.

February 21, 1936. Barbara C. Jordan born. Served in Congress for a number of years. Died January 17, 1996.

February 21, 1940. In step with the anniversary of the old style death of the author of *Dead Souls* eighty-eight years previously and on the twenty-fourth anniversary of the Battle of Verdun—where sacrifice is still given—SS Brigadier General Glücks will direct fifteen large concentration camps, five hundred auxillary ones, and issue monthly orders for the "Final Solution" and "extermination through labor." It's estimated that two million died at Auschwitz alone. Glücks made major general and was awarded the German Cross in *silver*. Where Hitler was born on April 20, 1889, Glücks was born two days later on April 22. Where Hitler committed suicide on April 30, 1945, Glücks is believed to have done the same on May 10, 1945—or he just disappeared on a day between the Lemuria spread.

February 21, 1944. Harilal, drunk, visited his mother's deathbed. Kasturbai died the following day, the Caristia. Mahatma Gandhi, a true crossroads being who gravitated toward the numbers twenty-one and twenty-two in his life, died on January 30, 1948, blessing his assassin. It would have been twenty-two days until February 21, or from January 31—the day of his cremation—twenty-one days to the Feralia and twenty-two until the Caristia. Ramakrishna, whose personal example demonstrated "the essential unity of all religions." was born on *February 18*, 1836, in Hooghly, India. He became a priest in a temple of Kali, the Hindu goddess of creation and destruction, early in his religious life. (See Luper-Kal, page 669.)

February 21, 1944. Eniwetok (Enewetak) Island seized this day by U.S. forces. It's my belief that the capture and the above event are related. My thinking concerning this will be made clearer in the last chapter.

February 21, 1946. Crews in the Royal Indian Navy mutinied for not enough of the bounty on this Feralia day in Bombay. They wanted more pay, better food, and made political demands. Rioting also broke out in Karachi and other Indian cities, using violence to protest British rule. (Two years before, Harilal, drunk, had to be escorted away from his mother's deathbed.) Anti-British rioting also took place in five *Egyptian* cities. Meanwhile in *Rome*, Pope Pius bestowed red hats on new cardinals. (It was the anniversary of Julius II's death; forty-four years previously, the lighter-than-air ship *Roma*, purchased from the Italian government, exploded in Virginia.) But perhaps we should begin on *February 18*, 1946, the Parentalia day and the anniversary of Michelangelo's death. A secret Consistory created thirty-two new cardinals. On *February 19* about three hundred Indians, some wearing the Royal Indian Navy uniform, burned the American flag on the streets of Bombay. All cardinals had now arrived in Rome. On *February 20*, Pope Pius rebuked "modern Imperialism." On *February 22*, the Caristia and the anniversary of Kasturbai's death two years before, Indian rioting still continued. In Bombay the mutineers *ran up* black surrender flags. In Rome, the cardinals who had received their red hats on the Feralia, received their rings and were told what churches were assigned to them. On *February 23*, fighting renewed in Bombay. On *February 24*, assurances were given to those Indian mutineers who had surrendered that no reprisals would be made. The Pope ended the week of Consistory ceremonies on *February 25* by asking the "world churchmen and diplomats to work for universal peace." Rioting that had begun in the Parentalia had resulted 228 deaths and 1,047 injured, not including those in Egypt.

February 21, 1948. President Truman started a five-day trip to Puerto Rico, the Virgin Islands, and *Cuba*, where he inspected the Guantanamo Bay Naval Base. (See February 13, 1885.)

February 21, 1952. A holiday and national *day of mourning* in Bangladesh had grown from the Bengali language movement in 1952. Note Bengali New Years: April 15 (4.5).

February 21, 1955. President Dwight David Eisenhower (445) proclaimed *May 21* as Armed Forces Day. Hermes, god of campaigns. Traditionally a date was issued by each administration. A Presidential Proclamation of May 17, 1989, covers the third Saturday in May (which it had been since 1950) in all following years.

February 21, 1956 (21). Russian-born Jake "Greasy Thumb" Guzik, a powerful man in the Chicago syndicate during the Capone era and for twenty-five years beyond, died of a heart attack while eating in a restaurant and making payoffs on the Feast of the Dead, seven days after the anniversary of the St. Valentine's Day Mass in 1929 (21).

Some thought Guzik *"was the only man Capone ever killed for out of friendship,"* and loyal to the last, Guzik is said to have helped support the prison-released, syphilitic-deteriorating Capone (Carl Sifakis, *The Encyclopedia of American Crime*. New York: Facts of File, Inc., 1982.)

In 1924, Guzik—overhearing a conversation of two mobsters who planned to ambush Capone—warned him. When later Guzik got beat up by "free-lance hijacker" Joe Howard, Guzik told Capone, who came to his friend's defense by putting six slugs into Howard's head.

Guzik was Jewish. More Italians came to his service than had ever been seen before in the temple. He was buried in an "ornate bronze coffin" which cost five thousand dollars, prompting a mobster to groan, "For that money, we could have buried him in a cadillac!"

February 21, 1957. The Spirit of St. Louis premiers. James Stewart stars as Lindbergh. (See: *February 13, 1929; February 13, 1935; February 14, 1929; February 14 and 15, 1764;* and *February 21, 1929.*)

February 21, 1961. G. Mennen Williams, assistant state secretary for African affairs, said in Nairobi, Kenya, that the Kennedy administration supported "Africa for the Africans." This caused a furor in Kenya and other places having white settlers.

February 21, 1965 (SY). Malcolm X assassinated. In Cheiro's *Book of Numbers,* Mercury is linked to the number 5, and each letter of the alphabet is associated with one number of 8. Thus M = 4, X = 5. Alex Haley, author of *Roots,* produced his first major work when he collaborated on *The Autobiography of Malcolm X.* February rightfully became Black History Month. When three Molotov cocktails were thrown at Malcolm X's home on *February 14,* half of it was destroyed. On Feralia Eve 1965, he later told the author of *Roots* that he believed the bombing was caused by a force much more sinister than Muslim fanatics. (Op. cit., Nash.)

"The more I keep thinking about what happened to me in France, I think I'm going to quit saying it's the Muslims," he told Haley. He very well could have been right considering 1) he had been refused entry to France when flying to Paris (remember it was Hermes who led the goddesses to the judgment of Paris) on February 9, 1965, as if a force were assuring that he would be back in the U.S.A. on the beginning day of the Parentalia; 2) he winged into New York City from London on the thirteenth; 3) he was scheduled to speak at the Audubon (suggesting bird, flight) Ballroom at *Washington* Heights (measurement), New York City, on the twenty-first.[332-A]

February 21, 1966. Washington. Jailed for spying for the Chinese, former CIA analyst Larry Chin killed himself in prison.

February 21, 1970. After an eleven-day offensive (and on the anniversary of the beginning of the battle of Verdun fifty-four years previously), pro-Communist Pathet Lao and North Vietnam forces regained the Plain of Jars. It was a sacrifice, the Jars being filled with the blood of more than five hundred troops (either dead or missing) of the garrison at Xieng Khouang airfield, during the withdrawal. The strategically located plain had been taken by

Laotian troops with U.S. air support in the fall of 1969.

February 21, 1971. Tornadoes (wind) struck Louisiana, Mississippi, and Texas. Ninety people were killed; more than five hundred were injured.

February 21, 1972. Harrisburg, Pennsylvania. The trial of the Reverend Philip Berrigan and six other "antiwar activists of the Catholic left" began. It was charged that they plotted to 1) kidnap Henry Kissinger, President Nixon's foreign policy adviser, 2) raid the draft boards, and 3) destroy Washington's heating tunnels. It was the eighty-seventh anniversary of the dedication of the Washington Monument.

February 21, 1972. President Richard M. Nixon arrived at Peking for historic talks. (Tricia Nixon Cox born February 21, 1946.) Was received by Chairman Mao Tse-tung and negotiated with Premier Chou En-lai.

February 21, 1974. One day after Patricia Hearst's twentieth birthday, the SLA demanded that four million dollars more be distributed in food to the poor in the San Francisco-Oakland area.

February 21, 1975. Sentencing took place for their part in the Watergate coverup for former President Nixon's Attorney General John Mitchell and top aides John Ehrlichman and H.R. Haldeman.

February 21, 1976. By invitation of the Chinese government, former President Richard M. Nixon began an eight-day visit to the People's Republic of China.

February 21, 1976. A Jakarta newspaper reported that five hundred corpses were found in four mass graves. These were the bodies of those who had belonged to pro-Indonesian factions in Timor and were thought to have been slain by Fretelin forces. (Op. cit., Leonard, Crippen, and Aronson.)

February 21, 1978. Hsinhua News Agency reported "Gang of Four" (of whom Mao Tse-tung's widow was one) would not be executed despite their "unrepentant" attitude.

February 21 obviously is connected to President Nixon. If he had not resigned, he would have become the second president to face impeachment proceedings, just as had President Johnson for firing Secretary of War Stanton on *February 21, 1868.*

The Feast of the Dead date in relation to Richard Nixon is particularly interesting on considering that when presidential candidate John F. Kennedy beat Nixon by more than one hundred and nineteen thousand votes on November 8, 1960, the democrats were accused of using a "cemetery vote" brought about by Chicago's mayor Richard Daley (born *May 15*, 1902, in Chicago). The Illinois victory gave twenty-seven electoral votes to Kennedy.

February 21, 1980. In protest of Soviet military presence, *merchants* closed their shops in Afghanistan's capital of Kabul, a city of one million. *Commerce* came to a halt. On *February 22*, the Soviets imposed martial law, but the strike spread to other cities with the reported deaths of three hundred civilians in the strike's first few days.

February 21, 1983. Former Vice President Mondale announced his candidacy for the Democratic presidential nomination. He later won this and then lost the election. (See *February 21, 1912*.)

February 21, 1989 (SY). Trial of Marine Lt. Col. Oliver North opened.

February 21, 1994. Aldrich Hazen Ames, a counter-intelligence officer of the CIA, and his wife were arrested separately in Virginia. Both were arraigned on *February 22* (2122) for selling information to the Soviet Union and then Russia over at least a nine-year period. Deception, judgment.[332-B]

On *February 21, 1967*, Senator Robert F. Kennedy had said the CIA *shouldn't be made a scapegoat* and that all relevant agencies had taken part in its funding decisions. Senator Ted Kennedy was born on *February 22, 1932*.

February 21, 1996. Jeanne Calment celebrated her 121st birthday. Born in Arles, France, in 1875, she is at this time the oldest person alive whose age can be documented. Carrie White died on *February 14, 1991*, at 117. She'd been a previous record holder in the *Guinness Book of World Records*.

On *February 21, 1963*, President John F. Kennedy sent to Congress the first presidential message on aging.

February 21-22, 1995. "The Night of Power" is observed. Ramadhan 21, 1415, Muslim calendar.

ST. PETER. Feast of St. Peter's Chair. February 22.[332-C]

AMERIGO VESPUCCI, who gave his name to America, died February 22, 1512, the Caristia. Born 1454, Florence, *Italy*.

GEORGE WASHINGTON, the father of his country, was born February 22, 1732. (New Style). 1732 - 1512 = 220. He died in 1799 on *December 14*, a date the English royal family later would identify as "Mausoleum Day."

JEFFERSON DAVIS was inaugurated as President of the Confederacy under permanent Confederate Constitution on February 22, 1862. On *February 4, 1861*, seven southern states formed the Confederacy. Five days later on *February 9*, Davis was unanimously elected president in voting by states. On *February 18, 1861*, he was inaugurated as provisional head of the Confederate States. On *May 21, 1861*, Richmond, Virginia, was designated as capital of the Confederacy. Presidents' Day, the third Monday in February, will always occur in the Parentalia

(15 - 21).[333]

It's said that the estate of Robert E. Lee was selected for Arlington National *Cemetery* because of his "treason." But then you've got to remember that the last sizable battle of the Civil War was fought at *Palm*ito Ranch on May 13 (equivalent to *February 21*, the old Feast of the Dead), 1865. It was won by Confederate troops led by Col. John Ford, a.k.a. RIP ("Rest in Peace") Ford. It seems likely that though the precipitating cause of the war was the secession of southern states, the real reason for over six hundred thousand deaths was the neglect of the ancient period. Memorial Day grew out of the Civil War.

Caristia and Terminalia[334]

February 22. St. Peter's Day Alsace. Snakes are driven away.

February 22, 1778. Rembrandt Peale born. Famous for "Porthole" portrait of George Washington. Son of Charles Willson Peale and last to paint Washington from life.

February 22, 1819. The Transcontinental Treaty, called simply "the Florida Treaty" by John Quincy Adams in his diary, was signed this date. At the time, Adams was U.S. Secretary of State. Under the treaty, western boundaries of the United States were described, and Spain ceded East Florida and West Florida (now Florida and the southern part of Alabama and Mississippi).[335]

February 22, 1821. U.S. and Spain exchange ratifications of the above treaty in the State Department. (Two snake-years later, Florida is admitted to union on March 3, 1845.) Known as "Old Man Eloquent," John Quincy Adams's motion in 1844 led to the repeal of the *twenty-first* (gag) rule (prevention of discussion of slavery in the House of Representatives). On February 21 (the anniversary of General Santa Anna's birthday), 1848, he fell unconscious from a cerebral stroke in Congress. He died two days later. Note Feralia-Caristia dates and recall the thirteen-twenty-one attached to Florida and Ponce de Leon, who was killed in a snake-year, three hundred years before the snake-year ratification in 1821. Compare the 21-22-23 February coincidence of John Quincy Adams to that of his father's death and Thomas Jefferson's. (See Book II, footnote 272.) Also Parentalia and/or Caristia dates tie into those of Aviles, Capone, and those of the Roosevelts to some extent.

February 22, 1827. Charles Willson Peale, father of Rembrandt Peale, died. (Born April 15, [4.5], 1741.) He had drawn seven portraits of Washington from life.

February 22, 1846. Liberty Bell had been repaired to ring for this celebration of Washington's birthday. It rang loud and true, then cracked irreparably, never to be rung again.[336]

February 22, 1847. After invading Mexico, General Zachary Taylor's forces were outflanked by those of General Santa Anna in the first day of Battle of Buena Vista in northeastern Mexico.

February 22, 1860. Dedication of equestrian statue of Washington at the Circle in Washington.

February 22, 1861. President-elect Lincoln is warned of an assassination plot against him.

February 22, 1881. One of two obelisks commonly referred to as C leopatra's Needle was officially presented to New York City this date. The other is on the Thames Embankment, London. Both are nearly twenty-one meters in height. The twenty-one dates concerning the English obelisk (see February 21, 1885) give a 2122 connection between the two.

February 22, 1889. Omnibus Bill, signed by President Cleveland, was an enabling act allowing for North Dakota, South Dakota, Montana, and Washington to be admitted to statehood.[337]

February 22, 1909. President Theodore Roosevelt (*associated with two deaths on the first full day of the Parentalia 1884*, a former assistant secretary of the navy, and an avenger of the Lupercalia sinking of the *Maine* in 1898) reviewed the "Great White Fleet" after its return from a world tour.

Note too it was TR who probably did more than any other president in getting the Panama Canal built after it was seen that the USS *Oregon*, named after the state admitted *February 14*, 1859, took so long to reach the Atlantic. One of the European cities he and his first wife visited on their honeymoon was Venice, Italy.

February 22, 1940. Tibetans are convinced of a boy's authenticity as a reincarnation of the thirteenth Dalai Lama. He ascends throne this date, becoming the fourteenth.

February 22, 1944. Kasturbia, the wife of Mahatma Gandhi, died in India. Mother's Day in India is established in her honor.

February 22, 1974. It was the 113th anniversary of the day President-elect Lincoln was warned of an assassination plot against himself. (see page 511.) At a line waiting to board Delta (Hermes persona) Flight 523 for Atlanta at Philadelphia airport, Samuel J. Byck shot and killed a security guard. He then ran aboard the plane, where he shot the pilot and co-pilot who couldn't respond to his orders for immediate takeoff. The co-pilot died. Sniper fire later hit Byck in the stomach and chest, whereupon he fired his own gun at his right temple. His plan had been to hijack the plane and force the crew to fly to Washington, D.C., where he would have taken control, crashing the plane into the White House to kill President

Nixon. (Op. cit., Sifakis.)

On *February 20*, the Feralia Eve two days previously (the 112th anniversary of William Wallace Lincoln's death at the White House [see page 399] and six years before Alice Roosevelt Longworth—"the other Washington Monument"—will die [see pages 526-527]), Byck made out his will leaving a dollar apiece to each of his children, who "have each other and they deserve each other." That his attempt to assassinate Nixon and Byck's own death took place on the Caristia is intriguing, since Nixon is linked to the Feralia. See *February 21*, 1972, 1976, and 1978.

February 22, 1985. Ceremony honoring symbolic billionth vehicle (Caristia) driven across Golden Gate Bridge. San Francisco County, the smallest in California, is *forty-five* square miles.

February 23, 1836. General Santa Anna's Mexican army lay siege to the Alamo.

February 23, 1847. U.S. Forces, better disciplined and better equipped, route those of General Santa Anna, whose withdrawal leaves U.S. control of northern Mexico.

February 23, 1848. John Quincy Adams died of a stroke, occurring on *February 21* when he became outraged by the proposal that U.S. generals were to be awarded honorary swords for their part in the Mexican War. He was buried at Quincy, Massachusetts.

February 23, 1861. President-elect Lincoln arrives safely at Washington.

February 23, 1930. Horst Wessel, a former Brownshirt, had fallen in love with a prostitute and moved into her apartment. On this date, he got into an argument with her pimp who was accompanied by several Red Front militants. Wessel was shot in the mouth and killed: Terminalia. When propaganda minister Joseph Goebbels heard that Wessel had written a poem titled "Up with the Flag," he turned the nonpolitical killing into "blood witness for the movement." Wessel became a party martyr and the poem was set to music, becoming the "Horst Wessel Song," the second German national anthem. (Christian Zentner and Friedemann Bedürftig (editors), translation edited by Amy Hackett, *Encyclopedia of the Third Reich*, two volumes. New York: Macmillan Publishing Co., 1991; Op. cit., Wallechinsky.) See *February 23*, 1945.

February 23, 1942. While President Franklin Roosevelt, associated with the Lupercalia, made a "fireside chat" (eloquence) to the nation, a Japanese submarine fired fifteen to twenty-five shells at Bankline Oil Refinery, twelve miles west of Santa Barbara, California. Damage estimated to be no more than five hundred dollars; there were no casualties reported. It was the first attack on American mainland.

February 23, 1945. Terminalia. Five marines and one navy pharmacist mate planted the U.S. flag on top of Mt. Surabachi, Iwo Jima. This was a landmark or boundary. The island was returned to Japan on June 26, 1968, so the U.S. flag no longer flies there; however, on top of the mountain there still remains a small white *stone* monument to the fifth Marine Division and its twenty-eighth Battalion which took the slope. Marine Amphibious Corp V had three divisions: the third, fourth, and fifth. The *fourth* and *fifth* made the landing on February 19, followed a few days later by the third, which had been kept in reserve. Curiously Louis L. Snyder[338-A] says the island wasn't taken until March 15, the Ides; others say it was March 16. Individual pockets of resistance weren't completely wiped out until March 26, 1945. The taking of the eight-square-mile island was hotly *contested*, making it one of the fiercest battles in World War II.

Chapter Thirty-six

February 21, 1944. It's the anniversary of the dedication of the Washington Monument. Harilal, drunk, has to be escorted from his mother's deathbed on the Feralia, the Feast of the Dead, the All-Soul's Day in Roman antiquity. She died the following day, the Caristia, the anniversary of George Washington's birth. Mohandas Gandhi gravitated toward the numbers twenty-one and twenty-two all his life. January 30, 1948 (twenty-two days until the Feralia), Gandhi is assassinated. On January 31, his body is cremated (twenty-one days before the Feralia).

February 21, 1944. After facing suicidal attacks by the Japanese, U.S. forces captured Eniwetok (Enewetak) Island. Population evacuated in 1947. During the following eleven years, forty-three atomic tests were conducted, including the detonation of the first hydrogen bomb by the U.S. at Eniwetok on November 1, 1952.

November 1, 1952. It's All Saints' Day. Centuries before this, it had been held on May 13 (the day in mythology Persephone is led by Hermes from the world of the dead back to earth). Before that, it had been February 21, the ancient Feralia. All Souls' Day falls on November 2, or November 3 if the second falls on a Sunday. (See May 13.) This detonation was reported officially by President Eisenhower on February 2, 1954.

May 21, 1956 (21). It's the beginning of the Mercury period. The first airplane hydrogen bomb was dropped by the U.S. on Namu, Bikini Atoll, in the Pacific. Thirty-five years previously (May 21, 1921), Andrei Sakharov, collaborator on the first Soviet atomic and hydrogen bombs, was born in Moscow.

May 15, 1957 (22). It's the anniversary of the celebration in ancient Rome to Mercury and Maia. A British megaton-range explosion (their first and said to have been a hydrogen bomb) occurs in the area of Christmas Island (Christ, son of Mary), whose discoverer was killed on St. Valentine's Day (45) and buried at sea on February 21, 1779.

February 13, 1960. Scientists detonated France's first atomic bomb in the Sahara. France then became the fourth nuclear power.338-B It was the forty-fourth day, the Ides, the beginning of the Parentalia.

February 18, 1967. J. Robert Oppenheimer, the father of the atom bomb, died within the Parentalia. Born April 22, 1904, the anniversary of the birth of SS Major General Richard Glücks, who on February 21, 1940, told Himmler the Auschwitz barracks would soon be ready. Andrei Sakharov died on Mausoleum Day, December 14, 1989 (SY).

April 19, 1979. Newspapers revealed that Gordon Dean, the Chairman of the Atomic Energy Commission at the time of the May 27, 1953, testing, wrote in his diary that President Eisenhower told the AEC to keep the public confused on atomic testing and fallout. Most important to remember—though peace later came—the atomic bombs were dropped in the year

'45.

April Dates and Occurrences

April	Month four, Hermes' number. April 1 to May 15 is forty-five days.
April 1	Forty-five days since Lupercalia, except in leap year.
April 1	April Fool's Day (Hermes' trickery). Believed to have had its beginning in 1564 with France's Reformed *Calendar*, which confused everybody as did Julius Caesar's Calendar changes in 46 B.C.
April 1, 1865	Union troops defeat Confederates at Five (5) Forks.
April 1, 1873	Sergei Rachmaninov born.
April 2, 1865	Petersburg taken (see page 338).
April 4, 1841	President William Henry Harrison died (see page 419).
April 4, 1846	U.S.A. and Mexican patrols clash (Book II, page 398).
April 4, 1864	*Royal Standard* hit iceberg (see page 406).
April 4, 1897	Mae Capone born (see page 350).
April 4, 19684-4.	"I have a dream" Martin Luther King, Jr., assassinated at Memphis (an abbreviation for funerary complex of Pepi I), Tennessee. Compare to 1965 Feralia death of Malcolm X.
April 5, 1732	George Washington christened.338-C
April 5, 1964	General of the Army MacArthur faded away (4-5). "Old soldiers never die." See April 19, 1951.
April 5, 1968	Rioting in U.S. following King's assassination.
April 5, 1976	The Hermetic Howard Hughes died (see page 418).

April 6, 1814	Napoleon overthrown in France.
April 6, 1841	John Tyler sworn in as president. "His Accidency" had fifteen children, more siblings than any other president. (See page 607, footnote 11.)
April 6, 1909	Robert E. Peary (born May 6, 1856) generally thought of being first to reach North Pole.
April 6, 1917	(SY). U.S. declared war on Germany. War not declared on Austria-Hungary until *December 7*, 1917.
April 8, 1513	Ponce de Leon landed in Florida.
April 9, 1626	Sir Francis Bacon died. Statesman, writer, scientist. Born January 22, 1561, the youngest of eight children.
April 9, 1747	The last person to be beheaded in England was Simon, Lord Lovat.
April 9, 1865	Lee surrendered at Appomattox (pages 338-339).
April 9, 1942	HMS *Hermes* sunk by Japanese dive bombers.
April 10, 1585	Pope Gregory XIII died. Under him, the Gregorian calendar.
April 10, 1865	George Duren died (page 338).
April 10, 1870	Lenin born (Julian calendar) (page 466). Under Lenin Soviet calendar adjusted to Gregorian by making February 1 into February 14, 1918 (St. Valentine's Day).
April 10, 1912	*Titanic* began maiden voyage (page 405).
April 10, 1963	U.S. nuclear submarine *Thresher* with 129 aboard is lost about two hundred miles off New England coast.
April 11, 1989	(SY). Mutilated bodies found at Matamoros (page 398).
April 12, 1861	First shots fired at Fort Sumter, the Federal fort on an island off Charleston, South Carolina, shouldn't have surprised the Union too much. In an ordinance of December 20, 1860—widely circulated in the Charleston *Mercury* at the time—South Carolina declared the Union dissolved. Mercury 4.
April 12, 1865	Lee's men lay down arms (pages 338-339).
April 12, 1981	Joe Louis died.
April 13, 1743	(New Style). Thomas Jefferson born.
April 13, 1992	Water floods heart of Chicago (page 408-409).
April 14, 1865	Lincoln shot (pages 339-340).
April 14, 1907	Francois Duvalier born. A graduate of the Haiti School of Medicine, he later became a member of Le Groupe des Griots, who espoused voodoo and black nationalism in Haitian culture. In keeping with

voodoo 21 (3 x 7), the two most important dates in his life were multiples of 7: his birth *April 14* and his death *April 21* (1971). Moreover, his regime lasted for fourteen years. See May 21, 1968.

April 14, 1912	*Titanic* hit iceberg (page 405).
April 14, 1944	Freighter *Fort Stikene* carrying munitions exploded in Bombay, killing eight hundred ashore.
April 14, 1994	Two U.S. Army Black Hawk helicopters were mistakenly shot down by two U.S. Air Force F-15C warplanes. Twenty-six U.N. representatives died, including fifteen Americans.
April 15 (4.5)	The witches' radius recurs as the Federal Income Tax deadline for filing income-tax returns. When April 15 occurs on a Saturday or Sunday, the deadline is extended.
April 15, 1452	Birth of Leonardo da Vinci (page 1).
April 15, 1741	Birth of Charles Willson Peale, who drew seven portraits of Washington from life. Washington, of course, born on February 22. Charles Willson Peale died on February 22, 1827. His son, Rembrandt Peale, who was the last to paint Washington from life, was born on February 22, 1778. Raphael Peale born February 17, 1774. *Peale.*
April 15, 1804	Thomas Keats, John Keats's father, thrown from a horse and died. In last years at Clarke Academy in London, John Keats began a translation of Virgil's *Aeneid. Shakespeare.* Ea in Assyro-Babl. mythology was a giver of arts and sciences. According to one story, he was the creator of mankind. Eden (Eaden?).
April 15, 1811	Siamese twins born in Bangesau, Siam. They were joined at the waist and brought to Boston, Massachusetts in 1829. They were exhibited in the U.S. and Europe. Each married and had children. (Op. cit. Kane.)
April 15, 1850	San Francisco incorporated as a city.
April 15, 1861	Lincoln called out Union troops. In a Proclamation, Lincoln asked states for a militia of seventy-five thousand men to put down the rebellion. To complete the line of 9 (4.5 + 4.5) and in commemoration of this first action:
April 15, 1865	Abraham Lincoln died. Nine years later:
April 15, 1874	Lord Randolph Churchill married Jenny Jerome of

	Brooklyn, New York. Winston Spencer Churchill was their first child. He hated to sleep in Lincoln's room at the White House when visiting President Franklin Delano Roosevelt.
April 15, 1912	The *Titanic* sank.
April 15, 1921	In a lecture on "relativity" to members of the science faculty and students at Columbia University, Professor Albert Einstein "called time the fourth dimension."
April 15, 1945	President Franklin Delano Roosevelt, who died April 12, was buried.
April 15, 1951	General MacArthur, having been relieved by President Truman on April 11, is visited by Emperor Hirohito.
April 15, 1959	Premier Fidel Castro began an eleven-day goodwill tour of the United States.
April 15, 1961	U.S.-made planes, said to have been flown by Cuban officers, bombed three Cuban bases.
April 15, 1967	Over one hundred thousand marchers met in front of U.N. Headquarters in New York to protest the Vietnam War.
April 15, 1967	Richard Speck found guilty of murdering eight nurses.
April 15, 1986	2:00 A.M. Libyan time, U.S. planes bombed Tripoli. Included were the barracks which Colonel Quaddafi used as his home, the port said to be used for terrorist training, and military portions of the airport. The Quaddafi family doctor reportedly said that the Colonel's infant adopted daughter was killed and two sons injured.
April 15, 1990	The Hermetic Greta Garbo died.
April 16, 1867	Wilbur Wright born.
April 16, 1957	John Torrio died.
April 17, 1421	Sea broke banks at Dort, Holland. An estimated one hundred thousand drowned.
April 17, 1506	Michelangelo fled from the Pope.
April 17, 1961	Invasion of the Bay of Pigs, Cuba.
April 18, 1480	Lucretia Borgia born in Rome.
April 18, 1506	Pope Julius II, from whom Michelangelo had fled the previous day, laid the stone for the new St. Peter's Church.
April 18, 1775	Famous ride of Paul Revere, called "Hermes of the American Revolution." Father named Apollos.

April 18, 1857	Agnostic Clarence Darrow born.
April 18, 1892	Final ghost dance performed at Chief Left Hand's Oklahoma camp.
April 18, 1906	San Francisco earthquake, the most destructive of this century in the U.S. Occurred at 5:13 A.M. It's said to have lasted forty-eight seconds. Fires spread and burned until April 21, when rain soaked the ashes. The next big earthquake in the area came October 17, 1989, an earth-snake year. Marina damaged. Section of San Francisco-Oakland Bay Bridge collapsed.
April 18, 1945	Ernie Pyle killed by Japanese gunfire.
April 18, 1955	Albert Einstein died.
April 18, 1983	Car-bomb nearly demolished U.S. Embassy in Beirut, Lebanon. Sixty-three killed, including seventeen Americans.
April 19, 1692	Bridget Bishop was supposed to have practiced witchcraft. She was the first of nineteen to be hanged.
April 19, 1721	Connected date to Boston smallpox epidemic.
April 19, 1775	Concord, Massachusetts, not far from Quincy, three Redcoats killed, eight wounded. Later writers Emerson, Hawthorne, Thoreau, and the Alcotts came to roost.
April 19, 1783	Eight years after the fighting at Lexington and Concord, Congress announced the end of the Revolutionary War.
April 19, 1824	Lord Byron, poet, died of fever at Missolonghi, Greece, where a statue now stands. Took Greeks' part against the Turks in the war.
April 19, 1847	Approximate time fourth rescue group questioned Keseberg about George Donner's money. Keseberg lied (pages 434-435).
April 19, 1861	Sixth Massachusetts Regiment attacked in Baltimore by mob supporting the South.
April 19, 1865	Body of Lincoln lies in Capitol rotunda.
April 19, 1882	Charles Darwin died. Born same day, month, and year as "honest ape."
April 19, 1892	Three million acres of land belonging to Arapaho and Cheyenne Indians opened up to thirty thousand homesteaders.
April 19, 1898	Congress adopted War Resolution recognizing Cuban Independence. President empowered to use armed force.
April 19, 1906	San Francisco fire—caused from earthquake—burns

on until twenty-first.

April 19, 1914	President Wilson asked and got authority from Congress to use armed force against Mexico's Huerta.
April 19, 1933	U.S. abandons gold standard. Price of silver goes up.
April 19, 1940	Armed Jews in Warsaw began resistance to German units preparing to liquidate ghettos. Resistance ended on May 16, 1943, after fifty thousand to sixty thousand Jews had died.
April 19, 1951	General MacArthur addressed joint session of Congress.
April 19, 1961	Castro forces win over invasion by exiles. Ninety invaders died; the rest were taken prisoners. John F. Kennedy was president. He had been born in Massachusetts on May 29, 1917.
April 19, 1967	*Surveyor 3*, a lunar probe by the U.S., made a perfect landing.
April 19, 1989	Explosion killed forty-seven aboard USS *Iowa* (see pages 616-617).
April 19, 1993	Eastern Iowa plane crash, killing all eight aboard, including South Dakota's governor.
April 19, 1993	Tanks breaking barriers in Waco, Texas, ended confrontation which began on February 28, 1993. Seventy or more perished, including children, in the fire.
April 19, 1995	Shortly after 9:00 A.M., a bomb blast ripped off the face of a nine-story Federal Building in Oklahoma City. Death toll 167. At least two hundred others injured.
April 20	Another Dies Mala or "Egyptian Day" in Middle Ages (Frewin, A., *The Book of Days*).
April 20, 1889	Born on a Dies Mala day, Adolf Hitler committed suicide on the day of Walpurgis Night, 1945.
April 21, 753 B.C.	Tradition holds that Romulus established Rome at this time. Celebration held on April 21.
April 21, 1519	Cortez landed at what is now Vera Cruz. Aztec year of 1 Reed.
April 21, 1836	Mexico defeated at Battle of San Jacinto, Texas. Texan forces commanded by Sam Houston, known earlier to Indians as the Raven.
April 21, 1898	U.S. declared a state of war existed with Spain from this date.
April 21, 1910	Mark Twain died. After the Civil War, Mark Twain had the inspiration of publishing Ulysses S. Grant's

memoirs. General Grant, needing the money badly, agreed to this. But one can only wonder, Grant being an old soldier, if Grant might have had some qualms about this since Clemens had been a deserter from the Confederate Army.

April 21, 1914	U.S. Navy had been sent to Vera Cruz. Germany had been using this port to get supplies to Huerta, the Mexican dictator. U.S. Marines captured the city this date, the anniversary of Cortez's landing. American losses: four dead, twenty wounded.
April 21, 1918	The Red Baron died. Born May 2, 1892.
April 21, 1926	Queen Elizabeth II born. Fire starting in royal chapel burns exactly *forty-five* years after she married Philip, a Greek prince. She was coronated in 1953, a snake-year. Queen Elizabeth I, the daughter of Henry VIII, was born on September 7 (MP), 1533, the snake-year Pizarro (cousin to 1-Reed Cortez of True Cross [Vera Cruz] above) ordered the strangling of the Inca leader at the square (page 612, footnote 50). Elizabeth I reigned 1558–1603, or forty-four to forty-five years. It was three hundred years after Elizabeth I's birth and the strangling at Cajamarca (marked box or coffin) and in the snake-year 1833 that John Marshall and George Watterston laid plans for financing the Washington Monument. George Washington was born in Virginia, named after the Virgin Queen, who was interested in everything to do with North America.
April 21, 1930	Fire killed 320-355 (depending on the source) at Ohio State Penitentiary.
April 21, 1962	President Kennedy opened Seattle's Century-21 Exposition by tapping a gold key at Palm Beach, Florida.
April 21, 1990	Public sees F-117A Stealth fighter for first time at Nellis Air Force Base, Nevada. Helen>Nell.
April 22, 1721	HMS *Seahorse* brought smallpox to Boston, Massachusetts. April records scanty. My belief: This date is connected to April 19, three days earlier.
April 22, 1870	Lenin born (New Style). Died January 21, 1924. Remains have been viewed by more people than those of any other person in history.
April 22, 1889	Major General Richard Glücks born at Düsseldorf. On *February 21*, 1940, he informed Himmler the barracks at Auschwitz, "a damp, marshy town," would

574

	soon be ready for quarantine.
April 25, 1792	Following experiments on dead bodies in the hospital of Bicêtre, a guillotine was set up on the Place de Grève. A *highwayman* named Nicholas Jacques Pelletier was the first to be executed. April (fourth month), robber of travelers, dead bodies, decapitation; the guillotine was named after French physician (caduceus) Joseph-Ignace Guillotin (1738–1814), who was either born on *May* 26/28 or died then, depending on the source. With the Revolution, thousands were guillotined in France, over a thousand in Guadaloupe. The most famous to be executed were Louis XVI and his wife, Marie Antoinette, both connected to the number twenty-one. (See pages 622-623). Caesar said Mercury (Hermes) was the most popular god in Gaul, and beheading was considered an honorable form of death in ancient Greece and Rome. Note change of calendar in the Revolution, as if the calendar god were displeased.
April 26, 1564	William Shakespeare, by name Swan of Avon, baptized. Died April 23, 1616. Buried April 25, 1616.
April 26, 1865	Actor-assassin John Wilkes Booth died.
April 27, 1521	(SY) Magellan killed with clubs and arrows in Philippines. Had started out on September 20 (MP), 1519, from Seville with five ships. Discovered the strait from Atlantic to Pacific on October *21*, 1520. Eighteen men and only one ship—the first to circumnavigate the world—returned to Seville on September 6 (MP), 1522.
April 27, 1791	Samuel Morse born. (Morse code, message.)
April 27, 1822	Ulysses S. Grant born.
April 27, 1937	Dedication ceremony for Golden Gate Bridge. Opening day on May 27, 1937.
April 28, 1789	Mutiny on the *Bounty*.
April 28, 1945	Italian partisans kill Mussolini.
April 28, 1967	After refusing induction into the army, boxer Muhammad Ali was stripped of his World Heavyweight Champion Title (won *February 25*, 1964, in Miami) by the New York State Athletic Commission. He was indicted by a Federal Grand Jury in Houston on May 8, 1967. The following

month on June 20, the last day of the Mercury period, he was sentenced to five years imprisonment and fined ten thousand dollars.

April 29, 1901   Emperor Hirohito of Japan born.

April 30   Walpurgis Night held in Harz (AZ) mountains in Germany on Eve of May 1 (pages 496-497). April to May: 4-5. May 1, called Beltane in Irish mythology, is sacred to Bile, god of death. He is also father of Gaelic gods and men. (Squire, Charles, *Celtic Myth and Legend, Poetry and Romance*. London: Gresham Publishing Co., 191-. If April 15 = 4.5 (the radius of the coven circle with a 9-foot diameter), then April 30 = 9, the witches' diameter; May 15 = 13.5 (the time in February the Parentalia began—don't get "techal" on me now and be a nitpicker about units); and May 30, the traditional Memorial Day = 18 or 9, or 2 x 4.5.

April 30, 1789   George Washington was inaugurated as the first president of the United States at Federal Hall on Wall Street, New York.[339] Hermes, god of commerce, gambling.

April 30, 1792   Sandwich, John Montagu, the *fourth* earl, died on the day of Walpurgis Night, the Witches' diameter, the same as Hitler in '45. (Walpurgis Night is reputed to be the time when witches' power is at its height.) Sandwich (implying cook; phonetic sand-witch, water) was British first lord of the admiralty during the American Revolution. He was a rake, a reckless gambler, and possibly treacherous, given the name "Jemmy Twitcher," after a character in John Gay's *Beggar's Opera* (a story of thieves and highwaymen; Gay's best poem: *Trivia: or, The Art of Walking the Streets of London*). Sandwich is said to have invented the sandwich to save time at the gaming table. He was Captain Cook's patron, and Cook named the Sandwich (Hawaiian) Islands after him. (Cook was butchered on St. Valentine's Day; his body parts were cooked in the Parentalia and offered in high places as a sacrifice, to be recovered in part and parts and buried at sea on the Feast of the Dead.) Cook had also discovered Christmas Island on Christmas Eve 1777 (the year John Gay's *Polly*, a sequel to *The Beggar's Opera*, was produced). Almost one hundred years later in *1888* (May 11, the second Lemuria day), Irving Berlin (a.k.a. Ren G. May and composer of

"White Christmas") was born. Also in this year, Great Britain annexed Christmas Island and John Montague Druitt, one of the Jack-the-Ripper suspects (see also *February 13*, 1849), was found floating in the Thames. He supposedly has committed suicide by weighing himself down with rocks. Prior to this he'd found the legal profession was too hard to succeed in and became a teaching assistant at a Blackheath prep school run by George Valentine. It was a letter written to Valentine which was supposed to have implicated Druitt.

Yet it's curious, April 15 seen as 4.5 and April 30, the witches' diameter; Sandwich to Walpurgis; sandwitch to water; Valentine to St. Valentine's Day; and John Montagu to John Montague. The old prep school (at No. 9 Eliot Place) no longer exists, and the "semi-detached" now in its place in a row of fine Georgian houses looks like a "rotten tooth" overlooking Blackheath. (Cullen, Tom A., *When London Walked in Terror*. Boston: Houghton Mifflin Co., 1965.)

If the evening of April 30 is Walpurgis Night, the coven circle radius is April 15 (4.5), the time of marriage of the parents of Winston Churchill, who would later be Britain's first lord of the admiralty (as Sandwich had been; Neptune, guardian of the month of February) when the *Titanic* sank at 4.5 and Prime Minister when 1) Franklin Roosevelt was buried at 4.5 and 2) Hitler committed suicide on the day of Walpurgis Night in 1945. A sandwich you say. Enjoy!

April 30, 1798	U.S. Marine Corps placed under navy jurisdiction. From the Halls of Montezuma/ to the witches' coven-tree.
April 30, 1812	Louisiana (LI or LA), home of the Mardi Gras, became the eighteenth state. 4 x 4.5 = 18.
April 30, 1888	Worst hailstorm recorded occurred at Moradabad, India. Winds, toppling houses, and hailstones killed 246.
April 30, 1923	The fifth Earl of Carnarvon, who had died in Egypt on April 5, was buried at Highclere, Berkshire, England, in an unmarked grave overlooking his castle.
April 30, 1945	Note sequence: *April 28*, 1945, Mussolini shot;

Hirohito born *April 29*, 1901; and *April 30*, 1945, Hitler committed suicide in a bunker. At the time of Mussolini's death in 1945, Hirohito was one day short of being forty-four. At the time of Hitler's death, Hirohito was one day past his forty-fourth birthday. Do not forget four-term elected Roosevelt died in April (fourth month) 1945 and was buried at 4.5, when Lincoln died, Churchill's parents had married.

April 30, 1973   Making a television statement, President Nixon accepted "responsibility" for the Watergate bugging, but he insisted he wasn't personally involved.

April 30, 1975   Saigon fell. (Some give April 30, 1967, as the date Muhammad Ali was stripped of title for refusing induction for religious reasons. Hermes, god of boxers, peace. See April 28, 1967.)

April 30, 1991   A devastating cyclone hit Bangladesh causing death to tens of thousands and misery to many more.[340] Bengali New Year, according to one book, is April 15.

May Dates and Occurrences

May   Fifth month. Maia's month. Dedicated to the Virgin Mary by the Roman Catholic Church. Senior Citizen Month. Superstitions: It's unlucky to get married in the month of May. Cats born in May bring bad luck. Little good can come from Friday, May 13. There are those who feel that May was a period of lustration to some extent in antiquity. That may be. But May today—as I suspect in ancient times—carries the duality of death and rebirth. The Celtic May Day called Beltane actually begins at moonrise on May Day Eve, or Walpurgis Night, and used to end on May Day with human sacrifice by fire. Beltane means Bel's Fire. Thus if a May spring suggests rebirth, its flowers also lend a funereal aspect to the month, which far from diminishing as it progresses, picks up at *twenty-one* with the beginning of the Mercury period—when the duality of the Gemini twins starts and carries on into the next month—and *nine* days later, the traditional Memorial Day occurs.

May 1   May Day. Celebration of spring. Thomas Morton's Maypole (page 620, footnote 121).

May 1, 1707   Great Britain came into being when England, Wales,

	and Scotland formed a union.
May 1, 1886	Serialization of Robert Louis Stevenson's *Kidnapped*, published forty-five years before the Lindbergh baby's kidnapping (See page 477), May 21, 1908, and May 21, 1927.
May 1, 1893	(SY). Chicago Exposition opens (page 609, footnote 34).
May 1, 1898	Commodore George Dewey sailed into Manila Bay on flagship *Olympia*. Compare illustrious name *Olympia* at beginning of fifth month in Spanish-American War and name *Olympic*—the record-holder for carrying troops in World War I—to that of the ill-fated *Titanic* in fourth month 1912, sinking at 4.5. But most important to remember, it was the navy's Beltane *Olympia* of the Lupercalia War which was given the honor of bringing the remains of the Unknown Soldier home from France for interment in Arlington National Cemetery, arriving at Washington Navy Yard on November 9, 1921. Sgt. Edward S. Younger (a name in contrast to the *older* ones of the Parentalia) of the Fifty-ninth Infantry and the most decorated American enlisted man in World War I, selected one of four (the number of Hermes) caskets disinterred from the cemeteries of Belleau Wood, Bony, Romagne-sous-Montfaucon, and Thiacourt. This was done at Chalons-sur-Marne, where he signified his choice by laying a spray of white roses on it. The *Olympic*, the Navy's oldest steel ship afloat, is now a national shrine at Philadelphia (Constitutional Convention May 25, 1787) as is the Liberty Bell, which cracked while being tolled during the funeral procession of Chief Justice John Marshall. See May 15, 1938.
May 1, 1931	Empire State Building, then the world's tallest, dedicated.
May 1, 1975	May Day parade celebrating the fall of Saigon the previous day of Walpurgis, the anniversary of Hitler's death.
May 1–2, 1972	J. Edgar Hoover died (page 369).
May 2, 1863	General Jackson, riding a horse, mistakenly shot by own men. He died on May 10, 1863 (page 641).
May 2, 1863	The Red Baron born. A cavalryman before becoming a flyer, he died in 1918 on April 21, which later would become the birthdate of Elizabeth II, also fond

	of horses.
May 2, 1983	Most destructive U.S. earthquake in twelve years (pages 316-317).
May 4, 1865	4-5. Lincoln buried at Springfield, Illinois. He had died at 4.5, the witches' radius. Body on display in Capitol rotunda on *April 19*. Illinois tomb now has obelisk above it, linking it to the Washington obelisk (dedicated on *February 21*, 1885; Illinois, the twenty-first state). When a youth, Lincoln was kicked unconscious by a horse. A horse's hoof is the only thing which can withstand the river Styx.

On November 7, 1876, a crime having Hermetic overtones was committed. Thieves broke into Lincoln's tomb and partly pulled the casket out of its sarcophagus. They had planned to hide it in Indiana sand dunes. Then they would demand for its return 1) $200,000 in cash and 2) the release of Benjamin Boyd, a counterfeiter, then serving time in Joliet penitentiary. Trouble was a Pinkerton detective they'd taken into their confidence notified the Secret Service. The perps received a year in prison for breaking a lock, there being no laws on the book concerning body snatching. Later the Indiana legislature rectified this. In 1901, Lincoln's body was encased in a solid block of concrete. (Kane, Joseph Nathan, *Facts about the Presidents*. New York: H.W. Wilson Co., 1974.) (See pages 492-493).

	Carnarvon died at 5-4 (4-5); Carter buried in #45.
May 4, 1929	(SY). Audrey Hepburn born (pages 465-466).
May 4, 1970	National Guardsmen fired into a crowd, killing four students during anti-war demonstration at Kent State University in Ohio. On May 11, the middle Lemuria Day, New York's Mayor John Lindsay ordered flags flown half-staff for the dead. This created a blue-collar backlash.
May 5, 1818	Karl Marx born.
May 5, 1821	(SY). Napoleon died (pages 357-358).
May 5, 1827	Andrew Johnson married Eliza McCardle. Johnson succeeded the assassinated Lincoln. Later impeachment trial.
May 5, 1862	Battle of Puebla, Mexico. Cinco de Mayo (page 614, footnote 65).
May 5, 1865	First train robbery in the U.S. occurred near North

	Bend, Ohio.
May 5, 1866	Memorial Day's beginning, by one account, at Waterloo, New York.
May 5, 1902	In April (fourth month) steaming ventholes began to appear around Mt. *Pelée*. (Pelé: bald (-headed) in French.)
	By early May, ash and sulfurous fumes began to choke the air, agitating over a hundred fer-de-lance snakes, which slithered into St. Pierre's mulatto quarters and "killed fifty people and two hundred animals" before being killed themselves by street cats. (Op. cit., Wallechinsky.)
	On May 5, lava began to flow from "bald mountain." See page 614, footnote 65.
May 5, 1925	John T. Scopes arrested for teaching theory of evolution.
May 5, 1960	Anniversary of Karl Marx's birthday. Krushchev announced U-2 airplane invaded Russian airspace to spy on May Day. Both the incident and the dates were Hermetic.[341]
May 5, 1961	Riding in the Project Mercury capsule and reaching an altitude of 115 miles in a suborbital flight, Cdr. Alan Shepard, Jr., became the first U.S. astronaut.
May 6, 1856	Sigmund Freud born.
May 6, 1864	Generals Longstreet and Jenkins, riding horses, mistakenly shot by own men in Civil War. Jenkins died a few hours later. Longstreet convalesced and returned to duty (pages 640-641).
May 6, 1884	Investment firm of Grant and Ward went bankrupt. Ulysses S. Grant was nearly broke.
May 6, 1910	King Edward died. King George V succeeded (page 404).
May 6, 1937	*Hindenberg* crashed in flames, a "funeral pyre" as one writer put it (page 638, footnote 142).
May 6, 1994	$15 billion channel tunnel, the "Chunnel" from Folkstone, England, to Calaise, France, formally inaugurated by Queen Elizabeth and President of France. *Crossroads*.
May 7, 1915	Cunard liner *Lusitania* sunk by German submarine U20.
May 7, 1945	Germany surrendered (page 375).
May 7, 1954	Dien Bien Phu fell (page 423).
May 8, 1846	Battle of Palo Alto. May and Walker (page 398).
May 8, 1884	Harry S. Truman born. A walker. Underdog who

came from behind to win 1948 election (page 607, footnote 11).

May 8, 1902	On the eve of the first Lemuria Day, Mt. Pelée erupted. Next eruption: snake-year 1929.
May 8, 1963	Buddha's 2527th anniversary. Nine killed in Buddhist protest of South Vietnam (page 422).
May 9, 1800	John Brown, abolitionist, born. After the Civil War broke out, Northern troops and civilians sang, "John Brown's body lies a-mouldering in the grave," which is Hermetic. May 9 is the first Lemuria Day.
May 9, 1846	Battle of Resaca de la Palma. Shallow, snake-like ravine. "Serpentine" ponds. Sam Grant (pages 398-399).
May 9, 1857	(SY). Meerut, India. Eighty-five sepoys became *prisoners* when they refused to bite open Enfield-rifle cartridges greased with tallow made from beef and pork. Religious beliefs prevented Hindu sepoys from eating beef and Muslim sepoys from eating pork. The following day they were freed in a revolt that spread through northern and central India. European men, women, and children massacred. Thousands died, mainly Indians.
May 9, 1868	First called Fullers Crossing, then lakes Crossing, Reno, Nevada, came into being on this date. See May 15, 1905.
May 9, 1873	First in series of three Lemuria days. Anton Cermak, later to become Chicago's mayor, born in Czechoslovakia. Though not liking President-elect Franklin Roosevelt, Mayor Cermak went to Miami to butter him up (cunning). A bullet meant for Roosevelt struck Cermak down on the Lupercalia 1933. He died March 6 and was buried on March 10, 1933, the day of the very respectable earthquake, causing most deaths in Long Beach, California, and damaging the *Constitution*, now the oldest ship on active duty in any navy throughout the world. Note Cermak was a boundary crosser. He came from Europe to the United States. Though wounded in Miami, he was buried in Chicago. (page 613, footnote 62.)
May 9, 1874	Howard Carter, who with Lord Carnarvon uncovered King Tut's tomb, born on the first Lemuria Day. He died on March 2, 1939, and was buried in grave number 45 in block 12 at Putney Vale Cemetery in London.

May 9, 1926	*Byrd* and Bennett are first to fly over North Pole. Plane called *Josephine Ford*. Hermes, god of flight.
May 9, 11, 13	Lemuria in ancient Rome (page 655, footnote 210).
May 10	Confederate Memorial Day observed in North and South Carolina. Some other southern states observe Confederate Memorial Day, dedicated to the memory of the Confederates who fell in the Civil War, in April or May (four or five), Hermetic months. Exceptions are Kentucky and Tennessee, which observe it on June 3 (still within the MP).
May 10, 1869	(SY). First transcontinental railroad (page 40 and 430).
May 10–11, 1927	Lindbergh made flight from San Diego to New York. Sets record (page 476).
May 10, 1994	Nelson Mandela becomes first black president of South Africa. Crossroads.
May 11, 330	Second Lemuria Day. Constantinople, the "New Rome," officially inaugurated.
May 11, 1888	Irving Berlin (Isr*ae*l Ba*l*ine) born. Ren G. *May*. Died September 22, 1989 (SY). (page 373.)
May 11, 1996	Valujët DC-9 crashes in Florida Everglades, killing 109.
May 12, 1820	Florence Nightingale born.
May 12, 1925	The day before Persephone's Day, a snake was found in Dublin, Ireland. Legend has it St. Patrick banished all snakes from Ireland.
May 12, 1975	*MAYAguëz* captured by Cambodians (page 424).
May 13	Hermes leads Persephone back to Demeter (de Vries, Ad) to earth, land of the living. Persephone (Kore)— like Hermes with the caduceus—goes between two worlds and occasionally is depicted with a snake or snakes in her hand, indicating her chthonic nature. She is sometimes referred to as the "Black One," wife of the Lord of Riches, and her diamond necklaces are as endless as the strings of moving cars at night. Considering that a total of over six hundred thousand Confederate and Union soldiers died in the Civil War, it's eerily in accord that the last battle was *Palm*ito Ranch (near the mouth of the Rio Grande where Colonel "RIP" Ford led the Confederates to victory) on May 13, equivalent to the old Feast of the Dead. Fourth Infantry Ulysses S. Grant at the Battle of Resaca de la *Palma* (May 9, 1846) with its serpentine ponds; Hermes, *palm and peace*. Note too that

May 9 and 13 are Lemuria days. The Feralia was celebrated on February 21. Pope Boniface IV in the seventh century started All Saints' Day on May 13 to replace it. Gregory II later changed the date to November 1. Thus February 21 = May 13 = November 1 (or perhaps the ancient Feralia corresponds to Allhallows Eve now). One can't help wondering if, rather than distancing itself, the Church managed to multiply the Feralia by three with the main strength still in February. Some see May 13 as "Old May Day" prior to Gregorian calendar reform. Association of two dates is interesting.

May 13, 1607	The first English settlement in America was established at what is now the national shrine at Jamestown, Virginia. Alive it was, dead it is, and yet alive. One of the leaders in founding Jamestown was Bartholomew Gosnold (ol'n gods) who had struck westward from the Azores (AZ) and on May 14, 1602, sighted what became part of Massachusetts (now southern Maine). The following day, May 15 (Mercury and Maia), he went ashore, naming it Cape Cod (fish). Here now are three days in May, and on September 16 (MP), 1620, the *MAYflower* set out from Plymouth, England with colonists who eventually landed at what became Plymouth *Rock*. It's presumed that the township of April 19 fame in the next century got its name from Gosnold's ship *Concord*, which might be viewed a synchronicity of affinity of April and May.
May 13, 1717	Maria Theresa, Habsburg ruler born. Staunch Roman Catholic. She died on November 29, 1780, before her daughter Marie Antoinette was decapitated.
May 13, 1756	Sarah Strout, a fourth generation Strout and fourth child of a second marriage, was born. Died on March 25 (tombstone, M.C. Morse: March 21), 1821, a snake-year, fittingly both for Hermes and Persephone. Married Matthew Duran who fled from Halifax for some unknown reason. Previously he had sailed with fleet commanded by *Wolfe*. (Both Wolfe and French commander Montcalm were killed in the war.)
May 13, 1846	U.S. declared war against Mexico. Ended May 30 (MP), 1848.

May 13, 1858	The first known public use of the name "Nevada" appeared in the *New York Times* (Rocha, Guy Louis, "How Nevada became 'Nevada'." *Nevada* magazine, April 1996). The state was admitted Halloween day, 1864, the last state to enter the union before Lincoln's assassination.
May 13, 1862	Robert Smalls, impressed into Confederate service, and a black crew seized the *Planter*, a Confederate gunboat, and sailed it into the hands of the Union. Born a slave on April 5, 1839, the anniversary of George Washington's christening, he died on *February 22*, 1915.
May 13, 1884	Approval of Joint Resolution of Congress concerning dedication ceremonies at Washington Monument. This was supposed to have occurred on *February 22*, 1885 but took place on *February 21*, the culmination of the anniversary of the Feast of the Dead.
May 13, 1888	William *DeWolf* Hopper—who never ate a whopper—recited Ernest L. Thayer's "Casey at the Bat." Audience rose to its feet and applauded. Thereafter, Hopper read it an estimated fifteen thousand times, since no performance was complete without him doing so. Hermes, god of orators. Hedda Hopper, the gossip columnist, was his fifth wife.
May 13, 1889	Theodore Roosevelt became Civil Service Commissioner on Persephone's Day and left his office on May 5, 1895.
May 13, 1892?	Eva Marthina Fry born. If not then, she was still Hermes in spirit (page 306-307).
May 13, 1913	Idylle Cameron born. Stella, her mother, died on May 31, 1913. (page 448) For awhile brought up by *Cora* and Dougald. Then later adopted by Alex and May.
May 13, 1914	Joe Louis (LI) born in *Lexington*, Alabama. Became heavyweight boxing champion when he knocked out James J. Braddock in eighth round on June 22, 1937, in Chicago, Illinois.[342] Sleep, unconsciousness, and death are related. May 13 = February 21.
May 13, 1917	Miracle (magic) of Fatima occurred.
May 13, 1923	Nails Morton, part owner of a *flower* shop, was kicked in the head by a horse (death symbol) at Lincoln Riding Academy and died. Persephone had been picking *flowers* when she was abducted. She was led to her mother on May 13 by Hermes, her half

brother. The Lincoln Riding Academy was at 300 North Clark Street. (Compare to 2122 North Clark Street [St. Valentine's Day Massacre] and 2221 North Clark Street [mortuary rooms where bodies were taken] and 271 Clark Street where Bobby Franks' father formerly owned a pawnshop.)

May 13, 1927   "Black Friday" points to collapse of Germany economically, a factor contributing to World War II. A dearth of Chicago social functions. For some who are superstitious, Friday, May 13, is considered an extremely unlucky day.

May 13, 1929   Charles E. Synder, former head snake keeper at Bronx Zoo, died from a rattlesnake bite. Antivenin failed to save his life.

May 13, 1929   Beginning of conference of gangster bosses in Atlantic City (page 355). See May 26, 1978.

May 13, 1931   Wednesday. Jim Jones was born in Lynn, Indiana. Before moving to California, he was a pastor in *Indianapolis*, Indiana. Nine hundred and twelve died at Jonestown. "The whole town's talk'n about the Jones boy," the song goes.[343]

May 13, 1932   Colonel Lindbergh identified the remains of his son (found May 12) which were cremated. Two days later (May 15, 1932), Jack Lynch, who had taught Lindbergh to fly, was killed, along with W.A. Clark III, when a plane crashed in foothills near *Clemenceau, Arizona*. (*February 19, 1919*, and *February 14, 1912*; name Clark brings to mind the Clark Street address relating to February 14, 1929, slaughter in Chicago and the address where Nails Morton had died on May 13, 1923; Lindbergh had flown mail service from St. Louis to Chicago; May 21, the beginning of the Mercury period, 1924, Bobby Franks was kidnapped and murdered, like Lindbergh's son in 1932; Franks' body found on May 22, a day in ancient Greece Hermae busts were mutilated; on May 21, 1927, Lindbergh became a hero by soloing across the Atlantic; May 21, 1932, would have marked five years, but this date is usurped by Amelia Earhart, a woman now who solos across the Atlantic. Then about July 2, 1937, she disappears mysteriously in flight; Bruno Hauptmann convicted of murder of Charles A. Lindbergh, Jr., on the beginning day of the Parentalia 1935; Colonel Lindbergh was in Cuba (where the Lupercalia sinking occurred in 1898) on February 13, 1928, and at or near Cuba (Florida same difference in respect to Parentalia) on February 13, 1929; on *February 14*, 1929, both he and Al Capone were in Miami, as was President-elect Herbert Hoover and Cermak, who four years later will be connected to the Miami Lupercalia of FDR, who had strong Parentalia links to Theodore Roosevelt and family.

May 13, 1940   On this day (corresponding to the old Feast of the Dead in February), Winston Churchill, whose parents married at 4.5, spoke to the House of Commons: "I have nothing to offer but blood, toil, tears, and sweat...without victory, there is no survival."

May 13, 1944   Hitler gave okay for German withdrawal from U.S.S.R.

May 13, 1948   (Some sources give May 14). Lady Kathleen Kennedy Hartington, Lord Fitzwilliam, and two crew members were killed in airplane crash. Plane had taken off from Les Bourget airport near Paris when it later hit a storm and slammed into a mountain twenty-five miles south of Valence, France. Kathleen Kennedy was born in 1920 on the Feralia Eve. Patricia Hearst born February 20, 1954.

May 13, 1960   President Eisenhower nominated Major General William C. Westmoreland to become the U.S. Military Academy's 45th superintendent.

May 13, 1965   (SY). On this day (equivalent to *February 21*, the Feast of the Dead), Israel established diplomatic relations with West Germany.

May 13, 1971   Thirteen Black Panthers are acquitted on charges of conspiracy to bomb New York police stations, department stores, railroad tracks, and the city's Board of Education Office. On May 21, two New York policemen were fatally shot in Harlem by black terrorists.

May 13, 1978   On this last Lemuria day, Pope Paul VI presided over a requiem mass for Aldo Moro. The body of the former prime minister of Italy was found stuffed in the back seat or trunk (depending on the source) of a car four days earlier on May 9, the first Lemuria day and thought to have been the day of his death.

May 13, 1981   Wednesday. Pope John Paul II shot in Vatican Square and later recovered. Shooting was fifty years after the birth of Jim Jones. Replacing the ancient Feralia, May 13 at one time had been All Saints' Day.

May 13, 1985   A police helicopter, which might have been dubbed "Persephone-the-Destroyer," reportedly dropped a powerful plastic explosive (C-4) on a "radical group" under siege in Philadelphia. The bomb and fire caused eleven deaths (including four children) and the destruction of sixty-one homes.

May 14 33 A.D.   Christ's Ascension by "common acceptance." (Frewin, A., *The Book of Days*.) It's the eve of May 15.

May 14, 1572   Pope Gregory XIII (Gregorian calendar) elected pope.

May 14, 1686   Gabriel Daniel Fahrenheit was born in Danzig. Died in the Hague on September 16 (MP), 1736. Started the use of mercury instead of alcohol in thermometers.

May 14, 1969   (SY). William Hale Thompson, Chicago's mayor, born in Boston, Massachusetts. He grew up in Chicago and died there. Capone's office in the Lexington Hotel in 1928 had a picture of "Big Bill." See May 15, 1902.

May 14, 1904   Olympic games held in U.S. for first time. Occur every four years. Five connecting rings (pages 374 and 619, footnote 109).

May 14, 1948   Israel established. It is historically the Holy Land for Christians, Jews, and Muslims.

May 14, 1965   (SY). Queen Elizabeth II dedicated a shrine in memory of President John F. Kennedy and deeded to the U.S. people an acre of ground at Runnymede, site of the signing of the Magna Carta in 1215.

May 14, 1975   *Mayagüez* recaptured by U.S. Marines (page 424).

May 15   It's the forty-fifth day since the beginning of April. Celebration in ancient Rome for Mercury and Maia. Merchandise sprinkled with water. One text[344] stated that festival of the Fontanalia (Fontinalia) was held at this time to honor the spirits of springs, streams, and fountains. If correct, there might be a connection to Neptune and/or moon (Thoth), from which some ancients believed water originated.

May 15, 495 B.C.   Dedication of temple to Mercury near Circus Maximus. Worship of Mercury thought to have been introduced from southern Italy. 495 (9 x 55) reduces to immutable 9 (See Book I, footnote 7-C).

May 15	St. Dymphna's Day. Legend is that St. Dymphna was the daughter of a seventh century Irish king. Her father wanted to marry her. To escape the incestuous marriage, she fled to Geel, Belgium, where he eventually found and *beheaded* her. She has become a patron saint of the insane, who for centuries were brought to her tomb. There some in the town looked after them. Today there's a large sanitarium for the mentally ill in Geel, and many of its patients are cared for in the homes of residents, who are paid for this. Annually on May 15, a special church service is held and a procession moves through the streets carrying a stone from St. Dymphna's tomb. At one time, a stone from her tomb was applied to patients in belief it would help them. (op. cit., Thompson, S. and Carlson, B.) Stone, cure, decapitation, tomb, *prisoner* of mind, and May 15 all suggest Hermes.
May 15, 1536	Anne Boleyn, second wife of King Henry VIII, was found guilty of charges of adultery and incest and condemned to die. Four days later, she was *beheaded*. Her life was typically Hermes. Henry VIII's determination to marry her caused the break between the Church of England and the Roman Catholic Church. But the daughter she bore Henry on September 7 (MP), 1533 (SY), became Queen Elizabeth I.
May 15, 1602	Bartholomew Gosnold (anagram: ol'n gods) went ashore, naming Cape Cod (fish). Landfall May 14, 1602.
May 15, 1814	Zachary Taylor received the regular commission of major in the twenty-sixth U.S. Infantry.
May 15, 1829	Joseph Smith, prophet of the Mormon religion, and Oliver Cowdery were ordained and baptized under the hand of a messenger called John, "the same that is called John the Baptist in the New Testament." ("The Prophet Joseph Smith's Testimony," by Corporation of the Church of Jesus Christ of the Latter-day Saints, 1984.) See page 268, footnote 25A. John the Baptist is associated with decapitation, a violent end. Joseph Smith and his brother Hyrum were imprisoned in Carthage, Illinois. While awaiting trial, they were shot and killed on June 27, 1844, by an armed mob. Brigham Young became the next leader. Under his leadership the Latter-day Saints left Illinois and journeyed to the Rocky

Mountains. Two stones in silver bows—fastened to a breastplate—make up what is called the Urim and Thummim in this religion. It's curious that the LDS Mormon Stakes today provide probably the best overall documentation of birthdates, deaths of ancestors and deceased (in effect, Parentalia information) not only in North America but many other countries as well. The statue "Mercury the teetotaler" got its name from the Street of the Temperate. (Clara Erskine Clement, *The Eternal City*, Vol. I. London: Gay and Bird, 1901.)

May 15, 1856   Lyman Frank Baum born. Wrote *The Wonderful Wizard of Oz*. Died May 6, 1919.

May 15, 1873   Dannie Cameron born. Died May 21, 1894. When body found the following year in the Parentalia, his head was missing.

May 15, 1898   Theodore Roosevelt arrived at San Antonio, Texas, to join Rough Riders. When graduating from Harvard in 1880, he ranked *twenty-one* in a class of 177.

May 15, 1902   Lyman Gilmore was the first to fly by power, some say.

May 15, 1902   Richard Daley born in Chicago. He was elected Chicago's mayor in 1955, then reelected every four years through 1975.

May 15, 1905   Las Vegas, Nevada, born. Snake-year, snake-month. Date appropriate.

May 15, 1918   U.S. operated for U.S. Post Office the world's first regular air mail service. Date appropriate.

May 15, 1920   Memorial Amphitheatre at Arlington National Cemetery was dedicated as a place of assembly for Memorial Day services. If April 15 = 4.5, then May 15 = 13.5 or the time the Parentalia began in February.
Lincoln is connected to the cemetery at Gettysburg, while Washington and Lee are connected to the Arlington National Cemetery, which is semicircular in shape, suggesting the moon, Thoth, and perhaps 4.5 and 9. The cemetery lies in Arlington County, at one time called *Alexandria* County. The first soldier to be buried there was a Confederate prisoner who died in a nearby hospital. He was buried in 1864 on May 13, Persephone's Day. In 1865, it was the last day of battle.

May 15, 1927   Commander Pinedo (Italy) set down on lake near Chicago's Grant (21 class standing) Park, Illinois, (admitted as the 21st state). Al Capone, married to Mae (born on April 4), greeted him. Later Capone associated with St. Valentine's Day Massacre at 2122. Capone's father, by the way, became an American citizen on May 25, 1906.

May 15, 1929   Chemical fumes from X-ray films caused fire and explosion in Cleveland Clinic Hospital; 124 died.

May 15, 1938   Armistice Day made a legal holiday in the District of Columbia.

May 15, 1953   (SY). Appropriate event on anniversary of ancient celebration. *Rocky* Marciano (Rocco *Francis* Marchegiano [aea]), world heavyweight boxing champion was born September 1 (MP), 1923, Brockton, Massachusetts, not too far from Quincy. In championship fight in *Chicago*, he finished off Jersey Joe Walcott in the first round. It was Marciano's *forty-fourth* victory in his professional career. He was killed in an *airplane* crash near Newton, Iowa, on August 31 (MP), 1969. This is saying very pointedly that he was still *forty-five*. A suspicion only is that 1969 might have had more than the usual significance of a non-snake year, e.g., Mary Jo Kopechne-Ted Kennedy; Ho Chi Minh died.

May 15, 1953   (SY). British explode their first thermonuclear bomb near Christmas Island. Captain Cook connected to forty-five.

May 15, 1959   Announcement of end to military war trials in Cuba by Fidel Castro. Civilian courts, henceforth, would try war criminals.

May 15   Police Memorial Day or Peace Officers Day, an annual event. It began on May 14, 1962. Thereafter, it was observed on May 15. Interesting that this day was selected since Hermes is the embodiment of the union of two opposites: life and death, cops and robbers.

May 15, 1963   Alcatraz (AZ), the Rock, closed. Former inmate Al Capone connected to the forty-fifth day of the year. San Francisco County is *forty-five* square miles. The city of San Francisco was incorporated on April 15, 1850.

May 15, 1966   Anti-war demonstrations. Hermes, persona peace. April 15 (4.5), 1967: At New York over one hundred thousand marched and assembled in front of U.N. headquarters in protest of Vietnam War.

May 15, 1969	People's Park demonstration at Berkeley. People claimed a university-owned plot about four blocks from University of California campus. National Guard called in, and police used shotguns in fighting with about two thousand demonstrators.
May 15, 1972	U.S. presidential candidate George Wallace shot. For rest of life, paralyzed from waist down. Born August 25 (MP), 1919.
May 16, 1993	Seven killed at Carrillo's Club around 2:00 A.M. in Fresno, California. Two others wounded (page 317).
May 17, 1875	Aristides (Greek name) won first Kentucky Derby, now held on the first Saturday in May at Churchill Downs, Louisville, Kentucky.
May 18, 1910	Halley's comet passed over sun.
May 18, 1980	Mt. St. Helens erupted. Thirty-six people dead; twenty-three were missing. Thousands of animals killed. Millions of trees destroyed.
May 19, 1864	Nathaniel Hawthorne died in sleep. (page 611, footnote 47.)
May 19, 1890	Ho Chi Minh born (page 423).
May 19, 1925	Malcolm X (Malcolm Little; LI), U.S. Black Muslim leader, born. In prison for burglary 1946–1952. Awarded Harlem's Mosque No. 7, a pastorate second in importance only to Chicago's. Dictated *The Autobiography of Malcolm X* to Alex Haley (pages 326-327). Assassinated in New York City on February 21, 1965 (SY).
May 19, 1928?	Pol Pot, murderous Cambodian ruler, born.
May 19, 1935	Lawrence of Arabia died. Born in Wales on August 15, *1888*.
May 19, 1994	Jacqueline Kennedy Onassis died.
May 20, 1506	Christopher Columbus died in Spain.
May 20, 1916	Frances May Duren married Frank Chichester.
May 21	Beginning of one of two Mercury periods during the year. May 21 is also one of the four days designated the Agonalia (derived from agonia, a victim). Other days are December 11, January 9, and March 17. Little is known about this other than a ram was sacrificed to someone, according to one source.[345] Another text[346] states that on May 21 a sacrifice was made to Veiovis, an Italian god whose "attributes were early forgotten." In earlier times, he was

592

identified with Apollo, then Jupiter. In a later period, he was Dis (Hades), a god of expiation and *protector of criminals who had run away*. If there is such a thing then as a genetic relationship of behavior of the gods, Hermes would seem to have carried the same gene as his uncle. On the December 11 date, furthermore, a victim was offered to each of the seven hills of Rome. (See seven as sacrifice number: pages 482-483; 3 x 7 = 21.) May 21 was one of the Rosalia days, and currently on May 21 firewalking in honor of St. Helena and St. Constantine, mother and son, occurs at the Greek village of Ayia Eleni (footnote 207). Constantine painted crosses on horses' heads and men's shields before taking Rome on October 27, 312 (page 460).

The weeping willow is given as the flower for May 21. It symbolizes sadness, mourning. It is considered a funereal tree. The number 21 figures in some voodoo rites (See voodoo, page 274.)

May 21, 1382   A great earthquake occurred in England at nine o'clock. It was especially bad in Kent, where some churches sank into the ground and collapsed. It was considered an omen for over-careless to beware. A song written at the time is quoted in *The Book of Days* (Volume 1, Chambers, R., Philadelphia: J.B. Lippincott Company, 1899). it says—among other things—that people prayed to God while it lasted.

May 21, 1471   Henry VI murdered in Tower of London. Born December 6, 1421. Became king on September 1 (MP), 1422.

May 21, 1502   Island discovered. Named St. Helena since the Feast of St. Helena occurred on this day in the Eastern Church. Napoleon would die on this island on May 5, 1821. Memorial Day's beginning, by one account, at Waterloo, New York. *Important to keep in mind*: *May 21, the first day of the Mercury period, is associated with St. Helena and Emperor Constantine, her son.* It was he—in the early fourth century A.D.—who built the first St. Peter's Basilica. If credit is given to the person who contributed most to the building of the second St. Peter's basilica, it would have to be given to Pope Julius II, who died on *February 21* (the Feralia of ancient times), 1513. Michelangelo lamented that he had spent his youth chained to a tomb. Now

	recall that tradition holds that Rome, the home of the Parentalia, was established on *April 21*, 753 B.C.
May 21, 1542	Hernando de Soto died. (Had landed in Florida on May 30, 1539.) Buried on banks or in Mississippi River itself in Louisiana, the only state bisected by the river. De Soto is credited with having discovered the Mississippi River. Louisiana was admitted to the Union on the day of Walpurgis Night.
May 21, 1688	Alexander Pope born. Typically Hermes. Son of well-to-do merchant. Probably had tuberculosis infection (Pott's disease). Had curvature of the spine and stood only four feet six inches. Brilliant mind. Translated the *Iliad* and the *Odyssey*. Died May 30, 1744.
May 21, 1780	Elizabeth Gurney Fry born at Earlham, Norfolk, England. She spent most her life improving the condition of the poor. This applied especially to women in *prison*.
May 21, 1804	Cemetery Père La Chaise opened in Paris.
May 21, 1842	(Old Style) Nikolai Gogal received first copies of Part I of *Dead Souls* from binder. (page 6.)
May 21, 1856	Four to five years before the War between the States, a civil war erupted in the Kansas Territory. The Free State Party had received arms ("Beecher Bibles") from the north. The Border Ruffians, aided by the pro-slavers, sacked Lawrence. One man was killed, and homes were looted. The Free State Hotel was burned, and two newspapers were destroyed. Brooding over this, abolitionist John Brown led his four sons and two others to killing five pro-slavery colonists. This occurred about *midnight May* 24–25 and was called the Pottawatomie massacre. In 1859 Brown with thirteen white men and five blacks captured the U.S. arsenal at Harper's Ferry, hoping that slaves would join his group and "the army of emancipation" would grow. This didn't happen. Brown was hung on December 2, 1859. His defiance, however, hastened to bring the Civil War and emancipation. He'd been born on the first Lemuria Day May 9, 1800. So it's fitting that 1) Union soldiers sang the folk song: "John Brown's body lies a-mouldering in the grave," and 2) the day of the last battle of war would be in 1865 on May 13, and third Lemuria Day, at Palmito Ranch. (Palm branch: sacred to

Hermes/Mercury, and symbol of conquest, peace.) May 13 also linked to the Feralia, the Feast of the Dead, the last day. On emancipation, some blacks took the name of plantation owners or someone they respected: Washington, Brown, etc. Whether Jim Brown's forebears had done this is unknown. However, he's regarded as "the greatest ball carrier in the history of professional football." Born in 1936 on *February 17*, he becomes another fitting into Black History Month.

May 21, 1861   Richmond, Virginia, designated the Confederate capital.

May 21, 1868   At the Republican convention in Chicago on the first day of the Mercury period, Ulysses S. Grant was nominated for president. (See page 640).

May 21, 1871   Bloody Week in Paris began (May 21–28). About seventeen thousand killed in fighting and mass executions before revolt ended.

May 21, 1874   President and Mrs. Ulysses S. Grant's only daughter, Nellie, was married in the White House. The president spent part of the morning in his room crying over the loss of his daughter. (op. cit., Mirkin, Standford M.) Grant was a man of finely tuned sensibilities. See May 13. Alice Lee Roosevelt Longworth was married in the White House in the middle of the Parentalia.

May 21, 1881   Clara Barton organized the American Red Cross (RC = 21), a branch of the International Red Cross.

May 21, 1888   The first state crematory authorized at New York.

May 21, 1894   Dannie Cameron murdered. Number suggests 2122 (dead-living). Al Capone, connected to number 2122, will pass close to Dannie's grave. Blackjack (living-dead): John Dillinger, John F. Kennedy, Frank Chichester, or dice (luck), 21 combinations.

May 21, 1908   *Dr. Jekyll and Mr. Hide*, the first horror film, was released in Chicago. Note here duality suggested by Mercury date, Gemini, and the story itself. The opening of Golden Gate Bridge was changed from May 21 (the anniversary of Dannie Cameron's death in 1894) to May 27, 1937, with perhaps disastrous results. As if to compensate for this, the opening date of the Golden Gate International Exposition at Treasure Island was on *February 18*, 1939, the anniversary of the finding of Dannie's headless body by R.W. Flint, a name like in *Treasure Island* by Stevenson who, of course, wrote *Dr. Jekyll and Mr. Hide*. See page 628.

May 21, 1917   (SY). Actor Raymond Burr, best known for role of Perry Mason (crime and punishment), born in New Westminister, British Columbia. Died September 12 (MP), 1993. He starred in the film The Amazing *World of Psychic Phenomena* (1976).

May 21, 1921   Andrei Sakharov born in Moscow, Russia. Helped to produce the first Soviet atomic bomb and following that, the hydrogen bomb. Later he became a humanitarian. Died December 14, 1989 (SY).

May 21, 1924   Bobby Franks murdered. (*M* is the thirteenth letter of the alphabet. Persephone, who had been picking flowers when abducted, was returned to earth on May 13 from the underworld where she was queen, the goddess of death. She was led by Hermes.) Bobby Franks was last seen by a friend who was examining flowers. His body was found in a culvert between two lakes on May 22 (2122), a day in ancient Greek history when there had been mutilation of Hermae busts just before the ships sailed (water). There is also the suggestion of wind. Flight-death stuffed birds of Leopold.

May 21, 1924   Guissepe Zangara filed Declaration of Intention to become a U.S. citizen. On February 15, 1933, Zangara made an assassination attempt on President Roosevelt.

May 21, 1927   Lindbergh landed near Paris. Son later murdered. Note with most Hermetic people, it's as if something is given, and then something is taken away, or vice versa.

May 21, 1932   The same can be said of Amelia Earhart who became the first woman to solo across the Atlantic (remember Hermes soloed as a messenger most of the time) and arrived at the beginning of the Mercury period. Her mysterious disappearance on or around July 2, 1937, has never been solved.

May 21, 1941   (SY). *Robin Moor* was first U.S. ship sunk by a U-boat (U is the twenty-first letter of the alphabet) in World War II. Note German submarines attacking in groups were called wolf packs.

May 21, 1951   Chinese Communists used last of rations.

May 21, 1956   The first airborne hydrogen bomb detonated by U.S. over Bikini Atoll.

May 21, 1968	Voodoo 21? Attempt by exiles to invade Haiti and overthrow government of President (snake-doctor) Francoise Duvalier is smashed. Papa Doc died *April 21, 1971*. Born April 14, 1907.
May 21, 1968	The same day that the Haiti invasion was smashed the U.S. nuclear submarine *Scorpion* with ninety-nine aboard was lost. She got underway for Mediterranean deployment on the 1968 Lupercalia. Operating with the sixth fleet into May, her last position indicated was about fifty miles south of the Azores (AZ). Scorpion at Mercury's feet.
May 21, 1972	Laszlo Toth pulled out a hammer at St. Peter's Basilica and severely damaged Michelangelo's Pietà.
May 21, 1979	Dan White, a former San Francisco supervisor, was found guilty of voluntary manslaughter in the shooting deaths on November 17, 1978, of Mayor George Moscone and Supervisor Harvey Milk. The prosecution had asked the death sentence but the defense offered psychiatric support that the murders weren't premeditated. The verdict carried a maximum prison sentence of seven years eight months. Most gays and many others felt that had Supervisor Harvey Milk not been gay, White wouldn't have gotten off so easy, that indeed if Milk had not been involved at all, White would have drawn a stiffer sentence for shooting Mayor Moscone. (Compare to the swift trial and execution of Guissepe Zangara for shooting Chicago's Mayor Cermak in 1933.) It would appear that in some process of the trial there had been a slick treachery. Rightfully enraged that life could be held so cheap for some and not others, about five thousand demonstrators protested at city hall the evening of the day of the verdict. It was the eve of the anniversary the Hermae busts had been mutilated. At least twelve police cars were set on fire, and more than one hundred forty persons were injured. A bitter irony for White perhaps was that the publicity surrounding his killing of the two officials and the inappropriateness of the sentencing probably helped the gays as a whole.
May 21, 1991	Rajiv Gandhi, a pilot, murdered by a bomb, possibly with ruse of flowers (pages 419-420). The name *India* is Greek in origin.

May 21, 1994	Local plane crash has mystical relationship (page 557).
May 21, 1996	Seven Trappist monks beheaded by Armed Islamic Group in Algeria.
May 22, 415 B.C.	Mutilation of Hermae busts in Athens on eve of departure of fleet. (page 650, footnote 181-A.)
May 22, 337	Most sources say Constantine died (a few give May 21). Also most sources say Alexander defeated Darius in the spring 334 B.C. At least one (Op. cit., Mirkin, Stanford M.) gives date as May 22.
May 22, 1802	Martha Dandridge Custis Washington died. Born June 21, 1731. 2122. She'd married George, the Mercury checker.
May 22, 1814	Lewis Keseberg of Donner Party born in Prussia.
May 22	National Maritime Day. U.S.-made steamship *Savannah* set out of transatlantic voyage (travel) on May 22, 1819. Arrived at Liverpool (LI) on June 20. Odin, chief god of Viking mariners. Odin linked to Mercury.
May 22, 1844	Lewis Keseberg immigrated to United States.
May 22, 1859	Sir Arthur Conan Doyle born. Writer, crusader for spiritualism. Died in Crowborough, Sussex, on July 7, 1930. (pages 653-654, footnote 203.)
May 22, 1861	Thornberry Baily Brown was fired upon by Confederate pickets and became the first Union soldier killed by enemy action in the Civil War. The first soldier to be buried in Arlington Cemetery was a Confederate on May 13, 1864.
May 22, 1868	Great Train Robbery at Marshfield, Indiana. Train Indianapolis bound. See May 5, 1865.
May 22, 1924	Bobby Franks's body found (page 478).
May 22, 1933	Dillinger released from *Indiana* State Prison "about forty-five miles from Chicago's loop" (page 364). He was in prison on May 21. The pendulum swings back and forth on 2122. He died on July 22, 1934 at Chicago, *Illinois*—maybe not. (See pages 368-369.) Note too that after Leopold and Loeb had kidnapped Bobby Franks, they crossed over into Indiana with the boy—then possibly dead—and back again to Illinois to dispose of his body.
May 22, 1945	Possibly time gold of Troy disappeared.
May 23, 1868	Kit Carson died (page 614, footnote 67). Like Joseph Walker, he served as a guide for Fremont.

May 23, 1994	Jacqueline Kennedy Onassis, a Roman Catholic, was buried on the Roman Rosalia. (page 649.) Died two days before May 21 and buried two days after.
May 24, 1819	*Alexandrina* Victoria born. Empire Day, Great Britain.
May 24, 1844	Telegraphic message: "What has God wrought!" Samuel Morse born April 27, 1791. Died April 2, 1872, in New York City. Artist and inventor, therefore referred to as "the American Leonardo." Curiously the fourth and fifth months also were important in the life of da Vinci, who was born on April 15, 1452, and died on May 2, 1519.
May 24, 1993	Cardinal Posadas Ocampo plus six others killed in drug shootout at Guadalajara's international airport.
May 24, 25	Festival of the Holy Maries, France. Each year thousands of gypsies travel to the Provencal village of Les Saintes-Maries-de-la-Mer. On the twenty-fourth, they worship at the shrine of Saint Sara, black-faced and uncanonized, patroness of gypsies, and Egyptian handmaid of Marie Jacobé (sister of the Virgin Mary) and Marie Salomé (mother of the Apostles James and John). Legend has it that the three were shipwrecked off the Provencal Coast. Coming ashore at or near the site of the present village, the two Maries, attended by Sara, preached, worked, and converted gypsies, whose pagan altar became the first Christian shrine in France. On the twenty-fifth, the two Maries are celebrated. On both days the sea is blessed. The annual fête ends with games: horse races and bull ring.347-A

Though Neptune was seen in the company of other gods, he was coupled especially with Mercurious in 399 B.C. lectisternium. |
| May 25 | Believed by me, at least, to be a sacred day for Mercury. Pergamum Rosalia May 24–26. Mercury, god of graveyards. (See page 268.) |
| May 25, 1787 | First regular session of Constitutional Convention at Philadelphia. (Since the market place [Hermes, god of merchants] was the place people gathered in ancient times, it was on occasion used as a place of assembly.) Dates February 21, 1787, and May 14, 1787, lead to opening date of Constitutional |

Convention and Mercury period date (September 17, 1787) ended it. Philadelphia is the home of the cracked bell (John Marshall funeral procession) and shrine of the *Olympia* (associated with May 1), which had the distinction of carrying back from France the Unknown Soldier of World War I, now at Arlington National Cemetery.

May 25, 1803	Ralph Waldo Emerson born. Died at Concord, Massachusetts, on April 27, 1882.
May 25, 1810	One of two official days surrounding Argentine Independence. (See Book I, footnote 25.)
May 25, 1845	Honolulu. First meeting of Hawaiian legislature held.
May 25, 1876	Adam Worth stole "Noble Lady," a portrait (cut off at the knees) of Georgiana Spencer, Fifth Dutchess of Devonshire, from Agnew's Gallery. Worth might have been a model for Arthur Conan Doyle's Professor Moriarty.
May 25, 1878	John Scott Harrison died. He was the son of William Henry Harrison and the father of Benjamin Harrison, both presidents born in snake-years. William Henry Harrison died after a little over a month in office. Two other presidents born in snake-years—Franklin Roosevelt, and John F. Kennedy—also died in office; i.e., three out of five died in office. Lincoln, who lacked only two days technically of being a snake, was so close that it really doesn't make any difference.
May 25, 1889	Igor Sikorski born at Kieve, Russia. Developed first successful helicopter in 1939.
May 25, 1898	Gene Tunney born, heavyweight boxing champion.
May 25, 1906	Gabriele Capone, Al's barber parent, became a U.S. citizen.[347-B] He was born in Naples, Italy, an area near which the Mercury-Maia cult was strong in antiquity. Al Capone always insisted that he himself was born in America. (See page 350 and Book II, footnote 32-B.) It's curious then that the headstone over his grave read:

QUI RIPOSA

Alphonse Capone

Nato: January 17, 1899

Morto: January 25, 1947

John Torrio, described as "the first of the gang lords"

and the last of the twenty-one shaving-mugs, had a heart attack in a barber shop in Brooklyn (the city in which Al was born), New York, and died on the same day: April 16, 1957.

Mae Coughlin Capone, Al's widow, also died on April 16 (1986).[348]

May 25, 1935   Jesse Owens set field and track records. Performance at 1936 Olympics was embarrassing to Hitler.

May 25, 1961   President John F. Kennedy said to the Congress and the American people:
"I believe that this nation should commit
itself to achieving the goal, before
this decade is out, of landing a man on
the moon and returning him safely to earth."
Thoth (Hermes) is a moon god.

May 25, 1965   MP-SY. World-champion fighter Cassius Marcellus (Roman names) Clay, Jr. (born Louisville (LI), Kentucky, January 17, 1942) knocked out Sonny Liston (LI) in first round. Compare to first round, snake-year defeat of Jersey Joe Walcott on anniversary of Mercury festival, May 15, 1953. Hermes, patron of boxers. Some thought fight "fixed" or a "fraud." If so, it was typically Hermes. Fight at Lewiston, Maine, a short distance from Lisbon Falls (Durham now part of Liston Falls?). Clay later changed name to Mohammad Ali, and that's all right too since Mohammad the Prophet said the only metal allowed in amulets was silver. See April 30, 1967.

May 25, 1979   Chicago, Illinois. American Airlines crash killed 271 persons.

May 25, 1980   Tulsa, Oklahoma. Oral Roberts saw and talked with a nine-hundred-foot Jesus Christ.

May 25, 1990   Hearing of the Senate Armed Services Committee. Results of the Sandia National Laboratories tests (conducted at behest of the General Accounting Office) showed 1) that calcium, chlorine, steel-wool fibers, cleaning fluids, and other substances could be found in the sixteen-inch-gun turrets of the *Iowa*, *New Jersey*, and *Wisconsin*, and 2) that the Navy—on urging of Sandia—had run a further test, eventually showing that friction from overram could have caused the explosion of the USS *Iowa* on April 19 (the witches' day), 1989.

May 26, 1815   John Salmon Ford was born in the Greenville District
of South Carolina. In 1836 he went to Texas. He
served two years in the Texas army. On discharge, he
settled in San Augustine, Texas, where he practiced
medicine (caduceus) and was elected to the Texas
House of Representatives. (San Augustine was
named after St. Augustine of Hippo, as was St.
Augustine, Florida, connected to the Parentalia via
February [Aviles], by being the oldest city in the U.S.
and having the *oldest national cemetery*. Florida: 13-21.
Lincoln connected to Gettysburg Cemetery, Lee to
Arlington National Cemetery via land.) Ford served
as a regimental adjutant in the Mexican War, which
began on May 13 (equivalent to the old Feast of the
Dead) and ended in 1848 on May 30, a month and
day years later to become the traditional Memorial
Day. (Memorial Day was brought about by the Civil
War.) General Santa Anna, appointed generalissimo,
and later provisional president, led a 20,000-man
army against the forces of General Taylor in the
Mexican War at the Battle of Buena Vista on
February *22 and 23*, 1847. (Remember now Santa
Anna born on the Feast of the Dead, and General
Taylor will later become the presidential peer sacri-
fice at the Washington Monument, connected to
February 21 and 22. See Book I, page 3.) Part of
Ford's job as adjutant was to write the next of kin of
those killed. He finished each report by writing
"Rest in Peace." There were so many that he eventually shortened this to "R.I.P.," from which he
acquired the nickname Rip. In 1855, Ford helped
form the Know-Nothing party in Texas. This was the
year that the Know-Nothings in Washington stole
the Washington Monument on the Feast of the Dead.
Who then would have been considered by Parentalia
forces to be better qualified and worthy to win the
last battle of the Civil War at Palmito (palm: peace)
Ranch than General Slaughter's[349] Colonel Ford on
May 13, the equivalent of the Feast of the Dead, a
time of respect? May 13 is also the third Lemuria day.
Then too because of the uncertainty, life's a gamble.
Ford was "the most inveterate gambler" and hardest
cusser.

E. Kirby Smith was born in St. Augustine, Florida, on

May 16, 1824. He surrendered his troops—the last Confederate army—on May 26, 1865, Colonel John Salmon "RIP" Ford's birthday.

A salmon is a fish living in salt water and spawning in fresh water. By definition a ford is a shallow place in a stream, river, etc., which can be walked across, therefore, a crossroads. By extension, it is a transition or change. John Salmon Ford "rip"ped away at the dead, life-death, in the Mexican War. Lincoln was assassinated at Ford Theater, life-death. Robert Ford shot the unarmed Jessie James in the back of the head on April 3, 1882. Ford Island was bombed by the Japanese on December 7, 1941, life-death, peace-war. President Kennedy was assassinated in a Lincoln built by Ford. Gerald Ford succeeded the disgraced President Nixon, linked to February 21.

May 26, 1867	Queen Mary (Princess May) born (page 412).
May 26, 1868	Andrew Johnson, who became president at 4.5 acquitted by only one vote at impeachment proceedings. It all began when he dismissed Edwin M. Stanton, the secretary of war, on *February 21*, 1868, the Feralia.
May 26, 1889	Nellie Duren White born (Book I, page 37).
May 26, 1916	USS *Nevada* joined Atlantic Fleet at Newport, Rhode Island.
May 26, 1936	Queen Mary began maiden voyage (page 413).
May 26, 1978	First day of long Memorial Day weekend. Legalized casino gambling began in Atlantic City.
May 27, 1937	Golden Gate Bridge (travel, commerce) opened (pages 624-625).
May 28, 1888	(MP). The figure 8 is one of the symbols of the Egyptian god Thoth. James *Francis Thorpe born*. Retired 1929 (SY). Died 1953 (SY).
May 28, 1984	On this Memorial Day the remains of an Unknown American Serviceman of Vietnam War was entombed beside Unknowns of World War I and II and Korean War.
May 29, 1453	Constantinople captured by Turks. Some historians list this as the closing of the Middle Ages.
May 29, 1917	(MP-SY.) John F. Kennedy born (page 648) in Brookline, Massachusetts, not far from Quincy.

May 29, 1953	(MP-SY.) Sir Edmund Hillary, a New Zealander, and Tenzing Norkay, a Sherpa guide, became first to reach the summit of Mt. Everest, the highest recorded point in the world.
May 30, 1431	Joan of Arc burned at stake. See February 21, 1431.
May 30	Traditional Memorial Day is nine (necromancy number) days following May 21. May 30th first celebrated as Declaration or Memorial Day in most of U.S. in 1868.
May 30, 1806	Andrew Jackson (presidential term: 1829–1837) killed Charles Dickinson in a duel.
May 30, 1848	Rest in peace. U.S.A. war with Mexico ended (page 399). Had started May 13, 1846, Persephone's Day.
May 30, 1853	Joseph Fry born. Prospector, guide (page 305).
May 30, 1909	Benny Goodman born in Chicago. Clarinet is woodwind instrument with reed attached to mouthpiece.
May 30, 1912	Wilbur Wright, airplane pioneer, died of typhoid fever at age forty-five. It was on December 17, 1903 (December being equivalent to February), that Wilbur Wright ran along the tract at the base of Kill Devil Hill, steadying the wing of the *Flyer*, when Orville took off into the wind for a flight of twelve seconds over the sands of Kitty Hawk. Wilbur was born on April 16, 1867. Orville was born August 19, 1871, and died January 30, 1948, the same day as Mahatma Gandhi.
	(At his 1925 court martial, Billy Mitchell was found guilty of insubordination on *December 17*, thirteen years after Orville took off at the base of Kill Devil Hill. In World War I, General Pershing (whom I think is connected to *February 20, 21, and 22*) appointed Mitchell to be the aviation officer of the AEF. [See *February 21, 1922*.] Mitchell resigned from the army on *February 1*, 1926, and died on *February 19*, 1936. Being somewhat vindicated after death, Mitchell was typically Hermes: up, down, up, and so on.)
May 30, 1922	Dedication of Lincoln Memorial on the forty-fifth day following the anniversary of his death at 4.5.
May 30, 1958	Entombment of Unknown Soldiers of World War II and Korea at Arlington National Cemetery.
May 30, 1962	*Arizona* dedicated as national monument (page 484). *Twenty-one* is the difference in the number of deaths of Arizona (AZ) and Lusitania (LA).

May 31	Memorial Day (Day of Dead), Romania.
May 31, 1873	Possibly time site of Troy and treasure discovered. Compare to May 22, 1945.
May 31, 1889	Dam broke destroying Johnstown, Pennsylvania. About two thousand one hundred (estimates vary) lost their lives.
May 31, 1911	*Titanic* launched (apge 404).
May 31, 1913	Stella Cameron died (page 448).
May 31, 1918	U.S. troopship *President Lincoln* (empty) was torpedoed and sunk by U90 (2 x 45).
May 31, 1924	Leopold and Loeb confessed to murder (page 480).
May 31, 1929	Reindeer calf, described as "jet black," born in North Beverly, Massachusetts. (Frew, Andrew F.)
May 31, 1935	Earthquake demolished Indian city of Quetta. Over twenty thousand died.
May 31, 1962	*Adolf* Eichmann hung in Isra*e*l. Though *ae* may not be considered a dipthong in the word *Israel*, it's striking the dipthong means "cry out."
May 31, 1970	Death toll over fifty thousand after an earthquake in northern Peru on this date.

Book II
Notes

1.   Charlotte M. Yonge, *History of Christian Names*. London: MacMillan and Co., 1884.

2-A.   Malcolm X, *The Autobiography of Malcolm X*, as told to Alex Haley. New York: Ballantine Books, 1964. Malcolm X's daughter Qubilah Bahiyah Shabazz was four when she saw her father killed at the Audubon Ballroom. On January 12, 1995, she was arrested and indicted for plotting to hire a hit man to kill Louis Farrakhan, the Nation of Islam leader living in Chicago, who Malcolm X's family believes had a hand in the 1965 assassination.

2-B.   "As Maine goes, so goes the nation" was adapted in 1888 by the Republican Party as a political slogan following the election of Benjamin Harrison. (Gorton Carruth, *The Encyclopedia of American Facts and Dates*. New York: Harper & Row, 1987).

3.   Song: "I'm a Ding Dong Daddy (from Dumas)" by Phil Baxter.

4.   The name "Duran" is possibly derived from a small place in the county of Caithness, Scotland, called Duran, which is pronounced locally as "Dee-ran." "Has the thought struck you," the genealogist asked, "that the name Duran (d) might be French? Way back families with the name Durand fled France, these were the Huegenots, and went to England, Scotland, and Ireland where they settled. In some cases, the Durand name was shortened to Duran. I have books on Irish genealogy where the name is listed."

5.   Everett S. Stackpole, *History of Durham*. Lewiston: Lewiston Journal, 1899. C.E. Fisher and S.G. Fisher, *Soldiers, Sailors, and Patriots of the American Revolutionary War Maine*. Louisville: The National Society of the American Revolution, D-3: 96: CL-53.

6.   Actually it didn't go by the name of Durham at that time. By petition to the Commonwealth of Massachusetts, a plantation called Royalsborough (named after General Isaac Royall) was incorporated into a town called Durham. This passed the House of Representatives on February 16, 1789, and the Senate, February 17, 1789—four and five days before February 21. The townsmen first petitioned to have it called Sharon or Bristol, but for some unknown reason decided to call it Durham at the last minute, probably after the city and county in

England, where George Washington's forebears had come from. Duran and Durham sound very close, certainly the closest name in Stackpole's book, which estimated the populated at seven hundred. Yet at forty-one, Matthew was not the town's most prominent citizen.

7.   *Gore* could mean a triangular piece of land, or in Maine and Vermont, a "minor civil division."

8.   The children of Matthew and Sarah Duran are listed in E.S. Stackpole's *History of Durham*, page 177.

9.   "Get Me to the Church on Time." Words: Alan Jay Lerner. Music: Frederick Loewe.

10.   G. for middle name or possibly initial (also 1850 census); *Henry* given for middle name of LDS records.

11.   Born 1820. Family tradition is that Margaret Tyler was related to John Tyler, a.k.a., "His Accidency" since he succeeded President William H. Harrison, a snake, who died of pneumonia after only thirty-two days in office. (page 419.) Yet at the other level, I doubt if it was an accident. Tyler's term extended into March 1845, when he signed a joint resolution of Congress annexing Texas. Remember it was the month of April (fourth month 1841) that Tyler came into office. Harry Truman (born May 8, 1884, or 5-8-1884) succeeded Franklin Delano Roosevelt who died in the month of April 1945. Roosevelt, like Harrison, was a snake.

12.   Both 1900 and 1910 censuses give his birth year as 1857. Also death certificate where the informant was his daughter Nellie I. White, who said that George Duren was his father and Margaret Tyler (maiden name) his mother.

13.   Robert E. Bell, *Dictionary of Classical Mythology*. Santa Barbara: ABC-CLIO, Inc., 1982.

14.   Op. cit., C.J.S. Thompson.

15.   A cockade is a rosette (a small rose), a ribbon, a knot of ribbon, and the like, worn on the hat as a badge or decoration. It comes from the French *cocarde* which is derived from *coq*, cock. A cock, an emblem of vigilance, is sometimes depicted on Hermes' wrists. Roses wreathed the tombs of the dead on May 21 and 23—the Rosalia as it was called in ancient times. As if to make May conspicuous by its absence, it was the only month into which the Petersburg campaign didn't extend.

16.   It was a chance that Nellie Duren White ended up with this diary, yet her father was neither the oldest nor youngest child. Why didn't it go to one of the others? Could be that the diary was given directly to Daniel by his mother or passed on to him or his daughter by one of his brothers and sisters. Norm and Nell White had three daughters. Had Marilyn or Phyllis, instead of Norma Beth, got the diary, chances are I probably never would have known that George was in the Civil War and to send off to National Archives for his records. Phyllis died in her fifties from cancer, and I didn't keep in close touch with Marilyn.

17-A.   "Peace" is given under Hermes' persona.

17-B.   Albert Pike was born in Boston on December 29, 1809, the same year as Edgar Allan Poe whose parents performed on a Boston stage, the same year as Lincoln. In his time, Pike made a name for himself as a poet, soldier, lawyer, and mason. Apparently never able to sit around long, his life was full of "tireless endeavor." His biggest problem as a soldier (he'd been sent to command a cavalry troop in the Mexican War and was a Confederate officer for awhile in the Civil War) is that he'd get angry and argue with his superiors. He died in 1891 and probably would be completely forgotten today except that he'd written some Confederate verses for Dixie. The melody itself had been played by a band at the inauguration of Jefferson Davis as President of the Confederacy on *February 18*, 1861, and became the marching tune of Confederate soldiers in the war. Thus if Washington, Lincoln, Davis, and the blacks are linked to Parentalia (more widely the month of February), Dixie is too. Note that Pike's version appeared in the Natchez, Mississippi, *Courier* on May 30 (a day later to become the traditional Memorial Day), 1861.

18.   Served in War of 1812. His first wife, Jane Davis, died in 1821. He had nine children by her and six by Martha Whitmore. *The Strout Family of Maine*, conscientiously compiled by Captain M.C. Morse, Jr., of Brunswick, Maine (and in files of the Maine Historical Society, Portland, Maine), lists those of both marriages with the exception of Martha A. Duran, born October 27, 1831. Elsy (Elsey) Duran was born probably October 13, 1824, rather than October 31, 1831. Also John Duran and Martha Whitmore got married January 21, 1823, rather than December 8, 1823.

19.   "In east Bradford," the genealogist wrote, "not too far from several Duran families lived Daniel Chase, age 68 and family. Could your Daniel have been named after a good friend and neighbor instead of carrying a family name?" That just blew my connection to the Chase-Manhattan Bank.

20.   E. Lendell Cockrum, article "Galapagos Islands," in *Encyclopedia Americana*.

21.   As in Indianapolis (as well as Chicago) where there were slaughterhouses, there was slaughter in the Galápagos Islands. Six years after Darwin visited the archipelago in 1835, Herman Melville went to the islands on the whaler (slaughter) *Acushnet*, which had stopped on its voyage to capture giant turtles. Melville will later tell of his visit there in "Las Islas Encantadas," the enchanted or *bewitched* islands.

22.   Rodney Davies, *Fortune-Telling Numbers*. Northamptonshire, Great Britain: The Aquarian Press, 1986.

24.   Its cemetery is on a small hill that faces Black Butte to the south and Cameron Butte to the northwest. Dannie Cameron: *May 15*, 1873, to *May 21*, 1894. He had been dead (head missing) four to five years when Capone was born.

25.   The Alky-pony express.

26.   John B. Staigmiller, article "Moonshine Days," *A Century in the Foothills*. Montana: Fairfield Times Pub., 1976.

27.   Moonshine in another sense—not to forget that George and Elizabeth Chichester came from areas in or around Chicago. This is, of course, before Capone was born.

28. The first month of the ancient Egyptian year (September) was named for Theuth (Thoth). James Hastings, *Encyclopaedia of Religion and Ethics*. New York: Charles Scribner's Sons, 1908.

29. John Dee (455) was Queen Elizabeth's gifted astrologer. It was his advice that was taken when to attack the Spanish Armada. His psychic powers seem to have manifested themselves in the snake year 1581. At that time he made a diary entry on *May 25* as follows: "I had sight in Chrystallo offered me and I saw." Six metal-snake cycles later was the attack on Pearl Harbor.

30. Alexander Graham Bell applied for a patent of the first phase of his telephone (*message*, communication) on February 14, 1876, the year of the Centennial. The fact February 13 is the forty-fourth day of the year is curious too.

31. Fred D. Pasley, *Al Capone: The Biography of a Self-made Man*. New York: Books for Libraries Press, 1930.

32-A. The city in Italy John Torrio was born in is not far from Naples, some say. Most records forwarded from U.S. Immigration and Naturalization Service pertaining to John Torrio, a.k.a. Frank Langley, give his birth as January 20, 1882. A few, however, say February 19 or 20. U.S. Certificate of Naturalization describes eyes as "grey." (Al Capone's are described as "ice-grey".) He lived for awhile in St. Petersburg, Florida, where he owned real estate and was "a large contributor to the American Legion Hospital for Crippled Children." He visited Havana, Cuba, about 1925 or 1926. Though he died a natural death, there were several instances of gangland slayings (one thief by another) in the 1920s barbershops. These, in my opinion, have occult overtones. Torrio's death could have been tied in with this too.

32-B. As Capone's noriety spread, some said he'd been born in Italy, insinuating by this, "Well what can you expect?" But Capone always insisted he'd been born in Brooklyn, New York. May is a derivative of Margaret, meaning pearl. Dante called the moon *"La gran Margherita."* Capone married *Mae* Coughlin. In the song titled "Give Me the Moon over Brooklyn" (Jason Matthews and Terry Shand. Copyright 1945 by London Music Corp.), the woman referred to is Mazie, another derivative of Margaret. Note: 1) moon, and 2) az and ae. Maia possibly connected to Miami, near where Capone died in Mae's presence, among others. Song titled "Moon over Miami" (words by Edgar Leslie. Music by Joe Burke, 1935 [renewed] 1963 Ahlert-Burke Corp., Los Angeles, CA). Are moons and derivatives signature brush strokes of the artist, lunacy, or both? In Al Capone's office at the Lexington Hotel in 1928 were three pictures; one of Chicago's Mayor William "Big Bill" Thompson, a second of George Washington, and third of Abraham Lincoln. Hanging next to Lincoln's picture was a facsimile of the Gettysburg Address. Op. cit., Kobler. William Hale Thompson was born in Boston, Massachusetts, May 14, 1869 (SY). He grew up in Chicago and died there on March 19, 1944.

33. Robert J. Schoenberg, *Mr. Capone*. New York: William Morrow and Co., Inc., 1992.

34. Though dedicated on October 12, 1892, to commemorate the four hundredth anniversary of the discovery of America in 1492, it didn't formally open for visitors until May 1, 1893 (21). Note both the opening month and year were snake, and *four* (400) and *five* (May). Christopher Columbus was born in Italy. I

wouldn't become aware of Al Capone's involvement in the scheme of things until November 1992 (21). This was five hundred years after Columbus discovered America.

35.   John Kobler, Capone: *The Life and World of Al*. New York: G.P. Putnam's Sons, 1971.

36.   Op. cit., Schoenberg.

37.   Lena, a derivative of Helen. This snake year my sister Helen was born and died. Indira Gandhi, John F. Kennedy, and Ferdinand Marcos born.

38.   Note it will be the Hermetic Howard Hughes who produced the movie *Scarface* in 1932. I also had been called "scarface" a couple of times. I had been a licensed barber. My father cut his sons' hair, as well as his father, sons, and friends alike as a sideline. Got to Naples twice when sailing. Have been to Florida, New York, and Atlantic City, New Jersey.

39.   Illinois, where Lincoln is buried at Springfield, was organized as a territory in 1809, the year Lincoln was born. On August 5, 1833 (SY), Chicago was incorporated as a city. Previously mentioned is the fact that 1893 was both the snake year Capone's parents came to the United States and the Columbia Exposition was held in Chicago. When the Chicago Century of Progress Exposition took place in 1933–1934, I was four and five years old.

40.   Again, the twenty-first amendment repealed this. Though most books give the period of the Parentalia from February 13 to 21, one book gives it from February 18 to 21, or the same numbers as the Prohibition amendments. Ulysses S. Grant was a legal resident of Illinois when elected the eighteenth president. But remember his class standing at West Point was 21.

41.   The numbers 21 and 22 pop up again and again in relation to Al Capone, as well as the numbers 4 and 5. The name of the Four Deuces, where twelve unsolved murders had been committed, came from its street address: 2222 Wabash Avenue. Capone would open up a second-hand furniture shop. a business alibi for himself, at 2220, a corner of the Four Deuces. $(2222 + 2220 = 4442 \div 2 = 2221.)$ The North Clark Street garage would have dimensions: 40 feet wide by 150 feet long.

42.   Hermes, four in mythology, five in astrology. Roman V might also suggest linkage to Cernunnos, Celtic god of underworld, sometimes depicted as an old man with stag's antlers.

43.   The Mafia gangsters, of course, had roots in Sicily, where Persephone was worshiped in ancient times. Some stories say Persephone was picking violets and white lilies when Hades abducted her, others that it was narcissi put there by Zeus to aid Hades. In Greece the narcissus is a bloom that is purple and silver. The timeless custom of sending flowers to a funeral or grave is in accord with Persephone picking her own flowers. May 13 is the day in mythology Hermes led Persephone back to earth. Nails Morton died on May 13, 1923. The numbers 9 and 13, as well as sometimes 21, are necromancy numbers. The number of days counting 13 through 21 is nine. May 21 to May 30 is nine.

44.   Op. cit., Schoenberg.

45.   When working, he usually had a white carnation or a sprig of *lily* of the valley in his buttonhole. Op. cit., Kobler. Apparently one of O'Banion's favorite floral pieces was a *lyre*, frequently made of lilies and some other flowers.

46.   Op. cit., Schoenberg.

47.   In early 1924, Capone made his headquarters at the *Hawthorne* Hotel or Inn. Here he established his gambling operation. Ibid. Nathaniel Hawthorne was under the Hermes sphere of influence too, a more positive side. Born in *Salem*, Massachusetts on *July 4*, 1804, four to five years before Lincoln, Hawthorne died in his sleep on *May 19*, 1864. The name *Nathaniel* is Hebrew and means "gift of God." Nathaniel in the Bible was the fourth son of Jessie, the father of David, the eighth son. Hawthorne's father was a merchant ship's captain and died when his son was four. Nathaniel traveled back and forth from Massachusetts to Maine. His mother's name was Manning. The Mannings bring to mind, of course, DiManes; DiManes, Maine. The hawthorn, of the rose family, is a spiny shrub or tree having red berries. Someone has said the crown of Christ was made of hawthorn. "Who said that? You don't know? Well anyway if that's the case, maybe we should use it in our home for protection."
So it was hung in the entrances of many homes in merry ol' England and very possibly in Puritan New England as well to guard against witches. It has been called May, May-bush, May-tree, May-bloom, and May-flower (Mayflower?). The fact that it has been designated as a noun in one case and adjectives in others opens up the possibility that it might have been a subtle form of enchantment. Maybe da witches were one step ahead.

48.   Op. cit., Schoenberg.

49.   Years later when the Lindbergh baby was kidnapped. Capone, then in jail, offered to try to get the boy back, if they'd release him temporarily from jail to make contacts. Whether successful or not, he gave his word he'd return to complete his sentence. No federal court would consider this, and Lindbergh himself said, "I wouldn't ask for Capone's release even if it would save a life." Not even for his own son? What kind of man was this? I'm not with Capone, but there's a feeling that had the situation been reversed, Capone would have asked for Lindbergh's release. Perhaps this mind-set and high-mindedness in Lindbergh was why he lost his son.

50.   The palm is sacred to Hermes. There are about 2,780 known species of the family Palmae (*Arecaceae*). *Encyclopedia Americana*, ae-ae-ae.

51.   As a gambler himself (i.e., betting on horses, etc.), Al wasn't too lucky. Nor in some respects was he lucky in love, considering his scars and the way his life ended.

52.   The number 8 occurred in his identification numbers: Atlanta Penitentiary 40886 (another source gives this as 40822). Alcatraz: 85, cell 181.

53-A.   Note here that Hermes is most often a god of harmless deception, as in games, but not always.

53-B.   It's said Capone acquired syphilis from a blond, teenage, *Greek* mistress he had salvaged from a brothel. Capone apparently was scared of a needle entering his vein for withdrawal of blood for a Wasserman test, and neglected having one, even though his doctor explained the devastation caused by syphilis.

54.   Florida's state tree is the sabal *palm*. Capone was holed up or vacationing in Florida (Spanish: flowery) during the St. Valentine's Day Mass and the Obsequies Chic days which followed. Why had Capone returned to Florida from the Bahamas on *February 12*, the Parentalia Eve? He had to keep two appointments, destiny links, in my opinion. The first of these was at 12:00 noon the following day, or exactly when the celebration began in early Roman history (Florida in some respects similar to Italy). The second—establishing an alibi—was with the Dade County Solicitor at 12:30 on *February 14*, when he will be asked, among other things, his connections with Parker Henderson when the latter was running the *Ponce de Leon* Hotel. In April (fourth month), 1513, Ponce de Leon discovered Florida, some white beach. It's believed Florida got its name for *Pascua florida*, meaning Easter season. In 1521 (SY) Ponce de Leon returned to Florida, was shot by an Indian arrow, and died shortly after. Note here the 13 and 21 in Ponce de Leon's discovery and death, but where does the 15 come in? It represents both the Lupercalia and the day Menéndez de Avilés was born in Spain on February 15, 1519. Avilés established St. Augustine, the oldest city in the United States and which also now has the oldest documented national cemetery, thereby representing heritage and the Parentalia.

On Good Friday, April 21, 1419, in the Aztec year of 1 Reed, Cortés landed in what is known today as Vera Cruz (True Cross), Mexico. The Aztecs believed at first that Cortés was their god Quetzalcóatl. Cortés played the role and Aztec leader Montezuma was "mystified in inaction" (deception). In 1521, the same snake year that Ponce de Leon died, Cortés recaptured Tenochtitlán, the Aztec capital, which had been weakened by an epidemic. (pages 281-282.) On August 29 (MP) 1533 (SY), Francisco Pizzaro (a cousin to Cortés) ordered the Inca leader strangled at the square of Cajamarca (marked coffin). Cuzco fell in November. (page 431.) A gut feeling is that there are Hermetic and Parentalia links between Avilés, Balboa, Columbus, Cortés, de Leon, Pizzaro, de Soto, and possibly other explorers. Moreover, both Lincoln and Capone are Hermetic characters related to the Parentalia.

55.   George Moran was born in 1893 (SY) and died of lung cancer in Leavenworth penitentiary on February 25, 1957.

56.   Op. cit., Schoenberg.

57.   It's said that Reinhart H. Schwimmer wasn't a gangster but was attracted to that type of personality. He'd been out of work and frequently bragged about his mob connections. Since they later found a loaded gun in his Parkway apartment, it's likely he'd crossed the line or planned to. Or perhaps he really was innocent, representing the "1" in the address 2122. In Schwimmer too a variation of 2122 occurs. Article titled "Massacre Victims' Funerals to be Held" (*Chicago Sunday Tribune*, February 17, 1929) stated Dr. R.H. Schwimmer was to be buried in Rosehill Cemetery after services Tuesday in the chapel at 2221 Lincoln Avenue.

58-A.   Hermes was the "sacrificial herald of the gods," and it was a part of any herald's duty "to assist at sacrifices." Harry Thurston Peck, *Harper's Dictionary of Classical Literature and Antiquities*. New York: American Book Co., 1896.

58-B.   A yearly average of just over 7 percent of the homicides in the U.S. occurs in February, making it the least likely month to be murdered (*The Atlantic Monthly*, February 1995).

Vladmir Ilich Lenin had been dead five years and exactly one month when I was born. He died of a final stroke on January 21 (the anniversary of the guillotine death of Louis XVI), 1924. Some believe Lenin changed the world more than any man before him. It can't be disputed, however, that his remains have been viewed by more than any other in history, and so he attained a niche for himself in the Parentalia world. Most sources give his date of birth as April 22, 1870. The address at North Clark Street was, of course, 2122. Like Capone, Lenin was a fourth child.

58-C.   If this were the case, it was more like old wine poured into new bottles or vice versa. The gruesome foundation of the Valentines' beheading (persona Hermes) replaced the flagellation by priests of many who might have felt by being beaten they were showing atonement and so were deserving of the reward of fertility. This ironically squares somehow with the Catholic doctrine today of no birth control. St. Valentine's Day became a time in legend when birds choose their mates—an ethereal bliss which priests could stomach—and chocolates, the aphrodisiacs, were sent. To date it appears the sum total of the pluses and minuses, barring that someone doesn't prove someday that voluntary whippings do increase fertility, is that dogs and goats (both associated with Mercury/Hermes) benefitted by no longer being sacrificed.

59.   Op. cit., Kobler.

60.   Ibid.

61.   Ibid.

62.   The *Constitution*, now the oldest commissioned ship afloat in any of the world's navies, distinguished herself especially in this war and is considered a very lucky ship. Designed as a forty-four gun frigate (but often carried fifty), she had a *four hundred and fifty*-man crew. She was launched in *Boston* on October 21, 1797, a snake-year. As a result of public sentiment aroused by the poem "Old Ironsides," she was in 1833 (another snake-year) rebuilt and returned to service. Oliver Wendell Holmes, who wrote the poem, was born August 29 (MP), 1809, an earth-snake year, following the snake-year of her launching. On March 10, 1933, the *Constitution* had just been towed from San Pedro to her birth at Long Beach, California, dock when the late afternoon earthquake, shaking the docks, caused her crew on land to lose control. She then crashed into the pier. Several twenty-four-pounder cannons rocked out of position and the railing on one side stove in. Lucky as usual, there was only slight damage, and none of her seamen were hurt. It was this day Mayor Cermak, who had been shot in Miami, Florida, on the Lupercalia, was buried in Chicago. Dr. Thomas W. O'Conner, mayor of East Chicago, Indiana, was killed the previous day on March 9 when his auto was struck by a train. A curiosity of Miami (see page 645, footnote 160) is the coincidence of the name to the Miami tribe which claimed territory in part of Ohio, Illinois, Michigan, and all of Indiana. One of its heroes was Chief Little Turtle, a name about as Hermetic as you can get. The *Chicago Tribune* of March 12, 1933 (two days after the earthquake), shows a picture of part of the U.S. fleet passing in review "recently" off the coast of San Pedro (next to Long Beach). Since the

picture was taken on the foremast of the USS *Arizona*, she was not, ominously, in the picture. Capone had greeted the crew of the *Santa Maria II*, an amphibious plane, after the first *Santa Maria* (take the *r* out of Maria and you have Maia), burned appropriately on a lake in Arizona (admitted St. Valentine's Day, 1912) to delay arrival in Chicago until *May 15*, 1927. This might not seem so preposterous when you stop to consider that Columbus's *Santa Maria* never made it back from the New World, having run aground and wrecked at Hispaniola early on *Christmas Day* 1492. Then on *May 21*, 1927 (six days after the landing in Chicago by the *Santa Maria II*), Lindbergh landed near Paris, one day after the anniversary of Columbus's death.

63.   Hermes can prophesy only by signs, omens, and occurrences.

64.   Lincoln was five when this four-stanza poem was written.

65.   Four (4) years previously on May 5, 1862, the army of President Benito Juárez (AZ) and General Ignacio Zaragoza (AZ) defeated the forces sent by Napoleon III in the Battle of Puebla, Mexico, now celebrated as the holiday Cinco de Mayo. On May 5, 1902 (forty years after the Battle of Puebla), a stream of lava flowed down from Mt. Pelée on the French island of Martinique, covering a sugar factory and killing twenty-five. (Justine Glass, *They Foresaw the Future: The Story of Fulfilled Prophecy.* New York: Putnam, 1969). A few days later on May 9 (the anniversary of the Battle of Palo Alto on May 8, 1846), Pelée erupted, destroying the town of St. Pierre and killing about thirty thousand. Only three survived. One was a prisoner (Hermes, god of prisoners) locked in a cell for murder. Though badly burned, he survived for three days before rescue and was later pardoned. The second was a shoemaker (footprints, sandals) who survived above ground. The third was a young girl who took refuge in a cave. (Hermes, born in a cave.) The next eruption of Mt. Pelée occurred in 1929.

66.   Capone's eyes were described as "ice-gray, ice cold." Standing five feet ten inches and weighing 225 pounds, Capone was a large, beefy man with a broad neck, who had no compunction whatsoever about killing. Having a murderous temper, he often made quick and permanent work of anyone who spoke up to him. He was a monster. Since possibly the worst yours truly has killed was a mouse in a trap—and feeling squeamish—it amazes me that Capone and I are linked someway. Maybe not though. I'd think nothing of dispatching someone magically, if possible, and because both of us knew: The amount of evil/ Never changes/ Just winks/ And rearranges. Along these lines said Will Rogers: "You can't say that civilizations don't advance, for in every war they kill you a new way."

67.   Like Lincoln, Christopher Carson (trailbreaker, walker, messenger, and guide) was born in Kentucky in 1809 (December 24), eight snake cycles exactly before another person famous in Nevada history called Howard Hughes was born on December 24, 1905. Where Carson died on *May* 23 (MP), 1868, Hughes died on *April* 5, (4-5), 1976. Carson moved across a boundary at a very early age. His greatest military success was at Adobe *Walls*, Texas, on November 25, 1864, the same year Lincoln signed Nevada into being as a state. Nevada's capital, Carson City, is named for Kit Carson. Also born in 1809 (August 9) was W.B. Trout of Alamo fame.

68.   The *uraeus* (yu-reé-us), the headdress of Egyptian gods and kings, is a symbol of sovereignty. It has a serpent or sn*ake* (h*aje*) in front of it, suggesting sacredness

and spiritualism—not the worship of the snake but rather its depth in mystery, wisdom, quick retaliation, deadliness, etc., aren't things to be trifled with and are attributes we would expect divinities or God to have.

69.   *Uraeus* illustration (*Funk and Wagnalls Dictionary*, Charles Earle Funk, ed., New York: Funk and Wagnalls, 1954) seems to show more snakes (stylized) on headdress.

70.   *Strange Stories, Amazing Facts* (The Reader's Digest Association, Inc., 1976).

71.   Ibid.

72.   Thoth was a god of judgment, and there is the syncretic Thoth-Hermes.

73.   M.E. Neely Jr. and R.G. McMurty, *The Insanity File*. Southern Illinois University, 1986.

74.   Elton Trueblood, *Abraham Lincoln*. New York: Harper & Row, 1973.

75.   Stephen B. Oates, *Abraham Lincoln*. New York: Harper & Row, 1984.

76.   *New Larousse Encyclopedia of Mythology*. New York: Putnam, 1968.

77.   James Frazer, *The Golden Bough*, Part III. New York: St. Martin's Press, 1976.

78.   Walter Burkert, *Greek Religion*. Cambridge, Massachusetts: Harvard University Press, 1985.

79.   Chariots as well as wheels (indirectly) are associated with Hermes. Ixion was chained by Hermes to a wheel that rolls eternally. Robert E. Bell, *Dictionary of Classical Mythology*. Santa Barbara: ABC-CLIO, Inc., 1982.

80.   Interestingly one of the major leaders in the campaign to oust Al Capone from Florida was Carl Fisher who, like Capone, was a sixth-grade dropout. After building the Indianapolis Speedway, Fisher moved to Florida, where he remained a lush, a womanizer, and an inveterate gambler. He opposed Capone because he feared casinos, which he would not allow in his hotels, would draw gangsters. Op. cit., Schoenberg.

81.   John Toland, *The Dillinger Days*. New York: Random House, 1963.

82.   Less than a year before, Dillinger had completed navy boot camp at Great Lakes, Illinois. He was sent for duty aboard the USS *Utah* (BB-31) where he was a fireman third class. Within a month, he began to go AWOL and got punished for doing so. On December 4, 1923, when the *Utah* arrived at Boston, he jumped ship for good and was posted as a deserter. Though using his real name on entering the service, he gave a phony address. When returning home about four months after deserting, he told relatives and friends alike that he'd been honorably discharged for medical reasons. (Jay Robert Nash, *Encyclopedia of World Crime*. Wilmette, Illinois: CrimeBooks, 1989). Now here is what seems a psychic thread, though tenuous: The *Utah* (BB-31) was authorized by an act of congress, approved May 13 (*Persephone's Day*), 1908. Later Jim Jones, born on May 13, 1931, in Lynn, Indiana, will be pastor of churches in Indianapolis, Indiana, the city

where Dillinger had been born and entered the navy. Capone was connected to Chicago's *St. Valentine's Day* massacre, occurring on the *forty-fifth* day of the year, the anniversary of the day Arizona was admitted to the union. The USS *Utah* was named, of course, after the state, the *forty-fifth* admitted, having the topaz as a state gem and being nicknamed "The Beehive State." The USS *Arizona* and the USS *Utah* were the only two ships not refloated when sunk on December 7, 1941. Both Chicago and Indianapolis are strongly Hermetic cities. If Chicago can claim Capone, Indianapolis can point to Dillinger. Dillinger had a scar over his lip. Capone, of course, was called Scarface. Where Capone had used a baseball bat to beat to death three gangsters who betrayed him, Dillinger swung a bat and played second base for the St. Martinsville team in spring 1924, shortly marrying sixteen-year-old Beryl Hovious, a fan. It was while playing baseball too that he met Edgar Singleton who was one of the umpires for the team. Singleton, married and having several children, was an ex-con with a history of thefts.

83.   Op. cit., Toland.

84.   The year 1933 was 585 years after the Great Plague in 1348. When Kandice and Clarence moved to Nevada in 1992, she sent one book: a long-forgotten copy of The Decameron, I'd bought, signed, and dated November 5, 1947. Since it was only a cheap copy, I wondered why she even bothered. The postage was more than the book was worth. Later I'd realize that it had been forty-four to forty-five years at least since the book was purchased and perhaps forty-five years exactly. There seemed to be some mystical reason for this. But what? At the time, I'd been reading about Dillinger, who in the above instance wasn't unlike Ser Ciappelletto in the first tale, deceiving the holy friar. Was it this, the plague, the fact that the title of the book brought to mind the name Cameron, or something else?

85.   Jay Robert Nash, who spent several years researching two books on Dillinger (*Dillinger: Dead or Alive?* and *The Dillinger Dossier*), calls Toland's gum incident fiction. The boy had a favorite tricycle, and he was often seen sitting next to his father on a horse-drawn wagon in the streets of Indianapolis when groceries were being delivered. When Mollie died, furthermore, Audrey and her husband gave up their place to move in with her father so that she could look after the boy. (Op. cit., *Encyclopedia of World Crime*.) Dillinger obviously had affection for his father, Audrey, and other relatives, or he wouldn't have taken foolish chances to see them, to listen to their censure, when wanted by the police and FBI.

86.   Op. cit., Toland.

87.   Ibid.

88.   Anna Sage had come from Romania fifteen years previously. Convicted of "operating a disorderly house," she hoped to use her involvement at the Biograph as a bargaining chip. Though she was given five thousand dollars of the reward money, she was, nevertheless, deported and cursed Melvin Purvis for lying to her. Later at Bucharest, she threatened "to tell the story of the Dillinger shooting." She was murdered a short time later. (Op. cit., Nash.)

89.   Op. cit., Toland.

90.   On November 22, 1963, President Kennedy rode in a Lincoln limousine made by Ford Motor Company when one of the bullets fired hit his head from behind and

exited at the upper right front. Lee H. Oswald was arrested at the Texas Theater in Dallas. Later Oswald will be killed by Jack Ruby, who lived much of his life in Chicago. Indeed he was born there the year the first Memorial Day 500 was held in Indianapolis. He was tried and sentenced to death for shooting Oswald but died of cancer before his appeal for a new trial came back. Both John F. Kennedy and Dillinger died on the twenty-second of a month, strengthening the view that twenty-two is an unlucky number. Anna Sage and Polly Hamilton were involved in the world's oldest profession. One of the reports on the Kennedy assassination and aftermath clearly states that they tried hard to prove Lee Oswald and Jack Ruby were lovers. If they could have made this link, then it would have shown that every cloud does have a silver lining. After considerable time and money were spent at taxpayers' expense, the fishing expedition proved fruitless. Neither one was a fag and probably never even knew each other. Had Oswald and Ruby been homosexuals, it would have been emphasized over and over, but since they weren't, no one wrote after their names, NOT HOMOSEXUALS. Nor did the government do this later with their spy cases, such as the Walkers of the navy, Richard Miller of the FBI, Marine guard Clayton J. Longtree at the embassy in Moscow, or Aldrich Ames of the CIA and his wife. In 1989 there was an explosion aboard the USS *Iowa*. Forty-seven men were killed. More than likely, it was accidental, which suggests some sort of negligence, since most accidents are preventable.

Here was a tragedy, providing fuel for those who saw battleships as obsolete, a wasteful expenditure. It's obvious too that whether fair or not, the captain of the *Iowa* isn't going to come out of it without some sort of censure. As a battleship CO, he was probably in line to be admiral someday, but all that vanished instantly (see page 144). Enter the investigators, hot shots sent out to tie up the affair as quickly as possible. If they come up with some answer, they have accomplished what they were sent out to do. This report can make them look good. No answers can make them look like dummies and reflect on their fitness reports. They really don't know what the cause was, but until they can fix the blame, then firing on the other battleships has ceased. By lopping off the ship's captain and one or two other officers, the navy appears to have taken corrective action. In the meantime, third-hand information (talk is cheap aboard ship) is that one or two of the men involved in the explosion might have been homosexuals. So the witch hunt begins. The witch was dealt with in Chapter Twenty-five, with just as much logic—and perhaps more—than the navy used. In the *Iowa* incident, the scapegoat was the homosexual in general, though the navy really couldn't prove its case that the two men were. Now let us assume that one or more of the investigators is homophobic and makes the quantum leap that since these men might have been gays, all gays are sick enough to commit a heinous crime, even though this is rarely the case. But this is what the investigator wants to believe and so makes his case to the others, who go along with it because they don't want to appear soft on gays. The CID, or whatever it's called nowadays, is always listening.

It makes sense in the service for any G.I. to carry life insurance. Most have government life insurance, making a relative or relatives as beneficiaries. Whether nowadays you can designate somebody other than a relative, I'm not certain. But suppose you had a friend who had done you a favor or liked as a person, and you would like to see that friend come into some money if you died, sort of as a surprise. You could hardly take out government insurance on someone of the same sex and on the same ship, so you take out insurance other than government. But if early leaks which the navy allowed were true—that the Gunner's Mate Second Class was depressed over the breakup—why would he still have continued paying on the insurance if he planned to blow them up? Or if he had paid his premiums in advance, why not change the beneficiary? Besides that, why would he have wanted to kill the others to get even? They had nothing to do with it. But if we assume this is still possible, then by using the navy's standard of reaching, it would have been just as logical for anyone—of several married men—who had been cuckolded by a shipmate to kill himself and the shipmate, while seeing the other *forty-five* shipmates as persons who might have done it to him to if they had the chance. But why not leave the government life insurance to his wife as it was? This way no one would ever guess the reason. In 1844, a large gun burst aboard the warship *Princeton* during a firing demonstration. The explosion killed the Secretary of State and the Secretary of the Navy." (National Park sign, Fort Point, San Francisco.) You don't suppose? You don't suppose that maybe, just maybe, ... The *Iowa* incident was the Dreyfus soup warmed over.

> I wish I could not tell you,
> Of these things I see.
> But it's the true world that was,
> Is, and shall be.

The *Iowa* CO at the time of the incident waited until he retired from the navy on May 4, 1990 (4-5, the anniversary of the burial of Lincoln who died at 4.5), and then spoke out saying that the navy was mainly concerned with "getting [the investigation] over with" and had relied on "unsubstantiated third-party information, unsubstantiated reports and suppositions." How like Salem 19! On May 25 (a time in ancient Rome when maybe there was a festival to Mercury), 1990, the homosexual hypothesis was made to seem even more tenuous (see date May 25, 1990) at a hearing of the senate armed services committee. Previously to this too, the FBI said that their tests did not support the navy tests. This was a surprise, really, as I'd thought if it hadn't got the same result, it would have cooked its books to conform. Based on the results of tests, however, it was a logical decision. The likelihood of the cause of these explosions was not driven home fully to the navy before this. If so, it was foolishness to make the captain a scapegoat.

91.   Note here the interplay of the two cities.

Criminals both in Illinois and Indiana ("the crossroads of America") would often commit crimes in one state and then cross over to the other, either to flee prosecution or wait until things cooled off. Frank McErlane, of the Depression era, was called by the Illinois Association for Criminal Justice "the most brutal gunman who ever pulled a trigger in Chicago." Drunk one night in a Crown Point, Indiana, bar, McErlane was challenged by an equally drunk companion to show his skill with a revolver. He took up the challenge by shooting in the head and killing a complete stranger and random victim (certainly it can be said in extenuation and mitigation there was nothing personal in it), an attorney called Thad Fancher. To escape prosecution, McErlane beat the Indiana police to the state line. He avoided extradition for one year. When finally brought to trial, he was acquitted. The prosecution's star witness couldn't make it, having been axed in the head. Op. cit., Kobler.

92.   John Toland, *The Rising Sun: The Decline and Fall of the Japanese Empire, 1936–1945*. New York: Random House, 1970.

93.   Robin Lane Fox, *Alexander the Great*. London: Allen Lane, 1973.

618

94.   It seems more than coincidence that one of my brothers was named Robert Lee. His wife, a fine woman, was named Rhoda, which is derived from the Greek word meaning "rose."

95.   Peter Green, *Alexander the Great*. New York: Praeger Publishers, Inc., 1970.

96.   Roxane is derived from a Persian word meaning "dawn of day."

97.   From Greek *sophos*, meaning wisdom and skill.

98-A.   *The New Encyclopaedia Britannica.*

98-B.   The second in the *Iliad* trio of the "Greek Bible" readers was *Alexander* Pope, who translated both the *Iliad* and the *Odyssey*. Pope never married. Therefore, like Alexander the Great, the later Sophia and Heinrich Schliemann, there were either no descendants or they would die out. With some facility, Pope could read Greek, Latin, Italian, and French. Like many Hermetic characters who are either marred somewhat physically or mentally, he suffered from a curvature of the spine and headaches (believed now to have been Pott's disease) and stood only four foot six inches. Born in London on May 21 (Agonalia, and the beginning of the Mercury period), 1688, he died May 30 (which later became Memorial Day), 1744. Benny Goodman, by the way, was born in Chicago (not too far from Indianapolis) on May 30, 1909. He learned to play the clarinet, a woodwind instrument similar to a flute and with a single reed attached to its mouthpiece, as a boy.

99.   Lynn and Gray Poole, *One Passion, Two Loves*. New York: Thomas Y. Crowell Company, 1966.

100.   Dannie Cameron born on May 15, 1873.

101.   Irving, Stone, *The Greek Treasure*. Garden City, New York: Doubleday and Company, Inc., 1975.

102.   Nearly one hundred years to the day (April 19, 1989), an explosion occurred on the USS *Iowa*.

103.   Robert L. Fish, *The Gold of Troy*. New York: Doubleday and Co., 1980.

104.   Berlin at first was divided among four powers, and the Berlin Wall was a boundary or barrier that was eventually broken.

105.   Op. cit., Fish.

106.   Barbara Salsini, *Irving Berlin*. Charlotteville, New York: Story House Corp., 1972.

107.   The word douse comes from the Greek word *deuten*, which means divine. To divine means to know or foretell the unknown.

108.   Anne Neimark, *With This Gift: The Story of Edgar Cayce*. New York: Morrow, 1978.

109.   Athlon means contest. Hermes, god of contests.

110.   Editors of Time-Life Books, *A World of Luck*. Alexandria: Time-Life Books, 1991.

111.   Brad Steiger, *Psychic City: Chicago*. Garden City, New York: Doubleday and Company, Inc., 1976.

112.   See Camerons.

113.   See Strouts.

114.   *Encyclopedia Americana.*

115.   *Webster's Third New International Dictionary*, 1971.

116.   Syd Brown, "State of Sage," *Nevada* magazine, October 1992.

117.   Both she and I attended the University of California there, though at different times.

118.   Op. cit., Thompson.

119.   The etymology of *pearl* has not been settled. *Margarite* is Greek for pearl, and *May* is a derivative.

120.   "Battleship Row" is at the east side of Ford Island. Here were the battleships *Arizona, California, Maryland, Nevada, Oklahoma, Tennessee,* and *West Virginia.* There were also the repair ship *Vestal* and the fleet oiler *Neosho.* The *Pennsylvania* was in drydock. The *Utah* (formerly BB-31) was on the other side of Ford Island. On December 6, 1941, the repair ship *Vestal* was moored alongside the *Arizona* (BB 39) at berth F-7. Seven, in my reckoning, is a sacrifice number. The state of Arizona was admitted to the union on February 14, 1912. On February 13 in ancient Rome, there was a sacrifice at the grave of Tarpeia by one of the vestals. The *Vestal* survived World War II. In harmony with the Parentalia, the *Arizona* Memorial was dedicated on *May 30*, 1962.

121.   Quincy (quin: 5) had its early beginning with Thomas Morton, who branded as a "pagan" because he celebrated May Day at Merry Mount, was run out of Massachusetts and much later died in Maine. The fourth generation Adams in America became famous when John Adams, who was born in Quincy, became the second president of the United States. His son, also born in Quincy, will become the sixth president twenty-eight years later. 6 - 2 = 4.

122.   At 7:55 A.M. the first of 353 Japanese planes hit the harbor. Notice the absence of four in these numbers. The number five is believed to be bad luck at times, and again seven is a number of sacrifice. December 7 was called Dies Mala or the "Egyptian Day" in the middle ages and was considered unlucky. (Anthony Frewin, *The Book of Days*; wood engravings by Yvonne Skargon. London: Collins, 1979). But Hermes was the most cunning of the gods, and in the end, *December 7,* 1941, proved to be an even more unlucky day for Japan than the United States. Note here the similarity between the syncretic Thoth-Hermes (TH) and Territory of Hawaii (T.H.). On May 7, 1945, Germany was beaten. Shortly after, Japan was brought to her knees, smitten by a deadly snakebite of The Declining Sun (Apollo). Revenge is sweet for both gods and men. On December 7, 1787, Delaware was the first state to ratify the constitution. On December 7, 1815, Marshal Michel Ney, whom Napoleon called "the bravest of the brave" and who "commanded the Old Guard" at the Battle of Waterloo, was executed by a firing squad in Paris.

123.   The state of Nevada was the last state signed into being by President Lincoln before his assassination in 1865. He will be shot at Ford's Theater. The battleship *Nevada* will become battleborn at Ford Island in the spirit of seventy-six years after his assassination. Besides this, there's the similarity of the number four or its multiples. In threshold symbolism, a ford is the line between two realisms such as time and eternity (*From Here to Eternity*), consciousness and unconsciousness, sleeping and waking. Life-death, peace-war? (Fords Theater, Col. John Ford at Palmito Ranch, Ford Island.) Milton called Hermes' caduceus the "opiate rod" because it could bring sleep. Lincoln had no church affiliations. Of interest is that he prayed at the bedside of a dying confederate soldier. The two said the well-known prayer together: "Now I lay me down to sleep.." (Anthony S. Mercante, *Encyclopedia of World Mythology and Legend*. New York: Facts on File, 1988.

124.   "Can it, Hermes! Show more respect, or by Jove, I'll yet toss you into Tartarus."

125.   The word *coven* is said to come from the Latin root meaning "gathering" or "assembly." Traditionally a coven consists of thirteen, but this can vary. It's more important that the members can work in harmony in a "nine" (4 + 5) circle than their actual number. The "nine" is usually understood to mean nine feet in diameter. Twelve or thirteen members fitting into this space appear "to be the upper limit," Paul Hugli observed (*Witchcraft: What is it?* Dayton: P.P.I., Publishing Pámplet Publications, 1981). Margaret Murray, the famous Egyptologist, said that a coven is made up of twelve witches and a devil who is the leader. *The Witch Cult in Western Europe* (1921). This may have been in some cases sick and/or sensitive people with a leader who believed he was a devil and acted accordingly. But equally dangerous, it seems to me, is that any person with impressive credentials who's supposed to be an authority would generalize, leaving the impression that any non-Christian deity has to be the devil. Christians saw a parallel between the twelve and thirteen members, believing it to be a mocking of Christ and his twelve disciples. Since witchcraft is pre-Christian, it may be that originally thirteen was connected to thirteen lunar months. Ironically, it was rumored that Margaret Alice Murray herself was a witch who practiced witchcraft. (J. Gordon Melton and Isotta Poggi, *Magic, Witchcraft, and Paganism in America*. New York: Garland Pub. Inc., 1992) Born on July 13, 1863, in Calcutta (named for Kali), Murray died on November 13, 1963, charming more years out of life than reasonably might have been expected. It's doubtful if anyone knows for sure if witches actually exist, other than nominally, anymore than anyone knows with 100 percent certainty that Christ ever existed. But if so, exactly as portrayed? To take this reasoning one step further, supposing neither Christ nor witches ever existed. If this be true, the so-called witchcraft followers and Christians make not-so-strange bedfellows. Apparently witchcraft didn't always represent evil (black magic) nor does it today. Most so-called neo-Pagan groups, to my understanding from reading only, condemn sacrificing and are committed to healing and doing good. The numbers 12 (4+4+4) and 13 (4+4+5 or 8+5), a gathering, mixing clay with spittle to rub on a blind man's eyes, converting water to wine, etc., seem similar. There's logic then in seeing Jesus as a good witch, a word which comes from the old English *wicca*, pertaining to a worker of witchcraft or magic (miracle). Muhammad, as far as I know, claimed no miracles. However, he did say that silver was to be the only metal used in amulets. In what might be witchful thinking (though not necessarily so), others believe that *wicca* is derived from an old English word meaning "councilor." Or perhaps another word meaning "to bend." Still a third explanation is that it comes from the root word *wise*. so in the best connotation (greatly differing from the worst), witchcraft is wisdom to

influence events. The oldest pack of Tarot cards known to exist was that used in the fifteenth century. It consisted of thirteen cards. One card was that of an astrologer. The other twelve were signs of the zodiac. A variation of 13 is 31, and Halloween (a nine-letter word) is the Eve of All Saints' Day when Christians honor their worthy dead (martyrs and saints) on the first day of the eleventh month (1 + 11 = 12). Then there's the matter of Cotton Mather, the author of 444 published works (many on witchcraft), who was born on February 12, 1663, and died on February 13, 1728. Perhaps the appearance of both 12 and 13 can be associated with his character, which was consistent only in that he was forever the suffering hero. In his 1724 diary he wrote that "some, on purpose to affront me, call their Negroes by the name of 'Cotton Mather,' so that they may, with some shadow of truth, assert crimes as committed by one of that name, which the hearers take to be me." He was certain he was damned half the time, the other half, in religious ecstasy. He advised the judges to use caution in considering "spectral evidence" in the witchcraft trials. Indeed he felt justice could best be served not by punishment but by prayer and fasting. Then later he did a complete about face and praised the judges for their action—perhaps fearful that he himself would come under suspicion if he didn't. Whatever, it's clear that gossip and pernicious witchcraft are one and the same.

My purpose here, however, is to comment on numbers and the frequency of numbers. Nine, twelve, and thirteen, along with twenty-one, bring to mind the numbers of the Parentalia, and 12 and 13, recalling the time the Nevada became waterborne, suggest a fluctuation of a pointer. Roundness is suggested by a pearl, as well as kiva, and the pit dug for the Di Manes to go between the two worlds. The *Arizona* was the only battleship to have both the letters A and Z in her name, suggesting the alpha and omega, the beginning and the end. Hermes was/is a god of graveyards. The syncretic Hermanubis, burial rites, and that's exactly what the *Arizona* from the forty-fifth day now represents, a sepulcher. Hermes was a fertility god who brought souls back to be born. The number 9 could suggest the nine-month gestation period for humans, as well as the 4:5 (4 + 5 = 9) relationship of Apollo and Hermes. It's called the "esoteric number of initiation." There's disagreement among writers and theologians concerning the witch of Endor of whom Saul inquired. Some see her as a clever fake. Others say that she is allied somehow with the devil and that the spirit she called forth was really not Samuel's but that of the devil There are many opinions. About the only thing these experts can agree on is that four deaths were predicted for the following day: Saul's and that of his three sons (Jonathan, Abinadab, and Malchishua)). And they agree that Saul's armorbearer refused to kill Saul, who fell upon his own sword as did the armorbearer. But in my opinion, they all missed the important point, the omen-stamped significance of the number 4 and/or 5.

126. Though most textbooks give 12:00 noon as the beginning time. W. Warde Fowler (*The Roman Festivals of the Period of the Republic*. New York: Macmillan and Co., 1899) states it began in the sixth hour, which would have made the time even closer. Washington was the first president, Lincoln, the sixteenth. They're considered by most to be the two greatest. Lincoln's birthday on February 12 preceded the Parentalia by one day; Washington's on the 22nd (New Style) followed it by one. John Adams of Quincy and Thomas Jefferson were signers of the Declaration of Independence on July 4, 1776. Both became presidents. Each died on July 4, 1826, the *fiftieth* anniversary of the signing. Adams outlived Jefferson by *five* hours. Remember too that though it's said in mythology Hermes was born on the fourth

day, no month was specified. So it could have been on July 4. But skipping the month and dealing only with the day and year, we have a fourth day in 1776 (21). As a child, Louis XVI of France was told to be very careful on the twenty-first day of each month. Still the precautions he took did him no good. He and Marie Antoinette were arrested on June 21, 1791. France ended royalty as an institution and became a republic on September 21, 1792. Louis the sixteenth was guillotined (decapitation and calendar associated with Hermes) on January 21, 1793. In Hindu *Vedas*, 21 is considered a lucky number. Elsewhere it's called a number of "absolute truth." It's the name of a well-known card game. If the dealer has 21 in blackjack, you're dead. Las Vegas, the gaming capital of the world where craps are shot (see Book I, footnote 24-B) and 21 are played, can be added to the AEA list. Still a further connection to the god of death and gambling is that on May 26 (the first day of the long Memorial Day weekend), 1978, legalized casino gambling began in Atlantic City, New Jersey. Derring-doer "Wild Bill" Hickok, born on May 27 (MP), 1837, in *Troy* Grove, Illinois (twenty-first state), had a life filled with close scrapes with death, including being sentenced to die by Confederates, whereupon he managed to escape. He had many notches on his gun. All his life he'd been a card player. During a poker game in Deadwood, Dakota Territory, in 1876, he was shot dead from behind by a vagrant named Jack McCall. The hand Hickok had been dealt was two pairs, aces and eights called then the "Dead Man's Hand." The aces, snake eyes? The eights, snakes? Equals $18 = 9 \; 9 \div 2 = 4.5$.

127.   The Duran family had roots in Massachusetts and Maine in the eighteenth and nineteenth centuries. A Snohomish, Washington, high-school class roster, beginning September 4, 1905, SY, shows Edith Duren, twelve; Fannie Duren, seventeen; and Nellie Duren, fifteen. Frances May (Fannie Mae) Duren married Frank Chichester on May 20, 1916, the same year the *Nevada* was commissioned. They lived in Nevada where their first child, Helen, was born and died in 1917, the year John F. Kennedy was born and Joseph P. Kennedy, his father, became employed by the Fore (phonetic four) River Shipyard at *Quincy* where the *Nevada* had been built previously. Rose and Joseph will have nine children: *four* boys and *five* girls.

Lincoln was shot at the Ford (phonetic four'd) Theater, and the Nevada will be bombed at Ford Island. Joseph P. Kennedy's son will be assassinated on November 22 (4), 1963, in a Lincoln built by Ford Motor Company. But in 1962 on April 21 (the anniversary date a state of war existed between the United States and Spain), President John F. Kennedy (vacationing at the family home in *Palm* Beach, Florida) pressed the golden key (Key, Francis Scott; Key West, southernmost city in the U.S., Spanish name for "Bone Island" [bones suggesting death]: Audubon [birds, *flying*] and Ernest Hemingway [writer]) that began the Century 21 Exposition in Seattle. This key, he said, had been used by seven presidents. Thus John F. Kennedy was closely linked to the number 2122. Both Florida and Cuba figure strongly in the Lupercalia. Lee H. Oswald, the assassinator of President John F. Kennedy (who ultimately was responsible for the failure at the Bay of Pigs when the fighting ended on April 19, an infamous day reminiscent of the USS *Iowa* and Waco, Texas), had supported the Fair Play for Cuba Committee. April 21 was also the anniversary of the founding of Rome, the death in a plane crash of the Red Baron, the birth of Queen Elizabeth II in 1926. On May 14, 1965 (SY and possibly the anniversary of Lady Kathleen Kennedy Hartington's death and that of Lord Fitzwilliam and two others in a plane crash in 1948), Queen Elizabeth deeded an acre of land at Runnymede, England (where King John signed the Magna Carta in 1215) to the American people and dedicated a shrine to the memory of President John F. Kennedy.

128-A.   LAT 20-58N, LONG 159-17W in 2600 FATHOMS.

128-B.   Rossell Hope Robbins, *The Encyclopedia of Witchcraft and Demonology*. New York: Crown Publishers Inc., 1959.

129-A.   Ola Elizabeth Winslow, *A Destroying Angel: The Conquest of Smallpox in Colonial Boston*. Boston: Houghton-Mifflin, 1974.

129-AA.   John S. Bowman (General Editor), *The World Almanac of the American West*. New York: Pharos Books, 1986. This was the second Indian chief called Left Hand. He succeeded Little Raven as the principal chief.

129-B.   Arthur M. Schlesinger (General Editor), *The Almanac of American History*. New York: Bramhall House, 1983.

129-BB.   At Massachusetts legislature. Roger Williams, born in England about 1603, was an advocate of religious and political freedom. He arrived at Nantuckett, Massachusetts, on February 5, 1631. In 1633 or 1634, he became minister of the church in Salem. Here he demanded that all churches become separate from the Church of England and stated that the royal charter for Massachusetts was invalid since the land hadn't been purchased from the Indians. He found himself in especially hot water when he added that King Charles I was an advocate of the anti-Christ, for which Williams later apologized. On April 30, 1635, more charges were brought against him. On October 9 he was convicted for his "newe and dangerous opinions" and sentenced to be banished. Before he could be sent back to England, he fled out of Massachusetts Bay Colony's jurisdiction. In 1636 Williams and a few others came to a place he called Providence and purchased land—later to be called Rhode Island—from the Narragansett Indians. It was ordered "no man should be molested for his conscience." Massachusetts remained hostile to the new colony. In 1683 Williams died. Salem, Massachusetts, where Williams aired his views which were offensive, would have its witchhunts in 1692. Had he lived there at that time, he most certainly would have been hung too. Thus he had our support on April 18, 1899.

129-C.   "The Crime of '73" occurred when a coinage act demonetized silver and made gold the sole monetary standard. To make matters worse, they had the gall to do it on February 12 (1873), the anniversary of Lincoln's birth. In annoyance again, the Territories Committee of the House of Representatives waited for Lincoln's birthday on February 12, 1896, to refuse to accept Arizona with its rich silver deposits for statehood, for it would strengthen the pro-silver forces in Congress. This was a temporary setback only. On February 14 (a difference perhaps to explain the two setbacks), 1912, Arizona was admitted. Nevada's capitol at Carson City is, of course, a *stone* structure with *Doric* columns and a *silver* dome.

On April 27, 1937, a ceremony to celebrate the dedication of the Golden Gate Bridge was held. The army sent a band and from nearby Fort Scott came two companies of soldiers who were 1) accused of ruining the bridge when they came, and 2) were captives of the spectators and speech-making dignitaries. Probably it never occurred to anyone attending that 1) the Hermetic Ulysses S. Grant had been born on the same day in 1822, a horse year; 2) he, as a lieutenant, designed a bridge at Knight's Ferry, Stanislaus county; and 3) died in 1885 on July 23, the anniversary of the ancient celebration to Neptune.

Certainly the association wasn't made that the federal government's credit during the Civil War was strengthened by the output of silver from Nevada's mines. When most dignitaries had made their speeches, Edward Stanley, a bridge worker nicknamed "Iron Horse Stanley," started to put in the rivet made from California gold, as all eyes focused on him. But damn! It wouldn't go in right. Particles splattered on nearby spectators. The head of the rivet fell off and disappeared. What remained was punched out, and it too vanished. To Stanley's embarrassment, the attempt had to be abandoned, and the bridge was completed for that day at least—which is probably all that mattered—with a steel rivet. On May 28, the great liners *Lurline* and *Santa Paula* left San Francisco Bay and were followed in by thirty-eight ships from the U.S. Navy. Among the many battleships and cruisers were the *NEVAda* (BB-36) and the *Quincy* (CA-39). From the *Lexington* (April 19, 1775), *Ranger*, and the *Saratoga* out in the Pacific flew 450 planes overhead (flight).

The Golden Gate Bridge (between San Francisco and Marin County) crosses a five-mile waterway leading from the Pacific Ocean to San Francisco. At 4,200 feet (measurement), it was then the longest suspension bridge in the world (contest) while the San Francisco-Oakland Bay Bridge, running part way through a tunnel blasted through rock at the old "Goat Island" (goat sacred to Hermes) was the longest stretch of navigable water ever bridged. As "every bridge requires a life," so a very old saying goes, a piece of derrick fell killing a man on October 21, 1936. Paint colored gold wasn't used because orange stood up better to weather and was easier to see in dense fog. But orange is almost midway in hue between red (like cinnabar) and yellow, like the sun. In preparation for the opening day, Girl and Boy Scouts planted—at both ends of the bridge—golden poppies and blue lupines, representing the state colors. But poppies are symbolic of dreams and death and *lupines are related to the underworld*. The bridge was completed on May 26, 1937, a *Wednesday*. Mrs. Frances Parrish, totally blind and led by a seeing-eye *dog*, was allowed to walk on the bridge that day. Nine days of formal festivities were planned from May 27 to June 2 to include sports events, contest (including beauty), parades with many horses (perhaps representing both Hermes and Poseidon) and pageants. But preliminary festivities actually began on May 25, the anniversary perhaps of an ancient Mercury celebration. There were two opening days for the public (travelers). The first on May 27 was for walkers; the second, May 28, for automobiles. Note the April dedication ceremony and the May opening days (4-5) and that the original opening day had been set for May 21 (*Chicago Tribune*, February 18, 1937). This was delayed to permit the arrival of naval vessels for the celebration. Still the circumstances in which this decision was sandwiched seem rather strange, as you will read later, again, Hermes, god of death and cemeteries. On May 30, a service was held on the bridge for the eleven, ten of whom lost their lives in the Parentalia during the construction. Hundreds of school children dropped a large wreath over the side, and tribute was to be made yearly thereafter honoring these dead. Monsignor William P. Sullivan said prayers and blessed the structure. On May 31, a Decoration Day Parade was held with the decorating of graves at the National Cemetery at the Presidio, from which can be seen the Golden Gate Bridge.

In 1929, the year I was born, Dr. F.H. *Red*ewill, a San Francisco urologist (caduceus), painted a picture of the bridge, which has a striking resemblance to the completed bridge. The general manager of the bridge project was James *Reed*, an echoing name from the Donner Party. The bridge has two cables, and strung down from these are suspenders, giving the impression of a lyre or harp, two instruments associated with (like the reed pipe) a wind deity. Mid-afternoon of the Pedestrian Day, a breeze began to blow. The "bridge that sings" surprised the crowd with its four harps, two from each of the bridge towers, making "unearthly" sounds. Chief Engineer Joseph Baermann Strauss (like in music) was president of the Strauss Bascule Bridge Company in *Chicago*. He'd built nearly four hundred bridges throughout the world, among which were the Arlington Memorial Bridge over the Potomac, bridges in Egypt (home of Thoth), and the bridge across the *Neva* river that led to the Czar's winter palace in Russia. Strauss, just over five feet tall, had a nervous breakdown for three months at the beginning of the construction. Tradition holds that he said the bridge would last forever. Unfortunately he didn't. On October 1, 1937 he resigned as bridge chief engineer, and within less than a year of accepting a *gold* pass from Bridge District to allow him to cross over the bridge as often as he liked free of charge, he was dead (May 18, 1938).

When the bridge was nearly finished, most of the filling in of the ground and construction of the seawall at Treasure (sudden wealth) Island (writer) was almost completed. Built of *rock* and sand and originally conceived to expand airport facilities (flight, travel, commerce), Treasure Island no doubt was connected to the bridge, a paralleling someway. But why or how? Note Alcatraz (derived from Spanish "Island of the Pelicans" [bird, flight], the "Rock" of thieves, and the likely or perhaps destined place for Chicago's Al Capone (associated with February 14) to be during most of the construction going on, lay between the Golden Gate Bridge and Treasure Island, home of the Golden Gate International Exposition in 1939. The fair commemorated the opening of the two bridges, as well as the Clipper Ship Bridge to the Far East, making Asia only a few days away.

In the Parentalia on February 16, 1932, the trial of the gate span suits opened. On February 22, 1933, the Caristia, the 201st anniversary of George Washington's birth, the day my father would die in 1958, dedication of the Veteran's Memorial building (past-present) took place in San Francisco, which was founded in 1776 (21), 2122. Four days later, the ground-breaking ceremony for the Golden Gate Bridge was held.

But February 26 was forty-four to forty-five years after my mother's birth in 1888 and the anniversary of her death four years previously.

Her mother (my maternal grandmother Annie Cameron Duren) was buried on October 21 (1912), later the month and day of the first bridge death in 1936. This was the month and day the *Constitution* (the survivor of the 1933 earthquake) was launched in 1797; the Aberfan, Wales, disaster (having mystical overtones) in 1966; and the day in 1986 President Ronald Reagan signed the "Titanic Maritime Memorial Act." Evan S. Connell, Jr. (article titled "San Francisco: The Golden Gate," *Holiday*, April 1961) spoke of San Francisco's "topaz lights" at night.

On *February 12*, 1937, memorial celebrations were held for Lincoln. On the night of the Lupercalia, *February 15* ("Fifteen men on the dead man's chest"), 1937, a *traveling* scaffold was installed at the Golden Gate Bridge. Though it operated okay the next day, a commission inspector felt it was unsafe and asked for a meeting with his superiors and Pacific Bridge representatives concerning this. It was *February 17*, the day the "Sea Devils" would begin to play at the Golden Gate theater, one in the cast being Ida *Lupino*. Shortly after 10:00 A.M. and just before the inspection was to be made, the scaffold collapsed with ten men falling to their death in the Parentalia, since the *2100* foot net fell into the bay. (But February 17

626

happened to be the anniversary of my paternal grandmother Elizabeth Mills Chichester's violent death in 1934 close to Topaz. Ralph, born on February *21*, the Feralia, would die on August *21*, 1939, when the Golden Gate International Exposition was going strong, while I, lacking three days of being ten on its opening in the Parentalia on February 18, 1939, would later visit it with Anita, my stepmother.) Later that morning of *February 17*, 1937, when the Bridge District was holding a meeting downtown to discuss the postponement from May 21 (the anniversary when my great uncle, the above Annie Cameron Duren's brother, died a violent, perhaps decapitating, death in Montana in 1894) to May 27 to allow for the arrival of one hundred and fifty naval ships from Pacific exercises, Strauss burst in on them with the news, whereupon the meeting immediately adjourned.

According to the "Table of Good and Bad Days" (Sophie Lasne and André Pascal Gualtier, *A Dictionary of Superstitions*. Englewood Cliffs, New Jersey, Prentice-Hill, Inc., 1984), February 17 is considered unlucky in a table of French origin and also a sixteenth century English table.

This makes sense since it lies in the middle of the Parentalia. (On February 17, 1979, two to three hundred thousand Chinese troops supported by artillery and aircraft invaded Vietnam. By March 15, 1979, the ides, China had withdrawn all forces.) Note. In ancient Rome, February 17 was the Festival of Quirinus (Quirinalia), god of assembly who was later identified with Romulus. However, one facet of Hermes/Mercury was that he was a god of agoras. (See February 23 concerning Terminus and Hermes.)

The changing of the date to wait for the naval vessels was in the bag even before the meeting, which was simply a formality. Still you can't help wondering had the directors not meddled with May 21, the beginning of the MP, on February 17 would the accident ever happened? Yet it wasn't this alone which tends to support my view but also the series of events that followed. Of course, nothing can be proved. The mystique is like a floater that moves back and forth in front of one's eye. A gnat which can't be ignored but which probably no one sees but that one person.

On *February 18*, 1937, seven marines (pertains to sea) were killed and twelve seriously wounded when a five-inch gun shell exploded on the USS *Wyoming* near San Clemete Island, fifty miles from *San Pedro*. (Recall the *February 21*, 1513, death of St. Peter's warring Julius II. In Alsace on *February 22*, Saint Peter's Day, snakes are driven away. Ibid.) This was the anniversary of the day Dannie Cameron's body had been found in 1895. On *February 19*, Haviside Company derrick #4 located the 2100 foot length of net a mile or so from the Gate and in five hundred feet of water.

When it was brought to the surface, a hand was sticking out. Neptune, guardian of the month of February, had yielded this second body. On shore, the search continued for the others, which were eventually found. On *February 20*, an explosion occurred at the *Walker* mine, Plumas (*plumas* Spanish for feathers; *la pluma*, the pen; Thoth, sometimes depicted with a pen in hand; Hermes, over miners; Quincy, county seat) County, high up in the Sierra at the side of the Feather River wonderland. Six lives were lost and five injured in the copper and *gold* mine owned by Anaconda (snake) Copper Co.

At dusk on the night of February 20 (the eve of the Feralia), the six bodies, in a strange funeral procession, swung high into the air over *nine* miles of suspended cable. (From article titled "Strange Aerial Funeral Held for Six Killed in California Mine Blast," by Stanley Bailey, *San Francisco Chronicle*, February 21, 1937). Also on this date, two earthquakes (Poseidon) shook Paso Robles, though no damage was reported. *February 21*, appropriately the Feralia. On *February 22*, America and San Francisco paid homage to Washington. A large parade was held in the morning. In the evening, a pageant and ball were held in the Civic Auditorium.

At the beginning of the Parentalia on *February 13*, 1939 (five days before the opening of the Golden Gate International Exposition at Treasure Island), J.M. Silvey (name suggesting silver; deceptive *cook Long* John *Silver* had leg missing [footprint]; Jim *Hawk*ins narrator in most of story; Stevenson fitting the Hermetic pattern in that he suffered from tuberculosis), committed suicide by jumping from the Golden Gate Bridge. He had been a former secretary of the San Jose Chamber of *Commerce*. The following day, *February 14*, Pope Pius XI was buried in a crypt in St. Peter's, built over a graveyard, and San Francisco began its premier festival. Compare to the Parentalia-Caristia opening-day weekend (February 20, 21, and 22) of the Panama-Pacific International Exposition of 1915 in San Francisco, named after an Italian. The discovery of San Francisco Bay was made in 1774 on All Souls Day by an exploration party of Gaspar de Portola. (Bolton, Herbert Eugene, *Anza's California Expedition*. Berkeley: 1930.)

On *February 21*, 1985, two nightgown-clad, elderly sisters were found slain in a Telegraph Hill apartment. It was believed that their deaths occurred at 10:00 P.M. on *February 20* when neighbors heard noise coming from the apartment. It was said the sisters had two things they prized in life: 1) their cats, and 2) the view of the crooked Lombard Street, the bay, and the Golden Gate Bridge. (From article titled "Telegraph Hill Murders" by Gary E. Swan, *San Francisco Chronicle*, February 22, 1985.)

On *February 22*, 1985, the car of Dr. Arthur Molinari, a dentist (Molar-nari; caduceus), was selected as the symbolic billionth, though Bridge District was certain only that the billionth car had passed over the bridge sometime in February. Still *February 22* was the Car-istia, the anniversary of George Washington's birth and my father's death.

According to an article appearing in the *San Francisco Chronicle* ("Tragic Story on the Ships That Failed," May 27, 1937), the *Rio de Janeiro* was probably the most famous ship of the Golden Gate wrecks. It hit Fort Point on *February 22*, 1901, and sank. One hundred twenty-eight perished. Her hull—at the time the article was published—hadn't been found, and the wealth of gold she carried could only be speculated. As if in a cabala, Treasure Island (remember Robert Louis Stevenson's island had its deaths) is the symbolic burial ground for the deaths (flight, speed, distance) from the bridge. The first known suicide was that of Harold B. Wobber, a forty-nine-year-old bargeman and World War I veteran, on August 7, 1937. Rather interesting in that he *traveled* to the bridgehead by bus; paid at the pedestrian turnstile, and *walked* across the bridge once with Professor Lewis Hastings (Hastings Cut-off, another name associated with the Donner Party) Naylor, whom he'd met on the bus. When they were returning from the Marin side, Mr. Wobber said without any theatrics: "This is where I get off. I'm going to jump," which he did.

In an on-going thing, there have been 971 suicides (figure from *Sacramento Bee* October 7, 1994) since the bridge was opened. It's said to account for 10 percent of the suicides yearly in San Francisco. "There's no doubt that there's some mystique to the bridge," Jerry Monge, a California Highway Patrol officer, is quoted as saying.

And poppies are symbolic of dreams and death, and lupines are related to the underworld.

Again, Poseidon over navigation and guardian of the month of February:

1) On February 28, 1849, the *California* was the first steamship to sail through the Golden Gate.

   "This day," said Oscar Winther (*Via Western Express and Stage Coach*. Stanford: Stanford University Press, 1945), marks the coming of the first Forty-niners."

2) On February 28, 1941 (SY), Treasure Island was leased from the city and county of San Francisco for conversion to a naval base. Robert Louis Bal*four* Stevenson's father, grandfather, and two uncles, by the way, had been civil engineers, specializing in lighthouse and harbor work. Shrines had been set up in seaports to Poseidon, the Equestrian, who, as previously stated, was guardian of *February, the month of purification*. The treasure in *Treasure Island* was, of course, sudden wealth (Hermes).

Elizabeth Mills Chichester born *February 4*, 1850. Died *February 17*, 1934. She and George Chichester, her husband, came from Chicago area and set up "station" at Coleville, California. Great wagons drawn by sixteen to twenty horses. George: sailor, teamster, died aboard ship or possibly in port at end of voyage.

Duncan Cameron born *February 21*, 1844 (1844 + 44 = 1888), according to two Montana newspapers). Sailor. Teamster. Experienced earthquake coming from North Dakota with family and three horses to Montana in 1889. Omnibus bill of *February 22*, 1889, enabled North Dakota, South Dakota, Montana, and Washington later to be admitted as states. Here is a suggestion of 2122.

Dannie Cameron born *May 15*, 1873. (Celebration in ancient Rome on *May 15* to Mercury and Maia. In 495 B.C., dedication on *May 15* to Mercury near Circus Maximus, a horseshoe-shaped stadium for horse and chariot racing [Hermes sometimes depicted as charioteer] and other athletic events. Poseidon, the creator of the horse in myth and over water in general—so important to the American West, also connected to Circus Maximus.) Cowboy with several horses of his own. "Killed" on *May 21* (1894), the beginning of the Mercury period, with possibly horse theft. Al Capone in early days of bootlegging will pass close to graveyard where Dannie is buried. Idylle Cameron, Dannie's niece, born on *May 13* (1913), a day in mythology when Hermes leads Persephone (Cora) back to earth. Another niece, born long after his death and at the beginning of Parentalia, will—without realizing the significance of this and what she's done—honor him by telling his story in *A Century in the Foothills*.

Margaret Tyler Duren died *February 21*, 1907 (U.S. Pension Agency, San Francisco). Related to "His Accidency." Wife of great grandfather clock. Mother-in-law of Annie Cameron Duren.

Margaret Cameron, wife of Duncan and mother of Annie and Dannie, died *February 27*, 1911. Thought to have psychic gift.

Margaret A. Cameron, daughter of horse-breaking team, born to tightly corsetted Cora (disguise as much as Trojan horse and to surprise of ranch hands) on *February 13*, 1918, the beginning day of the Feast of the Dead.

Ralph Chichester born February 21 (Feralia; Battle of Verdun began three years previously), 1919, died on August 21 (anniversary of the festival to Neptunus Equestris. See page 290, footnote 80-A). Death caused from fall from rodeo-string horse (horse associated with realm of the dead), spooked by a rattlesnake. Horse, snake, pile of rocks are persona Hermes. Water, horse, horse breaking are associations to Neptune, guardian of the month of February. Hawaii, surrounded by water and taking considerable travel to reach, was admitted to union on August 21, 1959, twenty years after Ralph died. Captain Cook, connected to Hawaii and the Parentalia, was buried at sea on the Feralia. U.S. entered World War II when Japanese planes bombed Pearl Harbor on December 7 (death anniversary of Captain Bligh, associated with Cook and Hawaiian Islands), 1941, a snake year. The second snake, representing the U.S., was President Franklin D. Roosevelt, elected to four terms. Hermes, persona peace, caused reconciliation in 1945. Charles Lindbergh—connected to May 21—died at Maui, Hawaii, on August 26 (MP), 1974.

Brent Chichester born *February 21*, 1929 (SY). In St. Valentine's Day Massacre: seven bodies, one for each day until *February 21*. Mother's death partly due to childbirth. Long Beach earthquake in 1933 like merry-go-round with horses going up and down. Broken bridle. Snorts, mustang, forever getting away and running back to ranch.

Near above brother—born ten years earlier—at time of accident and death. Attended funeral. The following year: horses and pack horse, travel, rattlesnake, wind, and range fire. Long before understanding significance, wrote, produced, and acted in one-man amateur, high-school show on *radio* about and on Valentine's Day. (Jacqueline Kennedy led millions of *television* viewers through the White House on *February 14*, 1962.) The experience of Jacqueline Kennedy (1929 earth-snake and recipient of snake bracelet in 1963) on November 22, 1963, was similar in some respects to mine thirteen years earlier in Korean November. If 1963 was fire-snake John F. Kennedy's and earth-snake Jacqueline's worst year, it was also mine.

When moving to San Francisco in 1963, I took a room in a small hotel on Grant Avenue. The fact that North Beach was predominately Italian hadn't any influence on my decision whatsoever, and it was while living here I applied for and got Coast Guard papers to sail. When sailing for twenty years and for a few years after retirement, I lived in Seattle. Then in 1996 I decided to move back to San Francisco. I had no idea that after a false start or two, I'd eventually return to the old hotel—the name now changed—nor that the same manager would still be here about 30 years later. For the first month and a half after moving in, I never made the association of the Parentalia to the Italian community.

As you recall, the name Grant is connected to the number 21. He had built a bridge himself. So if not realized at the time, it was appropriate that the Golden Gate bridge was dedicated April 27 on the anniversary of his birth and that he died in 1885 on July 23, the anniversary of Roman celebration for Neptune.

Not more than a block away from where I now live is the St. Francis of Assisi church, one of its sides beginning at the 1300 block of Grant Avenue. (On *February 24*, 1209, St. Francis had received additional revelations concerning his vocation.) At the opposite side is the *corso Cristóforo Colombo*. As I walked along it I recalled that Columbus was linked indirectly to the Feralia. (See *February 21*, 1429.) Two blocks north of the St. Francis of Assisi church is Washington (linked to *February 22*) Square. Then on Filbert and Powell (Dr. Powell had been a ship's surgeon and so linked to the caduceus and water) and opposite Washington Square on one side is the church of Sts. Peter and Paul. St. Peter is linked to *February 22*, and the Deposition of St. Peter and St. Paul connects both to this date. The church had been erected in 1922. On impulse I entered and inquired from an old man in the bookstore if any important dates concerning this church's history were in February. He said no, his face clearly registering: what kind of a question is that? I asked then if he knew what had been on the site before the church. He gave the names of a few businesses. My final question was to ask if there had been any graves or cemetery on or near the area. He looked at me as if I were something out of "Kindred Embraced" and replied an emphatic "no!" I bit off asking him then, "Why are you so shocked? Isn't the church in the business of burying people?" Thanking him, I left. The symbol of the Christian church—unless I'm mistaken—is a ship. Peter was a fisherman, and both Peter and Paul traveled. On the first Sunday in October those of Sicilian heritage gather at the church of Sts. Peter and Paul to ask the Madonna of the Candle to bless the local fishing fleet. The worshippers go down Columbus Avenue to pier 45, where the priest gives his blessing. In the other direction—just before Columbus Avenue begins—is an obelisk-like structure not too dissimilar from the Washington Monument (connected to *February 21* and *February 22*) called the Transamerica (Amerigo Vespucci died *February 22*, 1512) Pyramid. Curiously it sits where Merchant Street would have passed. One street adjacent to the huge office building is Washington. Once again, Washington was born on February 22.

Frances Duren Chichester. Died *February 26*, 1929. In only letter (written at Machias, Washington, on *April 18*, 1907) to have come down to me, she speaks of practicing elocution and visiting a cemetery with a friend (see pages 300-301). Among courses she'd later taken at Stanford were Roman language, Latin, and Greek (tragedy). The *February 26*, 1933 ground-breaking ceremony for the Golden Gate Bridge was the fourth anniversary of her death. Painted a creditable picture of herself on a horse and was a writer. She was born on *August 22*, 1888, while Anita, my stepmother, was born on *August 22*, 1903. (Anita had lived in San Francisco before going to Topaz. Loved horses, though breaking collarbone in fall from one, and dogs.) On *Wednesday, August 22*, 1934, Al Capone entered Alcatraz. The following day (August 23, the beginning of the Mercury period) Edward G. Robinson (who in "Little Caesar" plays a character fashioned after Al Capone) opened at the Paramount theater in *The Man with Two Faces*. I believe the Capone link to Dannie Cameron, myself, my mother, my stepmother, and possibly others in the family comes down from forebears in ancient history. Capone's parents had come from a "village about sixteen miles from the bay of Naples." Naples was one of two cities I'd visited in Italy, and in ancient times the Mercury-Maia cult was strong in this area and Pompeii (about fourteen miles from Naples), which suggests death, museum, preservation of the past, and excavation. The city's dead outlasted the people who lived there, as if there's something profound we haven't learned.

Frank Chichester died *February 22*, 1958. He'd gone to school in Oakland and so undoubtedly had been to San Francisco. Gave up wool-growing for cattle ranching. Horseman.

Anita Carmel Chichester. August 22, 1903–March 25, 1977. Stan Gentry, her grandson, recalls: "As I remember Anita telling it, she was not involved in the earthquake of 1906, but she remembered the fires. She (I think) said she was there."

Now I've said the date of the opening of the bridge was changed from May 21 (the anniversary of Dannie Cameron's death in 1894) to May 27, 1937, with perhaps disastrous results. As if to compensate for this, the opening date of the Golden Gate International Exposition at Treasure Island was on *February 18*, 1939, the anniversary of the finding of Dannie's headless body by R.W. Flint, a name like in Stevenson's *Treasure Island*. Again, it's possible that both Dannie Cameron and Elizabeth Mills Chichester were buried on the Feralia. The exposition closed, by the way, on October 6, 1939, and then reopened again in 1940 on May 25 (a month and day I believe is linked to Hermes) and closed for the last time on September 29, 1940.

California has fifty-eight counties. Twenty-seven (46.55 percent) of these, including San Francisco and Los Angeles counties, were created on February 18, 1850. This is the greatest percent of total counties created during the Parentalia for any state. Twenty-nine (50 percent) were created in February (one would expect only 8.3 percent). Forty-five (22.41 percent) were created in March or August (1 only). San Francisco, having a mainland area of *forty-five* square miles, is California's smallest county (measurement). Indeed San Francisco is second only to Rome in Parentalia aspects. Yet I doubt if ancient Rome—fearing the wrath of the Di Manes, would have sanctioned digging up bodies to be *housed* (interred) ten miles away as San Francisco did in 1937, the year young men played soccer with skulls, ten men fell to their death, and the ongoing suicidal Golden Gate bridge was opened. Colma, lying south and having a population of eleven hundred, is still close enough, however, for the Di Manes to come and go. It's estimated that two to three million are now buried there.

In 1993, three hundred bodies—thought to be Gold Rush workers—were uncovered when grounds near the Palace of the Legion of Honor were being restored. (Mungo, Ray, *San Francisco Confidential*. New York: Carol Publishing Group, 1995.)

On the *twenty-fourth of February* (the month of purification) 1977 (about forty years after the desecration of thousands of graves above), the Reverend Jim Jones (born on Persephone's day and a former Indianapolis pastor) was elected chairman of the San Francisco *Housing* Authority. A year later found that he had moved to another position: the high priest of death over the mass grave at Jonestown. The death toll of nine hundred twelve was a very pointed mocking of nine one one: Help!

The Trojan Horse was a symbol both for Poseidon (creator of the horse) and Hermes (who had dominion over it). It was Ulysses, the legendary grandson of Hermes, who supposedly suggested it to the Greeks. But Laocoön, a priest of Troy, warned that a gift of the wooden horse not be accepted. When Laocoön and his two sons were about to sacrifice to Poseidon, two sea serpents crushed them to death. The citizens of Troy misread this as a sign of Poseidon's disapproval of the advice, when actually Poseidon's anger was directed at Laocoön for revealing the truth.

Though Poseidon was later against Ulysses, whom Hermes supported, I believe the two gods' friendship was closer in general than the ancients realized:

1) It would have balanced the relationship Hermes had with Hades. Neptune is guardian of February. The old Pisces symbol (Pisces, the twelfth sign of the zodiac; February used to be the last month of the year) of two fish attached to a string and traveling in opposite directions could very well represent the Parentalia-Caristia. Life-death is common both to those who live on land as well as in water. Man's death (as well as mammals such as the whale and dolphin) at sea could involve both gods. In a way, life-death is the most basic commerce. The necromancy 9, furthermore, can be broken down into 2 x 4.5 (Hermes) or 3 x 3 (Neptune).

2) The ibis was sacred to Hermes in Greece. In Egypt it stood in *water* while being the first to greet the dawn. Hermes born at dawn. Dawn associations also in baboon, which usually begins chattering at sunrise and thus is called "Hailer of the Dawn." The dog-headed baboon assists Thoth in judgment scenes. (Elizabeth Goldsmith, *Ancient Pagan Symbols*. New York: G. P. Putnam's Sons, 1929.) The heron, sacred to Poseidon, is an ally of the crow (Op. cit., *Dictionary of Symbolism*.)

3) Thoth is connected to the moon, and Poseidon had links to it also. Because of moon-shaped mark of hooves, the horse was sacred to it, and the source of all water was thought to be the moon. Moonlight, tides. Hermes has a nocturnal aspect, as well as being associated with the dawn. The moon—in one sense—is one big rock. Hermes is connected to rock and Poseidon, water. Many believe that at the beginning of time the ocean water was pure, free of salt. The salt comes from river water passing over rocks. The salinity of the ocean increases each year, suggesting the bond between Hermes and Poseidon increases with it. Hence, washing-stone or Washington.

4) There's some thinking that both Hermes and Poseidon might have come to Greece via Mesopotamia, "the cradle of civilization." (William Sherwood Fox, *The Mythology of All Races*, Vol. 1. Boston: Marshall Jones Co., 1916.) Though Neptune was seen in the company of other gods in the lectisternium of 399 B.C. Roman history, he was coupled especially with Mercurius (Hermes). Since there's nothing existing this early to suggest Neptune was connected to the sea, W. Warde Fowler (op. cit.) comments that the coupling of the two gods need mean nothing more than they had come to Rome via Greek commerce. This could be true, or perhaps it's much too simplistic.

5) Both Poseidon and Hermes were cunning and associated with wind, horses, chariots, horse racing, and gambling. Poseidon, with brothers Zeus and Hades, shook lots in a helmet for lordships of the underworld, sea, and sky. Though dolphins, horses, and tridents are the usual Poseidon associations, there's also one to wolves, and possibly Hermes has an association to wolves too since they are said to be the ancestors of dogs. Folklore abounds in werewolves—in the light of the moon—which can be stopped with a silver bullet. Lupine, Lupino. On May 21 (the beginning of the Mercury period), 1924, Bobby Franks was killed. Wolf Lake is one of the many wolf names in the case. His funeral was held on May 25.

6) Poseidon was over naval engagements; Hermes, god of contests. Poseidon connected to seaports and was the most reliable protector of ships and sailors and so linked to commerce and travelers at sea, as was Hermes. Odin, linked by the Romans with Mercury, was the Viking mariner's chief deity.

7) The Reflecting Pool lies between the Parentalia markers of the Washington Monument and Lincoln Memorial. Water used in purification. Poseidon was the chief god at Corinth, Greece. Washington, D.C., on the left bank of the Potomac at junction with Anacostia River, and San Francisco are reminders.

If Christ is Hermes, then Poseidon would enter the picture as follows:

1) "And behold, the curtain of the temple was torn in two, from top to bottom; and the earth shook, and rocks split" (Mt 27: 51).

2) "And behold, there was a great earthquake; for an angel of the Lord descended from heaven and came and rolled back the stone, and sat upon it" (Mt 28: 02).

The date of the San Francisco disaster is usually given as April 18–19, 1906, though some fires burned into the twenty-first. The earthquake (Poseidon) occurred at 5:13 A.M. on Wednesday the eighteenth. Dawn was at 5:31 A.M. (U.S. Naval Observatory, Nautical Almanac Office, *Sunrise and Sunset Tables for Key Cities and Weather Stations of the U.S.* Detroit: Gale Research Co., 1977, error possible not exceeding two minutes [and generally less than one minute] in using tables.) On April 19, a break line was established at Van Ness by dynamiting and firing of houses (Hermes associated with fire) to check much of its spread.

Note the occurrence of important events especially in U.S. history of April 18 and April 19 and the fact that the fire wasn't completely extinguished until April 21 (the anniversary of the date Romulus, one of the twins suckled by a wolf [canine] established Rome) when a rain soaked the ashes. Cats and dogs, as witches' familiars, can stand for witches as rain-makers. Thus "it's raining cats and dogs." (See *April 19*, 1927.)

As messenger of the gods, Hermes represented Hades, Poseidon, and Zeus in sinking the *Titanic*.

The meeting to delay the May 21 opening of the Golden Gate Bridge occurred both in February and the Parentalia morning when ten men met their death in the sea.

April was probably the month the Isthmian Games were held in Corinth. Dedication date of the Golden Gate Bridge was April 27, 1937, the anniversary of *Ulysses* S. Grant's birthdate, and on May 25, 1937, a *fire* fanned by a high *wind* swept supply buildings at *Mare* Island and caused injury to *four* sailors. (Demeter changed herself into a mare to escape Poseidon, who covered her as a stallion.)

In the huge, opening-day parade on May 27, 1937, were a mounted cavalry band and mounted troops from Monterey. This was the first they'd been seen in San Francisco in a long time. The distinction of *walking* on the bridge before the opening day was given to a blind (both Poseidon and Hermes were protectors of the blind because of their sons: Poseidon, Polyphemus; Hermes, Daphnis) lady with a *guide* dog. The dog is man's best friend.

The Egyptians called the dog Hermes because of its philosophic nature and felt it characterized "the most logical of the gods." (Op. cit., Goldsmith.)

One day when living in San Francisco in the late 1960s, I was walking along the beach when a saddled horse with no rider in sight came trotting by. Figuring it belonged to a riding academy three miles away, I caught it (obviously no relation to Snorts) and rode it where the water lapped up on the sand back to the academy. When I got to the stables, a man came out gesticulating,

> "You're late! You're late! I had to wait. I'm going to have to charge you more money."
> "You're not charging me nothin'," I said, getting off and handing him the reins. "Your horse was trotting along the beach without a rider and I am just bringing him back to you."

He looked doubtful and asked,

> "Don't you know the horse would have come back by himself?"
> "Would he? Didn't know that." A big lie.

Though he looked very unhappy, Hermes and Poseidon must have been laughing, for not long after I got into the merchant marines.

129-D. In ancient Egypt, swineherds couldn't enter temples or marry other men's daughters. Nevertheless, there was a yearly sacrifice of pigs to Osiris and the moon. (*Funk and Wagnalls Standard Dictionary of Folklore Mythology and Legend*, Vol. Two. New York: Funk and Wagnalls Company, 1950.)

635

In some cases in antiquity, pigs were substituted for humans in sacrifice to gods of death. (Op. cit., Jobes.)

129-E.   Information on the investigation: footnote 90. Bibliography dealing with chapter on USS *Nevada*:

> (a) L.S. Davidson, Jr., *The Disturber*. New York: The Macmillan Co., 1964.
>
> (b) Alan F. Pater, *United States Battleships*. Beverly Hills: Monitor Book Co., 1968.
>
> (c) Bert Shanas, "Nevada Under Attack," *Nevada* magazine, December 1991.

Thanks is given to National Archives and Bureau of Ships for information on USS *Nevada*'s exact location and on her ship's bells.

Books differ as to whether Hermes was born on the fourth month (Op. cit., Peck; Oskar Seyffert, *A Dictionary of Classical Antiquities*. London: William Glaisher, Ltd., 1891) or the fourth day of the month (Op. cit, *The Oxford Classical Dictionary*; op. cit., Eliade).

The confusion might have come about in the former in that this or that region in antiquity the fourth month was named for Hermes or the fourth day sacred to him. The latter, however, are using *Hymn, Homeric, Merc.* as their reference. Both schools of thought agree that Hermes' number is four. Keeping this in mind as well as the stipulation that Hermes can only use signs and omens, I—perhaps a pedagogic ol' fool—find it uncanny that in translations of the *Homeric Hymn No. 4* the reference is line 19.

130.   N.C. Brooks, *A Complete History of the Mexican War 1846–1848*. Chicago: The Rio Grande Press, Inc., 1965.

131.   Traditionally palms are used in Christian churches on Palm Sunday and are blessed and given to the congregation. Then—especially in years past—they could be put to any number of uses, depending on the customs of the country. Two of these seem particularly relevant:

> 1) Decorations of graves.
>
> 2) Formerly, the palms were burned and the ashes were to be saved for use on Ash Wednesday, the beginning of Lent, the following year. Where the ashes are obtained now, I don't know, but the customs remain the same. The priest sprinkles or dabs the ashes of the heads of penitents and says, "Remember, man, that thou art ashes and to ashes thou shalt return." This, of course, pertains to Christianity. But now consider that the palm was sacred to Hermes, the picture of Christ as the good shepherd was taken from him, that he was the god of graveyards, the conductor of the souls of the dead, and Wednesday in astrology is assigned to him. Wednesday, after Woden.

The Eucharist wafer is sometimes stamped IHS. I assume the abbreviation comes from *in hoc signo vinces* (By this sign shall you conquer). Or does it mean "Invocation of the Holy Spirit"? Or perhaps, "Invocation of Hermes"? "Foul," you cry. "This is heresy and deceit." Ah, but what then were the grafting of Christian practices (Christmas, Easter, Halloween) on pagan timetables? Yet I doubt we're really much off in our beliefs. For I don't see Hermes as Satan but rather as a face of God.

In context with the wine-wafer rite, there's some truth in seeing Christianity as one of the world's oldest blood cults. Here a boundary is crossed. In *transubstan*tiation we drink Christ's blood and eat his body. Better to eat than be eaten, as in the legendary *Transyl*vania, a region in central *Roman*ia. The reality of life is that its not this simple; however, no one escapes without some sacrifice, freely offered (excluding suicide) or taken by "The Son of Man (who) cometh as a thief in the night." But bizarre extension of thought doesn't give us the right to sacrifice one another.

132-A.   David Nevin, *"The Mexican War"* from *The Old West*. Time-Life Books, Inc., 1978.

132-B.   Joseph E. Suppiger, *The Intimate Lincoln*. New York: University Press of America, 1985.

133.   George W. Olszewski, *Restoration of Ford's Theatre*, 1963, under direction of Conrad L. Wirth, National Park Service.

134.   Stephen B. Oates, *Abraham Lincoln, the Man Behind the Myths*. New York: Harper and Row.

135.   Carl Sandburg, *Abraham Lincoln, the Prairie Years and the War Years*. New York: Harcourt Brace Jovanovich, 1974.

136.   Jean H. Baker, *Mary Todd Lincoln*. New York: Norton Publishers, 1978.

137.   Justin G. and Linda L. Turner, *Mary Todd Lincoln: Her Life and Letters*. Knopf, 1972.

138-A.   Once a freighter captain decided to have a deck meal for the passengers. The other waiter stayed below to feed some officers, while I began to set up tables on deck. It was soon obvious as things whipped around that no one could eat out there. Certainly not passengers with a mean age of seventy. I went into the lounge where the captain was having cocktails with twelve passengers and two or three other officers and explained to him it was too windy outside. He then craned his neck around, glanced through one of the windows, and said he was sure the weather was just fine outside and to set up the meal as ordered. Having been made to appear rather stupid, I went outside again. If anything, things were getting worse, so I returned to the lounge door and caught the purser's attention, motioning to talk to him. He then went out on deck to see what the problem was. The wind by this time was such force that it was hard to walk and rain was pouring down. He returned to the lounge where the captain was regaling the passengers with sea stories, and told him point blank, "You can't have a deck lunch out there, Captain." Without missing a beat, the captain replied, "Well set it up below in the dining room."

Years later when the purser and I ran into one another on ships, we'd laugh about our *Titanic* captain, who often made snap and ill-considered decisions.

138-B. Both the *Titanic* and the *Olympic* were descended from the *Oceanic*, built in 1871, and considered the paragon for White Star liners to follow. Hermes is associated with disguise (the Trojan Horse via Ulysses) and forms of concealment such as darkness, clouds, mists, fogs, and icebergs. Hermes, the messenger and traveler, was the Iceman in the case of the *Titanic*, which sank in the Atlantic Ocean. *Oceanus* was the oldest of the Titans. Hermes can be thought of as a liar or protector, depending on your point of view, and lies to yourself can be damaging or protective. Honesty is a fine attribute, but no one could live long in this world by being completely honest. So as human beings, we take much from Hermes for survival.

138-C. Some ghetto American blacks were synchronized with the Olympians.

There was satisfaction and irony expressed in songs: a gloating joy that blacks hadn't lost a single girl or boy. (Wyn Craig Wade, *The Titanic: End of a Dream*. New York: Rawson Wade Publishers Inc., 1979.)

> *Freedom*
> I've traveled far,
> Have my dents,
> They no care *so long as*
> *I pays the rents.*

It wasn't just coincidence that Lincoln, who signed the Emancipation Proclamation, and the *Titanic* died at 4.5. As the *Titanic* had been polished to perfection from the *Olympic*, there was an irony that after the *Titanic* sank, the *Olympic* would be rebuilt to withstand flooding in six compartments. The *Olympic* became a troop ship in World War I. When attacked by U-103 by May 1918, she turned, rammed, and sank the German submarine. Thereafter, she was dubbed "Old Reliable."

By the end of World War I, she had become the record holder (Hermes, god of contest) for carrying troops. Finally, compare the name *Olympic* to *Olympia*, Commodore Dewey's flagship. Not one American life was lost in the seven-hour Battle of Manila Bay. See May 1, 1898.

139. J.P. Eaton and C.A. Hass, *Titanic Destination Disaster*. London: W.W. Norton & Co., 1987.

140. Other marriages and snake years: Heinrich and Sophia Schliemann (1869); Franklin and Eleanor Roosevelt (1905); Martin and Coretta King, Jr. (1953); John and Jacqueline Kennedy (1953).

141. Harold Nicolson, *King George the Fifth*. New York: Doubleday, 1953.

142. The German dirigible *Hindenberg* was launched in *April* 1936. Thirty-six died when it crashed in flames at Lakehurst, New Jersey, on May 6, 1937.

143. Other than flight association of any bird and Thoth being called a god of birds, I know of no specific example where the hawk is identified with Hermes in Greek or Roman mythology. This isn't saying there's no instance but that my knowledge goes only so far due to limited access to information and language barriers.

However, many books list the hawk as one of heaven's messenger birds. An American Indian tribe sees a similarity between Hermes and one of its gods who is represented by a hawk, and there's the case of Black Hawk, (pages 4 and 5). In Aztec religion (remember Good Friday, April 21, the year of 1 Reed when Cortés landed in Mexico. See Book II, footnotes 54 and 127) the hawk is a messenger of the gods. And curiously we find Wilbur Wright (who with his brother flew their plane at Kitty Hawk) died on May 30 (Memorial Day), 1912. (See Book II, footnote 189.)

144.   Like George V, George Duren kept a diary, at least during part of the Civil War.

145.   Five Forks is "about *fourteen* miles" southwest of Petersburg. This proved to be an unlucky time for Major General Warren who commanded the *fifth* corps. Because of dilatory behavior, he was relieved of his command. He had been wronged and would spend the rest of his life trying to clear his name. Unfortunately it took *fourteen* years before his case was brought before a board of inquiry ordered by President Hayes. The court eventually vindicated him, but sadly he died three months before this.

Information concerning his life can be read in Emerson G. Taylor's *Gouverneur Kemble Warren*, New York. Houghton Mifflin Co., 1932. On page *four* of this book it tells that he was the *fourth* of *twelve* children. On page 5, he is quoted as having written, "I look back and find that for *five* generations I can claim an honorable lineage antedating the old French Wars."

146.   The boy, born in the *fourth* month, had one parent called *Jesse*, after the father of David in the Bible. And David, of course, had been anointed by Samuel. Its other parent was called *Hannah*, after Samuel's mother who had petitioned the Lord for a son and then gave the boy for life to Him.

Curiously then the boy was born a *first* child and son, and when he later went to West Point, he would be called "Sam" for years, during which time he became the academy's best rider. Thus he had asked to be assigned to the cavalry but was sent instead to the *Fourth* Infantry. Recalling the year 1864, one of his staff members at the time said that he had seen Grant lose his temper only once. That was when Grant saw a teamster beating horses in the face. For the first six weeks of his life, he had no name at all, as if the artist couldn't decide what to call him. Finally his name was selected by lot and luck as Ulysses, after the world's most famous *traveler* who had been under the protection of Hermes. His mother, Hannah, remained a "strange and mystifying" figure throughout her life, seemingly unconcerned about Ulysses when as a small boy he was swinging on a horse's tail. She was pious and withdrawn, a woman of few words who never wept or laughed. Some have speculated she was simple-minded, that she and Ulysses never cared for one another. Others thought she acted as if she were "harboring a deep secret" which she kept to herself (W.E. Woodward, *Meet General Grant*. Horace Liveright Inc., 1928). But perhaps like the biblical Hannah, she had said, "Grant my wish O'Lord, and I will do this (or that) for the rest of my life." And he became "Sam" Grant (from U.S. Grant) his years at the academy. Jessie Root Grant and Hannah Simpson Grant also gave Ulysses the biblical name of Hiram at baptism. But through an error of his appointing congressman, Ulysses' official listing at West Point was Ulysses Simpson Grant. He eventually decided to accept this rather than fight an uphill battle for correction. Hiram then was dropped. His parents were married in 1821 (SY). So in a way, his class standing was the first echo of 21. The second came when—just after the Civil War broke out in 1861—he was appointed a colonel by the governor in the *Twenty-first* Illinois Volunteers. He was sworn in as president on March 4, 1869 (SY). It was the year the first transcontinental railroad was completed in the U.S. and the Suez Canal in Egypt. He was a sensitive man who hated the carnage of war. It's said that after some bloody battles, he retired to his tent, closed the flap, and lay down, trying to deal with it as best he could. He also had become a heavy drinker. But at his presidency, which was rocked with *scandals* of fraud, this tendency apparently disappeared. His two favorite topics were horses and the past war. Yet in 1878 when asked by Emperor Franz Joseph if he'd reviewed any troops in Paris, former President Grant replied, "No, I am fed up with these things; I always avoid meeting soldiers or generals because, although I was educated at the Military Academy of West Point, I never developed a taste for this profession." (Anatol Murad, *Franz Joseph I of Austria and His Empire*. New York: Twayne Publishers, 1968.)

Grant's wife, Julia Dent, was squint-eyed, giving her (some thought) a dented or slightly crazed appearance, and "Honest Ape," who though having storklike legs, looked almost simian (the evolutionary Charles Darwin and Lincoln were born on the same month and day, Thoth is sometimes depicted as a dog-headed baboon or an ibis-headed human). Very fitting too in this context (the *superlative writing* of the Gettysburg Address given at the graveyard dedication), he must have had a special feeling or concern for one of his sons who was born with a cleft palate and had a lisp. All this was in the days before corrective surgery. The pattern somehow is Hermes, born out later in the Kennedy child who was retarded and Al Capone's son who lost much of his hearing through disease.

Where Lincoln enjoyed a good dirty joke, Grant would get up and leave the room when one was being told, in what seemed an incongruity with his *cigar-smoking* and drinking history. He was also partial to flowers.

As had been Nails Morton and Deany O'Banion who bought into Schofield's flower business. (Morton later died when kicked by a horse at the Lincoln Riding Academy.) Even more curious in the Hermes-Grant relationship is the query that has come down from the *cigar-smoking* Groucho Marx, "Who's buried in Grant's tomb?"

It was if the artist, the god of horses, liked both Grant and Lee and couldn't make up his mind from one day to the next, or even when the war was over. He made Grant a first child and gave him the name Ulysses. But Robert Edward Lee would be a *fifth* child, the son of *"Light-Horse* Harry," a cavalry hero in the Revolutionary War. Grant will marry Julia Dent and have *four* children. But Lee will marry Mary Custis, whose father was a grandson of Martha Washington. Grant will grow up in *George*town, Ohio, and Lee in *Alexandria*, Virginia.

Lee also loved horses and animals and was an excellent rider in a surrounding where "good riding was common." The artist named Grant after the most famous traveler of all time and had the young boy swing on a horse's tail. Yet he gave Lee his beloved Traveller, the most famous mount in the Civil War. He also gave Lee the choice of commanding either the forces of the North or South before the war began. And when Lee had chosen, he was given two very competent lieutenant generals (now get this): Thomas *"Stonewall"* Jackson and James *Longstreet*, suggesting measure and road. All three generals were born in January: Lee, January 19, 1807; Longstreet, January 8, 1821 (SY); and Jackson, January 21, 1824. Both Jackson and Longstreet were riding horses when mistakenly shot by their own men: Jackson, *May 2*, 1863; Longstreet, *May 6*, 1864. (Riding with General Longstreet at the time was Brigadier General Micah Jenkins who was also shot and died within a few hours.) Jackson died from an amputation and pneumonia on May 10, 1863, eight days after being wounded. Longstreet returned to duty in October 1864.

Grant was the winning general, but the artist made Lee a better tactician than Grant and gave both Lee and Jackson adulation by their troops that Grant never had. And when the war was over, the artist made Grant a president and Lee a "Marble (stone) man," a legend even mothers in the North would name their sons after, as possibly one of my brothers was. At times it looked as if the artist had painted himself into a corner. Although Richmond, Virginia, has been designated the capital of the Confederacy on *May 21*, 1861, the overall signs were there long before the war ended what its outcome would be. Lee had come in second in class standing at West Point and received no demerits in four years. All things considered—including how he applied what he learned, how he behaved after the war—this was probably the best record ever. Nonetheless, the second status was an omen, as well as Grant's class standing of 21, the admission number of the state of Illinois where Lincoln is buried and the number of the Illinois regiment which Grant first commanded. The granddaddy of all 21s is December 21 (or February 21). Note also 1822 (2122) was Grant's birth, the year of the horse, which can be a symbol of death and/or victory. Legend is that Hermes was the grandfather of Odysseus (Ulysses), the shrewdest of the Greek leaders during the Trojan War. The wooden horse, which Ulysses suggested be built, finally brought the end to the Trojan War. Troy's Hector, "tamer of horses," was a loser.

In perhaps the most brilliant denouement ever written, Lee at Appomattox wanted his men to be able to take their horses and mules home with them, and Grant agreed to this. Hector was lamented for nine days. With his funeral, the *Iliad* ended. The *Odyssey* tells of Ulysses' long journey back to his home at Ithaca. Ulysses' trickery and craftiness linked him to Hermes, whose divinity was partly being god of contests. During the Trojan War, Poseidon and Athena favored the Greeks, who were traditionally sailors and sea people. But after it, both Poseidon and Athena turned against the Greeks. Only later did Athena's fondness for Ulysses return. In the meantime, Ulysses had blinded Cyclops Polyphemus, the son of Poseidon, to save his own life and that of his men. But Poseidon was implacable in his bitterness toward Ulysses, much like the South's feeling right after the Civil War. Damned Yankees! Damned Ulysses! Twenty-one Ulysses was much like Ulysses of the *Odyssey*. Had General Grant and his wife accepted the presidential invitation to accompany him and Mrs. Lincoln that night at Ford's Theater, their fate might have been similar to that of Major Rathbone and Clara. So luck was with Ulysses S. Grant too.

John J. Pershing was born on September 13 (MP), 1860, four-five years before the end of the Civil War. He was the first of nine children and ploughing at the time he heard of his appointment to West Point.

The one physical characteristic of Pershing which seems to stand out by his biographers was his cold, steely blue eyes, which were as arresting as those of Al

Capone, who started out in New York City. But Pershing's link is primarily to Ulysses S. Grant, whose class standing was 21.

At the time of Grant's death, Pershing was a senior cadet captain. It was the only time Pershing was at the Point that the cadet corps as a body left the military post. They crossed the Hudson to Garrison, where they stood at rigid attention in salute, a tribute to Grant as his funeral train passed for burial in New York City. (Frederick Palmer, *John J. Pershing, General of the Armies*. Harrisburg: Military Service Pub. Co., 1948.)

Where Grant, a horse in Chinese astrology, was unable to become a cavalryman on graduation from West Point, Pershing was, and pictures show him sitting very erect on a horse and leading a parade down New York's Fifth Avenue in 1918. It was in 1918 too he was promoted to general of the armies. (Note all the really big-shot generals and admirals have four or five stars.) Both Grant and Pershing saw service in Mexican wars. Pershing, as leader of the American Expeditionary Force (AEF) in Europe in World War I, is linked to Hermes, god of campaigns. But there were other links too.

In 1905 at the age of forty-four, he married the daughter of Senator Francis E. Warren. On August 27 (MP), 1915, when Pershing was in Texas, his wife and four children were living at the Presidio in San Francisco. Their quarters caught on fire and burned down. Four perished: his wife and three daughters. Why does this seem like an exacted sacrifice? Only one of the five survived: his son Warren, who was sent to *May* Pershing, his father's sister, in Lincoln, *Nebraska*. His wife's maiden-en name was Helen Frances Warren. He had been promoted from captain, over 852 officers who were his superiors in rank, to brigadier general by President Roosevelt in 1906. Then too, I'd been stationed at Letterman Army Hospital at the Presidio in 1950 when the Korean War broke out.

Biographer *Palmer* (Ibid) recalls a talk with Pershing at Walter *Reed* Hospital, where Pershing had referred to Caesar's commentaries, Caesar's bridge over the Rhine, and Roman wars.

Pershing had taught at a black school before going to West Point, but he got the nickname "Black Jack" when he was later assigned to a black regiment. But black-jack is a game where the object is to total 21. Lindbergh flew from New York and landed near Paris on May 21. Malcolm X, who knew how to pronounce Caesar, flew back from Europe and landed in New York on February 13, later to be assassinated on the twenty-first. Pershing died on July 15, 1948, the same year as Gandhi, who can also be associated with 21. Vladmir Lenin 2221 (2122).

In 1947 to 1950 I walked many times to the area where there still stood structures, with reflective colonnades in lagoons and with willow trees, from the Panama-Pacific International Exposition in 1915, where Pershing's wife and children had visited several times just before the fire.

It was at Darien (Panama) that Balboa's march inland began on September 6, 1513, with about one hundred and ninety men, one thousand native warriors and carriers, and a pack of *bloodhounds*. He and his men repulsed an Indian attack of about one thousand men on September 24.

On the twenty-fifth, he saw the waters of Mar Del Sur for the first time. On the twenty-ninth, he took possession of the sea and lands in the names of the king and queen of Castile. The name "Pacific" wasn't given to the ocean until seven years later by Magellan (*Encyclopedia Americana*).

The collective events below suggest a cabala spanning many centuries:

1) In my travels, I'd been through the Panama Canal several times.

2) Pershing's wife's maiden name (Helen Frances Warren) included my sister's name, my mother's name, and my brother's name. His sister's, May, is my mother's name.

3) I'd been stationed on an Army Hospital Ship going in and out of Fort Mason, California, when Pershing died in 1948.

4) Both Pershing and I were in the army and connected to horses.

5) The Liberty Bell had been brought from Philadelphia for the 1915 exposition. More importantly, it was the first international exposition which recognized man-flight, navigation of the air, a new triumph of travelers compared to the traveling and exploring of the earlier Balboa, and the commercial travels on the waterways of the Panama Canal, opened August 15, 1914.

6) Balboa had sailed from Antigua on September 1, 1513, a Mercury period that would last to the twenty-second.

7) The exposition had opened on February 20, a day Governor Johnson had declared a legal holiday. (Frank Morton Todd, *The Story of the Exposition*. New York: G.P. Putnam's Sons, 1921.)

February 20 was also a day in the Parentalia. The twenty-first, a Sunday, was the Feralia, and the twenty-second, Monday, was the Caristia and Washington's birthday. So there were three straight holidays for visitors.

8) Geographers call the isthmus of Panama "one of the great crossroads of the world." *Encyclopedia Americana*. Crossroads are very important here (Hermes, god of crossroads) as well as the beheading of Balboa and four of his alleged accomplices (January 12, 1519 at Acla, on the isthmus's northern coast). Decapitation, persona Hermes. That Captain Cook and four marines will die together in 1779 is an interesting similarity.

9) It was in 1513 that Ponce de Leon discovered Florida. Now we are tracing back in a different direction. Thirteen to twenty-one represents Ponce de Leon's discovery and death (as well as Magellan's permanent limp from a fight with Moors and his death in 1521), along with the Parentalia. February 14 (St. Valentine's Day), Captain Cook was slaughtered with four marines and Arizona was admitted as a state. February 14 (2122) Chicago's Al Capone in Florida. February 15, Franklin D. Roosevelt in Florida, Chicago's

mayor killed. December 7, Bligh (who had been with Captain Cook) died; Roosevelt president on December 7 when battleship *Arizona* sunk.

10) Magellan, who had named the ocean Balboa, discovered on October 21, 1520, the strait which was later named after him. He was killed by Filipinos on April 27, 1521 (SY). He had started out from Seville with five ships on September 20 (MP), 1519. September 6 (MP), 1522, only one ship (eighteen men) returned, after completing the first circumnavigation of the world. Clearly 2122 is linked to Magellan.

11) Ulysses S. Grant, born *April 27*, 1822, is linked to Magellan who died *April 27*, 1521 (2122).

12) *George Washington* Goethals, builder of the Panama Canal, died in New York City on January *21*, 1928.

147. Frequently similarities in the John F. Kennedy assassination to that of Abraham Lincoln are drawn. Strike out the *r* in Maria (Mary) and you have Maia. Mae and May are derived from Mary, as they are from Margaret.

148. Michael Davie, *Titanic the Death and Life of a Legend.* New York: Alfred A. Knopf, Inc., 1968. Details information concerning "Futility" and the *Royal Standard*.

149. At the Appomattox meeting, Lee didn't know how many men he still commanded, only that they were hungry. In a generous gesture, Grant gave him twenty-five thousand rations, all he could spare. This was almost double rations per man. It has been estimated (P. Batty and P. Parish, *The Divided Union.* Topsfield, Massachusetts: Salem House Publishers, 1987) that Lee had thirteen thousand troops.

150. *Webster's Third New International Dictionary*, 1971.

151. *Philip* is Greek for "lover of horses." Horse racing is called the "sport of kings." Philip II, king of Macedon, was Alexander the Great's father.

The seer Cheiro commented that April to July is a significant period for the royal family—the Hanoverians, or Windsors (the Wind soars). For the most part, my theory of a Hermes influence agrees with this. April is the fourth month; May, the fifth; and the first Mercury period is May 21 to June 20 (not named for Juno). The round wedding ring is worn around the fourth of "five fingers," or 4.5, and twice this is 9, the number of the span and the coven circle's diameter. So if you think you married a witch, you just might be right.

In 1992 (21) on November 20, the anniversary of the day Queen Elizabeth II married Philip *forty-five* years previously in 1947 (21), a fire severely damaged St. George's Hall, where the ceiling collapsed, and several other rooms at Windsor castle. (*Seattle Post-Intelligencer*, November 21, 1992, from article by Edith M. Lederer, The Associated Press.) It's been pointed out that man is the only animal which shares the possession of fire with the gods. It links him to the divine as it rises from lighted altars to heaven. (Op. cit., Eliade.) The fire started in the royal chapel.

152.   *Strange Stories, Amazing Facts.* The Reader's Digest Association, Inc., 1976. Under the Roman Empire, Hermes-Mercury was the most important god of all in Gaul, as well as small parts of Germany, where he was identified with Woden, the Teutonic god. (Charles Theodore Seltman, *The Twelve Olympians.* New York: Crowell, 1960.) Here is another link to Wednesday.

153.   Colin M. Wells, from "Nero," *Encyclopedia Americana.*

154.   Gérard Walter, translated by Sidney Shore, from "Nero," *Collier's Encyclopedia.*

155.   This eruption began, to my understanding, in September 1991.

156.   Alfred J. Kolatch, *The Jonathan David Dictionary of First Names.* Middle Village, New York: J. David Publishers, 1980.

157.   Alexandria had been a port of call two or three times when sailing.

158.   This was the year that *George* Chichester, whose roots are unknown, died aboard a ship in the Atlantic and whose body was brought across country for proper burial. His date of death was fifty-three years exactly before the assassination of President John F. Kennedy.

        George V, the husband of Queen Mary, was coronated in 1910. When the *Titanic* sank in 1912, he and Mary were king and queen of England. Their first child Edward abdicated the throne in 1936, the year the *Queen Mary* made her maiden voyage in the *fifth* month, as compared to the maiden voyage made by the *Titanic* in the fourth month twenty-four years earlier. Their second child, who will later become *George* VI, was born—to the family's horror—on what it termed "Mausoleum Day" (David Duff, *George and Elizabeth.* Oxford: Clio Press, 1983). December 14, 1895, was even a worse day to be born than Friday the thirteenth which preceded it. December *14* (5) was the day Prince Albert, Queen Victoria's consort, died in 1861. Victoria's eldest son nearly died of typhoid fever that day in 1871, and Alice, her second daughter, died of diphtheria on December 14, 1878. On April 14 (the anniversary of Lincoln being shot), 1912, the *Titanic* with the princess aboard hit an iceberg, the mausoleum Prince was sixteen and had eight months to go before his next birthday. Come to think of it, if I'd been Edward in 1936, I'd have abdicated quickly too with the Mausoleum Prince waiting in the aisle. This Edward VIII did, by the way, four days before his brother's birthday. The Mausoleum Prince was also linked to Hermes in that he was a stutterer. his life must have been pure hell in this respect, especially as King George VI, having to speak in front of people.

159.   Peter Eldin and Kim Bundell (illustrations), *Amazing Ghosts & Other Mysteries,* "The Mummy's Curse." New York: Sterling Pub. Co., 1988.

160.   Florida was admitted to the Union on March 3, 1845 (SY). California, another corner and seacoast state, on September 9 (MP), five years later, or 9-9-1850. The name Miami is believed to come from the Indian world *mayami* or *mayaimi*, meaning "big" or "sweetwater." *Maia* (Greek) has several meanings, a few of which are "old nurse," "midwife," and "foster mother." "Put them all together they spell mother," a word that meant the world to the Cubans.

161.   Mao Zedong and Huey Long were alike to some extent. Each was a water-snake born in 1893. Some thought both were tyrants. Each believed in "Share Our

Wealth." Long attacked Standard Oil Co. which had been started by John D. *Rockefeller* (an appropriate name considering the derivation of petroleum) and was largely controlled by his descendants. Though Zedong had many people gunning for him throughout his life, he lived to be an old man. Long, on the other hand, died on September 8 (MP), 1935, two days after being shot.

162.   Erwin Gustav Gudde, *1000 California Place Names*. Berkeley: University of California Press, 1959.

163.   Phil Townsend Hanna, *The Dictionary of California Land Names*. Los Angeles: Automobile Club of Southern California, 1946.

164.   Mercury (atomic number 80) was formerly called quicksilver or living silver. At room temperature it's the only element that is liquid. *Silvery*-white in color, it's extracted from *red* sulfide ore.

165.   William J. Duncan, R.M.S. *Queen Mary, Queen of the Queens*. Anderson, South Carolina: Droke House Inc., 1969.

166.   Thoth, whom the Greeks associated with Hermes, was, among other things, a moon god. As a reckoner of time, he was called "the measurer." *Tehu* in ancient Egyptian is "the moon as a measurer of time." Probably the ibis, *Tekh*, became a symbol for Thoth because the name sounded similar to *Tehu*. Budge, Sir E.A. Wallis, *The Book of the Dead*. New Hyde Park, New York: University Books, 1960.

167.   Kenneth Rose, *King George V*. New York: Publisher Knopf, 1983.

168.   Bacchante: A priestess of Bacchus. Dionysus, identified with Roman Bacchus, was a god of wine and vegetation in general. Hermes is linked to Dionysus not only as a half-brother but also because it was Hermes who tried to hide baby Dionysus from Hera.

169.   Op. cit. Eldin.

170.   Curacoa is an island seventeen miles north of Venezuela, having one of the largest oil refineries in the world. Once upon a time, as the story goes, it had a governor who was plagued with severe headaches which he felt were caused or aggravated by the glare of white houses and buildings. He decreed that thereafter none would be painted white and that softer hues were to be used. Today these are all colors of the rainbow and fit in well with the sunny climate, giving Curacoa a distinctive charm, linking it with the past. But a rainbow is also a short-lived herald, showing death has no respect for color and comes to us all who—in the end—are merely travelers. Only once did I make it to Curacoa. When the passenger ship tied up, someone said the city was over a hill or two down a path, within walking distance. So following the directions, I had no trouble finding my way there. Waiting until the last minute to return before sailing, I started back from the city but somehow got lost. Becoming anxious, I went up to a man mowing his lawn, told him what had happened, and asked if he could tell me where the ship was. He said he didn't know for sure but to jump into his car, and we'd look for it. I had spent everything, so certain I was that I knew my way back. I explained before we started I couldn't pay him. "Don't worry about it," he said. Anyway he got me back in time. If Hermes had once guarded wayfarers on the Roman road to Londinium, he was certainly with me that day, an ocean and centuries away.

171.   In 1888 Irishman W.B. Yeats (ea), a later Nobel Prize winner, became interested in theosophy, joining the "Hermetic Order of the Golden Dawn" in 1890.

               The planet Mercury (five) orbits the sun every *eighty-eight* days. This is the length of its year, and it could be called "Stone 588." The length of its day is fifty-nine days. Its mass relative to the earth is .05 and its maximum surface temperature is 400°C.

172.   The coat of arms of one of the most powerful, Fitzgerald, Irish feudal families was a *silver* shield with a *red* saltire.

173.   Nancy Gager Clinch, *The Kennedy Neurosis*. New York: Grosset and Dunlap, 1973.

174.   Honey was one of the sacrifices made to Hermes.

175.   This was about three months before the stock market crash. The four-stacker *Titanic* sailed on her fateful, maiden voyage on April (fourth month) 10, 1912, from Southampton, England. The three-stacker *Queen Mary* also used Southampton as a port. She sailed on her maiden voyage on May (fifth month) 26 (MP), 1936.

176.   Jacqueline Kennedy, Idanell (born 1919) and John Connolly. Special agent William R. *Greer* (the name of a navy LST I'd been on) was driving, and assistant agent Roy H. Kellerman was sitting on his right. In certain ways it was similar to the experience I and three others had thirteen years previously in Korea, November 1950. In both cases the man mortally shot was sitting next to a 1929 earth-snake, who wasn't physically harmed. Four witnesses stated that Kennedy was shot at 12:30 P.M.

177-A.   Ford Motor Co. introduced the Mercury in 1938 (21). Ford edged out Honda for first place in 1992 (21).

177-B.   Some believe to this day that the assassination attempt was meant against John Connolly (LA). Was his blooding a sacrifice? Certainly his life was mercurial with its ups and downs. He had become a multimillionaire and then lost most of it, filing for bankruptcy. Toward the end of his life he had become a partner in a group from Houston which wanted to build a *horse race* track. On May 17, 1993, he was admitted to a Houston hospital with pneumonia and pulmonary fibrosis. He died on June 15 (MP), 1993. It had been nearly thirty years since the fateful day in Dallas on November 22, 1963.

178.   The feather is emblematic of Ma_t, the female counterpart of Thoth, regarded as the inventor of all sciences and arts. Most students in the U.S. begin the fall term in the Mercury period.

179-A.   The president and his wife celebrated their tenth wedding anniversary on September 12, 1963. Jackie selected her own anniversary gift from a catalogue. This was a coiled serpent bracelet (C. David Heymann, *A Woman Named Jackie*. New York: Signet Book, 1989).

               Five months after my discharge on June 7, 1963, President Kennedy, the Commander in Chief of the Armed Forces, was assassinated in Dallas on November 22, 1963. I was a twenty-one to the President's twenty-second, but there was no knowledge of this then nor that Mercury takes on the number 5 with the declining sun's 4 (PT = 36; 3 + 6 = 9 ÷ 2 = 4.5 [Hermes' No.]; 109 ÷ 2 = 54.5 [/5 is death or negative aspect] and that things Hermetic are often synchronized among several people, sometimes tit for tat.

One example, Diem and his brother were killed when the U.S. withdrew its support of them. Was it "per Diem payment" or the "goblin universe" when Kennedy's assassination on the *twenty-second* was *twenty-one* days following the coup?

When Robert F. Kennedy's assassination was four to five years later? The fact was that had it been anybody else but the president, he might have lost his top secret clearance with his womanizing, though who knows with Hoover in the FBI. The crime wasn't so much John Kennedy's adultery as his hypocrisy.

When the airplane arrived, Jackie might have thought or said, "Here we are at Love Field, my love." When the motorcade had left, she might have thought or said, "We are no longer at Love Field, my love."

At the time of the assassination, I was *cutting hair*. Jackie will later testify before the Warren Commission that she was "trying to hold his hair on," but apparently there is no record of her doing this on film. I bore him no ill will consciously, and apparently Jackie didn't either on the surface. (See page 417.) Yet there's a biblical and perhaps arcane strangeness about this, the snake bracelet and all. It's as if someone were saying, "Whether or not you know the reason—or even wished it—I will look after your interest. You both symbolically were required to take part in it, one way or another."

Four to five years later, Robert F. Kennedy came to California, where I was living. It was important to participate by voting for him in the primary. Things happen for many in one stroke. The Lord walks and chews gum at the same time.

It's easy to dismiss all this as nonsense. While you're at it, discount the fact that Imelda Marcos and Jackie Kennedy were born in the same 1929, earth-snake year: Imelda, July 2, and Jackie, July 28. Each will be a patron of the arts, outlive her husband, and have a penchant for expensive clothes. In fact, Imelda had hundreds of pairs of shoes, which my mythological context is really not so strange, considering her husband had been a *walker* in the Bataan Death March.

John F. Kennedy and Ferdinand E. Marcos were born in the same year, 1917, fire-snake year: John, the first Mercury period on May 29, and Ferdinand, the second Mercury period on September 11. Both were World War II veterans and became leaders of their countries. Marcos, furthermore, was inaugurated as president of the Philippines on December 30, 1965 (SY), and died on September 28, 1989 (SY).

The Philippine government under Marcos was suspected of having Benigno Simeon Aquino, Jr., shot in the head when he got off an airplane at the Manila airport on August 21, 1983, or forty-four years to the day after Ralph Haven Chichester's death. 1939 = 22; 1983 = 21; 1993 = 22.

Perhaps most interesting of all this is that being in exile, Ferdinand Marcos had crossed a boundary to die. If he is not now buried in the Philippines, I have no doubt that he will be someday. But why did he select Honolulu for his exile? Assumptions are that 1) the U.S. would protect him since he doubtless knew where the bodies were buried; 2) it was a place that could support his lifestyle; 3) expert medical attention was available; 4) a large portion of the Hawaiian population was of Philippino extraction; 5) airplanes at the Honolulu airport came from and went to the Philippines everyday, so that by couriers he could keep his hand in Philippine politics; 6) cash assets.

Still his death-date of September 28, 1989 was two hundred years since Captain Cook had died on Hawaii. Pearl Harbor had been bombed four snake years previously on December 7, 1941, an act that brought the U.S. into the war on the side of the Philippines. Marcos had lived to hear of the forty-seven deaths on the *Iowa* on August 19, 1989. Nearly four years after his death, forty-seven more would die in the Sunset Limited's train accident in Alabama on September 22, 1993, at the border of the Mercury period.

On April 10, 1963, the year both father and son died, the U.S. nuclear submarine *Thresher*, with 129 aboard, was lost off the coast of New England. But George Duren—great grandfather clock—died on April 10, 1865, and was buried in New England.

On May 21, 1968, the U.S. nuclear submarine *Scorpion*, with 99 aboard, was lost near the Azores (AZ-ORES). But Dannie Cameron had been murdered on this date, the beginning of the Mercury period, in 1894. Bobby Franks, forty-four years before to the day, in 1924, and Lindbergh landed near Paris on May 21, 1927, the anniversary of day its Bloody week began.

After leaving Viking Press in 1977, Jackie Onassis began working for Doubleday and Company, becoming a senior editor in books on performing arts and Egyptian art and literature (Jackal-ine). Double any doubled number and the sum can be divided by four.

In February 1994, it was disclosed that Jackie had non-Hodgkins lymphoma, a cancer of the lymphatic system. Then I'd forgotten about her until it was announced on Wednesday, May 18, 1994, that she had returned to her Fifth Avenue apartment to die. The month she disclosed her illness seemed significant, as well as *Fifth* Avenue and the *fifth* month. I'm hoping she will make it until the twenty-first and am thinking, "Come on Jackie, you can do it." But it wasn't to be. If nothing else has been learned when disappointed in a date, another of equal importance will emerge. She died on Thursday evening (7:15 PDT; age sixty-four), May 19, the anniversary of Ho Chi Minh's birth. (See page 11.) She was buried on May 23, one of the Rosalia days in ancient time, next to her husband at Arlington (Li) National Cemetery.

179-B.   The APL freighter, loaded with ammunition and other supplies, went up the river to Saigon. We drew hazard duty pay because there was a possibility we might get hit by enemy fire or even stinkin' sitting in some bar downtown. The risk at the time being about as great as if...you were driving your car to work and had an accident.

Yes, I was in Nam, that godforsaken hole, fighting for my country. Where were you, buddy, when your country needed you? Everybody gotta get inta da act!

Still even with such vague and shadowy credentials, it's possible to see that Vietnam brought into sharp focus the link common to all wars, a humbling. Most who went there were without blemish, suitable for sacrifice to a god. By and large, stereotyped youth looking down its nose at people who had fought and lost battles in their minds, the weak ones. The most that could happen to the young bloods—which was considerable—was that they would lose their lives or be permanently maimed. What hadn't been bargained for, however, was that they could be caught up in a time warp of surviving. It was a nightmare where they hadn't *measured up* as they felt they should or, in the heat and passion of war, had committed or been an accessory to some despicable crime. "And the spirit of ruthless brutality will enter into every fiber," said President Wilson.

Mind you, in their prayers before going to Vietnam, they had plugged into machismo—John Wayne, popcorn, and wanting to be real men. So it came to pass that holes were poked into machismo, a hell of a reason to kill somebody.

Some returned, making the adjustment from G.I. to civilian, and fell quickly into the smugness of their old ways. The only way to maintain their sanity was to double-think. Many were especially bitter that nobody welcomed them home:

"Uh, what's your name?" Ha! Ha! "If I get a chance sometime, might look on the rolls to see if I can find you."

Some talked only to other Vietnam vets and licked each others' wounds, like dogs, a breed apart. Don't knock it when you've never been close to being there!

180.   Mom was a fan of the Scottish writer Robert Louis Stevenson, probably a part of her Cameron heritage. Also it will be learned later that Duncan Cameron had sold his ranch prior to November 16, 1901. So unless his family lived on there, Mom would have been twenty months or less in age at the time she visited.

181-A.   Notice here the suggestion of 2122 for Keseberg. The date of May 22 (415 B.C.) is given (James Trager, ed.).

The People's Chronology: A Year-by-Year Record of Human Events from Prehistory to the Present. New York: Holt, Rinehart, and Winston, 1979, as the date Hermae busts in Athens are found mutilated. This was on the eve of the departure of the armada to attack Sicily. The sacrilege was regarded as a very bad sign. Alcibiades—a joint commander of the expedition—was accused of the crime. He asked for immediate trial but was ordered to sail. When he reached Sicily, however, he was recalled home to stand trial. He fled to Sparta on the voyage home and learned that he had been condemned to death in absentia. An Athenian victory was of little use. The following year (414 B.C.) the Athenian commander was killed and the fleet defeated. Meanwhile Aristophanes' *The Birds* played back in Athens, which awaited news of its military expedition in Sicily.

181-B.   One of the idioms in Germany meaning "not to be quite sane" is *einen Vogel haben*. The literal translation is "to have a bird." (Op. cit., Biederman.)

182.C.   F. McGlashan, *History of Donner Party. Stanford*: Stanford University Press, 1940.

183-A.   Saturn identified with Greek god Kronos.

183-B. One superstition is that snow is caused by witches. (Biren Bonnerjea, *A Dictionary of Superstitions and Mythology*. Detroit: Singing Tree Press, 1969.)

Allhallow's Eve (Halloween) begins Hallow-tide, which takes in November 1 and November 2, but this is linked to May 13, the last day of the Lemuria, and thus to February 21, the Feralia. Samhain, October 31 (one of the Sabbats of the Wiccan year), is called "Feast of the Dead." (*Chase's 1966 Calendar of Events*. Chicago: Contemporary Books, Inc., 1995.) *Day of the Dead* (Mexico) November 1 and 2. Observance starts in last days of October. Sugar-skulled, round loaves of bread are sold in bakeries (Ibid.) Hermes is sometimes depicted as cook and, by extension, baker. There's the belief that the spirits of the dead are able to return at this time to visit friends and relatives. *El Día de Los Muertos* is celebrated in Los Angeles and other areas in the U.S. heavily populated with Mexican-Americans.

184. It's very important to remember that some dates and numbers dealing with the Donner Party will vary slightly with the source.

185. Though willow could be substituted for palm in the Jewish Feast of the Tabernacles, the alder was forbidden. (Ad de Vries, *Dictionary of Symbols and Imagery*. London: North-Holland Publishing Co., Ltd., 1974.)

In addition to Bran meaning raven or crow, it also means alder, which is described as a resurrection tree. Though Bran had good aspects, his side as a war god "delighted in carnage." It's said that the earth was laid to waste by him each winter. (Op. cit., Jobes.) As with Hermes, Bran is associated with decapitation. But it was his own, since before his death, he instructed his men to cut off his head.

186. This was the first symbolism suggesting a celebration of the dead. October 31 (Halloween) was the second.

187. The goose is associated with migration, snow, and winter. (Op. cit., Vries.)

188. They apparently can fly up to 70 percent more efficiently by catching the rising current from the winds of another bird. ("On the Wing" [condensed from National Wildlife, Bill Lawren], *Reader's Digest*, August 1992.) So besides flight and V (suggesting five, victory, peace), another connection to Hermes would be wind (wind, wing, win). The ring or roundness, as with all birds, is suggested by their flying above the earth. Some say birds were sacred to Thoth, and Hermes was given sovereignty over birds of omen.

General Charles Gordon wrote before going to Khartoum,

> ...all of a sudden from a large bush came peals of laughter. I felt put out; but it turned out to be birds, who laughed at us from the bushes for some time in a very rude way. They were a species of stork, and seemed in capital spirits and highly amused at anybody thinking of going up to Gondokoro with the hope of doing anything... (Richard A. Bermann, *The Mahdi of Allah*. New York: The Macmillan Co., 1932.)

In antiquity the stork had been used in sacrifice to Hermes, god of campaigns. Both the Mahdi of Allah and General Gordon were mystics. Since Gordon read his Bible, it's almost certain he made the following association: "Even the stork in the heavens knows her times..." (Jer 8: 7).

February 18, 1884, within the Parentalia, Gordon entered Khartoum. On January 26, 1885, the Mahdi's forces attacked and took the city. Though the Mahdi had given orders that Gordon was to be taken alive, his orders were not obeyed. Gordon's decapitated head was displayed on a spear in front of the Mahdi's tent. One wonders if for sanctioning that the Mahdi sealed his own doom, for four-five months later on June 22, 1885, the Mahdi died after a short illness.

The Greeks had long since noted that geese, cranes, and some other birds fly in the wedge formation, which they likened to their letter *D* or *delta* Δ, the fourth letter of their alphabet. Between the Greeks and Romans then is the suggestion of 45.

At John F. Kennedy's burial, fifty navy and air force jets (one for each state) flew overhead. The loss of the fallen leader was signified by an empty space in the final V formation. Following the fifty planes, Air Force One dipped its wings. (Jane M. Hatch, *The American Book of Days*. New York: H. W. Wilson Co., 1978.)

Note too, the suggestion of 2122: the twenty-one-gun salute; the day of his death the twenty-second.

In World War II, there was the famous V for victory sign of Winston Churchill. D-Day (44), "the longest day," measurement.

189.   Hawks, ducks, and geese are soul birds in Egyptian mythology. The name for hawk is related to the Greek word for *krikos* meaning "circle" or "ring," since the hawk wheels in flight. In Egyptian hieroglyphs, a five-pointed star is surrounded by a circle. This identifies the underworld, "the land of the dead." (Op. cit., Mircea.)

The hawk is identified with Hermes by some Indian tribes and religions. (Jamie Sams and David Carson, *Medicine Cards: The Discovery of Power through the Way of Animals*. Santa Fe: Bear & Co., 1988.)

The desecration of Black Hawk's grave possibly influenced the lives of six men in the Civil War. See pages 4 and 5.

190.   Op. cit., de Vries.

191.   Mable R. Gillis, *California*. New York: Hasting House, Pub., 1939.

192.   Iona and Peter Opie, *Children's Games in Street and Playground*, Oxford: Clarendon P.

193.   Notice in conquest of the New World (especially in Peru and Mexico) the significance of the horse in Hermetic context.

194.   Reasoning that since potatoes aren't mentioned in the Bible they must be unholy, there was at one time a condemnation of them in eighteenth century Scotland. (Anthony S. Mercante, *Encyclopedia of World Mythology and Legend*. New York: Facts of File, 1988.)

195-A.   Emily Lawless, "With the Wild Geese."

195-B.   Robert J. Myers, *Celebrations*. Garden City, New York: Doubleday and Co., Inc., 1972.

196.   Thomas W.H. Fitzgerald, *Ireland and Her People*. Chicago: Fitzgerald Book Co. 1909–1911.

197.   Another source says seventeen.

198.   Zoeth Skinner Eldrege, *History of California*. New York: Century History Co., 1915.

199.   Ibid.

200.   Op. cit., Donald Ungent.

201-A.   If we can think of HMS as Hermes, why not USS for Ulysses?

201-B.   One of the many derivatives of Dannie's mother's name (also *Margaret* Tyler Duren) besides Maggie is May or Mae. *Margaret* in Greek means pearl. Dante refers to the moon as being "la gran Margherita," so we're possibly back to Thoth again, the moon god, Mary Moon, May, and "Mary's month."

202.   Thanks is given to cousin Margaret A. Kodalen for permission to quote her words concerning Duncan A. Cameron, Sr., and family from *A Century in the Foothills*. Letter postmarked October 21, 1992. She married Kenneth L. Kodalen. They live in Great Falls, Montana, and have a son named Robert.

203.   Sir Arthur Conan Doyle was born in Edinburgh, Scotland, on May 22, 1859, the year Charles Darwin published his *Origin of the Species*.

The fifth month and the twenty-second day suggest a Hermes influence. He was educated at *Stone*yhurst College. After becoming an M.D. (caduceus), he sailed two trips as a ship's doctor. (Traveler. The Pleiades, of which Maia is one, rise and begin the season when the weather is most favorable [May] for navigation.) His first voyage was on a whaler (Herman Melville sailed on a whaler also and dedicated *Moby Dick* to Nathaniel Hawthorne) called the *Hope*, which happened to be the name of the second ship (an army hospital ship) I sailed on. His second voyage was on the *MAY*umba and a very uncomfortable one, while the *Comfort* was the first ship I went aboard.

A Study in Scarlet was his first novel. (Remember: Nathaniel Hawthorne wrote *The Scarlet Letter*. Cinnabar is red and from it is extracted *silver*-white mercury.) In it Conan Doyle first introduced the detective Sherrin*ford* Holmes, a name Doyle changed to Sherlock Holmes (SH: HIS: HERMES). Holmes and Dr. Watson lived at 221B Baker Street. (2 + 2 + 1 = 5); or it can be looked at as [22]1 or 2[21].) Thus we have *A* in *The Scarlet Letter*; and *B* from the Baker Street address in *A Study in Scarlet*. Besides, the number 221 lacks only one number in 2122.

Doyle's second novel pertaining to Holmes was called *The Sign of the Four*. After its success, Conan Doyle gave up medicine and devoted his full time to writing.

The Silver Mirror was just one of many stories he wrote. He admired and was greatly influenced by Edgar Allan Poe. In *The Ring of Thoth*, the otherwise very proper doctor dealt with necrophilia and so outdid Poe in perverse themes. It's my purpose only, however, to call attention to the symbolism of *SH, SCARLET, SILVER, FOUR,* and *THOTH.* Doyle's son died in World War I, and the author believed that he could receive messages from him. He then became a crusader for spiritualism. He died in *Crow*borough, Sussex, England. Montana, the fourth largest state with motto "Oro Y Plata" ("Gold and Silver," has part of the *Rocky* Mountains and part of Yellow*stone* Park. It also has some Crow Indians. The Sioux Indians, of which the Crow are part, called themselves Dakota, and of course my mother had been born in the Dakota Territory.

CROWBOROUGH	SUSSEX
CROW (4)	SIOUX (5)

Sussex, a county in England, is divided into two parts: East Sussex, county town, Lewes; West Sussex, county town, *Chichester.*

204.   The name Cora comes from the Greek *kore* which means maiden, and Catherine (Katie, Kate, Kitty) comes from the Greek word *katharos,* meaning crystal. Some of the popularity of the name is believed to have dated from Cathariné, the maiden martyr of *Alexandria.* (Op. cit., Yonge.) Helena is the capital of Montana.

205.   Op. cit., *A Century in the Foothills,* article titled "The Cameron Hill Cemetery" by Jim Pilgeram.

206.   Op. cit., *A Century in the Foothills,* page 27.

207.   The Anastenaria (aea) is a Greek sect living in the Balkans. On May 21, a feast day in honor of St. *Helena* and St. Constantine, firewalking is performed. (*Strange Stories, Amazing Facts.* Pleasantville, New York: The Reader's Digest Association, Inc., 1989.)

At Ayia Eleni, the Greek village, a lamb is sacrificed before the firewalking begins. St. Constantine is said to have walked into a blazing church to save icons. Since the Anastenarides is an unorthodox Christian sect, the more orthodox church wishes it weren't so. Still this is part of life there and remains a tourist attraction. (Michael Sky, *Dancing with the Fire.* Santa Fe: Bear and Company Publishing, 1989.)

Recall that Constantine had built the first St. Peter's Church. Firewalking was practiced in ancient Rome; it is still performed in India where one of the goddesses usually honored is Kali. See Luper-Kal, Book II, page 669, and note under *February 21,* 1944 concerning Ramakrishna.

Perhaps two legs are reminiscent of the fire-sticks of Hermes—or footprints. Both fire and Dannie's name bring to mind 3 Daniel 24: 25:

> The King Nebuchadnezzar was astonished and rose up in haste. He said to his counselors, "Did we not cast three men bound into the fire?" They answered the king, "True, O king." He answered, "But I see *four* men loose, walking in the midst of the fire, and they are not hurt; and the appearance of the *fourth* is like a son of the gods."

208.   Sepharial, *The Kabala of Numbers*, Part I. North Hollywood: Newcastle Publishing Co., Inc., 1974.

209.   The French Revolutionary calendar (later replaced by the Gregorian calendar on January 1, 1806) gave September 22, 1792, as the official date of the republic's establishment. This was year one and September 22 was the autumnal equinox (*Encyclopedia Americana*).

210.   There were two general periods in the year when the spirits of the dead were believed to return to the earth. The nine-day Parentalia, the Feast of the Dead, in February, and three days in May, the ninth, eleventh, and thirteenth, called the Lemuria. The latter began at midnight (in contrast to 12:00 noon for the Parentalia), and each household father threw black beans behind himself repeating two incantations nine times each to send the spirits away. It was required that the ceremonies be performed *barefoot*. (James Hastings, *Encyclopedia of Religion and Ethics*. New York: Charles Scribner's Sons, 1908.)

211.   The *Great Fall Tribune*, January 14, 1933; *Cascade Courier*, January 26, 1933.

212.   Georges, Dumézil, *Archaic Roman Religion*, Volume Two. Chicago: University of Chicago Press, 1970.

Not to be confused with the Coliseum. There were three circuses in ancient Rome. These were horseshoe-shaped stadiums in which chariot races were run. The largest, oldest, and most famous of these was the Circus Maximus, which is said to have been able to seat two hundred and fifty thousand. Hermes is sometimes depicted as a charioteer.

Note here a Hermes link to Poseidon (Hippios, the Equestrian) who was also celebrated at the Isthmian Games (Corinth, Greece), where horse and chariot races and athletic contests were held.

I had no sooner finished writing about number 495 when I came across it the same day in another place. Even then it might have been ignored had there not been the association to Massachusetts. A character called Carrington in the book (William Martin, *Back Bay*. New York: Pocket Books, 1979) says that since everything starts in Los Angeles and flows east; a wall might be built along Route 495 to protect Boston from the "cultural onslaught."

It's clear from any map that Route (road, highway) 495 is a good demarcation—as if fixed and named by Hermes himself—for Boston, Quincy, Lexington, Concord, and other cities. (Note Lexington and Concord associated with *April 19, 1775*.) The book had to do with a mystery surrounding a Golden Eagle Tea Set, presented to George Washington when he visited Boston in 1789. The set had been made by Paul Revere, who hadn't previously come to mind as being under Hermes' sway. Revere was born in Boston on January 1, 1735. He died there in 1818 on May 10, the Eve of the Second Lemuria Day. Though he was a gifted artisan, he was also a forger, and it's clear he was under a strong Hermes influence.

Under Apollos (Joseph Conrad, born December 3, 1857 [SY], had a father called Apollo), his father, young Paul Revere began an apprenticeship that led to him becoming a superb *artist* in working *silver*. In 1757 he married Sarah Orne, by whom he had eight children. She "shuffled off this mortal coil" in the snake month and year of May (3), 1773, and he married Rachel *Walker* five months later on October 10. They in turn had eight children. The family of eighteen was probably never invited out to dinner.

Whether "Paul Revere's Ride" on *April* 18, 1775, is historically accurate isn't important. What is, is that it was the work of a poet (eloquence) that turned Revere into a hero. And hero (protector), messenger, speed, horse, silver, eloquence, and artist are associations to Mercury, quicksilver.

The name, breed, and color of Paul Revere's horse, to whom we owe so much as a nation, are unknown. It just seemed to disappear in history. You don't suppose his family got so hungry it could eat a horse?

Everyone knows, however, the Lone Ranger's horse was pure white and called Silver, and when he said "Hi-ho Silver," he meant "quick Silver" and "Tonto be pronto."

213.   Alfred Alge, ae ae, and Dannie Cameron, ae ae, are possibly part of this.

214.   Though Dannie might have been dead at the time, there was still a beheading (decapitation, persona Hermes). The fire in Elizabeth's case is suggestive of Hermes' fire-sticks.

215.   Information from *Progressive Men of Montana*, 1902. My understanding from this is that Duncan McRay died in 1887 and that Christie McRay died in 1880. But it's possible the writer could have confused these dates with those of Duncan Cameron, Sr.'s parents.

216.   Information about birthplace of father (Dougal or Dugald) is taken from Duncan A. Cameron, Sr.'s death certificate.

217.   Arbitrary. Spelled in various records also as McLocklin, McLacklan, McLauclin, and McLaughlin. McLachlan spelling was taken from *Great Falls Daily Tribune*, March 3, 1911. Curiously, one of the pall bearers at Margaret's funeral was one George Chichester, though my grandfather died the previous year.

218.   According to death certificates, Margaret Cameron died at 12:00 P.M. (noon) on February 27, 1911, and Duncan Cameron, Sr., on January 13 (Friday), 1933. Date of birth on Duncan Cameron's death certificate is given as "February 1844." The age is figured as "88 years, 11 months, and 1 day," suggesting a birthdate of February 12, 1844. The year 1844 seems to square with an 1881 census. But an article in the *Great Falls Daily Tribune* on February 23, 1902, says that he'd just sold his ranch and planned to retire. This would have meant he was fifty-eight, if born in 1844. It was surprising that as a farmer he could do this so early. A third date (*Progressive Men in Montana*) for his birth is January 4, 1833. The year 1833 is obviously wrong, made clear by 1844 being given in censuses, birth certificate, newspaper articles, and more recently in a letter dated December 21, 1994, to me from the secretary of Solomon Lodge, Port Hawkesbury, Nova Scotia, Canada. It reads in part as follows:

In the absence of modern documentation, my research so far is confined to the Register of all members past and present. Within this Register is the following information:

DUNCAN CAMERON   Age 33 years

Farmer of West Bay, Inverness County, Cape Breton.

Raised in Solomon Lodge No. 46,

Port Hawkesbury, N. S.

Date January 22, 1877

From this information his year of birth would be 1844...Sorry I can't be more helpful re., place and date of birth.

But the January 1877 date suggests a birthdate on or before January 22, 1844, which might be January 4, or age might have been figured roughly for some reason and he might have been born in February.

The information below is taken from 1881 census, Black River, Richmond Co., Cape Breton, Nova Scotia:

DUNCAN CAMERON	37	Presbyterian	Married
MARGARET	38	"	Married
ANN	15	"	
ALEXANDER	11	"	
ARCHIBALD	8	"	
HUGH	4	"	
ALLAN	1	"	

219.   Op. cit., de Vries. In mythology, May 13 was the day Hermes brought Persephone back from Hades to Demeter. Persephone (Cora) was Demeter's daughter, who was stolen away by Hades. When Demeter discovered this, she refused to plant or see that things grew. In time all on earth would have died. Eventually a deal was struck between Zeus and Hades where Persephone could return to earth and her mother for two-thirds of each year, but she had to return to rule the underworld with Hades one-third of it. She is sometimes shown with a snake or snakes in hand. The snake is aptly described as "the most spiritual of all creatures." Perhaps in this sense, the correspondence of the snake as Christ equals the fish. (Ibid.) Both Hermes and Christ have links to the three worlds. The nine (diameter) of the coven circle is the same as the length of the Parentalia, so it seems possible that at the root of magic is the belief of a power beyond. The transition from death to afterlife is magic and thus Thoth and Hermes. If there's no such thing as an afterlife, then probably there's no such thing as magic. Houdini might have reasoned this when he said he would try to communicate after his death.

220. The color of Lent, Ash Wednesday. (Persephone was picking violets and white lilies when she was carried off by Hades. So violet is a flower of death and mourning. Op. cit., Vries.) The owner of the vessel was a Captain Grant. Coincidentally on May 9, 1846 (the first day of the Lemuria), young Ulysses S. Grant was fighting in the battle of Resaca de la Palma. Buried palm leaves at one time being used for Ash Wednesday. Ashes too are symbolic of mourning and affliction. 1846 was the year the Donner Party set out.

221. Exception: Numbers on one page stood out. Daphna Moore, *The Rabbi's Tarot*. St. Paul: Llewellyn Pub., 1989. In the "Wheel of Fortune," 45 is the number assigned to man. It's curious that before reading this I'd assigned 45 to Hermes, who happened to be the friendliest of the gods to man.

222. Aleister Crowley, *The Book of Thoth*. York Beach, Maine: Samuel Weiser, Inc., 1991.

223. *Webster's Third New International Dictionary*, 1971.

224. In a Greek city in Asia Minor, the Apostle Paul helped a cripple who'd never walked to *walk*. Because of this and Paul's great *eloquence*, the people believed he was Hermes, a tremendous compliment. Not taking it as such, Paul was rankled and tore his garments. Not long after, Paul was stoned, close "to becoming submerged in a stoneheap" and was mistaken for dead. Act 14: 8–19 and Op. cit., Seltman.

225. The Greeks felt that burial was absolutely necessary because those who weren't buried couldn't pass the river that went around the kingdom of death and thus were doomed to wander in weariness with no place to rest. It was the sacred duty to bury the dead, even a stranger. Creon of Thebes had ruled that none who fought against Thebes would be given a burial, which included Antigone's brother. Antigone, defying Creon's edict, buried her brother, explaining that though she'd disobeyed Creon's ruling, there was a higher, unwritten law of heaven that must not be disobeyed. Op. cit., Hamilton.

> When it was evening, there came a rich man from Arimathea, named Joseph, who also was a disciple of Jesus. He went to Pilate and asked for the body of Jesus. Then Pilate ordered it to be given to him. And Joseph took the body, and wrapped it in a clean linen shroud, and laid it in his own new tomb, which he had *hewn in rock*; and he rolled a great stone to the door of the tomb, and departed (Mt 27: 57–60).

> Another of the disciples said to him, "Lord, let me first go and bury my father." But Jesus said to him, "Follow me, and leave the dead to bury their own dead" (Mt. 8: 21, 22).

Creon or Hitler can be visualized saying the above. But it's completely out of character for Jesus, who's otherwise a caring, kind, and loving person. Therefore, it seems possible that the statement is inaccurate or incomplete. What with all the editing and amending of the Bible, something might have been deleted, similar to the following:

And the disciple replied, "Lord, in all good conscience and decency, I can't do this, for it's disobeying the commandment of honoring my father."

And Jesus said, "Verily I say unto you, many will be sorely tested between two rights. If it's not within their power to determine between them, those who have made the wrong choice will not be judged too harshly. Go and bury your father and return with haste."

226.   Ass: an animal related to a *horse*. Jesus is *traveling* on Palm Sunday. (Hermes, the lonely traveler.) Four-five days later he will be crucified.

227.   Scarlet: bright red. Cinnabar: bright red.

228.   Irony: Hermes tells the future by lots, like shepherds. Both Hermes and Christ are depicted as the Good Shepherd.

229.   Since the beheading of John the Baptist fit Hermes' persona, why wasn't Christ beheaded? There's a symbolic suggestion of this in that he was crucified at Golgatha, the place of the skull. It was written that not a bone in his body would be broken. Defiling the body of the god of wayfarers by breaking his legs wouldn't have been proper.

230.   Easter Island was named for the Easter Sunday it was discovered in 1772. It's famous now for over six hundred stone statues which were there long before the discovery. Captain *Cook* visited it and later discovered Christmas Island. Beheaded on St. Valentine's Day. Feralia burial at sea.

231.   A legend in Winchester, England, was that a thief was about to be hung. Because of his great reverence for the Virgin Mary, however, she appeared and held him up so that he escaped the hanging. Late in the fifteenth century, a group of pictures was painted in the Lady Chapel at the east end of Winchester Cathedral. One of these clearly shows the thief being rescued. Op. cit., Seltman.

232.   Joseph Campbell, *The Way of the Animal Powers*, Vol I. New York: Harper and Row, 1988.

233.   This doesn't sound good for Bran, but the price for any and all immortality is to be a death god.

234.   Op. cit., *Complete Atlas of the British Isles*.

235.   Editors of Time-Life Books, *Psychic Powers*. Alexandria: Time-Life Books, 1987.

236.   A similarity of name to Helen of Troy. The violent eruption of Mt. St. Helens (named after Lord St. Helens) occurred on May 18, 1980. It caused widespread destruction and killed thirty-six. Twenty-three were missing.

237.   Thomas Gifford, *The Assassini*. New York: Bantam Books, 1990.

In ancient times, the horse was symbolic of magic, witches, death, omens, and clairvoyance. Though St. Constantine may not have this in mind, some might argue that the efficacy was still there. Consider this in context with:

1) The Trojan horse.

2) Alexander the Great (pages 370-371).

3) "Go into the village opposite, where on entering you will find a colt tied, on which no one has ever yet sat; untie it and bring it here. If any one asked you, 'Why are you untying it?' you shall say this, 'The Lord has need of it'" (Lk 19: 30, 31).

4) "The Midnight Ride of Paul Revere," whom the witches chose.

5) Some horse carcasses still lay rotting when Lincoln gave the Gettysburg Address. When younger, he had been kicked unconscious by a horse, and Grant had swung on a horse's tail.

6) The horsemanship of Lee and Grant. Remember, at Appomattox, Lee's concern that his men be able to take their horses and mules.

7) Dannie Cameron. (page 443).

8) Edgar Cayce. (pages 373-374).

9) Ralph Chichester. (pages 66-67).

10) Queen Elizabeth II. (page 407).

11) Jacqueline Kennedy. (page 416).

238-A.   *Queen Mary*. London: The Shipbuilder Press, June 1936.

"The panel in the 1st Class Swimming Pool is no longer in its original location, and I am not aware of whether it was broken, stolen or sold following the ship's arrival in Long Beach," wrote William M. Winberg, historian, *Queen Mary & Spruce Goose* Entertainment Center. Research and letter dated April 2, 1992, is acknowledged with thanks.

238-B.   When going into the army in 1947, I and two others were sent from the induction center at San Pedro to Hollywood where Ronald Reagan, playing the part of a sergeant, and Eve Arden were on set at Warner Brothers filming *The Voice of the Turtle*. Our being there was a publicity stunt to show that Ronald Reagan believed young men between the ages of eighteen to twenty-one should join the U.S. Army for three years. Years later after working with the Poverty Program in San Francisco for three months, I quit: disillusionment. It had grand ideas but very little money to accomplish much other than paying the salaries of the workers. Still in three months, I saw enough "crazies," many of whom for which life was a living hell, on the streets to know they needed help, that it was very important they be seen by a psychiatrist or psychologist once a week.

Still later when I was in the merchant marines and had no worries concerning my own medical status, Reagan cut off the mental health programs. But how could he expect a dishwasher, say, who was earning two hundred dollars a month to be able to pay fifty dollars a week to see a doctor, which he really needed to do? Since Reagan had no obvious mental problems, he couldn't relate to this, or only that in seeming to be a "bleeding heart" didn't fit in with his masculinity. More than anything he'd ever done or would do, I hated the man for this and cursed him, as had thousands of others, the voice of the turtle. On March 31, 1981, Reagan was shot by John W. Hinckley, who was later found not guilty because of insanity and admitted to a mental institution. I doubt, however, that any of us would have wanted him to get Alzheimer's disease. Yet it strikes me as an ironic retribution his mind will be turned to stone, but not before getting on the bandwagon for victims of Alzheimer's, a cost he and his family wouldn't have—comparatively—much to worry about.

Reagan's inability to relate to problems he himself didn't have—"there but for the grace of god go I"—flawed him for any consideration of greatness.

239-A.   Dean R. Koontz, *Cold Fire*. New York: The Berkeley Pub. Group, 1991.

239-B.   Being too old to want to stay up until the witching hour, I first performed a simple, innocuous ritual between 6:00 to 7:00 P.M., give or take fifteen minutes, on December 23, 1991. Though not asking for death and destruction specifically, I would be lying if saying I didn't want some sign of power.

At 4:15 the following morning near Spokane, nineteen cars derailed from a 108-car train (travel) headed for Pasco. There were no injuries. Since the Burlington Northern Railroad wasn't the Great Northern, whose goat or ram I had prayed to in Myrtle Edwards Park, I could attach no significance to the accident. The idea occurred, however, that there might have been one car from Great Northern, as trains sometimes pulls cars from other railways. But even if there had been one or two, I felt it was too far-fetched to pursue. It was the Burlington Northern Railroad, not the Great Northern Railway. Yet even after dismissing the idea, it kept coming back. On the off chance that there still might be some connection, I decided to write to the Burlington Northern Seattle Office at 999 Third Avenue. Burlington Northern Railroad was created on March 2, 1970, from a merger of four railways:

1)   *Great Northern.*

2)   Northern Pacific.

3)   *Chicago*, Burlington, and *Quincy*. This included Colorado and Southern Railway and Fortworth and Denver Railway. (I was disappointed at first to read this was Quincy, Illinois. Later I was reassured of being on the right track when reading that the first railroad opened in the U.S. on October 7, 1826. [Granite Railway Company, *The First Railroad In America: A History of the Origin and Development of the Granite Railway at Quincy, Massachusetts*. Boston: Private Printing, 1926. Since it was the beginning of a whole new era of transportation, I don't believe it was just one more coincidence with all the other things which had occurred at Quincy, Massachusetts.)

4)   Spokane, Portland, and Seattle Railway.

There is, of course, a Hermetic association to railroad—travel, speed, wind (the Burlington *Zephr* of the 1930s), commerce. The metal rails are like two parallel snakes (as are the parallel bars of the gymnast). These in turn are supported by (cross) ties or *sleepers*. The locomotives pull rolling stock. BNR is an American railroad. ABNR in an anagram for Bran, the Celtic god whose name means raven. In some esoteric way, it all seemed connected.

A search of the papers showed that the accident described was the second in a series of three that occurred within about a week to Burlington Northern Railroad. On Monday, December 23, 1991, at 12:30 A.M., a Burlington Northern southbound train was derailed. No injuries, butane-filled tanker cars burned near Lakewood and residents within a half-mile radius were evacuated from their homes. Then on Sunday afternoon December 29, 1991, an eleven-year-old boy was killed in Everett when he tried to crawl over a Burlington Northern car or coupling that suddenly began to move.

My responsibility for anyone or more of these three accidents is doubtful. Yet why the gravitation of mind process toward these accidents? Why not all train wrecks instead of a few?

A vague suspicion is hardly an adequate reason to go to the nearest police station and confess all, a process I hardly understand myself. The upshot would be a ride in a patrol car to Harborview Hospital for a consult with a psychiatrist who would quickly point out with steel-trap logic: 1) some accidents have occurred out of state where I wasn't; 2) the times given for alleged mental activities don't correspond exactly to the hours of the accident, and 3) authorities—in some cases—have already determined the cause.

On February 15, 1996 (the night before being one of mental activity), I heard, with only vague attention, the tail end of a newscast. A freight train had lost its brakes and slammed into an office building, causing injury to nine. Forget it. The following day when walking through Seattle Center, one date on a flagpole attracted my attention when walking by, though I don't look at these: May 11, 1858, Minnesota was admitted. May 11 is the second Lemuria Day. So what? About ten or fifteen minutes later when passing a newspaper vending machine, I noticed the wreck had taken place at St. Paul, Minnesota. As I had other things to do for an hour or two (namely to walk down to Myrtle Edwards Park and then to lower Kinnear Park), I decided to buy the newspaper on my way back. But when going to do so later, the older newspaper had been replaced. I could not seem to locate the article. Then later I found it—as if it were sitting purposely to be found—in only two or three pages left of a *Seattle-Post Intelligencer* on a bus's seat.

The night of February 15–16, 1996, was also one of mental activity. Then on February 16 at about 5:45 P.M., an Amtrak passenger train bound for Chicago and a local commuter train crashed head-on, killing eleven. In each case, I'd felt a link to these wrecks *before* seeing the calling cards of "Burlington Northern" and "St. Paul" (whom I never liked, nor did St. Peter) and in the second wreck at Silver Springs, Maryland.

In my case, there's probably not a thing to any of it. What's important, however, is the suggestion that the original idea of the coven—before it deteriorated in some cases—might have been to teach people who had fragmented, undisciplined, and undependable power to focus, to try to harness and control this.

Supposing there are people who are fragmented cases, who neither know what they're are doing nor understand that they are causing the problem. Would it not be better to try to control these wild forces? We would be fools, of course, to pump billions of dollars into trying to understand something which is nonexistent. We would be bigger fools if in the occurrence of some accidents we're like cattle going to a slaughter, never understanding nor having any way to prevent it.

I submit that the so-called miracles—if indeed they occurred—were due to a fragmented power, that the potential of becoming a miracle worker lay in the people before they ever entered the Church. In some cases, it would have happened whether they became converts or not. The Church just provided a means of focusing.

Far out? Perhaps. But the monasteries and the convents gave protection to a lot of sensitive and vulnerable people. Isolation, seclusion, abstinence, vows of silence, dietary control, etc., come very close to the profile I felt must be valid for the usual witch.

239-C.   Maybe it was just my imagination or I hadn't noticed them that closely before, but the ravens seemed fatter, larger, and more numerous than remembered. Then too, I read for the first time (*February 21*, 1993) that Hermes was given dominion over all birds of omen by Zeus. (Homer, *The Homeric Hymns.* translation by Thelma Sargent, New York: Norton, 1973.)

If the gravestone is connected to Hermes, then it follows the lapis manalis (see page 36) was also. There's a lapis-Hermes and a lapis-Christ.

Some believe Hermes is represented by half the fish symbol. He is and he isn't Christ, as Christ is known or revealed. Yet Hermes is a god of revelation. His so-called dual nature could be just another way of testing faith or a catalyst.

240.   As written previously, Anita was in her early old-age when I surprised her one Christmas with a German shepherd puppy. She commented that since Rocky was getting older, maybe it was a good thing to have a younger dog also to continue on with and soften the grief when Rocky would die. Rocky was run over a year or two later, and Chief lived to be eight. About sixteen years later when I visited Anita in Santa Rosa, California, she said she would always believe Rocky purposely had gotten himself killed. If somebody else had made such a remark, I might not have thought much about it. But it was strange coming from Anita. Was this some sort of prescience of the old and/or slightly daffy? Since animals give us so much pleasure, it's natural they take their toll on us mentally, the same as humans. Though she had come to love the second dog, there seemed to have been an underlying *mea culpa* for accepting the puppy, a feeling in doing so she had been disloyal to Rocky. And maybe too there was an underlying mixed feeling toward me in this respect for having brought her the puppy.

Could be Rocky was an old dog who had just gotten run over because he was slowing down. Could be he did commit suicide for the reason Anita thought: that he felt Chief had replaced him in Anita's heart.

There is now the symbolism of Topaz and surrounding area, and though a German shepherd may not be a wolf, it's so close that it really doesn't make much difference. Looking back, I'm not so certain it wasn't like she said. About a year or so after visiting her in Santa Rosa, she—who was born on August 22 like my mother—died of a brain tumor.

My father took me over to Kate's place one year when I'd first gone to the ranch. She was a cousin of some sort and old then when I was young. A remembrance now of her coming out of her small home to greet us. She had about fifteen or twenty beautiful collies she told to be quiet. My father spoke of her with respect, but one of my brothers later called her "Crazy Kate." I wish I'd gotten to know her.

241-A.   When the "Miracle in the Mountains" rescue of three cross-country skiers (Brigitte Schluger and Rob and Dee [455] Dubin lost *February 20* near Aspen, Colorado, in a blizzard) occurred, I decided not to use it, though here were lost people making footprints in the snow and fitting the Hermetic picture of wayfarers, athletes, and speed. Then in a picture (by Kent Meireis with the Carl Weiser article "Skier: I Felt Treated Like 'Roman Slave'," *USA Today*, March 4, 1993), Brigitte Schluger shows *five* bandaged fingers (two thumbs + three fingers). She is indignant by her treatment during the ordeal in the snow. When she suggested to be "younger Dubin" that he was going the wrong way, she is quoted as saying, "He told me, 'You shouldn't think so much.'" Yet in some mysterious way perhaps all roads lead to Rome. She says resentfully, "I just felt like this little Roman slave girl, and there's this guy on the cart behind going, 'Faster! Faster!' In a faxed statement, Dubin apologized to Brigitte but said polite conversation was "*sacrificed* to the need to survive" (eloquence).

241-B.   It was I who had the idea of going to the library just before one Christmas and running off copies of a perpetual calendar to send out as Christmas presents to relatives and friends. They'd only need one calendar for life. It was a real savings, and every time they used it, they'd be reminded of me!

242.   John DiGiovanni, Robert Kirkpatrick, Stephen Knapp, William Macko, and Monica Rodriguez Smith.

243.   In order to bring the Julian calendar into conformity with the seasons, 46 B.C. was given 445 days and so dubbed "the year of confusion." Had people designating *Anno Domini* been able to read the signs (see page 27), they might have realized that 445 is consistent with 45 and 44 B.C. The Julian calendar had one day inter-calculated every four years after February 24.

The calendar, as we know it today, owes its form to the papal bull of Gregory XIII on *February 24*, 1582. It seems reasonable to believe there's also another calendar—of time, events, and numbers that we don't understand and, for peace of mind, might not want to if we could.

244.   Shakespeare (aeeae) used Plutarch as his source for *Julius Caesar* (aea). Plutarch, though living for awhile in Rome, was a Greek born about 46, or ninety years after the Lupercalia in 44 B.C. So undoubtedly each had to do some educated guessing. This then is another:

When Caesar was offered the crown the first time, the crowed hissed, booed, and laughed. Noting the political wind, Caesar acted that he thought the same as the crowd. What was being foisted on him he certainly wanted nothing to do with.

This could only be interpreted by those who disliked him as shallow deviousness, hypocrisy. Hatred festered bringing about his assassination a month later.

Both Caesar and Lincoln were viewed as tyrants by some. In Caesar's case, it was true. There's little doubt Virginia state's motto *"Sic semper tyrannis,"* which Shakespearean actor John Wilkes Booth shouted, was adopted with Caesar, as well as others, in mind.

Two colleges of priests conducted the Lupercalia: one called *Fabiani,* and the other, *Quintiliania.* (Op. cit., *Lemprière's Write Large Classical Dictionary.*) The ceremony was religious and represented hundreds of years of history and tradition. Now the comparative upstart, both powerful and self-important, added a third group of priests called the *Julii,* after himself naturally. This was a very unpopular thing to have done, for it was perceived as just one more example of Caesar's vain glory, ambition, and highhandedness. Did it never stop? There were people before him, and there would be people after him. At the very least, he needed the prescription, the Rx, to have his mental glasses changed.

Mark Antony had nothing to do with Caesar's death, and he thought Brutus and Cassius were "butchers," which was true. Still Antony's friendship might have blinded him to Caesar's opportunism, which paradoxically Antony himself fell into after Caesar's death.

Caesar had named Octavian his successor. Sharing command in 42 B.C., Antony and Octavian defeated Brutus and Cassius, the assassins, at the battle of Philippi, Greece. Still later Antony and Cleopatra (a throne name of some Macedonian queens of Egypt) Philopater VII committed suicide. Tradition is that she died from the bite of an asp, in this case, the small delta was the mouth of the river of death for Cleopatra of Alexandria, the city named after the Macedonian born 356 B.C. Cleopatra was part Greek, Iranian, and Macedonian. Olympias, the mother of Alexander, had a collection of snakes, and Alexander's sister was also called Cleopatra. The Greek-Roman-Egyptian mysticism preceding the birth of Christ is inescapable in many ways. With Octavian, there came a peace—nearly unbroken—for two hundred years called *Pax Romana.* Hermes, persona peace.

Caesar's greatness didn't depend on William (illi) Shakespeare, but the world would be less aware of the Lupercalia had Shakespeare not written about it. He was possibly an instrument, noting a fact for a later period. Considering too the enormity of Shake-spear-ean works and the mystery surrounding him, the writer could very well have channeled, if such a thing exists.

"But one of the soldiers pierced his side with a *spear*" (Jn 19: 34). "And behold, the curtain of the temple was torn in two...and the earth shook" (*shake*) (Mt 27: 51). Hermes, god of writers, eloquence.

Anno Domini means in a specified year of the Christian era. Therefore 44 B.C. = 44(5), the suggestion of 45, and A.D. = 5. The 44 was the important thing of the Lupercalia, the small delta omens pointing to Christ's birth and later the cross.

Jesus was possibly crucified during the Parentalia or Caristia—a most likely day being February 14, which now has come down to mean the forty-fifth day.

245.   M. Cary, et. al., editor, *The Oxford Classical Dictionary*, Oxford: Clarendon Press, 1949.

665

246. Two festivals were held for Faunus: one on February 13, and the other, December 5 (Op. cit. Peck). The first was the beginning of the Parentalia. If December stood for this also, then December 7 would have represented the Lupercalia.

247. Op. cit., *Civilization of the Ancient Mediterranean*.

248. Op. cit., *Lemprière's* Dictionary, Writ Large.

249. Jesus can be associated with several caesars. Julius Caesar was born 100 B.C. and died forty-four years before his birth. Octavian died in the year 14. Tiberius was Jesus' contemporary when beginning his mission about 27. Tiberius died March 16, 37.

250. Edith Hamilton, *Mythology*. Boston: Little, Brown & Co., 1942.

251. *Meryre* sounds similar to the name *merthyr*, meaning graveyard, near Aberfan, Wales. See Chapter Twenty-five.

252. Op. cit., Steiger.

253. Kenneth Sydney Davis, *The Hero: Charles A. Lindbergh and the American Dream*. Garden City, New York: Doubleday, 1959.

254-A. Hal Higdon, *The Crime of the Century: The Leopold and Loeb Case*. New York: G.P. Putnam's Sons, 1975.

254-B. On the same day of the murder, Mrs. Jessie Creighton Woolworth, wife of F.W. Woolworth (wealth), died at Glen Cove, Long Island. Estate later valued at "over 21 million."

255. Note too the *L* in Lemures, the ghosts of the ancients who hadn't received a proper burial.

256. Op. cit., Eliade. Vol. 15.

257. Op. cit., Higdon. Pages 132 and 200.

258. Op. cit., Higdon.

259. In the 1941 Hollywood version *The Sea Wolf*, Edward G. Robinson played Wolf Larsen. Robinson had been born in *Roman*ia on December 12, 1893 (SY). Also starring in the film was London-born Ida *Lupino*, a name which sounds like lupine or wolf. Earlier Robinson had starred in *Little Caesar*, playing the part of Rico Bandello, a character loosely patterned after Al Capone.

London (John Chaney) was the illegitimate son of *Flora* Wellman and William Henry Chaney (ae), a *traveling astrologer*. When the baby was eight months old, she married John London, who had eleven children. John Chaney then got his new parent's name and the name Jack to avoid confusion. He had been a traveler, sailor, and writer. Today the "Square" in Oakland, California, is named after him. Among many stories Jack London wrote, besides *The Sea Wolf*, were *White Fang*, a story of a wolf, and *The Son of the Wolf*. Later in life, London had become a heavy drinker and committed suicide, as had Hitler. Nietzsche, who impressed London, went insane, dying possibly from the ravages of syphilis, as had Capone.

> "When you look into the abyss,
> The abyss looks back."

For most who are strongly Hermetic, a high price is exacted either before, during, or after achievement. To name just a few: Hemingway, Van Gogh, and O.J. Simpson—and probably William Shakespeare. In their way, they were seekers of the magic.

260.   Official notice of parole came 33 years, 275 days, and 18 hours after Bobby Franks died. *Time*, March 3, 1958.

261.   Op cit., Eliade.

262.   Roger G. Swearingen, *The Prose Writings of Robert Louis Stevenson*: A Guide. Hamden, Connecticut: Archon Books, 1980.

263.   May 21.   Weeping Willow is the birthday flower. Because of drooping, it symbolizes mourning. It is a funeral tree and one of two in front of Hades.

         May 22.   Willow, ancient symbol of mourning.

         May 24.   Wolf's bane is the birthday flower. It symbolizes misanthropy (distrust or hatred of all people).

         (Op. cit., Jobes).

In mythology there are numerous tales where flowers are associated with kidnapping, cruelty, death, sadness, etc. On May 24, friends of the Franks sent flowers to their desolated home. The funeral was held on May 25, possibly the anniversary of a Mercury festival in Rome. The coffin, as if in reminder of the Roman Rosalia, was covered with rosebuds and placed in a mausoleum in Rosehill Cemetery.

264.   What might be worth a passing thought is if there's some 45-echo or ripple affect, starting with the 13 through 21 period of February with emphasis on a 1(4)/1(5) linkage (some believe the Lupercalia was the beginning of Valentine's Day) and 21. This continues into March, April, and May. On March 15, Caesar was assassinated. It's reasonable to assume there was some preparation, plotting, or scheming on March 13 and 14. March 21 approximates the first day of spring.

April 14/15 represents both the end of Lincoln and the *Titanic*, and April 21, the founding of Rome.

More recently on April 14, 1994, two American F-15 fighter jets shot down two American helicopters over northern Iraq. The Pentagon (five) asked why at one level and eventually laid the "friendly fire" tragedy to rest, but it also should have wondered about the symbolism. The number 4 occurred twice: the month of April and the number of aircraft involved. The figures 14/15 occurs twice: the date and the F-15 designation, the date and the number of Americans killed. There were in all 26 (2 x 13) deaths: 3 Turkish officers, 2 British officers, 1 French officer, 5 Kurds, and 15 Americans. The shoot-downs represented flight-death. Black Hawk, the name of each helicopter, even sounds ominous. (Note: *Olympic* collided with HMS *Hawke*, causing delay on construction of *Titanic*; consider Black Hawk in relation to Lincoln of April 14.) Two missiles were fired, one being a side*wind*er, a heat-seeking missile, which suggests 1) snake, 2) wind, and 3) Mercury temperature (heat). The incident occurred in broad daylight and good weather, a lulling *deception*, also seen in safeguards not operating and possibly an error influenced by combat tension. Compare this to deception concerning Lincoln's protection, iceberg, and four wireless messages unheeded.

May 15, the Roman festival for Mercury and Maia. May 21 is the beginning of the Mercury period. May 30 was Memorial Day, where at the Indianapolis Speedway a record was broken (contest) and Henry *Ford* (to whom Dillinger would later write a note) was in attendance. Here again is the interplay of the two stockyard cities, one of which will be described as windy. Twenty-one (21) is a number of absolute truth, involving 1, 2, and 3. In the case of Bobby Franks, it involved 1, 2, and 3. And there's nothing more truthful (faithful) to life than death. They are husband and wife, though it's not worth my life to conjecture which is which nor my intention to get into bathos humor, flippancy, or morbidness, but to show a different perspective. Moreover, the truthfulness of death is being talked about, rather than its permanence. Truth isn't always beauty.

265-A.   A canary bird is a jailbird. Years ago some convicts had yellow uniforms. Their cells then were their cages. The death of Howard Carter's canary was thought to have been an omen. Though it'd been killed by a cobra, no one could figure out how the snake got through the wires of the cage.

265-B.   Reference is made to *The Greek Magical Papyri in Translation, Including the Demotic Spells*, edited by Hans Dieter Betz, Chicago, University of Chicago Press, 1992. What's interesting about this is that revealed in the "Binding Love Spell of Astrapsoukos" (Astrampsychos was the name of one or more Persian magicians) are four forms of Hermes:

> In the east: An ibis.
> In the west: A dog-faced baboon.
> In the north: A serpent.
> In the south: A wolf.

The Egyptian god Anubis, judge and protector of the dead, is sometimes identified with Hermes. There's the composite god Hermanubis. Anubis is usually described as jackal-headed and less frequently as dog-headed. Yet there are a few references to Anubis's head being like a wolf's. At Siut (Lycopolis), Egypt, Anubis was a cemetery god, subject to the city-deity Upawat, who is described as being a sun god and *wolf*. Here possibly is an Apollo/Hermes relationship, or 4:5. Anubis would have taken on the wolfish appearance from Upawat or Osiris (chief god of the underworld and said to be the father of Anubis), since the wolf, revered at Lycopolis, was believed on a much wider scale to be the transformation of Osiris.

Some of the statues of Hermes/Mercury in Egypt "represented him with the head of a dog." The dog, whom Hermes is said to have dominion over in *Homeric Hymn* No. 4, might well have meant *canis*, to include the dog, jackal, wolf, coyote, etc. Also in some societies, the wolf was associated with fugitives, exiles, and outlaws. Since Hermes was a god of thieves, the wolf symbolism is suggestive. *The*

668

Greek Magical Papyri in Translation was the first direct reference from older texts I'd come across to Hermes as a wolf, more often associated with Zeus, Apollo, and Mars. Since the ibis, the dog-faced baboon (a companion of Thoth and possibly associated with Anubis too), and the snake (the caduceus) are usually given or surmised about Thoth-Hermes, I have little doubt about the wolf being true. This now ties in with Romulus and Remus (the Capitoline wolf was a protector and nurturer, which happen to be qualities of Hermes.) Not to be forgotten too is that Romulus helped populate the first Rome with thieves, fugitives, and exiles.

Romulus had attracted citizens to Rome by making it a refuge for outlaws (*Encyclopedia Americana*). As stated previously, Hermes is seen as an Indo-European god. This becomes more curious when coupled with the fact that the great Indian goddess Kali was—in one form—a she-wolf and gave birth to a godly son "in the cave of the wolf." It's possible then that Lupercal is a corruption of Luper-Kal (wolf-Kali). (Op. cit., Walker).

Logically February 17, being part of the Parentalia, should relate to Hermes, but it's called the Festival of Quirinus, god of the assembly later identified with Romulus. Yet again, the marketplace—which Hermes was over in Greece—was used for assembly.

In alchemy, the wolf, with the dog, is the duality of the nature of Mercurious, "the philosophical mercury." (J.C. Cooper, *An Illustrated Encyclopaedia of Traditional Symbols*. London: Thames and Hudson Ltd., 1978.)

266.   Darrow once said hatred and malice masquerade under the *"nom de plume*: 'Justice.'" Sometimes beneath those who quote the Bible and speak of the Lord's justice there lies this too.

267.   Apparently the number 777 is linked to Hermes in Tarot. Janet and Stewart Farrar, *The Witches' God*. Custer, Washington: Phoenix Pub., 1989. Seven hundred seventy-seven vessels set out from the East Coast for San Francisco in 1849. (Op. cit., Hansen, Gladys, *San Francisco Almanac*.) Hermes persona: sudden wealth, gambling.

268.   Octavia Vivian, *Coretta*. Philadelphia: Fortress Press, 1970. "Bloody Sunday," March 7, 1965 (*Encyclopedia Americana*).

269.   Lusitania, a region in ancient Spain, probably took in what is now Portugal. The inhabitants were warlike, crude, rude, and lived mainly off plunder. Spartan-like in many ways, they never had more than one dish at a meal. Their clothes were commonly black, and they warmed themselves by heating stones in fires. Usually they took their sick and put them on high roads so that travelers passing through might treat or cure them. (Op. cit., *Lemprière's Classical Dictionary*.)

Though the Roman army defeated them with much difficulty, the Lusitanians were—in the end—losers, and so it's unclear why a Cunard luxury liner would be called the *Lusitania*.

270.   U.S. Department of Interior, NPS, GPO 1991-281-954/40026.

271.   Arizona (AZ), the Apache state, became the forty-eighth, entering the union on St. Valentine's Day, February 14, 1912 (12, the transposition of 21). This was the

anniversary of the date Captain Cook's body was decapitated and mutilated in the Hawaiian Islands.

272.   The Liberty Bell was among several that rang in Philadelphia on the Delaware River to proclaim the Declaration of Independence by the *thirteen* states. (The Parentalia began on the thirteenth.) But this was on July 8, four days after their signing on the fourth. Tradition is that the bell cracked when it rang during John Marshall's funeral procession (*Hermes, conductor of the dead*) and then again— irreparably and never to be rung after—on George Washington's birthday in 1846, which was twenty years after John Adams of *Quincy* and Thomas Jefferson *died* on July 4, 1826, the *fiftieth* anniversary of their signing.

273.   George Watterston (October 23, 1783–February 4, 1854) was born in New York harbor. (Note here *water*, which brings to mind the reflecting pool, and his death date of *February 4*.) His father for years had spelled the family name "Waterstone." After the library (temple of knowledge) burned to the ground in 1814, G. Watterston was appointed librarian. Thomas Jefferson donated his own collection, and Watterston, with only a small salary and one assistant, did all the work except for selecting additions, which was done by a congressional commit- tee. (Dumas Malone, *Dictionary of American Biography*. New York: Scribner's Sons, 1936, Neptune's Fountain before Library of Congress.

274.   Frank Freidell and Lonnelle Aikman, *G. Washington: Man and Monument*. Washington, D.C.: Washington National Monument Association with coopera- tion of National Geographic Society, 1965.)

275.   "The sum total of heavenly and earthly numbers is 55." See Book I, footnote 1-G.

276-A. Though the Lincoln Memorial in Washington, D.C., has Greek (Doric) columns, his tomb at Oak Ridge Cemetery, Springfield, Illinois, has an obelisk arising from it, suggesting Egypt, Thoth. Here again is another link between Lincoln and Washington, whose head might be that of the Great Sphinx at Giza, carved from a natural bluff of rock, which is *twenty-one* meters (*Encyclopedia Americana*) at its tallest point. Because of being used as a target in gun practice by the Mamluks, the Sphinx's head is damaged, pitted, but Washington's face was also pitted with smallpox scars, and he has a resemblance to the Sphinx. Southeast of the Sphinx lies Khufu, the first great pyramid. The U.S. dollar bill (money, a means of com- merce) has Washington on the front of it, and a pyramid on the back. The top of the pyramid is an eye. The eye of Ra?

276-B. To be more exact, *The World Book Encyclopedia* gives 34 feet 5½ inches for each side of the base of the pyramidion, 55 feet 1½ inches for each side of the monument's bottom, and 555 feet 5⅛ inches for its height. "The pyramidion rises 55 feet." The nine-inch cap of aluminum *protects* the tip.

277.   It was Jeanne Calment's tenth birthday. She was thirteen years old when Vincent Van Gogh, another Hermetic character, came to Arles to paint. She thought him to be "very ugly, ungracious, impolite, and not well." On February 21, 1996, Calment celebrated her 121st birthday, becoming the oldest person alive whose age can be verified by official documents.

278.	Both Frank and Frances will die in February. Frank on the twenty-second (1958), the day after the anniversary of Ralph's and my birthdays. Past-present, present-past, 2122. In some sort of reasoned symmetry, Ralph will die on August 21, the day before the anniversary of both our mother's and stepmother's birthday (Anita Carmel Chichester, 1903) on August 22. (Catholic Church: Feast of the Immaculate Heart of Mary, one day before the Mercury period begins.) 2122.

279-A.	Frank Chichester was born September (*ninth* month) 10, 1888. Frances Duren Chichester, August (*eighth* month) 22, 1888.

279-B.	Jean Pierre Vernant, *Myth and Thought among the Greeks*. Boston: Routledge and Kegan Paul, 1965.

280.	Several statues of Hermes have no arms. Some say that this was to show that the god of eloquence could overcome all by the power of word alone. Op. cit., *Lemprière's Classical Dictionary*.

281.	From my understanding, Hermes generally isn't thought of as a god to whom human victims were offered, though apparently at one time there was a few far-out cults in Greece who did sacrifice humans to him. The word *quetzal* can mean "bird," "flying," "precious," and *coatl*, "twin" or "snake." *Quetzalcóatl* could mean "bird snake" or "flying twin" (caduceus?), among other meanings. He was a god of death and resurrection who did not sacrifice human beings but only snakes, birds, and butterflies. One story is that before departing on a raft of snakes in the Atlantic, he promised to return to bring happiness. A raft will swing at times when it floats upon an ocean. Thus S-wings could also apply to Quetzalcóatl.

282.	Op. cit., Hastings.

283-A.	*Facts and Fallacies*. Pleasantville, New York: Reader's Digest Association, 1988.

283-B.	Richard B. Morris, *Encyclopedia of American History*. New York: Harper and Row, Publishers, 1976.

283-C.	George W. Nordham, George Washington: *Vignettes and Memorabilia*. Philadelphia: Dorrance and Co., 1977.

	The dedication of the temple to Mercury near the Circus Maximus (either existing at the time or built later) was on the Ides of May, 495 B.C., the time in ancient Rome there was a celebration to Mercury. 495 becomes 4(4 + 5)5 or 4(5 + 4)5 or 4(4.5 + 4.5)5. Man has four limbs, each having five digits. There's no way to divide May into two equal halves as was possible with April. However, $15/31 = 0.4839$ and $16/31 = 0.5161$. Thus 5.4839, having a 4, probably comes closer to representing Mercury than 5.5161.

283-D.	In February (24), 1582, Pope Gregory XIII announced the reform of the Julian *calendar* (named after Julius Caesar, connected to February 15, 44 B.C.), to be replaced by the Gregorian. The birthdate of Gregory *thirteen* is difficult to nail down as it's given variously as January 1, 1502, January 7, 1502, and June 7, 1502. All sources agree, however, that he was elected Pope on May *14*, 1572, and died on *April 10* (1585), a date unknown to me when writing about great grandfather clock. Pope Gregory had an illegitimate son.

283-E. The question has been raised that if there were really a curse, how come Howard Carter wasn't touched by it? The most convincing reason is given on page 9. It's surprising the connection—to my knowledge—hasn't been made until now. In another way, however, Howard Carter was cast perfectly into the blessing-curse (curse-blessing) far in advance, being a "mercurial" man who—though immensely talented and courageous—was stubborn, nervous, and high strung all his life. He has been described by Thomas Hoving (*Tutankhamun, the Untold Story.* New York: Simon and Schuster, 1978) as insensitive, tactless, lying or deceptive at times, among other things. He undermined himself and his own achievements with such negative aspects and so "tortured himself" as well as others.

Officially the dismantling of the Burial Chamber blocking (wall or door) occurred on February 17, 1923. Prior to this and after, Lord Carnarvon and Howard Carter had many arguments. Carnarvon, trying to put some of it behind them and to discuss the problems, visited Carter's home on February 23 (the day following the Caristia), 1923. This ended in heated words in which Carter told his patron, in no uncertain terms, to get out of his home and never come back. Indeed it can be said that Howard Carter had been insinuated into the blessing-curse far in advance of King Tut's desecration. On February 26, Lord Carnarvon and Howard together managed to lock up the tomb until the next season. When Carnarvon died on April 5, 1923, however, Howard became very depressed. Howard died in 1939. On February 22 (the anniversary of: the Deposition [disposition] of SS. Peter and Paul and Washington's birthday [New Style as opposed to Old Style], 1940, his books were auctioned at Sotheby's.

284-A. John S. Goff, Robert Todd Lincoln: *A Man in His Own Right.* Norman: University of Oklahoma Press, 1968.

284-B. Ruth W. Gregory, *Anniversaries and Holidays.* Chicago: American Library Association, 1975.

285. Brent Ashabranner and Jennifer Ashabranner (some of the photographs and historical ones), *A Memorial for Mr. Lincoln.* New York: Putnam, 1992.

286. Edward F. Concklin (under direction of Director of Public Buildings and Public Parks of National Capital), *The Lincoln Memorial, Washington.* Washington, D.C.: U.S. Government Printing Office, 1927.

287. The peace accord between Israel and Palestine on September 13 (MP), 1993, provided a basis for ending the *forty-five* years of hostility between them. Israel was established on May 14, 1948. Hermes, persona peace.

288. In Allhallows, the day following Halloween, there's the aspect of communing with the dead. Its original date was *May 13.* This was changed to November 1, and in 834 *Pope* Gregory IV extended it to include the entire Church. (Op. cit., Farrar.) But on *May 13:* Persephone returned from Hades, Reverend Jim Jones was born, the Miracle of Fatima occurred (a snake year), and *Pope* John Paul II was shot. May is the fifth month, and there seems to be a similar or parallel system of May 13–21 to that of the Parentalia at least and possibly to the entire months. February is a short month, and February 2 (Imbolg) is close to May 1. If you assume that many women would become pregnant right after marrying, those marrying in May would tend to have their babies in February.

The Parentalia could have been unlucky generally for birth and so the superstition against marrying in May. Consider once again Duncan Cameron's possible birth on February 21, Margaret Cameron's birth on February 13, Ralph's and Brent's on February 21, Idylle Cameron's on May 13, and Dannie Cameron's on May 15 and his death on May 21. (See pages 380-381, concerning Kathleen Kennedy Hartington and Patricia Hearst. Exception Jean Kennedy.)

289.   Whether superstition or fiction, I don't know. But it has been said Satan's power is weakest at midnight on December 21 of the winter solstice (Ed Kelleher and Harriette Vidal, *Prime Evil*. New York: Dorchester Publishing Co., 1988). This logic—to my thinking—is contrary to that of Yalda. The Yalda Iranian observance on December 21 sprang from the idea that Light and Good are the contrasts of Darkness and Evil. Since the winter solstice has the most darkness of any day throughout the year, it was considered extremely unlucky, a time to be wary and watchful. (*Chase's 1966 Calendar of Events*.) The winter solstice is the shortest day of the year and could be either December 21 *or* 22. Osiris's final entombment was December 21 (Op. cit., Farrar). There is the suggestion of Feralia-Caristia in this as well as the winter solstice. Zodiac's first confessed killings, by the way, were those of two teenagers in 1968 on December 20, the eve of the god's final entombment. It's believed early Christians thought the winter solstice to be December 25, which they set as the birth of Christ. December 25 also happened to be the date of birth of Mithra, the sun, the Persian God of Light. The summer solstice is June 21 *or* 22. The spring equinox occurs on March 20 or 21; the autumn equinox is on September 22 or 23. Briefly then there is a closeness or likeness of the number 2122, the North Clark Street address, in the solstices and equinoxes, as well as the Feralia-Caristia. These periods represent change, as most certainly the St. Valentine's Day Mass (an expiation of sorts) did. Al Capone, the "Little Caesar," is probably better known today worldwide than Julius Caesar, who turned down the crown at the Lupercalia. I don't believe this fame or notoriety was accidental or the fact that when George Washington was a youth, he played in Joseph Addison's Cato. His part was that of Juba, an adoptive son of *Cato*, who was an enemy of Julius Caesar. (Noemie Emery, *Washington*. New York: G.P. Putnam's Sons, 1976.)

290.   Halfway through reading Cliff Stoll's *The Cuckoo's Egg*, I realized this was a ready-made example of what was written previously:

> If Hermes is a god of derring-do,
> He's gotta be a god of detectives too.

Here was a composite of Hermes, siding with both sides in a computer game of trickery, deception, measurement. Patience and fortitude are part of cunning. In the end, he who is most cunning wins. Later I'd see that Stoll had selected arbitrarily the date of February 13 for the computer virus to erase itself. "Just a coincidence this happened to be the beginning of the Parentalia," you comment, Why then were Hess, Brysinski, and Carl found guilty of espionage on February 15, the Lupercalia? Stoll might be amused to read that—in my opinion—there was a cuckoo's egg within the cuckoo's egg. The game was even more complicated: 13 February = 44; 15 February = 46. 90 ÷ 2 = 45.

291.   Someday scientists will discover that all these years we should have been eating the plastic (since it's extremely high in roughage content) and throwing away the food. By doing this, billions in garbage-disposal waste could be saved each year. This then could be applied to what we owe. Rich-poor, young-old,

Republicans-Democrats alike, one nation indivisible, each doing his or her fair share to eliminate the national debt.

292. Both the banyan and bo are kinds of fig trees. Because a fig tree overshadowed the wolf cave where Romulus and Remus were born, the prosperity of Rome was predicted.

293-A. When proofreading, I wrote down the old page numbers and notations where to type in corrections later. One had been made as follows

261   (the 13th word before the had a baby)

The joke line never crossed by mind. The handwriting is exactly like mine except for a small difference in the "2" (I do at times write _____ or _____) and the way "baby" was written. Automatic writing?

Schizophrenia? A multiple personality? All this is possible. But it doesn't rule out—to my thinking—that though my room is always locked, someone or others can get in. Oh well, whoever you are, have a nice bray. Seattle's Capital Hill area has witches, I believe. The obvious attempts at harassment at times by some are red herrings possibly. Obvious causes of noises uncovered and explained, but very possibly for a few these simple ruses mask real paranormal power—to be used at other times—to throw off witch hunters and paranormal investigators.

293-B.

674

294. The years 1776/1777 were a 2122 sequence for Captain Cook as well as the forty-five-year-old General Washington, who by Christmas had already begun to see the first of some of his men's shoeless feet leave bloody footprints in the snow at Valley Forge. The misery was at its worst during the first two months the army was there. By "mid-February" (St. Valentine's Day?) 1788, food supplies had become adequate. (James Thomas Flexner, *Washington, The Indispensable Man*. Boston: Little, Brown, and Company, 1969.) And, of course, Cook died the following year.

295. The sandwich got its name from the fourth earl when he was at a gaming table (Hermes, god of gamblers) for twenty-four hours without any other food. Sandwich died in 1792 on April 30, the day of Walpurgis night. These facts are very consistent in Hermetic context with later events happening to Captain James (ae) Cook and especially in the period or days they took place. All things considered, it's more than just coincidence. On *February 13*, 1866 (21), at *Liberty*, Missouri, ten or so men pulled off what is thought to have been the first daylight, peacetime, bank robbery in *America* (*Encyclopedia Americana*, Joe B. Frantz, University of Texas). Remember too that a chisel and tongs had been stolen aboard the *Discovery* at Hawaii on February 13, 1779, and that Amerigo Vespucci died February 22, 1512. Jesse and Frank James are believed to have been among the group pulling the first bank robbery. Hermes, god of thieves. Jesse Woodson *James* was born September 5, (MP), 1847, and died April 3, 1882. Alexander (aeae) Franklin James was born on January 10, 1843 (i.e., he was four-five years older than Jesse), and died within the Parentalia on February 18, 1915. These were the most famous outlaws of the U.S. West. To some Jesse was a merciless killer. To ex-Confederates, he was a Robin Hood (HR) and indeed pretty much had assumed the status of a folk hero. As you recall, Hermes denied the theft of the cattle. Curiously Jesse took pains in most cases to write some newspaper to deny any involvement after a robbery. A bank was robbed in Gallatin, Missouri. A horse left behind was identified "as belonging to a young man named James" (*Encyclopedia Americana*). Was this a calling card or a mistake? Hermes, dominion over horses. But the thing that's hard to explain is that this robbery took place on *December 7*, 1869 (SY) (fifty-two years to the day after Vice Admiral William Bligh—connected to Hawaii—died) or exactly six snake cycles before the Japanese attack at Pearl Harbor. As you might recall, Jesse was shot treacherously in the back of the head by Bob Ford. And you might call the chair—Jesse was standing on one at the time while adjusting a picture—an island. Ford's accomplice was his brother Charles. Two pair (Hermes, god of gamblers): Jesse and Frank, Robert and Charles. Charles committed suicide within a year after Jesse was shot (Todd Ruthven, *Collier's Encyclopedia*), and Frank died a free man in the same room in which he had been born (*Encyclopedia Britannica*).

296. Robert Chambers, *The Book of Days*. London: W. And R. Chambers, Ltd., n.d.

Hermes, god of sleep, dreams.

297. Richard A. Hough, *The Last Voyage of Captain James Cook*. New York: William Morrow and Co., Inc., 1979.

298. Ibid.

299. Ibid.

300. In mythology, Mercury stole Vulcan's finest pair of tongs.

301.   Christopher Lloyd, *Captain Cook*. London: Faber and Faber Ltd., 1952.

302.   Daniel Conner and Lorraine Miller, *Master Mariner, Captain James Cook and the Peoples of the Pacific*. Seattle: University of Washington Press, 1978.

303.   Op. cit., Hough.

304.   Op. cit., Conner.

305.   Op. cit., Hough.

306-A. *Encyclopedia Americana*. Quotation and dates from contribution with "Bligh, William" by Robert G. Albion, Harvard University.

306-B. Ralph Martin, *Jennie: The Life of Lady Randolph Churchill*. Vol. Two, Englewood Cliffs, New Jersey: Prentice-Hall, Inc., 1971.

306-BB. His name was John Strange Churchill. The name Strange is thought to have been an indication that Randolph wasn't his father. Indeed the two brothers didn't look alike. Jack was born on *February 4*, 1880, thirty years to the day after my Grandmother Elizabeth, the daughter of Mary Moon Mills. According to Martin Gilbert (*Winston S. Churchill*, Vol. VIII, Houghton Mifflin Co., 1988), Winston—who was writing his memoirs—met with Ismay, Pownall, and Deakin in a working session as they dined at Hyde Park Gate every Friday in February 1947:

The meeting on *February 21*, 1947 (21), the Feast of the Dead, "was overshadowed" by Jack's worsening health. Jack had had a weak heart for years and was again struck down. On *February 22* (Caristia), Winston told Lord Moran, "Jack may go out with the tide." (Tide linked to the moon, water, and Neptune, guardian of the month of February.) On *February 23* (Terminalia), John Strange Churchill died. Winston's youngest daughter Mary had been married just twelve days before on *February 11* to Christopher Soames.

In connection to the Cuban link to the mystique, it's interesting that in 1895 Winston got permission to visit the battle scene in Cuba. It was there on his twenty-first birthday that he came under fire. Churchill and Theodore Roosevelt were egotists and much alike. This is probably why TR didn't like him.

306-BBB. Norman Lebrecht, *A Musical Book of Days*, New York: Universe Books, 1989.

306-C. Thomas Leonard, Cynthia Crippen, and Marc Aronson, *Day By Day: The Seventies*. Vol II, New York: Facts on File Publications, 1988.

307-A. Several saints and martyrs in the Christian world are called Valentine. February 14, according to Acta Sanctorum, is observed for seven of these. (Claudia de Lys, *A Treasury of American Superstitions*, New York: Philosophical Library Inc., 1984.

307-B. The date *February 14*, 1573, is used by James A. Michener (Caribbean, New York: Ballantine Books, 1989).

John Sugden (*Sir Francis Drake*. London: Barrie & Jenkins Ltd., 1990) states in a footnote that Spanish accounts put the happening at the last day of January, while the English place it in the middle of February. Apparently there are variations by biographers too. Sugden's account is that Francis Drake's men found "no more than two horse-loads of silver and some food." So that the English wouldn't suspect the Spanish were on to their ambush, the animals were sent forward. Whatever happened, there was deception by the Spaniards. The date is interesting too in that Sir Winston S. Churchill was a descendant of Sir Francis Drake.

308-A. Her gunnery record at the Battle of Santiago de Cuba was "pitiable." It wasn't so much the U.S. Navy won the war but rather the Spanish Navy lost it. (Brayton Harris, *The Age of Battleships*, 1890–1922. New York: Franklin Watts, 1965.) She was sold on the Ides of March 1956 to Massey Supply Corp., then resold and towed to Kawasaki, Japan, where she was scrapped.

308-B. Carol Felsenthal, *Alice Roosevelt Longworth*. New York: G. P. Putnam's Sons, 1988.

In Japan in all major temples on February 3 or 4, Setsubun (Bean-Throwing Festival) is held. This is in accordance with the lunar calendar and marks the last day of winter. Priest and celebrities, such as sumo wrestlers and actors, throw dried beans on the crowd, which hollers, "Fortune in, Devils out!" Beans which are caught are taken to their homes to drive out the devils. (Sue Ellen Thompson and Barbara W. Carlson, *Holidays, Festivals, and Celebrations of the World Dictionary*. Detroit: Omnigraphics, Inc., 1994.

To the day: twenty-nine years after the assassination of Grand Duke Sergei in Moscow, twenty-eight years after the marriage of Princess Alice in the White House (her only child committed suicide), twenty-five years after Geronimo's death, and one year after Theodore Roosevelt's sister Corinne died, that is *February 17, 1934*, grandmother Elizabeth Chichester died under suspicious circumstances, and her white house in Coleville, California burned to the ground. Her body was later found with its head crushed. On *February 17, 1937*, ten men fell to their deaths when a scaffold collapsed from the Golden Gate bridge, whose ground-breaking ceremony *February 26, 1933*, was on the anniversary of Frances Duren Chichester's death 4 years previously. On *February 17, 1970*, a San Francisco police station was bombed by agitators. Also on *February 17, 1970*, the Hawthorne Inn, renamed the Towne Hotel, burned down. This had once been Al Capone's headquarters in Cicero, and here he'd invited 3 Sicilians to a feast. Then long past midnight, he had them tied and gagged, whereupon he clubbed them to death with a baseball bat.

308-C. Theodore Roosevelt succeeded the assassinated McKinley to the presidency on September 14 (MP), 1901. His second term began on March 4, 1905. When seeking a third term on October 14, 1912, he was en route to make a political speech when a saloon keeper—opposed to Roosevelt's attempt at a third term—shot him in the chest. Although Roosevelt's shirt was covered with blood, he told his audience that he would deliver his speech or die. (Joseph Nathan Kane, *Facts about the Presidents*. New York: H.W. Wilson Co., 1989.) Such a stance might have been seen as showing great determination and courage in his day—maybe—but in the world today it would be viewed cynically. He talked for fifty minutes and then was taken to a hospital.

308-CC. On *February 14* especially (along with other days of the Parentalia), the image of a stringed instrument recurs, with death in some cases:

  1) A violin, shaped something like a gourd, has four strings over a sounding-board. In Hebrew, the cardinal number for 4 is *Arabo*. The heart (upside down) is a variation of the Arabic sign for 5.

677

Thus by picturing the sounding-board as the Arabic sign for 5, the total violin is 45, the number of St. Valentine's Day, "til death do us part." With its bow of horsehairs running across the strings, it produces crossroads music. Ridiculous? Then you might also include the wizards of "crossroad" puzzles, who are possibly programmed from God only knows where by dailies. In folklore, the fiddle is an instrument of magic, perhaps the devil. This isn't hard to believe when hearing a beginner or a virtuosos like Paganini who had superhuman dexterity and daredevilry, taking great risks. A primitive fiddle was used by North American Apaches, connected to February via Arizona and Geronimo—not to forget that Nero fiddled (harped) while Rome burned. Tradition required, among other things, that each member of the Habsburg family "either sing, act, dance, or play an instrument." (Egon Gartenberg, *Johann Strauss: The End of an Era*. University Park: Penn State University, 1974.) Maria Theresa (born *May 13*, 1717) played the string bass and her husband, the violin. Marie Antoinette, their daughter later to be decapitated, danced. Johann Strauss contributed *Kaiserwalzer* (Emperor Waltz) to the jubilee in *1888*, marking the fortieth anniversary of the reign of Emperor Franz Joseph I, two hundred years after Antonio Stradivari in *1666*, the year of the plague and London fire, affixed labels on violins of his own making, one of the three best called *The Messiah* (1716). Throughout his reign, Franz Joseph danced to Strauss waltzes, almost inseparable from stringed instruments. After the emperor's blooding on *February 18*, 1853 (see Book II, footnote 325), he saw one tragedy after another befall his family. The conclusion of World War I brought an end to the Habsburg empire.

And finally as my mind jumps from one subject to another, I can't help wondering if the subject matter will drive me insane—or even worse, if some wag will write in the margin, "No, but it has me!"

2) Wagner died on *February 13*, 1883. Cosima had to be pulled away from his body thirty hours later on *February 14*. She cut off all her hair and put it in his coffin before it was closed. Though she may not have thought it as such, the hairs were strings symbolically.

3) Violinist Jack Benny was born on *February 14*, 1894 (thirty-five years before the St. Valentine's Day Mass) in Chicago, "illinois(e)". He had a mincing walk. His sister's name was Florence. His wife's stage name was Mary Livingstone. He played in the movie *George Washington Slept Here*.

4) *Viola* Riddle Hoffa gave birth to James Hoffa on *February 14*, 1913, in Brazil, Indiana, "The Crossroads of America" state.

5) As with Hoffa's, the death of Bishop Pike, born the same day, seems mysterious.

6) Charles Walton, who lived in the Warwickshire village of Lower *Quinton*, was murdered on *February 14*, 1945, the day Dresden— the Florence of Germany—was being bombed. He was thought to have been a witch. The county of Warwickshire has the municipal borough of Stratford-on-the-Avon, birthplace of Shakespeare.

7)   Ann Frederick Funston's mother was the daughter of an Oakland violinist. The general heard the "Blue Danube" while sitting in a lobby in San Antonio (city founded *May 1*, 1718, Antony). "How beautiful it all is," he said and died a comparatively beautiful death. Johann Strauss I was an accomplished violinist and forbade his oldest son Johann to play the violin. Anna, the boy's mother, encouraged him to play it. *February 15*. 44 B.C. brings to mind the day Antony offered the crown to Caesar, who refused it and died on the Ides of March, later in 1835 to be the birthdate of Eduard Strauss, the least talented and the most problematic of the three sons. There was rivalry between Johann Strauss I, the old Waltz King, and Johann Strauss II, his son who would eventually surpass his father and wear the crown. Anna Strauss died on *February 23*, 1870, the day in 1917 General Funston's body arrived at San Francisco, the city of St. Francis. On *February 24* (the anniversary of the day in 1209 St. Francis of Assisi had a revelation to live in poverty and to preach) with water pouring down, Frederick Funston—who'd measured temperatures up to 165° Fahrenheit in Death Valley—was buried overlooking the Golden Gate (a translation from the Greek) and later the Golden Gate Bridge, when on *February 15*, 1937, the scaffold was erected, causing—in the middle of the Parentalia—the sacrifice of ten men. (See Book II, footnote 129-C.) But the bridge, a stringed instrument which sings "unearthly sounds," was built by Chief Engineer Joseph Strauss. Josef Strauss, the composer-violinist, had also been a chief engineer before giving up that career for music. He was born in 1827 on August 22, the day and month my mother and stepmother would later be born. He was the deepest, most gifted, most sensitive, and most vulnerable of the three Strauss brothers. He was described as both "romantic looking" and "chaotically pale," a nice way of saying death warmed over. As a boy, he wrote the sad and haunting poem: *Elegie, Der Totengräber* (The Grave-Digger). As a man, he had a nervous breakdown in Warsaw. He died about five months after his mother. Chief Engineer Joseph Strauss also had a nervous breakdown when the Golden Gate Bridge was being constructed and died in less than a year after it opened.

July 22, 1870, is usually given as the date of death of Josef Strauss. It is, however, sometimes given as July 21, the date forty-five years later that TR gave his speech at the Panama-Pacific Exposition with its symbolic death-life opening on *February 20, 21, 22*.

A third Strauss who might be mentioned at this time (see also *February 13*, 1867) is the merchant-manufacturer Levi Strauss who was born *February 26*, 1829.

309.   Helen Rex Keller, *The Dictionary of Dates*. New York: Macmillan, 1934.

310-A.   Ibid.

310-B.   He was brought up as a Roman Catholic. Choosing the Jesuit University at Santa Clara, he had thought of becoming a priest. After much study, he realized that he was very much at odds with the Church's teaching of birth control. In effect, he was questioning the doctrine of papal infallibility. He left the church then. He got a law degree from Yale and practiced law for a few years. In 1944 he joined the

Episcopal Church. On February 4, 1966, prior to returning to Cambridge, England, from the U.S., he received word that his son Jim Jr. had committed suicide in Manhattan (one source says by an overdose of pills, another that he shot himself). Burying his son, he returned to his Cambridge flat where strange things began to happen, which led him to pursue psychial research. Both sides of his family, incidentally, had some psychic ability. On February 20, postcards Jim Jr. collected appeared on the floor by the bishop's bed, arranged at a 140-degree angle. From February 22 to 24, his secretary's bangs—which Jim Jr. had hated— were singed gradually until gone. Safety pins were sprung open in an angle of 140 degrees. Milk soured and the heat would go up without explanation, etc. What did 140 mean? Was it exact? April 20? A day before or after (360/365)?

311.   Can be thought of as seven, if you want to count the four who were decapitated with Balboa.

312.   *Chicago.* The twenty-second letter in the Greek alphabet is CHI. This is transliterated to chu or X in English, German, and Latin. (Op. cit., Jobes.) And so significant to Malcolm X and me (Chi). Illinois was the twenty-first state admitted to the union. Thus Illinois, Chicago, becomes 2122.

313.   Nathan Miller, *FDR, an Intimate History.* Garden City, New York: Doubleday, 1983.

314.   Source of information concerning head nearly severed and pitchfork through neck is as follows: *Man Myth and Magic,* Richard Cavendish, editor in chief. New York: Marshal Cavendish, 1983.

         Another source (Jay Robert Nash, *Crime Chronology: A Worldwide Record 1900–1983.* New York: Facts on File Pub., 1984) states that a sickle blade was in Walton's throat, a pitchfork in his chest, and the sixteenth century killings were done this way on those accused of witchcraft. Be that as it may, the sickle is described as crescent shaped, and crescent means shaped like the *moon* in its first or last quarter. The sickle is associated with Hermes and Perseus, who used a curved sword or sickle to decapitate Medusa.

315.   Op. cit., Cavendish.

316.   In the moon is a dog acting as a messenger of death according to Devonshire folklore. Dogs—able to see the approaching Angel of Death—howl back at the moon. But moon, messenger, death, and dogs are persona Hermes.

         June 13, 1991. It was the U.S. Golf Open (contest) at Chaska, Minnesota. A violent thunderstorm came up, causing forty thousand spectators to seek shelter. Laughing while the wind blew and the rain fell, six joked under a *willow tree.* Suddenly a lightning bolt struck them. William Faden died instantly. Another man was seriously injured, and the other four—complaining of numbness in their legs—had to be taken to the hospital. Hermes, god of walkers.

317-A.   The subject of milk comes up at other times of the year when libations were poured to the three goddesses: *Cuba,* Cunina, and Rumina, who watched over infants in their cradles, taken to mean sleeping infants too. Infant, cradle, and sleep are associated with Hermes. But experts say the country of Cuba gets its name from vat or is associated with the cube.

317-B.   On May 15, rush-puppets called *Argei*, representing men bound hand and foot, were put into the Tiber. Fowler (Op. cit., Fowler.) stated that the common people believed these were substituted for human victims—probably old men. A priestess of Jupiter (father of Mercury) called the Flaminica Diales was present in mourning.

Be that as it may, the puppets were symbolic. Mourning and bound captives/prisoners sound like Anubis (syncretic Hermanubis. See Seal of the City of the Dead, Book II, page 492). Moreover, it's interesting that the Lupercalia custom will pop up again on this Mercury day. Was the Tiber then symbolic of the Styx in this case? The etymology and history of the word *Argei* are unknown. So why not look for the most obvious meaning that *Arg*, as in Argos and Argonauts, stands for travelers?

Some say Evander was the invention of Greek scholars who saw a similarity between the Lupercalia and the Arcadian celebrations to Pan. Evander was the son of Hermes (as was Pan by one account) and an Arcadian nymph, later called Carmenta by the Romans. Sixty years before the Trojan War, he led a Pelasgian group from Pallantium in Arcadia to Latium. From the word *Pallantium* was derived the name for the Palatine Hill. In mythology, Romulus and Remus were the sons of Mars and the disgraced vestal virgin Ilia (LI-LA). Either because she had forsaken her vows and/or because Amulius, usurper of Ilia's father's throne, wanted them dead, the twins were cast adrift in the surging Tiber and deposited at or near the Lupercalia cave where a she-wolf nourished them. Traditionally the wolf via the twins is associated with Mars. But a wolf can be associated with other gods too, such as Neptune, Apollo, and Dionysus. Through Egyptian (Anubis, Osiris) and Norse (Odin, two wolves typifying wind and storm) mythologies, a wolf inference can be given to Hermes-Mercury, a protector god who freed the shackled Mars and helped the young Dionysus, both half-brothers. Whether the story of Evander can be taken seriously or not, there's much elsewhere suggesting Hermes symbolism and persona: *travel* on the Tiber, the fig tree at the cave's entrance (*Mercury born in a cave*, the proverbial *Mercury fig*). The fig tree—thought to be a good omen—can also be associated with death, since Dionysus planted one at the gates of Hades) and the *twin contenders* (strife, the Gemini contenders ruled by the planet Mercury and symbolized by a capital *H*). Remus is killed by Romulus, who invites thieves—among others—to populate Rome and who—having become a despot—is later chopped up by his magistrates.

There's a duality to the Lupercalia. Life-death. Caesar at the *44* B.C. Lupercalia is killed on the Ides of *March*. The slaying of the goats and dogs represents both death and sacrifice, while regeneration is linked to the lashings by the februa for fertility. Two youths from noble families—perhaps standing for Romulus and Remus—were led forth. Whether or not they actively participated for selection, it was a *contest*. By one account, each youth clad in the skins of the sacrificed goats and dogs (Mercury animals) led a group of priests *running* through the *streets*, possibly at one point passing through a graveyard.

Finally by disregarding the position of the months at different periods in antiquity and accepting them as they have come down to us today on the *calendar*, we find March—named after the blustering Mars, god of war—sandwiched among those months of Mercury, persona peace. Thus the four: February, March, April, and May. This is not to say the months aren't identified with other gods too.

318.   Modern science begins with Galileo, who was born on the Lupercalia and who died in 1642, the year Sir Isaac Newton was born.

Science had two "miraculous years." (Milton Dank, *Albert Einstein*, New York: Watts, 1983.) The first occurred when Cambridge closed and Newton fled the plague to his mother's home where he did his most brilliant work in the year 1666. The second happened in the year 1905 when Einstein published his four papers.

Note both that this was a snake year and the occurrence of the numbers 4 and 5. A triple 6 number is mentioned, so it might be worth the time to look into what happened in the triple number years:

> 1555.   Nostradamus's *Centuries*, a series of prophecies, was published. The French astrologer and physician was born on December 14 (Mausoleum Day), 1503. He predicted the date and manner of his death which was due to natural causes.
>
> Philip II of Spain received the sovereignty of the Lower Countries in 1555. Remorseless in support of the Inquisition, he severely prose-cuted Hollanders who supported the reformation. Nearly 100,000 were said to have died. His second wife was "Bloody Mary." Where she has been christened on *February 21*, 1516, Philip—who later became King of Naples—was born on *May 21*, 1527. It was during his reign on November one (equal to the Feast of the Dead), 1570, that the North Sea broke through Holland's northwestern dikes, causing the death of 50,000. Holland had been at war with Spain, which blamed the All Saints' Day flooding on the heretic Calvanism of the Dutch. Philip II of Spain was also later Philip I of Portugal. This is curious in light of the earthquake and flooding in Lisbon, Portugal, on All Saints' Day in 1755, two hundred years after Philip II had become sovereign of the Low Countries.
>
> 1666.   Plague winding down from 1665. London fire from September 2–6 (MP). Newton, who was interested in astrology, did his most brilliant work. Antonio Stradivari, still a pupil of Nicolo Amati, began placing his own name on violins he'd made.
>
> 1777.   Discovery of Christmas Island by Captain Cook. (Two years later, Cook was slain on St. Valentine's Day and buried on the Feralia. Had visited Easter Island in 1774.) Young Alexander Hamilton joined General Washington's staff. Oriskany battle.
>
> 1888.   An altar to Mercury was discovered in 1888 near S. Martino ai Monti. Augustus dedicated this altar in 10 B.C. (Op. cit., Clement.)
>
> The Feralia-Caristia symbol was opened to the public (October 9). Though perhaps calling it the Washington Monument, only fools would really think of it as such.
>
> Discovery of the "Cliff Palace." The "Blizzard of 1888." Moradabad, India, had history's worst recorded hailstorm. Irving Berlin ("White Christmas" "Easter Parade"), T.S. Eliot, and Jim Thorpe born. Great Britain annexed Christmas Island. Congress authorized the second-

class battleship *Maine*. The Washington Monument was opened to the public. Quincy, Massachusetts incorporated as a city. Thomas P. Corbett—who had castrated himself and later became Lincoln's avenger—escaped from an insane asylum and then was seen no more after visiting an old friend. Jack the Ripper. Lawrence of Arabia born.

1999.   It's said Edgar Cayce predicted World War III will begin in this year.

319.   The *Maine* was laid down at New York Yard on October 17, 1888, launched on November 18, 1889.

There's a superstition that numbers unlucky for seafaring people are those having a "double 8, 5, or 7." Examples given: 1888, 1855, and 1877. (Cora Linn Daniels and C.M. Stevens, *Encyclopedia of Superstitions and Folklore*, Detroit: Gale Research Co. 1971.) Whether the superstition existed before the Maine was laid down is not known.

The "*Maine*'s hulk was finally floated on 2 February 1912 and towed out to sea where it was sunk in deep water in the Gulf of Mexico with appropriate military honors 16 March." (James L. Mooney, ed., *American Naval Fighting Ships*. Washington: Naval Historical Center, Dept. of the Navy.) Here's a synchronicity of sorts: It has been under water for thirteen (a necromancy number) years and brought to surface in February, the month guarded by Neptune and in which occurs the Lupercalia. It has a temporary life, transgressing natural and proper limits, and is returned to its grave one day following the Ides, a waterlogging. There's no certainty what caused the explosion on the *Maine*, but early investigators believed that it had been caused externally by a mine or something else. The Spanish government has always denied responsibility.

In 1978 a research team led by Admiral Hyman Rickover reexamined the evidence. The conclusion reached was that a fire smoldering in a coal bunker caused the explosion when it ignited gunpowder stored close by. This in turn detonated the forward magazines. (*Collier's Encyclopedia*, from article by George Harmon Knowles titled "Maine, Destruction of the [Feb. 15, 1898]".)

320.   Guiseppe Zangara was born in Italy on September 7 (MP), 1900. Like Capone's parents, he left from Naples. On May 21, 1924 (the beginning of the Mercury period and day Bobby Franks was murdered in Chicago), Zangara filed his declaration of intention to become a U.S. citizen. He was naturalized on September 11 (MP), 1929 (SY). Besides Mayor Cermak, there were four others wounded as follows:

   1)   Margaret Kruis, shot through the hand.

   2)   Russell Caldwell, struck in the head.

   3)   Joseph Gill, shot in the abdomen.

   4)   William Sinnott, New York detective, wounded in head.

Later President-elect Roosevelt will reveal (*Chicago Tribune* February 17, 1933) that the top of a hand on one of his bodyguards (Robert Clark of *Chicago*—shades of 2122 North Clark Street) had been grazed by a bullet. Clark had helped take Al Capone from Chicago to the Federal Penitentiary at Atlanta. On February 4 (the day Captain Cook had left Hawaii in 1779, later to return), Roosevelt had begun an eleven-day fishing trip on Vincent Astor's yacht in the Bahama and Florida waters. Roosevelt returned to Florida on February 15, but four years previously on February 12, 1929, Capone had also returned to Florida from the Bahamas.

The assassination attempt was on a Wednesday evening shortly after 9:00 P.M., thirty-five years to the day and hour when the USS Maine had been blown up in Havana harbor (9:40). Roosevelt was sworn in as president on March 4, 1933. The body of Mayor Anton Cermak (born Czechoslovakia May 9, 1873) crossed many state boundaries to be buried on March 10, in Chicago, *five days before the Ides*. It was also the day of the earthquake where Long Beach was hit hardest of the cities in southern California (see page 46). Lemuria Cermak was shot on the anniversary of when the *Maine* was blown up and buried on the earthquake day when the *Constitution* was slightly damaged. His death for Roosevelt's seemed like an exacted sacrifice. An irony was that when Cermak was wounded he said to Roosevelt, "I'm glad it was me instead of you." And Roosevelt probably thought: *So am I!*

For you see during the presidential election campaign, Cermak had been very vocal about being anti-Roosevelt. And only a few days before going to Florida, he'd commented to Paddy Bauler, a Chicago alderman, concerning Roosevelt, "I don't like the sonofabitch!" "Listen," Bauler told him, "for christsakes, you ain't got any money for the Chicago schoolteachers and this Roosevelt is the only one who can get it for you. You better go over there and kiss his ass or whatever you got to do. Only you better get the goddamn money for them teachers, or we ain't goin' to have a city that's worth runnin'." (Ted Morgan, *FDR, a Biography*. New York: Simon & Shuster, 1985.)

Zangara, a "have-not," short and hollow-eyed, hated all rulers, people who were rich and powerful. As if hearkening back distantly, vaguely, imperfectly to the Lupercalia, Rear Admiral Culveras was talking about the *Maine*, and the people in the crowd beat Zangara severely before his capture. The mockingbird is the state bird of Florida. Besides Florida's boot (inverted map) being suggestive of Italy's, it's interesting that Florida (58,644 square miles) is about half the size of Italy (116,330 square miles) and also nearly surrounded by water and phallic in appearance.

The number 21 surfaced to some extent in the three players' lives. Roosevelt was stricken with polio in 1921, and the twenty-first amendment was ratified on December 5, his first year in office. (Note December 5 and February 13 were two days of celebration in ancient Rome for Faunus or perhaps syncretic Pan-Faunus.) After being elected, Mayor Anton Cermak reduced salaries 21 percent, redeeming his campaign pledge. Zangara filed his declaration of intention to become a U.S. citizen on May 21, 1924. It was first believed likely by the *Chicago Tribune* that Zangara would be executed on March 21, 1933. But this proved to be off one day. In a swift justice, Zangara was electrocuted on March 20, the first day of spring and five days after the Ides of March.

321.   Also on this day, Canada unfurled a new red-and-white maple-leaf flag amidst a twenty-one-gun salute on Parliament Hill, Ottawa.

322.   *February 212*, Rome. Caracalla murdered his brother Geta. A bloody depression followed with about twenty thousand victims. (Jacques Legrand [conception and coordination] and Jerome Burne, ed., *Chronicle of World*. Mt. Kisko, New York: ECAM Publications, 1990.)

323-A.   Op. cit., Robbins.

684

323-B.   Robert Coughlan and the Editors of Time-Life Books, *The World of Michelangelo, 1475–1564*. New York: Time Incorporated, 1966.

323-C.   Pope Julius II had summoned Michelangelo to Rome and gave him the job of sculpturing his tomb. Then the Pope temporarily changed his mind and suggested Michelangelo do paintings on the vault of the Sistine Chapel. Michelangelo thought of himself as a sculptor and fled, hoping never to come across the Pope again, but the Pope was powerful and Michelangelo was sent back "with a rope around his neck." Julius II then pardoned him and gave him the new project of doing the bronze statue, which hadn't pleased Michelangelo since he preferred to work in stone. He asked the Pope if he wished to have a book in his left hand. Julius II replied, "A sword! I know nothing about letters, not I." Eventually the Pope was portrayed with keys of St. Peter (or a book and the keys of St. Peter in his left hand, and right, giving a benediction). At one point, the Pope asked, "That statue of yours, is it a blessing or cursing?" The rough estimate Michelangelo had given the Pope for the amount of money needed proved insufficient, and the sculptor suffered many hardships besides poverty. It's reasonable to assume that though he might have come to like the Pope later, he didn't at this time. Being mercurial, he must have cursed the Pope roundly under his breath. About three years after the bronze sculpture was set in place, Bologna was captured by enemies of the Pope. The statue was toppled to the pavement. The head was saved as a souvenir (decapitation), but the body was cast into a cannon and dubbed *la Giulia* (emasculation). Nearly four years Michelangelo spent on his back painting the ceiling of the Sistine Chapel, which is right next door to what is now the new St. Peter's Basilica. It's probable then that the chapel also had been built over the graveyard. Pope Julius's interest during this time eventually returned to the construction of his mausoleum, which took forty years to complete. Michelangelo lamented, "I lost my youth chained to this tomb." The bottom line: the graveyard below; the Feralia dates; the Pope's preoccupation with his tomb; Michelangelo's sorrow at being "chained to" to the tomb; his own sickness and death in a Parentalia period; and that on May 21, 1972, Laszlo Toth took a hammer to Michelangelo's stone Pietà, housed in the Basilica of St. Peters (Petra = rock), founded by Pope Julius II.

Obviously the Parentalia-Caristia was a real worry for the early Catholics, for they hoped the feast of St. Peter's Chair would replace the Caristia. It's hard to figure out, however, how "the Deposition of SS. Peter and Paul" really changed anything and to explain the fact that Pope Julius II, who laid the cornerstone for the second St. Peter's Church, died on the Feast of the Dead, February 21, 1513.

324.   J.C. Beaglehole, *The Life of Captain James Cook*, Stanford: Stanford University Press, 1974.

325.   On *February 18*, 1853, Emperor Franz Joseph was blooded by an assassin. This is counted as the beginning of a series of calamitous events that would "stalk" the emperor to his death. His brother Maximilian, "Emperor of Mexico," was killed by Juarez's firing squad. His brother's wife went insane. His son Rudolf, heir to the throne, committed suicide. His wife, Empress Elizabeth, was killed by a fanatic. In 1914 the successor to the throne, the Archduke Franz Ferdinand and his wife, were assassinated. Later the emperor made a declaration of war that led to the first World War. He died on November 21, 1916, at Schönbrunn Palace near Vienna. The Battle of Verdun was still going.
I was born exactly thirteen years after the day the battle began. Some say the

raven is a necromancy omen. This dates back to the Babylonian calendar where the raven governs the thirteenth month, which is variable. Odin fears his raven Memory will not return. (See Book I, footnote 1-J.)

The Church, largely responsible for phasing out the ancient practice in February of honoring the dead, will be accused in the following World War of not giving sufficient backing to the Jews and other minorities, the victims of gas attack, the Holocaust, Verdun Part II. Now the Holocaust is or will become simply honoring the dead who were killed and/or tortured by the Nazis. We all know what the reasoning was behind the Nazis, but at another level, it's unclear why the Jews and other minorities had to be the sacrifice. Maybe since all else has failed, the only thing we can really trust is our dead, an alliance of all nations must be formed to honor their dead during this ancient period. If there's this common bond to build on, then perhaps the world as a whole will be deemed worthy of receiving help to maintain the peace.

A.D. 494. Roman Lupercalia sacrifices last held. Op. cit., Milgate.

326.   Op. cit., Flexner.

327.   Ibid.

328.   *Chicago Daily Tribune* (by Associated Press), February 22, 1922.

329.   *Chicago Daily Tribune*, February 23, 1922, carries article titled "Italians Knew Roma's Defects, Article Hints" by Morrow Krum. In it he cites previous article by Kenneth L. Roberts (*Saturday Evening Post*, August 13, 1921), where Roberts claims the Italians refused to sail the ship over Mt. Vesuvius, apparently fearing the heat of the crater. However, Vesuvius is also a death symbol.

         Chicago Daily Tribune of February 22, 1922, described the misshapen mass of the *Roma* as a "funeral pyre" of intense heat.

330.   Stanford M. Mirkin, (*What Happened When*, Ives Washburn, Inc., 1966) states that the U.S. Navy's *Monitor* was ready for sea duty on *February 15*, 1862.

331.   *The Washington Post*, February 23, 1922.

332-A.   Overall the Parentalia-Caristia 1965 (21), a snake-year, was an eventful period for blacks.

         13th.   Malcolm X arrives at New York. Flight and travel.

         14th.   X's home damaged by three gasoline bombs on Valentine's Day.

         15th.   Nat (King) Cole died at age *forty-five*. Dr. Martin Luther King, Jr., led a voter registration march (walk) at Selma, Alabama.

         16th.   Four (4) arrested. Three members of a black terrorist group and a Canadian woman (some whites involved) in plot to dynamite freedom symbols.

         17th.   Brooklyn, New York. Four hundred black high school students threw bricks at store windows.

21st.	Malcolm X killed at Audubon Ballroom. A few hours later, a fire caused extensive damage to the apartment of X's friend Cassius (Roman name) Clay, heavyweight boxing champion. Arson ruled out. (Clay won title February 25, 1964, and lost it *February 15*, 1978, to Leon Spinks; in a rematch he regained title on September 15 [MP], 1978. Boxing, contest, and fire associated with Hermes. See May 25, 1965, and April 28, 1967. Later pendulum swings back with Parkinson's disease.)
22nd.	Elijah Mohammad denied he had anything to do with the slaying of Malcolm X.
23rd.	Terminalia. Fires burned Black Muslim headquarters in Harlem and San Francisco.

332-B. When Ames delivered a six-pound stack of secret documents to a KGB official in the Soviet Embassy in 1985, he was chief of the counterintelligence branch of the CIA's Soviet Division. On the basis of this information, Moscow arrested and executed ten or more Soviet and Soviet-bloc agents who worked for the CIA. Moreover, it appears that ninety-five CIA reports passed on to Pentagon officials and U.S. Presidents were influenced by the KGB. (Article by Tim Weiner, *Seattle PI*, November 10, 1995.)

332-C. It's believed that the feast of St. Peter's Chair provided a substitute for pagan rites (the Caristia) practiced on February 22. (Herbert Thurston and Donald Attwater, eds., *Butler's Lives of the Saints*, New York: P.J. Kennedy and Sons, 1956.)

As you recall, St. Peter and St. Paul didn't get along. So as the Caristia was a time when the living were to get together to settle their differences, "St. Peter's Chair at Rome" was also called "the Deposition of SS. Peter and Paul." There is some controversy about this and the date January 18 is also used as St. Peter's Chair. But February 22 is interesting in that Pope Julius II, who laid the cornerstone for the second St. Peter's at Rome, died on *February 21*, 1513. February 22 is celebrated as St. Peter's Day in Alsace when St. Peter is suppose to drive out the snakes. It's unknown by me, however, whether this celebration is for St. Peter, the apostle, or St. Peter Damian, who died on February 22, 1072, or both.

333. The fixed holidays (*Feriae stativae*) in Rome were *forty-five* in number and celebrated every year on a certain day. Op. cit., Peck.

334. In a very ancient calendar, February 23 was figured as the terminal or last day of the month. Romans had an elaborate procedure for setting a stone to mark a boundary, whatever time of the year this might have been. Those living near the boundary assembled. A hole was carefully prepared to receive the stone. This could include the blood of a sacrificial animal, incense, wine, honey, bits of the harvest, etc. The stone (or stones) once so consecrated was under the protection of Terminus, the Roman god of boundaries and landmarks. Woe unto him who removed it! He was cursed, and anyone could kill him with impunity. In later times the punishment of fines was substituted. The Terminalia was then a festival on February 23 to honor Terminus. Those on either side of a boundary gathered

with family and servants and put a bloodless offering to their side. Later times, a suckling pig or lamb was killed. The blood was sprinkled on the stone or stones. Afterward, they would join in a neighborhood feast. (Oskar Seyffert, *A Dictionary of Classical Antiquities, Mythology, Religion, Literature, and Art*, London: S. Sonnensehein, 1894.) Terminus was represented by a human head on a stone. There were, however, no arms or feet, implying that Terminus never moved from the guarded site. The representation is similar to the quadrangular pillar in Greece on which was usually the head of Hermes, placed in areas regarded as sacred or designating (probably originally) the bounds of property or home. The latter was also used as decorations in Roman homes. Hermes, it's said, needed no arms or legs because he could overcome all by eloquence alone. Though I'd reached the conclusion independently that Terminus represented a facet of the more complex god, others had seen the similarity before me. There is, furthermore, the superficial suggestion that *Turms*, the name given Mercury in Tuscanny, is close to terms. If—as I believe—Hermes-Mercury is linked to the Parentalia-Caristia, then the appropriateness of a Mercury-Terminus on February 23 is not too far-fetched.

335.   The treaty was ratified by Spain on *February 21*, 1821 (*Collier's Encyclopedia* from section "Adams-Onís Treaty" by Raymond Walters, Jr.).

John Quincy Adams, by the way, named his first son after George Washington. All along too, we are speaking of dates and calendars. Both Washington and Lenin fit into two calendars.

336.   Before this it had been rung for the funeral procession (Hermanubis over burial rites; Thoth-Hermes, god of reckoning, judgment) of Chief Justice John Marshall on July 8, 1835, when it cracked inexplicably. July 8 also happened to be the anniversary when in 1776 (21) several bells rang in Philadelphia to announce the first public reading of the Declaration of Independence.

337.   Frank Chichester died February 22, 1958. Frances Duren Chichester had been born in the Dakota Territory (North Dakota) on August 22, 1888. In 1889 she traveled with family from North Dakota to Montana, where she spent most of her early years. In 1905 she and her family were living in Washington.

338-A.   Louis L. Snyder, *Louis L. Snyder's Historical Guide to World War II*. Wesport, Connecticut: Greenwood Press, 1982.

338-B.   On June 17 (MP), 1967, Communist China announced that it had exploded its first hydrogen bomb. On May 18, 1974, India carried out an underground explosion, becoming the sixth nation with a nuclear bomb.

338-C.   Op. cit., Nordam.

339.   Joseph Nathan Kane, *Facts about the Presidents*. New York: H.W. Wilson Co., 1974.

340.   Officials said over one hundred thousand perished. More conservative estimates placed the figure between sixty thousand to seventy thousand. (To have some idea of the magnitude of human suffering, Hurricane Andrew on August 23,

1992—though terrible—caused the deaths of less than a hundred.) A few days after the catastrophe, Ali Akbar, a watchman friend living in Chittagong, wrote:

> You will be sorry to hear that a heavy flooding and tidal bore affect in the southern side of our country. Chittagong town is seriously affected. As per government account, about 5 lacks of people died. Most of the victims are children and women. Many dead body are also floating here and there around our house. There is no sign of my house where we lived. Jemid and Obaidul also in the same condition. We and our family members are somehow safe. After 7 days of the flooding, there are also 10 feet water in my house. The peoples are now suffering from diarrhea and other types of diseases. There is no supply of medicine here. Food is not available here. I am wonder how we save our life in the foodless situation.

Ali wrote again on May 22, 1991, as follows:

> Seven Fleet & Destroyer are now in Bay of Bengal waiting in the international line. U.S. Navy are now serving the distressed person with medicine, food, clothes, drinking water and other necessary goods. Bangladeshis have got their new life getting the historical service of U.S. Naval Force. They are distributing the relief materials among the people. The peoples of Bangladesh are thanking the Americans and telling among themselves "Americans are Great" in the world. Bangladesh has manpower only but have no such transportation facilities to reach the relief materials. Many men also had to die if the U.S. Navy did not arrive in Bangladesh. Now diarrhea is the main disease in the costal areas. Such type of tidal bore and flooding caused on 1960. I am unable to explain to you and such language are not known to me how we are passing our days.

The cyclone which hit on April 30, 1991, came just after the Persian Gulf War. President Bush ordered 7,550 marines and sailors sent to help in the relief effort. On *May 15*, 1991, eight U.S. warships arrived at Chittagong.

341.   President Eisenhower first denied it, and people believed "Ike" because he was "Ike." Then when it was clear the communists had irrefutable proof, Eisenhower backpeddled. In effect, he was admitting he'd lied both to the Russians and the American people. With this credibility gap—and the others to follow in the many years since—the blind patriotism of World War II and to some extent the years immediately following which President Kennedy hoped to evoke in his "ask not what your country can do for you, ask what you can do for your country" speech never returned. Of course our government was better than the communist governments throughout the world. That was never the question in anybody's mind, nor is it today. But after the U-2 plane mess, people began to wonder more actively: What can you believe?

342.   Hermes was "the especial patron of boxing." (*Harper's Dictionary of Classical Literature and Antiquities.*) See May 25, 1898; May 15, 1953; and May 25, 1965.

When comparing the birthdates of Joe Louis and Jimmy Hoffa, there seems to be some undefined relationship: Hoffa, February 14, 1913, and Louis, May 13, 1914. Valentine's Day—Persephone-Hermes.

When asked why he was at the trial of Jimmy Hoffa on July 15, 1957, Louis replied, "I'm just here to see what they are doing to my old friend Jimmy Hoffa." (Clark R. Mollenhoff, *Tentacles of Power: The Story of Jimmy Hoffa*, World Publishing Co., 1965.)

In the "Bumper Sticker" Epilogue (James R. Hoffa, *Hoffa the Real Story*, as told to Oscar Fraley, New York: Stein and Day Publishers, 1975), Fraley described Hoffa as a Caesar with more than one Brutus. Joe Louis wasn't one of these, though he did become a greeter at Caesar's Palace, Las Vegas, the city where he died on April 12, 1981. Born in the fifth month, he died in the fourth. Possibly too a Hermetic context might be given to Hoffa's end.

343.   "The Jones Boy" by Mann Curtis and Vic Mizzy. Copyright 1953 by George Pincus Music Co.

344.   Kay and Marshall Lee, eds., *The Illuminated Book of Days*, New York: G.P. Putnam's Sons, 1979. Another (Op. cit., Peck.) gives the date of October 13 for the Fontinalia, a festival in honor of Fontus, the Roman god of springs.

345.   Michael Grant and Rachel Kitzinger, *Civilization of the Ancient Mediterranean*, "Roman Cults" by John Ferguson, New York: Charles Scribner's Sons, 1988.

346.   Op. cit., Peck.

347-A.   Dorothy Gladys Spicer, *Festivals of Western Europe*, New York: H. W. Wilson Co., 1958.

347-B.   Op. cit., Bergreen.

348.   Ibid.

349.   Union General Lew Wallace invited Confederate General Slaughter (who took Colonel Ford with him) to a meeting at Point Isabel on March 11, 1865. At the meeting Wallace stated that the Rio Grande fighting was useless slaughter since it would have no effect on the war's outcome. This is interesting in that Wallace would write *Ben-Hur: A Tale of Christ* and later die on the Lupercalia (see *February 15*, 1905). Slaughter apparently hadn't wanted to fight this last battle and wanted to retreat, but Ford was insistent. Note too that Ford was riding around on a horse (a death symbol), and the horses were exhausted. The observation is made (John Salmon Ford, *Rip Ford's Texas*, Austin: University of Texas Press, 1963) that the Palmito Ranch battle was the last of the war, and it was possible "the first blood of the war was spilt in Zapata County, Texas." If so, Zapata might suggest Hermes' sandals. *Rip Ford's Texas* quotes from Bancroft's *History of the North Mexican States and Texas*: "Meantime on May 13, the engagement above alluded to, the last in the war, was fought near the old battlefield of Palo Alto, the scene of Taylor's victory over Arista."

Bibliography

Aaron, David. *Crossing by Night*. New York: Avon Books, 1993.

Adkins, Lesley and Adkins, Roy A. *Handbook to Life in Ancient Rome*. New York: Facts on File Inc, 1994

Akbar, Ali. 2 letters in May 1991. Chittagong, Bangladesh.

Aken, A.R.A. Van. *The Encyclopedia of Classical Mythology*. New Jersey: Prentice Hall, Inc., 1965.

Albion, Robert G. "Blight William." *Encyclopedia Americana*.

Albion, Robert Greenhalgh. *Forrestal and the Navy*. New York: Columbia University Press, 1962.

Allardice, Bruce S. *More Generals in Gray*. Baton Rouge and London: Louisiana State University Press.

Almanacs:

1)	*The World Almanac and Encyclopedia.*
2)	*The World Almanac and Book of Facts.*
3)	*Information Please Almanac.*
4)	*Reader's Digest Almanac and Yearbook.*
5)	*The CBS News Almanac.*
6)	*The New York Times Encyclopedia Almanac.*

Arizona (USS) Publication. U.S. Dept. of Interior, National Parks Service. GPO 1991 - 28 - 954/40026.

Arnold, Caroline. *The Golden Gate Bridge*. New York and London: Franklin Watts, 1986.

Ashabranner, Brent and Ashabranner, Jennifer (some of the photographs and historical ones). *A Memorial for Mr. Lincoln*. New York: Putnam, 1992.

Atcheson, Richard. "Night Thoughts on the Pietà." *Saturday Review*. June 17, 1972.

Atlantic Monthly, February 1995.

Bailey, Stanley. Article titled "Strange Aerial Funeral Held for Six Killed in California Mine Blast." *San Francisco Chronicle*. February 21, 1937.

Baker, Jean H. *Mary Todd Lincoln*. New York: Norton Pub., 1987.

Barthell, Edward E., Jr. *Gods and Goddesses of Ancient Greece*. Coral Gables, Florida: University of Miami Press, 1971.

Batty P. and Parish, P. *The Divided Union*. Topsfield, Massachusetts: Salem Publishers, 1987.

Baxter, Phil. "I'm a Ding Dong Daddy (from Dumas)." New York: Leo Feist Inc., Feist Building.

Beach, Edward L. *The Wreck of the Memphis*. New York * Chicago * San Francisco: Holt, Rinehart and Winston, 1966.

Beaglehole, J.C. *The Life of Captain James*. Stanford: Stanford University Press, 1974.

Beesley, Lawrence. *The Loss of the U.S. Titanic: Its Story and Its Lessons*. New York: Dover Publications, 1960.

Bell, Robert E. *Dictionary of Classical Mythology*. Santa Barbara: ABC-CLIO, Inc., 1982.

Bergreen, Laurence. *Capone, the Man and the Era*. New York: Simon and Schuster, 1994.

Bermann, Richard A. *The Mahdi of Allah*. Introduction by Winston S. Churchill. New York: the Macmillan Co., 1932.

Betz, Hans Dieter (editor). *The Greek Magical Papyri in Translation, Including Demotic Spells*. Chicago: University of Chicago Press, 1992.

Bible, Holy Bible. Revised Standard Version. Cleveland: World Publishing Co., 1962.

Biedermann, Hans. *Dictionary of Symbolism*. Translated by James Hulbert. New York: Facts on File Inc., 1992.

Blackerby, M. *Cosmic Keys: Fortunetelling for Fun and Self-discovery*. St. Paul: Llewellyn Publications, 1991.

Bland, Henry Meade. Article titled "Great Orations of the Expositions." *The Overland Monthly*. 66: 528-30. San Francisco: Overland Monthly Co., 1915.

Bodoff, Lippman. Article titled "God Tests Abraham—Abraham Tests God." *Bible Review*. Washington, D.C.: Biblical Archaeology Society, Oct/Nov 1993.

Bondurant, Joan V., "Gandhi, Mohandas Karamchand." *Encyclopedia Americana*.

Bonnerjea, Biren. *A Dictionary of Superstitions and Mythology.* London: Folk Press, Ltd. Detroit: reissued Singing Tree Press, 1969.

Bowman, John S. General Editor. *The World Almanac of the American West.* New York: The World Almanac, an Imprint of Pharos Books, 1986.

Brackman, Arnold C. *The Search for the Gold of Tutankhaman,* New York: Mason/ Charter, 1976.

Bray, Warwick. *Everyday Life of the Aztecs.* New York: Dorset Press, 1968.

Brodie, Fawn McKay. *Thomas Jefferson, an Intimate History.* New York: Norton, 1974.

Brooks, N.C. *A Complete History of the Mexican War 1846-1848.* Chicago: The Rio Grande Press, Inc., 1965.

Brooks, Tim & Marsh, Earle. *The Complete Dictionary to Prime Time Network and Cable TV Shows 1946-Present.* New York: Ballantine Books, 1995.

Broom, Jack. From article on Lotto. *Seattle Times.* 7-25-1992.

Brown, Allen. *Golden Gate.* Doubleday and Company, Inc. 1965.

Brown, Syd. "State of Sage." *Nevada* magazine. October 1992.

Brown, Weldon Amzy. *Prelude to Disaster: The American Role in Vietnam, 1940-1963.* Port Washington, New York: Kennikat Press, 1975.

Buckland, Raymond. *The Tree: The Complete Book of Saxon Witchcraft.* New York: S. Weiser, 1974.

Budge, E.A. Wallis, Sir. *The Book of the Dead.* New Hyde Park, New York: University Books, 1960.

Bunson, Margaret. *The Encyclopedia of Ancient Egypt.* New York: Facts on File, Inc., 1991.

Burke, Bernard, Sir. *The General Armory of England, Scotland, Ireland, and Wales.* London: Harrison and Sons, 1878.

Burkert, Walter. *Greek Religion.* Cambridge, Massachusetts: Harvard University Press, 1985.

Burt, R.A. *German Battleships 1897-1945.* London: Arms and Armour Press, 1989.

Cameron, Kenneth Neill. *Shelley: The Golden Years.* Cambridge, Massachusetts: Harvard University Press, 1974.

Campbell, Joseph, with Moyer, Bill. *The Power of Myth.* New York: Doubleday Pub., 1988.

Campbell, Joseph. *The Way of the Animal Powers.* Vol I. New York: Harper and Row, 1988.

Cannadine, David (editor). *Blood, Toil, Tears, and Sweat: The Speeches of Winston Churchill.* Boston: Houghton Mifflin Co., 1989.

Carlson, Helen S. *Nevada Place Names*. Reno: University of Nevada Press, 1974.

Carpenter, Allan. *The Encyclopedia of the Far West*. New York * Oxford: Facts on File, 1991.

Carpenter, Frank G. *Carp's Washington*. New York: McGraw-Hill Book Co., 1960.

Carruth, Gorton. *The Encyclopedia of American Facts and Dates*. New York: Harper and Row. 1987.

Carruth, Gorton. *The Encyclopedia of World Facts and Dates*. New York: Harper Collins Pub., 1993.

Carter, Michael. *Tutankhamun, The Golden Monarch*. New York: McKay, 1972.

Cary, M. (and others), editor. *The Oxford Classical Dictionary*. Oxford: Clarendon Press, 1949.

"Cascade Courier." Montana: January 26, 1933.

Cavendish, Richard, Editor in Chief. *Man Myth and Magic*. New York: Marshal Cavendish, 1983.

Chalekian, Harry A. From "Yesterday: Was the Garden of Eden Located in Nevada?" *Nevada* magazine. August 1993.

Chambers, Robert. *The Book of Days*. London * Edinburg: W. & R. Chambers, Ltd., 1863-64.

Chase's Annual Events: The Day-by-Day Directory to 1994. Chicago: Contemporary Books, 1993.

Chicago Daily Tribune. Article titled "Fighting Life of Army's Hero Ends in South." February 20, 1917.

Chicago Daily Tribune. February 22, 1922.

Chicago Daily Tribune. February 16, 1929. Article titled "'I detest men,' says Woman 100 Years Unmarried."

Chicago Daily Tribune. February 17, 1929. Article titled "Massacre Victims' Funeral to be Held Tuesday and Wednesday."

Chicago Daily Tribune. March 12, 1933. Fleet passing off coast of San Pedro, California.

Chicago Daily Tribune. February 18, 1937.

Chicago Daily Tribune. February 14, 1952. Mae Capone's home sold February 13, 1952.

Chichester, Anita. Letter written in 1963.

Chichester, Elsie. family history.

Chichester, Robert Lee, Jr., and Monica. Letters postmarked January 11, 1991.

Chichester, Terri. Letter postmarked 1 Mar 1991.

Churchill, Peregine, and Mitchell, Julian. *Jennie: Lady Randolph Churchill.* St. James Place, London: Collins, 1974.

Cirlot, J.E. *A Dictionary of Symbols* (translated by Jack Sage). New York: Rutledge and Kegan Paul, Philosophical Library Inc., 1962.

Clark, R. T. Runcle. *Myth and Symbol in Ancient Egypt.* Thames and Hudson, 1978.

Clinch, Nancy Gager. *The Kennedy Neurosis.* New York: Grosset and Dunlop, 1973.

Cockrum, E. Lendell. Article "Galapagos Islands." *Encyclopedia Americana.*

Coel, Margaret. *Chief Left Hand Southern Arapaho.* Norman: University of Oklahoma Press, 1981.

Cohen, Hennig, & Coffin, Tristram (editors). *The Folklore of American Holidays*, Detroit: Gale Research Co., 1987.

Cohn, Art. *The Joker Is Wild*, the story of Joe E. Louis. New York: Random House, 1955.

Complete Atlas of the British Isles. London: The Reader's Digest Association, September 1, 1983.

Complete Work of Michelangelo. New York: Renal and Co. in association with William Morrow Co., 1965.

Concklin, Edward F. (under direction of Director of Public Building and Parks of the National Capital). *The Lincoln Memorial.* Washington: U.S. Government Printing Office, 1927.

Connell, Evan S., Jr. "San Francisco: The Golden Gate." *Holiday.* April 1961.

Conner, Daniel & Miller, Lorraine. *Master Mariner, Captain James Cook and the Peoples of the Pacific.* Vancouver Museums and Planetarium. Seattle and London: University of Washington Press, 1978.

Cook, Adock, Charlesworth. *The Cambridge Ancient History.* Vol. VIII. Cambridge, England: Macmillan Co., 1930.

Cook, Jacob Ernest. Alexander Hamilton. New York: Charles Scribner's Sons, 1982.

Cooper, J.C. *An Illustrated Encyclopedia of Traditional Symbols.* London: Thames and Hudson, Ltd.

Cornell, James. *The Great International Disaster Book.* New York: Charles Scribner's Sons, 1982.

Cottrell, Philip L. *Events: A Chronicle of the Twentieth Century.* Oxford * New York: Oxford University Press, 1992.

Coughlan, Robert and the Editors of Time-Life Books. *The World of Michelangelo, 1475-1564.* New York: Time Incorporated, 1966.

Crowell, Chester T. Article titled "A Bath for the Washington Monument." *The Literary Digest.* V 118:35 N24 34.

Crowley, Aleister. *The Book of Thoth.* York Beach, Maine: Samuel Weiser Inc., 1991.

Cullen, Tom A. *When London Walked in Terror.* Boston: Houghton Mifflin Co., 1965.

Curtis, George Ticknor. *Life of James Buchanan.* Vol I. Franklin Square, New York: Harper and Brothers, 1883.

Curtis, Mann and Mizzy, Vic. "The Jones Boy." George Pincus Music Co., 1953.

Cusic, Don. *Cowboys and the Wildwest.* New York: Facts on File, Inc., 1994.

Czech, Danuta. *Auschwitz Chronicle: 1939-1945.* New York: Henry Holt and Company, 1990.

Daniels, Cora Linn and Stevens, C.M. *Encyclopedia of Superstitions and Folklore.* Detroit: Gale Research Co., 1971.

Dank, Milton. *Albert Einstein.* New York: Watts, 1983.

Darling, William, Sir. *A Book of Days.* London: The Richards Press, 1951.

Davidson, Jr., L.S. *The Disturber.* New York: Macmillan Co., 1964.

Davie, Michael. *Titanic the Death and Life of a Legend.* New York: Alfred A. Knopf, 1986.

Davies, Rodney. *Fortune-Telling Numbers.* Wellingborough, Northamptonshire, Great Britain: The Aquarian Press, 1986.

Davis, Kenneth Sydney. *The Hero: Charles A. Lindbergh and the American Dream.* Garden City, New York: Doubleday, 1959.

Decker, Karl and McSween, Angus. *Historic Arlington.* Washington, D.C.: Decker and McSween Pub. Co., 1892.

Dedication of the Washington National Monument. Published by order of Congress. Government Printing Office, 1885.

Deuterman, P.T. *Scorpion in the Sea.* Fairfax, Virginia: George Mason University Press, 1992.

Devlin, Christopher. *The Life of Robert Southwell: Poet and Martyr.* London * New York * Toronto: Longmans, Green and Co., 1956.

Dictionary of American Naval Fighting Ships. Mooney, James L., editor. Naval Historical Center, Dept. of the Navy.

Did You Know? London * New York * Montreal * Sydney * Capetown: Reader's Digest Association, Ltd., 1990.

Dillon, Richard H. *Humbugs and Heroes: A Gallery of California Pioneers.* Garden City, New York: Doubleday, 1970.

Duff, David. *George and Elizabeth*. Oxford, England: Clio Press, 1983.

Dumézil, Georges. *Archaic Roman Religion*. Volume Two. University of Chicago Press, 1970.

Duncan, William J. R.M.S. *Queen Mary, Queen of Queens*. Anderson, South Carolina: Droke House Inc., 1969.

Dunkling, Leslie. *A Dictionary of Days*. New York * Oxford: Facts on File Publications, 1988.

Durant, Will. *The Story of Civilization: Caesar and Christ*. New York: Simon and Schuster, 1944.

Duran, George. *Civil War Diary*.

Dwyer, Jim; Kocieniewski, David; Murphy, Deidre; and Tyre, Peg. "Two Seconds Under the World." Condensation: *Reader's Digest*. February 1995. "The Bomb that Shook the World."

Eaton, J. P. and Hass, Charles A. *Titanic, Triumph and Tragedy*. New York: Norton, 1986.

Eaton, J. P. and Hass, Charles A. *Titanic Destination Disaster*. London * New York: W.W. Norton and Company, 1987.

Eden Area Historical Committee. *A Century in the Foothills 1876-1976*. Montana: Fairfield Times, June 1976.

Editors of Time-Life Books. *A World of Luck*. Alexandria, Virginia: Time-Life Books, 1991.

Editors of Time-Life Books. *Psychic Powers*. Alexandria, Virginia. Time-Life Books, 1987

Eldin, Peter and Blundell, Kin (illustrations). *Amazing Ghosts and Other Mysteries*, "The Mummy's Curse." New York: Sterling Pub., 1988.

Eldredge, Zoeth Skinner. *History of California*. New York: Century History Co., 1915.

Eliade, Mircea, editor in chief. *The Encyclopedia of Religion*. New York: Macmillan, 1987.

Emery, Noemie. *Washington*. New York: G.P. Putnam's Sons, 1976.

Encyclopedias:

> *Academic American Encyclopedia*. Danbury, Connecticut: Grolier, Inc. 1990.

> *Encyclopedia Americana*. Danbury, Connecticut: Grolier, Inc., 1990.

> *The New Encyclopaedia Britannica*, Chicago: 1992.

> *Collier's Encyclopedia*. London * New York: Macmillan, 1988.

> *The World Book Encyclopedia*. Chicago: World Book, 1991.

Encyclopedia of World Mythology and Legend. New York * Oxford: Facts on File, 1988.

Erickson, Carolly. *Bloody Mary*. Garden City, New York: Doubleday and Co., Inc., 1978.

Espenshade, A. Howry. *Pennsylvania Place Names*. Harrisburg, Pennsylvania: The Evangilical Press, 1925.

Evans, Arthur. *Witchcraft and the Gay Counterculture*. Boston: Fag Rag Books, 1978.

Facts and Fallacies. Pleasantville, New York: Reader's Digest Association, 1988.

Fairbairn, James. *Fairbairn's Crests of the Leading Families in Great Britain and Ireland*. Baltimore: Genealogical Pub., 1963.

Fairclough, Melvyn. *The Ripper and the Royals*. London: Gerald Duckworth & Co., 1991.

Fallows, James. Article titled "Vatican City." *National Geographic*. December 1985.

Farnell, Lewis Richard. *The Cults of the Greeks*. Oxford: Clarendon Press, 1909.

Farrar, Janet and Farrar, Stewart. *Eight Sabbats for Witches*. Custer, Washington: Phoenix Pub. Inc., 1988.

Farrar, James and Stewart. *The Witches' God*. Custer, Washington: Phoenix Pub., 1989.

Federal Writers' Project. *Washington: City and Capital*. Washington, D.C.: U.S. Government Printing Office, 1937.

Fellman, Michael. *Citizen Sherman*. New York: Random House, 1995.

Felsenthal, Carol. *Alice Roosevelt Longworth*. New York: G.P. Putnam's Sons, 1988.

Fines, John. *Who's Who in the Middle Ages*. London: Anthony Blond Ltd., 1970.

Fish, Robert L. *The Gold of Troy*. New York: Doubleday and Co., 1980.

Fisher, C.E. and Fisher, S.G. *Soldiers, Sailors, and Patriots of the American Revolutionary War Maine*. The National Society of the American Revolution. Louisville, Kentucky.

Fitgerald, Randy. "Welfare for Illegal Aliens." *Reader's Digest*. June 1994.

Fitzgerald, Thomas W.H. *Ireland and Her People*. Chicago: Fitzgerald Book Co., 1909-1911.

Flexner, James Thomas. *Washington the Indispensable Man*. Boston * Toronto: Little, Brown, and Co., 1969, 1973, 1974.

Flexner, Stuart and Flexner, Doris. *The Pessimist's Guide to History*. New York: Avon Books, 1992.

Ford, John Salmon. *RIP Ford's Texas*. Austin: University of Texas Press, 1963.

Ford, Velma. Article titled "History of Lyon County" in *Nevada: The Silver State*. Carson City, Nevada: Western States Historical Publishers, Inc., 1970.

Fowler, W. Warde. *The Roman Festivals of the Period of the Republic.* New York: Macmillan and Co., 1899.

Fowler. W. Warde. *The Religious Experience of the Roman People.* London: Macmillan and Co., Ltd., 1911.

Fox, Robin Lane. *Alexander the Great.* London: Allen Lane, 1973.

Fox, W.S. (Greek and Roman). *The Mythology of All Races.* Vol I. Editor: Gray, Louis H., Boston: Marshal Jones Co., 1916.

Frank, Buddy. Article titled 'Back to Bonanza.' *Nevada* magazine. Nov/Dec 1993.

Frankland, Noble (general editor). *The Encyclopedia of Twentieth Century Warfare.* New York: Crown Publishers, 1989.

Frantz, Joseph B. "James, Jessie Woodson." *Encyclopedia Americana.*

Frazer, James. *The Golden Bough.* Part III. St. Martin's, New York.

Frazer, Frank and Aikman, Lonnelle. G. *Washington: Man and Monument,* Washington National Monument Association with cooperation of the National Geographic Society, 1965.

Fresno Bee. October 20, 1991, Fresno, California.

Frew, Andrew F. *Frew's Daily Archives.* Jefferson, North Carolina * London: McFarland and Co., 1984.

Frewin, Anthony. *Book of Days.* Wood engravings by Yvonne Skargon. London: Collins, 1979.

Fry, Burton C. Excerpts of letter written in 1963.

Fry. Page from family Bible.

Funk and Wagnalls Standard Dictionary of Folklore Mythology and Legend. Vol. II. New York: Funk and Wagnalls Co., 1950.

Gallen, David. *Malcolm X: As They Knew Him.* New York: Carroll and Graf, 1992.

Gardner, Jane F. *Roman Myths.* London: Pub. for Trustees of British Museum by British Museum Press, 1993.

Gartenberg, Egon. *Johann Strauss: The End of An Era.* University Park and London: Penn State University Press, 1974.

Gibbons, Floyd. *The Red Knight of Germany.* Garden City, New York: Garden City Pub. Co., 1927.

Gifford, Thomas. *The Assassini.* New York: Bantam Books, 1990.

Gilbert, Martin. *Winston S. Churchill.* Vol. VIII. Boston: Houghton, Mifflin Co., 1988.

Gillis, Mable R. California State Librarian. *California* (Federal Writers' Project). New York: Hastings House Pub., 1939.

Gittings, Robert. *John Keats*. Boston * Toronto: Little, Brown and Co., 1968.

Glass, Justine. *They Foresaw the Future*. New York: Putnam, 1969.

Goff, John S. *Robert Todd Lincoln: A Man in His Own Right*. Norman University of Oklahoma Press, 1968, 1969.

Goldscheider, Ludwig. *Michelangello*. London: The Phaidon Press, 1964.

Goldsmith, Elizabeth. *Ancient Pagan Symbols*. New York * London: G. P. Putnam's Sons, 1929.

Granite Railway Company. *The First Railroad in America*. Massachusetts: Private Printing, 1926.

Grant, Michael, and Kitzinger, Rachel, editors. *Civilization of the Ancient Mediterranean*. "Roman Cults" by John Ferguson. New York: Charles Scribner's Sons, 1988.

Graves, Robert. The Greek Myths. Vol. One. New York: George Braziller, Inc., 1955.

Great Falls Tribune. Great Falls, Montana: January 1, 1895; February 23, 1895; February 23, 1902; and January 14, 1933.

Green, Peter. *Alexander the Great*. New York: Praeger Publishers, Inc., 1970.

Gregory, Ruth W. *Anniversaries and Holidays*. Chicago: American Library Association, 1975.

Gudde, Erwin Gustav. *1000 California Place Names*. Berkeley: University of California Press, 1959.

Guerber, H.A. *Myths of Greece and Rome*. New York: American Book Co., 1893.

Guiley, Rosemary Ellen. *The Encyclopedia of Ghosts and Spirits*. New York * Oxford: Facts on File, 1992.

Guirand, F. and Pierre, A.V. "Roman Mythology" in *Larousse Encyclopedia of Mythology*. London: Batchword Press Ltd., 1959.

Haley, Alex. *Roots*. Boston: G.K. Hall, 1979.

Hamilton, Edith. *Mythology*. Boston: Little, Brown, & Co., 1942.

Hanchett, William. "Gettysburg Address." *Encyclopedia Americana*.

Hanna, Phil Townsend. *The Dictionary of California Land Names*. Los Angeles: Automobile Club of Southern California, 1946.

Hansen, Gladys, editor. *San Francisco Bay and Its Cities*. New York: Hasting House Pub. Inc., 1973.

Harder, Kelsie B. *Illustrated Dictionary of Place Names United States and Canada*. New York: Van Nostrand Rheinhold Co., 1976.

Harris, Brayton. *The Age of Battleships, 1890-1922*. New York: Franklin Watts, Inc., 1965.

Harrison, Jane Ellen. *Mythology*. Massachusetts: The Plimpton Press.

Hart, George. *A Dictionary of Egyptian Gods and Goddesses*. London * Boston * Henley: Routledge and Kegan Paul, 1986.

Hartley, Christine. Article titled "Tarot." *Man Myth and Magic*.

Hastings, James. *Encyclopaedia of Religion and Ethics*. New York: Charles Scribner's Sons, 1908.

Hatch, Jane M. (compiler and editor). *The American Book of Days*. New York: H.W. Wilson Co., 1978.

Helena Daily Herald. February 25, 1895. Helena, Montana.

Herbert-Brown, Geraldine. *Ovid and the Fasti: An Historical Study*. Oxford: Clarendon Press, 1994.

Heymann, C. David. *A Woman Named Jackie*. New York: Signet Book, New American Library Pub., 1989.

Hibbert, Christopher. *Rome: the biography of a city*. New York * London: W.W. Norton and Co., 1985.

Higdon, Hal. *The Crime of the Century: The Leopold and Loeb Case*. New York: G. P. Putnam's Sons, 1975.

Hill, Douglas. Article titled "Serpent." *Man Myth and Magic*. Cavendish, Richard, editor in chief. Pub: Marshall Cavendish, 1983.

Hiller, B.B. *Teenage Mutant Ninja Turtles*. 1990, Northshore Investments Ltd. Characters copyrighted 1989 by Mirage Studios. New York: Dell Publishing.

Hochman, Stanley. *Yesterday and Today*. New York: McGraw-Hill Book Company, 1979.

Hoffa, James R. *Hoffa the Real Story*, as told to Oscar Fraley. New York: Stein and Day Publishers, 1975.

Homer. *The Homeric Hymns*, translated by Boer, Charles. Chicago: The Swallow Press, Inc., 1970.

Homer. *The Homeric Hymns*, translated by Sargent, Thelma. New York: Norton, 1973.

Hough, Richard A. *The Last Voyage of Captain James Cook*. New York: William Morrow and Co., Inc., 1979.

Hough, Richard. *Winston and Clementine: The Triumph of the Churchills*. London, New York, Toronto, Sydney, Auckland: Bantam Press, 1990.

Hoving, Thomas. *Tutankhamun, The Untold Story*. New York: Simon and Schuster, 1978.

Howard, O.O. *General Taylor* (The Great Commander Series). New York: D. Appleton and Co.

Hugli, Paul. *Witchcraft: What is it?* Dayton, Ohio: P.P.I. - Publishing Pamphlet Publications.

Huxley, Francis. From articles titled "Voodoo" and "Zombie". *Man Myth and Magic*. op. cit..

Jackson, Donald and Twohig, Dorothy (editors). *The Diaries of George Washington*. Charlottesville: University Press of Virginia, 1976-1979.

James, T.G.H. Howard Carter: *The Path to Tutankhamun*. New York and London: Kegan Paul International, 1992.

Jobes, Gertrude. *Dictionary of Mythology, Folklore and Symbols*. New York: Scarecrow Press, 1961-1962.

Johnson, Allen (editor). *Dictionary of American Biography*, "Black Hawk." New York: Charles Scribner's Sons, 1957.

Johnson, David E. *From Day to Day: A Calendar of Notable Birthdays and Events*. Metuchen, New Jersey and London: The Scarecrow Press Inc., 1990.

Jones, Merlin. "Haunted Places." Boca Raton, Florida: Globe Mini Mag. Globe Communications Corp., 1992.

Jung, C.G. *The Collected Works of C.G. Jung*. Editors: Herbert Read, Michael Fordham, Gerhard Adler. New York: Pantheon Books, 1953.

Kane, Joseph Nathan. *Facts About the Presidents*. New York: H.W. Wilson Co., 1974.

Kane, Joseph; Anzovin, Steven; and Podell; Janet. *Facts About the States*. New York: H.W. Wilson Co., 1989.

Kane, Joseph Nathan. *Famous First Facts*. New York: H.W. Wilson Co., 1981.

Kane, Joseph Nathan. *The American Counties*. New York: Scarecrow Press Inc., 1960.

Keegan, John (general editor). *The Rand McNally Encyclopedia of World War II*. Chicago * New York * London: Bison Book, Rand McNally and Co., 1977.

Kelleher, Ed and Vidal, Harriette. *Prime Evil*. New York: Dorchester Publishing Co., 1988.

Keller, Helen Rex. *The Dictionary of Dates*. New York: Macmillan Co., 1934.

Kelly, Aidan; Dresser, Peter; Ross, Linda M. *Religious Holidays and Celebrations*. Detroit: Omnigraphics Inc., 1993.

Key, Francis Scott. "The Star-Spangled Banner."

Kirkendall, Richard S. Editor. *The Harry S. Truman Encyclopedia*. Boston: G.K. Hall and Co., 1989.

Klein, Philip Shriver. *President James Buchanan*. University Park, Pennsylvania: Penn State University Press, 1962.

Knowles, George Harmon. "Maine, Destruction of the (February 15, 1898)." *Collier's Encyclopedia*.

Kobler, John. Capone: *The Life and World of Al*. New York: G.P. Putnam's Sons, 1971.

Kodalen, Margaret (Peggy) Cameron, from (1) "The Unsolved Case of Dannie Cameron," and (2) "Duncan A. Cameron, Sr." *A Century in the Foothills 1876-1976*. Montana: Fairfield Times Pub., 1976.

Kodalen, Margaret Cameron and Penman, Lois Ziegler from "Story of Dougald H. and Cora D. Edwards Cameron and Parker A. And Berthe E. Edwards Zeigler." *A Century in the Foothills 1876-1976*. ibid.

Kolatch, Alfred J. *The Jonathan David Dictionary of First Names*. Middle Village, New York: J. David Publishers, 1980.

Koontz, Dean R. *Cold Fire*. Nkui, Inc., cover illustrations copyrighted 1991 by Don Brautigam. New York: The Berkeley Pub Group, 1991.

Krum, Morrow. "Italians Knew Roma's Defects, Article Hints" (cites previous article by Kenneth L. Roberts, *Saturday Evening Post*. August 13, 1921). Chicago Daily Tribune, February 23, 1922.

L'Amour, Louis. *The Haunted Mesa*. Toronto, New York: Bantam Books, 1987.

Lasne, Sophie and Gaultier, André Pascal. *A Dictionary of Superstitions*, translated by Amy Reynolds. Englewood Cliffs, New Jersey: Prentice-Hall, Inc., 1984.

Lawless, Emily. "With the Wild Geese."

Lawren, Bill. *On the Wing* (condensed from "National Widelife.") *Reader's Digest*. August 1992.

Lawson, John Cuthert. *Modern Greek Folklore and Ancient Greek Religion*. New Hyde Park, New York: University Books, 1964.

Leach, M. *Standard Dictionary of Folklore, Mythology and Legend*. Funk and Wagnalls Co., 1950.

Leach, Marjorie. *Guide to the Gods*. Santa Barbara, California: ABC-CLIO, 1992.

Lebrecht, Norman. *A Musical Book of Dates*. New York: Universe Books, 1989.

Lederer, Edith M. The Associated Press, from article in *Seattle Post-Intelligencer*. November 21, 1992.

Lee, Kay and Marshall (editors). *The Illuminated Book of Days.* New York: G. P. Putnam's Sons, 1979.

Legrand, Jacques (conception and coordination) and Burne, Jerome, editor. *Chronicle of World.* Mt. Kisko, New York: ECAM Publications, 1990.

Lemprière's Classical Writ Large Dictionary, 1984, Rewood Burn, Trowbride, Wilts, Great Britain.

Leonard, Thomas; Crippen, Cynthia; Aronson, Marc. *Day By Day: The Seventies.* Vol. II. New York: Facts on File Publications, 1988.

Leopold, Nathan F. *Life Plus 90 Years,* Introduction by Erle Stanley Gardner. Garden City, New York: Doubleday, 1958.

Lerner, Alan Jay (words) and Loewe, Frederick (music). "Get Me to the Church on Time."

Leslie, Anita. *Lady Randolph Churchill.* New York: Charles Scribner's Sons, 1969.

Leslie, Edgar (words) and Burke, Joe (music). "Moon Over Miami." Copyright 1935. Los Angeles: Ahlert-Burke Corp., (renewed) 1963.

Linton, Calvin D. (editor). *The American Almanac.* New York: Thomas Nelson, Inc., 1977.

Little, Bentley. *The Revelation.* New York: St. Martin's Press, 1989.

Line, David and Julia. *Fortune-Telling By Dice.* Wellingborough, Northamptonshire, New York: 1987.

Liungman, Carl G. *Dictionary of Symbols.* Santa Barbara, California: ABC-CLIO.

Lloyd, Christopher. *Captain Cook.* London: Faber and Faber, Ltd., 1952.

Long, E.B. and Long, Barbara. *The Civil War Day by Day.* Doubleday and Co., Inc., 1971.

Lorant, Stefan. *The Life and Times of Theodore Roosevelt.* Garden City, New York: Doubleday and Co., Inc., 1959.

Lynch, Don. Article titled "The Paiute Messiah" in *Nevada.* June 1992.

Lys, Claudia de. *A Treasury of American Superstitions.* New York: Philosophical Library Inc., 1984.

Mabee, Carleton. *The American Leonardo, A Life of Samuel F.B. Morse.* New York: A.A. Knopf, 1943.

MacFarlane, Gwyn. *Alexander Fleming, the Man and the Myth.* Cambridge, Massachusetts: Harvard University Press, 1984.

Madariaga, Salvador de. *Christopher Columbus.* New York: Macmillan Co., 1940.

Malcolm X. *The Autobiography of Malcolm X,* as told to Alex Haley, copyright 1964, copyright 1965, by Alex Haley and Betty Shabazz. New York: Ballantine Books.

Malone, Dumas, editor. *Dictionary of American Biography*. Copyright 1936 by Council of Learned Societies. New York: Scribner's Sons.

Man Myth and Magic. Article titled "Leafing through the Occult."

Marn, John R. Letter dated February 17, 1993, from Belt, Montana.

Marn, Shirley (Cameron). From article "Daniel Cameron." *A Century in the Foothills 1876-1976*, op. cit..

Martelli, George. Jemmy Twitcher, *A Life of the Fourth Earl of Sandwich 1718-1792*. London: Jonathan Cape, 1962.

Martin, Ralph G. *Jennie: The Life of Lady Randolph Churchill*. Vol. Two. Englewood Cliffs, New Jersey: Prentice-Hall, Inc., 1971.

Martin, William. *Back Bay*. New York: Pocket Books, 1979.

Matthews, Jason and Shand, Terry. "Give Me the Moon Over Brooklyn." London Music Corp., 1945.

Matthew, John, editor. *The World Atlas of Divination*. Boston: Bulfinch Press, 1993.

Matthews, Rupert. *The Supernatural*. Illustrations by Peter Dennis. New York: Bookwright Press, 1989.

McGlashan, C.F. *History of Donner Party*. Stanford, California: Stanford University Press, 1940.

McLeave, Hugh. *Rogues in the Gallery*, The Modern Plague of Art Thefts, Boston: D.R. Godine, 1981.

McLynn, Frank. Robert Louis Stevenson. London: Hutchinson, 1993.

McPhaul, Jack. *Johnny Torrio, First of the Gang Lords*. New Rochelle, New York: Arlington House, 1970.

Melton, J. Gordon and Poggi, Isotta. *Magic, Witchcraft, and Paganism in America*. New York * London: Garland Pub. Inc., 1992.

Mercante, Anthony S. *Encyclopedia of World Mythology and Legend*. New York * Oxford: Facts on File, 1988.

Merritt, Jeffrie D. *Day By Day: The Fifties*. New York: Facts on File, 1979.

Michelmore, Peter. Article titled "Inside Hurricane Andrew." *The Reader's Digest*. January 1993.

Michener, James A. *Caribbean*. New York: Ballantine Books, 1989.

Miller, Nathan. *FDR, An Intimate History*. Garden City, New York: Doubleday, 1983.

Millgate, Linda. *The Almanac of Dates*. New York * London: Harcourt Brace Jovanovitch, 1977.

Mirkin, Stanford M. *What Happened When*. New York: I. Washburn, 1966.

Mollenhoff, Clark R. *Tentacles of Power, The Story of Jimmy Hoffa*. World Publishing Co., 1965.

Montrose, P. "Oh! My Darling Clementine." New York: Robbins Music Corporation, 1942.

Mooney, James L., editor. *American Naval Fighting Ships*. Washington: Naval Historical Center. Dept. of the Navy.

Moore, Daphna. *The Rabbi's Tarot*. St. Paul, Minnesota: Llewellyn Pub., 1989.

Moore, David, editor. *Nevada*. Letter dated Oct. 16, 1995.

Moorthy, M. Letter dated June 18, 1982. Madras, India.

Moreno, Richard. Article titled "Wed and Wild." *Nevada*. Jan/Feb 1994.

Morgan, Ted. *Churchill: Young Man in a Hurry 1874-1915*. New York: Simon and Schuster, 1982.

Morgan, Ted. *FDR, A Biography*. New York: Simon and Schuster, 1985.

Morris, Richard B. Encyclopedia of American History. New York: Harper and Row Publishers, 1976.

Morison, Samuel Eliot. *The Rising Sun in the Pacific*. Vol 3. Boston: Little Brown and Co., 1948.

Mormon Stakes Records. West Seattle, Washington.

Morse, M.C., Jr., Capt. *The Strout Family of Maine*. Vol. I. Portland, Maine: Files of Maine Historical Society.

Murad, Anatol. *Franz Joseph I of Austria and His Empire*. New York: Twayne Publishers, 1968.

Murray, Alexander S. *Manual of Mythology*. New York: Tudor Publishing Co., 1935.

Murray, Margaret. *The Witch Cult in Western Europe*. 1921.

Myers, Robert J. (with the editors of Hallmark cards). *Celebrations*. Illustrations by Bill Greer. Garden City, New York: Doubleday and Co., Inc., 1972.

Nardo, Don. *The Irish Potato Famine*. Illustrations by McGovern, Brian. San Diego: Lucent Books, 1990.

Nash, Jay Robert. *Crime Chronology: A Worldwide Record 1900-1983*. New York: Facts on File Pub., 1984.

706

Nash, Jay Robert, editor in chief. *Encyclopedia of World Crime*. Wilmette, Illinois: CrimeBook, 1989 and 1990.

National Archives. Information on George Duren and family. USS *Nevada*.

National Archives and Records Administration. Washington, D.C. A special thanks for answering many inquiries.

National Cyclopaedia of American Biography. Article "Mary Walker." New York: James T. White and Co., 1906.

Navy Department. *Dictionary of American Naval Fighting Ships*. Volume I. Part-A. Vol III. Washington, D.C.: United States Government Printing Office.

Neely, M.E. and McMurty, R.G. *The Insanity File*. Southern Illinois University, 1986.

Neimark, Anne. *With This Gift: The Story of Edgar Cayce*. New York: Morrow, 1978.

Nettleship, Henry and Sandys, J.E. *Dictionary of Classical Antiquities*. Ohio: World Publishing Co., 1956.

Nevada. Article titled "A Spiritual Celebration." August 1995.

Nevada State Library and Archives. Letter dated Dec 14, 1995, from LaBonge, Deanna, Library Assistant, giving dates of birth of H.M. Yerington.

Nevin, David (text). *The Mexican War* from *The Old West*. Time-Life Books, Inc., 1978.

New Catholic Encyclopedia. Vol XIV. Washington, D.C.: The Catholic University of America, 1976.

New Larousse Encyclopedia of Mythology. New York: Putnam, 1968.

Newsweek. Item concerning Bess Truman's death. Nov 1, 1982.

Nicolson, Harold. *King George the Fifth*. New York: Doubleday and Co., Inc., 1953.

Nordam, George W. *George Washington: Vignettes and Memorabilia*. Philadelphia and Ardmore, Pennsylvania: Dorrance and Co., 1977.

Oates, Stephen B. *Abraham Lincoln, The Man Behind the Myths*. New York: Harper and Row, 1984.

O'Brien, Mark. "Golden Spike Breaks Off, Vanishes." *San Francisco Chronicle*, April 28, 1937.

Olszewski, George J. *Restoration of Ford's Theatre*. Under Conrad L. Wirth, Director National Park Service. U.S. Dept. of Interior. National Capital Region. 1963

Opie, Iona and Peter. *Children's Games in Street and Playground*. Oxford: Clarendon P., 1969.

Otto, Walter F. *The Homeric Gods*. New York: Pantheon Books Inc., 1954.

Ovid. *Fasti*. 2.527 - 539.

Oxford Classical Dictionary. Oxford: Clarendon Press, 1949.

Paletta, Lu Ann and Worth, Fred L. *The World Almanac of Presidential Facts*. New York: World Almanac, 1988.

Palmer, Frederick. *John J. Pershing, General of the Armies*. Harrisburg, Pennsylvania: Military Service Pub. Co., 1948.

Parker, Thomas and Nelson, Douglass. *Day By Day: The Sixties*. Vol I and II. New York: Facts on File Publications, 1983.

Pasley, Fred D. *Al Capone: The Biography of a Self-Made Man*. Freeport, New York: Books for Libraries Press, 1930.

Pastene, Jerome. *Three Quarter Time*. New York: Abelard Press, 1951.

Pater, Alan F. *The United States Battleships*. Beverly Hills, California: Monitor Book Co., 1968.

Pearce, Alfred John. *The Text-Book of Astrology*. Washington: American Federation of Astrologers, 1970.

Peck, Harry T. *Harper's Dictionary for Classical Literature and Antiquities*. New York: American Book Co., 1896.

Pelling, Henry. *Winston Churchill*. London: Macmillan, 1974.

Pelta, Kathy. *Bridging the Golden Gate*. Minnesota: Lerner Pub. Co. 1987.

Perowne, Stewart. *Roman Mythology*. Copyright 1969. New York: Peter Bedrick Books, 1983.

Peter, Laurence J. *Peter's Almanac*. New York: William Morrow and Co., Inc., 1982.

Peticus, A.H. *The Gods of Olympos*. Translated by Katherine A. Raleigh. New York: Cassell Publishing Co., 1892.

Pike, Donald G. (text) and Muench, David (photos). *Anasazi, Ancient People of the Rock*. Palo Alto, California: American West Pub. Co.

Pilgeram, Jim. From "The Cameron Hill Cemetery." *A Century in the Foothills 1876-1976*. Op. cit..

Pinsent, John. *Greek Mythology*. New York: Peter Bedrick Books, 1982.

Poole, Lynn and Gary. *One Passion, Two Loves*. New York: Thomas Y. Crowell Company, 1966.

Potter, Neil and Frost, Jack. *The Queen Mary*. New York: John Day Co., 1961.

Progressive Men of Montana. Chicago: A.W. Bowen and Co.

Queen Mary. Souvenir number of "The Shipbuilder and Marine Engine-Builder." New Castle-on-Tyne, England: The Shipbuilder Press, Townville House, June 1936.

Raymond, Henry J. *The Life and Public Services of Abraham Lincoln.* New York: Derby and Miller, 1865.

Radford, E. and M.A. *Encyclopedia of Superstition.* (Edited by Christine Hole.) Hutchinson of London, 1961.

Reader's Digest Book of Facts. Pleasantville, New York * Montreal: The Reader's Digest Association Inc.

Reeves, Nicholas. *The Complete Tutankhamun.* London: Thames and Hudson, Ltd., 1990.

Reit, Seymour. *The Day They Stole the Mona Lisa.* New York: Summit Books. 1981.

Robbins, Rossell Hope. *The Encyclopedia of Witchcraft and Demonology.* New York: Crown Publishers Inc., 1959.

Rocha, Guy Louis. "How Nevada Became 'Nevada.'" *Nevada* magazine. April 1996.

Roosevelt, Nicholas. *Theodore Roosevelt, the Man as I Knew Him.* New York: Dodd, Mead, and Co., 1967.

Rose, H.J. *The Religion in Greece and Rome.* New York: Harper Torchbooks, Harper and Brothers, 1959.

Rose, Kenneth. *King George V.* Distributed by Random House. New York: Knoph, 1983, 1984.

Ross, Walter S. *The Last Hero: Charles A. Lindbergh.* New York: Harper and Row. 1976.

Rumi, Mevlana Jelalu'ddin. "Come, come, whoever you are." etc.

Ryan, Cornelius. *The Longest Day.* (Quote from S/Sgt. Alfred Eigenberg.) Simon and Schuster, 1959.

Sacramento Bee. 10/07/94. Byline: Associated Press. "More Leaping off S.F. Bridge—'Mystique' Draws the Despondent."

Salsini, Barbara. *Irving Berlin.* Charlottesville, New York: Story House Corp., 1972.

Sams, Jamie and Carson, David; Werneke, Angela (illustrations). *Medicine Cards: the discovery of power through the ways of animals.* Santa Fe, New Mexico: Bear & Co., 1988.

San Francisco Chronicle. Concerning Pershing. August 30, 1915.

San Francisco Chronicle. "General Gomez is Joined by Regulars." Feb. 14, 1917.

San Francisco Chronicle. "Fighting General Answers to Taps." Feb. 20, 1917.

San Francisco Chronicle. "Funston's Body to Lie in State in City Hall." Feb. 21, 1917.

San Francisco Chronicle. "City Bows at Bier of Her Dead Hero." Feb. 24, 1917.

San Francisco Chronicle. "Taps Sounded for Major-General Frederick Funston." Feb. 25, 1917.

San Francisco Chronicle. "The Tragic Story of the Ships that Failed." May 27, 1937.

Sandburg, Carl. *Abraham Lincoln, the Prairie Years and the War Years.* Copyright 1966. New York: Harcourt Brace Jovanovich, 1974.

Sanders, Robyn. Excerpts from letters dated: March 18, 1991; March 27, 1991; April 13, 1991; June 22, 1991; July 28, 1991; April 23, 1992; February 10, 1993.

Schaeffer, Claude F.A. Article titled "Secrets from Syrian Hills." *National Geographic Magazine.* July 1933.

Schlesinger, Arthur M., Jr., general editor. *The Almanac of American History.* New York: Bramhall House, 1983.

Schoenberg, Robert J. *Mr. Capone.* New York: William Morrow, 1992.

Seattle Times. Concerning weather. December 28, 1990.

Seltman, Charles Theodore. *The Twelve Olympians.* New York: Crowell, 1960.

Sepharial. *The Kabala of Numbers.* Part I. North Hollywood, California: New Castle Publishing Co., 1974.

Seward, Robert. *Dictionary of American Biography*, under "Scott, Winfield." New York: Charles Scribner's Sons, 1935.

Seyfert, Oskar. *A Dictionary of Classical Antiquities.* London: William Glaisher, Ltd., 1891.

Shanas, Bert. 'Nevada Under Attack.' *Nevada. Dec. 1991.*

Shelley, Percy. "Queen Mab."

Shepherd, Jack. *The Adams Chronicles.* Boston * Toronto: Little, Brown, & Co.

Shultz, Sigfried. Article titled "Europe in Grip of Record Cold; Many Are Dead." *Chicago Daily Tribune.* Feb. 12, 1929.

Sifakis, Carl. *Encyclopedia of Assassinations.* New York * Oxford: Facts on File, Inc., 1991.

Sifakis, Carl. *The Encyclopedia of American Crime.* New York: Facts on File, Inc., 1982.

Sky, Michael. *Dancing With the Fire.* Sante Fe, New Mexico: Bear and Co. Publishing, 1989.

Smith, Elsdon C. *American Surnames.* Philadelphia: Chilton Book Co., 1969.

Smith, Frank. *A Genealogical Gazetteer of England.* Baltimore: Genealogical Pub. Co., 1968.

Smith, William, and Anthon, Charles (editors). *Dictionary of Greek and Roman Antiquities*. New York: Harper and Brothers, 1878.

Smythe, Donald. *Guerrilla Warrior: The Early Life of John J. Pershing*. New York: Charles Scribner's Sons, 1973.

Snyder, Louis L. *Encyclopedia of the Third Reich*. New York: McGraw-Hill Book Co., 1976.

Snyder, Louis L. Louis L. *Snyder's Historical Guide to World War II*. Westport, Connecticut and London, England: Greenwood Press, 1982.

Spence, Lewis. *An Encyclopaedia of Occultism*. New Hyde Park, New York: University Books, 1960.

Spicer, Dorothy Gladys. *Festivals of Western Europe*. New York: H.W. Wilson Co., 1958

Squire, Charles. *Celtic Myth and Legend, Poetry and Romance*. London: Gresham Pub. Co., 191?.

Stackpole, Everett S. *History of Durham, Maine*. Lewiston, Maine: Lewiston Journal, 1899.

Staigmiller, John B. Article titled "Moonshine Days." *A Century in the Foothills 1876-1976*. Op. cit..

Steiger, Brad. *Psychic City: Chicago*. Garden City, New York: Doubleday and Co., Inc., 1976.

Steward, George R. *American Place-Names*. New York: Oxford University Press, 1970.

Stoll, Clifford. *The Cuckoo's Egg*. New York: Doubleday, 1989.

Stone, Irving. *The Greek Treasure*. Garden City, New York: Doubleday and Co., Inc., 1975.

Strange Stories, *Amazing Facts*. The Reader's Digest Association, Inc., 1976.

Stringfellow, William and Towne, Anthony. *The Bishop Pike Affair*. New York * Evanstown * London: Harper and Row.

Sturluson, Snorri. "The Deluding of Gylfi" (from Icelandic).

Sugden, John. *Sir Francis Drake*. London: Barrie and Jenkins, Ltd., 1990.

Sunrise and Sunset Tables for Key Cities and Weather Stations of the U.S. (U.S. Naval Observatory, Nautical Almanac Office.) Detroit: Gale Research Co., 1977.

Suppiger, Joseph E. *The Intimate Lincoln*. Landham * New York * London: University Press of America, 1985.

Swan, Gary E. "Telegraph Hill Murders." *San Francisco Chronicle*. Feb. 22, 1985.

Swearingen, Roger G. *The Prose Writings of Robert Louis Stevenson: A Guide*. Hamden, Connecticut: Archon Books, 1980.

Taylor, Emerson G. *Gouverneur Kemble Warren*. New York: Houghton Mifflin Co., 1932.

Taylor, Tim. *The Book of Presidents*. New York: Arno Press.

Thompson, C.J.S. *The Hand of Destiny: the Folklore and Superstitions of Everyday Life*. Detroit: Singing Tree Press, 1970.

Thompson, Sue Ellen and Carlson, Barbara W. *Holidays, Festivals, and Celebrations of the World Dictionary*. Detroit: Omnigraphics, 1994.

Thornton, J. Quinn. *The California Tragedy*. By Joseph A. Sullivan. Oakland, California: Bio Books.

Thurston, Herbert and Attwater, Donald (editors and revision). *Butler's Lives of the Saints*. New York: P. J. Kennedy and Sons, 1956.

Time magazine. March 3, 1958.

Todd, Frank Morton. *The Story of the Exposition*. New York * London: G.P. Putnam's Sons, the Knickerbocker Press, 1921.

Todd, Ruthven. "James, Jessie Woodson." *Collier's Encyclopedia*.

Toland, John. *The Dillinger Days*. New York: Random House, 1963.

Toland, John. *The Rising Sun: The Decline and Fall of the Japanese Empire, 1936-1945*. New York: Random House, 1970.

Trager, James (editor). *The People's Chronology*. New York: Holt, Rinehart and Winston, 1979.

Troyat, Henri. *Divided Soul: The Life of Gogol*. Translated from French by Nancy Amphoux. New York: Double Day and Co., 1973.

Trueblood, Elton. *Abraham Lincoln*. New York: Harper & Row. 1973.

Turner, Justin G. and Linda L. *Mary Todd Lincoln: Her Life and Letters*. Knopf, 1972.

Ungent, Donald. From section on "Potato." *Encyclopedia Americana*.

U.S. Dept. of Interior. NPS. GPO - 281-954/40026. USS *Arizona* Memorial.

Vandiver, Frank E. *Black Jack: The Life and Times of John J. Pershing*. Vol I. College Station and London: Texas A & M University Press, 1977.

Van Straalen, Alice. *The Book of Holidays Around the World*. New York: Dutton, 1986.

Vernant, Jean Pierre. *Myth and Thought Among the Greeks*. Boston * London: Routledge and Kegan Paul, 1965.

Vidal, Gore. *Creation*. New York: Ballantine Books, 1981.

Vincent, Benjamin. *Haydn's Dictionary of Dates and Universal Information*. New York: G. P. Putnam's Sons, 1898.

Vivian, Octavia. *Coretta, the story of Mrs. Martin Luther King, Jr.* Philadelphia: Fortress Press, 1970.

Von der Porten, Edward P. *The German Navy in World War II.* New York: Thomas Y. Crowell Co., 1969.

Vries, Ad de. *Dictionary of Symbols and Imagery.* Amsterdam * London: North-Holland Publishing Co., 1974.

Wade, Wynn Craig. *The Titanic: End of a Dream.* New York: Rawson Wade Publishers, Inc., 1979.

Walker, Barbara G. *The Woman's Encyclopedia of Myths and Secrets.* San Francisco: Harper and Row Pub., 1983.

Wallechinsky, David. *People's Almanac Presents the Twentieth Century.* Boston * New York * Toronto * London: Little, Brown and Co., 1995.

Walter, Gérard. Translated by Sidney Shore. From "Nero." *Collier's Encyclopedia.*

Weber, Gerda and Hermann. *Lenin, Life, and Works.* Edited and translated by Martin McCauley. New York: Facts on File, 1980.

Walters, H.B. *A Classical Dictionary.* Cambridge: at University Press, 1916.

Walters, Raymond Jr. "Adams-Onís Treaty." *Collier's Encyclopedia.*

Washington Post. Article on St. Valentine's Day. Feb. 14, 1917.

Washington Post. Feb. 23, 1922.

Webster, Donovan. Article titled "The Soldiers Moved On. The War Moved On. The Bombs Stayed." *Smithsonian.* Feb. 1994.

Webster's Third New International Dictionary. 1971.

Wechsberg, Joseph. *The Waltz Emperors.* New York: G. P. Putnam's Sons, 1973.

Weiner, Tim. (*New York Times.*) Article titled "95 CIA Reports Tainted by KGB." *Seattle Post-Intelligencer.* Nov. 10, 1995.

Weiser, Carl. Article "Skier: I Felt Treated Like 'Roman Slave.'" *USA Today.* March 4, 1993.

White, Suzanne. *The New Astrology.* New York: St. Martin's Press. 1986.

Whittick, Arnold. *Symbols, Signs and Their Meaning.* London: Leonard Hill Ltd., 1960.

Widbrodt, Norma Beth. Excerpts from letter telling of Camerons from Isle of Skye and Daniel Chase and Ida Duren.

Williams, Ben Ames. *Leave Her to Heaven.* Boston: Houghton Mifflin Company, 1944.

Williams, Neville. *Chronology of the Modern World.* London: Barrie and Rockliff, 1966.

Wilson, Colin. *A Criminal History of Mankind*. London: Granada Publishing Ltd., 1984.

Winberg, William M., Historian. *Queen Mary and Spruce Goose* Entertainment Center. Letter dated April 2, 1992.

Wincour, Jack (editor). *The Story of the Titanic as Told by Its Survivors*. New York: Dover Pub. Inc., 1960.

Winslow, Ola Elizabeth. *A Destroying Angel: The Conquest of Smallpox in Colonial Boston*. Boston: Houghton-Mifflin, 1974.

Winstone, H.V.F. *Howard Carter and the discovery of the tomb of Tutankhamun*. London: Constable, 1991.

Winter, C.W.R. *The Queen Mary: Her Early Years Recalled*. New York: W. W. Norton.

Woodward, W.E. *Meet General Grant*. Horace Liverright Inc., The Literary Guild, 1928.

Writers' Program (Nev.). *Nevada: A Guide to the Silver State*. Portland, Oregon: Binsford and Mort, 1940.

Wyndham, Francis and King, David. *Trotsky*. London: Allen Lane the Penguin Press, 1972.

Yonge, Charlotte Mary. *Christian Names*. London: Macmillan, 1884.

Zentner, Christian and Bedürftig, Friedemann (editors). Translation edited by Hackett, Amy. *The Encyclopedia of the Third Reich*. Two volumes. New York: Macmillan Publishing Co., 1991.